Lecture Notes in Computer Science 3317

Commenced Publication in 1973
Founding and Former Series Editors:
Gerhard Goos, Juris Hartmanis, and Jan van

Michael Domaratzki   Alexander Okhotin
Kai Salomaa   Sheng Yu (Eds.)

Implementation and Application of Automata

9th International Conference, CIAA 2004
Kingston, Canada, July 22-24, 2004
Revised Selected Papers

 Springer

Volume Editors

Michael Domaratzki
Acadia University, Jodrey School of Computer Science
Wolfville, Nova Scotia B4P 2R6 , Canada
E-mail: mike.domaratzki@acadiau.ca

Alexander Okhotin
Kai Salomaa
Queen's University, School of Computing
Kingston, Ontario K7L 3N6, Canada
E-mail: {okhotin, ksalomaa}@cs.queensu.ca

Sheng Yu
University of Western Ontario, Department of Computer Science
London, Ontario N6A 5B7, Canada
E-mail: syu@csd.uwo.ca

Library of Congress Control Number: 2004117401

CR Subject Classification (1998): F.1.1, F.1.2, F.4.2, F.4.3, F.2

ISSN 0302-9743
ISBN 3-540-24318-6 Springer Berlin Heidelberg New York

Springer is a part of Springer Science+Business Media

springeronline.com

© Springer-Verlag Berlin Heidelberg 2005
Printed in Germany

Typesetting: Camera-ready by author, data conversion by Scientific Publishing Services, Chennai, India
Printed on acid-free paper   SPIN: 11376019   06/3142   5 4 3 2 1 0

Preface

This volume of Lecture Notes in Computer Science contains the revised versions of the papers presented at the 9th International Conference on Implementation and Application of Automata, CIAA 2004. Also included are the extended abstracts of the posters accepted to the conference.

The conference was held at Queen's University in Kingston, Ontario, Canada on July 22–24, 2004. As for its predecessors, the theme of CIAA 2004 was the implementation of automata and grammars of all types and their application in other fields. The topics of the papers presented at the conference range from applications of automata in natural language and speech processing to protein sequencing and gene compression, and from state complexity and new algorithms for automata operations to applications of quantum finite automata.

The 25 regular papers and 14 poster papers were selected from 62 submissions to the conference. Each submitted paper was evaluated by at least three Program Committee members, with the help of external referees. Based on the referee reports, the paper "Substitutions, Trajectories and Noisy Channels" by L. Kari, S. Konstantinidis and P. Sosík was chosen as the winner of the CIAA 2004 Best Paper Award. The award is sponsored by the University of California at Santa Barbara.

The authors of the papers presented here come from the following countries and regions: Austria, Canada, Czech Republic, Finland, France, Germany, Hong Kong, Netherlands, Portugal, Russia, Slovakia, South Africa, Spain, UK, and USA.

It is a pleasure for the editors to thank the members of the Program Committee and the external referees for reviewing the papers and maintaining the high standard of the CIAA conferences. We are grateful to all the contributors to the conference, in particular to the invited speakers, for making CIAA 2004 a scientific success.

We are grateful to the conference sponsors for their generous financial support. For help with the local arrangements, we thank Nancy Barker, Michelle Crane, Lynda Moulton, Sandra Pryal and Amber Simpson. Thanks are due to the School of Computing systems group for arranging Internet access for the conference participants.

Finally, we are indebted to Ms. Christine Günther and Mrs. Anna Kramer from Springer for the efficient collaboration in producing this volume.

September 2004

M. Domaratzki
A. Okhotin
K. Salomaa
S. Yu

Organization

Invited Speakers

Oscar H. Ibarra	University of California, Santa Barbara, USA
Jeffrey O. Shallit	University of Waterloo, Canada

Program Committee

B. Boigelot	Université de Liege, Belgium
J. Brzozowski	University of Waterloo, Canada
C. Câmpeanu	University of Prince Edward Island, Canada
J.-M. Champarnaud	Université de Rouen, France
J. Gruska	Masaryk University, Czech Republic
T. Harju	University of Turku, Finland
M. Holzer	Technische Universität München, Germany
J. Hromkovič	ETH Zürich, Switzerland
O. Ibarra	University of California, Santa Barbara, USA
M. Ito	Kyoto Sangyo University, Japan
T. Jiang	University of California, Riverside, USA
J. Karhumäki	University of Turku, Finland
L. Karttunen	Palo Alto Research Center, USA
N. Klarlund	Bell Labs, New Jersey, USA
W. Kuich	Technische Universität Wien, Austria
C. Martín-Vide	Rovira i Virgili University, Spain
D. Maurel	Université de Tours, France
M. Mohri	Courant Institute of Mathematical Sciences, USA
F. Neven	Limburgs Universitair Centrum, Belgium
Gh. Păun	Romanian Academy, Romania
J.-E. Pin	CNRS and Université Paris 7, France
B. Ravikumar	Sonoma State University, USA
G. Rozenberg	Leiden University, The Netherlands, and University of Colorado, Boulder, USA
K. Salomaa	Queen's University, Canada, *co-chair*
K. Sutner	Carnegie Mellon University, USA
W. Thomas	RWTH Aachen, Germany
B. Watson	Technische Universiteit Eindhoven, The Netherlands, and University of Pretoria, South Africa
D. Wood	Hong Kong University of Science and Technology, Hong Kong, China
H.-C. Yen	National Taiwan University, Taiwan
S. Yu	University of Western Ontario, Canada, *co-chair*

Organizing Committee

M. Domaratzki   Acadia University, Canada
A. Okhotin   Queen's University, Canada
K. Salomaa   Queen's University, Canada, *chair*

Sponsors

- School of Computing, Queen's University
- Office of Research Services, Queen's University
- Communications and Information Technology Ontario (CITO)
- European Association for Theoretical Computer Science (EATCS)

Additional Referees

Abdullah Arslan	Jarkko Kari	Dirk Nowotka
Geert Jan Bex	Satoshi Kobayashi	Alexander Okhotin
Béatrice Bouchou	Mojmír Kretínský	Friedrich Otto
Cristian S. Calude	Antonín Kučera	Michael Palis
Ivana Černá	Michal Kunc	Andrei Păun
Christian Choffrut	Joachim Kupke	Mathieu Raffinot
Fabien Coulon	Sylvain Lombardy	Philipp Rohde
Zhe Dang	Wim Martens	Nicolae Santean
Stéphane Demri	Alexandru Mateescu	Sebastian Seibert
Michael Domaratzki	Giancarlo Mauri	Benjamin Steinberg
Horváth Géza	Ian McQuillan	Stijn van Summeren
Peter Habermehl	Koji Nakano	Mikhail V. Volkov
Maia Hoeberechts	Gonzalo Navarro	

Table of Contents

Poster Papers

Automata-Theoretic Techniques for Analyzing Infinite-State Systems*

Oscar H. Ibarra

Department of Computer Science,
University of California,
Santa Barbara, California 93106, USA
ibarra@cs.ucsb.edu

Automata theory tries to answer questions concerning machine models and the languages they define. Classical questions like the relationships between finite/pushdown automata and regular/context-free languages, their closure and decidable properties are standard material in many undergraduate theory courses. New questions that arise from real-world applications, such as in verification, internet/web services, and molecular computing are providing interesting and challenging problems to automata theorists. In this talk, I will present some automata-theoretic and related techniques for analyzing various forms of restricted infinite-state systems in the areas of formal verification, e-services, and membrane systems.

---

* This research was supported in part by NSF Grants IIS-0101134 and CCR02-08595.

M. Domaratzki et al. (Eds.): CIAA 2004, LNCS 3317, p. 1, 2005.

Enumerating Regular Expressions and Their Languages

Jonathan Lee[*] and Jeffrey Shallit[**]

School of Computer Science, University of Waterloo,
Waterloo, ON N2L 3G1, Canada
jwlee@alumni.uwaterloo.ca
shallit@graceland.uwaterloo.ca

Abstract. We discuss enumeration of regular expressions and the distinct languages they represent.

1 Introduction

Regular expressions have been studied for almost fifty years, yet many interesting and challenging problems about them remain unsolved. By a regular expression, we mean a string over the alphabet

$$\Sigma \cup \{+, *, (,), \epsilon, \emptyset\}$$

that represents a regular language. For example, (0+10)*(1+ϵ) represents the language of all strings over $\{0,1\}$ that do not contain two consecutive 1's.

We would like to enumerate valid regular expressions and the distinct languages they represent. Enumeration of regular languages is, generally speaking, a difficult problem. For example, define $G_k(n)$ to be the number of distinct languages accepted by nondeterministic finite automata with n states over a k-letter input alphabet. The following problem, studied by Domaratzki, Kisman, and Shallit [2], seems very difficult:

Find good upper and lower bounds for $G_k(n)$.

The analogous problem for regular expressions, however, is somewhat easier. Strangely enough, it does not seem to have been studied previously. We define $R_k(n)$ to be the number of distinct languages specified by regular expressions of length n over a k-letter alphabet. The "length" of a regular expression can be defined in several different ways [3]:

- *Ordinary length*: total number of symbols, including parentheses, $\emptyset$, ϵ, etc., counted with multiplicity.
  - (0+10)*(1+ϵ) has ordinary length 12

---

[*] Research of this author supported by an NSERC Undergraduate Student Research Award.

[**] Research of this author supported in part by NSERC.

M. Domaratzki et al. (Eds.): CIAA 2004, LNCS 3317, pp. 2–22, 2005.

– *Reverse polish length*: number of symbols in a reverse polish equivalent, including a symbol • for concatenation
– Equivalently, number of nodes in a syntax tree for the expression

- (0+10)*(1+ϵ) in reverse polish would be 010•+*ϵ+•
- This has reverse polish length 10

– *Alphabetic length*: number of symbols from Σ, not including ϵ, $\emptyset$, parens, operators

- (0+10)*(1+ϵ) has alphabetic length 4

2   Valid Regular Expressions

In this section we introduce our basic method by counting the number of valid regular expressions of (ordinary) length n. Let $S_k(n)$ be the number of such expressions over an alphabet Σ of size k. Since a regular expression is defined over the alphabet $\{\epsilon, \emptyset, (,), +, *\} \cup \Sigma$, we immediately get the trivial upper bound $R_k(n) \leq S_k(n) \leq (k+6)^n$. To improve our estimate for $S_k(n)$, it becomes necessary to state more precisely what a valid regular expression is.

There is some ambiguity about the definition of a valid regular expression. For example, is the empty expression valid? How about () or a**? The first two, for example, generate errors in Grail version 2.5 [7].

Surprisingly, very few textbooks, if any, define valid regular expressions properly or formally. For example, using the definition given in Martin [6–p. 86], the expression 00 is not valid, since it is not fully parenthesized. (To be fair, after the definition it is implied that parentheses can be omitted in some cases, but no formal definition of when this can be done is given.)

Probably the best way to define valid regular expressions is with a grammar. We now present a grammar for valid regular expressions:

$$S \rightarrow E_+ \mid E_\bullet \mid G$$
$$E_+ \rightarrow E_+ + F \mid F + F$$
$$F \rightarrow E_\bullet \mid G$$
$$E_\bullet \rightarrow E_\bullet G \mid GG$$
$$G \rightarrow E_* \mid C \mid P$$
$$C \rightarrow \emptyset \mid \epsilon \mid a \quad (a \in \Sigma)$$
$$E_* \rightarrow G *$$
$$P \rightarrow (S)$$

The meaning of the variables is as follows:

– S generates all regular expressions
– E_+ generates all unparenthesized expressions where the last operator was +
– $E_\bullet$ generates all unparenthesized expressions where the last operator was · (implicit concatenation)

- E_* generates all unparenthesized expressions where the last operator was $*$ (Kleene closure)
- C generates all unparenthesized expressions where there was no last operator (i.e., the constants)
- P generates all parenthesized expressions

Here by "parenthesized" we mean there is at least one pair of enclosing parentheses. Note this grammar allows $a * *$ but disallows $()$.

We claim this grammar is unambiguous. Because of this, we can apply the Chomsky-Schützenberger theorem [1], which states that if a language is generated by an unambiguous CFG, then the generating function

$$f(x) = \sum_{i \geq 0} |L \cap \Sigma^i| x^i$$

is algebraic over $\mathbb{Q}(x)$.

So we look at the "commutative image" of this grammar, which replaces each terminal by x, each occurrence of the empty string ϵ by 1, and each occurrence of $|$ by $+$. This gives the following system of equations:

$$S = E_+ + E_\bullet + G$$
$$E_+ = E_+ F x + F^2 x$$
$$F = E_\bullet + G$$
$$E_\bullet = E_\bullet G + G^2$$
$$G = E_* + C + P$$
$$C = (k+2)x \quad (k = |\Sigma|)$$
$$E_* = Gx$$
$$P = Sx^2$$

Now we can use Gröbner bases to find the algebraic equation satisfied by S. It is

$$(x^2 + x^3)S^2 + ((k+3)x^2 + (k+3)x - 1)S + (k+2)x = 0.$$

Solving for S, we get

$$S = \frac{-(k+3)x^2 - (k+3)x + 1 - \sqrt{D}}{2(x^2 + x^3)}.$$

where the discriminant

$$D = (k+1)^2 x^4 + 2(k^2 + 4k + 5)x^3 + (k+1)(k+3)x^2 - 2(k+3)x + 1.$$

We can expand this as a power series to get a generating function enumerating the regular expressions of length n. For example, for $k = 2$, we have

$$S = 4x + 20x^2 + 120x^3 + 716x^4 + 4356x^5 + 26880x^6 + \cdots.$$

(The 20 regular expressions of length 2 are

Table 1. Number of Valid Regular Expressions

$k =$	1	2	3	4
$n = 1$	3	4	5	6
2	12	20	30	42
3	60	120	210	336
4	297	716	1465	2682
5	1509	4356	10375	21666
6	7800	26880	74340	176736
7	40962	168068	538540	1455018
8	218052	1063156	3940280	12080862

  − yz
  − $y*$

where $y, z \in \{\epsilon, \emptyset, \mathsf{a}, \mathsf{b}\}$.)

The number $S_k(n)$ of valid regular expressions of length n with alphabet size k is summarized in Table 1.

The asymptotic growth rate of the coefficients of the generating function for S depends on the reciprocal of the smallest zero of the discriminant D [5]. This smallest zero is, as $k \to \infty$, asymptotically equal to

$$\frac{1}{k} - \frac{6}{k^2} + \frac{42}{k^3} - \frac{1319}{4k^4} + \frac{22463}{8k^5} - \cdots,$$

and its reciprocal is

$$k + 6 - \frac{6}{k} - \frac{167}{4k^2} - \frac{2615}{8k^3} - \cdots.$$

For $k = 1$ this the smallest zero is about .16246250262 and for $k = 2$ it is about .13755127577.

Using Darboux's method, we can prove

Theorem 1. *We have $S_k(n) \sim c_k \alpha_k^n n^{-3/2}$ for some constant c_k, where $\alpha_1 \doteq 6.1552665$ and $\alpha_2 \doteq 7.2700161767$.*

While we have counted valid regular expressions with n symbols, we are still a long way from counting the distinct languages they represent. This is because using our definition, many languages are double-counted. To improve the bound, we can attempt to improve the grammar to weed out evidently uninteresting regular expressions, such as those containing redundant parentheses.

An unambiguous grammar for regular expressions without redundant parentheses is as follows:

$$S \to E_+ \mid E_\bullet \mid E_* \mid C$$
$$E_+ \to E_+ + F \mid F + F$$
$$F \to E_\bullet \mid E_* \mid C$$
$$E_\bullet \to E_\bullet G \mid GG$$
$$G \to (E_+) \mid E_* \mid C$$

$$C \to \emptyset \mid \epsilon \mid a \quad (a \in \Sigma)$$
$$E_* \to (E_+)* \mid (E_\bullet)* \mid E_** \mid C*$$

We can mimic the analysis given for the previous grammar. For $k = 2$, we get the equation $(x^9 + x^6)S^4 + (2x^6 + 5x^5 + x^3)S^3 + (5x^4 + 5x^3 + 5x^2 - x)S^2 + (8x^2 + 5x - 1)S + 4x = 0$ which has the power series solution

$$S = 4 + 20x^2 + 116x^3 + 660x^4 + 3780x^5 + 21844x^6 + \cdots .$$

The discriminant is a polynomial of degree 30, the smallest positive root is .146378001, and the asymptotic growth rate is $O(6.832^n)$.

Maple worksheets for these examples are available at
http://www.cs.uwaterloo.ca/~shallit/papers.html .

Using more complicated grammars, we can dramatically improve these bounds; we do this in Section 5. For now, however, we turn to lower bounds.

3   Lower Bounds

We now turn to lower bounds on $R_k(n)$.

In the unary case ($k = 1$), we can argue as follows: consider any subset of $\{\epsilon, a, a^2, \ldots, a^{t-1}\}$. Such a subset can be denoted by a regular expression of (ordinary) length at most $t(t+1)/2$. Since there are 2^t distinct subsets, this gives a lower bound of $R_1(n) \geq 2^{\sqrt{2n}-1}$. Similarly, when $k \geq 2$, there are k^n distinct strings of length n, so $R_k(n) \geq k^n$.

However, these naive bounds can be improved somewhat using a grammar-based approach.

Consider a regular expression of the form

$$x_1(\epsilon + x_2(\epsilon + x_3(\epsilon + ...)))$$

where the x_i denote nonempty words. Every distinct choice of the x_i specifies a distinct language. Such expressions can be generated by the grammar

$$S \to Y \mid Y(\epsilon + S)$$
$$Y \to aY \mid a, \qquad a \in \Sigma$$

which has the commutative image

$$S = Y + YSx^4$$
$$Y = kxY + kx.$$

The solution to this system is

$$S = \frac{kx}{1 - kx - kx^5}.$$

Once again, the asymptotic behavior of the coefficients of the power series for S depend on the zeros of $1 - kx - kx^5$. The smallest (indeed, the only) real root is, asymptotically as $k \to \infty$, given by

$$\sum_{i \geq 0} \frac{(-1)^i \binom{5i}{i}}{4i+1} k^{-(4i+1)} = \frac{1}{k} - \frac{1}{k^5} + \frac{5}{k^9} - \frac{35}{k^{13}} + \cdots .$$

The reciprocal of this series is

$$\sum_{i \geq 0} \frac{4\binom{5i+5}{i+1}}{5(5i+4)} k^{1-4i} = k + \frac{1}{k^3} - \frac{4}{k^7} + \frac{26}{k^{11}} - \frac{204}{k^{15}} + \frac{1771}{k^{19}} - \cdots .$$

For $k = 1$ the only real root of $1 - kx - kx^5$ is approximately $.754877666$ and for $k = 2$ it is about $.4756527435$. Thus we have

Theorem 2. $R_1(n) = \Omega(1.3247^n)$ and $R_2(n) = \Omega(2.102374^n)$.

We now turn to improving these lower bounds.

4   Better Lower Bounds

4.1   Trie Representations of Finite Languages

We begin by describing how to represent non-empty finite languages not containing ϵ via a trie structure; an example is given Fig. 1.

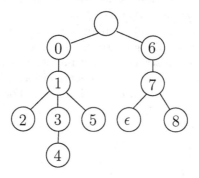

Fig. 1. Trie representation for `01(2+34+5)+6(ϵ+7)`

Algorithm 1 below takes as input a finite non-empty language L not containing ϵ and returns a trie in our desired format. The words in such a language L correspond to the leaf nodes of the trie for L; moreover, the concatenation of labels from the root to a leaf node gives an expression for the word associated with that leaf node. For regular languages L_1 and L_2, we write $L_2^{-1}L_1$ to denote the left quotient of L_1 by L_2; formally

$$L_2^{-1}L_1 = \{x \: : \: \text{there exists } y \in L_2 \text{ such that } yx \in L_1\}.$$

Algorithm 1 CREATE-TRIE(L)

Require: $\epsilon \notin L$, $L \neq \emptyset$
1: create a tree T with an unlabelled root
2: **for all** $a \in \Sigma$ such that $a^{-1}L \neq \emptyset$ **do**
3:     add the subtree returned by CREATE-TRIE-HELP($\{a\}^{-1}L$, a) as a child of the
       root of T
4: **end for**
5: return T

Algorithm 2 CREATE-TRIE-HELP(L, a)

1: create a tree T with a root labelled a
2: **if** $L \neq \{\epsilon\}$ **then** {need to create children}
3:     **for all** $b \in \Sigma$ such that $b^{-1}L \neq \emptyset$ **do**
4:         add the subtree returned by CREATE-TRIE-HELP($\{b\}^{-1}L$, b) as a child of
           the root of T
5:     **end for**
6:     **if** $\epsilon \in L$ **then**
7:         add a node labelled ϵ as a child of the root of T
8:     **end if**
9: **end if**
10: return T

4.2   Star-Free Regular Expressions

We begin with the simple problem of counting the number of regular languages that may be specified by regular expressions of length n.

We develop lower bounds by specifying a context-free grammar that generates regular expressions, factoring out common prefixes in a style similar to Horner's rule. In fact, the grammar is designed so that if r is a regular expression generated by the grammar, then the structure of r mimics that of the trie for $L(r)$ — nodes with a single child correspond to concatenations while nodes with multiple children correspond to concatenations with a union. For notational convenience, we take our alphabet to be $\Sigma = \{a_0, a_1, \ldots, a_{k-1}\}$, where $k \geq 1$ denotes our alphabet size.

$$S \rightarrow Y \mid Z$$
$$E \rightarrow Y \mid (Z) \mid (\epsilon + S)$$
$$Y \rightarrow P_i \text{ for } 0 \leq i < k$$
$$Z \rightarrow P_{n_0} + P_{n_1} + \cdots + P_{n_t} \text{ where } 0 \leq n_0 < n_1 < \cdots < n_t < k \text{ for } t > 0$$
$$P_i \rightarrow a_i \mid a_i E \text{ for } 0 \leq i < k$$

The set of regular languages represented corresponds to all non-empty finite languages over Σ not containing the empty string ϵ. We briefly describe the non-terminals:

S generates all non-empty finite languages not containing ϵ — this corresponds to Algorithm 1.

E generates all non-empty finite languages containing at least one word other than ϵ — this corresponds to line 2 of Algorithm 2.

Y generates all non-empty finite languages (not containing ϵ) whose words all begin with the same letter — this corresponds to line 2 of Algorithm 1 and line 3 of Algorithm 2 when the body of the for loop is executed only once.

Z generates all non-empty finite languages (not containing ϵ) whose words do not all begin with the same letter — this corresponds to line 2 of Algorithm 1 and line 3 of Algorithm 2 when the body of the for loop is executed more than once.

P_i generates all non-empty finite languages (not containing ϵ) whose words all begin with a_i — this corresponds to line 1 of Algorithm 2.

We remark that this grammar is unambiguous and that no regular language is represented more than once; this should be clear from the relationship between regular expressions generated by the grammar and their respective tries.

(Note that it is possible to slightly optimize this grammar in the case of ordinary length to generate expressions such as $0 + 00$ in lieu of $0(\epsilon + 0)$, but as it results in marginal improvements to the lower bound at the cost of greatly complicating the grammar, we do not do so here.)

To obtain bounds, we make use of the following result adapted from Klarner and Woodworth [5].

Theorem 3. *Suppose it is known that the coefficients of an algebraic power series $F(x)$ grow at a rate of $\Omega(\alpha^n)$ and $O(\beta^n)$ for $\alpha < \beta$. Suppose also there is a polynomial $P \in \mathbb{Z}[x,y]$ such that $P(x,F) = 0$ and whose discriminant δ with respect to y has only one root γ in the interval $[1/\beta, 1/\alpha]$. Then modulo some sub-exponential growth rate, the coefficients of $F(x)$ grow asymptotically like $1/\gamma^n$.*

Proof. We may assume that F has a radius of convergence $0 < R < \infty$. Klarner and Woodworth deduce that R is a singularity of F, so it suffices to show that γ is the smallest positive singularity of F; that is, R. Suppose there exists a smallest positive singularity $\gamma' < \gamma$. By assumption, $\gamma' < 1/\beta$ so $1/\gamma' > \beta$. However, γ' determines the radius of convergence of F, contradicting the fact that the coefficient growth is $O(\beta^n)$. It remains to show that γ is indeed a singularity. Since the coefficient growth is $\Omega(\alpha^n)$, there must be a singularity less than $1/\alpha$. By assumption, this must be γ. $\blacksquare$

Table 2 lists the lower bounds obtained through this grammar.

Remark 1. By virtue of Theorem 3, these lower bounds were obtained by bootstrapping off the trivial bounds of $\Omega(k^n)$, $\Omega(k^{n/2})$ and $\Omega(k^n)$ for the ordinary, reverse polish and alphabetic length cases, respectively.

Asymptotic Analysis for Alphabetic Length. We first state a version of the Lagrange implicit function theorem as a simplification of [4–Theorem 1.2.4]. If $f(t)$ is a power series in t, we write $[t^n]f(t)$ to denote the coefficient of t^n in $f(t)$.

Table 2. Lower bounds for $R_k(n)$ with respect to length measure and alphabet size

	ordinary	reverse polish	alphabetic
1	$\Omega(1.3247^n)$	$\Omega(1.2720^n)$	$\Omega(2^n)$
2	$\Omega(2.5676^n)$	$\Omega(2.1532^n)$	$\Omega(6.8284^n)$
3	$\Omega(3.6130^n)$	$\Omega(2.7176^n)$	$\Omega(11.1961^n)$
4	$\Omega(4.6260^n)$	$\Omega(3.1806^n)$	$\Omega(15.5307^n)$
5	$\Omega(5.6264^n)$	$\Omega(3.5834^n)$	$\Omega(19.8548^n)$
6	$\Omega(6.6215^n)$	$\Omega(3.9451^n)$	$\Omega(24.1740^n)$

Lemma 1. *Let R be a commutative ring of characteristic 0 and take $\phi(\lambda) \in R[[\lambda]]$ such that $[\lambda^0]\phi$ is invertible. Then there exists a unique formal power series $w(t) \in R[[t]]$ such that $[t^0]w = 0$ and $w = t\phi(w)$. For $n \geq 1$,*

$$[t^n]w(t) = \frac{1}{n}[\lambda^{n-1}]\phi^n(\lambda).$$

Due to the simplicity of alphabetic length, the problem of enumerating regular languages in this case may be interpreted as doing so for rooted k-ary trees, where each internal node is marked with one of two possible colours. We thus investigate how our lower bound varies with k.

More specifically, consider a regular expression r generated by the grammar from the previous section and its associated trie. Colour each node with a child labelled ϵ black and all other nodes white. After deleting all nodes marked ϵ, call the resultant tree $T(r)$. This operation is reversible, and shows that we may put the expressions of alphabetic length n in correspondence with the k-ary rooted trees with $n + 1$ vertices where every non-root internal node may assume one of two colours. In order to estimate the latter, we first prove a basic result:

Lemma 2. *There are $\frac{1}{n}\binom{kn}{n-1}$ k-ary trees of n nodes. Moreover, the expected number of leaf nodes among k-ary trees of n nodes is asymptotic to $(1 - 1/k)^k n$ as $n \to \infty$.*

Proof. Fix $k \geq 1$. For $n \geq 1$, let a_n denote the number of k-ary rooted trees with n vertices and consider the generating series:

$$f(t) = \sum_{n \geq 1} a_n t^n.$$

By the recursive structure of k-ary trees, we have the recurrence:

$$f(t) = t(1 + f(t))^k.$$

Thus, by the Lagrange implicit function theorem, we have

$$a_n = [t^n]f(t)$$
$$= \frac{1}{n}[\lambda^{n-1}](1 + \lambda)^{kn}$$
$$= \frac{1}{n}\binom{kn}{n-1}.$$

We now calculate the number of leaf nodes among all k-ary rooted trees with n vertices. Let $b_{n,m}$ denote the number of k-ary rooted trees with n vertices and m leaf nodes and c_n the number of leaf nodes among all k-ary rooted trees with n vertices. Consider the bivariate generating series:

$$g(s,t) = \sum_{n,m \geq 1} b_{n,m} s^m t^n \,.$$

By the recursive structure of k-ary trees, we have the recurrence:

$$g(s,t) = t(s - 1 + (1 + g(s,t))^k)\,.$$

The Lagrange implicit function theorem once again yields

$$
\begin{aligned}
c_n &= \frac{\partial}{\partial s}[t^n]g(s,t)\Big|_{s=1} \\
&= \frac{\partial}{\partial s}\frac{1}{n}[\lambda^{n-1}](s - 1 + (1 + g(s,t))^k)^n\Big|_{s=1} \\
&= \frac{1}{n}[\lambda^{n-1}]\frac{\partial}{\partial s}(s - 1 + (1 + \lambda)^k)^n\Big|_{s=1} \\
&= [\lambda^{n-1}](1 + \lambda)^{k(n-1)} \\
&= \binom{k(n-1)}{n-1}.
\end{aligned}
$$

Thus, the expected number of leaf nodes among n-node trees is

$$
\begin{aligned}
\frac{c_n}{a_n} &= \frac{n\binom{k(n-1)}{n-1}}{\binom{kn}{n-1}} \\
&= \frac{n(kn - n + 1)(kn - n) \cdots (kn - k - n + 2)}{(kn)(kn - 1) \cdots (kn - k + 1)} \\
&\sim n\left(\frac{k - 1}{k}\right)^k \quad \text{as } n \to \infty \text{ for fixed } k. \qquad \blacksquare
\end{aligned}
$$

We wish to find a bound on the expected number of subsets of non-root internal nodes among all k-ary rooted trees with n nodes, where a subset corresponds to those nodes marked black. Fix $k \geq 2$. Since the map $x \mapsto 2^x$ is convex, for every $\varepsilon > 0$ and sufficiently large n, Jensen's inequality (e.g., [8–Thm. 3.3]) applied to the lemma above implies the following lower bound on the number of subsets:

$$2^{(1 - (1 - 1/k)^k - \varepsilon)n}\,.$$

Since $-(1 - 1/k)^k > -1/e$ for $k \geq 1$, we may choose $\varepsilon > 0$ such that

$$-(1 - 1/k)^k - \varepsilon > -1/e\,.$$

This yields a lower bound of

$$2^{(1 - 1/e)n}\,.$$

Assuming $k \geq 2$, we now estimate $\binom{kn}{n-1}$. By Stirling's formula, we have that as $n \to \infty$,

$$
\binom{kn}{n-1} = \frac{(kn)!}{n! \, ((k-1)n)!} \frac{n}{(k-1)n + 1}
$$

$$
\sim \frac{\sqrt{2\pi kn} \, (kn/e)^{kn}}{\sqrt{2\pi n} \, (n/e)^n \, \sqrt{2\pi(k-1)n} \, ((k-1)n/e)^{(k-1)n}} \frac{n}{(k-1)n + 1}
$$

$$
= \Theta \left(\left(\frac{k^k}{(k-1)^{k-1}} \right)^n \right).
$$

Putting our two bounds together, we have the following lower bound as $n \to \infty$ on the number of star-free regular expressions of alphabetic length n:

$$
\Omega \left(\left(\frac{2^{(1-1/e)} k^k}{(k-1)^{k-1}} \right)^n \right) \quad \text{where the implied constants depend only on } k.
$$

4.3   General Regular Languages

We now turn our attention to enumerating regular languages in general; that is, we allow for regular expressions with Kleene stars.

Our grammars for this section are based on the those for the star-free cases. Due to the difficulty of avoiding specifying duplicate regular languages, we settle for a "small" subset of regular languages. For simplicity, we only consider taking the Kleene star closure of singleton alphabet symbols.

Recall the trie representation of a star-free regular expression written in our common prefix notation. With this representation, we may mark nodes with stars while satisfying the following conditions:

- each starred symbol must have a non-starred parent other than the root;
- a starred symbol may not have a sibling or an identically-labelled parent (disregarding the lack of star) with its own sibling; and
- a starred symbol may not have an identically-labelled child (disregarding the lack of star).

The first condition eliminates duplicates such as

$$
0*11*0*1*0* \leftrightarrow 0*1*0*11*0*;
$$

the second eliminates those such as

$$
01* \leftrightarrow 0(\epsilon + 11*) \text{ and } 0(1 + 2*1) \leftrightarrow 02*1
$$

and the third eliminates those such as

$$
0*0 \leftrightarrow 00*.
$$

In this manner, we end up with starred tries such as in Fig. 2.

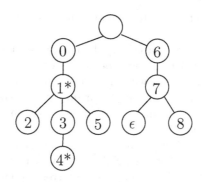

Fig. 2. Trie representation for `01*(2+34*+5)+6(ε+7)`

Algorithm 3 CREATE-STAR-TRIE(L)

Require: $\epsilon \notin L$, $L \neq \emptyset$
1: create a tree T with an unlabelled root
2: **for all** $a \in \Sigma$ such that $\{a\}^{-1}L \neq \emptyset$ **do**
3:      add the subtree returned by CREATE-STAR-TRIE-HELP($\{a\}^{-1}L, a$) as a child of the root of T
4: **end for**
5: return T

Algorithm 4 CREATE-STAR-TRIE-HELP(L, a)

1: create a tree T with a root labelled a
2: **if** exists $b \in \Sigma$ such that $\{b^n\}^{-1}L \cap (\epsilon + (\Sigma \setminus \{b\})\Sigma^*) \neq \emptyset$ for all $n \geq 0$ **then** {need a starred child labelled b^*}
3:      attach a child labelled b^* to the root of T
4:      **if** $L \neq b^*$ **then** {starred child will be an internal node}
5:          **for all** $c \in \Sigma \setminus \{b\}$ such that $\{c\}^{-1}L \neq \emptyset$ **do** {determine children}
6:              add the subtree returned by CREATE-STAR-TRIE-HELP($\{c\}^{-1}L, c$) as a child of the node labelled b^*
7:          **end for**
8:          **if** $b \in L$ **then**
9:              add a node labelled ϵ as a child of the node labelled b^*
10:          **end if**
11:      **end if**
12: **else**
13:      **for all** $b \in \Sigma$ such that $\{b\}^{-1}L \neq \emptyset$ **do** {need an unstarred child labelled b}
14:          add the subtree returned by CREATE-STAR-TRIE-HELP($\{b\}^{-1}L, b$) as a child of the root of T
15:      **end for**
16: **end if**
17: **if** $\epsilon \in L$ and the root of T has at least one unstarred child **then**
18:      add a node labelled ϵ as a child of the root of T
19: **end if**
20: return T

Algorithm 3 illustrates how to recreate such a starred trie from the language it specifies.

Let T be any starred trie satisfying the conditions above. Then T represents a regular expression, which in turn specifies a certain language. We now show that when the algorithm is run with that language as input, it returns the trie T by arguing that at each step of the algorithm when a particular node (matched with language L if the root and aL otherwise) is being processed, the correct children are determined.

We first consider children of the root. By the original trie construction (for finite languages without ϵ), no such children may be labelled ϵ. Thus, by the first star condition, the only children may be unstarred alphabet symbols. Thus, line 2 of Algorithm 3 suffices to find all children of the root correctly.

Now consider a non-root internal node, say labelled a. By the third star condition, a starred node may not have a child labelled with the same alphabet symbol, so if a has a child labelled b^*, then

$$\{b^n\}^{-1}L \cap (\epsilon + (\Sigma \setminus \{b\})\Sigma^*) \text{ is non-empty for all } n \geq 0.$$

Conversely, by the second condition, a starred node may not have an identically-labelled parent that has ϵ as a sibling, so if

$$\{b^n\}^{-1}L \cap (\epsilon + (\Sigma \setminus \{b\})\Sigma^*)$$

is non-empty for all $n \geq 0$, then a must have a child labelled b^*. By the second star condition, a starred node may not have siblings, so the algorithm need not check for other children once a starred child is found. This shows that line 2 of Algorithm 4 correctly finds all children in the case of a starred child.

Assuming a has a starred child b^*, then by the third condition, line 5 of Algorithm 4 correctly determines all children of b^*.

Otherwise, a has no starred children, and line 13 of Algorithm 4 suffices to find all children.

We give a grammar that generates expressions meeting these conditions. As before, we take our alphabet to be $\{a_0, a_1, \ldots, a_{k-1}\}$.

$$S \to Y \mid Z$$

$$E \to Y \mid (Z) \mid (\epsilon + Y') \mid (\epsilon + Z)$$
$$E_i \to Y_i \mid (Z_i) \mid (\epsilon + Y_i') \mid (\epsilon + Z_i) \text{ for } 0 \leq i < k$$

$$Y \to P_i \text{ for } 0 \leq i < k$$
$$Y' \to P_i' \text{ for } 0 \leq i < k$$
$$Y_i \to P_j \text{ for } 0 \leq i, j < k \text{ and } i \neq j$$
$$Y_i' \to P_j' \text{ for } 0 \leq i, j < k \text{ and } i \neq j$$

$$Z \to P_{n_0}' + P_{n_1}' + \cdots + P_{n_t}' \text{ where } 0 \leq n_0 < n_1 < \cdots < n_t < k \text{ for } t > 0$$
$$Z_i \to P_{n_0}' + P_{n_1}' + \cdots + P_{n_t}' \text{ as above, but with } n_j \neq i \text{ for all } 0 \leq j \leq t$$

$$P_i \to a_i \mid a_i E \mid a_i a_j^* \mid a_i a_j^* E_j \text{ for } 0 \le i, j < k$$
$$P_i' \to a_i \mid a_i E \mid a_i a_j^* \mid a_i a_j^* E_j \text{ for } 0 \le i, j < k \text{ and } i \ne j$$

We describe the non-terminals.

S generates all expressions — this corresponds to Algorithm 3.

E, E_i generate expressions that may be concatenated to non-starred and starred alphabet symbols, respectively. The non-terminal E corresponds to lines 2 and 13 while E_i corresponds to line 5 of Algorithm 4. These act the same as S except for the introduction of parentheses to take precedence into account and restriction that no prefixes of the form $\epsilon + aa^*$ are generated, used to implement the second condition.

Additionally, E_i has the restriction that its first alphabet symbol produced may not be a_i — this is used to implement the third condition.

Y, Y', Y_i, Y_i' generate expressions whose prefix is an alphabet symbol. As a whole, these non-terminals correspond to Algorithm 4, and may be considered degenerate cases of Z and Z_i; that is, trivial unions.

The tick-mark signifies that expressions of the form aa^* for $a \in \Sigma$ are disallowed, used to implement the second condition. The subscripted i signifies that the initial alphabet symbol may not be a_i, used to implement the third condition.

Z, Z_i generate non-trivial unions of expressions beginning with distinct alphabet symbols — Z corresponds to line 2 of Algorithm 3 and line 13 of Algorithm 4, while Z_i corresponds to line 5 of Algorithm 4.

The subscripted i signifies that none of initial alphabet symbols may be a_i, used to implement the third condition.

P_i, P_i' generate expressions beginning with the specified alphabet symbol a_i. They correspond to line 1 of Algorithm 4.

The tick-mark signifies that expressions may not have the prefix $a_i a_i^*$, used to implement the second condition.

Since the algorithm correctly returns a trie when run on the language represented by the trie, the correspondence between the algorithm and the grammar gives us the following result.

Theorem 4. *The grammar above is unambiguous and the generated regular expressions represent distinct regular languages.*

Table 3. Improved lower bounds for $R_k(n)$ with respect to length measure and alphabet size

	ordinary	reverse polish	alphabetic
1	$\Omega(1.3247^n)$	$\Omega(1.2720^n)$	$\Omega(2^n)$
2	$\Omega(2.7799^n)$	$\Omega(2.2140^n)$	$\Omega(7.4140^n)$
3	$\Omega(3.9582^n)$	$\Omega(2.8065^n)$	$\Omega(12.5367^n)$
4	$\Omega(5.0629^n)$	$\Omega(3.2860^n)$	$\Omega(17.6695^n)$
5	$\Omega(6.1319^n)$	$\Omega(3.6998^n)$	$\Omega(22.8082^n)$
6	$\Omega(7.1804^n)$	$\Omega(4.0693^n)$	$\Omega(27.9500^n)$

Table 3 lists the improved lower bounds for $R_k(n)$.

Remark 2. These lower bounds were obtained via Theorem 3, boot-strapping off the bounds in Table 2.

5   Better Upper Bounds

Turning our attention back to upper bounds, we develop grammars for regular expressions such that every regular language is represented by at least one shortest regular expression generated by the grammar, where a regular expression R of length n is said to be shortest if there are no expressions R' of length less than n with $L(R) = L(R')$.

In increasing order of precedence, the operations on regular languages are union, concatenation and Kleene-star closure, which we denote by the symbols $+$, $\bullet$ and $*$, respectively. In our grammars for this section, we will denote these by the non-terminals A, B and C, respectively.

As $+$ and $\bullet$ are associative, we will consider them to be variadic operators taking at least 2 arguments and impose the condition that in any parse tree (see Fig. 3), neither of them are permitted to have themselves as children.

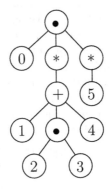

Fig. 3. Parse tree for 0(1+23+4)*5*

Taking into mind associativity, we start with the following unambiguous grammar as our basis for regular expressions — note that this is different from the grammar given previously.

$S \rightarrow A \mid B \mid C \mid D \mid \epsilon \mid \emptyset$ (start symbol)

$A \rightarrow A_0 + A_0 \mid A_0 + A$ (union)
$A_0 \rightarrow B \mid C \mid D \mid \epsilon$

$B \rightarrow B_0 B_0 \mid B_0 B$ (concatenation)
$B_0 \rightarrow (A) \mid C \mid D$

$C \rightarrow (A)^* \mid (B)^* \mid D^*$ (Kleene-star closure)

$D \rightarrow a$ for $a \in \Sigma$ (alphabet symbols) .

We claim that each regular language has at least one shortest regular expression that is generated by the grammar; our immediate aim is to modify the grammar to generate fewer regular expressions per regular language while still generating at least one shortest one.

There are a few possible optimizations for removing duplicate regular languages.

- In all cases, by the commutativity of $+$ (viewed as a variadic operator), we may impose the condition that its operands appear in the following order:
  1. the symbol ϵ;
  2. starred expressions (those generated by C);
  3. concatenated expressions (those generated by B); then
  4. singleton alphabet symbols (those generated by D).
  Also, given that for languages $L_1, L_2, \ldots, L_n$ we have

$$(L_1 + L_2 + \cdots L_n)^* = (L_1^* + L_2^* + \cdots + L_n^*),$$

  we impose the restriction that whenever $+$ is an operand of $*$, none of its own operands may be $*$ or ϵ. Otherwise, at most one operand may be ϵ, provided none of the other operands are $*$. These conditions prevent expressions such as $(a^*)^*$, $(\epsilon + a)^*$ and $\epsilon + a^*$ when a^* will suffice.
  We implement these two conditions by modifying the "A"-productions to:

$$A \rightarrow \epsilon + A_B \mid C + A_C \mid B + A_B \mid D + A_D \quad \text{(union)}$$
$$A' \rightarrow B + A_B \mid D + A_D$$
$$A_C \rightarrow C \mid C + A_C \mid A_B$$
$$A_B \rightarrow B \mid B + A_D \mid A_D$$
$$A_D \rightarrow D \mid D + A_D.$$

In addition, we modify the "C"-production to:

$$C \rightarrow (A')^* \mid (B)^* \mid D^* \quad \text{(Kleene-star closure)}.$$

- In the unary cases, by the commutativity of $\bullet$ (viewed as a variadic operator), we may impose a similar condition as for $+$; namely, that its operands appear in the following order:
  1. starred expressions (those generated by C);
  2. united expressions (those generated by A); then
  3. single alphabet symbols (those generated by D).
  We also impose the condition that at most one such operand may be a starred expression. For if we have an operand of the form a^* for $a \in \Sigma$, all other starred expressions are redundant. Otherwise, due to precedence, we may assume we have operands of the form (r_1) and (r_2) for regular expressions r_1 and r_2, so with respect to ordinary length,

$$|(r_1 + r_2)^*| = |(r_1)^*(r_2)^*| - 2.$$

Note that in the alphabetic and reverse polish length cases, this condition is implied by the one we will state next.

We implement these conditions by modifying the "B"-productions to:

$$B \to CB_A \mid (A)B_A \mid DB_D \qquad \text{(concatenation)}$$
$$B_A \to (A) \mid (A)B_A \mid B_D$$
$$B_D \to D \mid DB_D.$$

- In the alphabetic and reverse polish measure of length cases, we impose the restriction that no two adjacent operands of •, the concatenation operator, are starred expressions. For if r_1, r_2 denote regular expressions, then $r_1^* r_2^* = (r_1 + r_2)^*$. Furthermore, with respect to alphabetic length,

$$|(r_1 + r_2)^*| = |r_1^* r_2^*|;$$

and with respect to reverse polish length,

$$|(r_1 + r_2)^*| = |r_1^* r_2^*| - 1.$$

We implement these conditions by modifying the "B"-productions to:

$$B = (A)B_0 \mid CB_1 \mid DB_0 \qquad \text{(concatenation)}$$
$$B_0 = (A) \mid C \mid D \mid (A)B_0 \mid CB_1 \mid DB_0$$
$$B_1 = (A) \mid D \mid AB_0 \mid DB_0.$$

With these enhancements, we obtain improved upper bounds on $R_k(n)$, as listed in Table 4.

Remark 3. In the case of reverse polish length, the least positive root was less than $1/(k+4)$, meaning it could be safely ignored by Theorem 3. In the ordinary unary case, the bound was boot-strapped from the bound obtained from relaxing the operand ordering of $+$; in the ordinary non-unary cases, the restriction disallowing ϵ and starred expressions to be siblings was dropped due to apparent computational infeasibility.

By discarding the productions for the non-terminal C altogether, we obtain upper bounds for the star-free analogue of $R_k(n)$, as shown in Table 5.

Table 4. Improved upper bounds for $R_k(n)$ with respect to length measure and alphabet size

	ordinary	reverse polish	alphabetic
1	$O(2.9090^n)$	$O(2.7037^n)$	$O(21.7527^n)$
2	$O(4.2198^n)$	$O(3.9675^n)$	$O(62.9522^n)$
3	$O(5.3182^n)$	$O(4.6899^n)$	$O(94.4282^n)$
4	$O(6.4068^n)$	$O(5.2957^n)$	$O(125.9043^n)$
5	$O(7.4736^n)$	$O(5.8276^n)$	$O(157.3804^n)$
6	$O(8.5261^n)$	$O(6.3074^n)$	$O(188.8564^n)$

Table 5. Improved upper bounds for star-free $R_k(n)$ with respect to length measure and alphabet size

	ordinary	reverse polish	alphabetic
1	$O(2.4702^n)$	$O(2.4495^n)$	$O(14.6032^n)$
2	$O(3.5051^n)$	$O(3.3096^n)$	$O(29.2063^n)$
3	$O(4.5681^n)$	$O(3.9837^n)$	$O(43.8095^n)$
4	$O(5.6208^n)$	$O(4.5579^n)$	$O(58.4126^n)$
5	$O(6.6629^n)$	$O(5.0670^n)$	$O(73.0158^n)$
6	$O(7.6969^n)$	$O(5.5292^n)$	$O(87.6189^n)$

Remark 4. For the unary reverse polish and alphabetic length cases, it can be shown directly that the lower bounds given in Table 2 are indeed upper bounds as well.

6   Exact Enumerations

Tables 6 to 11 give exact numbers for the number of regular languages representable by a regular expression of length n, but not by any of length less than n.

Table 6. Star-free ordinary cases

	1	2	3	4
1	3	4	5	6
2	1	4	9	16
3	2	11	33	74
4	3	28	117	336
5	3	63	391	1474
6	5	156	1350	6560
7	5	358	4546	28861
8	8	888	15753	128720
9	9	2194	55053	578033
10	14	5665	196185	

Table 7. Star-free reverse polish cases

	1	2	3	4
1	3	4	5	6
3	2	7	15	26
5	3	25	85	202
7	5	109	589	1917
9	9	514	4512	20251
11	14	2641	37477	
13	24	14354	328718	
15	41	81325	231152	
17	71	475936		
19	118			

Table 8. Star-free alphabetic cases

	1	2	3	4
0	2	2	2	2
1	2	4	6	8
2	4	24	60	112
3	8	182	806	2164
4	16	1652	13182	51008
5	32	16854	242070	1346924
6	64	186114		

Table 9. General ordinary cases

	1	2	3	4
1	3	4	5	6
2	2	6	12	20
3	3	17	48	102
4	4	48	192	520
5	5	134	760	2628
6	9	397	3090	13482
7	12	1151	12442	68747
8	17	3442	51044	354500
9	25	10527	211812	
10	33	32731	891228	

Table 10. General reverse polish cases

	1	2	3	4
1	3	4	5	6
2	1	2	3	4
3	2	7	15	26
4	2	13	33	62
5	3	32	106	244
6	4	90	361	920
7	6	189	1012	3133
8	7	580	3859	13529
9	11	1347	11655	48388
10	15	3978	43431	208634

We explain how these numbers were obtained. Using the upper bound grammars described previously, a dynamic programming approach was taken to produce (in order of increasing regular expression size) the regular expressions generated by each non-terminal. To account for duplicates, each regular expression was transformed into a DFA, minimized and relabelled via a breadth-first search to produce a canonical representation. Using these representations as hashes, any regular expression matching a previous one generated by the same non-terminal was simply ignored.

Table 11. General alphabetic cases

	1	2	3	4
0	2	2	2	2
1	3	6	9	12
2	6	56	150	288
3	14	612	3232	9312
4	30	7923	82614	357911
5	72	114554		
6	155	1768133		
7	343			
8	731			
9	1600			
10	3407			

A   Commutative Images

We provide the commutative images for the grammars described. We do not explicitly provide images for the star-free cases, as they may be obtained from those below by simply ignoring the images of sentential forms containing a star.

We also set one of $\delta_o, \delta_r, \delta_a$ to 1, depending on whether the ordinary, reverse polish or alphabetic case is being considered, respectively — all others are set to 0. As usual, k denotes the alphabet size.

A.1   Lower Bounds

$$S = Y + Z$$
$$E = Y + Zx^{2\delta_o} + Y'x^{4\delta_o+2\delta_r} + Zx^{4\delta_o+2\delta_r}$$
$$E_N = Y_N + Z_N x^{2\delta_o} + Y'_N x^{4\delta_o+2\delta_r} + Z_N x^{4\delta_o+2\delta_r}$$
$$Y = kP_N$$
$$Y' = kP'_N$$
$$Y_N = (k-1)P_N$$
$$Y'_N = (k-1)P'_N$$
$$Z = \sum_{i=2}^{k} \binom{k}{i} P'^i_N x^{(\delta_o+\delta_r)(i-1)}$$
$$Z_N = \sum_{i=2}^{k-1} \binom{k-1}{i} P'^i_N x^{(\delta_o+\delta_r)(i-1)}$$
$$P_N = x + Ex^{1+\delta_r} + kx^{2+\delta_o+2\delta_r} + kE_N x^{2+\delta_o+3\delta_r}$$
$$P'_N = x + Ex^{1+\delta_r} + (k-1)x^{2+\delta_o+2\delta_r} + (k-1)E_N x^{2+\delta_o+3\delta_r} \, .$$

A.2   Upper Bounds

$$S = A + B + C + D + 2(\delta_o + \delta_r)x \qquad \text{(start symbol)}$$
$$A = A_B x^{2(\delta_o + \delta_r)} + CA_C x^{\delta_o + \delta_r} + BA_B x^{\delta_o + \delta_r} + DA_D x^{\delta_o + \delta_r} \qquad \text{(union)}$$
$$A' = BA_B x^{\delta_o + \delta_r} + DA_D x^{\delta_o + \delta_r}$$
$$A_C = C + CA_C x^{\delta_o + \delta_r} + A_B$$
$$A_B = B + BA_D x^{\delta_o + \delta_r} + A_D$$
$$A_D = D + DA_D x^{\delta_o + \delta_r}$$
$$C = A' x^{3\delta_o + \delta_r} + B x^{3\delta_o + \delta_r} + D x^{\delta_o + \delta_r} \qquad \text{(Kleene-star closure)}$$
$$D = kx \qquad \text{(alphabet symbols)}$$

In the unary cases:

$$B = CB_A x^{\delta_r} + AB_A x^{2\delta_o + \delta_r} + DB_D x^{\delta_r} \qquad \text{(concatenation)}$$
$$B_A = Ax^{2\delta_o} + AB_A x^{2\delta_o + \delta_r} + B_D$$
$$B_D = D + DB_D x^{\delta_r}$$

In the ordinary, non-unary cases:

$$B = AB_0 x^2 + CB_0 + DB_0 \qquad \text{(concatenation)}$$
$$B_0 = Ax^2 + C + D + AB_0 x^2 + CB_0 + DB_0$$

In the non-ordinary, non-unary cases:

$$B = AB_0 x^{\delta_r} + CB_1 + DB_0 \qquad \text{(concatenation)}$$
$$B_0 = A + C + D + AB_0 x^{\delta_r} + CB_1 x^{\delta_r} + DB_0 x^{\delta_r}$$
$$B_1 = A + D + AB_0 x^{\delta_r} + DB_0 x^{\delta_r}$$

References

1. N. Chomsky and M. P. Schützenberger. The algebraic theory of context-free languages. In P. Braffort and D. Hirschberg, editors, *Computer Programming and Formal Systems*, pp. 118–161. North Holland, Amsterdam, 1963.
2. M. Domaratzki, D. Kisman, and J. Shallit. On the number of distinct languages accepted by finite automata with n states. *J. Automata, Languages, and Combinatorics* **7** (2002), 469–486.
3. K. Ellul, B. Krawetz, J. Shallit, and M.-w. Wang. Regular expressions: new results and open problems. To appear, *J. Autom. Lang. Combin.*, 2003.
4. I. P. Goulden and D. M. Jackson. *Combinatorial Enumeration*. Wiley, 1983.
5. D. A. Klarner and P. Woodworth. Asymptotics for coefficients of algebraic functions. *Aequationes Math.* **23** (1981), 236–241.
6. J. C. Martin. *Introduction to Languages and the Theory of Computation*. McGraw-Hill, 3rd edition, 2003.
7. D. Raymond and D. Wood. *Grail*: a C++ library for automata and expressions. *J. Symbolic Comput.* **17** (1994), 341–350.
8. W. Rudin. *Real and Complex Analysis*. McGraw-Hill, 1966.

A General Weighted Grammar Library

Cyril Allauzen[1], Mehryar Mohri[2], and Brian Roark[3,*]

[1] AT&T Labs – Research, 180 Park Avenue, Florham Park, NJ 07932-0971
allauzen@research.att.com
[2] Department of Computer Science, Courant Institute of Mathematical Sciences,
New York University, 719 Broadway, New York, NY 10003
mohri@cs.nyu.edu
[3] Center for Spoken Language Understanding,
OGI School of Science & Engineering, Oregon Health & Science University,
20000 NW Walker Road, Beaverton, Oregon 97006
roark@cslu.ogi.edu

Abstract. We present a general weighted grammar software library, the *GRM Library*, that can be used in a variety of applications in text, speech, and biosequence processing. The underlying algorithms were designed to support a wide variety of semirings and the representation and use of very large grammars and automata of several hundred million rules or transitions. We describe several algorithms and utilities of this library and point out in each case their application to several text and speech processing tasks.

1   Introduction

The statistical methods used in text and speech processing [19] or in bioinformatics [10] require the representation and use of models that are given as weighted automata either directly or as a result of the approximation and compilation of more powerful grammars such as probabilistic context-free grammars. In all cases, the weights play a crucial role in their definition and use, in particular because they can be used to rank alternative sequences.

This constituted our original motivation for the creation of a general *weighted* grammar library and the design of essential algorithms for creating, modifying, compiling, and approximating large weighted statistical or rule-based grammars. The algorithms of our software library, *GRM Library*, were designed to support a wide variety of semirings, thus weight sets. While keeping a high degree of generality, the algorithms were also designed to be very efficient to support the representation and use of grammars and automata of several hundred million rules or transitions. The representations and functions of a general weighted-transducer library (the FSM library [18]), served as the basis for the design of the GRM library.

---

* Much of this work was done while the last two authors were affiliated with AT&T Labs – Research.

M. Domaratzki et al. (Eds.): CIAA 2004, LNCS 3317, pp. 23–34, 2005.

Another motivation for the design of the GRM library was the need for general text and automata processing algorithms, which, in many cases, constitute the first step of the creation of a statistical grammar. An example is the requirement to compute from the input, the counts of some fixed sequences to create statistical language models. When the input is not just text, but a collection of weighted automata output by a speech recognizer or an information extraction system, novel algorithms and utilities are needed.

In the following, we describe several algorithms and utilities of the GRM library and point out in each case their application to several text and speech processing tasks. Some of the algorithms and utilities of an older version of this library, e.g., the algorithms and utilities for the compilation of weighted context-dependent rules, were presented elsewhere [16]. Here we describe three categories of algorithms and utilities of the library: local grammar and text processing utilities, context-free grammar compilation and approximation, and statistical language modeling algorithms and tools.

2   Design

The core foundation of the GRM library is the FSM library [18]. Both libraries are implemented in C and share the same data representations, the same binary file format and the same command-line interface style. In the FSM library, the memory representation of a weighted automaton or transducer is determined by the use of an FSM class that defines methods for accessing and modifying it. The efficient implementation of several algorithms required the definition of new FSM classes in the GRM library: the *edit*, *replace* and *failure* classes. The latter will be described in this article, the reader can refer to the documentation for the other classes.

3   Local Grammars and Text Processing

The GRM library includes several utilities for text processing. This section briefly reviews the relevant utilities.

3.1   Failure Transitions

There exists a general technique for representing the transitions of automata in an implicit manner, which can lead to substantial savings in space. The method is based on the use of *failure transitions*. A failure transition is a specific type of transitions with the semantic of 'otherwise': it is taken when no regular transition with the desired input label is found. Failure transitions were popularized by [1] and are used to represent local grammars (see section 3.2) and backoff language models (see section 5.3).

The use of failure transitions is made possible in the GRM library through a dedicated FSM class, the *failure class*. The utility grmfailure can convert a regular FSM representation to a failure class representation by interpreting transitions labeled with the symbol phi specified by the option -p as failure transitions:

```
grmfailure -p phi A.fsm > A.failure.fsm
```

3.2   Local Grammars

Algorithm. Let A be a deterministic finite automaton and let $L(A)$ be the regular language accepted by A. An algorithm constructing a compact representation of the deterministic automaton representing $\Sigma^*L(A)$ using failure transitions was given by [15]. This algorithm can be seen as an extension to the case of an arbitrary deterministic automaton A of the classical algorithms of [13, 1] which were designed for a string or a tree. When A is a tree, its complexity coincides with that of [1]: it is linear in the sum of the lengths of the strings accepted by A.

Utility. The algorithm of [15] was implemented in the GRM Library. The utility grmlocalgrammar takes as input a deterministic finite automaton A and returns a deterministic finite automaton recognizing $\Sigma^*L(A)$ represented with failure transitions. The symbol used to label the failure transitions can be specified through the option -p:

```
grmlocalgrammar -p phi A.fsm > sigma-star.A.fsm
```

Examples and Applications. A deterministic finite automaton A is given by Figure 1(a) and the corresponding automaton recognizing $\Sigma^*L(A)$ is given by Figure 1(b), the failure transitions being labeled with ϕ. The main applications of local grammars are string-matching [1, 15] and disambiguation as a first step before part-of-speech tagging or parsing [14].

3.3   Weighted Suffix Automata

Algorithms. The *suffix automaton* of a string u is the minimal deterministic finite automaton recognizing the set of suffixes of u [5, 8]. Its size is linear in

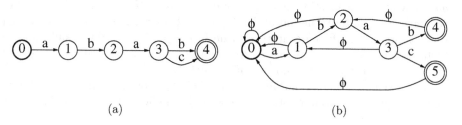

(a)   (b)

Fig. 1. (a) A deterministic finite automaton A and (b) a deterministic automaton recognizing $\Sigma^*L(A)$ where transitions labeled with ϕ are failure transitions

the length of u, n. More precisely, its number of states is between n and $2n - 1$ and its number of transitions between $n + 1$ and $3n - 2$. This automaton can be obtained by minimizing the suffix trie of u. A crucial advantage of suffix automata is that, unlike suffix trees, they do not require the use of 'compact' transitions (transitions labeled with strings) for the size to be linear in $|u|$. In [8], the notion of *weighted suffix automaton* was introduced. It is defined over the tropical semiring and has the same topology as the suffix automaton. Let $SA(u)$ be the weighted suffix automaton of a string u and let x be a suffix of u. The weight associated by $SA(u)$ to x is the position of the suffix x in u. A string x is a factor of u iff it is the label of a path π in $SA(u)$ starting from the initial state. The weight of π gives the position of the first occurrence of x in u. A weighted suffix automaton can be built by an on-line algorithm deriving $SA(u\sigma)$ from $SA(u)$ for $\sigma \in \Sigma$. This algorithm is based on the definition of failure transitions similar to the suffix links defined in a suffix tree. The complexity of the on-line construction algorithm is $O(\log(|\Sigma|)|u|)$ in time and $O(|u|)$ in space.

The *weighted suffix oracle* $SO(u)$ of a string u is an approximation of the suffix automaton recognizing a superset of the set of suffixes of u [2]. It has exactly $|u| + 1$ states and at most $2|u| - 1$ transitions. The weight associated by $SO(u)$ to a string x is the position in u where x would occurs if x was a suffix of u. The construction algorithm is a simplified version of the on-line construction algorithm of the suffix automaton, its complexity is $O(\log(|\Sigma|)|u|)$ in time and $O(|u|)$ in space.

Utilities. The on-line construction algorithms of the weighted suffix automaton and oracle have been implemented in the GRM library and can be invoked through the `grmsuffix` command-line utility:

```
grmsuffix A.fsm > suffix.fsm
grmsuffix -o A.fsm > oracle_suffix.fsm
```

This utility takes as input a string represented by a finite automaton and returns the weighted suffix automaton of that string. When the -o option is used, the weighted suffix oracle is returned instead.

Examples and Applications. The weighted suffix automaton $SA(abbab)$ of the string $abbab$ is given by Figure 2(b). The weight associated by $SA(abbab)$ to ab is 3, which is the position in $abbab$ where ab occurs as a suffix, and the weight of the path starting from the initial state and labeled with ab is 0, which is indeed the position of the first occurrence of ab in $abbab$. The weighted suffix oracle $SO(abbab)$ of $abbab$ is given Figure 2(c). Note that the string $abab$ is recognized by $SO(abbab)$ although it is not a suffix of $abbab$.

The (weighted) suffix automaton can be used for indexing [6,8], string-matching [9,4] and compression [8]. The main application of the suffix oracle is string-matching [2].

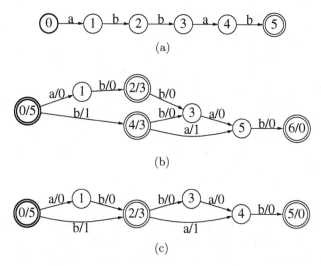

Fig. 2. (a) A string u represented by a finite automaton. (b) The weighted suffix automaton of u. (c) The weighted suffix oracle of u

4   Context-Free Grammars

The GRM library includes several utilities for reading, compiling, and approximating context-free grammars (CFGs) into finite automata. This section briefly reviews the relevant utilities of the GRM library.

4.1   Textual and Binary Representations

A textual representation of a weighted context-free grammar can be used directly as input to the GRM utilities. The following illustrates that representation in the case of a simple CFG.

CFG rules	cfg.txt
$Z\ .1 \rightarrow XY$	Z .1 X Y
$X\ .2 \rightarrow aY$	X .2 a Y
$Y\ .3 \rightarrow bX\ \mid .4\ c$	Y .3 b X $\mid$ .4 c

The textual representation is a straightforward translation of the classical way a CFG is written. Since, by definition, the first symbol of each rule is a nonterminal, there is no need to keep the arrow symbol for indicating the rule derivation. The second symbol of each line is the weight associated to the rule (in the case of weighted CFGs). The weights can be elements of an arbitrary semiring.

For efficiency purposes, this textual representation can be turned into a binary format using the utility **grmread**. The following is a command line sequence that generates the binary representation **cfg.bin** of the CFG **cfg.txt** where the file **labels** is a user-defined association between the symbols (terminal and nonterminal) and some numbers associated with them.

```
grmread -i labels -w cfg.txt >cfg.bin
```

The flag -w indicates that the input CFG is weighted. In the GRM library, the current binary representation is in fact that of a weighted transducer, see Figure 3(a). There are several reasons that motivated that choice. First, this representation makes it natural to apply grammar operations such as union or concatenation directly at the binary level. Secondly, and perhaps more importantly, the use of general determinization and minimization algorithms with this representation increase the sharing (*factoring*) among grammar rules that start or end the same way, which improves dramatically the time and space needed for the grammar compilation.

4.2   Compilation and Regular Approximation

When the input weighted context-free grammar is *strongly regular*, it can be compiled by the GRM library into an equivalent weighted automaton using the utility grmcfcompile. A CFG is strongly regular when the rules of each set M of mutually recursive nonterminals are either all right-linear or all left-linear (nonterminals that do not belong to M are considered as terminals for deciding if a rule of M is right- or left-linear). The following illustrates the use of the GRM utility grmcfcompile for compiling a CFG given by the binary representation cfg.bin.

```
grmcfcompile -i labels -s Z cfg.bin >cfg.fsm
```

Figure 3(b) shows the result of the compilation of that grammar. The CFG compilation of the GRM library produces an FSM that can be expanded on-demand. The FSM returned by grmcfcompile is a delayed acceptor, thus, its states and transitions are expanded as required by the FSM operation that is applied to it.

Not all weighted CFGs are strongly regular and thus can be compiled into weighted automata using grmcfcompile. We have designed an efficient context-free approximation algorithm that transforms any context-free grammar into one that is strongly regular [17]. The algorithm is based on a simple transformation that applies to any context-free grammar. The resulting grammar contains

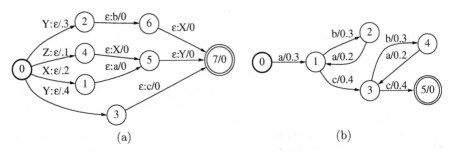

(a)   (b)

Fig. 3. (a) Binary representation of the context-free grammar G. (b) Compilation of G into a weighted automaton

at most one new nonterminal for any nonterminal symbol of the input grammar. The result thus remains readable and if necessary modifiable. A mapping from an arbitrary CFG generating a regular language into a corresponding finite automaton cannot be realized by any algorithm [24]. Thus, in general, our approximation cannot guarantee that the language is preserved when the grammar already generates a regular language (neither can any other approximation). However, this is guaranteed when the grammar is strongly regular.

The GRM utility `grmcfapproximate` takes as input the binary representation of a CFG and produces the textual representation of a strongly regular grammar approximating the input. The approximation creates new non-terminal symbols. The option `-o olab` specifies a new symbols file to be created, `olab`, containing the original and the new symbols. The following illustrates the use of `grmcfapproximate`.

```
grmcfapproximate -i lab -o nlab cfg.bin >ncfg.txt
grmread -i nlab ncfg.txt | grmcfcompile -i nlab -s E >cfg.fsm
```

cfg.txt	ncfg.txt		cfg.fsm
	E' eps	T T	
E E + T	T' eps	T' * F	
E T	F' eps	F' T'	
T T * F	E E	T F	
T F	E' + T	F' T'	
F (E)	T' E'	F (E	
F a	E T	E') F'	
	T' E'	F a F'	

The grammar `cfg.txt` above represents a simple grammar of arithmetic expressions. When applied to `cfg.txt`, `grmcfapproximate` returns the strongly regular grammar `ncfg.txt` that can be compiled into the automaton `cfg.fsm` represented by the figure.

5   Statistical Language Models

The GRM library includes utilities for counting n-gram occurrences in corpora of text or speech, and for estimating and representing n-gram language models based upon these counts. The use of weighted finite-state transducers allows for an efficient algorithm for computing the expected value of n-gram sequences given a weighted automaton. Failure transitions provide a natural automata encoding of stochastic language models in the tropical semiring. Some of the algorithmic details related to these utilities are presented in [3]. Here we give a brief tutorial on their use.

5.1   Corpora

For counting purposes, a corpus is a collection (or archive) of weighted automata in the log semiring. A corpus of strings can be compiled into such an archive with the FSM library utility `farcompilestrings`. A collection of word lattices (acyclic weighted graphs of alternative word strings, e.g. output from a speech recognizer) can be simply concatenated together to form an archive. For posterior counts from word lattices, weights should be pushed toward the initial state and the total cost should be removed, using `fsmpush`.

5.2   Counting

We define the *expected count* (the *count* for short) $c(x)$ of the sequence x in A as: $c(x) = \sum_{u \in \Sigma^*} |u|_x [\![A]\!](u)$, where $|u|_x$ denotes the number of occurrences of x in the string u, and $[\![A]\!](u)$ the weight associated to u by A. The transducer of Figure 4 can be used to provide the count of x in A through composition with A, projection onto output labels, and epsilon-removal. While we have been mentioning just acyclic automata, e.g., strings and lattices, the algorithm can count from cyclic weighted automata, provided that cycle weights are less than one, a requirement for A to represent a distribution. There exists a general algorithm for computing efficiently higher order moments of the distributions of the counts of a sequence x in a weighted automaton A [7].

The utility `grmcount` takes an archive of weighted automata and produces a count automaton as shown in figure 5. Optional arguments include the n-gram order, and the start and final symbols, which are represented by <s> and </s> respectively in the examples of this Section. These symbols are automatically appended by `grmcount` to the beginning and end of each automaton to be counted.

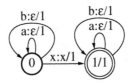

Fig. 4. Counting transducer for sequence x

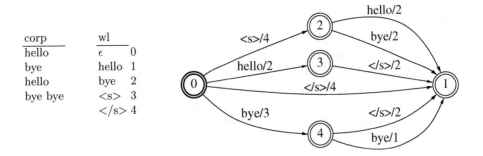

Fig. 5. Example corpus and count automata resulting from the command: `farcompilestrings -i wl corp | grmcount -n2 -s"<s>" -f"</s>" -i wl>bg.fsm`

In addition to `grmcount`, the utility `grmmerge` is provided, which takes k count files of the format produced by `grmcount`, and combines the counts into a single file of the same format. This allows counting to be parallelized, and the results combined. These counting utilities are used as follows:

```
grmcount -n2 -s3 -f4 foo.far > foo.2g.counts.fsm
grmmerge foo.counts.fsm bar.counts.fsm > foobar.counts.fsm
```

5.3   Creating a Backoff Model from Counts

The counts described in the previous section can be used in a variety of applications, e.g., to compute expected counts and gradients for machine learning algorithms. They can also be used to produce n-gram backoff language models, commonly used in many natural language processing applications, e.g., automatic speech recognition, speech synthesis, information retrieval, or machine translation.

An n-gram model is based on the Markovian assumption that the probability of the occurrence of a word only depends on the $n - 1$ preceding words. Thus,

$$\mathbf{P}(w) = \prod_{i=1}^{k} \mathbf{P}(w_i \mid h_i) \tag{1}$$

where the conditioning history h_i has length at most $n-1$: $|h_i| \leq n-1$. Let $c(hw)$ denote the count of n-gram hw and let $\widehat{\mathbf{P}}(w \mid h)$ be the maximum likelihood probability of w given h, estimated from counts. $\widehat{\mathbf{P}}$ is often adjusted to reserve some probability mass for unseen n-gram sequences. Denote by $\widetilde{\mathbf{P}}(w \mid h)$ the adjusted conditional probability. For all n-grams $h = wh'$ where $h \in \Sigma^k$ for some $k \geq 1$, we refer to h' as the Katz backoff n-gram of h [11]. Conditional probabilities in a backoff model are of the form:

$$\mathbf{P}(w \mid h) = \begin{cases} \widetilde{\mathbf{P}}(w \mid h) & \text{if } c(hw) > 0 \\ \alpha_h \mathbf{P}(w \mid h') & \text{otherwise} \end{cases} \tag{2}$$

where α_h is a factor that ensures a normalized model. In practice, for numerical stability, negative log probabilities are used. Furthermore, when the Viterbi approximation is used, which is common in speech processing applications, then an n-gram language model is represented by a weighted automaton over the tropical semiring. The utility `grmmake` takes counts in the format produced by `grmcount` and produces a backoff model in the tropical semiring:

```
grmmake foo.2g.counts.fsm > foo.2g.lm.fsm
```

Figure 6 shows the bigram language model in the tropical semiring that results from the counts in Figure 5. The smoothing technique that is used by default is Katz backoff [11], but the utility also provides for alternative estimation methods, such as absolute discounting [20] and Kneser-Ney smoothing [12]. Backoff transitions are naturally represented as failure transitions, but the

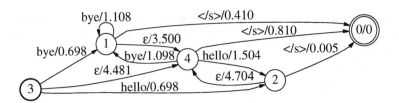

Fig. 6. Bigram language model with ε backoff arcs

grmmake utility produces them with ε-transitions, a convenient off-line approximation of the failure-function representation.

The utility grmshrink takes a model output from grmmake and removes transitions when their absence results in a change to the model of magnitude less than some threshold. Two methods are provided, the weighted difference method [21] and the relative entropy method [22]. The utility grmconvert converts a model output from grmmake or grmshrink to a failure class model or an interpolated model. Also, an exact off-line model can be produced from grmconvert, using ε-transitions instead of failure transitions, as detailed in [3]. These utilities are used as follows:

```
grmshrink -c 4 foo.2g.lm.fsm > foo.2g.s4.lm.fsm
grmconvert -t failure foo.2g.lm.fsm >foo.fail.2g.lm.fsm
```

5.4   Comparison with Other Utilities

The statistical language modeling utilities of the GRM library are similar in many ways to those of the SRI Language Modeling Toolkit (SRILM toolkit) [23], but there are some key differences. The SRILM toolkit provides a large variety of scripts and utilities for not only counting and creating language models, but also for the use and manipulation of these models. Since the models produced by the GRM library are in the format used by the FSM library, they can be readily used and manipulated with existing FSM utilities. Hence additional utilities are not part of the core GRM library.

For example, to score a string with a language model, the string must simply be encoded as an automaton (*farcompilestrings*) and intersected with the model (*fsmintersect*). Many of the same modeling options are provided by the utilities in both the SRILM toolkit and the GRM library, as well as count merging and model pruning capabilities. Class-based modeling is included explicitly in the SRILM toolkit, but, as shown in [3], general class-based models can be straightforwardly represented with the GRM library, without requiring additional utilities, through the use of weighted transducers. With such an approach, classes can be (weighted) regular languages, rather than just a finite set of words or a finite list of sequences of words.

The GRM library provides some features that are not covered by the SRILM Toolkit. It allows for counting from weighted automata, e.g., word lattices, which is crucial in a number of text and speech processing applications. Also, the use of failure transitions for the representation of language models and its off-line approximation based on ϵ-transitions provide efficient and useful encodings for intersection and composition with other finite automata and finite-state transducers. Finally the GRM's tight coupling with the FSM library allows one to benefit from the wide range of utilities of that library. In reverse, some of the features provided by the SRILM Toolkit, e.g., different discounting methods such as that of Witten-Bell are not provided by the current release of the GRM library but are likely to be available in future versions. The SRILM Toolkit also provides a utility for converting its models to and from that of the FSM library.

6   Conclusion

We presented a general weighted grammar library and emphasized its use in several text and speech processing applications. The binary executables of the library are available for download from the following URL:

http://www.research.att.com/sw/tools/grm/

The GRM algorithms and utilities can be used in a similar way in many computational biology applications.

Acknowledgements

We thank our colleagues Donald Hindle, Mark-Jan Nederhof, Fernando Pereira, Michael Riley, and Richard Sproat for their help and contributions to various aspects of the design of GRM library.

References

1. A. V. Aho and M. J. Corasick. Efficient string matching: An aid to bibliographic search. *Communications of the ACM*, 18(6):333–340, 1975.
2. C. Allauzen, M. Crochemore, and M. Raffinot. Efficient experimental string matching by weak factor recognition. In *Proceedings of CPM 2001*, volume 2089 of *Lecture Notes in Computer Science*, pages 51–72, 2001.
3. C. Allauzen, M. Mohri, and B. Roark. Generalized algorithms for constructing language models. In *Proceedings of ACL 2003)*, pages 40–47, 2003.
4. C. Allauzen and M. Raffinot. Simple optimal string matching. *Journal of Algorithms*, 36(1):102–116, 2000.
5. A. Blumer, J. Blumer, A. Ehrenfeucht, D. Haussler, and J. I. Seiferas. The smallest automaton recognizing the subwords of a text. *Theoretical Computer Science*, 40(1):31–55, 1985.
6. A. Blumer, J. Blumer, D. Haussler, R. M. McConnel, and A. Ehrenfeucht. Complete inverted files for efficient text retrieval and analysis. *Journal of the ACM*, 34(3):578–595, 1987.
7. C. Cortes and M. Mohri. Distribution Kernels Based on Moments of Counts. In *Proceedings of the Twenty-First International Conference on Machine Learning (ICML 2004)*, Banff, Alberta, Canada, July 2004.
8. M. Crochemore. Transducers and repetitions. *Theoretical Computer Science*, 45(1):63–86, 1986.

9. M. Crochemore, A. Czumaj, L. Gasieniec, S. Jarominek, T. Lecroq, W. Plandowski, and W. Rytter. Speeding up two string-matching algorithms. *Algorithmica*, 12(4/5):247–267, 1994.

10. R. Durbin, S. Eddy, A. Krogh, and G. Mitchison. *Biological Sequence Analysis: Probabilistic Models of Proteins and Nucleic Acids*. Cambridge University Press, Cambridge UK, 1998.

11. S. M. Katz. Estimation of probabilities from sparse data for the language model component of a speech recogniser. *IEEE Transactions on Acoustic, Speech, and Signal Processing*, 35(3):400–401, 1987.

12. R. Kneser and H. Ney. Improved backing-off for m-gram language modeling. In *Proceedings of ICASSP*, volume 1, pages 181–184, 1995.

13. D. E. Knuth, J. H. Morris, Jr., and V. R. Pratt. Fast pattern matching in strings. *SIAM Journal on Computing*, 6(2):323–350, 1977.

14. M. Mohri. Syntactic analysis by local grammars automata: an efficient algorithm. In *Proceedings of the International Conference on Computational Lexicography (COMPLEX 94)*. Linguistic Institute, Hungarian Academy of Science, 1994.

15. M. Mohri. String-matching with automata. *Nordic Journal of Computing*, 2(2):217–231, 1997.

16. M. Mohri. *Robustness in Language and Speech Technology*, chapter Weighted Grammar Tools: the GRM Library, pages 165–186. Kluwer, 2001.

17. M. Mohri and M.-J. Nederhof. *Robustness in Language and Speech Technology*, chapter Regular Approximation of Context-Free Grammars through Transformation, pages 153–163. Kluwer, 2001.

18. M. Mohri, F. C. N. Pereira, and M. Riley. The design principles of a weighted finite-state transducer library. *Theoretical Computer Science*, 231:17–32, January 2000. http://www.research.att.com/sw/tools/fsm.

19. M. Mohri, F. C. N. Pereira, and M. Riley. Weighted Finite-State Transducers in Speech Recognition. *Computer Speech and Language*, 16(1):69–88, 2002.

20. H. Ney, U. Essen, and R. Kneser. On structuring probabilistic dependences in stochastic language modeling. *Computer Speech and Language*, 8(1):1–38, 1994.

21. K. Seymore and R. Rosenfeld. Scalable backoff language models. In *Proceedings of ICSLP*, volume 1, pages 232–235, Philadelphia, Pennsylvania, 1996.

22. A. Stolcke. Entropy-based pruning of backoff language models. In *Proc. DARPA Broadcast News Transcription and Understanding Workshop*, pages 270–274, 1998.

23. A. Stolcke. SRILM – an extensible language modeling toolkit. In *Proc. Intl. Conf. on Spoken Language Processing (ICSLP'2002)*, volume 2, pages 901–904, 2002.

24. J. Ullian. Partial algorithm problems for context free languages. *Information and Control*, 11:80–101, 1967.

On the Complexity of Hopcroft's State Minimization Algorithm

Jean Berstel[1] and Olivier Carton[2]

[1] Institut Gaspard Monge,
Université de Marne-la-Vallée
http://www-igm.univ-mlv.fr/~berstel
[2] LIAFA, Université Paris 7
http://www.liafa.jussieu.fr/~carton

Abstract. Hopcroft's algorithm for minimizing a deterministic automaton has complexity $O(n \log n)$. We show that this complexity bound is tight. More precisely, we provide a family of automata of size $n = 2^k$ on which the algorithm runs in time $k2^k$. These automata have a very simple structure and are built over a one-letter alphabet. Their sets of final states are defined by de Bruijn words.

1 Introduction

Efficient state minimization algorithms are an important issue for tools involving finite state automata, as they arise e.g. in computational linguistics. The elementary minimization algorithm usually credited to Moore (see also [1]) has been improved by Hopcroft [2]. In the special case of finite sets, minimal automata can be constructed and maintained even more efficiently (see [3, 4] and [5] for a recent survey). Extensions to more general situations of Hopcroft's algorithm are considered in [6, 7, 8].

Hopcroft's algorithm is known to run in time $O(n \log n)$ for an automaton with n states. We show here that this bound is tight, that is that this running time is reached for an infinite family of automata. For that purpose we define a class of automata over a unary alphabet. These automata have a very simple structure since they are just made of a single cycle. The final states of these automata are defined by a pattern given by de Bruijn words. The simple structure of the automaton and the special layout of the final states allows us to control precisely how some particular execution of the algorithm runs.

We should point out that Hopcroft's algorithm has a degree of freedom because, in each step of its main loop, it allows a free choice of a set of states to be processed. Hopcroft has proved that any sequence of choices can be processed in time $O(n \log n)$. Our family of examples results in showing that there exists some "unlucky" sequence of choices that slows down the computation to achieve the lower bound $\Omega(n \log n)$. Partial results on another family of examples have been obtained in [9].

M. Domaratzki et al. (Eds.): CIAA 2004, LNCS 3317, pp. 35–44, 2005.

The paper is organized as follows. After some general definitions we outline Hopcroft's algorithm. We next present de Bruijn words, and then introduce our family of automata. These are simply one letter automata with $n = 2^k$ states organized as a cycle. The key property is the choice of final states. Exactly one half of the states are final, and they are chosen according to the occurrence of the symbol 1 in a de Bruijn word of order k.

Given such a cyclic automaton, we next present the strategy used to choose the sets in Hopcroft's algorithm. We then prove that this choice indeed leads to a running time in $O(n \log n)$. It should be observed that minization of one-letter automata can be performed in linear time by another algorithm [7].

2   Minimal Automaton

In this section, we fix some notation and we give some basic definitions.

We only use deterministic and complete automata. An *automaton* $\mathcal{A}$ over a finite alphabet A is composed of a finite state set Q, a distinguished state called the initial state, a set $F \subseteq Q$ of final states, and of a next-state function $Q \times A \to Q$ that maps (q, a) to a state denoted by $q \cdot a$.

A *partition* of a set Q is a family $\{Q_1, \ldots, Q_n\}$ of nonempty subsets of Q that are pairwise disjoint (that is $Q_i \cap Q_j = \emptyset$ for $i \neq j$) and cover Q, (that is $Q = Q_1 \cup \cdots \cup Q_n$). The subsets Q_i are called the *classes* of the partition.

If Q is the state set of an automaton $\mathcal{A}$, a *congruence* of $\mathcal{A}$ is a partition which is compatible with the transitions of $\mathcal{A}$. This means that if q and q' are in the same class, then $q \cdot a$ and $q' \cdot a$ are also in the same class for any $q, q' \in Q$ and any $a \in A$.

A partition of Q *saturates* a subset F of Q if F is the union of some of its classes. This also means that in a class either all elements or none belong to F. A partition $\{Q_1, \ldots, Q_n\}$ is *coarser* than a partition $\{Q'_1, \ldots, Q'_m\}$ if the partition $\{Q'_1, \ldots, Q'_m\}$ saturates each class Q_i. This relation defines a partial order on partitions.

It is well known that any regular set L of finite words is accepted by a unique minimal deterministic automaton.

It should be noticed that the minimal automaton of $\mathcal{A}$ does not depend on the initial state of $\mathcal{A}$ as long as any state is reachable from it. In what follows, we often omit to specify the initial state since it does not matter.

3   Hopcroft's Algorithm

Hopcroft [2] has given an algorithm that computes the minimal automaton of a given deterministic automaton. The running time of the algorithm is $O(|A| \times n \log n)$ where $|A|$ is the cardinality of the alphabet and n is the number of states of the given automaton. The algorithm has been described and re-described several times [2, 10, 11, 12, 13, 14].

The algorithm is outlined below, and it is explained then in some more detail.

It is convenient to use the shorthand $T^c = Q \setminus T$ when T is a subset of the set Q of states. We denote by $\min(B, C)$ the set of smaller size of the two sets B and C, and any one of them if they have the same size.

```
1:  P ← {F, Fᶜ}
2:  for all a ∈ A do
3:      Add((min(F, Fᶜ), a), S)
4:  while S ≠ ∅ do
5:      (C, a) ← Some(S)                    ▷ takes some element in S
6:      for each B ∈ P split by (C, a) do
7:          B′, B″ ← Split(B, C, a)
8:          Replace B by B′ and B″ in P
9:          for all b ∈ A do
10:             if (B, b) ∈ S then
11:                 Replace (B, b) by (B′, b) and (B″, b) in S
12:             else
13:                 Add((min(B′, B″), b), S)
```

Algorithm 1. Hopcroft Minimization

Given a deterministic automaton $\mathcal{A}$, Hopcroft's algorithm computes the coarsest congruence which saturates the set F of final states. It starts from the partition $\{F, F^c\}$ which obviously saturates F and refines it until it gets a congruence. These refinements of the partition are always obtained by splitting some class into two classes.

Before explaining the algorithm in more detail, some notation is needed. For a set B of states, we note by $B \cdot a$ the set $\{q \cdot a \mid q \in B\}$. Let B and C be two sets of states and let a be a letter. We say that the pair (C, a) *splits* the set B if both sets $(B \cdot a) \cap C$ and $(B \cdot a) \cap C^c$ are nonempty. In that case, the set B is split into the two sets $B' = \{q \in B \mid q \cdot a \in C\}$ and $B'' = \{q \in B \mid q \cdot a \notin C\}$ that we call the *resulting sets*. Note that a partition $\{Q_1, \ldots, Q_n\}$ is a congruence if and only if for any $1 \leq i, j \leq n$ and any $a \in A$, the pair (Q_i, a) does not split Q_j.

The algorithm proceeds as follows. It maintains a current partition $\mathcal{P} = \{B_1, \ldots, B_n\}$ and a current set $\mathcal{S}$ of pairs (C, a) where C is a class of $\mathcal{P}$ and a is a letter that remain to be processed. The set $\mathcal{S}$ is called the *waiting* set. The algorithm stops when the waiting set $\mathcal{S}$ becomes empty. When it stops, the partition $\mathcal{P}$ is the coarsest congruence that saturates F. The starting partition is the partition $\{F, F^c\}$ and the starting set $\mathcal{S}$ contains all pairs $(\min(F, F^c), a)$ for $a \in A$.

The main loop of the algorithm takes one pair (C, a) out of the waiting set $\mathcal{S}$ and performs the following actions. Each class B of the current partition (including the class C) is checked whether it is split by the pair (C, a). If (C, a) does not split B, then nothing is done. Otherwise, the class B is replaced in the partition $\mathcal{P}$ by the two resulting sets B' and B'' of the split. For each letter b, if the pair (B, b) is in $\mathcal{S}$, it is replaced in $\mathcal{S}$ by the two pairs (B', b) and (B'', b), otherwise only the pair $(\min(B', B''), b)$ is added to $\mathcal{S}$.

The main ingredient in the analysis of the running time of the algorithm is that the splitting of all classes of the current partition according to a pair (C, a) takes a time proportional to the size of C. Therefore, the global running time of the algorithm is proportional to the sum of the sizes of the classes processed in the main loop. Note that a pair which is added to the waiting set $\mathcal{S}$ is not necessarily processed later because it can be split by the processing of another pair before it is considered.

It should be noted that the algorithm is not really deterministic because it has not been specified which pair (C, a) is taken from $\mathcal{S}$ to be processed at each iteration of the main loop. This means that for a given automaton, there are many executions of the algorithm. It turns out that all of them produce the right partition of the states. However, different executions may give rise to different sequences of splitting and also to different running time. Hopcroft has proved that the running time of any execution is bounded by $O(|A| \times n \log n)$.

In this paper, we show that this bound is tight. More precisely, we show that there exist automata over a one-letter alphabet and of size n and there exist executions on these automata that give a running time of magnitude $O(n \log n)$. Actually, we will not give automata for all integers n but those of the form 2^k.

4   De Bruijn Words

The family of automata that we use to show the lower bound on the running time of Hopcroft's algorithm are based of de Bruijn words. We recall their definition.

Let $w = w_1 \ldots w_m$ a word of length m. By a slight abuse, we use the notation w_i even if the integer i is greater than m. We denote by w_i the letter $w_{i'}$ where i' is the unique integer such that $1 \leq i' \leq m$ and $i' = i \mod m$. A *circular occurrence* of a word $u = u_1 \ldots u_p$ of length p in w is an integer k in the interval $[1; m]$ such that $w_{k+i-1} = u_i$ for each i in $[1; p]$.

A *de Bruijn word* of order n over the alphabet B is a word w such that each word of length n over B has exactly one circular occurrence in w. Since there are $|B|^n$ words of length n, the length of a de Bruijn word of order n is $|B|^n$.

Set for instance the alphabet $B = \{0, 1\}$. The word $w = 1100$ is a de Bruijn word of order 2 since each of the words $\{00, 01, 10, 11\}$ has a circular occurrence in w. The word $w = 11101000$ is a de Bruijn word of order 3.

De Bruijn words are widely investigated (see for instance [15]). It is well known that for any alphabet, there are de Bruijn words for all orders. We recall here a short proof of this fact. Let B be a fixed alphabet and let n be a fixed integer. We recall the definition of the *de Bruijn graph* $\mathcal{B}_n$ of order n. Its vertex set is the set B^{n-1} of all words of length $n - 1$. The edges of $\mathcal{B}_n$ are the pairs of the form (bu, ua) for $u \in B^{n-2}$ and $a, b \in B$. This graph is often presented as a labeled graph where each edge (bu, ua) is labeled by the letter a. Note that the function which maps each word $w = bua$ of length n to the edge (bu, ua) is one to one. Therefore, a de Bruijn word of order n corresponds to an Eulerian circuit in $\mathcal{B}_n$. Since there are exactly $|B|$ edges entering and leaving each vertex of $\mathcal{B}_n$, the graph $\mathcal{B}_n$ has Eulerian circuits [15] and there are de Bruijn words of order n. In Fig. 1 below we show the de Bruijn graph of order 4. Taking an Eulerian circuit from it, one obtains the de Bruijn word $w = 0000100110101111$ of order 4.

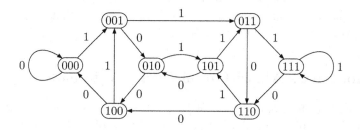

Fig. 1. The de Bruijn graph of order 4 over the alphabet $\{0, 1\}$

5   Cyclic Automata

In what follows, we only consider de Bruijn words over the binary alphabet $\mathbb{B} = \{0, 1\}$. Let w be a de Bruijn word of order n. Recall that the length of w is 2^n. We define an automaton $\mathcal{A}_w$ over the unary alphabet $\{a\}$ as follows. The state set of $\mathcal{A}_w$ is $\{1, \ldots, 2^n\}$ and the next state function is defined by $i \cdot a = i+1$ for $i < 2^n$ and $2^n \cdot a = 1$. Note that the underlying labeled graph of $\mathcal{A}_w$ is just a cycle of length 2^n. The final states really depend on w. The set of final states of $\mathcal{A}_w$ is $F = \{1 \leq i \leq 2^n \mid w_i = 1\}$.

For a word u over $\mathbb{B}$, we define a subset Q_u of states of $\mathcal{A}_w$. By definition the set Q_u is the set of positions of circular occurrences of u in w. If the length of u is n, the set Q_u is a singleton since the de Bruijn word w has exactly one circular occurrence of u. More generally, if the length of u is less than n, the cardinality of Q_u is $2^{n-|u|}$ since there are as many circular occurrences of u as there are words v such that $|uv| = n$. If u is the empty word, then Q_u is by convention the set Q of all states of $\mathcal{A}_w$. By definition, the set F of final states of $\mathcal{A}_w$ is Q_1 while its complement F^c is Q_0.

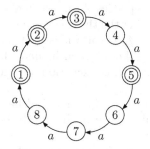

Fig. 2. Cyclic automaton $\mathcal{A}_w$ for $w = 11101000$

Let w be the de Bruijn word 11101000. The automaton $\mathcal{A}_w$ is pictured in Fig. 2. The sets Q_1, Q_{01} and Q_{011} of states are respectively $\{1,2,3,5\}$, $\{4,8\}$ and $\{8\}$.

Since any circular occurrence of u in w is followed by either 0 or 1, the equality $Q_u = Q_{u0} \cup Q_{u1}$ holds. If a word $u = bu'$ has a circular occurrence k in w, its suffix u' has a circular occurrence $k+1$ in w. If follows that if u is factorized $u = bu'$ where $b \in \mathbb{B}$, then $Q_u \cdot a \subset Q_{u'}$.

6   Hopcroft's Algorithm on Cyclic Automata

We claim that the running time of Hopcroft's algorithm on a cyclic automaton $\mathcal{A}_w$ may be of order $n2^n$. Before giving the proof of this claim, we give an example of an execution on the automaton pictured in Fig. 2. Since cyclic automata are over the unary alphabet $A = \{a\}$, we merely say that a class C splits a class B to mean that the pair (C, a) splits the class B.

- The starting partition is $\mathcal{P} = \{F, F^c\} = \{Q_0, Q_1\}$ and $\mathcal{S} = \{Q_1\}$.
- The class Q_1 is processed.
  - The class Q_0 is split into Q_{00} and Q_{01}, and Q_{01} is added to $\mathcal{S}$.
  - The class Q_1 is split into Q_{10} and Q_{11}, and Q_{11} is added to $\mathcal{S}$.
  Then $\mathcal{P} = \{Q_{00}, Q_{01}, Q_{10}, Q_{11}\}$ and $\mathcal{S} = \{Q_{01}, Q_{11}\}$.
- The class Q_{01} is processed.
  - The class Q_{00} is split into Q_{000} and Q_{001}, and Q_{001} is added to $\mathcal{S}$.
  - The class Q_{10} is split into Q_{100} and Q_{101}, and Q_{101} is added to $\mathcal{S}$.
  Then $\mathcal{P} = \{Q_{000}, Q_{001}, Q_{01}, Q_{100}, Q_{101}, Q_{11}\}$ and $\mathcal{S} = \{Q_{11}, Q_{001}, Q_{101}\}$.
- The class Q_{11} is processed.
  - The class Q_{01} is split into Q_{010} and Q_{011}, and Q_{011} is added to $\mathcal{S}$.
  - The class Q_{11} is split into Q_{110} and Q_{111}, and Q_{111} is added to $\mathcal{S}$.
  Then $\mathcal{P} = \{Q_{000}, Q_{001}, Q_{010}, Q_{011}, Q_{100}, Q_{101}, Q_{110}, Q_{111}\}$ and $\mathcal{S} = \{Q_{001}, Q_{011}, Q_{101}, Q_{111}\}$.
- Classes $Q_{001}, Q_{011}, Q_{101}, Q_{111}$ are processed but this gives no further splitting since the partition is made of singletons.

Let us point out some properties of this particular execution of the algorithm. The classes that appear during the the execution are all of the form Q_u for some word u. Every time a class Q_u is split, it is split into the classes Q_{u0} and Q_{u1}. Since these two classes have the same cardinality, the algorithm may either add one or another one to $\mathcal{S}$. In this execution we have always assumed that it chooses Q_{u1}.

When the algorithm processes Q_{01}, it could have chosen to process Q_{11} instead. The algorithm would have run differently because the class Q_{01} would have been split by Q_{11}.

We now describe the worst case strategy which we use to prove that the $O(n \log n)$ bound of Hopcroft's algorithm is tight. Given n and the automaton

$\mathcal{A}_w$, we construct a sequence $(\mathcal{P}_k, \mathcal{S}_k)$ for $k = 1, \ldots, n$ where $\mathcal{P}_k$ and $\mathcal{S}_k$ are the partition and the waiting set given by

$$\mathcal{P}_k = \{Q_u \mid u \in \mathbb{B}^k\} \quad \text{and} \quad \mathcal{S}_k = \{Q_v \mid v \in \mathbb{B}^{k-1}1\}.$$

In particular, $\mathcal{P}_1 = \{Q_0, Q_1\}$ is the starting partition of Hopcroft's algorithm and $\mathcal{S}_1 = \{Q_1\}$ is the starting content of the waiting set. The pair $(\mathcal{P}_{k+1}, \mathcal{S}_{k+1})$ is obtained from the pair $(\mathcal{P}_k, \mathcal{S}_k)$ by obeying to the following strategy: choose the sets Q_v of $\mathcal{S}_k$ in such an order that Q_v does not split any set in the current waiting set $\mathcal{S}$.

More precisely, a linear order $<$ on $\mathcal{S}_k$ is said to be *non-splitting* if whenever $Q_{v'}$ splits Q_v then $Q_v < Q_{v'}$. In other terms the strategy we choose is to process sets in $\mathcal{S}_k$ in some order which avoids splitting. We call such a strategy a *non-splitting strategy*. We will see in Proposition 1 that during this process, each removal of an element of $\mathcal{S}_k$ contributes to two elements in $\mathcal{S}_{k+1}$. It happens, as we will prove, that the new sets are not split by the currently processed set either. We will see in Proposition 2 that non-splitting orders do exist.

The transition from $(\mathcal{P}_k, \mathcal{S}_k)$ to $(\mathcal{P}_{k+1}, \mathcal{S}_{k+1})$ involves 2^{k-1} iterations of the main loop of the algorithm. Each iteration removes one set from the waiting set, and as we will show splits exactly two sets in the current partition and adds exactly two sets to the waiting set. These latter sets are of the form Q_v for $v \in \mathbb{B}^k1$.

Proposition 1. *If Hopcroft's algorithm starts from $(\mathcal{P}_k, \mathcal{S}_k)$ and processes the sets in $\mathcal{S}_k$ in a non-splitting order, it yields the pair $(\mathcal{P}_{k+1}, \mathcal{S}_{k+1})$.*

Proposition 2. *Each $\mathcal{S}_k$ admits non-splitting orders.*

We start with several lemmas. Some properties of the splitting of the sets of the form Q_u are needed. They are stated in the following lemma.

Lemma 1. *Let u and v be two words of length smaller than n. The pair (Q_v, a) splits Q_u if and only if there are $b \in \mathbb{B}$ and $s \in \mathbb{B}^+$ such that $us = bv$. If (Q_v, a) splits Q_u, the resulting sets are Q_{us} and $Q_u \setminus Q_{us}$. In particular if $|u| > |v|$, then Q_v does not split Q_u.*

Proof. Assume that $u = bu'$ where $b \in \mathbb{B}$. Then the inclusion $Q_u \cdot a \subset Q_{u'}$ holds. Therefore if v is not equal to $u's$ for some $s \in \mathbb{B}^*$, the intersection $(Q_u \cdot a) \cap Q_v$ is empty and (Q_v, a) does not split Q_u. Assume now that $v = u's$ for some s. If s is the empty word, the intersection $(Q_u \cdot a) \cap Q_v^c$ is empty and (Q_v, a) does not split Q_u. It follows that s is not empty and that $us = bv$. $\square$

Corollary 1. *If u and v are two words of the same length, the pair (Q_v, a) splits Q_u if and only if there are $b, b' \in \mathbb{B}$ such that $ub' = bv$. If (Q_v, a) splits Q_u, the resulting sets are Q_{u0} and Q_{u1}.*

In other terms, if u and v are two words of the same length k, then Q_v splits Q_u iff there is an edge (u, v) in the de Bruijn graph $\mathcal{B}_{k+1}$.

We are now ready for the proof of Proposition 1.

Proof. (of Proposition 1) We consider how the execution goes according to our non-splitting strategy from the pair $(\mathcal{P}_k, \mathcal{S}_k)$ to the pair $(\mathcal{P}_{k+1}, \mathcal{S}_{k+1})$. We denote by $\mathcal{P}$ and $\mathcal{S}$ the current values of the partition and of the waiting set when we process the classes in $\mathcal{S}_k$ in a fixed non-splitting order. At the beginning of the execution, $\mathcal{P} = \mathcal{P}_k$ and $\mathcal{S} = \mathcal{S}_k$ and at the end $\mathcal{P} = \mathcal{P}_{k+1}$ and $\mathcal{S} = \mathcal{S}_{k+1}$. By Corollary 1, each class Q_u of $\mathcal{P}_k$ is split by exactly one class Q_v in $\mathcal{S}_k$ and each class Q_v splits two classes Q_u and $Q_{u'}$ in $\mathcal{P}_k$. Moreover, Q_v does not split any other class in the current partition. By the choice of the ordering, both classes Q_u and $Q_{u'}$ do not belong to $\mathcal{S}$ when Q_v is processed. The class Q_u is split into the classes Q_{u0} and Q_{u1}. Since these two classes have the same cardinality, either Q_{u0} or Q_{u1} may be added to $\mathcal{S}$. Similarly the class $Q_{u'}$ is split into the classes $Q_{u'0}$ and $Q_{u'1}$. The execution of our strategy adds the classes Q_{u1} and $Q_{u'1}$ to the set $\mathcal{S}$. The execution continues until all classes in $\mathcal{S}_k$ have been processed. While this is done, classes Q_{u1} for $u \in \mathbb{B}^k$ are added to $\mathcal{S}$. When all classes Q_u from $\mathcal{S}_k$ have been processed, the partition $\mathcal{P}$ and the set $\mathcal{S}$ are $\mathcal{P}_{k+1}$ and $\mathcal{S}_{k+1}$. $\qquad\square$

We now proceed to proof of the existence of non-splitting orders on $\mathcal{S}_k$.

Proof. (of Proposition 2) Let $G_k = (V_k, E_k)$ be the graph where the vertex set is $V_k = \mathbb{B}^{k-1}1$ and the set of edges is $E_k = \{(u, v) \mid Q_v \text{ splits } Q_u\}$. By Corollary 1, the graph G_k is actually the subgraph of the de Bruijn $\mathcal{B}_{k+1}$ defined by the set V_k of vertices. The main property of that graph G_k is to be almost acyclic: For each $k \geq 0$, the only cycle in G_k is the edge $(1^k, 1^k)$.

It is easy to see that if there is a path of length ℓ from some node to v in G, then the word v belongs to $\mathbb{B}^{k-\ell-1}1^{\ell+1}$. It follows from the claim that the vertex 1^k is the only vertex which can appear in a cycle.

Since this graph is acyclic, the words of $\mathbb{B}^{k-1}1$ can be topologically ordered. Thus a non-splitting order on $\mathcal{S}_k$ is defined by $Q_u < Q_v$ iff $u < v$ in the previous topological order. $\qquad\square$

The graph G_3 of the previous proof is pictured in Fig. 3.

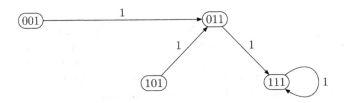

Fig. 3. The graph G_3

Let us come back to the execution given at the beginning of that section. After Q_1 is processed, the partition $\mathcal{P}$ and the set $\mathcal{S}$ are $\mathcal{P} = \{Q_{00}, Q_{01}, Q_{10}, Q_{11}\}$ and $\mathcal{S} = \{Q_{01}, Q_{11}\}$. The class Q_{11} splits the class Q_{01} while the class Q_{01} does not split the class Q_{11}. A non-splitting order on $\mathcal{S}_2$ is given by $Q_{01} < Q_{11}$. The class

Q_{01} is therefore processed before the class Q_{11}. The partition $\mathcal{P}$ and the set $\mathcal{S}$ become $\mathcal{P} = \{Q_u \mid u \in \mathbb{B}^3\}$ and $\mathcal{S} = \{Q_{u1} \mid u \in \mathbb{B}^2\}$.

We finally analyze the running time of the algorithm. The following result shows that the $O(n \log n)$ upper bound of the running time of Hopcroft's algorithm is tight.

Theorem 1. *The non-splitting strategy requires $n2^n$ operations for the minimization of the automaton $\mathcal{A}_w$ of size 2^n for any de Bruijn word w of order n.*

Proof. The time needed to process a class C is proportional to the size of C. In the execution that we give the algorithm processes all classes Q_{u1} for $|u| < n$. Summing all the sizes, we get that the running time of the algorithm is $n2^n$ whereas the size of the automaton $\mathcal{A}_w$ is 2^n.   □

7   Conclusion

We have shown that Hopcroft's algorithm may have executions running in time $O(n \log n)$. These executions run on the cyclic automata that we have defined. It is not very difficult to see that there are also executions that run in linear time for the same automata. It is still open whether there are automata on which all executions of Hopcroft's algorithm do not run in linear time.

These different executions depend on the choice of the class which is processed at each iteration of the main loop of the algorithm. Defining strategies which specify which class is processed might be of interest from a theoretical and practical point of view.

Acknowledgment. We would like to thank Luc Boasson and Isabelle Fagnot for fruitful discussions and the anonymous referees for their helpful comments.

References

1. Hopcroft, J.E., Ullman, J.D.: Formal Languages and their Relation to Automata. Addison-Wesley (1969)
2. Hopcroft, J.E.: An $n \log n$ algorithm for minimizing states in a finite automaton. In Kohavi, Z., Paz, A., eds.: Theory of Machines and Computations, Academic Press (1971) 189–196
3. Krivol, S.L.: Algorithms for minimization of finite acyclic automata and pattern matching in terms. Cybernetics **27** (1991) 324– 331 translated from Kibernetika, No 3, May-June 1991, pp. 11–16.
4. Revuz, D.: Minimisation of acyclic deterministic automata in linear time. Theoret. Comput. Sci. **92** (1992) 181–189
5. Daciuk, J.: Comparison of construction algorithms for minimal, acyclic, deterministic finite-state automata from sets of strings. In Champarnaud, J.M., Maurel, D., eds.: 7th Implementation and Application of Automata (CIAA 2002). Volume 2608 of Lect. Notes in Comput. Sci., Springer Verlag (2002) 255–261
6. Cardon, A., Crochemore, M.: Partitioning a graph in $O(|A| \log_2 |V|)$. Theoret. Comput. Sci. **19** (1982) 85–98

7. Paige, R., Tarjan, R.E., Bonic, R.: A linear time solution for the single function coarsest partition problem. Theoret. Comput. Sci. **40** (1985) 67–84
8. Paige, R., Tarjan, R.E.: Three partition refinement algorithms. SIAM J. Comput. **18** (1987) 973–989
9. Gai, A.T.: Algorithmes de partionnement : minimisation d'automates et applications aux graphes. Mémoire de DEA, Université Montpellier II (2003)
10. Gries, D.: Describing an algorithm by Hopcroft. Acta Inform. **2** (1973) 97–109
11. Aho, A., Hopcroft, J., Ullman, J.: The Design and Analysis of Computer Algorithms. Addison-Wesley (1974)
12. Beauquier, D., Berstel, J., Chrétienne, P.: Éléments d'algorithmique. Masson (1992)
13. Blum, N.: A $O(n \log n)$ implementation of the standard method for minimizing n-state finite automata. Inform. Proc. Letters **57** (1996) 65–69
14. Knuutila, T.: Re-describing an algorithm by Hopcroft. Theoret. Comput. Sci. **250** (2001) 333–363
15. Tutte, W.T.: Graph Theory. Volume 21 of Encyclopedia of Mathematics and its Applications. Addison-Wesley (1984)

Implementation of Catalytic P Systems

Aneta Binder, Rudolf Freund, Georg Lojka, and Marion Oswald

Faculty of Informatics, Vienna University of Technology,
Favoritenstr. 9-11, A-1040 Wien, Austria
{ani, rudi, georg, marion}@emcc.at

Abstract. Taking advantage of the weak determinism inherent to the simulation of deterministic register machines by catalytic P systems, we present an efficient implementation of such P systems.

1 Introduction

In the original paper (see [12]) introducing membrane systems (P systems) as a symbol manipulating model, catalysts as well as priority relations on the rules were used to prove them to be computationally complete (see [14] for a comprehensive overview and [18] for actual developments in the area); in [16] it was shown that a priority relation on the rules is not necessary to obtain this universality result. The best results on the number of catalysts known so far can be found in [7] (the results needed in this paper will be cited in Section 3).

When going to implement catalytic P systems (which notion was introduced by Ibarra in [3]) we can take advantage of a kind of "weak" determinism - introduced as k-determinism in [11] - allowing for an efficient simulation of deterministic register machines. In order to figure out which set of rules has to be applied to the current configuration, we only have to make a look-ahead of bounded depth k, i.e., we consider all possible continuations making (at most) k further steps in the catalytic P system. For every successful computation of the underlying deterministic register machine, at each step in the simulating catalytic P system, there exists exactly one set of rules to be applied determined by this look-ahead of depth k. Based on this theoretical background we present an efficient implementation of catalytic P systems that can compute any partial recursive function $f : N^\alpha \to N^\beta$ (where N denotes the set of non-negative integers) using only one membrane and $\alpha + 3$ catalysts. This implementation allowed us to easily verify the complicated construction given in the theoretical proof for the simulation of register machines; moreover, its user-friendly interface and visualization of the derivation steps and the configurations during any computation in an arbitrary k-deterministic catalytic P system make it a useful tool for introducing P systems to students.

In the following section, after some prerequisites we define the variant of register machines the simulation results for catalytic P systems are based on. In Section 3, we define catalytic P systems and introduce the notion of k-determinism; moreover, we prove the main theoretical result the implementation is based on.

M. Domaratzki et al. (Eds.): CIAA 2004, LNCS 3317, pp. 45–56, 2005.

In Section 4, we describe the tool implemented for simulating k-deterministic catalytic P systems, and finally we give a short conclusion.

2   Definitions

Let $m \geq 2$ and let k, l be two positive integers not greater than m; then we define:

$$l \ominus_m k := \begin{cases} l - k & \text{for } l > k \\ l - k + m & \text{for } l \leq k \end{cases}$$

2.1   Register Machines

In this subsection we briefly recall the concept of Minsky's register machine (e.g., see [10]). Such an abstract machine uses a finite number of registers for storing arbitrarily large non-negative integers and runs a program consisting of numbered instructions of various simple types. Several variants of the machine with different numbers of registers and different instruction sets were shown to be computationally complete (e.g., see [10] for some original definitions and proofs as well as [5], [6], and [8] for the definitions and results we use in this paper).

A *deterministic n-register machine* is a construct $M = (n, P, i, h)$ where

- n is the number of registers,
- P is a set of labelled instructions of the form $j : (op(r), k, l)$, where $op(r)$ is an operation on register r of M, j, k, l are labels from the set $Lab(M)$ (which numbers the instructions of the program of M represented by P),
- i is the initial label, and
- h is the final label.

The machine is capable of the following instructions:

$(A(r), k, k)$:   Add one to the contents of register r and proceed to instruction k.

$(S(r), k, l)$:   If register r is not empty then subtract one from its contents and go to instruction k, otherwise proceed to instruction l.

$Halt$:   Stop the machine. This additional instruction can only be assigned to the final label h.

Deterministic n-register machines can be used to compute any partial recursive function $f : \mathbf{N}^\alpha \to \mathbf{N}^\beta$; starting with $(n_1, ..., n_\alpha) \in \mathbf{N}^\alpha$ in registers 1 to α, M has computed $f(n_1, ..., n_\alpha) = (r_1, ..., r_\beta)$ if it halts in the final label h with registers 1 to β containing r_1 to r_β. If the final label cannot be reached, $f(n_1, ..., n_\alpha)$ remains undefined.

The results proved in [5] as well as in [6] and [8] immediately lead us to the following result (using a slightly different definition for the result of a computation):

Proposition 1. For any partial recursive function $f : \mathbf{N}^\alpha \to \mathbf{N}^\beta$ there exists a deterministic $(\alpha + 2 + \beta)$-register machine M computing f in such a way that, when starting with $(n_1, ..., n_\alpha) \in \mathbf{N}^\alpha$ in registers 1 to α, M has computed $f(n_1, ..., n_\alpha) = (r_1, ..., r_\beta)$ if it halts in the final label h with registers $\alpha + 3$ to $\alpha + 2 + \beta$ containing r_1 to r_β, and all other registers being empty; if the final label cannot be reached, $f(n_1, ..., n_\alpha)$ remains undefined.

3   Catalytic P Systems

The standard type of membrane systems (P systems) has been studied in many papers and several monographs; we refer to [4], [12], [13], and [14] for motivation and examples as well as to [18] for an up-to-date bibliography. In the definition of a (special variant of a) catalytic P system (catalytic P systems first were considered in [3]) below we omit some ingredients (like priority relations on the rules) not needed in the following.

3.1   Definition

A *catalytic P system (of degree d, d ≥ 1)* is a construct

$$\Pi = (V, C, T_1, T_2, \mu, w_0, \ldots, w_d, R_0, \ldots, R_d, i_0) \text{ where}$$

1. V is an alphabet; its elements are called *objects*;
2. $C \subseteq V$ is a set of *catalysts*;
3. $T_1 \subseteq V - C$ is the input alphabet;
4. $T_2 \subseteq V - C$ is the output alphabet;
5. μ is a membrane structure consisting of $d + 1$ membranes (usually labelled with i and represented by corresponding brackets $[_i$ and $]_i$, $0 \le i \le d$);
6. w_i, $0 \le i \le d$, are strings over V associated with the regions $0, \ldots, d$ of μ; they represent multisets of objects from V, the objects from C appearing at most once in each region of μ;
7. R_i, $0 \le i \le d$, are finite sets of catalytic *evolution rules* over V associated with the regions $0, \ldots, d$ of μ; these catalytic evolution rules are of the form $ca \rightarrow cv$, where c is a catalyst, a is an object from $V - C$, and v is a string from $((V - C) \times \{here, out, in\})^*$;
8. i_0 is a number between 0 and d and it specifies the *input/output* membrane of Π.

The membrane structure and the multisets represented by w_i, $0 \le i \le d$, in Π constitute the *initial configuration* of the system; the input vector is given by the corresponding multiset of symbols over T_1 in membrane i_0. A transition between configurations is governed by the application of the evolution rules which is done in parallel: all objects, from all membranes, which *can be* the subject of local evolution rules *have to* evolve simultaneously.

The system continues parallel steps until there remain no applicable rules in any region of Π; then the system halts. We consider the number of objects from T_2 contained in the output membrane i_0 at the moment when the system halts as the *result* of the underlying computation of Π.

3.2 k-Determinism

To represent a computation in a catalytic P system we will now, following the definition given in [14], use the notion of a computation tree:

The *computation tree* of a catalytic P system is a rooted labelled maximal tree, where the root node of the tree corresponds to the initial configuration of the system. The children of a node are configurations that follow in a one-step transition. Nodes are labelled by configurations and edges are labelled by sets of applicable rules. We say that a computation halts if it represents a finite branch in the computation tree.

To be more efficient in an implementation, we only consider catalytic P systems having the specific feature that we do not have to expand the complete computation tree during the simulation, but rather "look ahead" in the computation tree at most k steps for some fixed k to be able to exclude the paths which would lead to an infinite loop (because of containing a special symbol #, the trap symbol, for which always rules have to be present to guarantee that a configuration containing at least one such symbol can never be part of a halting computation) and choose the (only) path which may lead to a successful continuation (i.e., possibly being part of a halting computation).

For $k \geq 0$, the notion of k-*determinism* for catalytic P systems is defined as follows:

$k = 0$: A catalytic P system is called *deterministic* (is called 0-*deterministic*, is said to have a *level of look-ahead* 0), if at any step of a computation, there exists at most one configuration derivable from the current one. If at some stage of the computation the trap symbol # appears in the current configuration, we stop the computation without getting a result.

$k = 1$: A catalytic P system is called 1-*deterministic* (is said to have a level of *look-ahead* 1), if at any step of a computation, either
- there is no configuration derivable from the current one, i.e., the computation halts (and yields a result) **or**
- all configurations derivable from the current one contain the trap symbol # (hence, we stop without continuing the computation, no result is obtained) **or**
- there exists exactly one configuration which is derivable from the current one and does not contain the trap symbol #. As configurations containing the trap symbol can never lead to a halting computation (and therefore can never yield a result), the only reasonable continuation is the configuration not containing the trap symbol.

$k > 1$: For $k > 1$, a catalytic P system is called k-*deterministic* (is said to have a *level of look-ahead* k) if the following condition holds: At any moment of a computation, either
- the computation halts (and yields a result) **or**
- for any arbitrary configuration derivable from the current one we make $k - 1$ further steps and for all these branches of depth $k - 1$ we end up with a configuration containing the trap symbol # (hence, we stop without continuing the computation, no result is obtained) **or**

- for exactly one configuration c derivable from the current one there is at least one branch of the computation tree which cannot be continued (and therefore will yield a result at the end of this branch) or is of depth $k - 1$, with the root being this configuration, and the trap symbol # does not appear in any of the configurations along this branch. This uniquely determined configuration c is chosen for continuing the computation.

In each step of a computation in a k-deterministic P system there exists exactly one uniquely determined set of rules to be applied for possibly continuing the computation: either this set is empty, i.e., we stop (getting a result only in the case that we halt), or we continue with applying a non-empty set yielding the uniquely determined configuration possibly being part of a successful halting computation.

Following the proofs elaborated in [7] (by using Proposition 1) as well as in [11] we now show that any partial recursive function $f : \mathbf{N}^\alpha \to \mathbf{N}^\beta$ can be computed by a 4-deterministic catalytic P system with only one membrane and with only $\alpha + 3$ catalysts:

Theorem 2. *For each partial recursive function* $f : N^\alpha \to N^\beta$ *there is a catalytic P system* $\Pi = (V, C, T_1, T_2, [_0]_0, w, R, 0)$ *with* $\alpha + 3$ *catalysts and with the objects* $o_a \in T_1$ *satisfying the following conditions: For any arbitrary* $(x_1, ..., x_\alpha) \in N^\alpha$, *denote*

$$\Pi_{(x_1,...,x_\alpha)} = (V, C, T_1, T_2, [_0]_0, wo_1^{x_1}...o_\alpha^{x_\alpha}, R, 0).$$

The system $\Pi_{(x_1,...,x_\alpha)}$ *halts if and only if* $f(x_1, ..., x_\alpha)$ *is defined, and if it halts, then in the skin membrane, besides the catalysts, only the terminal symbols* $o_{\alpha+3}$ *to* $o_{\alpha+2+\beta}$ *appear with multiplicities* $y_1, ..., y_\beta$ *representing the output vector* $f(x_1, ..., x_\alpha) = (y_1, ..., y_\beta)$. *Moreover, the catalytic P system* Π *is 4-deterministic.*

Proof. Consider a (deterministic) register machine M as defined above with m' registers, the last β registers being special output registers which are never decremented. (From the result stated in Proposition 1 we know that $m' = \alpha + 2 + \beta$ is sufficient). Now let $m = m' - \beta$ and let P be a program which computes the function f such that the initial instruction has the label 1 and the halting instruction has the label n. The input values $x_1, ..., x_\alpha$ are expected to be in the first α registers and the output values from $f(x_1, ..., x_\alpha)$ are expected to be in registers $m + 1$ to m'. Moreover, without loss of generality, we may assume that at the beginning of a computation all the registers except possibly the registers 1 to α contain zero.

We now construct the P system

$$\Pi = (V, C, \{o_k \mid 1 \le k \le \alpha\}, \{o_k \mid m+1 \le k \le m'\}, [_0]_0, w, R, 0) \text{ with}$$

$$V = \{\#\} \cup \{c_i, c_i', c_i'' \mid 1 \le i \le m\} \cup \{c_{m+1}\} \cup \{o_k \mid 1 \le k \le m'\}$$
$$\cup \left\{p_n^{\langle h,1 \rangle} \mid 1 \le h \le m\right\} \cup \left\{p_j^{\langle h,1 \rangle} \mid 1 \le h \le m, \ j : (A(a), k, k) \in P\right\}$$
$$\cup \left\{p_j^{\langle h,1 \rangle} \mid 1 \le h \le m, \ j : (S(a), k, l) \in P\right\}$$
$$\cup \left\{p_j^{\langle h,l \rangle} \mid 2 \le h < m, \ 1 \le l \le 4, \ j : (S(a), k, l) \in P\right\}$$
$$\cup \left\{p_j', p_j'', \bar{p}_j, \bar{p}_j', \bar{p}_j'', \hat{p}_j, \hat{p}_j', \hat{p}_j'' \mid j : (S(a), k, l) \in P\right\},$$

the set of catalysts

$$C = \{c_i \mid 1 \le i \le m+1\},$$

the initial multiset

$$w = c_1 \ldots c_m c_{m+1} p_1^{\langle 1,1 \rangle} \ldots p_1^{\langle m,1 \rangle}$$

(for any arbitrary $(x_1, \ldots, x_\alpha) \in \mathbf{N}_0^\alpha$, the initial multiset of the corresponding system $\Pi_{(x_1, \ldots, x_\alpha)}$ therefore is $c_1 \ldots c_m c_{m+1} p_1^{\langle 1,1 \rangle} \ldots p_1^{\langle m,1 \rangle} o_1^{x_1} \ldots o_\alpha^{x_\alpha}$), as well as the following set of catalytic rules R :

$$R = \{c_{m+1} x \to c_{m+1} \# \mid x \in V - (C \cup \{o_k \mid 1 \le k \le m'\} \cup$$
$$\{\bar{p}_j', \hat{p}_j' \mid j : (S(a), k, l) \in P\})\}$$
$$\cup \left\{c_{m \ominus_m h} p_n^{\langle h,1 \rangle} \to c_{m \ominus_m h} \mid 1 \le h \le m\right\}$$
$$\cup \left\{c_{m \ominus_m h} p_j^{\langle h,1 \rangle} \to c_{m \ominus_m h} \mid 1 \le h < m, \ 1 \le a \le m',\right.$$
$$j : (A(a), k, k) \in P\Big\}$$
$$\cup \left\{c_m p_j^{\langle m,1 \rangle} \to c_m p_k^{\langle 1,1 \rangle} \ldots p_k^{\langle m,1 \rangle} o_a \mid 1 \le a \le m', j : (A(a), k, k) \in P\right\}$$
$$\cup \left\{c_{a \ominus_m h} p_j^{\langle h,l \rangle} \to c_{a \ominus_m h} p_j^{\langle h,l+1 \rangle} \mid 2 \le h < m, \ 1 \le a \le m,\right.$$
$$1 \le l \le 3, \ j : (S(a), k, l) \in P\Big\}$$
$$\cup \left\{c_{a \ominus_m h} p_j^{\langle h,4 \rangle} \to c_{a \ominus_m h} \mid 2 \le h < m, \ 1 \le a \le m, j : (S(a), k, l) \in P\right\}$$
$$\cup \left\{c_a p_j^{\langle m,1 \rangle} \to c_a \hat{p}_j \hat{p}_j', c_a p_j^{\langle m,1 \rangle} \to c_a \bar{p}_j \bar{p}_j' \bar{p}_j'',\right.$$
$$c_a o_a \to c_a c_a', c_a c_a' \to c_a c_a'', c_{a \ominus_m 1} c_a'' \to c_{a \ominus_m 1},$$
$$c_a \hat{p}_j' \to c_a \#, c_{a \ominus_m 1} \hat{p}_j' \to c_{a \ominus_m 1} \hat{p}_j'', c_a \hat{p}_j'' \to c_a p_k^{\langle 1,1 \rangle} \ldots p_k^{\langle m,1 \rangle},$$
$$c_a \bar{p}_j \to c_a, c_{a \ominus_m 1} \bar{p}_j'' \to c_{a \ominus_m 1} \bar{p}_j'', c_{a \ominus_m 1} \bar{p}_j'' \to c_{a \ominus_m 1} \bar{p}_j',$$
$$c_a p_j' \to c_a p_l^{\langle 1,1 \rangle} \ldots p_l^{\langle m,1 \rangle} \mid 1 \le a \le m, \ j : (S(a), k, l) \in P\Big\}$$
$$\cup \left\{c_{a \ominus_m 1} y \to c_{a \ominus_m 1} \mid y \in \left\{p_j^{\langle 1,1 \rangle}, \hat{p}_j, \bar{p}_j'\right\}, 1 \le a \le m,\right.$$
$$j : (S(a), k, l) \in P\Big\}.$$

The set of rules R depends on the instructions of P; the halting instruction as well as each add-instruction is simulated in one step, whereas each subtract-instruction is simulated in four steps; in more detail, the simulation works as follows:

1. Every simulation of a rule starts with the program labels $p_1^{\langle 1,1\rangle}, ..., p_1^{\langle m,1\rangle}$. The halting instruction eliminates the final labels $p_n^{\langle 1,1\rangle}, ..., p_n^{\langle m,1\rangle}$ by using the rules $c_{m\ominus_m h} p_n^{\langle h,1\rangle} \to c_{m\ominus_m h}$, $1 \le h \le m$.

2. Each add-instruction $j : (A(a), k, k) \in P$, $1 \le a \le m'$, is simulated in one step by using the catalytic rules $c_{m\ominus_m h} p_j^{\langle h,1\rangle} \to c_{m\ominus_m h}$, $1 \le h < m$, as well as $c_m p_j^{\langle m,1\rangle} \to c_m p_k^{\langle 1,1\rangle} ... p_k^{\langle m,1\rangle} o_a$. Observe that by definition $a \ominus_m m = a$ for all a with $1 \le a \le m$.

3. Each subtract-instruction $j : (S(a), k, l) \in P$ is simulated in the four steps that are shown in the following table:

simulation of the subtract-instruction $j : (S(a), k, l)$ if	
a. register a is not empty	**b.** register a is empty
$c_a p_j^{\langle m,1\rangle} \to c_a \hat{p}_j \hat{p}_j'$	$c_a p_j^{\langle m,1\rangle} \to c_a \bar{p}_j \bar{p}_j' \bar{p}_j''$
$c_{a\ominus_m 1} p_j^{\langle 1,1\rangle} \to c_{a\ominus_m 1}$	$c_{a\ominus_m 1} p_j^{\langle 1,1\rangle} \to c_{a\ominus_m 1}$
$c_a o_a \to c_a c_a'$	$c_a \bar{p}_j \to c_a$
$\langle c_a \hat{p}_j' \to c_a \# \rangle$	
$c_{a\ominus_m 1} \hat{p}_j \to c_{a\ominus_m 1}$	$c_{a\ominus_m 1} \bar{p}_j'' \to c_{a\ominus_m 1} p_j''$
$c_a c_a' \to c_a c_a''$	
	$\langle c_a o_a \to c_a c_a' \rangle$
$c_{a\ominus_m 1} \hat{p}_j' \to c_{a\ominus_m 1} \hat{p}_j''$	$c_{a\ominus_m 1} p_j'' \to c_{a\ominus_m 1} p_j'$
$c_a \hat{p}_j'' \to c_a p_k^{\langle 1,1\rangle} ... p_k^{\langle m,1\rangle}$	$c_a p_j' \to c_a p_l^{\langle 1,1\rangle} ... p_l^{\langle m,1\rangle}$
$c_{a\ominus_m 1} c_a'' \to c_{a\ominus_m 1}$	$c_{a\ominus_m 1} \bar{p}_j' \to c_{a\ominus_m 1}$

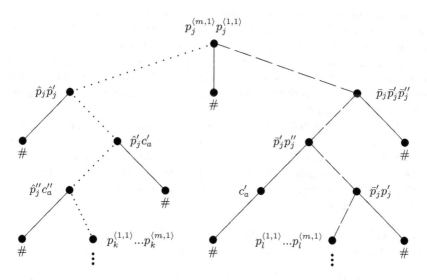

Fig. 1. Schematic representaion of the computation subtree

In order to argue that we only have to make a look-ahead of depth 4 to find out the correct set of catalytic rules for a successful continuation of the computation in Π, we give a schematic representation of the computation subtree of this situation for a subtract-instruction in Fig. 1, where we omit any objects that might also be part of the respective configuration, but do not appear in the table given above, and we also omit to include the catalysts c_a and $c_{a\ominus_m 1}$, respectively, as they are contained in all configurations; moreover, we represent all misleading configurations by # only.

It follows from the explanations given above that at most four steps are needed until the trap symbol # finally appears after having made a wrong non-deterministic decision. Consequently, the constructed catalytic P system Π is 4-deterministic.   □

4   Implementation

Only a few variants of P systems have been implemented so far (e.g., see [1], [2], and [17]). Usually, the main difficulty is how to choose a branch of the computation tree possibly leading to a result in a halting computation.

The main feature used in our implementation is the k-determinism of the underlying model of P systems which at any step of the computation allows for a deterministic continuation of the computation, i.e., the next configuration (if it exists) is uniquely determined (after having checked all branches of depth at most k, starting from the current configuration) and at the same time we are also able to state the set of productions leading to this uniquely determined configuration.

Based on the theoretical background elaborated in the preceding section, we implemented a simulation tool for k-deterministic catalytic P systems; the program was written in Java 2.0 (to be platform-independent) and was tested with several examples (e.g., see below for a very simple one; other examples based on the general simulation procedures described in the proof of Theorem 2 were chosen, too, in order to verify the given construction) showing efficient run-time behaviour on standard PCs.

The first screenshot (see Fig. 2) shows how arbitrary membrane structures can be edited. In the example we see the membrane structure $[_0[_1]_1[_2[_3]_3[_4]_4]_2]_0$; the outermost membrane - labelled by 0 - is called skin (membrane).

The following screenshots show the initialization of the system (Fig. 3) and the editing of the catalytic rules (Fig. 4). For showing the main features of the tool, we here refer to the catalytic P system

$$\Pi = (V, \{c_1, c_2, c_3\}, \{a_0\}, \{b_0\}, [_0]_0, c_1 c_2 c_3 X_4 X_5, R, 0) \text{ with}$$
$$V = \{X_i \mid 0 \le i \le 7\} \cup \{a_0, b_0, \#, c_1, c_2, c_3\}$$

which by adding the input $a_0{}^n$ computes $b_0{}^{2n}$ using the following rules in R:

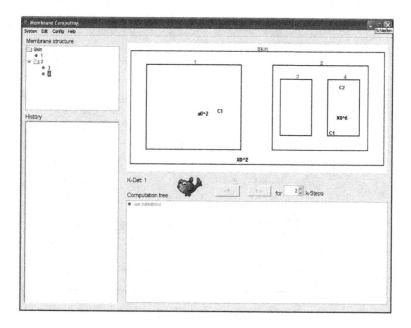

Fig. 2. Editing the membrane structure

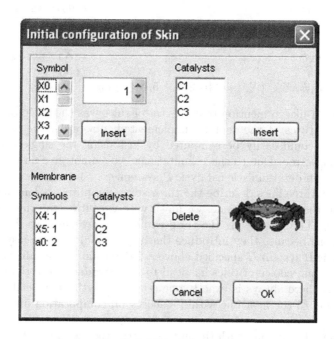

Fig. 3. Initial configuration

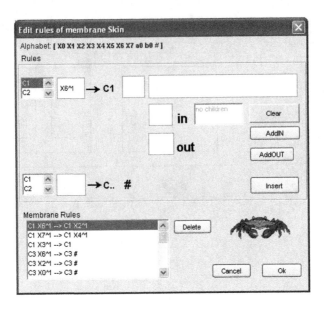

Fig. 4. Editing rules

$$c_1 X_5 \to c_1 X_6 X_7 b_0 b_0 \qquad\qquad c_2 X_4 \to c_2$$
$$c_1 X_6 \to c_1 X_2 \qquad\qquad c_2 a_0 \to c_2, c_2 X_7 \to c_2 \#$$
$$c_1 X_7 \to c_1 X_4 \qquad\qquad c_2 X_2 \to c_2 X_5$$
$$c_1 X_5 \to c_1 X_0 X_1 \qquad\qquad c_2 X_4 \to c_2$$
$$c_1 a_0 \to c_1 \# \qquad\qquad c_2 X_0 \to c_2 X_3$$
$$c_1 X_3 \to c_1 \qquad\qquad c_2 X_1 \to c_2$$
$$c_3 X \to c_3 \#, X \in \{X_i \mid i \in \{0,2,3,4,5,6\}\} \cup \{\#\}$$

We should like to mention that this set of rules was chosen in order to show the main features of the tool we implemented; obviously, the same function $a_0{}^n \mapsto b_0{}^{2n}$ could easily be computed by just using the single catalytic rule $c_1 a_0 \to c_1 b_0 b_0$, too. Due to space limitations, we cannot give an example of an inherently non-deterministic catalytic P system.

The first three lines describe the three steps computed as long as there still is an a_0 in the skin membrane; we finish with executing the rules depicted in lines 4 to 6. The rules using the third catalyst c_3 are never used in successful computations because they introduce the trap symbol $\#$. It is easy to see that the catalytic P system Π specified above is 2-deterministic, as after at most two steps the wrong choice of rules has lead to the introduction of the trap symbol $\#$, whereas there always is exactly one set of catalytic rules leading from one configuration to the next one within a successful computation until the system halts.

For example, starting with the input $a_0{}^2$, the tool computes the correct output value $b_0{}^4$ halting in the final configuration as depicted in Fig. 5:

Moreover, the screenshot above also shows that the tool computes every branch of the computation tree until the trap symbol appears, which allows the user to check the correct working of the catalytic P system.

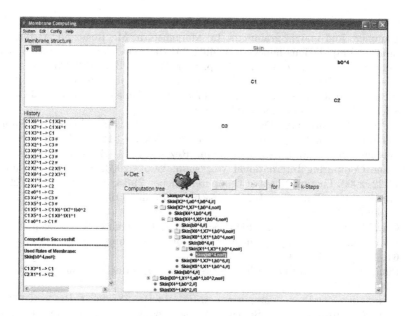

Fig. 5. Final configuration

5   Conclusion

In this paper we have presented an implementation of catalytic P systems which turned out to be quite efficient due to the k-deterministic simulation of deterministic register machines. The idea of k-determinism can also be used for obtaining more efficient implementations of several other variants of P systems; such implementations will be part of future research.

References

1. Arroyo, F., Luengo, C., Baranda, A.V., de Mingo, L.F.: A software simulation of transition P systems in Haskell. In: [15] 19–32
2. Ciobanu, G., Wenyuan, G.: P systems running on a cluster of computers. In: [9] 123–139
3. Dang, Z., Egecioglu, O., Ibarra, O. H., Saxena, G.: Characterizations of catalytic membrane computing systems. In: Rovan, B., Vojtás, P. (eds.): 28th International Symposium on Mathematical Foundations of Computer Science 2003, MFCS 2003, Bratislava, Slovakia, August 25-29, 2003. Lecture Notes in Computer Science **2747**, Springer, Berlin (2003) 480–489
4. Dassow, J., Păun, Gh.: On the power of membrane computing. Journal of Universal Computer Science **5**, 2 (1999) 33–49
5. Freund, R., Oswald, M.: GP systems with forbidding context. Fundamenta Informaticae **49**, 1–3 (2002) 81–102

6. Freund, R., Păun, Gh.: On the number of non-terminals in graph-controlled, programmed, and matrix grammars. In: Margenstern, M., Rogozhin, Y. (eds.): Machines, Computations and Universality. 3rd Internat. Conf., MCU 2001. Lecture Notes in Computer Science **2055**, Springer, Berlin (2001) 214–225

7. Freund, R., Kari, L., Oswald, M., Sosík, P.: Computationally universal P systems without priorities: two catalysts are sufficient. To appear in Theoretical Computer Science. Preversion downloadable at [18]

8. Freund, R., Păun, Gh.: From regulated rewriting to computing with membranes: collapsing hierarchies. Theoretical Computer Science **312** (2004) 143–188

9. Martín-Vide, C., Mauri, G., Păun, Gh., Rozenberg, G., Salomaa, A. (eds.): Membrane Computing International Workshop, WMC 2003, Tarragona, Spain, July 17-22, 2003. Lecture Notes in Computer Science **2933**, Springer, Berlin (2004)

10. Minsky, M. L.: Finite and Infinite Machines. Prentice Hall, Englewood Cliffs, New Jersey (1967)

11. Oswald, M.: P Automata. PhD thesis. Vienna University of Technology (2003)

12. Păun, Gh.: Computing with membranes. Journal of Computer and System Sciences **61**, 1 (2000) 108–143

13. Păun, Gh.: Computing with membranes: an introduction. Bulletin EATCS **67** (1999) 139–152

14. Păun, Gh.: Membrane Computing: an Introduction. Springer, Berlin (2002)

15. Păun, Gh., Rozenberg, G., Salomaa, A., Zandron, C. (eds.): Membrane Computing. International Workshop, WMC-CdeA 2002, Curtea de Argeş, Romania, August 2002. Lecture Notes in Computer Science **2597**, Springer, Berlin (2003)

16. Sosík, P., Freund, R.: P systems without priorities are computationally universal. In: [15] 400–409

17. Syropoulos, A., Mamatas, E. G., Allilomes, P. C., Sotiriades, K. T.: A distributed simulation of transition P systems. In: [9] 357–368

18. The P Systems Web Page. http://psystems.disco.unimib.it

Code Selection by Tree Series Transducers

Björn Borchardt*

Dresden University of Technology,
Department of Computer Science, 01062 Dresden, Germany
borchard@tcs.inf.tu-dresden.de

Abstract. In this paper we model code selection by tree series transducers. We are given an intermediate representation of some compiler as well as a machine grammar with weights, which reflect the number of machine cycles of the instructions. The derivations of the machine grammar are machine codes. In general, a machine grammar is ambiguous and hence there might exist more than one derivation of an intermediate code. We show how to filter out a cheapest such derivation and thereby perform tree parsing and tree pattern matching using tree series transducers.

1   Introduction

In this paper we model code selection (cf. [GG78]) by tree series transducers (for short: trstr's). In general, a machine grammar is ambiguous and hence, for some intermediate representation (for short: IR) there might exist several machine codes. We would like to find a cheapest machine code, i.e., a machine code with the least number of machine cycles. To visualize this, let us consider the following example (cf. [GL97]): for the C-expression $(f + i)$, where f and i are of type `float` and `int`, respectively, a cheapest machine code for an Intel iapX86 instruction set should be generated. All floating point operations are performed in an internal format. There are several possibilities for encoding $(f + i)$ in the Intel instruction set: first both f and i are loaded and converted into the internal format and then put into registers, from which the floating point addition finally takes its arguments. Alternatively, only f is loaded and converted into the internal format and put into a register; the floating point addition then would take i from the memory and implicitly perform the loading and converting, or vice versa. It turns out that the second of these alternatives is best.

In this paper we follow and extend the approach of [FSW94], in which techniques of tree automata (e.g., subset construction) are applied to code selection. We generate the cheapest machine code by using the more powerful model of trstr's (cf. [EFV02]). This gives us the chance to describe the cheapest machine code as output of a sequence of trstr's. Let us therefore briefly recall the concept of (polynomial, top-down) trstr's. Basically, trstr's generalize tree transducers (for short: trtr's) by associating to every transition a weight, which is taken from

---

* Financially supported by the German Research Foundation (DFG, grant GK 334/3).

M. Domaratzki et al. (Eds.): CIAA 2004, LNCS 3317, pp. 57–67, 2005.

a semiring. The tree transformation of a trstr is similar to that of classical trtr, but additionally weights are accumulated: the weights of the transitions of a run on an input tree s are multiplied and finally the weights of all accepting runs which translate s to the same output tree t are summed up. Hence s is transformed by M into the tree series $\tau_M(s)$. The support of $\tau_M(s)$ can be considered as the set of output trees and $(\tau_M(s))(t)$ denotes the weight of the transformation from s to t. We note that trstr's also cover (top-down) finite state weighted tree automata (for short: w-fta, cf. [BR82]).

We select the cheapest machine code by modeling the given machine grammar G by a regular, weighted tree grammar. Then the trstr M_G^{TP} translates the given IR s into the tree series $\tau_{M_G^{\mathrm{TP}}}(s)$. Each tree of the support of this tree series uniquely corresponds to a machine code, i.e., a derivation of the associated regular, weighted tree grammar, and the coefficient of such an output tree is the number of required machine cycles of the corresponding machine code, i.e., the weight of the corresponding derivation (tree parsing; also cf. [GG78]). The cheapest machine code of s then can be found by searching in the tree series $\tau_{M_G^{\mathrm{TP}}}(s)$ for a tree with minimal weight. We also show how to compute this minimal weight by providing the w-fta M_G^{mincost}. Moreover, we would like to find all occurrences of the right hand side of a rule r of G in s (tree pattern matching; also cf. [HO82]). Therefore we present the w-fta $M_{\tilde{r}}^{\mathrm{PM}}$, which generates the set of all occurrences of the right hand side of r in the input tree.

Let us point out the two main improvements to [FSW94]. There tree parsing is done by representing machine code as a computation of tree automata, while we generate the machine code explicitly. Moreover, tree pattern matching is solved in the aforementioned paper by deciding, whether or not a pattern is contained in the input tree, whereas we compute all the references on the occurrences of the pattern in the input tree.

This paper is organized as follows: in Sect. 2 we recall basic concepts, while the code selection problem is attacked in Sect. 3. We conclude this paper in Sect. 4 by stating open problems.

2   Preliminaries

2.1   Notions on Trees

Throughout this paper $\mathbb{N}$ and $\mathbb{N}_+$ denote the sets of all non-negative integers and all positive integers, respectively. Moreover, for every $i, j \in \mathbb{N}$, $[i, j] = \{n \in \mathbb{N} \mid i \leq n \leq j\}$. We abbreviate $[1, i]$ by $[i]$. Also, let $x_1, x_2, \ldots$ be variables, $X = \{x_1, x_2, \ldots\}$, and $X_n = \{x_1, \ldots, x_n\}$ for every $n \in \mathbb{N}$. A *ranked alphabet* is a tuple (Σ, rk) consisting of a non-empty, finite set Σ being disjoint with X and a rank mapping $\mathrm{rk} : \Sigma \to \mathbb{N}$. We always assume the rank mapping to be implicitly given and write Σ rather than (Σ, rk). Moreover, let $\Sigma^{(k)} = \{\sigma \in \Sigma \mid \mathrm{rk}(\sigma) = k\}$ for every $k \in \mathbb{N}$ and let $\mathrm{maxrk}(\Sigma) \in \mathbb{N} = \max\{k \in \mathbb{N} \mid \Sigma^{(k)} \neq \emptyset\}$. Now let $X' \subseteq X$. The set of *trees over Σ (indexed by X')* is denoted by $T_\Sigma(X')$ and defined to be the smallest subset T of $(\Sigma \cup X' \cup \{(,), ,\})^*$ satisfying (i) $X' \subseteq T$

and (ii) given $k \in \mathbb{N}$, $\sigma \in \Sigma^{(k)}$, and $t_1, \ldots, t_k \in T$, then $\sigma(t_1, \ldots, t_k) \in T$. As usual, we set $T_\Sigma = T_\Sigma(\emptyset)$. We will be short in notation and write $s = \sigma(s_1, \ldots, s_k) \in T_\Sigma(X')$ as a shorthand for "there exist $k \in \mathbb{N}$, $\sigma \in \Sigma^{(k)}$, and $s_1, \ldots, s_k \in T_\Sigma(X')$". To define the tree substitution let $t \in T_\Sigma(X_n)$ for some $n \in \mathbb{N}$ and $s_1, \ldots, s_n \in T_\Sigma(X)$. Then $t[s_1, \ldots, s_n] \in T_\Sigma(X)$ is obtained from t by replacing simultaneously every occurrence of every variable $x_i \in X_n$ by s_i.

Let us now define some properties of a tree $s \in T_\Sigma(X')$. The *number* $\#_{X'}(s) \in \mathbb{N}$ *of occurrences of elements of* X' *in* s and the set $\mathrm{pos}(s) \in \mathfrak{P}(\mathbb{N}^*)$ *of positions of* s are given by $\#_{X'}(s) = 1$ and $\mathrm{pos}(s) = \{\varepsilon\}$ if $s \in X'$, and $\#_{X'}(s) = \sum_{i \in [k]} \#_{X'}(s_i)$ and $\mathrm{pos}(s) = \{\varepsilon\} \cup \{i.o \mid i \in [k], o \in \mathrm{pos}(s_i)\}$ provided that $s = \sigma(s_1, \ldots, s_k) \in T_\Sigma(X')$. Further, for every $i \in \mathbb{N}$ the *position* $o(s, i) \in \mathrm{pos}(s)$ *of the* ith *occurrence of an element of* X' *in* s is $o(s, 1) = \varepsilon$ provided that $s \in X'$, $o(s, i) = j.o(s_j, i')$ if $s = \sigma(s_1, \ldots, s_k) \in T_\Sigma(X')$ and there exist an $i' \in \mathbb{N}$ and a $j \in [k]$ such that $j = \sum_{l \in [j-1]} \#_{X'}(s_l) + i'$; otherwise $o(s, i)$ is undefined. Further, for every $o \in \mathrm{pos}(s)$ the *subtree* $s|_o \in T_\Sigma$ *of* s *at position* o is defined by $s|_o = s$ and provided that $o = \varepsilon$ and if $o = i.o'$ for some $i \in [k]$ and $o' \in \mathrm{pos}(s_i)$ then $s|_o = s_i|_{o'}$. We call s a *subtree of* t, denoted by $s \leq t$ if $s = t|_o$ for some $o \in \mathrm{pos}(t)$. Finally, for every $o \in \mathrm{pos}(s)$ the *label* $\mathrm{lab}_s(o) \in \Sigma$ *of* s *at position* o is given by $\mathrm{lab}_s(o) = s$ provided that $s \in X'$, $\mathrm{lab}_s(o) = \sigma$ if $s = \sigma(s_1, \ldots, s_k) \in T_\Sigma(X')$ and $o = \varepsilon$, and $\mathrm{lab}_s(o) = \mathrm{lab}_{s_i}(o')$, if $s = \sigma(s_1, \ldots, s_k) \in T_\Sigma(X')$ and $o = i.o'$ for some $i \in [k]$ and $o' \in \mathrm{pos}(s_i)$.

For a given $n \in \mathbb{N}$ and ranked alphabet Σ, a *pattern* (also: *(Σ-n-) context*) is a tree $C \in (X_n)$ such that every variable $x_i \in X_n$ occurs precisely once in C. The class of all Σ-n-contexts is denoted by $C_\Sigma(X_n)$. If $C \in C_\Sigma(X_n)$, $t \in T_\Sigma$, and $o \in \mathrm{pos}(t)$, then C *is a pattern of* t *at position* o, if $t|_o = C[t_1, \ldots, t_n]$ for some trees $t_1, \ldots, t_n \in T_\Sigma$. Finally, $\mathrm{occ}_C(t)$ is the set of all $o \in \mathrm{pos}(t)$ of t such that C is a pattern of t at o.

2.2   Semirings

A *semiring* is tuple $\mathcal{A} = (A, \oplus, \odot, \mathbf{0}, \mathbf{1})$ satisfying the following conditions: (i) $(A, \oplus, \mathbf{0})$ is a commutative monoid (i.e., $\oplus$ is a binary, associative, commutative operation on A with the neutral element $\mathbf{0}$), (ii) $(A, \odot, \mathbf{1})$ is a monoid, (iii) $\odot$ distributes over $\oplus$, (i.e., $a \odot (b \oplus c) = (a \odot b) \oplus (a \odot c)$ and $(a \oplus b) \odot c = (a \odot c) \oplus (b \odot c)$ for every $a, b, c \in A$), and (iv) $\mathbf{0}$ is absorptive (i.e., $\mathbf{0} \odot a = \mathbf{0} = a \odot \mathbf{0}$ for every $a \in A$). For a finite index set $I = \{i_1, \ldots, i_n\}$ and semiring elements $a_{i_j} \in A$ for every $j \in [n]$ we write $\bigoplus_{i \in I} a_i$ for $a_{i_1} \oplus \cdots \oplus a_{i_n}$ provided that $I \neq \emptyset$. For the sake of completeness we set $\bigoplus_{i \in I} a_i = \mathbf{0}$ if $I = \emptyset$. Throughout this paper let $\mathcal{A} = (A, \oplus, \odot, \mathbf{0}, \mathbf{1})$ be a semiring. In this paper we make us of the Boolean semiring $\mathrm{Bool} = (\{0, 1\}, \vee, \wedge, 0, 1)$, the Tropical semiring $\mathrm{Trop} = (\mathbb{N} \cup \{+\infty\}, \min, +, +\infty, 0)$, and for a (not necessarily finite) alphabet Σ the language semiring $\mathrm{Lang}_\Sigma = (\mathfrak{P}(\Sigma), \cup, ., \emptyset, \{\varepsilon\})$.

2.3   Tree Series and Tree Series Substitution

Let Σ be a ranked alphabet and $X' \subseteq X$. A *(formal) tree series (over* Σ *and* $\mathcal{A}$*)* is a total mapping $S : T_\Sigma(X') \rightarrow A$. The image $S(t) \in A$ is called *coefficient of*

$t \in T_\Sigma(X')$, and as usual, we write (S, t) rather than $S(t)$. The tree series, which maps every $t \in T_\Sigma(X')$ to $\mathbf{0}$, is denoted by $\widetilde{\mathbf{0}}$. The *support of S* is defined to be the set $\mathrm{supp}(S) = \{t \in T_\Sigma(X') \mid (S, t) \neq \mathbf{0}\}$. We will be short in notation and write $\bigoplus_{t \in \mathrm{supp}(S)}(S, t)\, t$ to denote $\bigoplus_{t \in T_\Sigma}(S, t)\, t$. The tree series S is called *polynomial*, if its support is finite. Further, $A\langle\!\langle T_\Sigma(X')\rangle\!\rangle$ and $A\langle T_\Sigma(X')\rangle$ are the *classes of all tree series* and *of all polynomial tree series over Σ and A*, respectively. The sum of two tree series $S, T \in A\langle\!\langle T_\Sigma(X')\rangle\!\rangle$ is denoted by $S + T$ and defined by pointwise addition, i.e. $(S + T, s) = (S, s) \oplus (T, s)$ for every $s \in T_\Sigma(X')$.

To define the tree series substitution (cf. [EFV02]) let $T \in A\langle T_\Sigma(X_k)\rangle$ and $\boldsymbol{S} = (S_1, \ldots, S_k) \in A\langle T_\Sigma\rangle^k$ for some $k \in \mathbb{N}$. Then for every $s \in T_\Sigma$

$$(T \leftarrow \boldsymbol{S}, s) = \bigoplus_{\substack{t \in \mathrm{supp}(T) \\ (\forall i \in [k]): t_i \in \mathrm{supp}(S_i) \\ s = t[t_1, \ldots, t_k]}} (T, t) \odot (S_1, t_1) \odot \cdots \odot (S_k, t_k) \ .$$

2.4   Regular, Weighted Tree Grammars

Definition 1 (cf. [AB87]). *A regular, weighted tree grammar is defined to be a 6-tuple $G = (\mathcal{N}, \Sigma, I, \mathcal{R}, A, \mathrm{wt})$ satisfying $\mathcal{N} \cap \Sigma = \emptyset$, where $\mathcal{N}$ and Σ are ranked alphabets (of non-terminals and terminals, respectively) with $\mathcal{N} = \mathcal{N}^{(0)}$, $I \in \mathcal{N}$ (the initial non-terminal), $\mathcal{R}$ is a finite set (of rules) $N \to s$, where $N \in \mathcal{N}$, $s \in T_\Sigma(\mathcal{N}) \backslash \mathcal{N}$, and $\mathrm{wt} : \mathcal{R} \to A$ is the weight mapping. Let $r = (N \to s) \in \mathcal{R}$ be a rule. The type of r is $\mathrm{type}(r) = (N_1, \ldots, N_n) \to N$, where $(N_1, \ldots, N_n) \in \mathcal{N}^n$ is the sequence of non-terminals, which is obtained by reading the leaves of s from left to right and omitting all terminals. Moreover, we denote the right hand side s of r by $\mathrm{RHS}(r)$ and define the set $\mathrm{RHS}(G) = \{\mathrm{RHS}(r) \mid r \in \mathcal{R}\}$.*

In order to define the semantics of a regular, weighted tree grammar G let us introduce the notation $\widetilde{r}$ for some rule $r \in \mathcal{R}$ of type $(N_1, \ldots, N_n) \to N$: we define $\widetilde{r} \in C_\Sigma(X_n)$ as the context, which is obtained from $\mathrm{RHS}(r)$ by replacing N_i by x_i for every $i \in [n]$. Moreover, let $\Delta(G) = \{r^{(n)} \mid r \in \mathcal{R}, \mathrm{type}(r) = (N_1, \ldots, N_n) \to N\}$ be a ranked alphabet. An *N-derivation (tree) of $s \in T_\Sigma$* (with respect to G) is a tree $\psi = r(\psi_1, \ldots, \psi_n) \in T_{\Delta(G)}$ such that $r \in \mathcal{R}$ is of type $(N_1, \ldots, N_n) \to N$ and there exist trees $s_1, \ldots, s_n \in T_\Sigma$ with $s = \widetilde{r}[s_1, \ldots, s_n]$ and ψ_i is an N_i-derivation of s_i for every $i \in [n]$. An *I-derivation of s* is also called a *derivation (tree)* (also: *abstract syntax tree*) of s. The set of all derivations of s with respect to G is denoted by $\mathrm{der}_G(s)$. The weight of an N-derivation $r(\psi_1, \ldots, \psi_n)$ where $r \in \mathcal{R}$ is of type $(N_1, \ldots, N_n) \to N$ and ψ_i is a N_i-derivation for every $i \in [n]$ is defined by $\mathrm{wt}(r(\psi_1, \ldots, \psi_n)) = \mathrm{wt}(r) \odot \mathrm{wt}(\psi_1) \odot \cdots \odot \mathrm{wt}(\psi_n)$.

2.5   Tree Series Transducer

Let us now recall the definition of trstr's. Being more precise, we instantiate the concept of trstr's introduced in [EFV02]: for our purposes it suffices to consider top-down trstr, which is reflected in Condition (b) of the next paragraph; also, we restrict the devices to polynomial trstr', i.e., the weight of every transition is a polynomial tree series.

The transitions of a trstr and their weights are coded in a *tree representation* (*over a non-empty ranked alphabet* $Q = Q^{(1)}$ *of states, ranked alphabets* Σ *and* Δ (*of input and output symbols, respectively*), *and* $\mathcal{A}$), *which is a family* $\mu = (\mu_k : \Sigma^{(k)} \rightarrow A\langle T_\Delta(X)\rangle^{Q \times Q(X_k)^*} \mid k \in \mathbb{N})$ *of mappings such that*

(a) *for every* $\sigma \in \Sigma^{(k)}$ *there exist only finitely many indices* $(q, w) \in Q \times Q(X_k)^*$ *satisfying* $\mu_k(\sigma) \neq \widetilde{\mathbf{0}}$ *and*
(b) *for every* $\sigma \in \Sigma^{(k)}$ *and* $(q, w) \in Q \times Q(X_k)^*$ *it holds that* $\mathrm{supp}(\mu_k(\sigma)_{q,w}) \subseteq C_\Sigma(X_l)$, *where* l *denotes the length of* w.

The semantics of a trstr is defined in terms of the mapping $h_\mu : T_\Sigma \rightarrow A\langle T_\Delta\rangle^Q$, given for every $s = \sigma(s_1, \ldots, s_k) \in T_\Sigma$ and $q \in Q$ by

$$h_\mu(s)_q = \bigoplus_{w = q_1(x_{i_1})\ldots q_l(x_{i_l}) \in Q(X_k)^*} \mu_k(\sigma)_{q,w} \leftarrow \left(h_\mu(s_{i_1})_{q_1}, \ldots, h_\mu(s_{i_l})_{q_l}\right) .$$

Definition 2 (cf. [EFV02]). *A (polynomial, top-down) tree series transducer (for short: trstr) is a tuple* $M = (Q, \Sigma, \Delta, Q_d, \mathcal{A}, \mu)$, *where* $Q = Q^{(1)}$, Σ, *and* Δ *are ranked alphabets,* $Q_d \subseteq Q$, *and* μ *is a tree representation over* Q, Σ, Δ, *and* $\mathcal{A}$. *Moreover,* M *is called tree transducer (for short: trtr), if* $\mathcal{A} = \mathrm{Bool}$, *and it is called (finite state) weighted tree automaton (for short: w-fta) if* $\Sigma = \Delta$ *and for every* $k \in \mathbb{N}$, $\sigma \in \Sigma^{(k)}$, $q \in Q$, *and* $w \in Q(X_k)^*$ *it holds that* $\mu_k(\sigma)_{q,w} = a\, \sigma(x_1, \ldots, x_k)$ *for some* $a \in A$ *provided that* $w = q_1(x_1)\ldots q_k(x_k)$, *and* $\mu_k(\sigma)_{q,w} = \widetilde{\mathbf{0}}$ *otherwise. The semantics of* M *is a mapping* $\tau_M : T_\Sigma \rightarrow A\langle T_\Delta\rangle$, *which is defined for every* $s \in T_\Sigma$ *by* $\tau_M(s) = \bigoplus_{q \in Q_d} h_\mu(s)_q$.

As usual, we simplify notations for a trtr by writing $M = (Q, \Sigma, \Delta, F, \mu)$ rather than $M = (Q, \Sigma, \Delta, F, \mathrm{Bool}, \mu)$ and identifying every tree series occurring in the syntax or semantics of M with its support. Moreover, the generation of the output tree by a w-fta is superfluous. Further, if $\mu_k(\sigma)_{q,w} \neq \widetilde{\mathbf{0}}$, then w is of type $q_1(x_1)\ldots q_k(x_k)$. In particular, $\mu_k(\sigma)_{q,w}$ with w not being of the aforementioned type do not contribute to any generated tree series. We therefore shorten notation by writing $M = (Q, \Sigma, Q_d, \mathcal{A}, \mu)$ and $\mu_k(\sigma)_{q,(q_1,\ldots,q_k)} = a$ rather than $M = (Q, \Sigma, \Sigma, Q_d, \mathcal{A}, \mu)$ and $\mu_k(\sigma)_{q,(q_1(x_1),\ldots,q_k(x_k))} = a\, \sigma(x_1, \ldots, x_k)$, respectively. Also, in the accepted tree series $\tau_M(s)$ we omit the output tree, i.e., a stands for $a\, s$. Hence, every input tree is accepted by a w-fta with a semiring element. Thus the semantics of M also can be considered as a tree series, which we denote by S_M.

3   Code Selection

For the rest of this section let $G = (\mathcal{N}, \Sigma, I, \mathcal{R}, \mathrm{Trop}, \mathrm{wt})$ be a regular, weighted tree grammar and $s \in T_\Sigma$.

3.1   Tree Parsing

In this section we generate a representation of all derivations of s together with their costs, i.e. we solve the (extended) tree parsing problem (cf. [GG78]):

> **(Extended) Tree Parsing Problem:** Compute explicitly $\mathrm{der}_G(s)$ and the weight of every $\psi \in \mathrm{der}_G(s)$.

Therefore we define the trstr M_G^{TP}. This trstr generates for every input tree t a tree series the support of which uniquely corresponds to $\mathrm{der}_G(t)$. Moreover, the coefficient of a tree contained in $\mathrm{supp}(\tau_{M_G^{\mathrm{TP}}})$ is the weight of the corresponding derivation.

Let us first show, how we represent a derivation $\psi \in \mathrm{der}_G(s)$. We introduce for every $k \in [0, \mathrm{maxrk}(\Sigma)]$ a symbol e_k. The pseudo-code tree also contains nodes the label of which represents a rule $r \in \mathcal{R}$ and the rank of which equals the rank of the topmost element of $\mathrm{RHS}(r)$: $\Delta_{\mathrm{pseu}} = \{e_k^{(k)} \mid k \in [0, \mathrm{maxrk}(\Sigma)]\} \cup \{r_{\mathrm{pseu}}^{(k)} \mid r \in \mathcal{R}, k = \mathrm{rk}(\mathrm{lab}_{\mathrm{RHS}(r)}(\varepsilon))\}$. By definition it holds that $\psi = r(\psi_1, \ldots, \psi_n)$ for some $r \in \mathcal{R}$, $n \in \mathbb{N}$, and $\psi_1, \ldots, \psi_n \in \mathrm{der}_G$. The *pseudo-code tree of* ψ is inductively defined to be the tree $\mathrm{pseu}(\psi) = C_r[\mathrm{pseu}(\psi_1), \ldots, \mathrm{pseu}(\psi_n)] \in T_{\Delta_{\mathrm{pseu}}}$, where $C_r \in C_{\Delta_{\mathrm{pseu}}}(X_n)$ is a context satisfying $\mathrm{pos}(C_r) = \mathrm{pos}(\widetilde{r})$ $(= \mathrm{pos}(\mathrm{RHS}(r)))$ and for every $o \in \mathrm{pos}(C)$,

$$
\mathrm{lab}_{C_r}(o) = \begin{cases} r_{\mathrm{pseu}} & , \text{if } o = \varepsilon \\ e_k & , \text{if } o \neq \varepsilon \text{ and } \mathrm{lab}_{\widetilde{r}}(o) \in \Sigma^{(k)} \text{ for some } k \in \mathbb{N} \\ \mathrm{lab}_{\widetilde{r}}(o) & , \text{otherwise} . \end{cases}
$$

Clearly, from the pseudo-code tree the original computation ψ can be inductively reobtained by replacing the context C_r by the n-ary label r.

Let us now present the trstr M_G^{TP}, which solves the tree parsing problem. It traverses the input tree s and successively replaces patterns of s corresponding to a right hand side of some $r \in \mathcal{R}$ by C_r also checking, whether the "connecting" non-terminals are of appropriate type. Hence the states of M_G^{TP} are all the proper subtrees of trees contained in $\mathrm{RHS}(G)$ as well as the initial non-terminal I. The transitions are defined in the obvious way, where the weight of the rule r is assigned to the transition, which consumes the topmost element of $\mathrm{RHS}(r)$.

Definition 3. *The trstr* $M_G^{\mathrm{TP}} = (Q, \Sigma, \Delta, F, \mathcal{A}, \mu)$ *is defined by* $Q = \{I\} \cup \{t' \in T_\Sigma(\mathcal{N}) \mid (\exists t \in \mathrm{RHS}(G)) : t' < t\}$, $\Delta = \Delta_{\mathrm{pseu}}$, $Q_d = \{I\}$, $\mathcal{A} = \mathrm{Trop}$, *and for every* $k \in \mathbb{N}$, $\sigma \in \Sigma^{(k)}$, $w = q_1(x_{i_1}) \ldots q_l(x_{i_l}) \in Q(X_k)^*$, *and* $q \in Q$ *it holds that*

$$
\mu_k(\sigma)_{q,w} = \begin{cases} \mathrm{wt}(r) \, r_{\mathrm{pseu}}(x_1, \ldots, x_k) & , \text{if } w = q_1(x_1) \ldots q_k(x_k), \\ & \quad r = (q \to \sigma(q_1, \ldots, q_k)) \in \mathcal{R} \\ 0 \, e_k(x_1, \ldots, x_k) & , \text{if } w = q_1(x_1) \ldots q_k(x_k), \\ & \quad q = \sigma(q_1, \ldots, q_k) \\ \widetilde{+\infty} & , \text{otherwise} . \end{cases}
$$

Lemma 1. *It holds that* $\tau_{M_G^{\mathrm{TP}}}(s) = \bigoplus_{\psi \in \mathrm{der}_G(s)} \mathrm{wt}(\psi)\ \mathrm{pseu}(\psi).$

Example 1. Let us consider the regular, weighted tree grammar G given by $\mathcal{N} = \{I, A, B\}$, $\Sigma = \{\sigma^{(2)}, \alpha^{(0)}\}$, and $\mathcal{R} = \{r_1, r_2, r_3, r_4\}$, where

$$
\begin{array}{llll}
r_1 : I \to \sigma(\sigma(A, A), A) & \mathrm{wt}(r_1) = 3, & r_3 : I \to \sigma(B, \alpha) & \mathrm{wt}(r_3) = 2, \\
r_2 : A \to \alpha & \mathrm{wt}(r_2) = 1, & r_4 : B \to \sigma(A, A) & \mathrm{wt}(r_4) = 3.
\end{array}
$$

According to Definition 3 the set of states of M_G^{TP} is $Q = \{I, A, B, \alpha, \sigma(A, A)\}$, where I is the unique designated state. Moreover,

$$
\begin{array}{lll}
r_1 : & \mu_2(\sigma)_{I,\, \sigma(A,A)(x_1)\, A(x_2)} & = 3\ (r_1)_{\mathrm{pseu}}(x_1, x_2), \\
 & \mu_2(\sigma)_{\sigma(A,A),\, A(x_1)\, A(x_2)} & = 0\ e_2(x_1, x_2), \\[4pt]
r_2 : & \mu_0(\alpha)_{A,\, ()} & = 1\ (r_2)_{\mathrm{pseu}}, \\[4pt]
r_3 : & \mu_2(\sigma)_{I,\, B(x_1)\, \alpha(x_2)} & = 2\ (r_3)_{\mathrm{pseu}}(x_1, x_2), \\
 & \mu_0(\alpha)_{\alpha,\, ()} & = 0\ e_0, \\[4pt]
r_4 : & \mu_2(\sigma)_{B,\, A(x_1)\, A(x_2)} & = 3\ (r_4)_{\mathrm{pseu}}(x_1, x_2),
\end{array}
$$

and the not yet defined entries of the tree representation μ are set $\widetilde{+\infty}$. Let us consider the input tree $s = \sigma(\sigma(\alpha, \alpha), \alpha)$. Clearly, $\mathrm{der}_G(s) = \{\psi_1, \psi_2\}$, where $\psi_1 = r_1(r_2, r_2, r_2)$, $\mathrm{wt}(\psi_1) = 6$, $\psi_2 = r_3(r_4(r_2, r_2))$, and $\mathrm{wt}(\psi_2) = 7$. Let us now compute $\tau_{M_G^{\mathrm{TP}}}(s)$. For this purpose we calculate the characteristic vector $h_\mu(s)$ of s, which is shown in the following table, where t_1 and t_2 denote the trees $\mathrm{pseu}(\psi_1) = (r_1)_{\mathrm{pseu}}(e_2((r_2)_{\mathrm{pseu}}, (r_2)_{\mathrm{pseu}}), (r_2)_{\mathrm{pseu}})$ and $\mathrm{pseu}(\psi_2) = (r_3)_{\mathrm{pseu}}((r_4)_{\mathrm{pseu}}((r_2)_{\mathrm{pseu}}, (r_2)_{\mathrm{pseu}}), e_0)$, respectively.

$h_\mu(t)_q$	α	$\sigma(\alpha, \alpha)$	s
I	$\widetilde{+\infty}$	$\widetilde{+\infty}$	$\min\{6\,t_1, 7\,t_2\}$
A	$1\,(r_2)_{\mathrm{pseu}}$	$\widetilde{+\infty}$	$\widetilde{+\infty}$
B	$\widetilde{+\infty}$	$5\,(r_4)_{\mathrm{pseu}}((r_2)_{\mathrm{pseu}}, (r_2)_{\mathrm{pseu}})$	$\widetilde{+\infty}$
α	$0\,e_0$	$\widetilde{+\infty}$	$\widetilde{+\infty}$
$\sigma(A, A)$	$\widetilde{+\infty}$	$2\,e_2((r_2)_{\mathrm{pseu}}, (r_2)_{\mathrm{pseu}})$	$\widetilde{+\infty}$

Consequently, $\tau_{M_G^{\mathrm{TP}}}(s) = h_\mu(s)_I = \min\{6\ \mathrm{pseu}(\psi_1), 7\ \mathrm{pseu}(\psi_2)\}$.

3.2 Cost of a Cheapest Derivation

Now we compute the weight of a cheapest derivation of s with respect to G by the w-fta M_G^{mincost}, which works very similar to M_G^{TP}. Rather than replacing input symbols it just copies them. Moreover, it accumulates in every run the weight of a derivation of the input tree. Since a w-fta finally sums up (in Trop: takes the minimum) over the weights of all successful runs, M_G^{mincost} indeed computes the minimum of the weights of all derivations of the input tree.

Definition 4. *The w-fta* $M_G^{\mathrm{mincost}} = (Q, \Sigma, Q_d, \mathcal{A}, \mu)$ *is defined by* $Q = \{I\} \cup \{t' \in T_\Sigma(\mathcal{N}) \mid (\exists t \in \mathrm{RHS}(G)) : t' < t\}$, $Q_d = \{I\}$, $\mathcal{A} = \mathrm{Trop}$, *and for every*

$k \in \mathbb{N}$, $\sigma \in \Sigma^{(k)}$, $\mathbf{q} = (q_1, \ldots, q_k) \in Q^k$, and $q \in Q$ it holds that

$$\mu_k(\sigma)_{q,\mathbf{q}} = \begin{cases} \mathrm{wt}(r) & , \text{ if } r = (q \to \sigma(q_1, \ldots, q_k)) \in \mathcal{R} \\ 0 & , \text{ if } q = \sigma(q_1, \ldots, q_k) \\ +\infty & , \text{ otherwise .} \end{cases}$$

Lemma 2. *It holds that* $(S_{M_G^{\mathrm{mincost}}}, s) = \min\{\mathrm{wt}(\psi) \in \mathbb{N} \mid \psi \in \mathrm{der}_G(s)\}$.

The pseudo-code tree of a derivation having minimal weight is obtained by searching in $\tau_{M_G^{\mathrm{TP}}}(s)$ for an output tree with the coefficient $(S_{M_G^{\mathrm{mincost}}}, s)$.

3.3   Obtaining the Cheapest Machine Code

In this section we translate each pseudo-code tree $\mathrm{pseu}(\psi)$ into its corresponding machine code ψ by the trtr M_G^{trans}. Clearly, the input ranked alphabet of this trtr is Δ_{pseu} and its output ranked alphabet is $\Delta(G) = \{r^{(n)} \mid r \in \mathcal{R}, \mathrm{type}(r) = (N_1, \ldots, N_n) \to N\}$. Now let us show the states and transitions of M_G^{trans}. For this purpose let us consider the pseudo-code tree $\mathrm{pseu}(\psi) = C_r[\mathrm{pseu}(\psi_1), \ldots, \mathrm{pseu}(\psi_n)]$ for some rule $r \in \mathcal{R}$ of type $N \to (N_1, \ldots, N_n)$ and N_i-derivation ψ_i for every $i \in [n]$. The trtr M_G^{trans} should generate for this particular input tree the set $\{r(\psi_1, \ldots, \psi_n)\}$. By traversing $\mathrm{pseu}(\psi)$ the device consumes the topmost symbol r_{pseu}, generates $\{r(x_1, \ldots, x_n)\}$, and changes to $w = q_1(x_1) \ldots q_l(x_l)$. Since M_G^{trans} should substitute each of the variables x_i of $\{r(x_1, \ldots, x_n)\}$ by $\{\psi_i\}$ (which is generated by the "subrun" on $\mathrm{pseu}(\psi_i)$), the automaton has to traverse C_r to the node at position $o(C_r, i)$ when fulfilling the computation of $q_i(x_i)$. Therefore all the tuples (t, i) are states of M_G^{trans} where t is a subtree C_r for some rule r of G and i is a positive integer such that t contains at least i variables. Further, $(I, 1)$ is a state. In particular, it is the unique designated state of M_G^{trans}. The transitions are defined according to the aforementioned procedure.

Definition 5. *Let* $M_G^{\mathrm{trans}} = (Q, \Sigma, \Delta, Q_d, \mu)$ *be the trtr which is given by* $Q = \{(I, 1)\} \cup \{(t, i) \mid (\exists i \in \mathbb{N}_+)(\exists r \in \mathcal{R}) : t < C_r, o(t, i) \text{ defined}\}$, $\Delta = \Delta(G)$, *and* $Q_d = \{(I, 1)\}$. *Moreover, for every* $k \in \mathbb{N}$, $q \in Q$, *and* $\sigma \in \Sigma^{(k)}$, $w = (q_1(x_{i_1}), \ldots, q_l(x_{i_l}))$, *it holds that*

$\mu_k(\sigma)_{q,w}$

$$= \begin{cases} \{r(x_1, \ldots, x_l)\} & , \text{ if } (\exists r = N \to t \in \mathcal{R}), (\forall j \in [l]), (\exists j' \in [l]) : \\ & \qquad C_r = \sigma(C_r|_1, \ldots, C_r|_k) \in C_\Sigma(X_l), q = (N, 1), \\ & \qquad (q_j = (C_r|_{i_j}, j') \iff o(C_r, j) = i_j.o(C_r|_{i_j}, j')) \\[2mm] \{x_1\} & , \text{ if } (\exists t \in T_\Sigma(X_l)), (\exists i \in [k]), (\exists j, j' \in \mathbb{N}) : \\ & \qquad \sigma = e_k, t = \sigma(t|_1, \ldots, t|_k), q = (t, j), l = 1, \\ & \qquad (q_1 = (t|_{i_1}, j') \iff o(t, j) = i_1.o(t|_{i_1}, j')) \\[2mm] \emptyset & , \text{ otherwise .} \end{cases}$$

Lemma 3. *For every* $\psi \in \mathrm{der}_G(s)$ *it holds that* $\tau_{M_G^{\mathrm{trans}}}(\mathrm{pseu}(\psi)) = \{\psi\}$.

Example 2. Let us reconsider the regular, weighted tree grammar G of Example 1. According to Definition 5 the set of states of M_G^{trans} is given by $Q = \{(I,1), (A,1), (B,1), (e_2(A,A),1), (e_2(A,A),2)\}$, where $(I,1)$ is the unique designated state. The transitions having a weight different from $\emptyset$ are

$$C_{r_1}: \quad \mu_2((r_1)_{\mathrm{pseu}})_{(I,1),\,(e_2(A,A),1)(x_1).(e_2(A,A),2)(x_1).(A,1)(x_2)}$$
$$= \{r_1(x_1, x_2, x_3)\},$$
$$\mu_2(e_2)_{(e_2(A,A),1),\,(A,1)(x_1)} = \{x_1\},$$
$$\mu_2(e_2)_{(e_2(A,A),2),\,(A,1)(x_2)} = \{x_1\},$$
$$C_{r_2}: \quad \mu_0((r_2)_{\mathrm{pseu}})_{(A,1),\,()} = \{r_2\},$$
$$C_{r_3}: \quad \mu_2((r_3)_{\mathrm{pseu}})_{(I,1),\,(B,1)(x_1)} = \{r_3(x_1)\},$$
$$C_{r_4}: \quad \mu_2((r_4)_{\mathrm{pseu}})_{(B,1),\,(A,1)(x_1).(A,1)(x_1)} = \{r_4(x_1, x_2)\}.$$

Let us now consider $\mathrm{pseu}(\psi_1) = (r_1)_{\mathrm{pseu}}(e_2((r_2)_{\mathrm{pseu}}, (r_2)_{\mathrm{pseu}}), (r_2)_{\mathrm{pseu}})$, which we generated in Example 1. The following table shows all the intermediates steps of the translation of M_G^{trans} from $\mathrm{pseu}(\psi_1)$ to $\{\psi_1\}$.

$h_\mu(t)_q$	$(r_2)_{\mathrm{pseu}}$	$e_2((r_2)_{\mathrm{pseu}}, (r_2)_{\mathrm{pseu}})$	$\mathrm{pseu}(\psi_1)$
$(I,1)$	$\emptyset$	$\emptyset$	$\{r_1(r_2, r_2, r_2)\}$
$(A,1)$	$\{r_2\}$	$\emptyset$	$\emptyset$
$(B,1)$	$\emptyset$	$\emptyset$	$\emptyset$
$(e_2(A,A),1)$	$\emptyset$	$\{r_2\}$	$\emptyset$
$(e_2(A,A),1)$	$\emptyset$	$\{r_2\}$	$\emptyset$

In particular, $\tau_{M_G^{\mathrm{trans}}}(\psi_1) = h_\mu(\mathrm{pseu}(\psi_1))_{(I,1)} = \{r_1(r_2, r_2, r_2)\} = \{\psi_1\}$.

3.4 Tree Pattern Matching

In this section we attack the tree pattern matching problem, i.e., for a given pattern $C \notin X$ we generate the set $\mathrm{occ}_C(s)$ of occurrences of the pattern C in an input tree $s \in T_\Sigma$ (cf. [HO82]).

> **Tree Pattern Matching Problem:** Let $s \in T_\Sigma$ and $C \in C_\Sigma(X_n) \setminus X_n$ for some $n \in \mathbb{N}$. Compute the set $\mathrm{occ}_C(s)$.

The tree pattern matching problem is solved by the w-fta M_C^{PM} over $\mathrm{Lang}_{\mathbb{N}}$. By letting M_C^{PM} run on the input tree $s \in T_\Sigma$ we obtain a set containing an element $o \in \mathrm{occ}_C(s)$. How is this o computed? The automaton traverses s starting at its root as far as it assumes an occurrence of C. It also outputs as a weight the set containing the position of s, at which it assumes the copy of C. By consuming the top-most symbol of this assumed occurrence of C it changes the state keeping the information that it just has consumed the root of C. Now M_C^{PM} either meets the whole pattern C and consumes it without changing the up to now generated output or it stops. Clearly, if the w-fta has consumed a copy of C, then it has to consume the subtrees of s at the open position of the copy of C and keep the information that a pattern C was found. The traversing of s up to the occurrence of C is done in a state C, while the consumption of the pattern C is done in the states $t < C$, $t \notin X$. The traversing of the subtrees at the open positions of C is done in the state $\perp$.

Definition 6. *Let $n \in \mathbb{N}$. Moreover, let $C \in C_\Sigma(X_n) \setminus X_n$. The w-fta $M_C^{\mathrm{PM}} = (Q, \Sigma, Q_d, \mathcal{A}, \mu)$ is defined by $Q = \{\perp\} \cup \{t \in T_\Sigma(X_n) \setminus X_n \mid t \leq C\}$, $Q_d = \{C\}$, $\mathcal{A} = \mathrm{Lang}_{\mathbb{N}}$, and for every $k \in \mathbb{N}$, $\sigma \in \Sigma^{(k)}$, $\boldsymbol{q} = (q_1, \ldots, q_k) \in Q^k$, $q \in Q$, and $l \in [k]$ by*

$$\mu_k(\sigma)_{q,\boldsymbol{q}}$$

$$= \begin{cases} \{\varepsilon\} & , \textit{if } \big((\forall i \in [k]) : q = q_i = \perp\big) \textit{ or} \\ & \quad \big((\exists I \subseteq [k]), (\forall i \in I), (\forall j \in [k] \setminus I), (\exists T_i, T_j \in T_\Delta(X_n)) : \\ & \quad T_i = \mathrm{lab}_i(q) \in X_n, T_j = q_j, q = \sigma(T_1, \ldots, T_k), q_i = \perp, \\ & \quad q_j \in T_\Sigma(X_n)\big) \\ \{l\} & , \textit{if } (\forall i \in [k] \setminus \{l\}) : q_l = C = q, q_i = \perp, \\ \emptyset & , \textit{otherwise } . \end{cases}$$

Lemma 4. *For every $n \in \mathbb{N}$ and $C \in C_\Sigma(X_n) \setminus X_n$, $(S_{M_C^{\mathrm{PM}}}, s) = \mathrm{occ}_C(s)$.*

4   Conclusion and Open Problems

We extended the techniques of [FSW94] for code selection by using trstr's rather than tree automata and represented the cheapest machine code as output of a sequence of trstr's. Thereby we solved the tree parsing and the tree pattern matching problems by trstr's. It remains to "optimize", i.e., determinize and minimize these devices. In particular, it is an interesting question under which conditions trstr's over Trop can be determinized and minimized.

Acknowledgment

I would like to thank the unknown referees as well as Heiko Vogler, Andreas Maletti, and Janis Voigtländer for their helpful comments on previous versions of this paper.

References

[AB87]   A. Alexandrakis and S. Bozapalidis. Weighted grammars and Kleenes theorem. *Information Processing Letters*, 24(1):1–4, January 1987.

[BR82]   J. Berstel and C. Reutenauer. Recognizable formal power series on trees. *Theoretical Computer Science*, 18(2):115–148, 1982.

[EFV02] J. Engelfriet, Z. Fülöp, and H. Vogler. Bottom-up and top-down tree series transformations. *J. Automata, Languages and Combinatorics*, 7:11–70, 2002.

[FSW94] C. Ferdinand, H. Seidl, and R. Wilhelm. Tree automata for code selection. *Acta Informatica*, 31(8):741–760, 1994.

[GG78] R.S. Glanville and S.L. Graham. A new method for compiler code generation. In *Proceedings of the 5th ACM Symposium on Principles of Programming Languages*, pages 231–240, 1978.

[GL97] K.J. Gough and J. Ledermann. Optimal code-selection using MBURG. Presented to the 20th Australian Computer Science Conference, Sydney, 1997.

[HO82] C. Hoffmann and M.J. O'Donnell. Pattern matching in trees. *J. ACM*, 29:68–95, 1982.

Some Non-semi-decidability Problems for Linear and Deterministic Context-Free Languages

Henning Bordihn[1], Markus Holzer[2], and Martin Kutrib[3]

[1] Institut für Informatik, Universität Potsdam,
August-Bebel-Straße 89, D-14482 Potsdam, Germany
henning@cs.uni-potsdam.de
[2] Institut für Informatik, Technische Universität München,
Boltzmannstraße 3, D-85748 Garching bei München, Germany
holzer@informatik.tu-muenchen.de
[3] Institut für Informatik, Universität Giessen,
Arndtstraße 2, D-35392 Giessen, Germany
kutrib@informatik.uni-giessen.de

Abstract. We investigate the operation problem for linear and deterministic context-free languages: Fix an operation on formal languages. Given linear (deterministic, respectively) context-free languages, is the application of this operation to the given languages still a linear (deterministic, respectively) context-free language? Besides the classical operations, for which the linear and deterministic context-free languages are not closed, we also consider the recently introduced root and power operation. We show non-semi-decidability for all of the aforementioned operations, if the underlying alphabet contains at least two letters. The non-semi-decidability and thus the undecidability for the power operation solves an open problem stated in [4].

1 Introduction

Elementary undecidable questions for formal language families appeared first in [3], where it was shown that the family of languages defined by context-free grammars is too wide to admit a decidable theory for language equivalence. The same holds true even in the case when restricting to linear context-free grammars, but in contrast deterministic context-free language equivalence was recently shown to be decidable [17]. Additional results show that, e.g., inclusion, intersection emptiness, inherent ambiguity, and regularity for context-free languages are undecidable, too. On the other hand some related questions such as, membership, non-emptiness, and finiteness are decidable and obey fast sequential algorithms. Similar results hold true for linear context-free languages, while for the family of regular languages all of the above mentioned problems are well known to be decidable. In fact, many of the fundamental works on particular language families include results as to whether certain common questions are de-

M. Domaratzki et al. (Eds.): CIAA 2004, LNCS 3317, pp. 68–79, 2005.
© Springer-Verlag Berlin Heidelberg 2005

cidable or semi-decidable. In particular, (un)decidability results for sub-families of context-free languages are abundant, see, e.g., [7, 8, 9, 10, 11, 15].

Another important class of decision problems can be stated as follows. Fix a family of languages and operations thereon. Is it decidable or semi-decidable, given languages from this family, whether or not the application of the operation to the given languages leads out of this family? In the forthcoming this problem is referred to the *operation problem*. From an implementation point of view, the operation problem is related to the question whether, e.g., a parser or acceptor for a given language can be decomposed in several simpler automata. Advantages of simpler automata, whose result after applying the operation is equivalent to the given device, are obvious. For example, the total size of the simpler devices could be smaller than the given automaton, the verification is easier, etc. Therefore, there is a natural interest in efficient decomposition algorithms. From this point of view, the complexity of the converse question, whether the composition of languages yields a given language, is interesting. The operation problem can be seen as a weaker class of such problems. Of course, the operation problem makes only sense for language operations under which the family under consideration is *not* closed, since the aforementioned problem becomes trivially decidable otherwise. For instance, for context-free languages it is well known that the operation problems with respect to intersection and complementation are both undecidable. In fact, most of the undecidability results for context-free languages can be obtained from the fact that the calculations, i.e., the valid computations, of a given Turing machine can be identified with the intersection of two context-free languages [12], while the invalid computations can be identified with a context-free language. A closer look on these proofs reveals that in fact linear context-free languages are sufficient for the description of valid and invalid computations [2, 13]. Moreover, by using this technique it is shown that the problems under consideration are not even semi-decidable.

The aim of the present paper is just about to complete the picture afforded by the above decision problem for the family of linear and deterministic context-free languages. Besides the classical Boolean operations union, intersection, and complementation, we also consider concatenation, Kleene star, non-erasing homomorphism, non-erasing substitution, and shuffle, and moreover, the recently introduced operations root, and power [6]. For all of the above mentioned operations we prove non-semi-decidability, which implies undecidability, whenever the language family under consideration is not closed with respect to the studied operation. The technical depth of our results varies from immediate to more subtle constructions. Indeed, we use the two major techniques developed in the literature, namely (in)valid computations and Post's Correspondence Problem (PCP). The difficulty, when working with linear and deterministic context-free languages is that some of the "context-free" tricks are *a priori* unusable. A typical example arises with the power operation: The standard PCP construction clashes with the linear context-free property in case of having no solutions, because of the inherent copy feature of the power operation—compare with [4], where the decidability status of the linear context-freeness of the power of linear context-free languages was stated as an open problem.

2   Preliminaries

Concerning our notation, we have the following conventions: V^+ denotes the set of nonempty words over alphabet V; if the empty word λ is included, then we use the notation V^*. The mirror image of a string w is denoted by $\tilde{w}$, its length by $|w|$. Generally, for a singleton $\{a\}$ we simply write a. Moreover, the reader is assumed to be familiar with basic concepts of formal language theory, in particular with the definition of linear context-free grammars as well as deterministic pushdown automata, as contained, e.g., in [13, 16, 18]. A language is *linear context free*, if it is generated by some linear context-free grammar. A language is *deterministic context free*, if there is a deterministic pushdown automaton, where acceptance is defined to be by final state, that accepts the language.

In the following, we exploit the following property of all context-free, hence, of all linear and deterministic context-free languages.

Lemma 1 (Bader, Moura [1]). *For any context-free language L, there exists a natural number k, such that for all words z in L, if d positions in z are "distinguished" and e positions are "excluded," with $d > k^{e+1}$, then there are words u, v, w, x, and y such that $z = uvwxy$ and (1) vx contains at least one distinguished position and no excluded positions, (2) if r is the number of distinguished positions and s is the number of excluded positions in vwx, then $r \leq k^{s+1}$, and (3) word uv^iwx^iy is in L for all $i \geq 0$.*

Finally, we recall some notations on computability theory. A problem (or language) is called *decidable*, if there is a Turing machine, that will halt on all inputs and, given an encoding of any instance of the question, will return the answer "yes" or "no" for the instance. The problem is *semi-decidable*, if the Turing machine halts on all instances for which the answer is "yes," and it is *not semi-decidable*, if no such Turing machine exists that solves the task. For example, the equivalence and non-equivalence of two linear languages given by linear context-free grammars are undecidable. But it is easy to see that the non-equivalence is semi-decidable.

We will use the set of (in)valid computations of a Turing as a tool to prove some of our non-semi-decidability results. Basically, a *valid computation* is a word built from a sequence of configurations of a deterministic Turing machine M with one single tape and one single read-write head. The sequence of configurations is passed through during an accepting computation. Without loss of generality, one can assume that any accepting computation of M has at least three and, in general, an odd number of steps. So, it is represented by a sequence of configurations of even length. Moreover, it is assumed that a configuration is halting if and only if it is accepting. The language accepted by some Turing machine M is denoted by $L(M)$. In what follows, the set of valid computations $\mathrm{VALC}(M)$ is now defined to be the set of words of the form $w_0\$w_2\$\ldots\$w_{2k}\#\tilde{w}_{2k+1}\$\ldots\$\tilde{w}_3\$\tilde{w}_1$, where w_i are configurations $\$, \#$ are symbols not appearing in w_i, w_0 is an initial configuration, w_{2k+1} is an accepting configuration, and w_{i+1} is the successor configuration of w_i, with $0 \leq i \leq 2k$. The set of *invalid computations* $\mathrm{INVALC}(M)$ is the complement of $\mathrm{VALC}(M)$ with respect to the coding alphabet.

3   Results

In this section we consider the decision problem of the families of linear and deterministic context-free languages with respect to Boolean operations, catenation, Kleene star, non-erasing homomorphism and substitution, shuffle, root, and power. It is worth mentioning, that all of the aforementioned operations induce decidable problems, if one considers context-free languages over a one-letter alphabet only. This is due to the fact that from a context-free grammar with one-letter terminal alphabet one can effectively construct an equivalent regular grammar, and *one-letter* regular languages are closed under the above mentioned operations [13], except for the power operation. The power operation problem for one-letter regular languages was shown to be decidable [5], but the decidability status for regular languages in general is still an open problem [14]. Since the family of linear context-free languages is closed under homomorphisms and inverse homomorphism, easy encodings to binary input alphabet can be applied. Thus, the non-semi-decidability results already hold whenever the linear context-free language has a terminal alphabet with at least two letters. Since deterministic context-free languages are not closed under homomorphism in general, the above given argument does not apply. Nevertheless, one can reduce the alphabet size to two letters in the deterministic context-free case. Let $V = \{a_1, \ldots, a_n\}$ with $n \geq 3$ and define the encoding $h : V^* \to \{a, b\}^*$ by $h(a_i) = ab^i a$, for $1 \leq i \leq n$. Obviously, the deterministic context-free languages are closed under this form of encoding. Thus, with respect to alphabet size our results are optimal for both linear and deterministic context-free languages.

3.1   Boolean Operations

The family of linear context-free languages is closed under union, but not closed under intersection and complementation, whereas the deterministic context-free languages are closed under complementation, but neither under union nor under intersection. The first goal is to show that it is not semi-decidable whether the application of one of the Boolean non-closure operations yields a language from the same family.

Theorem 2. *(1) Given two linear context-free languages L_1 and L_2, it is not semi-decidable whether the intersection $L_1 \cap L_2$ or whether the complement of L_1 is linear context free. (2) Given two deterministic context-free languages L_1 and L_2, it is not semi-decidable whether the intersection $L_1 \cap L_2$ or whether the union $L_1 \cup L_2$ is deterministic context free.*

Proof. In contrast to the assertion, assume the intersection problem is semi-decidable. Then let M be an arbitrary Turing machine. In [2] it has been shown that VALC(M) is the intersection of two linear context-free languages, and the grammars for these languages can be effectively constructed from M. Taking a closer look at the proof shows that the languages are also deterministic context free, such that the deterministic pushdown acceptors can be effectively constructed. Therefore, two deterministic or linear context-free languages L_1 and L_2

can be effectively constructed such that $\text{VALC}(M) = L_1 \cap L_2$. Due to the assumption, it is semi-decidable whether $L_1 \cap L_2$ is deterministic or linear context free, i.e., whether $\text{VALC}(M)$ is deterministic or linear context free. Another result in [2] says that the valid computations of an arbitrary Turing machine are context free if and only if the language accepted by the Turing machine is finite. In fact, if $L(M)$ is finite, then $\text{VALC}(M)$ is finite and, hence, deterministic and linear context free. If, conversely, $\text{VALC}(M)$ is deterministic or linear context free, then it is context free and, thus, $L(M)$ is finite. Therefore, due to the assumption, it is semi-decidable whether $L(M)$ is finite. This is a contradiction since the finiteness of recursively enumerable languages is not semi-decidable.

Now assume, the complementation problem for linear context-free languages is semi-decidable. In [13] it has been shown that a linear context-free grammar for the language $\text{INVALC}(M)$ can be effectively constructed. So, the semi-decidability of the linearity of the complement of the language $\text{INVALC}(M)$ yields the semi-decidability of the linearity of $\text{VALC}(M)$. This implies the semi-decidability of the finiteness for the language $L(M)$, a contradiction.

The non-semi-decidability of the union problem for deterministic context-free languages follows from the closure under complementation and the observation that $\overline{L}_1 \cup \overline{L}_2$ is deterministic context free if and only if $L_1 \cap L_2$ is deterministic context free. □

3.2   Concatenation and Kleene Star

Next we consider concatenation and Kleene star, both operations under which deterministic and linear context-free languages are not closed. A known fact about linear context-free languages is the undecidability of regularity. Exploiting the notion of invalid computations and the fact that they are linear context-free languages, it can be seen that the property is not even semi-decidable. If the language $L(M)$ of some Turing machine M is finite, then $\text{VALC}(M)$ is finite and, hence, regular. Since regular languages are closed under complementation, in this case the language $\text{INVALC}(M)$ must be regular, too. Conversely, let $\text{INVALC}(M)$ be a regular language. This implies that $\text{VALC}(M)$ must be regular and, hence, context free. Thus the finiteness of $L(M)$ follows.

The following valuable result has been shown in [10].

Theorem 3 (Greibach [10]). *Let R and S be two linear context-free languages over some alphabet V and $c \notin V$ be a new symbol. The concatenation RcS is linear context free if and only if at least one of R and S is regular.*

Theorem 4. *(1) Given two linear context-free languages, it is not semi-decidable whether their concatenation or whether their iteration closure is linear context free. (2) Given two deterministic context-free languages, it is not semi-decidable whether their concatenation or whether their iteration closure is deterministic context free.*

Proof. (1) Let L be an arbitrary linear context-free language over some alphabet V. Then a linear context-free grammar for the language $L_1 = Lc$, where $c \notin V$ is a new symbol, can be effectively constructed.

Set $L_2 = L$ and consider the concatenation $L_1 \cdot L_2$. Since $L_1 \cdot L_2 = LcL$, by Theorem 3 the regularity of L could be semi-decided, if the linearity of the concatenation is semi-decidable.

Assume now the linearity of $(Lc)^*$ is semi-decidable. In order to obtain a contradiction, it suffices to show that $(Lc)^*$ is linear context free if and only if L is regular.

Let L be regular, then Lc is regular. Since the regular languages are closed under Kleene star, $(Lc)^*$ must be regular and, hence, linear context free. Conversely, let $(Lc)^*$ be linear context free. Since the linear context-free languages are closed under intersection with regular sets, the intersection $(Lc)^* \cap V^* c V^* c$ is linear, too. Then together with the closure of linear context-free languages under gsm-mappings, the linearity of LcL follows. Now Theorem 3 implies the regularity of L.

(2) Let L_1 and L_2 be two arbitrary deterministic context-free languages over some alphabet V and $c \notin V$ be a new symbol. The marked union $cL_1 \cup L_2$ is clearly a deterministic context-free language. Now we consider the concatenation $L = \{c, c^2\} \cdot (cL_1 \cup L_2)$ and assume that it is semi-decidable whether L is deterministic context free. In order to obtain a contradiction to Theorem 2 it suffices to show that L is deterministic context free if and only if $L_1 \cup L_2$ is deterministic context free.

Assume $L_1 \cup L_2$ is deterministic context free. Then there exists a deterministic pushdown acceptor for the language. An acceptor for the language L works as follows: At the beginning it reads the symbols c. If it finds one symbol, then it simulates the acceptor for L_2. If it finds two symbols, then it simulates the acceptor for $L_1 \cup L_2$. If it finds three symbols, then it simulates the acceptor for L_1. In any other case it rejects the input. Conversely, assume now $L_1 \cup L_2$ is not deterministic context free. If L is deterministic context free, then $L \cap c^2 V^* = c^2(L_1 \cup L_2)$ would be deterministic context free. This implies that $L_1 \cup L_2$ is deterministic context free by the closure under fixed word quotient. This is a contradiction to our assumption.

Now set $L = c^2 L_1 \cup c L_2 \cup \{c\}$. In order to prove the second part of the theorem it suffices to show that L^* is deterministic context free if and only if $L_1 \cup L_2$ is deterministic context free. If $L_1 \cup L_2$ is deterministic context free, then a deterministic pushdown acceptor for L^* can be constructed similarly to the construction given in the first part of the proof. If, conversely, L^* is deterministic context free, then $L^* \cap c^2 V^+ = c^2((L_1 \cup L_2) \setminus \{\lambda\})$ is deterministic context free. This implies that $L_1 \cup L_2$ is deterministic context free.   □

3.3   Non-erasing Substitution and Non-erasing Homomorphism

Let V be some alphabet. For all symbols $a \in V$, let $s(a)$ be some language over some alphabet V_a, and denote the union $\bigcup_{a \in V} V_a$ by U. A mapping $s : V^* \to 2^{U^*}$ is a *substitution*, if it satisfies $s(\lambda) = \{\lambda\}$ and $s(aw) = s(a)s(w)$, for all $a \in V$ and $w \in V^*$. Here 2^{U^*} denotes the powerset of U^*. The mapping is extended to languages in the usual way: $s(L) = \bigcup_{w \in L} s(w)$. A substitution is said to be *non-erasing*, if the empty word does not belong to any of the languages $s(a)$, it is *linear*, if all languages $s(a)$ are linear context free, it is *regular*, if all languages $s(a)$ are regular. If all languages $s(a)$ are singletons, then the substitution is said to be a *homomorphism*. It is well known that the linear context-free languages are closed under arbitrary (erasing) homomorphisms and gsm-mappings, but not closed under linear non-erasing substitutions. The deterministic context-free languages are not closed under substitution and homomorphisms, even if the homomorphisms are non-erasing.

Theorem 5. *(1) Given a linear context-free language L and a non-erasing linear substitution s, it is not semi-decidable whether $s(L)$ is linear context free. (2) Given a deterministic context-free language L and a non-erasing homomorphism h, it is not semi-decidable whether $h(L)$ is deterministic context free.*

The previous theorem can be strengthened to regular languages in the following way. The regular languages are closed under arbitrary regular substitutions but are not closed under non-erasing linear substitutions. Moreover, it is not semi-decidable for an arbitrary regular language L and an arbitrary non-erasing linear substitution s whether $s(L)$ is regular or linear context free or not at all. The theorem can be strengthened furthermore to marked substitutions, since we have shown the non-semi-decidability of the marked concatenation.

3.4   Shuffle

The next results concern the shuffle operation, which is defined as follows. Let V be some alphabet and x and y be two words over V. The *shuffle* of x and y is the set $\{ x_1 y_1 x_2 y_2 \ldots x_n y_n \mid x = x_1 \ldots x_n, y = y_1 \ldots y_n, x_i, y_i \in V^*, 1 \le i \le n, n \ge 1 \}$ and is denoted by $x \uplus y$. The shuffle of two languages $L_1, L_2 \subseteq V^*$ is $\{ w \in V^* \mid w \in x \uplus y \text{ for some } x \in L_1 \text{ and } y \in L_2 \}$. The families in question are not closed under the shuffle operation. For example, consider the deterministic linear context-free languages $L_1 = \{ a^n c^n \mid n \ge 0 \}$ and $L_2 = \{ b^n d^n \mid n \ge 0 \}$, whose shuffle is a non-context-free language, since $(L_1 \uplus L_2) \cap a^* b^* c^* d^*$ equals $\{ a^n b^m c^n d^m \mid m, n \ge 0 \}$, and both families in question are closed under intersection with regular languages. The following theorems show that shuffle for deterministic and linear context-free languages is not semi-decidable.

Theorem 6. *(1) Given two linear context-free languages, it is not semi-decidable whether their shuffle is linear context free. (2) Given two deterministic context-free languages, it is not semi-decidable whether their shuffle is deterministic context free.*

Proof. (1) For an arbitrary linear language L over some alphabet V, let L' be the primed copy of L over the disjoint primed copy V' of V. Assume contrarily to the assertion that the linearity of $L \uplus L'$ can be semi-decided. In order to obtain a contradiction, it suffices to show that $L \uplus L'$ is linear context free if and only if L is regular.

Let L be regular, then L' is regular. Since the regular languages are closed under shuffle, $L \uplus L'$ must be regular and, hence, linear context free. Conversely, let $L \sqcup\!\!\sqcup L'$ be linear context free. Then the intersection $(L \sqcup\!\!\sqcup L') \cap V^* V'^*$ is linear context free. Since V and V' are disjoint, this intersection represents the concatenation $L \cdot L'$, which must be linear context free, too. Since the linear context-free languages are closed under inverse homomorphisms, we obtain the linearity of the marked concatenation LcL', where $c \notin V \cup V'$ is a new symbol. Now Theorem 3 implies the regularity of L.

(2) Let L_1 and L_2 be two arbitrary deterministic context-free languages over some alphabet V and $c \notin V$. The marked union $cL_1 \cup L_2$ is a deterministic context-free language. Now we consider the shuffle $L = c^* \sqcup\!\!\sqcup (cL_1 \cup L_2)$.

If L is deterministic context free, then $L \cap cV^* = c(L_1 \cup L_2)$ is deterministic context free, which implies that $L_1 \cup L_2$ is deterministic context free. Conversely, if $L_1 \cup L_2$ is deterministic context free, then a deterministic pushdown acceptor M for L can be constructed as follows: If M starts reading a symbol not equal to c, then it simulates a modified acceptor for L_2, otherwise a modified acceptor for $L_1 \cup L_2$. The modifications are such that further input symbols c are ignored. So, the semi-decidability of the shuffle would imply the semi-decidability of the union. □

3.5   Root and Power

In the following we turn to use Post's Correspondence Problem (PCP) for proving non-semi-decidability. On the one hand, this makes the construction of a linear context-free grammar easier whose root or power is not linear context free anymore. On the other hand, it makes the argumentation for the non-semi-decidability more involved. First we consider the root operation.

The *root* of a word w, denoted by $\sqrt{w}$, is the unique primitive word v such that $w = v^n$, for some positive integer n. A word v is *primitive* if and only if v is not the power of another, different word. The root of a language L is $\sqrt{L} = \{\sqrt{w} \mid w \in L \text{ and } w \neq \lambda\}$. The families in question are not closed under the root operation. Consider, e.g., the linear context-free language $L = \{a^p ba^q ca^r \#a^s ba^r ca^p \# \mid p, q, r, s \geq 0\}$, which is also deterministic context free and whose root obeys $\sqrt{L} \cap a^* ba^* ca^* \# = \{a^n ba^n ca^n \# \mid n \geq 1\}$, which is a non-context-free language.

Theorem 7. *(1) Given a linear context-free language L, it is not semi-decidable whether $\sqrt{L}$ is linear context free or whether it is context free. (2) Given a deterministic context-free language L, it is not semi-decidable whether $\sqrt{L}$ is deterministic context free or whether it is context free.*

Proof. We show the first part only. The proof for the deterministic case is similarly. So, let $\{(u_1, v_1), (u_2, v_2), \ldots, (u_n, v_n)\} \subseteq \{a, b\}^+ \times \{a, b\}^+$ be a finite set of pairs, an instance of Post's Correspondence Problem. We consider the linear context-free grammar $G = (\{S, S', A, B, C, D\}, \{a, b, \$, \#\}, P, S)$, where P is the union of the following sets of productions:

$$P_1 = \{S \to \$S'\} \cup \{S' \to u_i S' \tilde{v}_i \mid 1 \leq i \leq n\} \cup \{S' \to \#A\#\},$$
$$P_2 = \{A \to xA \mid x \in \{a, b\}\} \cup \{A \to Ax \mid x \in \{a, b\}\} \cup \{A \to \#B\#\},$$

$$P_3 = \{B \to aBa, B \to bBb\}\} \cup \{B \to \$C\$\},$$
$$P_4 = \{C \to xC \mid x \in \{a, b\}\} \cup \{C \to \#D\},$$
$$P_5 = \{D \to aDa, D \to bDb\} \cup \{D \to \#\}.$$

The derivation process starts with an application of P_1 generating a sentential form $\$u_{i_1}u_{i_2}\ldots u_{i_k}\#A\#\tilde{v}_{i_k}\ldots\tilde{v}_{i_2}\tilde{v}_{i_1}$. The occurrence of A can then be replaced by productions in P_2 leading to $\$u_{i_1}u_{i_2}\ldots u_{i_k}\#y_1\#B\#y_3\#\tilde{v}_{i_k}\ldots\tilde{v}_{i_2}\tilde{v}_{i_1}$, for some y_1 and y_3 in $\{a,b\}^*$. Then the only way to get rid of the nonterminal B is applying P_3, which results in $\$u_{i_1}u_{i_2}\ldots u_{i_k}\#y_1\#w\$C\$\tilde{w}\#y_3\#\tilde{v}_{i_k}\ldots\tilde{v}_{i_2}\tilde{v}_{i_1}$, for some $w \in \{a,b\}^*$. After further derivation steps using productions from P_4 and P_5 in sequence a terminal string of the following form is obtained, with y_2 and z over alphabet $\{a,b\}$: $\$u_{i_1}u_{i_2}\ldots u_{i_k}\#y_1\#w\$y_2\#z\#\tilde{z}\$\tilde{w}\#y_3\#\tilde{v}_{i_k}\ldots\tilde{v}_{i_2}\tilde{v}_{i_1}$ Observe, that any terminating derivation starting off with axiom S is of this form. Thus, the language $L(G)$ consists only of those words x, for which there is a partition $x = x_1x_2x_3$, with $x_i \in \${a,b}^*\#\{a,b\}^*\#\{a,b\}^*$, for $1 \leq i \leq 3$. Therefore, $\sqrt{L} \subseteq \bigcup_{i \in \{1,3\}}(\${a,b}^*\#\{a,b\}^*\#\{a,b\}^*)^i$.

First, let us consider $L' = \sqrt{L} \cap (\${a,b}^+\#\{a,b\}^+\#\{a,b\}^+)$. If $L' \neq \emptyset$, then there is a terminal word in $L(G)$, as given above, such that $u_{i_1}\ldots u_{i_k} = y_2 = \tilde{w}$ and $w = \tilde{z} = \tilde{v}_{i_k}\ldots\tilde{v}_{i_2}\tilde{v}_{i_1}$. In conclusion, the mirror image of $u_{i_1}\ldots u_{i_k}$ is equal to $\tilde{v}_{i_k}\ldots\tilde{v}_{i_2}\tilde{v}_{i_1}$, that is, there is a solution of the PCP for the given instance. Moreover, the equation $y_1 = z = y_3$ must hold true. Conversely, if there is a solution to the PCP, then there are appropriate w, z, y_1, y_2, y_3 such that there exists a word in L'. Hence, we have

$$L' = \{\ \$x\#x\#\tilde{x} \mid x = u_{i_1}u_{i_2}\ldots u_{i_k} \text{ where } i_1 i_2 \ldots i_k \text{ is a solution of the PCP}\ \},$$

and L' is empty if and only if there is no solution of the PCP for the given instance. Now let z be a solution of the PCP for the given instance. Then every power of z is a solution, too. Assume that L' is linear context free and let k be the constant of Lemma 1 of Bader and Moura. Consider the string $\alpha = \$z^s\#z^s\#\tilde{z}^s$, with $s = k^{3+1}$, which is an element of L'. Let all positions occupied by the first z^s be *distinguished*, and all letters $\$$ and $\#$ are *excluded*. Then there is a factorization $\alpha = uvwxy$ according to Lemma 1. The pumping on α can be performed only in a way such that at most two substrings of the form z^s or $\tilde{z}^s$ are modified and, therefore, at least one of them remains unchanged. This yields a string, which is not of the appropriate form. Therefore, language L' is not (linear) context free.

Now let us consider $\sqrt{L}$. If the PCP has a solution for the given instance, then $\sqrt{L}$ is not linear context free, since the language family under consideration is closed with respect to the intersection with regular sets, and L' is not even context free as seen above. Otherwise, we find $\sqrt{L} = L(G)$, since L' is empty if and only if there is no solution to the PCP, and therefore $\sqrt{L}$ is linear context free in the non-solution case. This proves the non-semi-decidability, since verifying that a given PCP instance has *no* solution is not semi-decidable.   □

In the remainder of this subsection we consider the power operation. For any language L, the *power of L* is the set $\mathrm{pow}(L) = \{\ w^i \mid i \geq 0,\ w \in L\ \} = \bigcup_{w \in L} w^*$. Clearly, $\mathrm{pow}(L)$ is a subset of $L^* = \bigcup_{i \geq 0} L^i$. The families in question are not closed under the power operation. Consider, e.g., the language defined by the regular expression a^+b, its power is the non-context-free language $\bigcup_{i>0}(a^i b)^*$. In the forthcoming we prove, that the linearity of the power of linear context-free languages is non-semi-decidable. The proof for the context-free case does not transfer to the cases in question here because it employs the closure of the family of context-free languages under Kleene star. In the following, we give a more or less far-reaching modification of that reduction, adapting it to deterministic and linear context-free languages.

Theorem 8. *(1) Given a linear context-free language L, it is not semi-decidable whether $\mathrm{pow}(L)$ is linear context free or context free. (2) Given a deterministic context-free language, it is not semi-decidable whether $\mathrm{pow}(L)$ is deterministic context free or context free.*

Proof. We show the first part only. The proof for the deterministic case is similarly. Let $\{(u_1, v_1), (u_2, v_2), \ldots, (u_n, v_n)\} \subseteq \{a, b\}^+ \times \{a, b\}^+$ be a finite set of pairs, an instance of Post's Correspondence Problem. Furthermore, let $T = \{a, b, \#, \$, @\}$. Let $G_0 = (\{S, A, B, C, D, S', A', B', C', D'\}, T, P, S)$ be a linear context-free grammar, where P is the union of the following sets of productions:

$$P_1 = \{S \to \lambda, S \to S'\}$$
$$\cup \{S' \to xS' \mid x \in T\} \cup \{S' \to S'x \mid x \in T\} \cup \{S' \to \$A\$\},$$
$$P_2 = \{A \to aAa, A \to bAb\},$$
$$P_3 = \{A \to aBb, A \to bBa\} \cup \{B \to xBy \mid x, y \in \{a, b\}\},$$
$$P_4 = \{A \to aC, A \to bC, B \to C\} \cup \{C \to aC, C \to bC\},$$
$$P_5 = \{A \to Da, A \to Db, B \to D\} \cup \{D \to Da, D \to Db\},$$
$$P_6 = \{B \to @A'@, C \to @A'@, D \to @A'@\},$$
$$P_7 = \{A' \to aA'a, A \to bA'b\},$$
$$P_8 = \{A' \to aB'b, A \to bB'a\} \cup \{B' \to xB'y \mid x, y \in \{a, b\}\},$$
$$P_9 = \{A' \to aC', A' \to bC', B' \to C'\} \cup \{C' \to aC', C' \to bC'\},$$
$$P_{10} = \{A' \to D'a, A' \to D'b, B' \to D'\} \cup \{D' \to D'a, D' \to D'b\},$$
$$P_{11} = \{B' \to \#, C' \to \#, D' \to \#\}.$$

The derivation process starts off with an application of P_1 generating only λ or the set $T^*\$A\$T^*$. The nonterminal A can be replaced by productions in P_2 followed by exactly one A-production in P_3, P_4 or P_5. Note that there is no other way to get rid of the nonterminal A. After further derivation steps using productions from P_3, P_4 or P_5, from the nonterminal A a string of one of the following forms is obtained: (i) $z_1 B z_2$ with $z_1, z_2 \in \{a, b\}^*$ and $|z_1| = |z_2|$, $z_2 \neq \tilde{z}_1$, (ii) $z_1 C z_2$ with $z_1, z_2 \in \{a, b\}^*$ and $|z_1| > |z_2|$, and (iii) $z_1 D z_2$ with $z_1, z_2 \in \{a, b\}^*$ and $|z_1| < |z_2|$. The application of P_6 yields the set of sentential forms $T^*\{\$w_1@A'@w_2\$ \mid w_1, w_2 \in \{a, b\}^* \text{ and } w_2 \neq \tilde{w}_1\}T^*$. Now, analogous derivations dealing with the primed nonterminals can be performed, such that the language.

$L_0 = T^*\{\$w_1@z_1\#z_2@w_2\$ \mid w_1, w_2, z_1, z_2 \in \{a,b\}^*, w_2 \neq \tilde{w}_1, z_2 \neq \tilde{z}_1\}T^* \cup \{\lambda\}$
is generated by G_0. Next, let G_1 be the linear context-free grammar $G_1 = (\{S, E, E'\}, T, R, S)$ with

$$R = \{S \to \$E\$\} \cup \{E \to u_i E \tilde{v}_i \mid 1 \leq i \leq n\} \cup \{E \to u_i@E'@\tilde{v}_i \mid 1 \leq i \leq n\}$$
$$\cup \{E' \to u_i E' \tilde{v}_i \mid 1 \leq i \leq n\} \cup \{E' \to u_i\#\tilde{v}_i \mid 1 \leq i \leq n\}$$

generating the language

$$L_1 = \{\$u_{i_1}u_{i_2}\ldots u_{i_\ell}@u_{j_1}u_{j_2}\ldots u_{j_m}\#\tilde{v}_{j_m}\ldots\tilde{v}_{j_2}\tilde{v}_{j_1}@\tilde{v}_{i_\ell}\ldots\tilde{v}_{i_2}\tilde{v}_{i_1}\$ \mid$$
$$\ell, m \geq 1, 1 \leq i_k \leq n \text{ for } 1 \leq k \leq \ell, 1 \leq j_k \leq n \text{ for } 1 \leq k \leq m\}.$$

Since the family of linear context-free languages is closed under union, the language $L = L_0 \cup L_1$ is linear context free. Assume that the PCP does *not* have a solution for the given instance. Then $L_1 \subseteq L_0$ holds. Hence $L = L_0$ in this case. Since L_0 is the set of all strings over the alphabet T containing at least one infix of the form $\$w_1@z_1\#z_2@w_2\$$ with $w_1, w_2, z_1, z_2 \in \{a,b\}^*$, $w_2 \neq \tilde{w}_1$ and $z_2 \neq \tilde{z}_1$, we have $\mathrm{pow}(L_0) = L_0$, and L_0 is linear context free. Hence, $\mathrm{pow}(L)$ is linear context free if there is no solution for the instance of the PCP.

Now, let z be a solution of the PCP for the given instance. Then, every power of z is a solution, too. Assume that $\mathrm{pow}(L)$ is linear context free and let k be the constant of Lemma 1, the pumping lemma by Bader and Moura. Consider the string $\alpha = (\$z^s@z\#\tilde{z}@\tilde{z}^s\$)^3$ with $s = k^{6|z|+16}$, which is an element of $\mathrm{pow}(L)$. Let all positions occupied by letters of some z^s or $\tilde{z}^s$ be *distinguished*, whereas all remaining positions are *excluded*. Note that $6|z| + 15$ positions are excluded and $6|z|k^{6|z|+15+1}$ positions are distinguished, such that the constraint on the relation between the number of excluded and distinguished positions is obeyed. So there is a factorization $\alpha = uvwxy$. The pumping on α can be performed only in a way such that at most two substrings of the form z^s or $\tilde{z}^s$ are modified and, therefore, at least one of them remains unchanged. This yields a string of the form $\$w_1@z\#\tilde{z}@w_2\$\$w_3@z\#\tilde{z}@w_4\$\$w_5@z\#\tilde{z}@w_6\$$, where (1) $(w_1, w_2) = (z^s, \tilde{z}^s)$ (component wise) but (w_3, w_4) or (w_5, w_6) is not equal to $(z^s, \tilde{z}^s)$, or (2) $(w_3, w_4) = (z^s, \tilde{z}^s)$ but (w_1, w_2) or (w_5, w_6) is not equal to $(z^s, \tilde{z}^s)$, or (3) $(w_5, w_6) = (z^s, \tilde{z}^s)$ but (w_1, w_2) or (w_3, w_4) is not equal to $(z^s, \tilde{z}^s)$. Obviously, a string with this property belongs neither to L_0 nor to $\mathrm{pow}(L_1)$, thus it does not belong to $\mathrm{pow}(L)$, a contradiction.

Thus, we have shown that the Post's Correspondence Problem for a given instance has *no* solution if and only if $\mathrm{pow}(L)$ is linear context free. Since verifying that PCP has *no* solution is not semi-decidable, the stated claim follows.   □

4   Conclusions

We have considered the operation problem for deterministic and linear context-free languages, i.e., we fix an operation on formal languages, and ask the following question: Is it decidable or semi-decidable, given languages from the language family under consideration, whether or not the application of the operation to the given languages leads out of this family? It is worth mentioning that the non-semi-decidabilities of the operation problem with respect to the power operation solve an open problem recently stated in [4]. Moreover, observe that the regularity of the power of general regular languages is still an open problem—for some further reading we refer to [5] and [14].

Another point of interest could be the investigation of the border between decidability and undecidability of the operation problem for linear and deterministic context-free languages. Are there some nontrivial operations for which the problem is decidable? Can we characterize these cases?

References

1. Ch. Bader and A. Moura. A generalization of Ogden's lemma. *Journal of the ACM*, 29:404–407, 1982.
2. B. S. Baker and R. V. Book. Reversal-bounded multipushdown machines. *Journal of Computer and System Sciences*, 8:315–332, 1974.
3. Y. Bar-Hillel, M. Perles, and E. Shamir. On formal properties of simple phrase structure grammars. *Zeitschrift für Phonetik, Sprachwissenschaft und Kommunikationsforschung*, 14:143–177, 1961.
4. H. Bordihn. Context-freeness of the power of context-free languages is undecidable. *Theoretical Computer Science*, 2003. To appear.
5. T. Cachat. The power of one-letter rational languages. In *Developments in Language Theory*, LNCS 2295, Springer, 2001, pages 145–154.
6. H. Calbrix and M. Nivat. Prefix and period languages and rational ω-languages. In *Developments in Language Theory II. At the Crossroads of Mathematics, Computer Science and Biology*, World Scientific, 1996, pages 341–349.
7. S. Ginsburg and G. F. Rose. Some recursively unsolvable problem in ALGOL-like languages. *Journal of the ACM*, 10:29–47, 1963.
8. S. Ginsburg and E. H. Spanier. Bounded ALGOL-like languages. *Transactions of the American Matematical Society*, 113:333–368, 1964.
9. S. A. Greibach. The undecidability of ambiguity problem for minimal linear grammars. *Information and Control*, 6:117–125, 1963.
10. S. A. Greibach. The unsolvability of the recognition of linear context-free languages. *Journal of the ACM*, 13:582–587, 1966.
11. M. Gross. Inherent ambiguity of minimal linear grammars. *Information and Control*, 7(3):366–368, 1963.
12. J. Hartmanis. Context-free languages and Turing machine computations. In *Proceedings of Symposia in Applied Mathematics*, volume 19, Providence, Rhode Island, 1967. American Mathematical Society.
13. J. E. Hopcroft and J. D. Ullman. *Introduction to Automata Theory, Languages and Computation*. Addison-Wesley, 1979.
14. S. Horváth, P. Leupold, and G. Lischke. Roots and powers of regular languages. In *Developments in Language Theory*, LNCS 2450, Springer, 2002, pages 269–281.
15. R. McNaughton. Parenthesis grammars. *Journal of the ACM*, 14:490–500, 1967.
16. A. Salomaa. *Formal Languages*. ACM Monograph Series. Academic Press, 1973.
17. G. Sénizergues. L(A)=L(B)? Decidability results from complete formal systems. *Theoretical Computer Science*, 251:1–166, January 2003.
18. D. Wood. *Theory of Computation*. John Wiley & Sons, 1987.

Brute Force Determinization of NFAs by Means of State Covers

Jean-Marc Champarnaud, Fabien Coulon, and Thomas Paranthoën

LIFAR, University of Rouen
{jean-marc.champarnaud, fabien.coulon, thomas.paranthoen}@univ-rouen.fr

Abstract. Finite automata determinization is a critical operation for numerous practical applications such as regular expression search. Algorithms have to deal with the possible blow up of determinization. There exist solutions to control the space and time complexity like the so called "*on the fly*" determinization. Another solution consists in performing brute force determinization, which is robust and technically fast, although *a priori* its space complexity constitutes a weakness. However, one can reduce this complexity by perfoming a partial brute force determinization. This paper provides optimizations that consist in detecting classes of unreachable states and transitions of the subset automaton, which leads in average to an exponential reduction of the complexity of brute force and partial brute force determinization.

1   Introduction and Notation

Finite automata determinization is a critical operation for numerous practical applications such as regular expression search, *e.g.* Prosite and Swiss-prot patterns [1] in biology, or the family of grep commands in text manipulation systems [7].

Let $\mathcal{A} = < Q, \Sigma, \delta, I, F >$ be a nondeterministic automaton, where Q is the set of states, I (resp. F) is the set of initial (resp. final) states, δ is the *transition function* defined from $Q \times \Sigma$ into 2^Q. A *computation* of the word $a_1 \cdots a_k$ in $\mathcal{A}$ is a sequence $P_1, \ldots, P_{k+1}$ of subsets of Q such that $P_{l+1} = \delta(P_l, a_l)$ for all l. The determinization of $\mathcal{A}$ consists in precomputing $\delta(P, a)$ for all $P \subseteq Q$ and $a \in \Sigma$, which enables to parse a text of length n within time $\mathcal{O}(n)$. Determinization *by reachability* consists in computing $\delta(P, a)$ only for *reachable* subsets P, that is, subsets that can be reached at the end of some computation starting in I. On the contrary, *brute force* determinization consists in precomputing $\delta(P, a)$ for all subsets P and letters a.

In most cases, one can proceed to a simple incremental determinization by reachability. Unfortunately, the number of reachable subsets is potentially exponential, which can make determinization practically untractable. Moreover, the size of the structure used to store subsets that have been already parsed constitutes an obstacle. Indeed, this structure has to provide a fast testing procedure for membership and hence must be stored in memory. It is usually a list, a binary search tree, a trie, combined or not with a hashing table [10, 3, 8].

There are several known solutions to deal with the exponential blow up of determinization, including the so-called *on the fly* determinization used in *grep*,

M. Domaratzki et al. (Eds.): CIAA 2004, LNCS 3317, pp. 80–89, 2005.
© Springer-Verlag Berlin Heidelberg 2005

and the partial brute force determinization. The latter is a trade off between parsing time and determinization complexity. This trade off consists in splitting the set of states into several blocks $Q_1, \ldots, Q_r$. Then one precomputes $\delta(P_j, a)$ for all $P_j \subseteq Q_j$, $1 \leq j \leq r$. Yet, given a subset P of Q, one can recover $\delta(P, a)$ as $\cup_j \delta(P \cap Q_j)$ during the parse of the text. This is described by Wu and Manber in [13]. Moreover, brute force determinization has an efficient bitwise implementation [12, 8]. Indeed, subsets of Q are coded bitwise (one bit codes for the presence of one element of Q), and the deterministic transition table is an array indexed on subsets of Q. Each union is performed bitwise.

However, brute force determinization carries on a huge amount of useless precalculus. Navarro and Raffinot recently proposed a first improvement in [11] by dividing the complexity by the size of the alphabet using *position automata* [9] (or *Glushkov automata*). The *position automaton* obtained from an n-long regular expression is an $(n + 1)$-state automaton without epsilon transitions. A *position automaton* is homogeneous, in the sense that, all the transitions entering a given state are labelled by the same letter, so that one can represent such an automaton by labelling states instead of transitions. Hence we have a unique transition function $\delta : Q \mapsto 2^Q$ and a state partitioning with respect to their labels: we note Q_a the set of states labelled by a. The technique of Navarro and Raffinot consists in precomputing $\delta(P)$ for all $P \subseteq Q$. Then $\delta(P, a)$ can be recovered during the parse as $\delta(P) \cap Q_a$. So the precalculus needs a space $2^{|Q|}$ instead of $|\Sigma|2^{|Q|}$ for the "naive" brute force determinization.

We proposed a second improvement in [4], simply by considering that reachable subsets of a position automaton are necessarily contained in one Q_a. Hence the parse of the text can be done as soon as one knows every $\delta(P)$ for P contained in some Q_a. The space complexity of the precalculus is then reduced to $\sum_a 2^{|Q_a|}$, which is in average exponentially smaller than the latter.

The present paper no longer considers position automata. It aims, for general automata, to extend the idea of performing brute force determinization on blocks rather than on the complete automaton. We propose different techniques, either polynomial or not, for computing partitionings or covers $(Q_1, \ldots, Q_r)$, such that each reachable subset P is contained in one Q_j. When applied to position automata, these covers reveal to be at least as efficient as the symbol partitioning mentioned above. The tests we have carried out show that they are indeed much more efficient for reducing the space complexity of brute force determinization.

The paper is organized as follows. Section 2 describes our technique based on the notion of deterministic covers, whose practical computing is described in Section 3. Then we present experimental results in Section 4.

2   Deterministic Covering Automata

Many transitions outgoing from unreachable subsets are calculated in vain during a brute force determinization. In this section, we consider the problem of detecting subsets that are *a priori* known to be unreachable.

In the following, $\mathcal{A} =< Q, \Sigma, \delta, I, T >$ stands for an NFA, and we note $n = |Q|$. Let $\mathcal{R} = \{R_1, R_2, \ldots, R_k\}$ be a collection of non empty subsets of Q. If $\bigcup_{1 \le i \le k} R_i = Q$, then $\mathcal{R}$ is said to be a *cover* of Q. If $\mathcal{R}$ is a cover and satisfies $R_i \cap R_j = \emptyset$ ($\forall i, j$), then $\mathcal{R}$ is a *partitioning* of Q.

Definition 1 (Deterministic Cover). *A cover* $\mathcal{R} = \{R_1, \ldots, R_k\}$ *of* Q *is a deterministic cover of* $\mathcal{A}$ *if:*

1. $(\exists R_0 \in \mathcal{R})$ $I \subseteq R_0$,
2. $(\forall R \in \mathcal{R})(\forall a \in \Sigma)(\exists R' \in \mathcal{R})$ $\delta(R, a) \subseteq R'$.

A deterministic cover provides additional information about which subsets are visited during a simulation of the automaton: being in a subset of a block R, we know that one can go in some block R' by a symbol a and nowhere else. This behaviour can be modelled by a super-automaton:

Definition 2. *Let* $\mathcal{R}$ *be a deterministic cover of* $\mathcal{A}$. *We get a* covering *automaton*[1] $< \mathcal{R}, \Sigma, \Delta, \mathcal{I} >$ *of* $\mathcal{A}$ *by letting:* $\Delta(R, a) = \{R' \mid \delta(R, a) \subseteq R'\}$, *and* $\mathcal{I} = \{R \mid I \subseteq R\}$.

This super-automaton is not necessarily deterministic. We call deterministic covering automaton *any automaton obtained from the latter by keeping only one element in each* $\Delta(R, a)$, *and one element in* $\mathcal{I}$.

The elements kept for getting a deterministic covering automaton can be chosen arbitrarily, since we only need that there exists one R' such that $\delta(R, a) \subseteq R'$. Covering automata do not have final states since their purpose is just to describe transitions of the original automaton.

For example, consider the automaton at left of Figure 1. The cover $\{B_1, B_2\}$ with $B_1 = \{0, 1, 2\}$ and $B_2 = \{2, 3, 4\}$ is deterministic. One associated covering automaton is drawn at right.

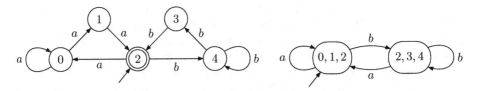

Fig. 1. An automaton recognizing $(a^3 a^* + b^3 b^*)^*$, and one of its covering automata

We easily see that every subset of the subset automaton is contained in one block of the deterministic cover. This gives an upper bound for the number of reachable subsets in the subset automaton:

---

[1] Let us mention that the covering automata introduced by this definition are not related to the covering automata for a finite language L due to Câmpeanu, Păun and Yu in [2].

Proposition 1. *Let $\mathcal{A} = <Q, \Sigma, \delta, I, T>$ be an NFA and $\mathcal{R} = \{R_1, R_2, \ldots, R_k\}$ be a deterministic cover of $\mathcal{A}$. The size of the subset automaton is lower than $\sum_{i=1}^{k} 2^{|R_i|}$.*

A brute force determinization does not take this bound into account and creates the 2^n subsets in vain. On the contrary, the brute force determinization technique that we present fits the bound.

Consider a deterministic cover $\mathcal{R} = \{R_1, R_2, \ldots, R_k\}$ of $\mathcal{A}$ and one associated deterministic covering automaton $< \mathcal{R}, \Sigma, \Delta, \{R_{init}\} >$.

We build a deterministic automaton related to the cover $\mathcal{R}$ by the following way. The deterministic transitions are stored in k tables $(C[i])_{i=1,\ldots,k}$. Each table $C[i]$ contains $|\Sigma|$ tables $(C[i][a])_{a \in \Sigma}$. Each table $C[i][a]$ is made of $2^{|R_i|}$ entries. And we let:

$$(\forall P \in R_i)(\forall a \in \Sigma) \quad C[i][a][P] = \delta(P, a)$$

The simulation of the automaton is carried out by the following way. The current state of our system is a couple (i, P) where $P \subseteq R_i$. The initial state is $(init, I)$, then each transition is given by the transition function δ' defined by $\delta'((i, P), a) = (\Delta(i, a), C[i][a][P])$. The couple we get is a state of the system since $C[i][a][P] = \delta(P, a) \subseteq \Delta(i, a)$.

For each i, the table $C[i]$ contains the transitions of $2^{|R_i|}$ subsets. Hence,

Proposition 2. *The tables $(C[i])_{i=1,\ldots,k}$ are computed and stored with a complexity lower than*

$$n|\Sigma| \sum_{i=1}^{k} 2^{|R_i|}$$

Using these tables, each transition of the subset automaton can be calculated in time $\mathcal{O}(n)$.

The $\mathcal{O}(n)$ time complexity is due to the manipulation of a state number. Indeed, states rank from 0 to $2^n - 1$, so that storing a state number requires n bits in the worst case. However in practice, the memory limitation implies that a table index can always be stored in a processor register.

3 Computing a Deterministic Cover

We focus now on the existence and the practical calculus of deterministic covers.

3.1 The Maximal Cover

Definition 3. *Let $\mathcal{D}$ be the set of reachable subsets of $\mathcal{A}$. The* maximal cover *of $\mathcal{A}$ is the set of all maximal elements of $\mathcal{D}$ with respect to inclusion.*

Clearly, the maximal cover of $\mathcal{A}$ is a deterministic cover. In practice, this cover is obtained as the fixed point of the sequence $(\mathcal{R}_i)$ defined in the following way:

The collection $\mathcal{R}_0$ contains initially the only block I. The collection $\mathcal{R}_{i+1}$ is deduced from $\mathcal{R}_i$ as follows:

$$\mathcal{R}'_{i+1} = \mathcal{R}_i \cup \{\delta(R, a) \mid R \in \mathcal{R}_i,\ a \in \Sigma\}$$

Then, $\mathcal{R}_{i+1}$ is obtained from $\mathcal{R}'_{i+1}$ by keeping only subsets that are maximal for inclusion. The sequence $(\mathcal{R}_i)$ converges to the maximal cover of $\mathcal{A}$.

The maximal cover can be exponentially greater than the automaton:

Proposition 3. *If $|\Sigma| \geq 2$, then for all n, there exists an automaton $\mathcal{A}_n$ such that its maximal cover is made up of $\binom{n}{\lfloor \frac{n}{2} \rfloor}$ blocks.*

Proof. We build an n-state automaton $\mathcal{A}_n =< Q_n, \Sigma, \delta_n, I_n, F_n >$ whose maximal cover contains $\binom{n}{\lfloor \frac{n}{2} \rfloor}$ blocks. We note $Q_n = \{1, \ldots, n\}$, and we let $I_n = \{1, \ldots, \lfloor \frac{n}{2} \rfloor\}$. Let $a, b \in \Sigma$, we let

$$\delta_n(q, a) = \begin{cases} 2 \text{ if } q = 1 \\ 1 \text{ if } q = 2 \\ q \text{ otherwise} \end{cases} \quad \text{and } \delta_n(q, b) = \begin{cases} q + 1 \text{ if } q < n \\ 1 \text{ if } q = n \end{cases}$$

The mappings $q \mapsto \delta_n(q, a)$ and $q \mapsto \delta_n(q, b)$ are permutations of Q_n, respectively the transposition $(1, 2)$ and the cycle $(1, 2, \ldots, n)$. Yet, these two permutations are generators of the symmetric group of degree n. Hence, the reachable subsets of $\mathcal{A}_n$ are all permutations of I, that is, all subsets of cardinality $\lfloor \frac{n}{2} \rfloor$.

The algorithm for computing a maximal cover is as follows:

Algorithm 1 Maximal Cover($\mathcal{A}$)

1: Let $\mathcal{R}$ contain the only block I, and mark I.
2: **while** there exists a marked block in $\mathcal{R}$ **do**
3:    pick a marked block R in $\mathcal{R}$ and unmark it
4:    **for** $a \in \Sigma$ **do**
5:        $P \leftarrow \delta(R, a)$
6:        **if** P is not included in any block of $\mathcal{R}$ **then**
7:            remove blocks of $\mathcal{R}$ that are included in P
8:            add P to $\mathcal{R}$ and mark it
9:        **end if**
10:   **end for**
11: **end while**

All the following cover algorithms have been implemented using the same schema.

3.2   Other Covers

Different techniques can provide deterministic covers with a polynomial complexity. But those covers may contain larger blocks than blocks of the maximal cover.

The Optimal Partitioning. Among deterministic covers, the class of covers that are just partitionings can be easily studied. We refer to these covers as *deterministic partitionings*. There exists a unique optimal deterministic partitioning that can be calculated by an algorithm similar to the latter one, but whose complexity is polynomial.

Consider the partitioning of Q obtained as the fixed point of the sequence $(\mathcal{P}_i)$ defined in the following way. The collection $\mathcal{P}_0$ contains initially the block I and all singletons of $Q \setminus I$. The collection $\mathcal{P}_{i+1}$ is deduced from $\mathcal{P}_i$ as the finest partitioning that is compatible with $\mathcal{P}_i$ and with each block $\delta(B, a)$, $(B \in \mathcal{P}_i$, $a \in \Sigma)$. That is, let first $\mathcal{P}_{i+1} \leftarrow \mathcal{P}_i$. For all couples of blocks B_1, B_2 in $\mathcal{P}_i$ that intersect a same block $\delta(B, a)$, B_1 and B_2 are removed and replaced by $B_1 \cup B_2$. This operation is repeated until all blocks $\delta(B, a)$, $(B \in \mathcal{P}_i$, $a \in \Sigma)$ are included in a block $B \in \mathcal{P}_{i+1}$.

The sequence $(\mathcal{P}_i)_i$ converges toward a deterministic partitioning of $\mathcal{A}$. On the other hand, since the partitioning $\mathcal{P}_{i+1}$ is obtained by merging elements of $\mathcal{P}_i$, the sequence reaches its fixed point at least at $\mathcal{P}_n$. As a result:

Proposition 4. *The fixed point of the sequence $(\mathcal{P}_i)_i$ is a deterministic partitioning finer than any other deterministic partitioning of $\mathcal{A}$. Hence, it is called the* optimal deterministic partitioning. *Moreover, it can be calculated in time $|\Sigma| n^3$.*

Proof. The partitioning $\mathcal{P}_0$ is clearly finer than any deterministic partitioning, and $\mathcal{P}_i$ inherits this property from $\mathcal{P}_{i+1}$ for all i. Indeed, $\mathcal{P}_{i+1}$ is the finest partitioning that is compatible with $\mathcal{P}_i$ and all $\delta(\mathcal{P}_i, a)$. On the other hand, a deterministic partitioning $\mathcal{P}$ is compatible with itself and all $\delta(\mathcal{P}, a)$. If $\mathcal{P}$ is coarser than $\mathcal{P}_i$, then $\mathcal{P}$ is compatible with $\mathcal{P}_i$ and all $\delta(\mathcal{P}_i, a)$, hence $\mathcal{P}$ is coarser than $\mathcal{P}_{i+1}$.

The Neighbourhood Cover. We propose a first polynomial heuristic providing covers that are not just partitionings.

Definition 4. *Let q be a state, the* left language *of q is the set of labels of paths starting in an initial state and ending in q. It is denoted $\overleftarrow{\mathcal{L}}(q)$.*

Definition 5. *Consider the non oriented graph $\mathcal{G} = \,< Q, G >$ whose vertices are the states of $\mathcal{A}$, and whose set of edges G is defined by*

$$(q, p) \in G \iff \overleftarrow{\mathcal{L}}(q) \cap \overleftarrow{\mathcal{L}}(p) \neq \emptyset$$

Proposition 5. *The graph $\mathcal{G}$ can be calculated in time $\mathcal{O}(n^4)$. Let $q, p \in Q$, the edge (q, p) is in G if and only if there exists a reachable subset P of $\mathcal{A}$ that contains q and p.*

Definition 6. *We denote $\mathcal{V}(p) = \{p\} \cup \{q \in Q \mid (q, p) \in G\}$ the neighbourhood of a state p.*

Proposition 6. *If the automaton $\mathcal{A}$ is complete and has just one initial state $(I = \{i_0\})$, then the cover $\mathcal{R} = \{\mathcal{V}(p) \mid p \in Q\}$ is deterministic and can be computed in time $\mathcal{O}(n^4)$.*

Proof. Let p be a state of $\mathcal{A}$ and $a \in \Sigma$, there exists $p' \in \delta(p, a)$ since the automaton is complete. It is sufficient to prove that $\delta(\mathcal{V}(p), a) \subseteq \mathcal{V}(p')$. So, let $q \in \delta(\mathcal{V}(p), a)$. We have $q' = \delta(q, a)$ for some $q \in \mathcal{V}(p)$. Hence, there exists a word w contained in $\overleftarrow{\mathcal{L}}(p) \cap \overleftarrow{\mathcal{L}}(q)$, which implies $wa \in \overleftarrow{\mathcal{L}}(p') \cap \overleftarrow{\mathcal{L}}(q')$, thus $(q', p') \in G$ or $q' = p'$, and finally $q' \in \mathcal{V}(p')$.

The Merging Cover. We present a second cover calculus whose complexity is polynomial.

Here is the general description of the algorithm: initially, we have the cover $\mathcal{R}$ made up of I and the singletons of $Q \setminus I$. As long as the cover $\mathcal{R}$ is not deterministic, there exists a block P and a letter a such that $\delta(P, a)$ is included in no block. The algorithm picks a block $R \in \mathcal{R}$ and replaces it by $R \cup \delta(P, a)$. This operation is repeated until one gets a deterministic cover. The blocks of the cover $\mathcal{R}$ are numbered from 1 to n. The ith block is noted B_i.

Algorithm 2 Merging Cover $(\mathcal{A})$

1: The cover $\mathcal{R}$ is made up of I and the singletons of $Q \setminus I$
2: Mark all blocks $B_1, \ldots, B_n$
3: **while** there exists a marked block in $\mathcal{R}$ **do**
4:     pick a marked block B_i in $\mathcal{R}$ and unmark it
5:     **for** $a \in \Sigma$ **do**
6:         $P \leftarrow \delta(B_i, a)$
7:         **if** P is not included in any bloc of $\mathcal{R}$ **then**
8:             pick a bloc B_j such that $B_j \cap P \neq \emptyset$
9:             $B_j \leftarrow B_j \cup P$
10:           mark B_j
11:           remove blocks B_k ($k \neq j$) that are included in B_j
12:         **end if**
13:     **end for**
14: **end while**

During the running of the algorithm, the number of blocks is n, and each iteration raises strictly the size of a given block. Hence, such an algorithm ends within n^2 iterations. The algorithm efficiency depends on the technique used to pick the block B_j at line 8.

The objective is to generate small blocks. A technique likely to be efficient consists in picking the block B_j such that $B_j \cup P$ is the smallest possible.

This choice can be performed in time n^2. Hence,

Proposition 7. *The merging cover of $\mathcal{A}$ is deterministic and can be calculated in time $\mathcal{O}(n^4)$.*

4   Experimental Results

4.1   Implementation

Three algorithms have been implemented for computing a deterministic cover of an NFA: the maximal cover algorithm, the merging cover algorithm and the optimal partitioning algorithm. They are deduced from an unique scheme described in Section 3.1 for the case of maximal cover algorithm. The implementation of the algorithms must fit with the theoretical complexities given previously. Consequently, a marked block should be accessed in constant time, which is achieved by representing a cover by a double linked list.

4.2   Performance Tests

Tests have been carried out from two different sets of regular expressions, and from random NFAs. In the first set (RandExpr), regular expressions are randomly built on an alphabet of size 4. In the second one (RandText), they are built from words randomly picked in the text "Alice's adventures in wonderland". The random NFAs (RandNFAs) are generated as described in [5]. As usually, each random regular expression is prefixed by $\Sigma^\star$ in order to perform pattern matching over a text.

We define the space requirement of a cover as the number of states of the deterministic automaton related to this cover. The distribution of the space requirement of the covers obtained by each algorithm applied on each random object is illustrated in the following figures. On these figures, for each algorithm, a graph gives the number of regular expressions (or random NFAs) whose cover leads to a given space requirement. Each graph have been made from 10 000 random regular expressions (or random NFAs).

The Figures 2, 3 and 4 give the logarithm of the space requirement of the covers obtained respectively from the optimal partitioning algorithm (b), the maximal cover algorithm (d) and the merging cover algorithm (c).

The following observations can be made about the space distribution:

- For all algorithms the space distribution is better in the case of RandExpr and RandText than in the case of RandNFAs. Moreover it is better in the case of RandText than in the case of RandExpr.
- The distribution of the maximal cover gives informations about the size of the subsets obtained during a determinization by reachability. The larger the space requirement is, the larger is the size of the subsets.
- In the case of RandomNFAs, since the reachable subsets are large ones (see [5]), the space requirement of all covers is important.
- In the case of RandExpr, since both alphabet and words used to build these expressions are small, the distribution of the optimal partitioning is similar to the distribution of the symbol partitioning.
- In the case of RandText, the distribution of the merging cover is similar to the distribution of the maximal cover. Both of these two distributions are closer to the space requirement of the determinization by reachability; the reason is that the size of reachable subsets is small.

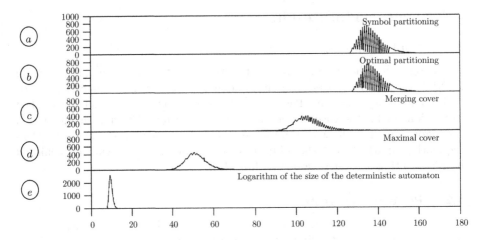

Fig. 2. Case of `RandExpr` expressions of size 500 (on an alphabet of size 4)

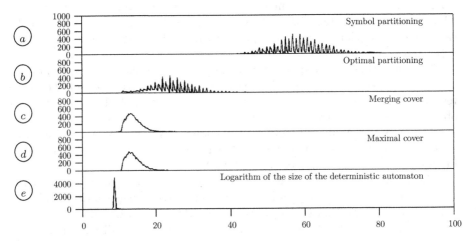

Fig. 3. Case of `RandText` expressions of size approximately 500

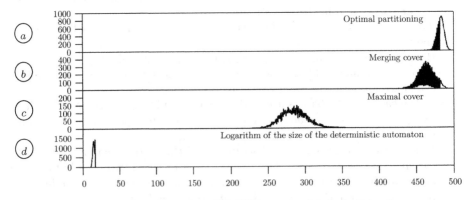

Fig. 4. Case of random 500-NFAs on an alphabet of size 2

5   Conclusion

Deterministic covers enable a consequent reduction of brute force determinization complexity, so that we can reasonably handle 500-long regular expressions on text (Figure 3). We expect them also to reduce the complexity of determinization by reachability. The first optimization described in paper [4] has been implemented in the software CCP [6]. We shall soon design a new version implementing improvements of this paper.

References

1. A. Bairoch and R. Apweiler. The SWISS-PROT protein sequence database and its supplement TrEMBL in 2000. *Nucleic Acids Research*, 28(1):45–48, 2000.
2. C. Campeanu, A. Paun, and S. Yu. An efficient algorithm for constructing minimal cover automata for finite languages. *Int. Journal of Foundations of Computer Science*, 13(1):83–97, 2002.
3. J.-M. Champarnaud. Subset construction complexity for homogeneous automata, position automata and ZPC-structures. *Theoret. Comp. Sc.*, 267(1-2):17–34, 2001.
4. J.-M. Champarnaud, F. Coulon, and T. Paranthoën. Compact and fast algorithms for safe regular expression search. *Intern. J. of Computer. Math.*, 81(4):383–401, 2004.
5. J.-M. Champarnaud, G. Hansel, T. Paranthoën, and D. Ziadi. Nfas random generation models. In *Proceedings of DCFS 2002*, 2002.
6. F. Coulon. CCP software. http://www.univ-rouen.fr/LIFAR/aia/ccp.html.
7. J.E.F. Friedl. *Mastering Regular Expressions, Second edition*. O'Reilly, 2002.
8. J. Glenn and W.I. Gasarch. Implementing WS1S via finite automata: Performance issues. In *Lecture Notes in Computer Science, Workshop on Implementing Automata*, volume 1260, pages 75–86. Springer, 1997.
9. V-M. Glushkov. The abstract theory of automata. *Russian Mathematical Surveys*, 16:1–53, 1961.
10. J.H. Johnson and D. Wood. Instruction computation in subset construction. In D.R. Raymond, D. Wood, and S. Yu, editors, *Lecture Notes in Computer Science*, volume 1260, pages 64–71. Springer, 1997.
11. G. Navarro and M. Raffinot. Compact DFA representation for fast regular expression search. In G. S. Brodal, D. Frigioni, and A. Marchetti-Spacamella, editors, *Lecture Notes in Computer Science*, number 2141, pages 1–12. Springer-Verlag, Berlin, 2001.
12. G. Navarro and M. Raffinot. *Flexible Pattern Matching in Strings – Practical on-line search algorithms for texts and biological sequences*. Cambridge University Press, 2002. ISBN 0-521-81307-7.
13. S. Wu and U. Manber. Fast text searching algorithm allowing errors. *CACM*, 35(10):83–91, October 1992.

Computing the Follow Automaton of an Expression

Jean-Marc Champarnaud[1], Florent Nicart[1,2], and Djelloul Ziadi[1]

[1] L.I.F.A.R, Université de Rouen
{jmc, nicart, ziadi}@dir.univ-rouen.fr
[2] XRCE, Xerox Research Center Europe, 38240 Meylan
florent.nicart@xrce.xerox.com

Abstract. Small nondeterministic recognizers are very useful in practical applications based on regular expression searching. The follow automaton, recently introduced by Ilie and Yu, is such a small recognizer, since it is a quotient of the position automaton. The aim of this paper is to present an efficient computation of this quotient, based on specific properties of the $\mathcal{ZPC}$-structure of the expression. The motivation is twofold. Since this structure is already a basic tool for computing the position automaton, Antimirov's automaton and Hromkovic's automaton, the design of an algorithm for computing the follow automaton via this structure makes it easier to compare all these small recognizers. Secondly such an algorithm provides a straightforward alternative to the rather sophisticated handling of ε-transitions used in the original algorithm.

1 Introduction

Regular expressions are a very convenient formalism used in a wide range of applications like regular expression searching, text processing or natural language processing. Since they are fully equivalent, finite automata are their natural implementation. Simple and very efficient, regular expressions and their finite automata are integrated into many computer science applications such as grep, perl, flex, etc. Thus, computing small finite state automata from regular expressions is a challenging problem.

The position automaton of a regular expression [8, 14] is of particular interest. Let $|E|$ be the size of the expression E, i.e. the number of nodes of its syntax tree and let $||E||$ be the number of occurrences of symbols in E. The position automaton of E has $||E|| + 1$ states. It can be built in $O(|E|^3)$ time by a naive algorithm and in $O(|E|^2)$ time by optimized implementations based on expression transformation [2], lazy evaluation [7], or implicit structure computation [17, 15]. Moreover, it has been proved that quotients of this automaton can be computed with the same quadratic time complexity. Champarnaud and Ziadi have shown that Antimirov's automaton [1] is such a quotient; they have used the notion of canonical derivative to design a quadratic algorithm to compute it [4]. More recently, Ilie and Yu [12] have introduced the follow automaton of a regular expression E. There exists an equivalence relation over the set of positions of E,

M. Domaratzki et al. (Eds.): CIAA 2004, LNCS 3317, pp. 90–101, 2005.

called the follow relation and denoted by $\equiv_f$, such that the follow automaton is the quotient of the position automaton by the relation $\equiv_f$.

Our aim is to design an efficient computation of this quotient, based on specific properties of the $\mathcal{ZPC}$-structure of the expression [17, 15]. The motivation is twofold. First this structure is already a basic tool for computing not only the position automaton and Antimirov's automaton, but also Hromkovic's automaton [10, 9] which focuses on the reduction of the number of transitions. An algorithm based on the $\mathcal{ZPC}$-structure for computing the follow automaton makes it easier to compare all these small recognizers. Secondly such an algorithm provides a straightforward alternative to the rather sophisticated handling of ε-transitions used in the original algorithm.

In our approach, the expression is first normalized; the normalization that we consider includes size reduction (elimination of redundant ϵ's, $\emptyset$'s and $*$'s) as well as Star Normal Form transformation [2] and its time complexity is linear w.r.t. the size $|E|$ of the expression. Then its $\mathcal{ZPC}$-structure is built in linear time and space w.r.t. $|E|$. We prove that, as far as the expression is a normalized one, the set of follow links of the $\mathcal{ZPC}$-structure has specific properties. It allows us to compute the follow relation via a simple marking of the nodes of the $\mathcal{ZPC}$-structure, hence with a linear time complexity w.r.t. $|E|$. Finally we present a new algorithm to compute the follow automaton of a regular expression, with an $O(c \times |E|)$ time complexity, where c is the index of the relation $\equiv_f$. It turns out that this algorithm is about three times faster than the original one.

Next section gathers definitions concerning expressions and automata and a short description of classical constructions (position automaton, $\mathcal{ZPC}$-structure and follow automaton). Section 3 presents the specific properties of the $\mathcal{ZPC}$-structure of a normalized expression and the new algorithm to build the follow automaton. Experimental tests are reported in Section 4.

2   Preliminaries

In this section we first recall some basic definitions and properties about regular expressions and finite automata. For more details, we refer to [11] and [16].

2.1   Regular Expressions and Finite Automata

Let Σ be a non-empty finite set of symbols, called an *alphabet*. The set of all the words over Σ is denoted by Σ^*. The *empty word* is denoted by ε. A *language* over Σ is a subset of Σ^*. *Regular expressions* over an alphabet Σ are inductively defined as usually. We will write $Sym(E) = \text{'+'}$ (resp. '$\cdot$', '$*$') if $E = F+G$ (resp. $E = FG$, $E = F^*$). We call *alphabetic width* of E, denoted by $||E||$, the number of occurrences of symbols of Σ in E whereas we call *size* of E, denoted by $|E|$, the number of nodes of the syntax tree of E. For all integer j, $1 \leq j \leq ||E||$, if x is the jth alphabetic symbol in E, the pair (x, j) (written x_j) is called a *position* of E. The set of all the positions of E is denoted by $Pos(E)$. An expression E is said to be *linear* over Σ if and only if every symbol of Σ occurs at most one time in E. The *linearized version* of E is the expression $\overline{E}$ deduced from E by replacing the symbol x in position j by x_j, for all j, $1 \leq j \leq ||E||$. We denote by h the mapping from $Pos(E)$ to Σ induced by the linearization of E. An expression E is said to be *nullable* if and only if $\varepsilon \in L(E)$. We set $Null(E) = \{\varepsilon\}$ if $\varepsilon \in L(E)$ and $\emptyset$ otherwise.

In practical applications, it is usual to preprocess the input expression in order to reduce its size and to make its size proportional to its alphabetic width. We will consider the following definition [12]:

Definition 1. *Given a regular expression E, an equivalent reduced expression can be computed in linear time by applying the following rules to every node ν of the syntax tree of E:*
a) $\emptyset$-reduction: if $L(\nu) = \emptyset$, the subtree rooted by ν is replaced by $\emptyset$. At the end, E contains no $\emptyset$ or equals to $\emptyset$.
b) ε-reduction: if $L(\nu) = \{\varepsilon\}$, the subtree rooted by ν is replace by ε. Then, if the parent node is labelled by '·', it is replaced by the other child. If it is labelled by '', it is replaced by the child. If it is labelled by '+' and if ε belongs to the language of the other child, then the parent is replaced by its child.*
*c) *-reduction: every vertex labelled with '*' such that parent node is also labelled by '*' is replaced by the child.*

An automaton is a quintuple $\mathcal{A} = (Q, \Sigma, \delta, I, F)$ where Q is a finite set of states, Σ is the alphabet, $\delta \subseteq Q \times \Sigma \times Q$ is the transition mapping, $I \subseteq Q$ is the set of initial states and $F \subseteq Q$ is the set of final states. An ε-automaton is an automaton with $\delta \subseteq Q \times (\Sigma \cup \varepsilon) \times Q$.

2.2   Classical Constructions

The Position Automaton. The position automaton [8, 14] of a regular expression E, denoted by $\mathcal{P}_E$, is related to specific subsets of $Pos(E)$. If E is linear, the following subsets of Σ are computed: $First(E)$ (resp. $Last(E)$), the set of symbols that match the first (resp. last) symbol of some word in $L(E)$, and, for all x in Σ, $Follow(E, x)$, the set of symbols that follow the symbol x in some word of $L(E)$. The functions $First$, $Last$ and $Follow$ can be inductively computed. The set of states of the position automaton of E is $Pos(E)$ added with a specific position denoted by 0. The following notation will be used: $Pos_0(E) = Pos(E) \cup \{0\}$; the set $Last_0(E)$ is equal to $Last(E)$ if $Null(E) = \emptyset$ and to $Last(E) \cup \{0\}$ otherwise; the set $Follow_0(E, x)$ is equal to $Follow(E, x)$ if $x \in Pos(E)$ and to $First(E)$ if $x = 0$. It is easy to see that the position automaton of a regular expression E is such that $\mathcal{P}_E = (Pos_0(E), \Sigma, \delta, \{0\}, Last_0(E))$, with $\delta(x, a) = \{y \mid y \in Follow_0(E, x) \text{ and } h(y) = a\}$, $\forall x \in Pos_0(E)$, $\forall a \in \Sigma$.

Remark 1. *We consider the expression $E_0 = \$E$ where $\$ \notin \Sigma$. Then $Pos(E_0) = Pos_0(E)$, $Last(E_0) = Last_0(E)$ and, for all $x \in Pos(E_0)$, $Follow(E_0, x) = Follow_0(E, x)$. Hence an equivalent definition of the position automaton of E: $\mathcal{P}_E = (Pos(E_0), \Sigma, \delta, \{0\}, Last(E_0))$, with $\delta(x, a) = \{y \mid y \in Follow(E_0, x) \text{ and } h(y) = a\}$, $\forall x \in Pos(E_0)$, $\forall a \in \Sigma$.*

Definition 2. *Two positions x and y of a regular expression E are said to be Last-equivalent in E ($x \sim_E y$) if and only if $x \in Last(E) \Leftrightarrow y \in Last(E)$.*

Definition 3. *A regular expression E is said to be in Star Normal Form (E is in SNF) if and only if for every expression F such that F^* is a subexpression of E, the following property holds: $\forall x \in Last(F)$, $Follow(F, x) \cap First(F) = \emptyset$.*

It was shown in [2] that any regular expression can be turned into Star Normal Form in linear time.

The $\mathcal{ZPC}$-Structure. The $\mathcal{ZPC}$-structure of a regular expression [17, 15] is a linear space and time representation of the position automaton that is based on two state forests connected by a set of links. Let us briefly recall how to convert a regular expression into its $\mathcal{ZPC}$-structure (see Figure 1). More details can be found in [3, 6].

1. We perform a depth-first traversal of the syntax tree $T(\overline{E})$ of $\overline{E}$ in order to add specific links from each leaf to its successor and from each node to its leftmost leaf and to its rightmost leaf. These specific links allow us to directly access to the set of positions of each node.
2. We create two copies of the tree $T(\overline{E})$, respectively denoted by $Lasts(E)$ and $Firsts(E)$.
3. For each node $A = B \cdot C$ of $Lasts(E)$, if C is not nullable, we disable the connection to B, and we update the leftmost leaf pointer of A.
4. For each node $A = B \cdot C$ of $Firsts(E)$, if B is not nullable, we disable the connection to C, and we update the rightmost leaf pointer of A.
5. For every node $A = B \cdot C$, we create a *follow link* from B in $Lasts(E)$ to C in $Firsts(E)$. It encodes the set of transitions associated with $Last(B) \times First(C)$.
6. For every node $A = B^*$, we create a follow link from B in $Lasts(E)$ to A in $Firsts(E)$ It encodes the set of transitions associated with $Last(B) \times First(B)$.

It has been shown in [17, 15] that the $\mathcal{ZPC}$-structure of a regular expression requires $O(|E|)$ space, can be built in $O(|E|)$ time and converted into a position automaton in $O(|E|^2)$ time. A follow link is said to be *redundant* if and only if the set of transitions it encodes is included into the set of transitions encoded by another follow link. Redundant follow links may be eliminated in linear time w.r.t. $|E|$.

The Follow Automaton. The inductive construction of the ε-automaton $\mathcal{A}_f^\varepsilon(E)$ of a regular expression E is defined by Ilie and Yu in [12]. Its computation is in $O(|E|)$ time; see Section 5 for more details. The *follow automaton* $\mathcal{A}_f(E)$ (see Figure 2) is produced by eliminating ε-transitions from $\mathcal{A}_f^\varepsilon(E)$, which can be performed in $O(|E|^2)$ time. Let $\equiv_f \subseteq (Pos_0(E))^2$ be the equivalence relation defined by

$$x \equiv_f y \Leftrightarrow Follow_0(E, x) = Follow_0(E, y) \text{ and } x \in Last_0(E) \Leftrightarrow y \in Last_0(E)$$

Then $\mathcal{A}_f(E)$ is a quotient of the position automaton: $\mathcal{A}_f(E) \simeq \mathcal{P}_E/_{\equiv_f}$.

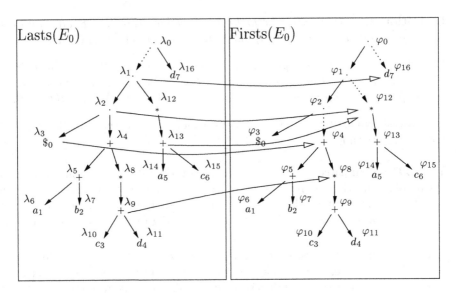

Fig. 1. The $\mathcal{ZPC}$-structure of $E_0 = \$ \cdot ((a+b) + (c+d)^*) \cdot (a+c)^* \cdot d$

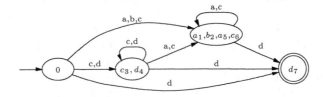

Fig. 2. The follow automaton of $E = ((a+b) + (c+d)^*) \cdot (a+c)^* \cdot d$

Following Definition 2 and Remark 1, we will rather consider the relation $\equiv_f \subseteq (Pos(E_0))^2$ such that $x \equiv_f y \Leftrightarrow Follow(E_0, x) = Follow(E_0, y) \wedge x \sim_{E_0} y$. Indeed, this definition is more convenient when working on a $\mathcal{ZPC}$-structure since it allows us to express properties directly on the basic sets of the expression E_0.

3   From a $\mathcal{ZPC}$-Structure to a Follow Automaton

Our aim is to provide an efficient algorithm to compute a follow automaton. We first introduce normalized expressions and prove some of their properties. Then we describe an efficient computation of the relation $\equiv_f$ over the $\mathcal{ZPC}$-structure of a normalized expression. Finally we show how the transition function of the follow automaton can be deduced from the $\mathcal{ZPC}$-structure.

3.1   Normalized Expressions

Definition 4. *A regular expression E is said to be normalized if the following conditions hold:*

1. *The expression E is a reduced one (according to Definition 1).*
2. *The operation '·' is assumed to be left associative when building the syntax tree of the expression.*
3. *The expression E is in SNF.*

Here is a detailed list of properties of normalized expressions. Let H be a subexpression of a normalized expression E. Then the following properties hold:

a. If $H = F + G$, then $F \neq \emptyset$ and $G \neq \emptyset$.
b. If $H = F + \varepsilon$, then $Null(F) = \emptyset$.
c. If $H = F \cdot G$, then $F \neq \emptyset$, $G \neq \emptyset$, $F \neq \varepsilon$ and $G \neq \varepsilon$.
d. If $H = F \cdot G$, then $Sym(G) \neq$ '·'.
e. If H^* is a subexpression of E, then for all $x \in Last(H)$, $Follow(H, x) \cap First(H) = \emptyset$.

Properties (a), (b) and (c) come from the fact E is reduced. Property (d) comes from the fact the operation '·' is left associative. Property (e) is a consequence of the fact E is in SNF. It is straightforward to check that given a regular expression E' of size s', it is possible to construct an equivalent normalized expression E in $O(s')$ time and space. Therefore we can assume that all regular expressions are normalized. We now state two useful propositions. The first one addresses arbitrary regular expressions; the second one addresses normalized expressions.

Proposition 1. *Let x and y be two Last-equivalent positions of a regular expression E. If E is in SNF, for all H such that H^* is a subexpression of E, it holds: $Follow(F^*, x) = Follow(F^*, y) \Leftrightarrow Follow(F, x) = Follow(F, y)$.*

Proposition 2. *Let E be a normalized expression such that $E = F \cdot G$ and let x and y be two positions of E such that $x \in Last(F)$, $y \in Last(G)$ and $Follow(E, x) = Follow(E, y)$. Then G is such that $G = H^*$.*

3.2   Computation of $\equiv_f$ over the $\mathcal{ZPC}$-Structure

Let E be a regular expression and let us consider its $\mathcal{ZPC}$-structure. We denote by λ_F (resp. φ_F) the root of the tree associated with the subexpression F in $Lasts(E)$ (resp. $Firsts(E)$). Let x be a position of E. In order to shorten notation, the node associated with x in $Lasts(E)$ is denoted by x too. In the tree that contains x there is a unique path from the root to x. We consider the reverse path $\pi(x) = \lambda_{i_1}\lambda_{i_2}...\lambda_{i_p}$, with $\lambda_{i_1} = x$. We will denote $Colast(E) = Pos(E) \backslash Last(E)$.

Definition 5. *Let E be a regular expression and x a position of E. We denote by $\Delta_E(x)$ the set of nodes of $Firsts(E)$ that are head of a follow link whose tail belongs to the path $\pi(x)$. We have:*
$$\Delta_E(x) = \{follow(\lambda) \mid \lambda \in \pi(x) \text{ and } (\lambda, follow(\lambda)) \text{ is a follow link}\}$$

Let x and y be two positions of an arbitrary regular expression. It is easy to check that $\Delta_E(x) = \Delta_E(y) \Rightarrow x \equiv_f y$. We are going to show that, as far as normalized expressions are concerned, the inverse also holds, i.e.: $x \equiv_f y \Rightarrow \Delta_E(x) = \Delta_E(y)$.

Theorem 1. *Let x and y be two positions of a normalized expression E. It holds: $(Follow(E, x) = Follow(E, y) \wedge x \sim_E y) \Leftrightarrow \Delta_E(x) = \Delta_E(y)$.*

Proof is by induction on the size of E. Theorem 1 allows us to compute the relation $\equiv_f$ over the $\mathcal{ZPC}$-structure of a normalized expression. We now see how it can be achieved efficiently. Let x be in $Pos(E)$. We denote by $D_E(x)$ the head of the lower follow link having its tail on the path $\pi(x)$. We write $D_E(x) = \perp$ if there exists no such follow link. More precisely $D_E(x)$ can be recursively computed as follows.

Proposition 3. *The lower follow link of a regular expression E is such that:*
1. *Case $E = F + G$:*
If $x \in Pos(F)$, then $D_E(x) = D_F(x)$.
If $x \in Pos(G)$, then $D_E(x) = D_G(x)$.
2. *Case $E = F \cdot G$:*
If $x \in Colast(F)$, then $D_E(x) = D_F(x)$.
If $x \in Last(F)$, then $D_E(x) = D_F(x)$ if $D_F(x) \neq \perp$ and φ_G otherwise.
If $x \in Pos(G)$, then $D_E(x) = D_G(x)$.
3. *Case $E = F^*$:*
If $x \in Colast(F)$, then $D_E(x) = D_F(x)$.
If $x \in Last(F)$, then $D_E(x) = D_F(x)$ if $D_F(x) \neq \perp$ and φ_G otherwise.

Theorem 2. *Let x and y be two positions of a normalized expression E. It holds: $D_E(x) = D_E(y) \Leftrightarrow \Delta_E(x) = \Delta_E(y)$.*

3.3 Algorithms

Let E be a normalized regular expression and $E_0 = \$E$. Theorem 2 leads to the Algorithm 1 that computes the relation $\equiv_f$ of E via the $\mathcal{ZPC}$-structure of $E_0 = \$E$, and hence the set Q_f of states of the follow automaton of E. On the other hand, Algorithm 2 computes the set of transitions of the follow automaton.

Algorithm 1. Since the expression E is normalized, the expression E_0 is normalized too, as far as the syntax tree of E_0 satisfies left associativity of '·' operation. Thus, according to Theorem 2, it comes: $x \equiv_f y \Leftrightarrow D_{E_0}(x) = D_{E_0}(y)$.

The Algorithm 1 is based on a marking of the positions of $Lasts(E_0)$ (see Figure 3). The set Q_f is initialized to $\emptyset$ and the call $Marking(\lambda_E, \phi_0)$ is performed. Every position x is marked with the head of the lower follow link whose tail is on the path $\pi(x)$. Two positions in E_0 are $\equiv_f$-equivalent iff they have an identical marking. The predicate $broken(\lambda)$ is true iff λ is not connected to its parent in $Lasts(E_0)$. The procedure $Marking$ performs a prefix traversal of $Lasts(E_0)$. The marking $D(\lambda)$ of the node λ is equal to $\varphi = follow(\lambda)$ if there exists a follow link (λ, φ) and to the marking of its parent otherwise.

The set of classes of $\equiv_f$ is the set of markings of the positions of E_0. The computation of the set of transitions is facilitated by the use of a class representative, such as the least leaf (w.r.t. the order of the traversal) with a given marking. It can be achieved by a marking of the nodes of $Firsts(E_0)$ that is not

Algorithm 1 Computes the set Q_f of states of the follow automaton.

Procedure $Marking(\lambda$: node, parent_mark: node)
  if $follow(\lambda) = \bot$ **then**
    $D(\lambda) \leftarrow parent\_mark$
  else
    $D(\lambda) \leftarrow follow(\lambda)$
  end if
  $leftson \leftarrow left(\lambda)$
  if $leftson \neq \bot$ **then**
    if $broken(leftson)$ **then**
      $Marking(leftson, \bot)$
    else
      $Marking(leftson, D(\lambda))$
    end if
  end if
  $rightson \leftarrow right(\lambda)$
  if $rightson \neq \bot$ **then**
    $Marking(rightson, D(\lambda))$
  end if
  if $leftson = \bot \wedge rightson = \bot$ **then** {case of a node}
    if $(D(\lambda),.) \notin Q_f$ **then**
      $Q_f \leftarrow Q_f \cup (D(\lambda), \lambda)$
    end if
  end if

Algorithm 2 Computes the set δ_f of transitions of the follow automaton.

Procedure Transitions()
  for all $(D(x), x) \in Q_f$ **do**
    for all $y \in Targets(x)$ **do**
      $\delta_f \leftarrow \delta_f \cup \{((D(x), x), h(y), (D(y), .))\}$
    end for
  end for
Function Targets($\lambda : node$)
  $T \leftarrow \emptyset$
  repeat
    $\phi = follow(\lambda)$
    if $\phi \neq \bot$ **then**
      $T \leftarrow T \cup First(\phi)$
    end if
    if $broken(\lambda)$ **then**
      $\lambda \leftarrow \bot$
    else
      $\lambda \leftarrow parent(\lambda)$
    end if
  until $\lambda = \bot$
  return T

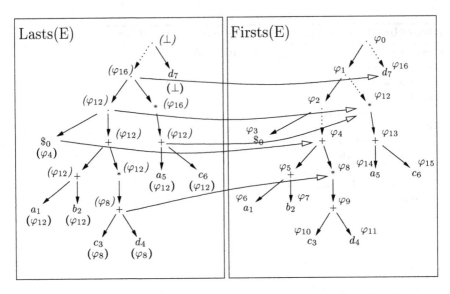

Fig. 3. Computation of the set of states according to Algorithm 1

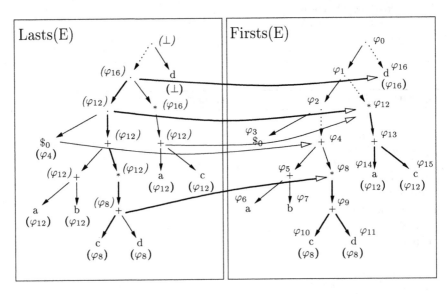

Fig. 4. Computation of the transitions of the state (φ_8, c_3) according to the Algorithm 2

detailed here. Finally we get: $Q_f = \{(\varphi, x) \mid \varphi \in Firsts(E_0), x \in Pos(E_0), x$ *is the least position s.t.* $D(x) = \varphi\}$. At the end of the execution, every position in $Lasts(E_0)$ is marked with the head of its associated lower follow link. Therefore two positions in E_0 are equivalent iff they get an identical marking by the Algorithm 1. Moreover the Algorithm 1 has an $O(|E|)$ time complexity.

Algorithm 2. The Algorithm 2 computes the set of transitions of the follow automaton of E (see Figure 4). There exists a transition $((\varphi, x), h(y), (\varphi', x'))$ from (φ, x) to (φ', x') in Q_f iff $(x, h(y), y)$ is a transition of the position automaton and $D(y) = \varphi'$. The function $Targets$ computes the set T of targets of the transitions coming from the state (φ, x). For each follow link $(\lambda_1, \varphi_1 = follow(\lambda_1))$ such that λ_1 belongs to the path $\pi(x)$, the sets $First(\varphi_1)$ and T are merged in linear time. Moreover, since the expression E_0 is in SNF, the successive $First(\varphi_1)$ sets are disjoint. Therefore, for each state (φ, x), the computation of T is linear. Hence the Algorithm 2 has an $O(c \times |E|)$ time complexity. Finally we get the following proposition:

Proposition 4. *The follow automaton of a normalized regular expression can be computed from its $\mathcal{ZPC}$-structure by the Algorithms 1 and 2, with an $O(c \times |E|)$ time complexity, where c is the index of the relation $\equiv_f$.*

4   Experimental Results

The two algorithms have been coded in $C++$ using the STL (Standard Template Library) and the general design is object oriented. Both of the algorithms benefit from the same implementation of automata. Automata are represented by a data structure that allows fast insertion of states and transitions and a variant has been designed for the epsilon follow automaton that carries some optimizations.

The modus operandi is the following. For every regular expression, the two algorithms have been run one thousand times in order to have measurable times. The function clock() as been used since it provides the real CPU time of a process. All the tests have been run under Linux on a Pentium II 300 Mhz computer with 192 MB memory. The Figure 5 gives the running time (in seconds) versus the length of the expressions.

1. Randomly generated regular expressions: we used an home made random expression generator to produce 1000 expressions of length 30 to 240 with a step of 30. See Figure 5.(a) for the results.
2. Families of regular expressions: we have tested some families of regular expressions proposed by Ilie and Yu [13].
    - Family 1: we consider the expressions inductively defined by $E_1 = (a_1 + \epsilon)^*$ and $E_{i+1} = (E_i + F_i)^*$ where F_i is obtained from E_i by replacing each a_j by $a_{j+|E_i|}$. See Figure 5.(b) for the results.
    - Family 2: we consider the expressions of the form $E_n = a_1 \cdot (b_1 + \cdots + b_n)^* + a_2 \cdot (b_1 + \cdots + b_n)^* + \cdots + a_n \cdot (b_1 + \cdots + b_n)^*$. We generate expressions up to $n = 30$. See Figure 5.(c) for the results.
    - Family 3: we consider the expressions of the form $E_{n,m} = (a_1 + a_2 + \cdots + a_n) \cdot (a_1 + a_2 + \cdots + a_n + b_1 + \cdots + b_m)^*$. We generate a set of regular expressions for length from 20 to 150 by step of 10 and for each length l, we consider all the possible values of n and m such that $l = 2n + m$. See Figure 5.(d) for the results.

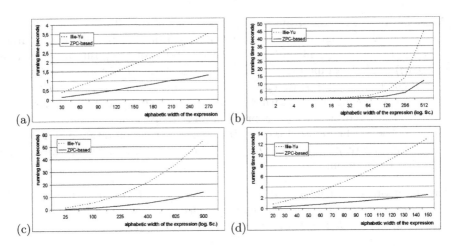

Fig. 5. Running time of the two algorithms: (a) Randomly generated expressions, (b) Family 1, (c) Familiy 2 and (d) Family 3

5   Conclusion

Experimental tests show that the ε-free algorithm for computing the follow automaton is about three times faster than the original one. Moreover it is quite easy to implement it from the $\mathcal{ZPC}$-structure. This new construction should facilitate the study of the properties of the follow automaton and its comparison with other small NFAs such as Antimirov's automaton and Hromkovic's automaton.

References

1. Antimirov V., *Partial derivatives of regular expressions and finite automaton constructions*, Theoret. Comput. Sci., 155, 2917–319, 1996.
2. Brüggemann-Klein A., *Regular Expressions into Finite Automata*, Theoret. Comput. Sci., 120, 197–213, 1993.
3. Champarnaud J.-M., *Subset Construction Complexity for Homogeneous Automata, Position Automata and ZPC-Structures*, Theoret. Comput. Sci., 267, 17–34, 2001.
4. Champarnaud J.-M. and D. Ziadi, *Computing the Equation Automaton of a Regular Expression in $O(s^2)$ Space and Time*, in CPM'2001, Lecture Notes in Computer Science, A. Amir and G. M. Landau eds., Springer-Verlag, 2089(2001), 157–168.
5. Champarnaud J.-M. and D. Ziadi, *From c-continuations to new quadratic algorithms for automaton synthesis*, Intern. Journ. of Alg. and Comp., 11-6, 707–735, 2001.
6. Champarnaud J.-M., *Evaluation of three implicit structures to implement nondeterministic automata from regular expressions*, Intern. J. of Foundations of Comp. Sc., 13-1, 99-113, 2002.
7. Chang C.-H. and Paige R., *From Regular Expressions to DFA's Using Compressed NFA's*, Theoret. Comput. Sci., 178, 1–36, 1997.

8. Glushkov V.M., *The Abstract Theory of Automata*, Russian Math. Surveys, 16, 1–53, 1961.

9. Hagenah C. and Muscholl A., *Computing ε-free NFAs from regular expressions in* $O(n \log^2(n))$ *time*, Theoret. Inform. Appl. 34(4), 2000, 257–277.

10. Hromkovic J., Seibert S., Wilke T., *Translating regular expressions into small ε-free nondeterministic finite automata*, J. Comput. System Sci, 62(4), 2001, 565–588.

11. J.E. Hopcroft and J.D. Ullman, *Introduction to Automata Theory, Languages and Computation*, Addison-Wesley, Reading, MA, 1979.

12. Ilie L. and Yu S., *Constructing NFAs by optimal use of positions in regular expressions*, in: A. Apostolico, M. Takeda, eds., Proc. of CPM'02, Lecture Notes in Computer Science 2373, Springer-Verlag, 279–288, 2002.

13. Ilie L. and Yu S., *Algorithms for Computing Small NFAs*, in: K. Diks, W. Ritter, eds., Proc. of MFCS'02, Lecture Notes in Computer Science 2420, Springer-Verlag, 328–340, 2002.

14. McNaughton R., Yamada H., *Regular Expressions and State Graphs For Automata*, IEEE Trans. on Electronic Computers, 9-1, 39–47, 1960.

15. Ponty J.-L., Ziadi D. and Champarnaud J.-M., *A new Quadratic Algorithm to Convert a Regular Expression into an Automaton*, in: D. Raymond, D. Wood, S. Yu eds., Proc. of WIA'96, Lecture Notes in Computer Science 1260, Springer-Verlag, 109-110, 1997.

16. S. Yu, *Regular languages*, in: G. Rozenberg, A. Salomaa, Handbook of Formal Languages, Vol. I, Springer-Verlag, Berlin, 41–110, 1997.

17. Ziadi D., Ponty J.-L. and Champarnaud J.-M., *Passage d'une expression rationnelle à un automate fini non-déterministe*, Journées Montoises (1995), Bull. Belg. Math. Soc. 4, 177-203, 1997.

Viral Gene Compression: Complexity and Verification[*]

Mark Daley[1,2] and Ian McQuillan[2]

[1] University of Saskatchewan, Saskatoon, Saskatchewan, Canada
daley@cs.usask.ca
[2] University of Western Ontario, London Ontario, Canada
{imcquill, daley}@csd.uwo.ca

Abstract. The smallest known biological organisms are, by far, the viruses. One of the unique adaptations that many viruses have aquired is the compression of the genes in their genomes. In this paper we study a formalized model of gene compression in viruses. Specifically, we define a set of constraints that describe viral gene compression strategies and investigate the properties of these constraints from the point of view of genomes as languages. We pay special attention to the finite case (representing real viral genomes) and describe a metric for measuring the level of compression in a real viral genome. An efficient algorithm for establishing this metric is given along with applications to real genomes including automated classification of viruses and prediction of horizontal gene transfer between host and virus.

1 Introduction

In contrast to the lengthy, often redundant, genomes of higher organisms, the genomes of viruses are extremely efficient in the encoding of their genes. Where mammalian genomes, for example, possess lengthy introns which code for no genes at all, any given segment of a viral genome may be a coding region for several genes. In addition to prefix and suffix overlap of viral genes, some genes may also be encoded in a retrograde fashion (that is, the gene would be read in a direction opposite to other genes). These systems provide evidence that viruses have evolved a special type of information compression technique. Studying this natural compression system in a rigorous setting could yield insight into the structure of viral genomes and may contribute to a basis for classifying such structures.

In this paper, we will specifically consider the types of compression seen in two small double-stranded DNA virus families, Papillomavirus and Polyomavirus, and single-stranded RNA viruses from the Bornavirus, Coronavirus and, to a lesser extent, the Filovirus and Retrovirus families.

---

[*] This research was funded in part by institutional grants of the University of Saskatchewan (M. Daley), the University of Western Ontario (M. Daley) and the Natural Science and Engineering Research Council of Canada (M. Daley and H. Jürgensen).

M. Domaratzki et al. (Eds.): CIAA 2004, LNCS 3317, pp. 102–112, 2005.

The importance of this genetic compression becomes obvious when considering the structure of viruses. Viruses generally consist of two principal components: a protein capsid, and genetic material inside the capsid. The capsid serves as protection for the genetic material and also as a mechanism for inserting the genetic material into a host cell. The genetic material may consist of single- or double-stranded DNA or RNA and, in some rare cases, a mixture of the former possibly also including proteins.

The need for compression stems from the fact that the size of the capsid limits the amount of room for genetic information inside the virus. In the case of Polyomaviruses, the genome is constrained to be approximately 5kbp (5,000 basepairs) of DNA (compare to the human genome of size 3,150,000 kb), yet still manages to encode 6 distinct genes.

We exposit here a formal model of the viral compression techniques in terms of constraints on languages. For example, we would say that a language satisfies the "viral overlapping compression" property if some prefix of some word in the language is also a suffix of some other word in the language. We can likewise define constraints for other viral compression techniques, including retrograde encodings. We will focus here on deterministic modeling of the gene-level mechanics, in contrast to the probabilistic analysis of [8], which addresses gene compression from the point of view of evolutionary pressures and constraints on entire genomes.

The organization of the paper is as follows: In section 2 we consider basic notation and prerequisites. In section 3 we define formal versions of the basic viral compression techniques and investigate relationships and dependencies between them. We consider also the question of for which families of languages it is possible to decide these properties. Section 4 focuses on the finitary case of the problem as this is the most interesting from the point of view of applied viral genetics. We present efficient algorithms to decide each of the properties for real viral genomes. Section 5 contains our conclusions and a discussion of practical applications.

2   Notation and Prerequisites

For a general introduction to virology, we refer the reader to [3] and [10]; for formal language theory preliminaries, we refer to [9]. Let Σ be a finite alphabet. We denote, by Σ^* and Σ^+, the sets of words and non-empty words, respectively, over Σ and the empty word by λ. A language L is any subset of Σ^*. For a word $w \in \Sigma^*$, we denote the length of w by $|w|$ and the reversal of w by w^R. Let $\mathbb{N}$ be the set of positive integers. Furthermore, for $k \in \mathbb{N}$, define $\Sigma^{\geq k} = \{w \in \Sigma^* \mid |w| \geq k\}$.

A *full trio* is a language family closed under homomorphism, inverse homomorphism and intersection with regular sets. A full trio is also referred to as a cone. It is known that every full trio is closed under arbitrary a-transductions[1] and hence arbitrary gsm mappings. We refer to [1, 4] for the theory of AFL's.

---

[1] An a-transducer is also referred to as a rational transducer.

For a binary relation $\varrho \subseteq \Sigma^* \times \Sigma^*$ and a language $L \subseteq \Sigma^*$, we define

$$\varrho(s) = \{t \in \Sigma^* \mid (s,t) \in \varrho\},$$
$$\varrho(L) = \{t \in \Sigma^* \mid s \in L, (s,t) \in \varrho\},$$
$$\varrho^R = \{(s,t^R) \mid (s,t), \in \varrho\},$$
$$\varrho^{-1} = \{(t,s) \mid (s,t) \in \varrho\},$$
$$\varrho^{-R} = (\varrho^{-1})^R.$$

We will consider the following well-known relations. Let $w, v \in \Sigma^*$.

1. prefix order: $w \leq_p v$ (or $(w,v) \in \leq_p$) if and only if $v = wx$ for some $x \in \Sigma^*$.
2. suffix order: $w \leq_s v$ (or $(w,v) \in \leq_s$) if and only if $v = xw$ for some $x \in \Sigma^*$.
3. infix order: $w \leq_i v$ (or $(w,v) \in \leq_i$) if and only if $v = xwy$ for some $x, y \in \Sigma^*$.

Also, for each of the relations above, we prepend the word "proper", which will be denoted by $<_p, <_s, <_i$ where we enforce that $x, y \in \Sigma^+$ above.

For example, $\leq_p (L) = \{w \in \Sigma^* \mid v \leq_p w, v \in L\}$ and $\leq_i^{-R} (L) = \{w \in \Sigma^* \mid xw^R y \in L, x, y \in \Sigma^*\}$.

3   Viral Properties

Before formally stating the definitions of the viral properties, we will define the following sets which will be used for the conditions.

Let $L \subseteq \Sigma^*$ be a language, and let $n \in \mathbb{N}$ such that $1 \leq n \leq 6$ and let $k \in \mathbb{N}$. Then we define the following sets:

$$U(1, L, k) = \{w \in \Sigma^* \mid \exists u \in \Sigma^{\geq k}, x \in \Sigma^+, v \in \Sigma^*, xu \in L, w = uv\},$$
$$U(2, L, k) = \{w \in \Sigma^* \mid \exists v \in \Sigma^{\geq k}, y \in \Sigma^+, u \in \Sigma^*, vy \in L, w = uv\},$$
$$U(3, L, k) = U(1, L, k) \cup U(2, L, k),$$
$$U(4, L, k) = \{w \in \Sigma^* \mid \exists u, v \in \Sigma^{\geq k}, x, y \in \Sigma^+, xu \in L \wedge vy \in L, w = uv\},$$
$$U(5, L, k) = \{w \in \Sigma^{\geq k} \mid \exists u, v \in \Sigma^*, uw^R v \in L\},$$
$$U(6, L, k) = \{w \in \Sigma^{\geq k} \mid \exists u, v \in \Sigma^*, uw^R v \in L^+\}.$$

Furthermore, for each i, $1 \leq i \leq 6$, $k \in \mathbb{N}$ and $L \subseteq \Sigma^*$, let $Z(i, L, k) = U(i, L, k) \cap L$.

So, for example, $Z(i, L, k)$ consists of all words $w \in L$ such that there exists a word u of length at least k, a non-empty word x and a word v whereby xu is in L and $w = uv$ which is also in L.

We now define the properties that we will study.

Definition 1. *Let $L \subseteq \Sigma^*$, let n satisfy $1 \leq n \leq 6$ and let $k, l \in \mathbb{N}$. We say that L satisfies condition $W(n, k, l)$ if $|Z(n, L, k)| \geq l$.*

We also call condition $W(1, k, l)$ the l-weak k-prefix overlapping property, condition $W(2, k, l)$ the l-weak k-suffix overlapping property, condition $W(3, k, l)$

the *l-weak k-overlapping property*, condition $W(4, k, l)$ the *l-weak k-double-sided overlapping property*, condition $W(5, k, l)$ the *l-weak k-retrograde overlapping property* and condition $W(6, k, l)$ the *l-weak k-concatenated retrograde overlapping property*.

For example, a language L satisfies $W(1, k, l)$ if and only if there exists l distinct words $w \in L$ whereby $w = uv$ for some $u, v, x \in \Sigma^*$, with u of length at least k, x non-empty and $xu \in L$.

We also define a strong version of the properties above.

Definition 2. *Let $L \subseteq \Sigma^*$, let n satisfy $1 \le n \le 6$ and let $k \in \mathbb{N}$. We say that L satisfies condition $V(n, k)$ if $L \subseteq U(n, L, k)$. Equivalently, L satisfies condition $V(n, k)$ if and only if $L = Z(n, L, k)$.*

We also refer to each of these properties by replacing the prefix "*l-weak*" of each condition above with "strong".[2]

We now consider the relationships of these properties to each other. The following is immediate from the definitions.

Lemma 1. *Let i, j satisfy $1 \le i, j \le 6$, $k, l \in \mathbb{N}$ and let $L \subseteq \Sigma^*$. Then the following are true:*

1. *If $U(i, L, k) \subseteq U(j, L, k)$ then both L satisfies $V(i, k)$ implies L satisfies $V(j, k)$ and L satisfies $W(i, k, l)$ implies L satisfies $W(j, k, l)$.*
2. *If $|L \cap \Sigma^{\ge k}| \ge l$, then L satisfies $V(i, k)$ implies L satisfies $W(i, k, l)$.*
3. *If $L \cap \Sigma^{\le k} \ne \emptyset$, then L does not satisfy $V(i, k)$.*

Also, we note the following:

Lemma 2. *Let $L \subseteq \Sigma^*, k \in \mathbb{N}$. Then the following are true:*

1. *$U(4, l, k) \subseteq U(i, l, k)$, for each $i \in \{1, 2, 3\}$,*
2. *$U(5, l, k) \subseteq U(6, l, k)$,*
3. *$Z(1, L, k)^R = Z(2, L^R, k)$ and thus $|Z(1, L, k)| = |Z(2, L^R, k)|$.*

Proof. The first three statements are straightforward. For the fourth statement, let $z \in Z(1, L, k)^R$. Thus, $z^R = uv \in L, xu \in L, u \in \Sigma^{\ge k}, x \in \Sigma^+, v \in \Sigma^*$. Then $z = v^R u^R \in L^R, u^R x^R \in L^R$ and $z \in Z(2, L^R, k)$. Conversely, let $z \in Z(2, L^R, k)$. Thus, $z = uv, vy \in L^R, v \in \Sigma^{\ge k}, y \in \Sigma^+, u \in \Sigma^*$. Then $v^R u^R, y^R v^R \in L, v^R u^R \in Z(1, L, k)$ and $z = uv \in Z(1, L, k)^R$. □

Combining Lemma 1, 2, we obtain:

Proposition 1. *Let $L \subseteq \Sigma^*, k, l \in \mathbb{N}$. Then the following statements are true:*

1. *L satisfies $W(1, k, l)$ or $W(2, k, l)$ implies L satisfies $W(3, k, l)$,*
2. *L satisfies $V(1, k)$ or $V(2, k)$ implies L satisfies $V(3, k)$,*

---

[2] While prefix/suffix overlap compression is very common in viruses, it is not often the case that *every* gene will have some overlap; hence the motivation to study "weakened" versions of these operations.

3. L satisfies $W(4, k, l)$ implies L satisfies $W(1, k, l)$, $W(2, k, l)$ and $W(3, k, l)$,
4. L satisfies $V(4, k)$ implies L satisfies $V(1, k)$, $V(2, k)$ and $V(3, k)$,
5. L satisfies $W(5, k, l)$ implies L satisfies $W(6, k, l)$,
6. L satisfies $V(5, k)$ implies L satisfies $V(6, k)$.
7. L (respectively L^R) satisfies $W(1, k, l)$ iff L^R (resp. L) satisfies $W(2, k, l)$,
8. L (respectively L^R) satisfies $V(1, k)$ iff L^R (resp. L) satisfies $V(2, k)$.

We see, however that if $L_1 = \{abc, aa\}$ and $L_2 = \{abc, cc\}$, then $Z(1, L_1, 1) = \{aa, abc\}$, $Z_2(2, L_1, 1) = \{aa\}$, $Z(1, L_2, 1) = \{cc\}$ and also $Z(2, L_2, 1) = \{abc, cc\}$. So, in general, there are languages satisfying $W(1, k, l)$ (respectively $V(1, k)$) but not $W(2, k, l)$ (respectively $V(2, k)$) and there are languages satisfying $W(2, k, l)$ (respectively $V(2, k)$) but not $W(1, k, l)$ (respectively $V(1, k)$). We note also that, since $Z(3, L_1, 1) = Z(1, L_1, 1) \cup Z(2, L_1, 1)$ and $Z(3, L_2, 1) = Z(1, L_2, 1) \cup Z(2, L_2, 1)$, there are languages satisfying $W(3, k, l)$ (respectively $V(3, k)$) but not $W(1, k, l)$ (respectively $(V(1, k)$) and there are languages satisfying $W(3, k, l)$ (respectively $V(3, k)$) but not $W(2, k, l)$ (respectively $V(2, k)$). Additionally, $Z(4, L_1, 1) = \{aa\}$ and $Z(4, L_2, 1) = \{cc\}$. Thus, in general, there are languages satisfying $W(1, k, l)$ (respectively $V(1, k)$) but not satisfying $W(4, k, l)$ (respectively $V(4, k)$), there are languages satisfying $W(2, k, l)$ (respectively $V(2, k)$) but not satisfying $W(4, k, l)$ (respectively $V(4, k)$) and there are languages satisfying $W(3, k, l)$ (respectively $V(3, k)$) but not satisfying $W(4, k, l)$ (respectively $V(4, k)$. Further, let $L_3 = \{a, b, c, abc\}$. Then $Z(5, L_3, 1) = \{a, b, c\}$ but $Z(6, L_3, 1) = L_3$ and so, in general, there are languages satisfying $W(6, k, l)$ (respectively $V(6, k, l)$) but not $W(5, k, l)$ (respectively $V(6, k, l)$).

We also define the following sets which we will use for a characterization.

$$C(1, L, k) = \leq_p (<_s^{-1}(L) \cap \Sigma^{\geq k}),$$
$$C(2, L, k) = \leq_s (<_p^{-1}(L) \cap \Sigma^{\geq k}),$$
$$C(3, L, k) = C(1, L, k) \cup C(2, L, k),$$
$$C(4, L, k) = (<_s^{-1}(L) \cap \Sigma^{\geq k}) \cdot (<_p^{-1}(L) \cap \Sigma^{\geq k}),$$
$$C(5, L, k) = \leq_i^{-R}(L) \cap \Sigma^{\geq k},$$
$$C(6, L, k) = \leq_i^{-R}(L^+) \cap \Sigma^{\geq k}.$$

Proposition 2. Let i satisfy $1 \leq i \leq 6$, let $k \in \mathbb{N}$ and let $L \subseteq \Sigma^*$. Then $U(i, L, k) = C(i, L, k)$.

Proof. Let $i = 1$. "$\subseteq$" Let $w \in U(1, L, k)$. Thus, there exists $u \in \Sigma^{\geq k}, v \in \Sigma^*, x \in \Sigma^+, xu \in L, w = uv$. Therefore, $u \in <_s^{-1}(L) \cap \Sigma^{\geq k}$ and $w \in \leq_p (<_s^{-1}(L) \cap \Sigma^{\geq k})$.

"$\supseteq$" Let $w \in \leq_p (<_s^{-1}(L) \cap \Sigma^{\geq k})$. Thus, there exists $u, v \in \Sigma^*$ such that $w = uv$ with $u \in <_s^{-1}(L) \cap \Sigma^{\geq k}$. Hence, there exists $x \in \Sigma^+$ such that $xu \in L$.

Let $i = 2$. "$\subseteq$" Let $w \in U(2, L, k)$. Thus, there exists $v \in \Sigma^{\geq k}, u \in \Sigma^*, y \in \Sigma^+, vy \in L, w = uv$. Therefore, $v \in <_p^{-1}(L) \cap \Sigma^{\geq k}$ and $w \in \leq_s (<_p^{-1}(L) \cap \Sigma^{\geq k})$.

"$\supseteq$" Let $w \in \leq_s (<_p^{-1}(L) \cap \Sigma^{\geq k})$. Thus, there exists $u, v \in \Sigma^*$ such that $w = uv$ with $v \in <_p^{-1}(L) \cap \Sigma^{\geq k}$. Hence, there exists $x \in \Sigma^+$ such that $vx \in L$.

Let $i = 3$. Immediate from case 1, 2.

Let $i = 4$. "$\subseteq$" Let $w \in U(4, L, k)$. Thus, there exists $u, v \in \Sigma^{\geq k}, x, y \in \Sigma^+, w = uv, (xu \in L \wedge vy \in L)$. Therefore, $u \in <_s^{-1}(L) \cap \Sigma^{\geq k}, v \in <_p^{-1}(L) \cap \Sigma^{\geq k}$ and $w \in (<_s^{-1}(L) \cap \Sigma^{\geq k})(<_p^{-1}(L) \cap \Sigma^{\geq k})$.

"$\supseteq$" Let $w \in (<_s^{-1})(L) \cap \Sigma^{\geq k})(<_p^{-1}(L) \cap \Sigma^{\geq k})$. Thus, there exists $u \in <_s^{-1}(L) \cap \Sigma^{\geq k}, v \in <_p^{-1}(L) \cap \Sigma^{\geq k}$ with $w = uv$. Hence, there exists $x, y \in \Sigma^+$ such that $xu \in L$ and $vy \in L$.

Let $i = 5$. "$\subseteq$" Let $w \in U(5, L, k)$. Thus, there exists $u, v \in \Sigma^*$ with $uw^R v \in L$ and $w \in \Sigma^{\geq k}$. Then $w \in \leq_i^{-R}(L) \cap \Sigma^{\geq k}$.

"$\supseteq$" Let $w \in \leq_i^{-R}(L) \cap \Sigma^{\geq k}$. Then there exists u, v with $uw^R v \in L$ and $w \in \Sigma^{\geq k}$.

Let $i = 6$. "$\subseteq$" Let $w \in U(6, L, k)$. Thus, there exists $u, v \in \Sigma^*$ with $uw^R v \in L^+, w \in \Sigma^{\geq k}$. Then $w \in \leq_i^{-R}(L^+) \cap \Sigma^{\geq k}$.

"$\supseteq$" Let $w \in \leq_i^{-R}(L^+) \cap \Sigma^{\geq k}$. Then there exists u, v with $uw^R v \in L^+, w \in \Sigma^{\geq k}$. $\square$

This leads naturally to some decision problems. One would like to provide algorithms to test whether languages (or genomes) satisfy these properties. Namely, can we decide whether a given language satisfies one of the properties, depending on the language family that the given language is in? For each weak condition, this amounts to deciding whether $|Z(i, L, k)| \geq l$ and for each strong condition, it amounts to deciding whether $Z(i, L, k) = L$.

Proposition 3. *Let $\mathcal{L}_1, \mathcal{L}_2$ be language families effectively closed under intersection and the full trio operations with $\mathcal{L}_1$ being effectively semilinear and $\mathcal{L}_2$ having a decidable equality problem. Then the following are true:*

1. *For each $k, l \in \mathbb{N}$ and $i, 1 \leq i \leq 4$, it is decidable whether $L \in \mathcal{L}_1$ satisfies $W(i, k, l)$ and it is decidable whether $L \in \mathcal{L}_2$ satisfies $V(i, k)$.*
2. *If $\mathcal{L}_1, \mathcal{L}_2$ are also effectively closed under reversal, then it is decidable whether $L \in \mathcal{L}_1$ satisfies $W(5, k, l)$ and it is decidable whether $L \in \mathcal{L}_2$ satisfies $V(5, k)$.*
3. *If $\mathcal{L}_1, \mathcal{L}_2$ are also effectively closed under reversal and $+$, then it is decidable whether $L \in \mathcal{L}_1$ satisfies $W(6, k, l)$ and it is decidable whether $L \in \mathcal{L}_2$ satisfies $V(6, k)$.*

Proof. It is easy to construct a-transducers which output $\leq_p^{-1}(L), \leq_s^{-1}(L), <_p^{-1}(L), <_s^{-1}(L), \leq_p(L), \leq_s(L)$ for each L in $\mathcal{L}_1$ or $\mathcal{L}_2$. Also, every intersection-closed full trio is closed under union and concatenation since $L_1 \$ \Sigma^* \cap \Sigma^* \$ L_2$ is in $\mathcal{L}_1$ and $\mathcal{L}_2$, there is an a-transducer which outputs $L_1 \cup L_2$ and there is a homomorphism which outputs $L_1 L_2$. Thus, $Z(1, L, k), Z(2, L, k), Z(3, L, k), Z(4, L, k)$ are in $\mathcal{L}_1$ and $\mathcal{L}_2$. Additionally, if $\mathcal{L}_1, \mathcal{L}_2$ are closed under reversal, then $Z(5, L, k)$ is in $\mathcal{L}_1$ and $\mathcal{L}_2$ and if $\mathcal{L}_1, \mathcal{L}_2$ are closed under reversal and $+$, then $Z(6, L, k)$ is in $\mathcal{L}_1$ and $\mathcal{L}_2$. Since $\mathcal{L}_1$ is effectively semilinear, we can decide if $L \in \mathcal{L}_1$ is infinite [5] and if it is not, then we can effectively find the length of the longest word in L. Then, we can test membership of every word of length less than or equal to that length to determine whether $|Z(i, L, k)| \geq l$

(emptiness is always decidable for semilinear sets, and since $\mathcal{L}_1$ is closed under intersection with regular languages, we can decide whether $w \in L$ by testing whether $L \cap \{w\} \neq \emptyset$). Also, by the decidability of equality for $\mathcal{L}_2$, the proposition follows.   □

We denote by **NCM** the family of languages defined by one-way nondeterministic, reversal-bounded multicounter machines. It is known that **NCM** is an intersection and reversal closed full trio effectively closed under semilinearity [7]. Also, it is known that the family of regular languages is closed under all of the operations above and has a decidable equality problem.

Corollary 1. *For each $L \in$ **NCM**, each i, $1 \leq i \leq 5$ and each $k, l \in \mathbb{N}$, it is decidable whether L satisfies $W(i, k, l)$. In addition, for each $L \in$ **REG**, each i, $1 \leq i \leq 6$ and each $k, l \in \mathbb{N}$, it is decidable whether L satisfies $W(i, k, l)$ and $V(i, k)$.*

4   Computational Verification of Viral Properties

Ideally, one would like to apply the formal definitions given here to real viral genomes as a method for classifying viruses based on gene compression. In this section we will consider fast algorithms to do exactly this, and their complexity. Since all real viral genomes are finite, we will restrict ourselves to dealing with finite input languages here. We will describe algorithms which will verify each of the viral properties for a given input viral genome. A viral genome is a finite language in which the words are the genes of the virus.

For a finite language $L \subseteq \Sigma^+$, we let s_L be the sum of the lengths of every word of L (the length of the genome).

We recall a well-known and important result from [2]. A partial deterministic finite automaton is a deterministic finite automaton in which each state need not have a transition on every letter. The smallest partial DFA for a given regular language is the partial DFA that recognizes the language and has the smallest number of states. In [2], it is demonstrated that, for each word $w \in \Sigma^*$, the smallest partial DFA accepting $\leq_s^{-1}(w)$ is linear in the length of w. Precisely, it has at most $2|w| - 1$ states and $3|w| - 4$ transitions. Moreover, it is shown that the smallest partial DFA accepting $\leq_i^{-1}(w)$ is linear in the length of w. That is, if $|w| > 2$, then it has at most $2|w| - 2$ states and at most $3|w| - 4$ transitions. In addition, they show that for any w over a fixed finite alphabet Σ, both the smallest partial DFA accepting $\leq_s^{-1}(L)$ and the smallest DFA accepting $\leq_i^{-1}(L)$ can be built in time linear in the length of w.

Now, let $L = \{w_1, \ldots, w_m\} \subseteq \Sigma^+$. For our algorithms, we construct a method which we call $suffix\_dfa(L)$ which returns a DFA accepting $\leq_s^{-1}(L)$. Let $w = w_1 \# w_2 \# \cdots \# w_m \#$. Then $\leq_s^{-1}(w) = (\leq_s^{-1}(w_m \#)) \cup (\leq_s^{-1}(w_{m-1} \#) w_m \#) \cup \ldots \cup (\leq_s^{-1}(w_1 \#) w_2 \# w_3 \# \cdots w_m \#)$. Let $M = (Q, \Sigma \cup \{\#\}, q_0, F, \delta)$ be the smallest partial DFA accepting $\leq_s^{-1}(w)$. Thus, it is clear that for every $x \in \Sigma^*$, $x \in \leq_s^{-1}(L)$ if and only if $x \# v \in \leq_s^{-1}(w) = L(M)$, where $v \in (\Sigma \cup \{\#\})^*$. Moreover, since M is partial and the smallest DFA, for each $y \in (\Sigma \cup \{\#\})^*$,

$\delta(q_0, y)$ is defined if and only if $yu \in L(M)$ for some $u \in (\Sigma \cup \{\#\})^*$. Thus, for each $x \in \Sigma^*$, $x \in \leq_s^{-1}(L)$ if and only if $\delta(q_0, x\#)$ is defined. Hence, we transform M into a new DFA M' by making the new final state set F' to be the set of all states $q \in Q$ such that $\delta(q, \#)$ is defined, and by removing all transitions of the form $\delta(q, \#) = p$ for $p, q \in Q$. Let $w \in L(M')$. Then $w \in \Sigma^*$ since there are no transitions on $\#$ and necessarily $w\#$ is defined in M. Thus, $w\#v \in L(M)$ for some $v \in (\Sigma \cup \{\#\})^*$. Thus, $w \in \leq_s^{-1}(L)$. Conversely, let $w \in \leq_s^{-1}(L)$. Then $w\#v \in L(M)$ for some $v \in (\Sigma \cup \{\#\})^*$ and so $w \in L(M')$. Hence we see that $L(M') = \leq_s^{-1}(L)$ and M' can be constructed in linear time from M which is linear in $|w|$ which is linear in s_L. We note that $suffix\_dfa(\Sigma^{-1}L) = \leq_s^{-1}(L)$. Further, for a DFA $M = (Q, \Sigma, q_0, F, \delta)$ over Σ and $w \in \Sigma^*$, define $S_{M,k}(w) = \{q \in Q \mid \delta(q_0, w_1) = q, w_1 \leq_p w, |w_1| \geq k\}$. For each algorithm in this section, we assume that we have some encoding of L as input, whereby there is only one copy of each word given.

Algorithm 1 input: $k \in \mathbb{N}, L \subseteq \Sigma^+$, Σ fixed, L finite, returns: largest l_1, l_2, l_3 such that L satisfies $W(1, k, l_1), W(2, k, l_2)$ and $W(3, k, l_2)$

1: Let $l_1, l_2, l_3 := 0, v_1, v_2 := false$, if $k \geq s_L$, return.
2: Let $M = (Q_1, \Sigma \cup \{\#\}, q_0, F_1, \delta_1) := suffix\_dfa(\Sigma^{-1}L)$,
3: Let $M^R = (Q_2, \Sigma \cup \{\#\}, p_0, F_2, \delta_2) := suffix\_dfa((L\Sigma^{-1})^R)$
4: **for all** $w \in L$ **do**
5:     **if** $S_{M,k}(w) \cap F_1 \neq \emptyset$ **then**
6:         $v_1 := true, l_1 := l_1 + 1$
7:     **end if**
8:     **if** $S_{M^R,k}(w^R) \cap F_2 \neq \emptyset$ **then**
9:         $v_2 := true, l_2 := l_2 + 1$,
10:    **end if**
11:    **if** either v_1 or v_2 is true, **then**
12:        $l_3 := l_3 + 1, v_1 := false, v_2 := false$.
13:    **end if**
14: **end for**

We have discussed above how to perform the method $suffix\_dfa$. It is easy to pass in the reversal of a language to $suffix\_dfa$, in time linear in s_L. Then, in line 5 of Algorithm 1, we can check to see if the intersection is empty by keeping a counter starting at k and running w through the transition function of M, decreasing the counter at each step. Then, when the counter reaches 0, we test every state we hit on input w to see whether it is a final state. If it is, we increase l_1 and set v_1 indicating that $w \in Z(1, L, k)$. Also, in line 8, we are testing whether $w^R \in Z(1, L^R, k)$. Indeed, by Lemma 2(3), $w^R \in Z(1, L^R, k)$ if and only if $w \in Z(2, L, k)$. Thus, if this is true, we increase l_2 and set v_2 to true. In addition, $w \in Z(3, L, k)$ if and only if $w \in Z(1, L, k) \cup Z(2, L, k)$ and so we increase l_3 if and only if either v_1 or v_2 is true, and we reset each to false. In this way, when the method completes, l_1, l_2 and l_3 will be the maximum such that L satisfies $W(1, k, l_1), W(2, k, l_2)$ and $W(3, k, l_3)$, respectively. Furthermore, this method runs in time $O(s_L)$ time.

For the fourth property, our algorithm requires only a small modification. For a word w, let $w(i)$ be the ith position of w. This algorithm, for each word w,

---

Algorithm 2 input: $k \in \mathbb{N}, L \subseteq \Sigma^+$, Σ fixed, L finite, returns: the largest integer l_4 such that L satisfies $W(4, k, l_4)$

Let l_4, if $k \geq s_L$, return.
2: Let $M = (Q_1, \Sigma \cup \{\#\}, q_0, F_1, \delta_1) := \text{suffix\_dfa}(\Sigma^{-1}L)$,
   Let $M^R = (Q_2, \Sigma \cup \{\#\}, p_0, F_2, \delta_2) := \text{suffix\_dfa}((L\Sigma^{-1})^R)$
4: **for all** $w \in L$ **do**
   Let b_1, b_2 be bit vectors of length $|w|$ all initialized to 0, let $j := 0$,
6:   **while** $j \leq |w|$ **do**
      if $\delta(w(1) \cdots w(j)) \cap F_1 \neq \emptyset$ **then**
8:        set $b_1(j) := 1$,
      end if
10:      **if** $\delta(w(|w|) \cdots w(|w| - j + 1)) \cap F_2 \neq \emptyset$ **then**
         set $b_2(|w| - j + 1) := 1$,
12:      **end if**
         $j := j+1$,
14:   **end while**
      if there exists j such that $(k \leq j) \wedge (k \leq |w|-j+1) \wedge (b_1(j) = 1) \wedge (b_2(j+1) = 1)$
      then
16:      $l_4 := l_4 + 1$.
      end if
18: **end for**

---

remembers every position of w which has the prefix of that length in $<_s^{-1}(L)$ and it also remembers every position of w^R which has the prefix of that length in $<_s^{-1}(L^R)$. Then $w = uv$ for some u, v with $u \in <_s^{-1}(L), v^R \in <_s^{-1}(L^R)$ and $|u|, |v| \geq k$ if and only if statement 14 is true. Hence, upon completion, l_4 will be the largest integer such that L satisfies $W(4, k, l_4)$. Furthermore, this method also runs in $O(s_L)$ time.

Property 5 can also be verified easily. Indeed, w^R is defined if and only if

---

Algorithm 3 input: $k \in \mathbb{N}, L \subseteq \Sigma^+$, Σ fixed, L finite, returns: largest integer l_5 such that L satisfies $W(5, k, l_5)$

Let $l_5 := 0$, if $k \geq s_L$ then return.
2: Let $M = (Q, \Sigma \cup \{\#\}, q_0, F, \delta) := \text{suffix\_dfa}(L^R)$,
   for all $w \in L$ **do**
4:   **if** $\delta(q_0, w^R)$ is defined **then**
      let $l_5 := l_5 + 1$.
6:   **end if**
   end for

$w^R u \in \leq_s^{-1}(L)$ for some u if and only if $w^R \in \leq_i^{-1}(L)$. Hence we can decide this property in time $O(s_L)$.

For property 6, we note that a word $w \leq_i v \in L^+$ if and only if $w \in R = (\leq_i^{-1}(L)) \cup (\leq_s^{-1}(L)L^* \leq_p^{-1}(L))$. Moreover, it is easy to construct an NFA

$M = (Q, \Sigma, q_0, F, \delta)$ accepting R in linear time, with the number of states linear in s_L. In addition, it is well-known that we can test whether a word w is in the language generated by an NFA in time $O(|Q||w|)$ (see [6]). Thus, to find the largest integer l_6 such that L satisfies $W(6, k, l)$, we construct the NFA from L and decide membership of w^R for each $w \in L$. This takes time $O(|w_1||Q| + \cdots + |w_m||Q|) = O(|Q|s_L)$. Thus, one can decide whether a finite language L satisfies $W(6, k, l)$ in time $O(s_L^2)$.

Finally, the strong properties can also be verified straightforwardly using the algorithms presented above. Indeed, they are just a special case where $l = |L|$. We summarize the preceding thusly:

Proposition 4. *Let i satisfy $1 \leq i \leq 5$ and let Σ be some fixed alphabet. Then given a finite language $L \subseteq \Sigma^+$ as input without duplicates and $k \in \mathbb{N}$, we can both find the largest integer l such that L satisfies $W(i, k, l)$ and we can decide whether L satisfies $V(i, k)$ in time $O(s_L)$. Furthermore, we can both find the largest l whereby L satisfies $W(6, k, l)$ and we can decide whether L satisfies $V(6, k)$ in time $O(s_L^2)$.*

5   Conclusions and Discussion

We have presented here a formalization of the process of gene compression that occurs in many viral genomes. We have shown dependencies and relationships between these properties and demonstrated that, in general, most of the weak versions of the properties can be decided for languages defined by nondeterministic finite automata augmented with reversal-bounded counters while the strong versions can be decided for regular languages. Most significantly, we have given algorithms which can efficiently decide these properties for real viral genomes and provide information which is immediately useful to virologists.

These algorithms give us the ability to study the relative amount of gene compression between related viruses in a quantifiable way. It may be possible to infer evolutionary relationships between viruses using this information. The fact that genes overlap one another provides a very serious constraint for viral genome evolution. It is known that viruses occasionally aquire genes horizontally (that is, a gene from an infected host becomes part of the virus's own genome). Clearly, only those genes which meet very specific constraints (*e.g.* those that are "compressible" relative to the virus's genome) will be able to be incorporated into the virus. Using the algorithms presented here and real viral genome data, we can find target genes in the host organism which, due to their structure, have the greatest probability of being incorporated into the viral genome.

Finally, the formal properties here also present a framework for automated classification of a virus given only its genome. The family of Coronaviruses, for example, has a very regular genomic structure: a single strand of +-sense RNA of length 27-30kb. The beginning of this RNA strand always encodes a viral polymerase (often as part of a polyprotein) and the remainder encodes a series of "nested" genes. Each of these nested genes is a proper suffix of the previous gene.

This structure can obviously be formally encoded using the properties given here. Similar compression regularities can be found in other viral genomes and encoded using our properties. Classification of a new virus is then simply a matter of verifying compliance to our properties and then checking to see if this matches any known structures.

By formalizing this ancient form of data compression, we have provided tools which will allow for further insight in the molecular evolution of viruses and assist in the automated classification of new viruses by reference to only their genomes.

References

1. J. Berstel. *Transductions and Context-Free Languages*. B.B. Teubner, Stuttgart, 1979.
2. A. Blumer, J. Blumer, M.T. Chen, A. Ehrenfeucht, Haussler D., and J. Seiferas. The smallest automaton recognizing the subwords of a text. *Theoretical Computer Science*, 40(1):31–55, 1985.
3. A.J. Cann. *Principles of Molecular Virology, 3e*. Academic Press, San Diego, CA, 2001.
4. S. Ginsburg. *Algebraic and Automata-Theoretic Properties of Formal Languages*. North-Holland Publishing Company, Amsterdam, 1975.
5. S. Ginsburg and E.H. Spanier. Bounded algol-like languages. *Transactions of the American Mathematical Society*, 113(2):333–368, 1964.
6. J. Holub and B. Melichar. Implementation of nondeterministic finite automata for approximate pattern matching. In J.-M. Champarnaud, D. Maurel, and D. Ziadi, editors, *WIA '98, Lecture Notes in Computer Science*, volume 1660, pages 92–99. Springer-Verlag, 1999.
7. O. Ibarra. Reversal-bounded multicounter machines and their decision problems. *Journal of the ACM*, 25(1):116–133, 1978.
8. D.C. Krakauer. Evolutionary principles of genome compression. *Comments on Theoretical Biology*, 7(4):215–236, 2002.
9. A. Salomaa. *Formal Languages*. Academic Press, New York, 1973.
10. E.K. Wagner and M.J. Hewlett. *Basic Virology*. Blackwell Science, Malden, MA, 1999.

Concatenation State Machines and Simple Functions

Wojciech Debski[1] and Wojciech Fraczak[1,2]

[1] IDT Canada, Ottawa, Ontario, Canada
[2] Université du Québec en Outaouais, Gatineau, Québec, Canada

Abstract. We introduce a class of deterministic push-down transducers called *concatenation state machines* (CSM), and we study its semantic domain which is a class of partial mappings over finitely generated free monoids, called *simple functions*.

1 Introduction

IDT Canada, a subsidiary of Integrated Device Technology, recently developed a specialized programmable processing unit for real-time network packet filtering and classification, called *PAX.port*. In this paper we define a mathematical model for *PAX.port* hardware which we call a *concatenation state machine* (CSM).

A CSM can be seen as a pass-through device transforming a flow of input data into a flow of output data. More formally, a concatenation state machine M defines a partial mapping $|M| : \Sigma^* \mapsto \Omega^*$ where Σ and Ω are two finite alphabets. We demonstrate that there is a strong correlation between CSM and *simple languages* as defined in [1]. Thus, a mapping which can be defined by a CSM will be called *"simple function"*.

The main result of the paper is the proof that a partial mapping $f : \Sigma^* \mapsto \Omega^*$ is a simple function if and only if there exists a finite set G of classifiers (classifiers are mappings defined on prefix codes and they constitute a monoid with respect to *classifier concatenation*) such that all quotients of f are included in G^*.

We end the paper with some results concerning the expressive power of simple functions.

2 Concatenation State Machine

Let Σ and Ω be two disjoint finite sets, called *input* and *output* alphabets, respectively. A Concatenation State Machine (CSM) is a rooted directed labeled graph with three types of vertices: *switch nodes, concatenation nodes*, and *accepting nodes*; such that:

- All edges outgoing from a switch node are labeled by different symbols of Σ.
- There are two ordered edges, *left* and *right*, outgoing from a concatenation node.
- Accepting nodes have no outgoing edges. An accepting node is labeled by an *accepting string* from Ω^*.

M. Domaratzki et al. (Eds.): CIAA 2004, LNCS 3317, pp. 113–124, 2005.

Consider the concatenation state machine in Figure 1. It is built over the input alphabet $\Sigma = \{a, b, c\}$, and the output alphabet $\Omega = \{\alpha, \beta, \gamma\}$. Switch nodes are represented by plain circles with outgoing edges labeled by letters of the input alphabet. Concatenation nodes are represented by rectangles with the *left* edge outgoing from the left, and the *right* edge outgoing from the right part of the node. Accepting nodes are represented by double circles marked by their labels which are words over the output alphabet Ω. The initial node of the CSM is distinguished by a short incoming arrow. Intuitively, a switch node can be seen

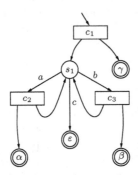

Fig. 1. Concatenation State Machine

as a state in the deterministic automaton. A concatenation node represents a "subroutine call" for the destination of the *left* edge; once the subroutine returns, we continue with the destination of the *right* edge. Accepting nodes are "return" instructions producing values defined by their labels.

Definition 1. *A CSM is a 9-uplet* $(\Sigma, \Omega, S, C, A, \eta_S, \eta_C, \lambda, i)$, *where:*

- Σ, Ω, S, C, A *are finite pairwise disjoint sets of* input symbols, output symbols, switch nodes, concatenation nodes, *and* accepting nodes, *respectively.*
- $\eta_S : (S, \Sigma) \mapsto (S \cup C \cup A)$, $\eta_C : (C, \{\texttt{left}, \texttt{right}\}) \mapsto (S \cup C \cup A)$, *and* $\lambda : A \mapsto \Omega^*$, *are partial mappings; and*
- $i \in (S \cup C \cup A)$ *is the* initial node.

A state of the concatenation state machine $M = (\Sigma, \Omega, S, C, A, \eta_S, \eta_C, \lambda, i)$, is defined by *execution stack* denoted `stack`. An execution stack is a list of nodes, i.e., `stack` $\in (S \cup C \cup A)^*$. The initial state of M consists of the execution stack containing one element, the initial node.

A CSM processes the nodes of the execution stack until the stack becomes empty. The machine runs the following execution loop. It pops the top node, s, of the stack. If s is an accepting node, $s \in A$, then the machine outputs $\lambda(s)$. If s is a switch node, $s \in S$, then the machine reads a new input symbol $a \in \Sigma$ and pushes the node $\eta_S(s, a)$ onto the top of the execution stack. If s is a concatenation node, $s \in C$, the machine pushes two nodes on the stack, first $\eta_S(s, \texttt{right})$ and then $\eta_S(s, \texttt{left})$, so node $\eta_S(s, \texttt{left})$ is on the top of the execution stack. If the execution stack is not empty, the execution loop continues. The pseudo-code defining the execution loop of a CSM $(\Sigma, \Omega, S, C, A, \eta_S, \eta_C, \lambda, i)$ is presented in Figure 2.

```
1   while (stack is not empty) do
2       s := pop(stack);   // pop the top of stack into an auxiliary variable s
3       if (s ∈ A) then
4           write(λ(s));
5       if (s ∈ S) then
6           read(a);   // read input symbol into an auxiliary variable a
7           push(ηS(s, a), stack);
8       if (s ∈ C) then
9           push(ηS(s, right), stack);
10          push(ηS(s, left), stack);
11  end while
```

Fig. 2. Pseudo-code for the execution loop of a CSM

For a given input w, M completes if its execution stack becomes empty after reading the whole input w. Then we say that M accepts w and the result of the acceptance, denoted by $|M|(w)$, is the concatenation of all outputs produced by $write()$. Otherwise we say that M is not defined on w, denoted by $|M|(w) = \emptyset$. M will reject input w if one of the partial mappings η_S, η_C, or λ, is called with arguments for which the mapping is not defined, or if w is too short and no new symbol can be read, or if w is too long and the execution stack becomes empty before reading the last symbol of w.

The CSM in Figure 1 can be described by $(\Sigma, \Omega, S, C, A, \eta_S, \eta_C, \lambda, i)$, where: $\Sigma = \{a, b, c\}$, $\Omega = \{\alpha, \beta, \gamma\}$, $S = \{s_1\}$, $C = \{c_1, c_2, c_3\}$, $A = \{a_1, a_2, a_3, a_4\}$, $\eta_S = \{(s_1, a) \mapsto c_2, (s_1, b) \mapsto c_3, (s_1, c) \mapsto a_2\}$, $\eta_C = \{c_1 \mapsto (s_1, a_4), c_2 \mapsto (a_1, s_1), c_3 \mapsto (s_1, a_3)\}$ (by $\eta_C : c \mapsto (x, y)$, for $c \in C$ and $x, y \in S \cup C \cup A$, we mean that $x = \eta_C(c, \texttt{left})$, $y = \eta_C(c, \texttt{right})$, and that both values are defined), $\lambda = \{a_1 \mapsto \alpha, a_2 \mapsto \varepsilon, a_3 \mapsto \beta, a_4 \mapsto \gamma\}$, and $i = c_1$. The execution steps of M on input word "bac" are: $(c_1) \xrightarrow{\eta_C(c_1)} (s_1, a_4) \xrightarrow{read(b)} (c_3, a_4) \xrightarrow{\eta_C(c_3)} (s_1, a_3, a_4) \xrightarrow{read(a)} (c_2, a_3, a_4) \xrightarrow{\eta_C(c_2)} (a_1, s_1, a_3, a_4) \xrightarrow{write(\alpha)} (s_1, a_3, a_4) \xrightarrow{read(c)} (a_2, a_3, a_4) \xrightarrow{write(\varepsilon)} (a_3, a_4) \xrightarrow{write(\beta)} (a_4) \xrightarrow{write(\gamma)} ()$. Thus, on input "$bac$", the CSM produces output string "$\alpha\beta\gamma$".

A concatenation state machine $M = (\Sigma, \Omega, S, C, A, \eta_S, \eta_C, \lambda, i)$ is called *trimmed* if:

- all nodes $S \cup C \cup A$ are accessible from i;
- from every switch node $s \in S$ there is a path to at least one accepting node $a \in A$;
- for every concatenation node $c \in C$, values $\eta_C(c, \texttt{left})$ and $\eta_C(c, \texttt{right})$ are both defined;
- there is no loop passing exclusively through concatenation nodes.

It is relatively easy to *trim* any concatenation state machine by removing all nodes which make the CSM non-trimmed. The trimmed CSM defines the same mapping from input strings into output strings as the original CSM.

3   Algebraic Definition of CSM

Let $u, w \in \Sigma^*$. We say that u is a *prefix* (initial segment) of w, denoted by $u \leq w$, if there exists a word $v \in \Sigma^*$ such that $uv = w$. If $u \leq w$ and $u \neq w$ then u is a *proper prefix* of w. A language $L \subset \Sigma^*$ is called a *prefix code* if L does not contain two words such that one is a proper prefix of the other.

Definition 2. *We call* classifier *any partial mapping* $f : \Sigma^* \mapsto \Omega^*$ *such that* $f^{-1}(\Omega^*)$ *is a prefix code.*

Classifiers, i.e., partial mappings defined on prefix codes, are particularly important to real-time network packet classification because a classification decision can be made on-line by looking into an initial segment of the packet. This eliminates the risk of having to change the decision later, when more bits arrive.

Proposition 1. *Every concatenation state machine defines a classifier.*

Proof. Since the execution of a concatenation state machine M is deterministic on the input word (read from left-to-right) and it stops once the execution stack becomes empty, M cannot accept an input word and its proper prefix at the same time. □

The classifier which is not defined for any input, i.e., such that its co-image of Ω^* is empty, will be called *empty classifier* and will be denoted by $\emptyset$. Classifiers which are defined (only) for the empty input word $\varepsilon \in \Sigma^*$, will be denoted by the result they produce, i.e., every output word $u \in \Omega^*$ defines classifier $u \stackrel{\text{def}}{=} \{\varepsilon \mapsto u\}$.

Definition 3. *Let* $f, g : \Sigma^* \mapsto \Omega^*$ *be two classifiers. Classifier concatenation,* fg, *is defined as:*

$$fg(w) \stackrel{\text{def}}{=} \{f(v_1)g(v_2) \in \Omega^* \mid w = v_1v_2 \text{ and } v_1 \in f^{-1}(\Omega^*)\} .$$

Since $f^{-1}(\Omega^*)$ *is a prefix code,* $fg(w)$ *is empty or a singleton set. Also, the co-image* $(fg)^{-1}(\Omega^*) = f^{-1}(\Omega^*)g^{-1}(\Omega^*)$ *is a prefix code. Thus* fg *is a classifier.*

Classifiers under *classifier concatenation* constitute a monoid with $\varepsilon : \{\varepsilon \mapsto \varepsilon\}$ as unit. Both, empty $\emptyset$ and unit ε classifiers, are called *trivial classifiers*. The monoid will be called *classifier monoid*.

Lemma 2. *Classifier monoid is a* cancellative *monoid, i.e., for every non-empty classifiers* f, g, g', h, *the equality* $fgh = fg'h$ *implies* $g = g'$.

Definition 4. *Let $\Sigma = \{a_1, \ldots, a_n\}$ be the input alphabet and $f_1, \ldots, f_n : \Sigma^* \mapsto \Omega^*$ be classifiers. Switch composition, $a_1 f_1 + \ldots + a_n f_n$, is defined as:*

$$(a_1 f_1 + \ldots + a_n f_n)(w) \stackrel{\text{def}}{=} f_i(v), \text{ where } w = a_i v, \text{ for some } i \in [1, n] \ .$$

Switch composition $a_1 f_1 + \ldots + a_n f_n$ yields a classifier.

Switch composition is an n-ary operation, where n is the size of the input alphabet. We allow abbreviated notation by omitting ε and terms with $\emptyset$. E.g., we will write $(a_1 + a_3 f_3)$ instead of $(a_1 \varepsilon + a_2 \emptyset + a_3 f_3 + a_4 \emptyset + \ldots + a_n \emptyset)$.

Definition 5. *Let $f : \Sigma^* \mapsto \Omega^*$ be a classifier and $v \in \Sigma^*$ an input word. Quotient, $v^{-1} f$, is defined as $(v^{-1} f)(w) \stackrel{\text{def}}{=} f(vw)$. Quotient $v^{-1} f$ yields a classifier. By $Q(f)$ we denote the set of all quotients of f, i.e., $Q(f) \stackrel{\text{def}}{=} \{w^{-1} f \mid w \in \Sigma^*\}$.*

3.1   Representation of CSM by Equations

Let $V = \{X_1, \ldots, X_n\}$ be an ordered set of *variables*. A system of equations over V is a vector $E = (E_1, \ldots, E_n)$, where E_i, for $i \in [1, n]$, is an expression of one of the following forms:

1. *Concatenation*: $X_i X_j$, for $i, j \in [1, n]$;
2. *Switch*: $a_1 X_{i_1} + \ldots + a_k X_{i_k}$, where $\{a_1, \ldots, a_k\} = \Sigma$ and $i_1, \ldots, i_k \in [1, n]$;
3. *Accepting string*: u, with $u \in \Omega^*$.

For example, let $\Sigma = \{0, 1\}$, $\Omega = \{a, b\}$, $V = \{X_1, X_2, X_3\}$, and $E = (X_2 X_2, 0 X_1 + 1 X_3, ab)$. This system of equations can also be written in a more familiar way:

$$\{X_1 = X_2 X_2, \ X_2 = 0 X_1 + 1 X_3, \ X_3 = ab\} \ .$$

A *solution* for a system of equations $(E_1, \ldots, E_n)$ over $\{X_1, \ldots, X_n\}$ is a vector $F = (f_1, \ldots, f_n)$ of classifiers such that $f_i = E_i[f_1/X_1, \ldots, f_n/X_n]$, for all $i \in [1, n]$. By $E_i[f_1/X_1, \ldots, f_n/X_n]$ we denote the expression E_i in which every occurrence of $X_1, \ldots, X_n$ is replaced by classifier $f_1, \ldots, f_n$, respectively.

We say that a system of equations is *proper* if it does not contain a loop over concatenation equations (i.e., the transitive closure of $\{(X_i, X_j) \mid E_i = X_j X_k \text{ or } E_i = X_k X_j\}$ is irreflexive).

Proposition 3. *Every proper system of equations has exactly one solution.*

Proposition 4. *Let f be a classifier. The two following statements are equivalent:*

1. *There is a concatenation state machine M implementing f.*
2. *There is a proper system of equations E whose solution includes f.*

Proof. There is a one-to-one correspondence between CSMs and systems of equations. The variables of a system of equations correspond to nodes of CSM: switch nodes are variables defined by switch expressions; concatenation nodes are variables defined by concatenation expressions, and accepting nodes are variables defined by the accepting string.   □

Sometimes, it is more natural to represent a system of equations using more general expressions allowing variables occurring as subexpressions to be substituted by their defining expressions. E.g., the system of three equations, $\{X_1 = X_2X_2,\ X_2 = 0X_1 + 1X_3,\ X_3 = ab\}$, could be represented by $\{X = 0XX + 1ab\}$, assuming we are interested in the solution for X_2. In the case of a proper system of equations, all the variables defined by concatenation expressions can always be eliminated. The resulting system of equations corresponds to a context-free grammar which is a *simple grammar* (i.e., $LL(1)$ grammar under Greibach normal form, [1, 2, 3]). The languages generated by simple grammars are called *simple languages* (or *s-languages* or $LL(0)$). Simple languages are precisely those languages which are recognized by *simple push-down automata* (deterministic push-down automata with one state). If the output alphabet is empty, $\Omega = \emptyset$, then concatenation state machines can be seen as a *simple push-down automata*. Therefore, the classifiers which can be defined by a CSM can be seen as a generalization of s-languages, and thus, they will be called *simple functions* (or *s-functions*). The immediate consequence of the above observations is the following proposition.

Proposition 5. *Let Σ and Ω be two disjoint alphabets. If a partial mapping $f : \Sigma^* \mapsto \Omega^*$ is an s-function, then there exists a simple language $L \subseteq (\Sigma \cup \Omega)^*$, such that*

$$\{(x, f(x)) \mid x \in \Sigma^*\} = \{(\pi_\Sigma(w), \pi_\Omega(w)) \mid w \in L\},$$

where π_Σ and π_Ω are projections of $(\Sigma \cup \Omega)^*$ onto Σ^* and Ω^*, respectively.

4   Characterization of Simple Functions

In [3] it was proved that a language L is an s-language if and only if the set $Q(L)$ of its quotients[1] is a subset of a free monoid generated by a finite set G of prefix codes, i.e., $Q(L) \subseteq G^*$. In this section we extend this result by providing a characterization theorem for s-functions.

A classifier is called *prime* if it is non-trivial and it cannot be represented as a concatenation of two non-trivial classifiers. Every non-trivial classifier f admits a (not necessarily unique) prime form, i.e., f can be expressed as a finite concatenation of prime classifiers, $f = p_1p_2 \ldots p_n$. The number of factors is bounded by $|w| + |f(w)|$ for any $w \in f^{-1}(\Omega^*)$.

Lemma 6. *Let f, g, h be non-empty classifiers and p, q prime classifiers such that $f = pg = qh$. If $p \neq q$ then p is an output letter ($p \in \Omega$) and $h = ph'$, or q is an output letter and $g = qg'$, for some classifiers h', g'.*

Proof. Since $f = pg = qh$, $f^{-1}(\Omega^*) = p^{-1}(\Omega^*)g^{-1}(\Omega^*) = q^{-1}(\Omega^*)h^{-1}(\Omega^*)$. Domains of classifiers are prefix codes, thus $p^{-1}(\Omega^*)P = q^{-1}(\Omega^*)$ (or, symmetrically, $q^{-1}(\Omega^*)P = p^{-1}(\Omega^*)$), for some prefix code $P \subset \Sigma^*$. Thus, every word

---

[1] A language L' is called *quotient* of $L \subseteq \Sigma^*$ if there exists a word w such that $L' = \{v \in \Sigma^* \mid wv \in L\}$. Intuitively, the quotients of L correspond to the states of the minimal deterministic automaton for L.

$w \in f^{-1}(\Omega^*)$ decomposes uniquely into $w = xyz$ with $x \in p^{-1}(\Omega^*)$, $y \in P$, and $z \in h^{-1}(\Omega^*)$. Then $Ph^{-1}(\Omega^*) = g^{-1}(\Omega^*)$.

Let $\Omega^{\otimes} \overset{\text{def}}{=} (\Omega \cup \overline{\Omega})^*_{/\{a\bar{a} = \bar{a}a = \varepsilon | a \in \Omega\}}$ be the free group, where $\overline{\Omega}$ is a copy of Ω with bijection $^{-} : \Omega \mapsto \overline{\Omega}$ playing the role of the inverse. Therefore, apart from monoid properties, i.e., $x(yz) = (xy)z$, $x\varepsilon = \varepsilon x = x$, we have $a\bar{a} = \bar{a}a = \varepsilon$, for every $a \in \Omega$. For example, $(ab\bar{c})^{-1} = c\bar{b}\bar{a}$, or $bc(abc)^{-1} = \bar{a}$.

Let $I \subseteq \Sigma^* \times \Omega^{\otimes}$ be defined by:

$$I \overset{\text{def}}{=} \{(y, (p(x))^{-1}(f(xyz)(h(z))^{-1})) \mid x \in p^{-1}(\Omega^*), y \in P, z \in h^{-1}(\Omega^*)\}.$$

Relation I is a function. Intuitively, $I : \Sigma^* \mapsto \Omega^{\otimes}$ defines an *imaginary classifier* over prefix code P representing the "gap" between output produced by p and h, i.e., $f = pIh$. I is called imaginary because it may yield an element from $\overline{\Omega}^+$ (i.e., non-empty string over $\overline{\Omega}$), in the case when the outputs of p and h overlap. Since the classifier monoid is cancellative we also have $pI = q$ and $Ih = g$.

There exists $(y, u) \in I$ such that $u \in \overline{\Omega}^+$, otherwise q is not prime or $p = q$. This means that every output produced by p must end by u^{-1}, i.e., $p = p'u'$ for $u' = u^{-1} \in \Omega^+$. Similarly, every output produced by h must start by u'. Since p is a prime classifier, $p' = \varepsilon$ and $u' \in \Omega$, i.e., $p \in \Omega$, and $h = ph'$, for some classifier h'.   □

Proposition 7. *Let p be a prime classifier and $a \in \Omega$ be an output symbol a. If $pa = aq$ (or $ap = qa$) for some classifier q, then q is a prime.*

Proof. If $p = a$ then $q = a$. Assume $p \neq a$. Since $pa = aq$ and p is prime, $\{\varepsilon\} \subseteq p(\Sigma^*) \subseteq a\Omega^* \cup \{\varepsilon\}$. Thus, $\{\varepsilon\} \subseteq q(\Sigma^*) \subseteq \Omega^*a \cup \{\varepsilon\}$. By contradiction, suppose that $q = q_1q_2$ is not prime. $\{\varepsilon\} \subseteq q_1(\Sigma^*)q_2(\Sigma^*) \subseteq \Omega^*a \cup \{\varepsilon\}$, implies $\{\varepsilon\} \subseteq q_i(\Sigma^*) \subseteq \Omega^*a \cup \{\varepsilon\}$, for $i \in [1,2]$. Therefore, $p_i \overset{\text{def}}{=} aq_ia^{-1}$, for $i \in [1,2]$, are well defined classifiers. Thus, we have $pa = aq = aq_1q_2 = aq_1a^{-1}aq_2a^{-1}a = p_1p_2a$ and, by Lemma 2, $p = p_1p_2$, which contradicts the assumption for p being a prime.   □

Let $p : \Sigma^* \mapsto \Omega^*$ be a prime classifier such that $\{\varepsilon\} \subseteq p(\Sigma^*) \subseteq \Omega^*a \cup \{\varepsilon\}$. The equation $ap = p'a$ is called *conjugation equation*, $p' \overset{\text{def}}{=} apa^{-1}$ is called the *left-conjugate* of p by a, and $p \overset{\text{def}}{=} a^{-1}p'a$ is called the *right-conjugate* of p' by a. We write $p \sim p'$ to denote that p is a (right- or left-) conjugate of p'. The equivalence relation on prime classifiers defined as the transitive and reflexive closure of $\sim$, will be denoted by $\simeq$. Notice that $p \simeq q$ if and only if there exists an output word $w \in \Omega^*$ such that $wp = qw$ or $pw = wq$.

Proposition 8. *For every prime classifier p, its equivalence class $[p]_\simeq \overset{\text{def}}{=} \{q \mid p \simeq q\}$ is finite.*

Proof. If $p(\Sigma^*) = \{\varepsilon\}$ then $[p]_\simeq = \{p\}$. Otherwise, we consider two cases: 1) There are the longest words w and u such that $wp = qw$ and $pu = uq'$. Clearly $[p]_\simeq$ contains no more elements than the length of wu plus one. 2) There are no such words. This implies that all non-empty words in $p(\Sigma^*)$ are a power of a unique primitive word w, [4]. Therefore, $[p]_{\simeq}$ contains no more elements than the length of w plus one.   □

Theorem 9. *Let $p = p_1 p_2 \ldots p_n$ and $q = q_1 q_2 \ldots q_m$ be two prime forms of two non-empty classifiers p and q. We have $p = q$ if and only if $p_1 p_2 \ldots p_n$ can be rewritten into $q_1 q_2 \ldots q_m$ in a finite number of steps using conjugation equations.*

Proof. If $p = p_1 p_2 \ldots p_n$ can be rewritten into $q = q_1 q_2 \ldots q_m$ by using conjugation equations, then, obviously $p = q$. The other implication is proved by induction. Assume $p_1 p_2 \ldots p_n = q_1 q_2 \ldots q_m$. If $n = 1$ or $m = 1$ then $n = m$ and $p_1 = q_1$. Let us now assume $n > 1$ and $m > 1$. If $p_1 = q_1$ then $p_2 \ldots p_n = q_2 \ldots q_m$ and induction can be applied. Otherwise, by Lemma 6, $p_1 = a \in \Omega$ (or $q_1 \in \Omega$) and $q_2 \ldots q_m = ah$, for some classifier h. Thus, by iterating Proposition 7 and Lemma 6, there exists $i \leq m$ such that $q_i = a$ and q_j has a right-conjugate q_j', for every $j \in [1, i)$. Therefore, $q_1 q_2 \ldots q_{i-1} q_i q_{i+1} \ldots q_m$ can be rewritten by using $i - 1$ conjugations into $a q_1' q_2' \ldots q_{i-1}' q_{i+1} \ldots q_m$, bringing us to the situation already considered, i.e., where $p_1 = q_1$.   □

The immediate consequences of Theorem 9 are that all prime forms of a non-empty classifier have the same length, and that they contain the same output symbols as prime factors occurring in the same order.

Proposition 10. *Every non-empty classifier admits a finite number of prime forms.*

Proof. By Lemma 6, if two prime forms for classifier f have output letters at the same positions, then the two forms are identical. In particular, if no prime factor is an output symbol, then the prime form is unique. In general, if a classifier has a prime form of length n, $f = p_1 p_2 \ldots p_n$, with k factors being output symbols, then f has at most $\binom{n}{k}$ prime forms.   □

Theorem 11. *Let $f : \Sigma^* \mapsto \Omega^*$ be a classifier. The two following statements are equivalent:*

1. *f is an s-function.*
2. *There exists a finite set G of classifiers such that $Q(f) \subseteq G^*$.*

Proof. If f is a simple function then there exists a system of equations whose solution $F = (f_1, \ldots, f_k)$ contains f and $Q(f) \subseteq \{f_1, f_2, \ldots, f_k, \emptyset\}^*$. Thus, 1 implies 2.

The other direction (2 implies 1) is less obvious. Let G be a finite set of classifiers such that $Q(f) \subseteq G^*$. Without loss of generality, we assume that G consists of primes. We define $H \stackrel{\text{def}}{=} \bigcup_{g \in Q(f)} \mathcal{P}(g)$, where by $\mathcal{P}(g)$ we denote the set of all prime factors occurring in at least one of the prime forms for g. Since for each $h \in H$ there exists $p \in G$ such that $p \simeq h$ (Theorem 9), $H \subseteq \bigcup_{p \in G} [p]_{\simeq}$. By Proposition 8 and that G is finite, $\bigcup_{p \in G} [p]_{\simeq}$ is finite. Thus, H is finite.

Firstly, we show that for every $h \in H$ and $a \in \Sigma$, $a^{-1}h \in H^* \cup \{\emptyset\}$. If h is an output letter, $h \in \Omega$, then the inclusion is valid. Assume $h \notin \Omega$. Since $h \in H$, there exists $w \in \Sigma^*$ such that $w^{-1}f = r_1 \ldots r_{i-1}r_i r_{i+1} \ldots r_m$ and $r_i = h$. Let $u \in (r_1 \ldots r_{i-1})^{-1}(\Omega^*) \subset \Sigma^*$ and $a \in \Sigma$ such that $a^{-1}h$ is non-trivial. We have

$$(wua)^{-1}f = r_1 \ldots r_{i-1}(u)(a^{-1}h)r_{i+1} \ldots r_m = \alpha_1 \ldots \alpha_l x_1 \ldots x_k r_{i+1} \ldots r_m$$

for $r_1 \ldots r_{i-1}(u) = \alpha_1 \ldots \alpha_l \in \Omega^*$ and some prime classifiers $x_1, \ldots, x_k$. By definition of H, $x_1, \ldots, x_k$ are all in H, therefore $a^{-1}h \in H^*$.

We can construct a system of equations over all elements of $H \cup \{f\}$. Let $\Sigma = \{a_1, \ldots, a_n\}$. If $h \in H$ is not an output letter than h is defined by switch equation $h = a_1(a_1^{-1}h) + \ldots + a_n(a_n^{-1}h)$, otherwise h is defined by an accepting equation. Since $f \in H^*$, f is simple (if f is not in H, we add a concatenation equation for f). $\qquad \square$

CSMs are powerful tools for implementing simple functions. One could ask a question about "normal form CSM", which would be used as a vehicle to compare s-functions. For example, let $f : \{0,1\}^* \mapsto \{a,b\}^* \overset{\text{def}}{=} \{0^n 1^{n+1} \mapsto a^n b^n \mid n \geq 0\}$, which can be defined as the solution for $\{X = 1 + 0aXb1\}$ and is represented by CSM in Figure 3. We could have represented f as the solution for $\{X =$

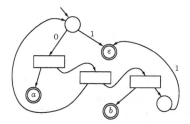

Fig. 3. CSM for $f = \{0^n 1^{n+1} \mapsto a^n b^n \mid n \geq 0\}$

$1 + 0aX1b\}$, in which case the final b would be produced after input symbol 1. The choice of *"producing output as soon as possible"*, as often adopted in the case of subsequential functions, e.g., [5], is not applicable here. In the case of our example this approach leads to an infinite CSM, corresponding to the following infinite system of equations: $\{X_0 = 1 + 0aX_1 1, \ X_1 = 1b + 0aX_2 1, \ \cdots, \ X_k = 1b^k + 0aX_{k+1}1, \ \cdots\}$, generating non context-free input/output language $L = \{(0a)^n 1 b^n 1^n \mid n \geq 0\}$.

Due to Theorem 11, we can easily establish a variety of *normal forms*, as long as we choose them from prime forms, which means that switch nodes are used only for representing primes. An effective method for calculating normal CSM (with output symbol prime factors moved to the right) is being developed. The algorithm combines the techniques for deciding the equivalence of simple grammars [6, 1] with the techniques from graph theory for finding D-articulation points [7, 8].

5   Simple Functions and Transducers

Simple functions are special cases of *transductions*, i.e., partial mappings from one free monoid into another. In this section we compare simple functions with transductions defined by transducers.

A *transducer* T is a 6-uple $(\Sigma, \Omega, Q, q_0, \delta, F)$ where Σ, Ω are two finite sets called *input* and *output alphabets* respectively, Q is a finite set of *states*, $q_0 \in Q$ is the *initial state*, δ is a finite subset of $Q \times \Sigma^* \times \Omega^* \times Q$ called *transition relation*, and $F \subseteq Q$ is the set of *final states*. A path $\pi \in \delta^*$ in T is a finite sequence of consecutive transitions, $\pi = (q_1, x_1, y_1, q_2)(q_2, x_2, y_2, q_3) \ldots (q_k, x_k, y_k, q_{k+1})$, which defines a pair of words $(x_1 x_2 \ldots x_k, y_1 y_2 \ldots y_k) \in \Sigma^* \times \Omega^*$. The semantics of a transducer is a relation over $\Sigma^* \times \Omega^*$ defined as the set of pairs of words generated by all paths from initial state q_0 to one of the final states $q_f \in F$. Such a relation is called *rational*. If a rational relation defines a partial mapping, then it is called *rational function*.

A *sequential transducer* is a transducer $(\Sigma, \Omega, Q, q_0, \delta, F,)$ defining a function, where δ is *deterministic on the input*, i.e., for every $p, q, q' \in Q$, $x, x' \in \Sigma^*$, and $y, y' \in \Omega^*$, if $(p, x, y, q) \in \delta$ and $(p, xx', y', q') \in \delta$ then $x' = \varepsilon$, $y = y'$, and $q = q'$. A *sequential function* is a rational function realized by some sequential transducer. Some authors call these functions *subsequential* [9, 10].

Simple functions are classifiers and thus they are defined on prefix codes. However, every language $L \subseteq \Sigma^*$ can be embedded into prefix code $L\$ \subseteq (\Sigma \cup \{\$\})^*$, by extending Σ by a new symbol $\$$ representing *end-of-word*. Therefore, from now on we assume that all mappings are on prefix codes explicitly or implicitly.

Proposition 12. *Every sequential function is simple.*

Proof. We suppose that f is defined on a prefix code, thus we can assume that no final state in a sequential transducer $T = (\Sigma, \Omega, Q, q_0, \delta, F,)$ defining f, has outgoing transitions. Also, we can suppose that every transition $(p, \alpha, \beta, q) \in \delta$ is such that $\alpha \in \Sigma \cup \{\varepsilon\}$. Construction of a CSM $(\Sigma, \Omega, S, C, A, \eta_S, \eta_C, \lambda, i)$ corresponding to T is straightforward. Intuitively, every final state $p \in F$ is transformed into an accepting node $a \in A$ with $\lambda(a) = \varepsilon$. Every state $p \in Q$ with a single outgoing transition $(p, \varepsilon, \beta, q) \in \delta$ is transformed into a concatenation node $c \in C$ and an accepting node $a \in A$ such that $\eta_C(c) = (a, q)$ and $\lambda(a) = \beta$. A state $p \in Q$ with k outgoing transitions $(p, \alpha_i, \beta_i, q_i)$, with $\alpha_i \in \Sigma$, is transformed into a switch node $s \in S$, k concatenation nodes $c_i \in C$, and k accepting nodes $a_i \in A$, such that $\eta_S(s, \alpha_i) = c_i$, $\eta_C(c_i) = (a_i, q_i)$, and $\lambda(a_i) = \beta_i$, for $i \in [1, k]$. □

Notice that if, in the construction of CSM for a sequential function f as described above, we reverse the *left* and *right* edges of the concatenation nodes (i.e., instead of $\eta_C(c) = (x, y)$ we put $\eta_C(c) = (y, x)$), then the resulting CSM will implement the reverse of f, i.e., $R_\Omega \circ f$, where $R_\Omega : \Omega^* \mapsto \Omega^*$ is the *reverse* function i.e., $R_\Omega \overset{\text{def}}{=} \{w \mapsto \tilde{w} \mid w \in \Omega^*\}$ with $\tilde{w}$ being the mirror of w.

Proposition 13. *There are some simple functions which are not rational.*

Proof. Function $f = \{a^n b^{n+1} \rightarrow x^n \mid n \geq 0\}$ is simple because it can be defined as the solution for $X = b + aXbc$, with $\Sigma = \{a, b\}$ and $\Omega = \{x\}$. The function is not rational because its domain $\{a^n b^{n+1} \mid n \geq 0\}$ is not a regular language. Another example of a simple function which is not rational is the reverse function R_Ω, whenever Ω has more than one symbol. □

Proposition 14. *There are some rational functions which are not simple.*

Proof. Function $f = \{a^n b \mapsto x^n, a^n c \mapsto y^n \mid n \geq 0\}$ is rational. It can be realized by a four state (non sequential) transducer. $Q(f) \supseteq \{a^{-k} f \mid k \geq 0\}$ and $a^{-k} f = \{a^n b \mapsto x^{n+k}, a^n c \mapsto y^{n+k} \mid n \geq 0\}$. Since $a^{-k} f$ are all different primes, there is no finite set of classifiers G such that $Q(f) \subseteq G^*$. Thus, by Theorem 11, f is not simple. □

Unlike rational functions, simple functions are not closed by functional composition. Even a composition of a simple function and a sequential function may yield a non simple function. The intersection of a rational and a simple language is not always simple. Language $a^n (b + c)^n$, for $n > 0$, is simple and language $a^* b^* + a^* c^*$ is rational. The intersection of these two languages, $a^n b^n + a^n c^n$, for $n > 0$, is not simple. Thus the composition of the identities on both languages (that is the identity on their intersection), is not a simple function.

We will say that a classifier is k-simple if it can be defined as the functional composition of k simple functions.

Proposition 15. *The class of rational functions is a strict subclass of 2-simple functions.*

Proof. Every rational function $f : \Sigma^* \mapsto \Omega^*$ can be represented as a composition $f = r \circ l$ of a *right-sequential* function $r : \Delta^* \mapsto \Omega^*$ and a sequential function $l : \Sigma^* \mapsto \Delta^*$, for some alphabet Δ, [10]. Function r is right-sequential if $r = R_\Omega \circ r' \circ R_\Delta$ for some sequential function $r' : \Delta^* \mapsto \Omega^*$, where R_Ω and R_Δ are reverse functions. Thus $f = R_\Omega \circ r' \circ R_\Delta \circ l = (R_\Omega \circ r') \circ (R_\Delta \circ l)$, where $(R_\Omega \circ r')$ and $(R_\Delta \circ l)$ are simple functions. □

There are still many questions concerning simple functions and the hierarchy of k-simple functions that we have yet to answer. For example, are the sequential functions those classifiers which are simple and rational at the same time? Palindrome characteristic function $\mathcal{P} \overset{\text{def}}{=} \{w \mapsto \varepsilon \mid w = \tilde{w}\}$ is 3-simple, however is it 2-simple? Is the hierarchy of k-simple functions proper?

6   Final Remarks

Concatenation state machines are playing an important role in a real-time network packet classification using *PAX.port* hardware. This study was conducted in order to better understand the power and the limitations of the *PAX.port* solution. Initially, *PAX.port* was designed as a compact interpreter for sequential transducers, where concatenation nodes were designed in order to compress the memory requirements. It turned out that the introduction of concatenation nodes extended the expressive power of the device. The partial mappings which can be defined by concatenation state machines are called *simple functions* as they are a natural extension of *simple languages.*

In the paper we introduced the notion of *classifiers* as partial mappings on words whose domains are prefix codes. Such classifiers, together with the *classifier concatenation*, constitute a monoid. We proved that a classifier $f : \Sigma^* \mapsto \Omega^*$ is a simple function if and only if there exists a finite set G of classifiers such that all quotients of f, $Q(f) \stackrel{\text{def}}{=} \{w^{-1}f \mid w \in \Sigma^*\}$, are included in G^*. This result as well as other properties of the classifier monoid proved in the paper, have many practical applications, e.g., the elaboration of an effective method to calculate a unique normal form for concatenation state machines.

References

1. Korenjak, A.J., Hopcroft, J.E.: Simple deterministic languages. In: Proc. IEEE 7th Annual Symposium on Switching and Automata Theory. IEEE Symposium on Foundations of Computer Science (1966) 36–46
2. Autebert, J.M., Berstel, J., Boasson, L.: Context-free languages and pushdown automata. In Salomaa, A., Rozenberg, G., eds.: Handbook of Formal Languages. Volume 1, Word Language Grammar. Springer-Verlag, Berlin (1997) 111–174
3. Fraczak, W., Podolak, A.: A characterization of s-languages. Information Processing Letters **89** (2004) 65–70
4. Berstel, J., Perrin, D.: Theory of Codes. Academic Press (1985)
5. Mohri, M.: Minimization algorithms for sequential transducers. Theoretical Computer Science **234** (2000) 177–201
6. Caucal, D.: A fast algorithm to decide on simple grammars equivalence. In: Optimal Algorithms. Volume 401 of LNCS. Springer (1989)
7. Czyzowicz, J., Fraczak, W., Pelc, A., Rytter, W.: Prime decompositions of regular prefix codes. In: Implementation and Application of Automata, CIAA 2002. Volume 2608 of LNCS. Springer, Tours, France (2003) 85–94
8. Tarjan, R.: Finding dominators in directed graphs. SIAM Journal on Computing **3** (1974) 62–89
9. Eilenberg, S.: Automata, Languages, and Machines. Volume A. Academic Press (1974)
10. Berstel, J.: Transductions and Context-Free Languages. Teubner (1979)

FIRE Station: An Environment for Manipulating Finite Automata and Regular Expression Views

Michiel Frishert, Loek Cleophas, and Bruce W. Watson

Technische Universiteit Eindhoven,
Department of Mathematics and Computer Science,
P.O.Box 513, NL-5600 MB Eindhoven, The Netherlands
michiel@michielfrishert.com, loek@loekcleophas.com,
bruce@bruce-watson.com

Abstract. We discuss a new tool, FIRE STATION, for the visualization, exploration and manipulation of regular languages and their various representations, including regular expressions and finite state automata.

1 Introduction

A regular language can be expressed in many forms; for example as a set of strings (if the language is finite), a regular expression, a parse tree or as a finite state automaton. The latter two also define relations between regular languages: in a parse tree, the language of each node is defined by its operator and the language of each of its children; and in a finite state automaton, the regular language of each state is its right-linear language. The goal for our new tool FIRE STATION has been to visualize the various representations of regular languages, and the relationships between them. FIRE STATION is designed as a framework so that visualization of other algorithms can be added easily.

FIRE STATION uses graphs to visualize regular languages, their properties and their interconnecting relationships. Each regular language is represented by a node in the graph. Binary relationships between regular languages are represented as edges between the nodes. Properties of regular languages are visualized in several other ways: node color, node shape, node symbols, etc. Figure 1, for example, shows how FIRE STATION displays the parse tree of regular expression abc along with all (deterministic) derivatives of abc and derivatives of its subexpressions. The solid, straight lines form the parse graph, while the curved, dashed lines represent the derivative relations.

2 Concepts

There exists a large number of functions on regular languages, yielding different binary relationships between regular languages. We split these relationships into

M. Domaratzki et al. (Eds.): CIAA 2004, LNCS 3317, pp. 125–133, 2005.
© Springer-Verlag Berlin Heidelberg 2005

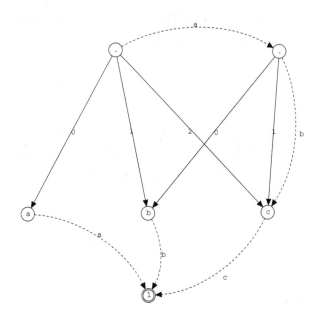

Fig. 1. Parse Trees for *abc* and its derivatives in FIRE STATION

so-called *layers*. Each layer represents one particular algorithm working on regular expressions, and is visually represented by edges of a particular color or line style.

Two constructions for which relationships between regular languages follow naturally from their algorithms are parse trees and (partial) derivatives automata. In a parse tree, the language of a particular node in the tree is defined by its subtree. In a derivatives automaton, the regular expression represented by a state in the automaton is known inherently from the derivatives algorithm, since the state is representative for that regular expression (see [1] and [2]).

It has been a goal in FIRE STATION to ensure that for each and every node, the regular expression (in the form of a parse tree) is known. Although it comes naturally for the derivatives algorithm, it will require some additional work on the implementation of future layers. We justify this effort because it provides us with sufficient information that all operations can always be performed at the regular expression level. Why this can be benificial is best shown by example. For example, if we have two states from two different automata and want to compute the intersecting automaton (the automaton recognizing the regular language that is the intersection of the regular languages of those two automaton states), then there are algorithms to compute this automaton. However, if we have the regular expressions for the nodes to be intersected, then we can create the regular expression of the intersection and compute the new automaton from that regular expression. In this manner we have greater control of the way the automaton for the intersection is created.

3   Layers

3.1   Parse Tree Layer

The parse tree layer represents regular expressions in a n-ary tree structure. The more traditional binary tree allows a node to have two children, while a node in the n-ary tree has a set of any number of children. One big advantage of the n-ary tree is that it can be represented visually with greater efficiently because we generally need fewer nodes and edges. Also, certain algorithms work more efficiently with n-ary trees, examples of which are global common subexpression elimination and rewriting, which will be discussed below. All algorithms that traditionally use binary trees can be adapted to work on n-ary trees; we will, however, not go into details on how this is done here.

An optimization well known in the field of compilers is *global common subexpression elimination* (GCSE), which we have added to the parse tree layer. GCSE merges parse trees that are identical in form, that is, they represent the same regular expression. This transforms the parse tree into a directed acyclic graph (DAG), but since we still interpret the DAG as a tree, we will continue to refer to it as the parse tree layer. In Figure 2 we show an example of a tree with common subexpressions merged.

A second optimization applied to any subtree that is created on the parse tree is rewriting (see [3]): based on a given set of rewrite rules, an equivalent and more efficient regular expression is computed, and created instead. Rewrite

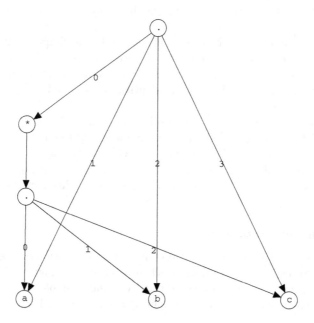

Fig. 2. Parse Tree after GCSE for $(abc)^* abc$

rules can be used for example to reduce using the identities: $\varepsilon \cdot E \rightarrow E$, or to remove redundancies such as: $((E)^*)^* \rightarrow E^*$.

Users can create new nodes on the parse tree layer in two ways. The first method is to enter a regular expression, which is parsed into a parse tree. The second method is to apply a regular operator to a node or set or list of nodes. The root node of the parse tree created by the first method, as well as the node created in the second method are called *user nodes*.

3.2   Nullable Layer

There are several useful properties of regular languages, each of which we represent by their own property layer. The nullable layer determines whether the regular language represented by a node contains the empty string. Nullability is what determines whether a state in an automaton is an accepting state, which is traditionally illustrated by two concentric circles. We adopt the same visual representation as illustrated in Figure 2.

3.3   Derivatives Layer

The parse tree layer along with the nullable layer provide sufficient information to compute Brzozowski's derivatives ([1]) for any node. The Derivatives Layer does just this. When a node is created on the parse tree layer, the derivatives layer computes all derivatives of the regular expression represented by the parse tree rooted at that node. For each of these derivatives, the regular expression is then created on the parse tree. For all new nodes that are created in this process, the derivatives layer again computes and creates derivatives nodes.

The computation of derivatives continues until all unique derivatives for the original regular expression have been computed. The computation is guaranteed to terminate because of the parse tree layer's elimination of common subexpressions. Reduction of derivatives by the identities is achieved using a set of rewrite rules on the parse tree layer.

Figure 3 shows an example of derivatives (dashed lines) and parse trees (solid lines) for each node. Note that we can add additional rewrite rules, which potentially leads to a smaller number of derivatives than Brzozowski's original algorithm. In similar vein to the derivatives layer, we compute Antimirov's partial derivatives (see [2]) on the partial derivatives layer, which is not shown here.

3.4   Equivalent States Layer

Using Watson's incremental algorithm for DFA minimization discussed in [4], the equivalent states layer determines which states are indistinguishable (describing the same regular language) on the derivatives and nullable layers. These nodes are connected by edges in the equivalent states graph, see Figure 4.

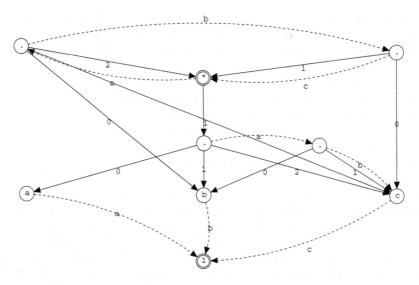

Fig. 3. Parse Trees for $(abc)^*$ and all its derivatives

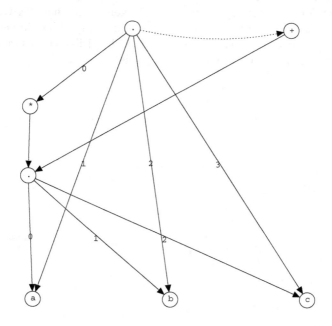

Fig. 4. The Equivalent States Layer illustrating that $(abc)^* abc$ is equal to $(abc)^+$

4   Graphs

Graphs are extracted from those layers that describe relations between regular expressions. Currently the only layer that does not describe relations between regular expressions is the nullable layer. The edges of the graphs are merged into one large graph, and a traditional node-and-edge layout algorithm is applied. Using this layout, we draw the graph for each layer succesively, using different colors.

Graph layout is preceded by two steps. In the first step, node visibility is determined. User nodes are considered to be of specific interest to the user, as they were explicitly created by the user, and therefore always made visible. The user can determine what other nodes are visible by changing the set of *node visibility graphs*; nodes that are reachable from a user node through the edges in the node visibility graphs are also made visible.

The second step preceeding graph layout is to determine which edges contribute to the layout of nodes. The user can control the set of *layout driving graphs*, and each layout driving graph contributes its edges to a grand *layout graph*, which contains all of the edges of the layout driving graphs (edges of which one or both nodes are invisible are not added to the layout graph).

The layout is performed on the layout graph. The layout algorithm is interchangable, in the sense that a new algorithm can easily be added to FIRE STATION, as long as it conforms to the interface specified by FIRE STATION. Currently FIRE STATIONuses the layered digraph layout algorithm described in chapter 9 of [5]. This algorithm is fairly generic in that it gives reasonable results in most cases, but is not optimized for any graph types in particular. The resulting node layout is used to render each of the visible graphs (again omitting edges of which one or both nodes are invisible).

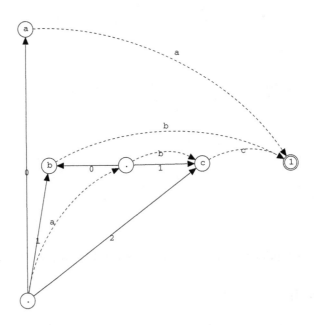

Fig. 5. Alternative Layout for Parse Trees and Derivatives for *abc*

Note that the node visibility graphs, layout driving graphs and visible graphs are independent of each other, meaning that, a graph can determine node visibility, while not being visible itself, or the graph is visible but doesn't influence node visibility. For example, the equivalent states layer shows which nodes have equivalent regular languages. Oftentimes we want to see whether two visible nodes are equal, however if a node is visible, we invisible nodes to remain invisible even though they might be equivalent, as to avoid cluttering our view. In the case of the parse graph, if we make its edges visible, but do not use it to determine nodes visibility, we end up with an incomplete parse graph; however we can then, for example, see which states in the derivatives automaton are in fact subexpressions of some other state in the automaton.

In Figure 1 we have already seen a traditional parse tree layout, with the edges for the derivatives added in, but not affecting layout. Figure 5 shows an alternative layout to Figure 1, with the edges of the derivatives graph (instead of the parse tree) driving the layout. All graphs are contributing to node visibility, making all nodes are visible. Note that for nodes with the concatenation operator, the parse tree edges are numbered because the layout sometimes does not (and cannot) retain the usual left-to-right order, see for example Figure 1.

5   Current Implementation

The current implementation is split into two parts: the core, named FIRE WORKS, consists of the layers framework, graph generation and graph layout algorithms. Currently, FIRE WORKS is implemented in high performance C++ code. FIRE STATION consists of FIRE WORKS with an added graphical user interface (GUI). The GUI code is written in the Objective-C language using Apple's Cocoa framework for OS X. Figure 6 shows a screenshot of FIRE STATION's GUI in action.

6   Future Work

There are many directions in which FIRE STATION can be extended. First and foremost, we have the ability to add more layers. We currently have plans to add a layer for the position automaton, as well as structures from the field of (multiple) string pattern matching, including directed acyclic word graphs, tries with failure functions and factor oracles.

Importing automata back into FIRE STATION is an important goal. Because of our goal of having a regular expression for each node, we need to recover a regular expression for each state in the automaton. The algorithms converting automata back to regular expressions that are currently available have the drawback that their regular expressions tend to blow up in size, and when then generating an automata from these computed regular expressions we end up with an automaton looking totally different from the original. (The exception is the position automaton, for which the regular expression can be recovered using the

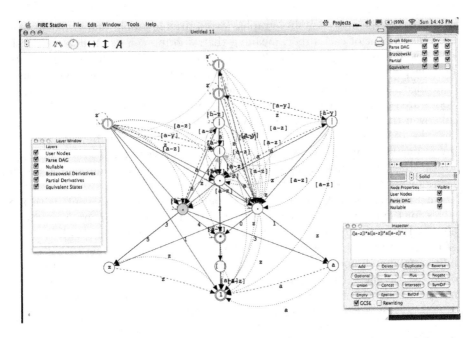

Fig. 6. FIRE STATION in Action

characteristics described in [6]). Better algorithms and heuristics will need to be developed for this extension to FIRE STATION to work well.

Export functionality will allow the use of computed automata and graphs outside of FIRE STATION. We are currently working on functionality to export to XML, the graphviz format and in the longer term to hardcoded automata (see [7]).

Another intended use for FIRE STATION is to simulate pattern matching. For this purpose, FIRE STATION functions as a typical software debugging application. Using breakpoints or by single-stepping through the matching process, the user can pinpoint problems with specific regular expressions. Such debugging of regular expressions can be useful in any situation where regular expressions are used, we specifically mention the fields of intrusion detection systems, text search and DNA search.

References

1. Brzozowski, J.A.: Derivatives of Regular Expressions. Journal of the ACM **11** (1964) 481–494

2. Antimirov, V.: Partial derivatives of regular expressions and finite automata constructions. In Mayr, E.W., Puech, C., eds.: STACS'95 (12th Annual Symposium on Theoretical Aspects of Computer Science). Springer, Berlin, Heidelberg (1995) 455–466

3. M.Frishert, L.Cleophas, B.W.Watson: The Effect of Rewriting Regular Expressions on Their Accepting Automata. In Ibarra, O.H., Dang, Z., eds.: Proceedings of CIAA 2003, Springer (2003) 304–305

4. Watson, B.: An incremental DFA minimization algorithm. In Karttunen, L., Koskenniemi, K., van Noord, G., eds.: proceedings of FSMNLP 2001, ESSLLI workshop, Helsinki (2001)

5. Battista, G.D., Eades, P., Tamassia, R., Tollis, I.G.: Graph Drawing: Algorithms for the Visualization of Graphs. Prentice-Hall (1999)

6. Caron, P., Ziadi, D.: Characterization of glushkov automata. Theor. Comput. Sci. **233** (2000) 75–90

7. Ngassam, E.K., Watson, B.W., Kourie, D.G.: Hardcoding finite state automata processing. In: Annual Conference of the South African Institute of Computer Scientists and Information Technologists, Proceedings, Fourways, South Africa (2003) 111–121

Finding Finite Automata That Certify Termination of String Rewriting

Alfons Geser[1,*], Dieter Hofbauer[2], Johannes Waldmann[3], and Hans Zantema[4]

[1] National Institute of Aerospace, 144 Research Drive,
Hampton, Virginia 23666, USA
geser@nianet.org
[2] Mühlengasse 16, D-34125 Kassel, Germany
dieter@theory.informatik.uni-kassel.de
[3] Hochschule für Technik, Wirtschaft und Kultur (FH) Leipzig,
Fb IMN, PF 30 11 66, D-04251 Leipzig, Germany
waldmann@imn.htwk-leipzig.de
[4] Department of Computer Science, Technische Universiteit Eindhoven,
P.O. Box 513, 5600 MB Eindhoven, The Netherlands
h.zantema@tue.nl

Abstract. We present a technique based on the construction of finite automata to prove termination of string rewriting systems. Using this technique the tools Matchbox and TORPA are able to prove termination of particular string rewriting systems completely automatically for which termination was considered to be very hard until recently.

1 Introduction

Consider a finite string over $\{a, b\}$ and only one rule: if $aabb$ occurs in the string than it may be replaced by $bbbaaa$. The goal is to prove *termination*: prove that application of this rule cannot go on forever. This is a surprisingly hard problem for which only ad hoc proofs were available until recently [11, 13]. A set of such string replacement rules is called a string rewriting system (SRS) or semi-Thue system. In this paper we describe a technique based on the construction of finite automata by which termination of such SRSs including this example $\{aabb \rightarrow bbbaaa\}$ can be proved fully automatically.

It is widely accepted that being able to prove termination of programs is highly desirable. String rewriting is one of the simplest paradigms having full computational power, and is extensively studied, e.g., in Book and Otto [3]. For instance, Turing machine computation is easily seen to be a special case of string rewriting. Therefore it is natural to consider techniques for automatically proving termination of SRSs. On the other hand string rewriting can be seen as a

---

* Partly supported by the National Aeronautics and Space Administration under NASA Contract No. NAS1-97046 while this author was in residence at the NIA.

M. Domaratzki et al. (Eds.): CIAA 2004, LNCS 3317, pp. 134–145, 2005.

special case of term rewriting, for which a wide range of termination techniques has been developed; for a recent overview see Zantema [14].

In order to prove termination of an SRS R, we construct an infinite SRS $\mathsf{match}(R)$, obtained from R by labelling the symbols by natural numbers. By construction, on the one hand, $\mathsf{match}(R)$-steps simulate R-steps, and on the other hand, every finite subsystem of $\mathsf{match}(R)$ terminates. Now we construct a finite automaton such that an accepting computation of s is transformed into an accepting computation of t whenever s rewrites to t by a $\mathsf{match}(R)$-step. This closure property entails that the simulation of an R-derivation involves only a finite subsystem of $\mathsf{match}(R)$. Termination of R follows. Since in this way a bound on the labels occurring in derivations is established, this is called the *match-bound* approach.

The inspiration of match-bounds was taken from Ravikumar's *change-bounds*. Ravikumar [10] proposes an infinite SRS similar to $\mathsf{match}(R)$, and shows that change-bounded length-preserving SRSs preserve regular languages. It is easy to see that change-bounds imply match-bounds, while also the converse can be proved to hold. However, in contrast to change-bounds, match-bounds work also for SRSs that do not preserve lengths.

An earlier version of the match-bound approach was presented before [5, 6]. Here we describe the basic approach in a more general setting. The reason for doing this is twofold: the presentation is more modular and therefore hopefully simpler, and this generalization can be used for variants and extensions of the method. Indeed in this new setting we are able to give short proofs of the main theorems.

Our main new contribution is to describe new algorithms to construct appropriate automata. In the earlier approach [5, 6] some of us described how a suitable rewriting closure of a language may effectively preserve regularity. The main algorithm then consisted of constructing an automaton that accepts exactly the desired rewriting closure. A drawback of this approach is that even for very small SRSs like $aabb \rightarrow bbbaaa$ intermediate automata with thousands of states are constructed, while the final automaton for this example consists only of 42 states.

In the new approach, the constructed automaton need no longer be *exact*: it may accept any superset of the desired rewriting closure. Therefore the new approach is called *approximate*. Like the exact approach, the approximate approach is correct: the constructed automaton certifies termination of the SRS. In contrast to the exact approach, it may fail. However, we have observed that the approximate approach often succeeds, and even yields the same automaton as the exact approach. The approximate approach is usually much more economical: all intermediate automata are no bigger than the final one. This efficiency allows one to solve examples that the exact approach, in spite of its completeness, could not handle within reasonable time and memory.

The match-bound technique is one of the few techniques that are able to prove termination on a given language: no infinite rewrite sequence exists starting with some string in the language. Most other techniques only prove (uniform) termination: no infinite rewrite sequence exists at all. Therefore it profits from the theory of *forward closures*, according to which full termination can be concluded from termination on a particular language.

Versions of the approximate approach have been implemented in three tools: `Matchbox`, `TORPA`, and `AProVE`. The tool `Matchbox` [12] was the first tool that implemented the match-bound approach, and it offers a variety of match-bound related computations. The tool `TORPA` [15] is a tool for proving termination of string rewriting by various techniques: polynomial interpretations, recursive path order, semantic labelling, dependency pairs and finally one particular version of match-bounds for forward closures. The tool `AProVE` [7] is a tool for proving termination of term rewriting mainly by dependency pairs, but also covering various other techniques. In the most recent version the approach using match-bounds for forward closures was copied from `TORPA`. In the category "string rewriting" in the termination competition of the 7th International Workshop on Termination in 2004 these three tools ranked third, first, and second, respectively.

The paper is organized as follows. In Section 2 the basic theory is presented, including preliminaries and all proofs, except for the proofs of forward closure theory. Next in Section 3 the various ways of finding compatible automata are discussed: the exact approach and the approximate approach. For the latter, two variants are discussed: the one that has been implemented in `TORPA`, and the one that has been implemented in `Matchbox`.

2   Basic Theory

A string rewrite system (SRS) over an alphabet Σ is a set $R \subseteq \Sigma^* \times \Sigma^*$. Elements $(\ell, r) \in R$ are called *rules* and are written as $\ell \to r$; the string ℓ is called the left hand side (lhs) and r is called the right hand side (rhs) of the rule. A string $s \in \Sigma^*$ rewrites to a string $t \in \Sigma^*$ with respect to an SRS R, written as $s \to_R t$ if strings $u, v \in \Sigma^*$ and a rule $\ell \to r \in R$ exist such that $s = u\ell v$ and $t = urv$. The reflexive transitive closure of $\to_R$ is written as $\to_R^*$. In this paper we consider both finite and infinite SRSs over both finite and infinite alphabets, on the other hand all automata we consider are finite.

A sequence $t_1, t_2, t_3, \ldots$ is called an R-*derivation* if $t_i \to_R t_{i+1}$ for all $i = 1, 2, 3, \ldots$. An SRS R is called *terminating* on a language $L \subseteq \Sigma^*$ if no infinite R-derivation $t_1, t_2, t_3, \ldots$ exists such that $t_1 \in L$. An SRS R is called *terminating* if no infinite R-derivation exists at all, i.e., it is terminating on Σ^*. Any SRS having an empty lhs is non-terminating, hence we generally assume that each lhs is non-empty.

For a map $h : \Sigma' \to \Sigma$ we reuse the notation h for its morphism extension $h : \Sigma'^* \to \Sigma^*$ by $h(\epsilon) = \epsilon$ and $h(uv) = h(u)h(v)$, and to languages over Σ' by $h(L) = \{h(u) \mid u \in L\}$.

Let R be an SRS over an alphabet Σ, and let $L \subseteq \Sigma^*$. Let R' be an SRS over an alphabet Σ', and let $L' \subseteq \Sigma'^*$. The triple (Σ', R', L') is called an *enrichment* of (Σ, R, L) by $h : \Sigma' \to \Sigma$ if $L = h(L')$ and

$$h(\ell') = \ell \wedge (\ell \to r) \in R \Rightarrow \exists r' \in \Sigma'^*. \, (\ell' \to r') \in R' \wedge h(r') = r$$

for all $\ell' \in \Sigma'^*$ and $(\ell \to r) \in R$. From the enrichment property, it follows that

$$h(s') \to_R t \Rightarrow \exists t' \in \Sigma'^*. \, s' \to_{R'} t' \wedge t = h(t')$$

for all $s', t' \in \Sigma'^*$, and so if R' terminates on L' then R terminates on L.

For an SRS R over an alphabet Σ for which all lhs's are non-empty we define the infinite SRS $\mathsf{match}(R)$ over $\Sigma \times \mathbf{N}$ to consist of all rules $(a_1, n_1) \cdots (a_p, n_p) \to (b_1, m_1) \cdots (b_q, m_q)$ for which $a_1 \cdots a_p \to b_1 \cdots b_q \in R$ and $m_i = 1 + \min_{j=1,\ldots,p} n_j$ for all $i = 1, \ldots, q$. For instance, if R contains the rule $aa \to aba$, then $(a, 3)(a, 1) \to (a, 2)(b, 2)(a, 2)$ is a rule of $\mathsf{match}(R)$.

We define $\mathsf{base} : \Sigma \times \mathbf{N} \to \Sigma$ by $\mathsf{base}((a, n)) = a$ for all $a \in \Sigma$, $n \in \mathbf{N}$, and $\mathsf{lift}_0 : \Sigma \to \Sigma \times \mathbf{N}$ by $\mathsf{lift}_0(a) = (a, 0)$ for all $a \in \Sigma$. By construction, $(\Sigma \times \mathbf{N}, \mathsf{match}(R), \mathsf{lift}_0(L))$ is an enrichment of (Σ, R, L) by base.

An SRS R' over Σ' is called *locally terminating* if for every finite alphabet $\Sigma'_0 \subseteq \Sigma'$ the SRS $R'_0 = \{ \ell' \to r' \in R' \mid \ell', r' \in \Sigma'^*_0 \}$ is terminating.

Theorem 1. *Let R be any finite SRS over Σ. Then $\mathsf{match}(R)$ is locally terminating.*

Proof. Let $\Sigma'_0 \subseteq \Sigma' = \Sigma \times \mathbf{N}$ be finite; we have to prove that R'_0 as defined above for $R' = \mathsf{match}(R)$ is terminating. Let n be the maximum value for which there is $a \in \Sigma$ such that $(a, n) \in \Sigma'_0$. Assume that R'_0 admits an infinite derivation, then there is also an infinite R'_0-derivation in which all symbols (a, k) satisfy $k \leq n$. Let m be a number such that for every rhs of R the length is less than m. Now for a symbol (a, k) define its weight $W((a, k)) = m^{n-k}$, and for a string of symbols the weight is the sum of the weights of the symbols. For every rule $\ell' \to r'$ in R'_0 we have $r' = (b_1, k), (b_2, k), \ldots, (b_q, k)$ while ℓ' contains a symbol $(a, k-1)$. Hence

$$W(\ell') \geq W((a, k-1)) = m^{n-k+1} > q \cdot m^{n-k} = W(r').$$

Hence in every step of the infinite derivation the weight in $\mathbf{N}$ strictly decreases, contradiction. □

Finiteness of R is not essential for validity of Theorem 1: using multisets easily a proof can be given not requiring finiteness. However, we intend to use Theorem 1 only for finite systems and we will use the present proof using weights to conclude a result on derivational complexity.

All automata we consider in this paper are standard non-deterministic finite-state automata. For two states p, q in an automaton A over Σ and a string $u \in \Sigma^*$ we write $p \xrightarrow{u}_A q$ if there is a path from p to q in A in which the transitions are successively labelled by the symbols in u. More precisely, the transition relation $\xrightarrow{a}_A$ for $a \in \Sigma$ is extended to Σ^* by defining inductively $p \xrightarrow{au}_A q$ if a state r exists such that $p \xrightarrow{a}_A r$ and $r \xrightarrow{u}_A q$, and $p \xrightarrow{\epsilon}_A p$ for all states p. Let A, L and R be a finite automaton, a language and an SRS over an alphabet Σ, respectively. Then A is called *compatible* with L and R if

- $L \subseteq L(A)$, and
- A is closed under R, i.e., if $\ell \to r \in R$ and $p \xrightarrow{\ell}_A q$ for two states p, q of A, then also $p \xrightarrow{r}_A q$.

A direct consequence of this definition is that if A is compatible with L and R, then we have $\to^*_R(L) \subseteq L(A)$, where the set of R-successors $\to^*_R(L)$ is defined by

$$\to^*_R(L) \;=\; \{u \mid \exists t \in L : t \to^*_R u\}.$$

If Σ is finite then such a compatible automaton trivially exists: take the automaton for Σ^* consisting of one state, and a-transitions from that state to itself for every $a \in \Sigma$. We will focus on finding finite compatible automata for infinite SRSs over infinite alphabets, starting from a language described by a finite automaton.

Theorem 2. *Let (Σ', R', L') be an enrichment of (Σ, R, L) by h, let R' be locally terminating, and assume that L' and R' admit a compatible finite automaton. Then R terminates on $h(L')$.*

Proof. Suppose there is an infinite R-derivation $u_1 \to_R u_2 \to_R u_3 \to_R \cdots$ for which $u_1 \in h(L')$. Then there exists $v_1 \in L'$ such that $h(v_1) = u_1$. By repeated application of the definition of enrichment this gives rise to an infinite R'-derivation $v_1 \to_{R'} v_2 \to_{R'} v_3 \to_{R'} \cdots$ for which $h(v_i) = u_i$ for $i = 1, 2, 3, \ldots$. Let A be a finite automaton compatible with L' and R'; let Σ'_0 be the finite set of transition labels occurring in A. Since $L' \subseteq L(A)$ we have $p_0 \xrightarrow{v_1}_A p_f$ for the initial state p_0 and a final state p_f, since A is closed under R' we obtain by induction on i that $p_0 \xrightarrow{v_i}_A p_f$ for all $i = 1, 2, 3, \ldots$. Hence for every rule $\ell' \to r' \in R'$ that is applied in the infinite derivation $v_1 \to_{R'} v_2 \to_{R'} v_3 \to_{R'} \cdots$ there are states p, q in A satisfying $p \xrightarrow{\ell'}_A q$ and $p \xrightarrow{r'}_A q$. Hence in the infinite derivation only rules from R'_0 are applied, contradicting the assumption that R' is locally terminating. $\qquad\square$

Theorem 2 will be used as follows. If termination of R on a language L over Σ has to be proved then we define $L_0 = \mathsf{lift}_0(L) = \{(s, 0) \mid s \in L\}$. By definition, $\mathsf{base}(L_0) = L$. Now according to Theorems 1 and 2 it suffices to find a compatible automaton for L_0 and $\mathsf{match}(R)$. Due to the form of the weights we used in the proof of Theorem 1 this does not only prove termination of R on L but even linear derivational complexity: there is a constant C such that every R-derivation starting in $s \in L$ has length at most $C \cdot |s|$.

To prove termination on Σ^* (usually simply called *termination*) we may apply this approach for $L = \Sigma^*$. However, by a result of Dershowitz [4] on forward closures, we may also choose another language for L that may be smaller. Thus we can prove termination for SRSs that do not satisfy linear derivational complexity, like $\{ab \to ba\}$ or $\{ab \to bba\}$.

We describe *forward closures* by rewriting using an extended SRS $R_\#$ [5,6]; this way we characterize termination on Σ^* by termination on a small regular set, which makes it amenable to automation. A self-contained presentation of this $R_\#$-approach including all proofs will appear in [16].

For an SRS R over an alphabet Σ we define the SRS $R_\#$ over $\Sigma \cup \{\#\}$ by

$$R_\# = R \cup \{ \ell_1 \# \to r \mid \ell \to r \in R \ \wedge \ \ell = \ell_1 \ell_2 \ \wedge \ \ell_1 \neq \epsilon \neq \ell_2 \}.$$

Write $\mathsf{rhs}(R)$ for the set of rhs's of R.

Theorem 3. *Let R be a finite SRS. Then R is terminating if and only if $R_\#$ is terminating on $\mathsf{rhs}(R) \cdot \{\#\}^*$.*

We omit the proof. Combining Theorems 1, 2, and 3 now for proving (uniform) termination of a finite SRS R it suffices to find a compatible automaton for $\mathsf{lift}_0(\mathsf{rhs}(R) \cdot \{\#\}^*)$ and $\mathsf{match}(R_\#)$.

3   Finding a Compatible Automaton

Due to the observations we made termination of an SRS can be proved by proving the existence of a finite automaton A compatible with a language L and a (usually infinite) SRS R. Such an automaton A is called *exact* if $L(A) = \to_R^*(L)$.

We describe two basic ways of constructing a compatible automaton: an *exact* approach that always yields an exact automaton in case of success, and an *approximate* approach that yields a compatible automaton that need not be exact. Each approach starts from an automaton that accepts L.

3.1   The Exact Approach

The exact approach is based on the notion of a *deleting* string rewriting system [8, 9]. A string rewriting system R over an alphabet Σ is called *deleting* if it has no empty lhs and there is an irreflexive partial order $>$ on Σ (a *precedence*) such that for each rule $\ell \to r$ in R and for each letter a in r, there is some letter b in ℓ with $b > a$.

Similar to the proof of Theorem 1 it is easy to see that every deleting string rewriting system over a finite alphabet is terminating. The class of deleting string rewriting systems enjoys the following strong effective decomposition property. An SRS is called context-free if every lhs has length at most 1.

Theorem 4 ([9]). *If R is a finite deleting string rewriting system over a finite alphabet Σ, then there are, effectively, an extended alphabet $\Gamma \supseteq \Sigma$, a terminating, context-free SRS T over Γ, and a context-free SRS C over Γ, such that for each language $L \subseteq \Sigma^*$, $\to_R^*(L) = \leftarrow_C^*(\to_T^*(L)) \cap \Sigma^*$.*

The exact approach consists of using this decomposition to construct an automaton that accepts $\to_R^*(L)$ from an automaton that accepts L. Let $\mathsf{match}_k(R)$ be the restriction of $\mathsf{match}(R)$ to the (finite) alphabet $\Sigma \times \{0, \ldots, k\}$. It is obvious that $\mathsf{match}_k(R)$ is deleting, so Theorem 4 applies. Now a finite automaton A_k is constructed such that $L(A_k) = \mathsf{base}(\to^*_{\mathsf{match}_k(R)}(\mathsf{lift}_0(L)))$. We do this construction successively for $k = 0, 1, 2, \ldots$. If some k is found that satisfies $L_k = L_{k+1}$ then A_k is the desired exact automaton compatible with $\mathsf{match}(R)$ and L.

The extended alphabet may turn out to be rather large (a few hundred letters even for small systems), so the automaton for $\to^*_T(L)$ has many states as well. We do not give details here; to give a flavor we sketch a small fragment of this approach as it occurs for computing A_2 for the single rule $aa \to aba$.

Let R be the SRS consisting of the rules $aa \to cdc, ac \to cdc, ca \to cdc, cc \to fgf$. This SRS is a renaming of (the accessible part–see [5,6]–of) the system $\mathsf{match}_2(\{aa \to aba\})$. Observe that R is deleting with $a > c > d > f > g$. Using Theorem 4 we get the decomposition $\Gamma = \Sigma \cup \{b, e, a_1, a_2, a_3, a_{22}, a_{32}, a_{11}, c_2\}$;

$$T = \begin{cases} a \to b, & a \to cda_2, & a \to cda_3, & a \to a_1dc, & c \to e, \\ c \to fgc_2, & a_2 \to fga_{22}, & a_3 \to fga_{32}, & a_1 \to a_{11}gc_2; \end{cases}$$

$$C = \begin{cases} c \to a_2b, & e \to a_2b, & c \to a_3c, & e \to a_3c, & c \to ca_1, \\ e \to ca_1, & f \to c_2e, & c_2 \to a_{22}b, & c_2 \to a_{32}c, & f \to ca_{11}. \end{cases}$$

Now let $L = \{a\}^*$. The automaton for $\to^*_T(L)$ is constructed by supplementing, as long as possible, a path $p \xrightarrow{r} q$ for each transition $p \xrightarrow{x} q$ and rule $x \to r$ in T.

For a better overview, we render the initial state in the center of the left figure without the looping transitions labelled by a and b.

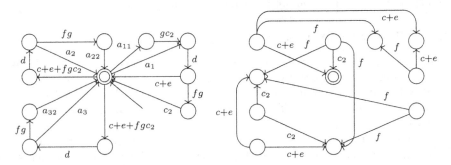

The automaton for $\leftarrow^*_C(\to^*_T(L))$ is obtained by adding, as long as possible, a transition $p \xrightarrow{x} q$ for each path $p \xrightarrow{r} q$ and rule $x \to r$ in C, see [1,2]. The result is given in the right figure, rendering only the new transitions. Finally, the automaton for $\to^*_R(L)$ is obtained by dropping all transitions labelled with $\Gamma \setminus \Sigma$ letters.

3.2 The Approximate Approach

The intermediate automata constructed during the exact approach may be much bigger than the final compatible automaton. For simple examples these intermediate automata may have thousands of nodes and may take minutes to compute.

We therefore introduce an approximate approach that avoids the construction of automata that are bigger than the result.

The basic idea of this approach is to start with an automaton that accepts exactly L, and then to add only states and transitions as needed for closure under rewriting. More precisely, the procedure systematically looks for counterexamples to closure under rewriting, i.e., for states p, q and rules $\ell \to r \in R$ such that $p \xrightarrow{\ell}_A q \wedge p \not\xrightarrow{r}_A q$. States and transitions are added to the automaton such that $p \xrightarrow{r}_A q$. The procedure repeats this step until either there are no counterexamples left, in which case the resulting automaton is compatible; or the resources are exceeded and the construction has failed.

There are various strategies how to add states and transitions suitably; we will describe two of them.

Our approach is currently restricted to the case where each right hand side is non-empty. Empty right hand sides can be included by automata having epsilon-transitions. Alternatively, empty right hand sides can be eliminated by preprocessing the SRS as we will see in an example.

The Strategy in TORPA [15]. If A has to be extended in order to satisfy $p \xrightarrow{r}_A q$ in TORPA this is done as follows. As stated above, we assume that r is non-empty, so we may write $r = au$ for $a \in \Sigma, u \in \Sigma^*$. It is checked whether a state n exists satisfying $n \xrightarrow{u}_A q$. If so, then only one single transition $p \xrightarrow{a}_A n$ is added. If not, then a completely fresh path from p to q is constructed: if $r = a_1 \cdots a_k$ then $k - 1$ fresh states $n_1, \ldots, n_{k-1}$ and k fresh transitions

$$p \xrightarrow{a_1}_A n_1, \quad n_1 \xrightarrow{a_2}_A n_2, \quad \ldots, \quad n_{k-2} \xrightarrow{a_{k-1}}_A n_{k-1}, \quad n_{k-1} \xrightarrow{a_k}_A q$$

are added. In both cases the extended automaton A indeed satisfies $p \xrightarrow{r}_A q$.

This strategy is particularly powerful for proving termination using $\mathsf{match}(R)$ and forward closures. As a simple example consider the SRS R consisting of the single rule $aba \to abbba$. Due to Theorem 3 termination of R may be proved by proving that $R_\#$ is terminating on $\{abbba\} \cdot \{\#\}^*$, where $R_\#$ consists of the rules

$$aba \to abbba, \ a\# \to abbba, \ ab\# \to abbba.$$

Due to Theorems 1 and 2 it now suffices to find a compatible automaton for $\{a_0b_0b_0b_0a_0\} \cdot \{\#_0\}^*$ and $\mathsf{match}(R_\#)$. Here we shortly write x_i rather than (x, i) for $x \in \{a, b, \#\}, i \in \mathbf{N}$, and $\mathsf{match}(R_\#)$ consists of the rules

$$
\begin{aligned}
a_ib_ja_k &\to a_mb_mb_mb_ma_m \quad \text{for } i, j, k, m \in \mathbf{N}, \ m = \min\{i, j, k\} + 1 \\
a_i\#_0 &\to a_1b_1b_1b_1a_1 \quad\quad \text{for } i \in \mathbf{N} \\
a_ib_j\#_0 &\to a_1b_1b_1b_1a_1 \quad\quad \text{for } i, j \in \mathbf{N}.
\end{aligned}
$$

Formally $\mathsf{match}(R_\#)$ also contains rules with $\#_i$ in the left hand side for $i > 0$, but it is easy to see that these will never be involved in derivations starting from a string not containing $\#_i$ for $i > 0$. This observation holds for every SRS, not only this example. Now the search for a compatible automaton may start. We start by the following automaton for $\{a_0b_0b_0b_0a_0\} \cdot \{\#_0\}^*$:

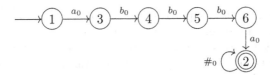

The numbering of the nodes is as generated in TORPA where the initial node is always 1 and the final node is always 2.

The first counterexample we find is $6 \overset{a_0 \#_0}{\to}_A 2$ for the rule $a_0 \#_0 \to a_1 b_1 b_1 b_1 a_1$ in $\mathsf{match}(R_\#)$. We have to construct a path from 6 to 2 labelled by $a_1 b_1 b_1 b_1 a_1$. As there is no path from any state to 2 labelled by $b_1 b_1 b_1 a_1$, a fresh path is added with the fresh states 7, 8, 9, 10 and transitions between them. The next counterexample is $10 \overset{a_1 \#_0}{\to}_A 2$ for the rule $a_1 \#_0 \to a_1 b_1 b_1 b_1 a_1$ of $\mathsf{match}(R_\#)$. Here a path from 10 to 2 labelled by $a_1 b_1 b_1 b_1 a_1$ has to be created. Since there is already a path from 7 to 2 labelled by $b_1 b_1 b_1 a_1$, only the single transition from 10 to 7 is added. There are no further counterexamples. This yields the following compatible automaton:

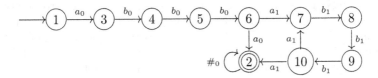

This simple strategy was found during a trial to reconstruct by pencil and paper the exact automaton for $\mathsf{match}(R_\#)$ for $R = \{aabb \to bbbaaa\}$ as it was given in [5, 6]. Using this strategy, TORPA generates the same automaton, only a few hundred times faster. Other, more involved strategies turned out unsatisfactory for forward closures.

The Strategy in Matchbox [12]. For a rule $\ell \to r \in R$ and states p, q in A for which $p \overset{\ell}{\to}_A q$ holds but not $p \overset{r}{\to}_A q$, this strategy considers all decompositions $r = xyz$ and states p', q' such that $p \overset{x}{\to}_A p'$ and $q' \overset{z}{\to}_A q$ and $y \neq \epsilon$. Then among all possibilities one is chosen for which y has minimal length, and a new path $p' \overset{y}{\to}_A q'$ is constructed.

The TORPA strategy can also be seen as a variant of this decomposition approach, constrained by $|x| = 0 \wedge (|y| = 1 \vee |z| = 0)$.

As an illustration of both strategies consider the automaton

$$\longrightarrow \boxed{1} \overset{a}{\to} \boxed{2} \overset{a}{\to} \boxed{3}$$

for $L = \{aa\}$ and the rule $aa \to aba$. Then a path $1 \overset{aba}{\to}_A 3$ has to be created. In the TORPA strategy it is observed that no state n exists satisfying $n \overset{ba}{\to}_A 3$. As a consequence two fresh states 4, 5 and three fresh transitions are created:

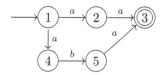

After this single step the automaton is closed under rewriting.

In contrast, in the `Matchbox` strategy no fresh states are required at all: by $1 \xrightarrow{a}_A 2$ and $2 \xrightarrow{a}_A 3$ only one fresh b-transition from 2 to 2 is added:

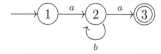

and again after a single step the automaton is closed under rewriting. This illustrates non-exactness of the `Matchbox` strategy: by the latter automaton A the string $abba$ is in $L(A)$ but not in $\to^*_R(L)$.

Similar non-exactness occurs in the `TORPA` strategy, for instance by starting from the automaton

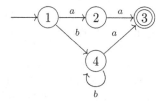

and the same rule $aa \to aba$ in the `TORPA` strategy the transition $1 \xrightarrow{a}_A 4$ is added, by which again the string $abba$ is in $L(A)$ but not in $\to^*_R(L)$.

We have experimented with several conceivable variants of such a strategy for re-using transitions. Roughly speaking in using forward closures the `TORPA`-strategy is often the most successful, while in not using forward closures the `Matchbox`-strategy is often more powerful. In any case, the order in which paths are handled strongly influences the process; and there does not seem to be a straightforward *complete* strategy: one that terminates in all cases where the exact computation is successful.

3.3   An Example with Empty Right Hand Sides

In an SRS one or more rules $\ell \to r$ may be replaced by $a\ell \to ar$ for all $a \in \Sigma$ without changing the termination behavior. As an example, consider the SRS R consisting of the rules

$$Ab \to baBA, \; Ba \to abAB, \; Aa \to \epsilon, \; Bb \to \epsilon.$$

Due to empty rhs's the approximate approach cannot be applied directly. However, by using the above observation termination of R may be concluded from termination of the SRS consisting of the rules

$$Ab \to baBA, \; Ba \to abAB, \quad aAa \to a, \; bAa \to b, \; AAa \to A, \; BAa \to B,$$

$$aBb \to a, \; bBb \to b, \; ABb \to A, \; BBb \to B.$$

This is easily proved using our approximate approach for forward closures by an automaton having only 14 states.

4   Conclusions

For an extensive class of string rewriting systems, termination can be shown by the construction of a compatible automaton, i.e., a finite automaton that has a suitable closure property. Whereas in theory the construction of an exact compatible automaton always succeeds if it exists, i.e., if the system is match-bounded, it may be prohibitively expensive. So we proposed an approximate approach that is more efficient but may fail. For instance, this new approach allows to prove termination of the single rule SRSs

$$\{babaa \to aaababab\}, \; \{babaa \to abaabbaba\}, \; \{baaabbaa \to aaabbaaabb\}$$

within fractions of seconds by automata having 72, 98 and 155 states, respectively. The exact approach, in contrast, fails due to lack of memory. All standard techniques for proving termination [14] fail, too, for these examples.

The notion of match-bounds was inspired by Ravikumar [10], who showed that *change-bounded* string rewriting preserves regularity of languages. Similar to $\mathsf{match}(R)$, he defined a related system over the alphabet $\Sigma \times \mathbf{N}$ to consist of all rules $(a_1, n_1) \cdots (a_p, n_p) \to (b_1, n_1 + 1) \cdots (b_p, n_p + 1)$ for which $a_1 \cdots a_p \to b_1 \cdots b_p$ is in the system R over Σ. This definition, however, is only meaningful for length-preserving systems, where $|\ell| = |r|$ for every rule $\ell \to r$. For this particular class of systems it can be shown that match-boundedness actually coincides with change-boundedness.

Presently we work on extending these techniques to term rewriting. To this end the automata are replaced by finite tree automata.

References

1. R. V. Book, M. Jantzen, and C. Wrathall. Monadic Thue systems. *Theoret. Comput. Sci.*, 19:231–251, 1982.
2. R. V. Book and F. Otto. Cancellation rules and extended word problems. *Inform. Process. Lett.*, 20:5–11, 1985.
3. R. V. Book and F. Otto. *String-Rewriting Systems.* Texts and Monographs in Computer Science. Springer-Verlag, New York, 1993.
4. N. Dershowitz. Termination of linear rewriting systems. In S. Even and O. Kariv (Eds.), *Proc. 8th Int. Coll. on Automata, Languages and Programming ICALP-81, Lecture Notes in Comput. Sci.* Vol. 115, pp. 448-458. Springer-Verlag, 1981.
5. A. Geser, D. Hofbauer and J. Waldmann. Match-bounded string rewriting systems. In B. Rovan and P. Vojtas (Eds.), *Proc. 28th Int. Symp. Mathematical Foundations of Computer Science MFCS-03, Lecture Notes in Comput. Sci.* Vol. 2747, pp. 449-459. Springer-Verlag, 2003.

6. A. Geser, D. Hofbauer and J. Waldmann. Match-bounded string rewriting systems. NIA Report 2003-09, National Institute of Aerospace, Hampton, VA, USA. Available at `http://research.nianet.org/~geser/papers/nia-matchbounded.html`. Accepted for *Appl. Algebra Engrg. Comm. Comput.*.

7. J. Giesl, R. Thiemann, P. Schneider-Kamp and S. Falke. Automated termination proofs with APROVE. In V. van Oostrom (Ed.), *Proc. 15th Int. Conf. Rewriting Techniques and Applications RTA-04, Lecture Notes in Comp. Sci.*, Springer, 2004. Tool and description available at `http://www-i2.informatik.rwth-aachen.de/APROVE/`.

8. T. N. Hibbard. Context-limited grammars. *J. ACM*, 21(3):446–453, 1974.

9. D. Hofbauer and J. Waldmann. Deleting string rewriting systems preserve regularity. In *Proc. 7th Int. Conf. Developments in Language Theory DLT-03, Lect. Notes Comp. Sci.*, Springer-Verlag, 2003. Accepted for *Theoret. Comput. Sci.*.

10. B. Ravikumar. Peg-solitaire, string rewriting systems and finite automata. In H.-W. Leong, H. Imai, and S. Jain (Eds.), *Proc. 8th Int. Symp. Algorithms and Computation ISAAC-97, Lecture Notes in Comput. Sci.* Vol. 1350, pp. 233–242. Springer-Verlag, 1997.

11. E. Tahhan Bittar. Complexité linéaire du problème de Zantema. *C. R. Acad. Sci. Paris Sér. I Inform. Théor.*, t. 323:1201–1206, 1996.

12. J. Waldmann. Matchbox: a tool for match-bounded string rewriting, In V. van Oostrom (Ed.), *Proc. 15th Int. Conf. Rewriting Techniques and Applications RTA-04, Lecture Notes in Comp. Sci.*, Springer, 2004. Tool and description available at `http://theo1.informatik.uni-leipzig.de/matchbox/`.

13. H. Zantema and A. Geser. A complete characterization of termination of $0^p1^q \rightarrow 1^r0^s$. *Appl. Algebra Engrg. Comm. Comput.*, 11(1):1–25, 2000.

14. H. Zantema. Termination. In *Term Rewriting Systems, by Terese*, pages 181–259. Cambridge University Press, 2003.

15. H. Zantema. TORPA: Termination of Rewriting Proved Automatically. In V. van Oostrom (Ed.), *Proc. 15th Int. Conf. Rewriting Techniques and Applications RTA-04, Lecture Notes in Comp. Sci.*, Springer, 2004. Tool and description available at `http://www.win.tue.nl/~hzantema/torpa.html`.

16. H. Zantema. Termination of string rewriting proved automatically. Accepted for *J. Automat. Reason.*, 2004.

Linear Encoding Scheme
for Weighted Finite Automata

Mathieu Giraud and Dominique Lavenier

IRISA / CNRS / Université de Rennes 1 35042 Rennes Cedex, France
{mgiraud, lavenier}@irisa.fr

Abstract. In this paper, we show that the linear encoding scheme efficiently implements weighted finite automata (WFA). WFA with t transitions can be hardwired with $\mathcal{O}(t)$ cells. They solve pattern matching problems in a pipelined way, parsing one character every clock cycle. With the massive parallelism of reconfigurable processors like FPGAs, a significant speed-up is obtained against software solutions.

1 Introduction

Weighted finite automata (WFA) are finite-state machines with weights on transitions. They have been widely used in image compression [1] or in speech recognition [2]. In Biology, searching genomic banks for patterns with error counting, or with arbitrary matrices of substitution scores, can be made using WFA. These applications involve sequential scans of large databases (today tens of gigabytes of data) whose size is increasing faster than CPU power.

Whereas efficient simulation of a non-deterministic finite automaton (NFA) can be achieved by first determinizing it (although leading to a potential exponential number of states), direct simulation of WFA is needed as they are not all determinizable [3]. Mark G. Eramian proposed in 2002 an algorithm in $\mathcal{O}(nt)$ time, where t is the number of transitions and n the length of the parsed sequence [4].

One can use dedicated hardware to accelerate parsing. Reetinder Sidhu and Viktor K. Prasanna proposed in 2001 an FPGA architecture to implement NFA [5]. This paper aims to extend their idea to WFA: we prove that WFA can be hardwired using a linear encoding scheme, providing a significant acceleration over software methods. In such a material implementation, space concerns become prominent and we need to ensure the WFA fits into FPGA devices. Thus, an estimation of the surface area will be conducted.

The rest of the paper is organized as follows. Section 2 provides background definitions about pattern matching and WFA. In Section 3, we show how to generalize the one-hot encoding scheme for NFA to the linear encoding scheme for WFA. Section 4 presents some experimental results comparing our method against software techniques.

M. Domaratzki et al. (Eds.): CIAA 2004, LNCS 3317, pp. 146–155, 2005.

2   Preliminaries

2.1   Continuous Pattern Matching

Let Σ be a finite alphabet. Elements of Σ are called characters. A word is a finite sequence of characters $w = w_1 w_2 \ldots w_n \in \Sigma^*$. A language $\mathcal{L}$ is a subset of Σ^*. Given a word w and a language $\mathcal{L}$, the problem of *continuous pattern matching* is to find all subwords v of w such that $v \in \mathcal{L}$.

Because this problem can have $\mathcal{O}(n^2)$ solutions (like a^* in the word a^n), we restrict it to find only all positions in the initial word which are terminating matching subwords, that is determining the set $\text{Pos}(\mathcal{L}, w) = \{ j \in [1; n] \mid \exists i \in [1; j], \; w_i w_{i+1} \ldots w_j \in \mathcal{L} \}$.

When $\mathcal{L}$ is a singleton or a finite dictionary, some indexing techniques can handle the continuous pattern matching. Here those techniques do not apply since $\mathcal{L}$ will be defined by a weighted finite automata.

2.2   Weighted Finite Automaton

Weighted finite automata (WFA) are finite-state machines describing languages of higher complexity than NFA [2, 4].

Let $(\mathbb{K}, \oplus, \otimes)$ be a semiring, where $\bar{0}$ and $\bar{1}$ are the identity elements for $\oplus$ and $\otimes$. A weighted finite automaton (WFA) is a 5-uple $\mathcal{A} = (Q, \Sigma, \delta, I, F)$, where Q is a finite set of states, Σ a finite alphabet, $\delta : Q \times \Sigma \times Q \mapsto \mathbb{K}$ the transition table, $I \subset Q$ and $F \subset Q$ the initial and final states set. The WFA $\mathcal{A}$ gives to every word $w = w_1 w_2 \ldots w_n$ a weight $W(w)$ defined by

$$W(w) = \bigoplus_{q_0 \in I, \; q_n \in F}^{q_1, \ldots, q_{n-1} \in Q} \delta(q_0, w_1, q_1) \otimes \delta(q_1, w_2, q_2) \otimes \ldots \otimes \delta(q_{n-1}, w_n, q_n).$$

This weight is the $\oplus$-sum (i.e. the sum according to $\oplus$) of all the weights on paths from an initial state to a final state labeled by w. Let us now define a recognizing set $\mathbb{J} \subset \mathbb{K}$. We say that the word w is recognized by $\mathcal{A}$ when $W(w) \in \mathbb{J}$.

If for every state q_1 and for every character α, there exists at most one state q_2 with $\delta(q_1, \alpha, q_2) \neq \bar{0}$, the WFA is said to be deterministic.

The nondeterministic finite automata (NFA) are only a particular case of WFA over the boolean semiring $(\{T, F\}, \vee, \wedge)$ with the recognizing set $\mathbb{J} = \{T\}$. In this case, a word w is recognized by $\mathcal{A}$ when there exists a path from a initial state to a final state labeled by w.

Other semirings are used like $(\mathbb{R}^+, +, \times)$ (probabilistic), $(\mathbb{R} \cup \{-\infty\}, \oplus_{\log}, +)$ (logarithm) and $(\mathbb{R} \cup \{-\infty\}, \max, +)$ (Viterbi's approximation). For practical use, we consider only a finite subset of the semiring $(\mathbb{Z} \cup \{-\infty\}, \max, +)$.

In that case and with the recognizing set $\mathbb{J} = \{x \in \mathbb{Z} \mid x \geq 0\}$, the WFA $\mathcal{A}_2$ represented in Fig. 1 recognizes the subset of $\mathcal{L}_1$ containing strictly more occurrences of b than c. This language $\mathcal{L}_2$ is not regular.

In the following, we want to solve on large databases the continuous pattern matching problem in which the language $\mathcal{L}$ is described by a WFA. The set $\text{Pos}(\mathcal{L}, w)$ will have the form $\{ j \in [1; n] \mid \exists i \in [1; j], \; W(w_i w_{i+1} \ldots w_j) \in \mathbb{J} \}$. The next section presents an hardware representation of WFA.

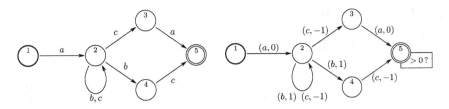

Fig. 1. On the left side, the NFA $\mathcal{A}_1$ recognizing the regular language $\mathcal{L}_1 = a\,(b|c)^*\,(ca\,|\,bc)$. On the right side, the WFA $\mathcal{A}_2$ over the semiring $(\mathbb{Z}\cup\{-\infty\}, \max, +)$. It recognizes the non-regular language $\mathcal{L}_2 = \{w \in \mathcal{L}_1 \mid |w|_b > |w|_c\}$

3   Linear Encoding Scheme for WFA

This section gives an overview of encoding schemes for finite-state machines, then describes the linear encoding scheme for WFA and its properties.

3.1   Encoding Schemes for Finite-State Machines

There are two major schemes to encode a finite state machine with $|Q|$ states in hardware, according to the representation of its states [6]:

- the *logarithmic scheme* uses a bit vector of size $\log_2 |Q|$ in binary encoding (natural, Gray, or any encoding tailored to a particular application). For $|Q| = 5$, one can have the values $\{000, 001, 011, 101, 111\}$;
- the *linear scheme* (or *one-hot scheme*) uses a bit vector of size $|Q|$ where only one bit is set to 1, like in the set $\{00001, 00010, 00100, 01000, 10000\}$.

Those schemes lead to different hardware implementations. The size of the logarithmic scheme merely depends on the logic part and can be reduced with a good numbering scheme. This approach is usual for a conventional serial machine, but is limited to deterministic automata.

On the other hand, there can be several states active at the same time in the linear encoding scheme, implementing a NFA in a *multi−hot* fashion. Sidhu and Prasanna showed that this representation is very effective to scan for a regular expression with an FPGA [5].

As the linear encoding scheme needs as many operators as the number of transitions, one could think that it is limited to implement automata with few transitions. However, it has be shown that, for common automata, the linear scheme is less power-consuming and even *smaller* than the logarithmic scheme [6].

3.2   Linear Encoding Scheme for WFA

Sidhu and Prasanna build an NFA from a regular expression describing it [5]. We present here a linear encoding scheme for WFA by giving another point of view: we directly map a given WFA into hardware.

Let $\mathcal{A} = (Q, \Sigma, \delta, I, F)$ a WFA over a semiring $\mathbb{K}$, as defined in section 2.2. We denote by k and p the number of bits needed to represent respectively the alphabet Σ and the weights in $\mathbb{K}$. Typical values are $k = 8$ for an ASCII text or $k = 5$ for amino acid patterns, and bit widths for the weight ranging from $p = 1$ to $p = 16$.

Principle. The hardware implementation can be viewed as a shift register, in which a weight with p bits is moving. For each state q, there will be a p-bit register. We call e_j^q its value at the clock cycle j.

- Each transition set from a state q' to a state q is materialized with an *evaluator* (left part of Fig. 2). It receives k bits (current character w_j) and generates the weight $\delta(q', w_j, q)$. In the general case, this evaluator will be a $\langle k \mapsto p \rangle$ function (k binary inputs, p binary outputs).
- This weight is aggregated with the weight at the previous state, giving the value $s_j^{q',q} = e_{j-1}^{q'} \otimes \delta(q', w_j, q)$.
- Each state is a register driven by the $\oplus$-sum of all the values at the outputs of its incoming transitions $s_j^{q',q}$ (right part of Fig. 2). At the following clock cycle, this $\oplus$-sum e_j^q will be given as input for other transitions.

The initialization phase of the automaton, not showed here, consists in setting all states to $\bar{0}$ except the initial states which are set to $\bar{1}$. Those initial states always receive an additional incoming transition whose weight is kept to $\bar{1}$.

The surface area needed by the WFA is here $\mathcal{O}(2^k pt)$, where t is the number of pairs (q', q) having a non-void transition $\delta(q', \alpha, q)$ for some α.

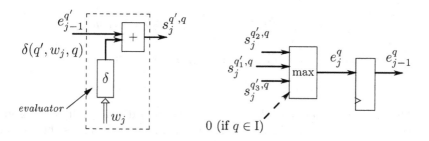

Fig. 2. Principle of linear encoding scheme for WFA over a finite subset of $(\mathbb{Z} \cup \{-\infty\}, \max, +)$. Here the identity elements are $\bar{0} = -\infty$ and $\bar{1} = 0$. The p bits representing the weight are a compound of $p - 1$ bits representing a two's complement integer, and 1 bit representing $-\infty$ (for the initialization, inexistent transitions, and overflows). As we consider only a finite subset of the semiring, one must ensure that the overflows are correctly handled. The overflow at $-\infty$ can be neglected, as it represents a weight which is very unlikely to participate to a final maximum. The overflow at $+\infty$ is detected at the output and gives a hit in the recognition. If there are cycles in the automaton, a reset of the whole automaton must follow the overflow at $+\infty$

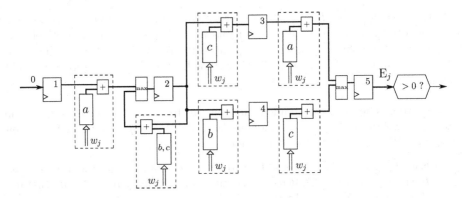

Fig. 3. Linear encoding scheme for the WFA $\mathcal{A}_2$

Values of States. The previous descriptions can be summarized to:

$$\begin{cases} e_0^q = \begin{cases} \bar{1} & \text{if } q \in I, \\ \bar{0} & \text{if } q \notin I, \end{cases} \\ s_j^{q',q} = e_{j-1}^{q'} \otimes \delta(q', w_j, q), \\ e_j^q = \begin{cases} \bar{1} \oplus (\oplus_{q' \in Q} \, s_j^{q',q}) & \text{if } q \in I, \\ \oplus_{q' \in Q} \, s_j^{q',q} & \text{if } q \notin I. \end{cases} \end{cases}$$

With this equation set, the following lemma holds:

Lemma. If q is a state and j an integer, one has

$$e_j^q = \oplus_{i=0}^{j} \; \oplus_{q_i \in I, q_j = q}^{q_{i+1}, \ldots, q_{j-1} \in Q} \; \otimes_{t=i}^{j-1} \delta(q_t, w_{t+1}, q_{t+1}).$$

Corollary. The $\oplus$-sum of all the weights at the final states is

$$E_j = \oplus_{q \in F} \, e_j^q = \oplus_{i=0}^{j} W(w_i w_{i+1} \ldots w_j).$$

The proof of the lemma, which relies on the right-distributivity of $\otimes$, is given in Appendix A. The corollary says that the final value E_j shows the $\oplus$-sum of all the weights of the words $w_i \ldots w_j$. Thus, if one could deduce from E_j if there is an i such that $W(w_i w_{i+1} \ldots w_j)$ is in $\mathbb{J}$, one would know if a word $w_i \ldots w_j$ has been recognized by checking if E_j is in $\mathbb{J}$. For this, we say now that $\mathbb{J}$ is a *good recognizing set* if it has the two following properties:

- $\forall a \in \mathbb{J}, \, \forall b \in \mathbb{K}, \, a \oplus b \in \mathbb{J}$,
- $\forall a \in \mathbb{K}, \, \forall b \in \mathbb{K}, \, a \oplus b \in \mathbb{J} \implies a \in \mathbb{J} \text{ or } b \in \mathbb{J}$.

With this definition, a direct consequence of the above corollary is:

Theorem. If $\mathbb{J}$ is a good recognizing set, then

$$E_j \in \mathbb{J} \iff j \in \text{Pos}(\mathcal{L}, w).$$

Therefore, if the hypothesis of the theorem holds, the continuous pattern matching problem is resolved by parsing one character on every clock cycle and by observing the value at the final states. In fact, the clock cycle time is in $\mathcal{O}(p \log d_{\max})$, where $d_{\max}$ is the maximum incoming degree of the states, but this is not a limitation for usual WFA.

- In the case of the NFA (boolean semiring $(\{T, F\}, \vee, \wedge)$), only one bit is needed to represent the weight: we fall back on the one-hot scheme. The subset $\mathbb{J} = \{T\}$ is a good recognizing set. Each evaluator $\langle k \mapsto 1 \rangle$ is reduced to a comparator ($w_i \in A$) for some subset $A \subset \Sigma$, the $\otimes$ is an AND gate and the $\oplus$ an OR gate.
- In the semiring $(\mathbb{Z}, \max, +)$, the only good recognizing sets are those of the form $\mathbb{J} = \{x \in \mathbb{Z}, x \geq x_0\}$ for some x_0. Those sets fit perfectly in the applications of WFA where the weight is a *score* compared to a threshold to know if a sequence was recognized.

4   Performance Evaluation

This section is about the performances of a real implementation of the linear encoding scheme described in section 3.2. Here the WFA are over a finite subset of $(\mathbb{Z}, \max, +)$. We begin by describing the context of use. As we use a low-cost FPGA chip and as the main constraint is about size, we need to know precisely the surface area taken by the WFA; this is done in section 4.2. In section 4.3, we compare the speed achieved against software techniques.

4.1   Context of Use

FPGAs. Field Programmable Gate Arrays (FPGAs) are reconfigurable chips composed by a matrix of interconnected logic cells [7]. The logic inside each cell as the interconnections can be configured in a few milliseconds, allowing to have a custom chip. The cost of such solutions is orders of magnitude below the cost of ASIC (Application Specific Integrated Circuits) full-custom chips.

Prototype Board. Our prototype board, which is part of the R-disk system [8] is devoted to filter large genomic databases on-the-fly. The board contains an hard disk and a low-cost FPGA which directly filters data from the disk. The total cost for the components is less than \$200. The FPGA is the Spartan-II from Xilinx. It contains 1176 cell logic blocs (CLB), each one having 4 look-up tables (LUT) of 16 bits. The LUTs can realize any $\langle 4 \mapsto 1 \rangle$ boolean function. Almost two thirds the of FPGA is devoted to the filter; that is a little more than 3000 LUTs. It operates at a clock frequency of 40 MHz.

4.2   Implementing the Linear Encoding Scheme on FPGAs

FPGA devices are well suited for the linear encoding scheme because of the high number of available registers and the local propagation of data without global control. Furthermore, the computation of transition weights fits perfectly into LUTs with 4 inputs.

Automaton type	Transitions logic	Weight operators	Total, by transition	Maximum number of transitions
NFA (1 bit)	$\langle 5 \mapsto 1 \rangle$ 2 LUTs	AND / OR $\leq$ 1 LUT	$\leq$ 3 LUTs	$\geq$ 1000
WFA, $\mathbb{Z}$ (p bits)	$\langle 5 \mapsto p \rangle$ $2p$ LUTs	max / + $\leq 3p$ LUTs	$\leq 5p$ LUTs	$\geq 600/p$

Fig. 4. Upper bound for the number of LUTs when $k = 5$. The last column shows the maximum number of transitions for a Spartan-II FPGA with 3000 LUTs

The regularity of the architecture allows a relative ease of programming. Our implementation, written in OCaml, translates WFA abstract descriptions into their representation in the hardware design language VHDL. One of the main issues with WFA is that their topology may change for each query. Design techniques with J-Bits [9] would allow a fast compilation of arbitrary WFA shapes, but they would need a custom place (& route) algorithm. The current slower solution is to perform a full compilation from VHDL for each query, the overhead due to compilation (4-5 minutes) being small compared to the performance gain when scanning large databases.

For the scanning of protein databases (alphabet with 5 bits), an automaton with q states and t transitions with a weight of p bits takes a surface area of $3pt + 2p(t - q)$ LUTs before compiler optimizations. The total area taken is less than $5pt$ LUTs. Thus WFA with 75 transitions and an 8-bit weight can be encoded.

To verify this bound, real FPGA experiments were done using the standard Xilinx framework. We run our method on two bench sets. The first one is random WFA, and results show that the real limit is beyond the 75 transitions (left part of Fig. 5). The other bench set is the PROSITE protein pattern bank [10], which contains about 1300 patterns that we translate into WFA to allow substitution errors. More than 98% of the PROSITE bank can be translated in the FPGA.

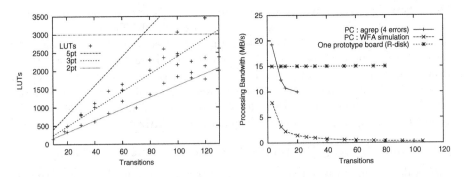

Fig. 5. Experimental results for the linear encoding scheme. The left part shows the LUT count for different WFA sizes. The right part compares the bandwidth processed by one prototype board with an FPGA against software solutions on a PC

4.3   Performance Comparison

Sidhu and Prasanna [5] showed that their FPGA realization is more effective than softwares like *agrep* if data is large enough. Their conclusions remain for WFA as they do even more operations (additions, maximums).

We compared our approach with some software techniques using WFA. The low-cost Spartan-II is compared against a Pentium IV 2 GHz with 728 MB RAM. This comparison is fair since the Spartan II was released in 2000 and the Pentium IV 2 GHz in 2001. Results are shown in the right part of Fig. 5.

The comparison with *agrep* [11] is for reference only, as this software only parse for regular expressions or for weighted expressions with a fixed score (with at most 4 substitution errors). When patterns are small and with no errors, data can be parsed through *agrep* at the disk rate. But those flows go down with errors and with larger patterns.

More interesting is the comparison against a software simulation of WFA, as in the algorithm described by Eramian in [4] that parses data in $\mathcal{O}(nt)$ time. Data rates go from 10 MB/s for small WFA down to less than 1 MB/s for WFA with more than 30 states.

On the contrary, our WFA implementation on the FPGA parses a constant bandwidth of data (which is now 15 MB/s), as far as the WFA fits into the available surface area of the FPGA. This bandwidth implies parsing less than one amino acid (5 bits) at the 40 MHz clock cycle of the FPGA, allowing to parse a character on every clock cycle. Experiment were done on real data (80-transition WFA, 34 GB canine DNA database). It takes more than 20 hours on a 2 GHz Pentium. On a single prototype R-disk board, it takes less than 45 minutes (5 minutes for compiling and 40 minutes for parsing).

5   Conclusion

Weighted finite automata can be effectively hardwired on FPGAs with the linear encoding scheme. That encoding is perfectly suited for standard FPGA devices and provides a significant speed-up over software implementations. To our knowledge, this is the first hardware realization of WFA.

The main current limitation with the linear encoding scheme is the size requirements of the targeted WFA. Currently, we can implement WFA with an 8-bit weight and more than 75 transitions. This limit is already pushed away by the next generation of FPGAs: in 2004, Xilinx sells the low-cost FPGAs Spartan-3 with more than 18,000 CLB, that is 15 times larger than the chip we use in our prototype board. The transition limit raises accordingly. If an higher number of transitions is available, one could distribute them among several automata, especially when one need to parse nucleic banks for protein patterns through six reading frames.

More generally, the speed-up obtained by such a spatial implementation [12] against software techniques will continue to increase, as it is easier to exploit more resources in a reconfigurable device than in a sequential CPU.

References

1. Culik II, K., Kari, J.: Image Compression Using Weighted Finite Automata. In: Mathematical Foundations of Computer Science (MFCS 93). Volume 711 of Lecture Notes in Computer Science. (1993) 392–402

2. Mohri, M., Pereira, F., Riley, M.: Weighted Automata in Text and Speech Processing. In Kornai, A., ed.: Extended Finite State Models of Language (ECAI 96). (1996) 46–50

3. Buchsbaum, A.L., Raffaele, G., Westbrook, J.R.: On the Determinization of Weighted Finite Automata. SIAM Journal on Computing **30** (2001) 1502 – 1531

4. Eramian, M.G.: Efficient Simulation of Nondeterministic Weighted Finite Automata. In: Fourth Workshop on Descriptional Complexity of Formal Systems (DCFS 02). (2002)

5. Sidhu, R., Prasanna, V.K.: Fast Regular Expression Matching using FPGAs. In: IEEE Symposium on Field Programmable Custom Computing Machines (FCCM 01). (2001)

6. Dunoyer, J., Ptrot, F., Jacomme, L.: Stratgies de codage des automates pour des applications basse consommation : exprimentation et interprtation. In: Journes d'tude Faible Tension et Faible Consommation (FTFC 97). (1997)

7. Sanchez, E.: Field Programmable Gate Array (FPGA) Circuits. Lecture Notes in Computer Science (1996) 1–18

8. Lavenier, D., Guyetant, S., Derrien, S., Rubini, S.: A reconfigurable parallel disk system for filtering genomic banks. In: Proc. Int. Conf. ERSA'03. (2003)

9. Guccione, S., Levi, D., Sundararajan, P.: JBits: A Javabased Interface for Reconfigurable Computing. In: 2nd Annual Military and Aerospace Applications of Programmable Devices and Technologies Conference (MAPLD). (1999)

10. Bucher, P., Bairoch, A.: A Generalized Profile Syntax for Biomolecular Sequences Motifs and its Function in Automatic Sequence Interpretation. In: Intelligent Systems for Molecular Biology (ISMB 94). (1994) 53–61

11. Wu, S., Manber, U.: Fast Text Searching Allowing Errors. Communications of the ACM **35** (1992) 83–91

12. DeHon, A.: Very Large Scale Spatial Computing. In: Third International Conference on Unconventional Models of Computation (UMC 02). (2002) 27–37

Appendix A

Proof of Lemma. Here we prove by induction on j the following property:

$$e_j^q = \oplus_{i=0}^{j} \; \oplus_{q_i \in I, q_j = q}^{q_{i+1}, \ldots, q_{j-1} \in Q} \; \otimes_{t=i}^{j-1} \; \delta(q_t, w_{t+1}, q_{t+1}).$$

At the cycle $j = 0$, the property is $e_0^q = \oplus_{q_0 \in I}^{q_0 = q} \bar{1}$, that is e_0^q equals $\bar{1}$ if $q \in I$ and $\bar{0}$ if $q \notin I$: the property is true. Assume that the induction is true until the cycle $j - 1$, with $j \geq 1$. Let q be a non-initial state. We compute the value e_j^q of the state q at the cycle j.

$$e_j^q = \oplus_{q' \in Q} \ s_j^{q',q}$$

$$= \oplus_{q' \in Q} \ \left[e_{j-1}^{q'} \otimes \delta(q', w_j, q) \right]$$

$$= \oplus_{q' \in Q} \ \left[\left(\oplus_{i=0}^{j-1} \ \oplus_{q_i \in I, q_{j-1}=q'}^{q_{i+1}, \ldots, q_{j-2} \in Q} \ \otimes_{t=i}^{j-2} \delta(q_t, w_{t+1}, q_{t+1}) \right) \otimes \delta(q', w_j, q) \right]$$

$$\qquad\qquad\qquad\qquad\qquad\qquad\qquad\qquad \textit{(hypothesis of induction)}$$

$$= \oplus_{q' \in Q} \ \oplus_{i=0}^{j-1} \ \oplus_{q_i \in I, q_{j-1}=q'}^{q_{i+1}, \ldots, q_{j-2} \in Q} \ \left[\left(\otimes_{t=i}^{j-2} \delta(q_t, w_{t+1}, q_{t+1}) \right) \otimes \delta(q', w_j, q) \right]$$

$$\qquad\qquad\qquad\qquad\qquad\qquad\qquad\qquad \textit{(right-distributivity of } \otimes\textit{)}$$

$$= \oplus_{q' \in Q} \ \oplus_{i=0}^{j-1} \ \oplus_{q_i \in I, q_{j-1}=q', q_j=q}^{q_{i+1}, \ldots, q_{j-1} \in Q} \ \left[\otimes_{t=i}^{j-1} \delta(q_t, w_{t+1}, q_{t+1}) \right]$$

$$= \oplus_{q' \in Q} \ \oplus_{i=0}^{j} \ \oplus_{q_i \in I, q_{j-1}=q', q_j=q}^{q_{i+1}, \ldots, q_{j-1} \in Q} \ \left[\otimes_{t=i}^{j-1} \delta(q_t, w_{t+1}, q_{t+1}) \right]$$

$$\qquad\qquad\qquad\qquad\qquad\qquad\qquad\qquad \textit{(because q is not initial)}$$

$$= \oplus_{i=0}^{j} \ \oplus_{q_i \in I, q_j=q}^{q_{i+1}, \ldots, q_{j-1} \in Q} \ \otimes_{t=i}^{j-1} \delta(q_t, w_{t+1}, q_{t+1})$$

Thus the property is true at the cycle j. If q is initial, the same result is obtained by a similar computation by adding a $\bar{1}$ to each term. By induction, the property is true for every cycle $j \geq 0$. $\square$

The Generalization of Generalized Automata: Expression Automata

Yo-Sub Han and Derick Wood

Department of Computer Science,
The Hong Kong University of Science and Technology, Hong Kong
{emmous, dwood}@cs.ust.hk

Abstract. We explore expression automata with respect to determinism, minimization and primeness. We define determinism of expression automata using prefix-freeness. This approach is, to some extent, similar to that of Giammarresi and Montalbano's definition of deterministic generalized automata. We prove that deterministic expression automata languages are a proper subfamily of the regular languages. We define the minimization of deterministic expression automata. Lastly, we discuss prime prefix-free regular languages.

Note that we have omitted almost all proofs in this preliminary version.

1   Introduction

Recently, there has been a resurgence of interest in finite-state automata that allow more complex transition labels. In particular, Giammarresi and Montalbano [4] have studied **generalized automata** (introduced by Eilenberg [3]) with respect to determinism. Generalized automata have strings (or **blocks**) as transition labels rather than merely characters or the null string. (They have also been called string or lazy automata.) Generalized automata allow us to more easily construct an automaton in many cases. For example, given the reserved words for C++ programs, construct a finite-state automaton that discovers all reserved words that appear in a specific C++ program or program segment. The use of generalized automata makes this task much simpler.

It is well known that generalized automata have the same expressive power as traditional finite-state automata. Indeed, we can transform any generalized automaton into a traditional finite-state automaton using **state expansion.** Giammarresi and Montalbano, however, took a different approach by defining **deterministic generalized automata (DGAs)** directly in terms of a local property which we introduce in Section 4.

Our goal is to re-examine the notion of **expression automata;** that is, finite-state automata whose transition labels are regular expressions over the input alphabet. We define **deterministic expression automata (DEAs)** by extending the applicability of prefix-freeness.

We first define traditional finite-state automata and generalized automata and their deterministic counterparts in Section 2 and formally define expression

M. Domaratzki et al. (Eds.): CIAA 2004, LNCS 3317, pp. 156–166, 2005.

automata in Section 3. In section 4, we define determinism based on prefix-freeness and investigate the relationship between deterministic expression automata and prefix-free regular languages. Then we consider minimization of deterministic expression automata, in Section 5, and introduce prime prefix-free regular languages in Section 6.

2   Preliminaries

Let Σ denote a finite alphabet of characters and Σ^* denote the set of all strings over Σ, where the elements of Σ^* are called strings or blocks. We call an element of Σ a character and an element of Σ^* a string. A language over Σ is a subset of Σ^*. The character $\emptyset$ denotes the empty language and the character λ denotes the null string.

Given two strings x and y in Σ^*, x is said to be a **prefix** of y if there is a string w such that $xw = y$ and we define x to be a **proper prefix** of y is $x \neq \lambda$ and $x \neq y$. Given a set X of strings over Σ, X is **prefix-free** if no string in X is proper prefix of any other string in X.

A traditional finite-state automaton A is specified by a tuple $(Q, \Sigma, \delta, s, F)$, where Q is a finite set of states, Σ is an input alphabet, $\delta \subseteq Q \times \Sigma \times Q$ is a (finite) set of transitions, $s \in Q$ is the start state and $F \subseteq Q$ is a set of final states. A string x over Σ is accepted by A if there is a labeled path from s to a state in F such that this path spells out the string x. Thus, the language $L(A)$ of a finite-state automaton A is the set of all strings that are spelled out by paths from s to a final state in F. Automata that do not have any **useless states;** that is states that do not appear on any path from the start state to some final state are called **trim** or **reduced** [3, 9].

Eilenberg [3] introduced **generalized automata,** an extension of traditional finite-state automata by allowing strings on the transitions. A generalized automaton A is specified by a tuple $(Q, \Sigma, \delta, s, F)$, where Q is a finite set of states, Σ is an input alphabet, $\delta \subseteq Q \times \Sigma^* \times Q$ is a finite set of block transitions, $s \in Q$ is the start state and $F \subseteq Q$ is a set of final states. Giammarresi and Montalbano [4] define a deterministic generalized automaton using a local notion of **prefix-freeness.** A generalized automaton A is deterministic if, for each state q in A, the following two conditions hold:

1. The set of all blocks in out-transitions from q is prefix-free.
2. For any two out-transitions (q, x, p) and (q, y, r) from q, if $x = y$, then we require that $p = r$.

Note that Giammarresi and Montalbano do not require condition 2 and, as a result, some DGAs are nondeterministic.

Since regular languages L are sets of strings, we can apply the notion of prefix-freeness to such sets.

Definition 1. *A (regular) language L over an alphabet Σ is prefix-free if, for all distinct strings x and y in L, x is not a prefix of y and y is not a prefix of x. A regular expression α is prefix-free if $L(\alpha)$ is prefix-free.*

Lemma 1. *A regular language L is prefix-free if and only if there is a trim deterministic finite-state automaton (DFA) A for L that has no out-transitions from any final state.*

3   Expression Automata

It is well known that regular expressions and (deterministic) finite-state automata have exactly the same expressive power [6, 12]. A finite-state automaton allows only a single character in a transition and a generalized automaton [3] allows a single string, possibly the null string, in a transition. It is natural to extend this notion to allow a regular expression in a transition, since a character and a string are also regular expressions. This concept was first considered by Brzozowski and McCluskey, Jr. [1].

Definition 2. *An **expression automaton** A is specified by a tuple $(Q, \Sigma, \delta, s, f)$, where Q is a finite set of states, Σ is an input alphabet, $\delta \subseteq Q \times \mathcal{R}_\Sigma \times Q$ is a finite set of expression transitions, where $\mathcal{R}_\Sigma$ is the set of all regular expressions over Σ, $s \in Q$ is the start state and $f \in Q$ is the final state. (Note that we need only have one final state.) We require that, for every pair p and q of states, there is exactly one expression transition (p, α, q) in δ, where α is a regular expression over Σ.*

We can also use the functional notation $\delta{:}Q \times Q \to \mathcal{R}_\Sigma$ that gives the equivalent representation. An expression transition (p, α, q) gives $\delta(p, q) = \alpha$. Note that δ contains exactly $|Q|^2$ transitions, one transition for each pair of states, and whenever $(p, \emptyset, q)$ is in δ, for some p and q in Q, A cannot move from p to q directly.

We generalize the notion of accepting transition sequences to accepting expression transition sequences and accepting language transition sequences.

Definition 3. *An **accepting expression transition sequence** is a transition sequence of the form:*

$$(p_0 = s, \alpha_1, p_1) \cdots (p_{m-1}, \alpha_m, p_m = f),$$

for some $m \geq 1$, where s and f are the start and final states, respectively.

*The second notion is an **accepting language transition sequence** of the form:*

$$(p_0 = s, L(\alpha_1), p_1) \cdots (p_{m-1}, L(\alpha_m), p_m = f),$$

for some $m \geq 1$, where s and f are the start and final states, respectively.

We include a proof sketch that every finite-state automaton can be converted into an equivalent expression automaton and conversely.

Lemma 2. *Every trim finite-state automaton can be converted into an equivalent trim expression automaton. Therefore, every regular language is an expression automaton language.*

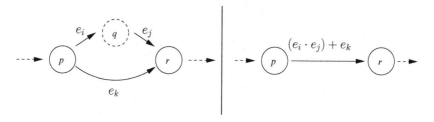

Fig. 1. An example of the state elimination of a state q

We next establish that we can convert every expression automaton A into an equivalent finite-state automaton; that is combining the two results, expression automata and finite-state automata have the same expressive power. We prove this fact by constructing a regular expression α such that $L(\alpha) = L(A)$. A trim expression automaton $A = (Q, \Sigma, \delta, s, f)$ is **non-returning** if $\delta(q, s) = \emptyset$, for all $q \in Q$. It is straightforward to show that any trim expression automaton A can be converted into a trim non-returning expression automaton for the same language $L(A)$.

We define the **state elimination** of $q \in Q \setminus \{s, f\}$ in A to be the bypassing of state q, q's in-transitions, q's out-transitions and q's self-looping transition with equivalent expression transition sequences. For each in-transition (p_i, α_i, q), $1 \le i \le m$, for some $m \ge 1$, for each out-transition (q, γ, r_j), $1 \le j \le n$, for some $n \ge 1$, and for the self-looping transition (q, β, q) in δ, construct a new transition $(p_i, \alpha_i \cdot \beta^* \cdot \gamma_j, r_j)$. Since there is always an existing transition (p, ν, r) in δ, for some expression ν, we merge two transitions to give the bypass transition $(p, (\alpha_i \cdot \beta^* \cdot \gamma_j) + \nu, r)$. We then remove q and all transitions into and out of q in δ. We denote the resulting expression automaton by $A_q = (Q \setminus \{q\}, \Sigma, \delta_q, s, f)$ after the state elimination of q. Thus, we have established the following state elimination result:

Lemma 3. *Let $A = (Q, \Sigma, \delta, s, f)$ be a trim and non-returning expression automaton with at least three states and q be a state in $Q \setminus \{s, f\}$. Define $A_q = (Q \setminus \{q\}, \Sigma, \delta_q, s, f)$ to be a trim and non-returning expression automaton such that, for all pairs p and r of states in $Q \setminus \{q\}$,*

$$\delta_q(p, r) = \delta(p, r) + (\delta(p, q) \cdot \delta(q, q)^* \cdot \delta(q, r)).$$

Then, $L(A_q) = L(A)$ and A_q is trim and non-returning.

The elimination of a state q preserves all the labeled paths from q's predecessors to its successors. Therefore, state elimination does not change the language accepted by the expression automaton A.

To complete the construction of an equivalent regular expression, we repeatedly eliminate one state at a time until $Q = \{s, f\}$. Thus, we are left with a trim and non-returning expression automaton $\bar{A}$, that has exactly two states s and f. Note that $\delta(s, s) = \emptyset$ and $\delta(f, s) = \emptyset$ since $\bar{A}$ is trim and non-

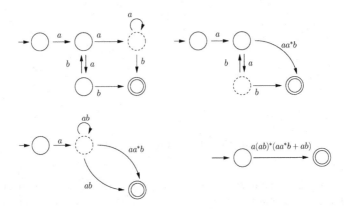

Fig. 2. An expression automaton for the regular language $L(a(ab)^*(aa^*b+ab))$ and its state eliminations

returning. Thus, only the transitions $\delta(s, f)$ and $\delta(f, f)$ can be nontrivial. Hence, $L(\bar{A}) = L(\delta(s, f) \cdot \delta(f, f)^*) = L(A)$. We have established the following result:

Theorem 1. *A language L is an expression automaton language if and only if L is a regular language.*

4   Deterministic Expression Automata

We now define **deterministic expression automata (DEAs)** and investigate their properties. A traditional finite-state automaton is **deterministic** if, for each state, the next state is uniquely determined by the current state and the current input character [12].

For an expression automaton, the situation is not as simple. When processing an input string with a given expression automaton and a given current state, we need to determine not only the next state but also an appropriate prefix of the remaining input string since each of the current state's out-transitions is labeled with a regular expression (or a regular language) instead of with a single character.

An expression automaton is deterministic if and only if, for each state p of the automaton, each two distinct out-transitions have disjoint regular languages and, in addition, each regular language is prefix-free. For example, the out-transition of the expression automaton in Figure 3(a) is not prefix-free, $L(a^*)$ is not prefix-free since a^i is a prefix of a^j, for all i and j such that $1 \le i \le j$; hence, this expression automaton is not deterministic. On the other hand, the expression automaton in Figure 3(b) is deterministic since $L(a^*b)$ is a prefix-free language. We give a formal definition as following.

Definition 4. *An expression automaton $A = (Q, \Sigma, \delta, s, f)$, where $|Q| = m$, is* **deterministic** *if and only if the following three conditions hold:*

(a)   (b)

Fig. 3. a. Example of non-prefix-freeness. b. Example of prefix-freeness

1. **Prefix-freeness:** *For each state $q \in Q$ and for q's out-transitions*

$$(q, \alpha_1, q_1), \ (q, \alpha_2, q_2), \ \ldots, \ (q, \alpha_m, q_m),$$

   $L(\alpha_1) \cup L(\alpha_2) \cup \cdots \cup L(\alpha_m)$ *is a prefix-free regular language.*
2. **Disjointness:** *For each state $q \in Q$ and for all pairs of out-transitions α_i and α_j, where $i \neq j$ and $1 \leq i, \ j \leq m$,*

$$L(\alpha_i) \cap L(\alpha_j) = \emptyset.$$

3. **Non-exiting:** *For all $q \in Q$, $\delta(f, q) = \emptyset$.*

We use the acronym DEA to denote deterministic expression automaton.

Lemma 4. *If a trim DEA $A = (Q, \Sigma, \delta, s, f)$ has at least three states, then, for any state $q \in Q \setminus \{s, f\}$, A_q is deterministic. However the converse does not hold.*

Proof. This result follows from Lemma 3 since the catenation of prefix-free languages is a prefix-free language.

   Therefore, state elimination for a DEA preserves determinism.

Lemma 5. *There exists a trim expression automaton A that is deterministic if and only if $L(A)$ is prefix-free.*

Lemma 5 demonstrates that the regular languages accepted by DEAs are prefix-free and conversely. Thus, DEA languages define a proper subfamily of the regular languages.

Theorem 2. *The family of prefix-free regular languages is closed under catenation and intersection but not under union, complement or star.*

These closure and nonclosure results can be proved straightforwardly.

5   Minimization of DEAs

It is natural to attempt to reduce the size of an automaton as much as possible to save space. There are well-known algorithms to truly minimize DFAs [5, 8] in that they give unique (up to renaming of states) minimal DFAs. Recently, Giammarresi and Montalbano [4] suggested a minimization algorithm for **deterministic generalized automata (DGAs)**. The technique does not however result in a unique minimal DGA. For a given DGA they introduce two operations in their quest for a minimal DGA. The first operation identifies indistinguishable states similar to minimization for DFAs and the second operation applies state elimination to reduce the number of states in a DGA (at the expense of increasing the label lengths of the transitions).

We define the minimization of a DEA as the transformation of a given DEA into a DEA with a smaller number of states. Note that, for all DEAs, we can construct an equivalent simple DEA, which consists of one start and one final states with one transition between them, from any DEA using a sequence of state eliminations.

Given a trim DEA $A = (Q, \Sigma, \delta, s, f)$, we define, for a state $q \in Q$, the **right language** $L_{\overrightarrow{q}}$ to be the set of strings defined by the trim DEA $A_{\overrightarrow{q}} = (Q', \Sigma', \delta', q, f)$, where $Q' \subseteq Q, \Sigma' \subseteq \Sigma, \delta' \subseteq \delta$. Similarly we define the **left language** $L_{\overleftarrow{q}}$ defined by the trim DEA $A_{\overleftarrow{q}} = (Q', \Sigma', \delta', s, q)$, where $Q' \subseteq Q, \Sigma' \subseteq \Sigma, \delta' \subseteq \delta$.

We define two distinct states p and q to be **indistinguishable** if $L_{\overrightarrow{p}} = L_{\overrightarrow{q}}$. We denote this indistinguishability by $p \sim q$. Note that if $p \sim q$, then there must exist a pair of indistinguishable states in the following states in a DFA. However, this property does not always hold for a DEA; see Fig. 4.

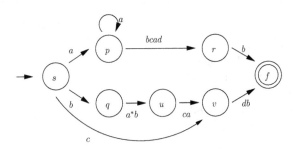

Fig. 4. An example of indistinguishable states. Note that r and u are distinguishable although $p \sim q$

Based on the notion of the right language, we define a minimal DEA as following.

Definition 5. *A trim DEA A is minimal if all states A are distinguishable from each other.*

Thus, we minimize a DEA by merging indistinguishable states. We now explain how to merge two indistinguishable states p and q to give one state p, say. The method is simple, we first remove state q and its out-transitions and

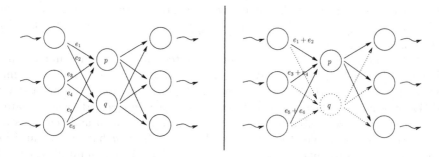

Fig. 5. An example of the merging two indistinguishable states p and q. The dotted lines show the removal of transitions

then redirect its in-transitions into state p. Once we have defined this micro-operation, we can repeat it wherever and whenever we find two indistinguishable states. Since there are only finitely many states, we can guarantee termination and minimality.

Now we need to prove that the micro-operation on $p \sim q$ in A does not change $L(A)$. Observe that since $L_{\overrightarrow{p}} = L_{\overrightarrow{q}}$, we can remove state q and its out-transitions and redirect q's in-transitions to be in-transitions of p. Now, let $L_{\overleftarrow{p}}$ and $L_{\overleftarrow{q}}$ be the left languages of p and q. Observe that redirecting q's in-transitions to be new in-transitions of p implies that the new left language of p is now $L_{\overleftarrow{p}} \cup L_{\overleftarrow{q}}$ whereas before the redirection the left language of p and q are $L_{\overleftarrow{p}}$ and $L_{\overleftarrow{q}}$. Moreover, since $L_{\overrightarrow{p}} = L_{\overrightarrow{q}}$, once q is removed the right

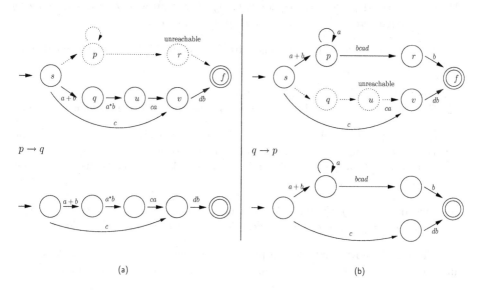

Fig. 6. Two different minimal DEAs for the DEA in Fig. 4

language of p is unchanged. Finally, we catenate the two languages to obtain $(L_{\overleftarrow{p}} \cup L_{\overleftarrow{q}}) \cdot L_{\overrightarrow{p}} = (L_{\overleftarrow{p}} \cdot L_{\overrightarrow{p}}) \cup (L_{\overleftarrow{q}} \cdot L_{\overrightarrow{p}}) = (L_{\overleftarrow{p}} \cdot L_{\overrightarrow{p}}) \cup (L_{\overleftarrow{q}} \cdot L_{\overrightarrow{q}})$, before the removal of q.

Note that, as with DGA, we cannot guarantee that we obtain a unique minimum DEA from a given DEA. We can only guarantee that we obtain a minimal DEA. For example, the automaton in Fig. 4 can be minimized in at least two different ways. As shown in Fig. 6(a), we merge p into q and remove state r which is now unreachable. In Fig. 6(b), we merge q into p and remove state u which is unreachable. But the second state v from q has an in-transition from s, which prevents v from being useless. The two minimizations result in two different minimal expression automata that have the same numbers of states.

6   Prime Prefix-Free Regular Languages

Assume that we have the regular expressions $\alpha_1 = b^*a^*$ and $\alpha_2 = a^*b^*$. Once we catenate them however, $\alpha_1 \cdot \alpha_2 = b^*a^*b^*$ and we have only three stars, b^*, a^* and b^*, instead of four stars. Prefix-freeness ensures that there is no such loss as a result of catenation. Similarly, any infinite regular language, can be split unboundedly often. For example, $L(a^*) = L(a^*) \cdot L(a^*) \cdot L(a^*) \cdots L(a^*)$.

These two examples have led us to investigate whether an unbounded split is possible for an infinite prefix-free regular language. There are some known results on the prime decomposition of finite languages and decomposition of regular languages [7, 10].

Definition 6. *A prefix-free regular language L is* **prime** *if $L \neq L_1 \cdot L_2$ for any two non-trivial prefix-free regular languages L_1 and L_2.*

We say a state b in a DFA A is a **bridge state** if the following conditions hold:

1. b is neither a start nor a final state.
2. For any string $w \in L(A)$, its path in A must pass through b at least once.

Then we partition A at b into two subautomata A_1 and A_2 such that all out-transitions from b belong to A_2 and make b to be the final state of A_1 and the start state of A_2, respectively. It ensures that A_1 defines a prefix-free regular language.

Theorem 3. *A prefix-free regular language L is a prime prefix-free regular language if and only if there is no bridge state in the minimal DFA A for L.*

Theorem 3 shows that a given prefix-free regular language L cannot be split unboundedly often because its minimal DFA has a finite number of states.

7   Conclusion

State elimination is a natural way to compute a regular expression from a given automaton that results in an automaton that we call an expression automaton. We have formally defined expression automata and DEAs based on the notion of prefix-freeness. In addition, we have shown that DEA languages are prefix-free regular languages and, therefore, they are a proper subfamily of regular languages.

We have studied the minimization of DEA and demonstrated that minimization is not unique in general. Since the regular expression equivalence problem is PSPACE-complete [11], we believe that the complexity of minimization is at least PSPACE-complete.

Acknowledgments

We are deeply grateful to Byron Choi for his helpful comments and hearty encouragement. We appreciate Wojciech Fraczak for providing an example to solidify the definition of bridge states in Section 6. We also discovered that the prime prefix-free regular language decomposition has been studied already by Czyzowicz et al. [2] while preparing the final version of this paper for the proceedings.

The authors were supported under the Research Grants Council Competitive Earmarked Research Grant HKUST6197/01E.

References

1. J. Brzozowski and E. McCluskey, Jr. Signal flow graph techniques for sequential circuit state diagrams. *IEEE Transactions on Electronic Computers*, EC-12:67–76, 1963.
2. J. Czyzowicz, W. Fraczak, A. Pelc, and W. Rytter. Linear-time prime decomposition of regular prefix codes. *International Journal of Foundations of Computer Science*, 14:1019–1032, 2003.
3. S. Eilenberg. *Automata, Languages, and Machines*, volume A. Academic Press, New York, NY, 1974.
4. D. Giammarresi and R. Montalbano. Deterministic generalized automata. *Theoretical Comput. Sci.*, 215:191–208, 1999.
5. J. Hopcroft. An $n \log n$ algorithm for minimizing the states in a finite automaton. In Z. Kohavi and A. Paz, editors, *Theory of Machines and Computations*, pages 189–196, New York, NY, 1971. Academic Press.
6. J. Hopcroft and J. Ullman. *Introduction to Automata Theory, Languages, and Computation*. Addison-Wesley, Reading, MA, 2 edition, 1979.
7. A. Mateescu, A. Salomaa, and S. Yu. Factorizations of languages and commutativity conditions. *Acta Cybernetica*, 15(3):339–351, 2002.
8. E. Moore. Gedanken experiments on sequential machines. In C. Shannon and J. McCarthy, editors, *Automata Studies*, pages 129–153, Princeton, NJ, 1956. Princeton University Press.

9. D. Perrin. Finite automata. In J. van Leeuwen, editor, *Formal Models and Semantics*, volume B of *Handbook of Theoretical Computer Science*, pages 1–57. The MIT Press, Cambridge, MA, 1990.

10. A. Salomaa and S. Yu. On the decomposition of finite languages. In G. Rozenberg and W. Thomas, editors, *Developments in Language Theory (DLT) 99*, pages 22–31. World Scientific, 2000.

11. L. Stockmeyer and A. Meyer. Word problems requiring exponential time. In *Proceedings of the Fifth Annual ACM Symposium on Theory of Computing*, pages 1–9, 1973.

12. D. Wood. *Theory of Computation*. John Wiley & Sons, Inc., New York, NY, 1987.

An Automata Approach to Match Gapped Sequence Tags Against Protein Database

Yonghua Han, Bin Ma, and Kaizhong Zhang

Department of Computer Science, University of Western Ontario,
London Ontario, N6A 5B7 Canada
{yhan2, bma, kzhang}@csd.uwo.ca

Abstract. Tandem mass spectrometry (MS/MS) is the most important method for the peptide and protein identification. One approach to interpret the MS/MS data is *de novo* sequencing, which is becoming more and more accurate and important. However *De novo* sequencing usually can only confidently determine partial sequences, while the undetermined parts are represented by "mass gaps". We call such a partially determined sequence a *gapped sequence tag*. When a gapped sequence tag is searched in a database for protein identification, the determined parts should match the database sequence exactly, while each mass gap should match a substring of amino acids whose masses total up to the value of the mass gap. In such a case, the standard string matching algorithm does not work any more. In this paper, we present a new efficient algorithm to find the matches of gapped sequence tags in a protein database.

1   Introduction

Proteins are essential to life, playing key roles in all biological processes. For example, enzymes that catalyze reactions are proteins and antibodies in an immune response are proteins. One of the first steps in understanding proteins is protein identification. Protein identification is to identify the primary structure of a protein, which is a chain of amino acids. There are 20 different amino acids, and therefore, the primary structure of a protein can be represented as a string over an alphabet of size 20. Protein identification is a fundamental problem in Proteomics. Nowadays, tandem mass spectrometry (MS/MS) is becoming the most important and standard technology for this importance protein identification problem [1]. In the current practice of protein identification using MS/MS, purified proteins are digested into short peptides with enzymes like trypsin. Then, tandem mass spectra are measured for the peptides with a tandem mass spectrometer. Fig. 1 shows an example of MS/MS spectrum. A peak in the MS/MS spectrum indicates the mass-to-charge ratio (m/z) of the type of ions that produce the peak, and the intensity of the peak indicates the number of the same type of ions detected. Finally the MS/MS spectra are interpreted by computer software to identify the amino acid sequences of the peptides and proteins.

Many algorithms have been developed and applied in software to interpret the MS/MS data. They can be grouped into two major approaches. The first

M. Domaratzki et al. (Eds.): CIAA 2004, LNCS 3317, pp. 167–177, 2005.

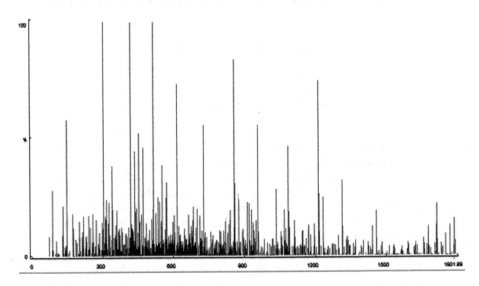

Fig. 1. An MS/MS spectrum

approach correlates MS/MS spectra with peptides in a protein database to find the best matches [10, 18, 19, 25]. We call this approach database search approach. Among the many software programs developed using this approach, Mascot [10] and Sequest [18] are the two most well-known programs.

The other approach is *de novo* sequencing [6, 8, 9, 11, 12, 13, 15, 20, 23, 24], which produces amino acid sequences of the peptides from the MS/MS data directly without the help of the protein database. *De novo* sequencing software often uses the mass difference between the peaks in an MS/MS spectrum to determine the amino acids of the peptide. Because the MS/MS spectra are always not perfect due to the impure sample, incomplete fragmentation and other factors in the MS/MS experiments, the mass difference between two peaks in an MS/MS spectrum may not indicate the mass of only one amino acid. Instead, it may be the sum of the mass of several amino acids. In this case, there can be several combinations of amino acids have the same mass. For example, mass(EE) = mass(GSN) = 258.1 Dalton. Even some single amino acids also have this kind of ambiguous mass, like mass(L) = mass(I) and mass(N) = mass(GG).

As a result, most *de novo* sequencing software cannot determine these ambiguous masses, therefore outputs erroneous results. We call this type of error same mass segments replacement, i.e., one segment of amino acids has the similar mass to another segment. There are some *de novo* sequencing software available, such as commercial software PEAKS [14] and free software Lutefisk [23, 24]. Both PEAKS and Lutefisk have their own mechanisms to reduce the effects of these errors. Lutefisk outputs a mass gap when it cannot confidently determine the sequence that fills the gap. One example output is

[258.1]TLMEYLE[114.0]PK,

where the mass gaps [258.1] and [114.0] represent two short segments of amino acids whose masses add up to 258.1 and 114.0 Dalton, respectively. We call such a sequence tag the *gapped sequence tag*.

A possible match of such a tag in the database is EETLMEYLENPK, as follows:

```
Tag:    [258.1]TLMEYLE[114.0]PK
Match:  [EE    ]TLMEYLE[N    ]PK,
```

where mass(EE) = 258.1 and mass(N)=114.0.

PEAKS uses different colors to represent different confidences on different amino acids in a sequence. PEAKS version 1.x outputs the low confidence level (< 80%) amino acids with black color, compared to the other colors (red, green, blue) for higher confidences (95%-100%, 90%-95%, 80-90%) [14]. [1] Here we use brackets for the low confidence level parts. For example, the output [GSN]TLMEYLE[GG]PK indicates that PEAKS is not confident at the two segments GSN and GG. Clearly, this [GSN]TLMEYLE[GG]PK can be converted to Lutefisk's output format by replacing GSN with the mass gap [258.1] and GG with [114.0].

The determined parts of sequence tags produced by Lutefisk and high confident parts of PEAKS are very likely the correct sequences. Therefore, when the gapped sequence tag is searched in a database, we require the determined parts to match exactly. However, the mass gaps should be matched by substrings whose total masses equal to the mass gaps.

2   Related Work

Software programs have been developed for the purpose of searching sequence tags in the database to identify peptides and proteins. MS-BLAST [22] uses a BLAST-like algorithm [4,5], which first finds a seed in the database, and then extends around the seed attempting to find a match. MS-BLAST can find approximate matches using a homology model. However, MS-BLAST does not accept inputs with mass gaps. When mass gaps are present in a query, MS-BLAST requires the user to find all possible exact matches of the tag, and then it uses all those possibilities as query and searches them all together simultaneously. This may create too many possible exact matches when there are very long mass gaps.

Another software program, OpenSea [21], considers the mass gaps and other *de novo* sequencing errors. But the mass gaps can only be matched by substrings with up to 3 amino acids. Therefore OpenSea does not work for long mass gaps either.

In this paper, we present our approach to match gapped sequence tags against database sequences. Our approach separates the query sequence tags into segments by mass gaps. A segment is a short run of amino acid sequence. We modify

---

[1] The color scheme has been changed slightly in later versions of the software.

Aho-Corasick automaton to find the exact matches of those segments, and a neat algorithm is used to assemble the exact matches together to get the match of the whole gapped sequence tag. We note that a straightforward assembly will not result into a linear running time as our algorithm does.

3   An Algorithm to Match Sequence Tags

In this section, we first describe our algorithm to match one gapped sequence tag against the protein database. Then by slightly modifications, we extend it to simultaneously match multiple gapped sequence tags against the database.

3.1   Problem Definition

In this section we define our problem more formally. Let Σ be an alphabet of constant size. Each letter a in Σ is associated with a mass $m(a)$. Let $s = s[1]s[2]\ldots s[k]$ be a string. $|s| = k$ denotes the length of the string, and $m(s) = \sum_{i=1}^{|s|} m(s[i])$.

A gapped sequence tag P is represented by m substrings, $p_1, p_2, \ldots, p_m$, and $m - 1$ mass gaps, $M_1, M_2, \ldots, M_{m-1}$. We want to find all the strings s in the database, such that, $s = p_1 q_1 p_2 \ldots q_{m-1} p_m$, and $m(q_j) = M_j$ for $j = 1, 2, \ldots, m - 1$. We use the notation $|P|$ to denote the total length of the m substrings, $p_1, p_2, \ldots,$ and p_m.

It is possible that a mass gap is at the beginning of or the end of a gapped tag. In such a case, we simply let p_1 or p_m to be null string that matches every position of the database.

Our idea is to use the standard algorithm for multiple string matching to find every occurrence of every substring p_i; and carefully assemble the occurrences together to get the match of the whole gapped sequence tag. The difficulty is that q_j can have variable lengths. However, as later shown in the paper, the constraint $m(q_j) = M_j$ allows us to do the assembly efficiently.

In the following section, we first briefly review the Aho-Corasick algorithm for multiple string matching.

3.2   Aho-Corasick Algorithm

As the extension of Knuth-Morris-Pratt algorithm [16], the Aho-Corasick algorithm is a widely used algorithm that finds all occurrences of multiple patterns in a text using an automaton in linear time. This algorithm serves as the basis for the UNIX tool fgrep, and has many applications in bioinformatics. For example, the Tandem Repeat Occurrence Locator (TROLL) [2] is an application developed on the basis of Aho-Corasick algorithm to find tandem repeats of pre-selected motifs from DNA sequence. Another application called CHAOS [7] using an algorithm including a simplified version of the Aho-Corasick algorithm to find local alignments, which are used as anchor points to improve the running time of DIALIGN [17], a slow but sensitive multiple-alignment tool.

An Aho-Corasick automaton can be constructed by the following two steps: firstly, construct a trie and goto functions from the multiple patterns to be searched. The goto function maps a pair (s, α), where s is a state and α is an input symbol, into a state or the message fail. Secondly, add failure and output functions. The failure function $f(s)$ maps a state into another state s'. $L(s')$ is the longest proper suffix of $L(s)$ such that $L(s)$ is a prefix of some pattern. An output function $out(s)$ gives the set of patterns matched when entering state s. The time complexity of the construction of Aho-Corasick automaton is linearly proportional to the total length of the patterns. The searching time is linear to the text size, and the $out(s)$ function will take $O(z)$ time, where z is the total number of occurrences of all the patterns. The details of constructing such an automaton and proof of time complexity can be found in [3].

However, the Aho-Corasick algorithm or its variances cannot apply to our problem directly. We need to modify it to allow mass gaps between matched segments.

3.3   Our Algorithm

The alphabet set Σ is 20 amino acid letters. We construct an extended Aho-Corasick automaton such that each state has 20 transitions according the segments in the sequence tag P. This automaton is a deterministic finite automaton, which contains five elements: $(Q, \Sigma, \sigma, q_0, F)$. Q is the set of states. Σ is an input alphabet, i.e., 20 amino acid letters. σ is a transition function: $\sigma : Q \times \Sigma \rightarrow Q$. q_0 is the start state, $q_0 \in Q$. The automaton is in the start state before the run of each protein sequence in the database. F is a set of final states, $F \in Q$. Each segment in the sequence tag will produce a final state while constructing the extended Aho-Corasick automaton. Entering a final state, the automaton will output matched position in the protein sequence and the number of segment in the sequence tag.

There are two special pair of amino acids (I,L) and (K,Q). I and L have the same mass, and K and Q have very similar mass. In most case, it is desired that they are not considered to be mismatch. So we have an option that make I and L have the same transition, K and Q have the same transition in each state according the passed parameters when constructing the automaton. For each protein sequence in the database, we will run this modified Aho-Corasick automaton to find all the segment matches of the sequence tag P.

When a segment match is found, it is attempted to assemble with other segment matches. For the joint of two adjacent segments, we need to compute the mass of the substring between the two occurrences of the two segments. Let T be the database string. Given any two positions i and j, it is possible to compute the total mass of substring $T[i..j]$ in $O(1)$ time by building a accumulated protein mass table while we read each amino acid from the database. Let $acm[i]$ be $m(T[1..i])$. Then $m(T[i..j]) = acm[j] - acm[i-1]$.

However, if we straightforwardly compute the mass value between every occurrence of segment p_i and segment p_{i+1}, the running time will be quadratic. Also, because a gap can be filled by substrings of variable lengths, a linear time algorithm cannot be achieved by trying every possible length of the substring.

The Segments Assembly Procedure. We use a set of queues $\{q_1, q_2, \ldots q_m\}$ to keep the matches that can be potentially parts of a whole tag match and discard the matches that do not have such a potential. Each q_i corresponds to the ith segment, p_i, of the gapped sequence tag. For the segment match of the first segment, p_1, we simply add the match to q_1. However, if p_i is matched at database position k for $i > 1$, before we add k to the queue q_i, we check whether there is a match of p_{i-1}, such that the two matches have a mass gap equal to M_{i-1} in between. This can be done by checking the queue q_{i-1}. Let k' be the first element in q_{i-1}. Let $M = m(T[(k' + |p_{i-1}|)..k])$, the mass gap between $k' + |p_{i-1}|$ and k.

There are three cases:

Case 1: $M < M_{i-1}$.
This means the occurrence of p_i at k cannot be joined with the occurrence of p_{i-1} at k'. Moreover, the former cannot be joined with any occurrences of p_{i-1} after k', because we use first-in-first-out queues. Therefore, we can safely discard k.

Case 2: $M > M_{i-1}$.
This means the occurrence of p_i at k cannot be joined with the occurrence of p_{i-1} at k'. Moreover, the latter cannot be joined with any occurrences of p_i after k, because we use first-in-first-out queues. Therefore, we can safely delete the occurrence of p_{i-1} at k' and continue to consider the next element in q_{i-1}.

Case 3: $M = M_{i-1}$.
This means the occurrence of p_i at k can be joined with the occurrence of p_{i-1} at k'. But the latter cannot be joined with any occurrences of p_i after k, because that will make the gap too large. Therefore, we can safely delete k' from q_{i-1} but add k to q_i.

Let i be the segment that matches the current database position k. Let $acm[k]$ be the accumulated mass of the database. Then our assembly process for this match is shown in Figure 2.

Lemma 1. *For any position k in q_i, there is a substring $T[j..k + |p_i|]$, such that $T[j..k + |p_i|]$ matches $p_1 M_1 ... p_{i-1} M_{i-1} p_i$. On the other hand, for every substring $T[j..k + |p_i|]$ that matches $p_1 M_1 ... p_{i-1} M_{i-1} p_i$, k is added into q_i once.*

Proof. We prove by induction on i. Obviously the lemma is true for $i = 1$ because of line 2 of Algorithm Assembly. Now suppose the lemma is true for $i = i_0$. We want to prove it is true for $i = i_0 + 1$.

When k is added into q_i in line 13, we know that k' was in q_{i-1}. By induction, we know that there is j such that $T[j..k' + |p_{i-1}|]$ matches $p_1 M_1 ... p_{i-1}$. Also we know by line 11 that the mass gap between the occurrence of p_{i-1} at k' and the occurrence of p_i at k is equal to M_{i-1}. Therefore, $T[j..k + |p_i|]$ matches $p_1 M_1 ... p_{i-1} M_{i-1} p_i$.

On the other hand, if k is such that $T[j..k + |p_i|]$ matches $p_1 M_1 ... p_{i-1} M_{i-1} p_i$, there must be k' that $T[j..k' + |p_{i-1}|]$ matches $p_1 M_1 ... p_{i-1}$. By induction, k' is added into q_{i-1}, and it is removed only when k was added into q_i in line 13.

Algorithm Assembly(i, k)
1   **if** $i = 1$
2   add k to q_1
3   **else**
4   **while** q_{i-1} is not empty **do**
5           $k' \leftarrow$ the first element of q_{i-1}
6   massDiff $\leftarrow (acm[k] - acm[k' + |p_{i-1}|])$
7   **if** massDiff $< M_{i-1}$
8   **break;**
9   **else if** massDiff $> M_{i-1}$
10   delete k' from q_{i-1}
11   **else**
12   delete k' from q_{i-1}
13   append k to q_i
14   **break;**
15   **if** q_m is not empty
16   output k as a match of the whole tag

Fig. 2. The procedure is called whenever the ith segment, p_i, is matched at the database position k. In the algorithm, $acm[k]$ is the accumulated mass of the database. q_i is a first-in-first-out queue

Lemma 2. *The Assembly procedure will be called $O(z)$ time, where z is the total number of occurrences of the segments in the database. The total time that the Assembly procedure takes is also $O(z)$.*

Proof. Because we only call the Assembly procedure whenever we find a match of a segment, the procedure is called $O(z)$ time.

Lines $1 - 2$ and $15 - 16$ of the Assembly procedure will take $O(1)$ time for each invocation of the procedure. And lines $5 - 14$ will take $O(1)$ time for each iteration of the while loop. Therefore, we only need to prove that the while loop is repeated $O(z)$ time in total.

We note that there is one element deleted from the queues every time the while loop is repeated, or the while will break in line 14. And we add at most one element into the queue when a match of a segment is found. Therefore, at most z elements will be added to the queues, and the total time of deletions can be at most z. Therefore, the while loop is repeated in total $O(z)$ time.

Theorem 1. *By using the automaton described above and calling the Assembly procedure whenever a segment match is found, all the matches of a gapped sequence tag can be found in $O(n + |P| + z)$ time, where n is the database size, $|P|$ is the total length of the segments in the queries, and z is the number of occurrences of the segments in the database.*

Proof. The correctness directly follows Lemma 1. For the time complexity, there are three main parts. First, constructing of the extended-AC automaton will take $O(|P|)$ time. Secondly, running the automaton against each amino acid letter in the protein database will take $O(n)$ time. Thirdly, assembling segments when a segment match is found in the database. From Lemma 2, the Assembly procedure will take $O(z)$ time in total.

Multiple Sequence Tags Match. The algorithm discussed above matches a mass gapped sequence tag against the database. It can be modified to adapt to multiple sequence tags. As mentioned in the first section of this paper, in an MS/MS experiment, a protein is digested into many peptides and each peptide will produce a corresponding MS/MS spectrum. The advantage of using multiple sequences is clear: even if some of the sequence tags produced by de novo sequencing software are wrong, the correct and partially correct sequence tags can still provide enough information to identify the protein. To adapt to multiple sequence tags, we need to the following modifications on our previous algorithm:

1. First, let the automaton include all the segments from all the sequence tags. That is, let $\mathcal{P} = \{P_1, P_2, \ldots, P_K\}$ be the set of input query sequence tags from *de novo* sequencing software. Then we include all the segments of all the P_i in the construction of the extended Aho-Corasick automaton. For example, if the query $\mathcal{P}$ contains three sequence tags: HGTVVLTALG[170.10]LK, [184.12]ELFR and [276.14]EFLSD[184.12]LHVLHSK. The automaton is constructed to search the sequence segments {HGTVVLTALG, LK, ELFR, EFLSD, LHVLFSK}.

2. The second modification is output function of the extended AC automaton. We have to modify the output to include the information of which sequence

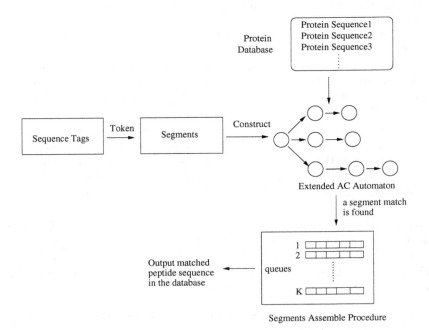

Fig. 3. The process overview of matching gapped sequence tags against a database

tag in the query and which segment in this sequence tag is matched as well as the segment match location in a protein sequence.

3. Third modification is about the queues implemented in segments assembly procedure. Instead of using one set of queues, we need K sets of queues. That is, $q_{i,j}$ corresponds to the jth segment of P_i. And whenever the jth segment of P_i is matched in the database position k, $q_{i,j-1}$ will be checked to determine whether k is inserted to $q_{i,j}$.

The rest of algorithm stays the same as before. It is easy to see the time complexity of matching multiple sequence tags is $O(n + |\mathcal{P}| + z)$, where $|\mathcal{P}|$ is the total length of the sequence segments in all $P_i \in \mathcal{P}$. The process is illustrated in Figure 3.

4   Experiments

We have implemented our algorithm into a Java program. We computed the *de novo* sequencing results of 54 Q-Tof MS/MS spectra, using PEAKS and Lutefisk, respectively. The 54 MS/MS spectra were obtained from the paper [14] of Ma *et al* and can be found at www.csd.uwo.ca/~bma/peaks. Both PEAKS and Lutefisk output some sequence tags completely correct and some sequences only partially correct. For example, PEAKS output [NGG]PVPKPK and Lutefisk output [228.11]PVPKPK while the correct peptide sequence is DIPVPKPK. The brackets in the PEAKS output indicates low confident level (lower than %80). We submitted each of the sequences to our program to search in Swiss-Prot protein database and examined whether the first match output by our program is the correct sequence. Lutefisk only outputs gapped sequence tags when it is not confident to some amino acids. PEAKS' output is also converted to gapped sequence tags by using the method discussed in the introduction.

Table 1 show the difference on the numbers (ratios) of correctly computed sequences before and after using our program on the two sets of data.

Table 1. A comparison of peptide identification before and after using our program

	PEAKS	Lutefisk
Before our program	22 (41%)	11 (20%)
After our program	36 (67%)	23 (42%)

A more interesting use of our program is protein identification with multiple sequence tags. The *de novo* sequencing results of the spectra for the same protein can be submitted to our programm together. The 26 spectra we used are in four groups, each for one of the four proteins, beta casein (bovine), myoglobin (horse), albumin (bovine), and cytochrome C (horse). By submitting each group of PEAKS (or Lutefisks) *de novo* sequencing results to our program, all of the four proteins can be correctly identified. The organisms of the proteins can also be identified except that beta casein (bovine) obtained the same score as beta casein (water buffalo). The reason is that the two proteins differ at only three amino acids, which are not covered by the peptides of the MS/MS spectra.

References

1. Aebersold, R.; Mann, M. "Mass spectrometry-based proteomics", *Nature* **2003, 422**, 198-207.
2. Adalberto T Castelo, Wellington Martins, Guang R. Gao, "TROLL-Tandem Repeat Occurrence Locator", *Bioinformatics* **2002, 18**:634-636.
3. Aho, V.A.; Corasick, J.M. "Efficient string matching: An aid to bibliographic search", *Communications of the ACM* **1975 18(6)**:333-340.
4. Altschul S.F. *et al.* "Basic local alignment search tool", *J. Mol. Biol.* **1990, 215**, 403-410.
5. Altschul, S.F. at. al. "Gapped BLAST and PSI-BLAST: a new generation of protein database search programs", *Nucleic Acids Res.* **1997, 25**, 3389-3402.
6. Bartels, C. "Fast algorithm for peptide sequencing by mass spectroscopy", *Biomed. Environ. Mass Spectrom.* **1990, 19**, 363-368.
7. Brudno, M. *et at.* "Fast and sensitive multiple alignment of large genomic sequences" *BMC Bioinformatics* **2003** 4:66.
8. Chen, T. *et al.* "A dynamic programming approach to *de novo* peptide sequencing via tandem mass spectrometry", *J. Comp. Biology* **2001, 8(3)**, 325-337.
9. Dančík, V. *et al.* "*De novo* protein sequencing via tandem mass-spectrometry", *J. Comp. Biology* **1999, 6**, 327-341.
10. Eng, J.K.; McCormack, A.L.; Yates, J.R. "An approach to correlate tandem mass spectral data of peptides with amino acid sequences in a protein database", *J. Am. Soc. Mass Spectrom.* **1994, 5**, 976-989.
11. Fernández-de-Cossio, J. at. al. "Automated interpretation of high-energy collision-induced dissociation spectra of singly-protonated peptides by "SeqMS", a software aid for *de novo* sequencing by MS/MS", *Rapid Commun. Mass Spectrom.* **1998, 12**, 1867-1878.
12. Hines, W.M. *et al.* "Pattern-based algorithm for peptide sequencing from tandem high energy collision-induced dissociation mass spectra", *J. Am. Sco. Mass. Spectrom.* **1992, 3**, 326-336.
13. Ma, B.; Tromp, J.; Li M. "PatternHunter: faster and more sensitive homology search", *Bioinformatics* **2002, 18(3)**, 440-445.
14. Ma B. *et al.* "PEAKS: powerful software for peptide *de novo* sequencing by MS/MS", *Commun. Mass Spectrom.* **2003, 17(20)**, 2337-2342.
15. Ma, B.; Zhang, K.; Liang C. "An effective algorithm for the peptide *de novo* sequencing from MS/MS spectrum", *CPM'03*, **2003**, 266-278.
16. Morris, J.H.; Pratt. V.P. "A linear pattern-matching algorithm" 1970 Report 40, University of California, Berkeley.
17. Morgenstern B "DIALIGN 2: improvement of the segment-tosegment approach to multiple sequence alignment" *Bioinformatics* **1999, 15**:211-218.
18. Perkins, D.N. *et al.* "Probability-based protein identification by searching sequence database using mass spectrometry data", *Electrophoresis* **1999, 20**, 3551-3567.
19. Pevzner, P.A.; Dančík, V.; Tang, C. "Mutation tolerant protein identification by mass spectrometry", *J. Comp. Biology* **2000, 6**, 777-787.
20. Sakurai, T. *et al.* "Paas3: A computer program to determine probable sequence of peptides from mass spectrometric data" *Biomed. Mass spectrum.* **1984, 11(8)**, 396-399.

21. Searle, B.C. *et al.* "High-throughput identification of proteins and unanticipated sequence modifications using a mass-based alignment algorithm for MS/MS *de Novo* sequencing results", to appear in *Anal. Chem.*.

22. Shevchenko, A. *et al.* "Charting the proteomes of organisms with unsequenced genomes by MALDI-quadrupole time-of-flight mass spectrometry and BLAST homology searching", *Anal Chem.* **2001, 73(9)**, 1917-26

23. Taylor, J.A.; Johnson, R.S. "Sequence database searches via *de novo* peptide sequencing by tandem mass spectrometry", *Rapid Commun. Mass Spectrom.* **1997, 11**, 1067-1075.

24. Taylor, J.A.; Johnson, RS. "Implementation and uses of automated *de novo* peptide sequencing by tandem mass spectrometry", *Anal. Chem.* **2001, 73**, 2594 - 2604.

25. Yates, J.R.I. *et al.* "Method to correlate tandem mass spectra of modified peptides to amino acid sequences in the protein database", *Anal. Chem.* **1995, 67**, 1426-36.

State Complexity of Concatenation and Complementation of Regular Languages

Jozef Jirásek[1], Galina Jirásková[2,*], and Alexander Szabari[1,2]

[1] Institute of Computer Science, P.J. Šafárik University,
Jesenná 5, 040 01 Košice, Slovakia
{jirasek, szabari}@science.upjs.sk
[2] Mathematical Institute, Slovak Academy of Sciences,
Grešákova 6, 040 01 Košice, Slovakia
jiraskov@saske.sk

Abstract. We investigate the state complexity of concatenation and the nondeterministic state complexity of complementation of regular languages. We show that the upper bounds on the state complexity of concatenation are also tight in the case that the first automaton has more than one accepting state. In the case of nondeterministic state complexity of complementation, we show that the entire range of complexities, up to the known upper bound can be produced.

1 Introduction

Finite automata are one of the simplest computational models. Despite their simplicity, some challenging problems concerning finite automata are still open. For instance, we recall the question of how many states are sufficient and necessary for two-way deterministic finite automata to simulate two-way nondeterministic finite automata. The importance of this problem is underlined by its relation to the well-known open question whether or not DLOGSPACE equals NLOGSPACE [23].

Recently, a renewed interest in regular languages and finite automata can be observed. For a discussion, the reader may refer to [13, 27]. Some aspects of this area are now intensively investigated. One such aspect is the state complexity of regular languages and their operations.

The state complexity of a regular language is the number of states of its minimal deterministic finite automaton (DFA). The nondeterministic state complexity of a regular language is the number of states of a minimum state nondeterministic finite automaton (NFA) accepting the language. The state complexity (the nondeterministic state complexity) of an operation on regular languages represented by DFAs (NFAs, respectively) is the number of states that are sufficient and necessary in the worst case for a DFA (an NFA, respectively) to accept the language resulting from the operation.

---

* Research supported by the VEGA grant No. 2/3164/23.

M. Domaratzki et al. (Eds.): CIAA 2004, LNCS 3317, pp. 178–189, 2005.

The state complexity of some operations on regular languages was investigated in [17, 1, 2]. Yu, Zhuang, and Salomaa [25] were the first to systematically study the complexity of regular language operations. Their paper was followed by several articles investigating the state complexity of finite language operations and unary language operations [3, 20, 21]. The nondeterministic state complexity of regular language operations was studied by Holzer and Kutrib in [9, 10, 11]. Further results on this topic are presented in [6, 4, 16] and state-of-the-art surveys for DFAs can be found in [29, 28].

In this paper, we investigate the state complexity of concatenation and the nondeterministic state complexity of complementation of regular languages. In the case of concatenation, we show that the upper bounds $m2^n - k2^{n-1}$ on the concatenation of an m-state DFA language and an n-state DFA language, where k is the number of accepting states in the m-state automaton, are tight for any integer k with $0 < k < m$. In the case of complementation, we show that for any positive integers n and m with $\log n \leq m \leq 2^n$, there is an n-state NFA language such that minimal NFAs for its complement have m states.

To prove the result on concatenation we show that a deterministic finite automaton is minimal. To obtain the result on complementation we use a fooling-set lower-bound technique known from communication complexity theory [12], cf. also [1, 2, 7].

The paper consists of five sections, including this introduction. The next section contains basic definitions and notations used throughout the paper. In Section 3 we present our result on concatenation. Section 4 deals with the problem of which kind of relations between the sizes of minimal NFAs for regular languages and minimal NFAs for their complements are possible. The last section contains some concluding remarks and open problems.

2   Preliminaries

In this section, we recall some basic definitions and notations. For further details, the reader may refer to [24, 26].

Let Σ be an alphabet and Σ^* the set of all strings over the alphabet Σ including the empty string ε. The power-set of a finite set A is denoted by 2^A and its maximum by $\max A$.

A *deterministic finite automaton* (DFA) is a 5-tuple $M = (Q, \Sigma, \delta, q_0, F)$, where Q is a finite set of states, Σ is a finite input alphabet, $\delta : Q \times \Sigma \to Q$ is the transition function, $q_0 \in Q$ is the initial state, and $F \subseteq Q$ is the set of accepting states. In this paper, all DFAs are assumed to be complete, i.e., the next state $\delta(q, a)$ is defined for any state q in Q and any symbol a in Σ. The transition function δ is extended to a function from $Q \times \Sigma^*$ to Q in the natural way. A string w in Σ^* is accepted by the DFA M if the state $\delta(q_0, w)$ is an accepting state of the DFA M.

A *nondeterministic finite automaton* (NFA) is a 5-tuple $M = (Q, \Sigma, \delta, q_0, F)$, where Q, Σ, q_0, and F are as above, and $\delta : Q \times \Sigma \to 2^Q$ is the transition function which can be naturally extended to the domain $Q \times \Sigma^*$. A string w in Σ^* is accepted by the NFA M if the set $\delta(q_0, w)$ contains an accepting state of the NFA M.

The *language accepted by* a finite automaton M, denoted $L(M)$, is the set of all strings accepted by the automaton M. Two automata are said to be *equivalent* if they accept the same language.

A DFA (an NFA) M is called *minimal* if all DFAs (all NFAs, respectively) that are equivalent to M have at least as many states as M. By a well-known result, each regular language has a unique minimal DFA, up to isomorphism. However, the same result does not hold for minimal NFAs.

Any nondeterministic finite automaton $M = (Q, \Sigma, \delta, q_0, F)$ can be converted to an equivalent deterministic finite automaton $M' = (2^Q, \Sigma, \delta', q_0', F')$ using an algorithm known as the "subset construction" [22] in the following way. Every state of the DFA M' is a subset of the state set Q. The initial state of the DFA M' is $\{q_0\}$. A state R in 2^Q is an accepting state of the DFA M' if it contains an accepting state of the NFA M. The transition function δ' is defined by $\delta'(R, a) = \bigcup_{r \in R} \delta(r, a)$ for any state R in 2^Q and any symbol a in Σ. The DFA M' need not be minimal since some of its states may be unreachable or equivalent.

3   Concatenation

We start our investigation with concatenation operation. The state complexity of concatenation of regular languages represented by deterministic finite automata was studied by Yu *et al.* [25]. They showed that $m2^n - k2^{n-1}$ states are sufficient for a DFA to accept the concatenation of an m-state DFA language and an n-state DFA language, where k is the number of the accepting states in the m-state DFA. In the case of $n = 1$, upper bound m was shown to be tight, even for a unary alphabet. In the case of $m = 1$ and $n \geq 2$, the worst case $2^n - 2^{n-1}$ was given by the concatenation of two binary languages. Otherwise, the upper bound $m2^n - 2^{n-1}$ was shown to be tight for a binary alphabet in [16]. In the case of unary languages, the upper bound on concatenation is mn and it is known to be tight if m and n are relatively prime [25]. The unary case when m and n are not necessarily relatively prime was studied by Pighizzini and Shallit in [20, 21]. In this case, the tight bounds are given by the number of states in the noncyclic and in the cyclic parts of the resulting automata. The next theorem shows that the upper bounds $m2^n - k2^{n-1}$ are also tight for any integer k with $0 < k < m$.

Theorem 1. *For any integers m, n, k such that $m \geq 2, n \geq 2$, and $0 < k < m$, there exist a DFA A of m states and k accepting states, and a DFA B of n states such that any DFA accepting the language $L(A)L(B)$ needs at least $m2^n - k2^{n-1}$ states.*

Proof. Let m, n, and k be arbitrary but fixed integers such that $m \geq 2, n \geq 2$, and $0 < k < m$. Let $\Sigma = \{a, b, c\}$.

Define an m-state DFA $A = (Q_A, \Sigma, \delta_A, q_0, F_A)$, where $Q_A = \{q_0, q_1, \ldots, q_{m-1}\}$, $F_A = \{q_{m-k}, q_{m-k+1}, \ldots, q_{m-1}\}$, and for any $i \in \{0, 1, \ldots, m-1\}$,

$$\delta_A(q_i, X) = \begin{cases} q_{i+1}, & \text{if } i < m - k \text{ and } X = a, \\ q_0, & \text{if } i \geq m - k \text{ and } X = a, \\ q_i, & \text{if } X = b, \\ q_{m-1}, & \text{if } i = 0 \text{ and } X = c, \\ q_{i-1}, & \text{if } i > 0 \text{ and } X = c. \end{cases}$$

Define an n-state DFA $B = (Q_B, \Sigma, \delta_B, 0, F_B)$, where $Q_B = \{0, 1, \ldots, n-1\}$, $F_B = \{n - 1\}$, and for any $i \in \{0, 1, \ldots, n-1\}$,

$$\delta_B(i, X) = \begin{cases} 1, & \text{if } i = 0 \text{ and } X = a, \\ i, & \text{if } i > 0 \text{ and } X = a, \\ i + 1, & \text{if } i < n - 1 \text{ and } X = b, \\ 0, & \text{if } i = n - 1 \text{ and } X = b, \\ i, & \text{if } X = c. \end{cases}$$

The DFA A and B are shown in Fig. 1 and Fig. 2, respectively.

We first describe an NFA accepting the language $L(A)L(B)$, then we construct an equivalent DFA, and show that the DFA has at least $m2^n - k2^{n-1}$ reachable states no two of which are equivalent.

Consider the NFA $C = (Q, \Sigma, \delta, q_0, \{n - 1\})$, where $Q = Q_A \cup Q_B$, and for any $q \in Q$ and any $X \in \Sigma$, $\delta(q, X) = \{\delta_A(q, X)\}$ if $q \in Q_A \setminus F_A$, $\delta(q, X) = \{\delta_A(q, X), \delta_B(0, X)\}$ if $q \in F_A$, and $\delta(q, X) = \{\delta_B(q, X)\}$ if $q \in Q_B$, see Fig. 3.

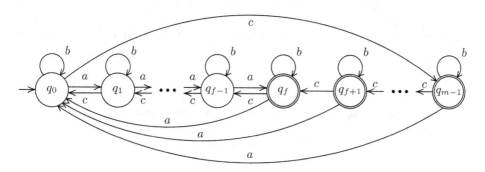

Fig. 1. The deterministic finite automaton A; $f = m - k$

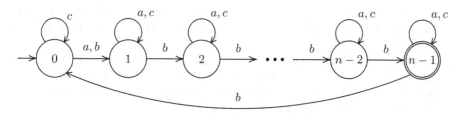

Fig. 2. The deterministic finite automaton B

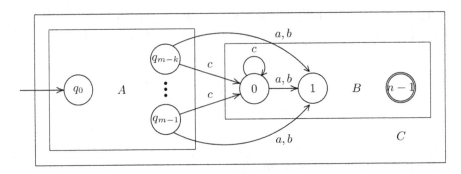

Fig. 3. The nondeterministic finite automaton C

Clearly, NFA C accepts the language $L(A)L(B)$. Let $C' = (2^Q, \Sigma, \delta', \{q_0\}, F')$ be the DFA obtained from the NFA C by the subset construction. Let $\mathcal{R}$ be the following system of sets: $\mathcal{R} = \{\{q\} \cup S \mid q \in Q_A \setminus F_A \text{ and } S \subseteq Q_B\}$ $\cup \{\{q\} \cup S \mid q \in F_A, S \subseteq Q_B, \text{ and } 0 \in S\}$, i.e., any set in $\mathcal{R}$ consists of exactly one state of Q_A and some states of Q_B, and if a set in $\mathcal{R}$ contains a state of F_A, then it also contains state 0. There are $m2^n - k2^{n-1}$ sets in $\mathcal{R}$. To prove the theorem it is sufficient to show that (I) any set in $\mathcal{R}$ is a reachable state of the DFA C' and (II) no two different states in $\mathcal{R}$ are equivalent.

We prove (I) by induction on the size of sets. The singletons $\{q_0\}, \{q_1\}, \ldots,$ $\{q_{m-k-1}\}$ are reachable since $\{q_i\} = \delta'(\{q_0\}, a^i)$ for $i = 0, 1, \ldots, m - k - 1$. Let $1 \leq t \leq n$ and assume that any set in $\mathcal{R}$ of size t is a reachable state of the DFA C'. Using this assumption we prove that any set $\{q_i, j_1, j_2, \ldots, j_t\}$, where $0 \leq j_1 < j_2 < \cdots < j_t < n$ if $0 \leq i < m - k$, and $0 = j_1 < j_2 < \cdots < j_t < n$ if $m - k \leq i < m$, is a reachable state of the DFA C'. There are two cases:

(i) $j_1 = 0$. Then we have $\{q_i, 0, j_2, j_3, \ldots, j_t\} = \delta'(\{q_0, j_2, j_3, \ldots, j_t\}, c^{m-i})$ for $i = 0, 1, \ldots, m - 2$, and $\{q_{m-1}, 0, j_2, j_3, \ldots, j_t\} = \delta'(\{q_0, j_2, j_3 \ldots, j_t\}, c^{m+1})$, where the set $\{q_0, j_2, j_3, \ldots, j_t\}$ is reachable by induction.

(ii) $j_1 \geq 1$ and $0 \leq i < m - k$. Then we have $\{q_i, j_1, j_2, \ldots, j_t\} = \delta'(\{q_0, 0, j_2 - j_1, j_3 - j_1, \ldots, j_t - j_1\}, b^{j_1} a^i)$, where the latter set is considered in case (i).

To prove (II) let $\{q_i\} \cup S$ and $\{q_l\} \cup T$ be two different states in $\mathcal{R}$ with $0 \leq i \leq l \leq m - 1$. There are two cases:

(i) $i < l$. Then the string $c^i a^{m-k} b^{n-1}$ is accepted by the DFA C' starting in state $\{q_i\} \cup S$ but it is not accepted by the DFA C' starting in state $\{q_l\} \cup T$.

(ii) $i = l$. Without loss of generality, there is a state j in Q_B such that $j \in S$ and $j \notin T$ (note that $j \geq 1$ if $m - k \leq i \leq m - 1$). Then the string b^{n-1-j} is accepted by the DFA C' starting in state $\{q_i\} \cup S$ but it is not accepted by the DFA C' starting in state $\{q_l\} \cup T$.

$\square$

4   Complementation

We now turn our attention to complementation operation. For DFAs, it is an efficient operation since to accept the complement we can simply exchange accepting and rejecting states. On the other hand, the complementation of NFAs is an expensive task. The upper bound on the size of an NFA accepting the complement of an n−state NFA language is 2^n and it is known to be tight for a binary alphabet [16]. For complementation of unary NFA languages a crucial role is played by the function $F(n) = \max\{\text{lcm}(x_1, \ldots, x_k) \mid x_1 + \ldots + x_k = n\}$. It is known that $F(n) \in e^{\Theta(\sqrt{n \ln n})}$ and that $O(F(n))$ states suffice to simulate any unary n−state NFA by a DFA [5]. This means that $O(F(n))$ states are sufficient for an NFA to accept the complement of an n−state unary NFA language. The lower bound is known to be $F(n-1) + 1$ in this case [16].

In this section, we deal with the question of which kind of relations between the nondeterministic complexity of a regular language and the nondeterministic complexity of its complement are possible. We provide a complete solution by showing that for any positive integers n and m with $\log n \le m \le 2^n$, there exists an n−state NFA language such that minimal NFAs for its complement have m states.

To obtain the above result we use a fooling-set lower-bound technique known from communication complexity theory [12]. Although lower bounds based on fooling sets may sometimes be exponentially smaller than the true bounds [14, 15], for some regular languages the lower bounds are tight [1, 2, 7]. In this section, the technique helps us to obtain tight lower bounds. After defining a fooling set, we give the lemma from [1] describing a fooling-set lower-bound technique. For the sake of completeness, we recall its proof here. Then, we give an example.

Definition 1. *A set of pairs of strings $\{(x_i, y_i) \mid i = 1, 2, \ldots, n\}$ is said to be a fooling set for a regular language L if for any i and j in $\{1, 2, \ldots, n\}$,*

(1) $x_i y_i \in L$, and
(2) if $i \ne j$ then $x_i y_j \notin L$ or $x_j y_i \notin L$.

Lemma 1 ([1]). *Let a set of pairs $\{(x_i, y_i) \mid i = 1, 2, \ldots, n\}$ be a fooling set for a regular language L. Then any NFA for the language L needs at least n states.*

Proof. Let $M = (Q, \Sigma, \delta, q_0, F)$ be any NFA accepting the language L. Since $x_i y_i \in L$, there is a state p_i in Q such that $p_i \in \delta(q_0, x_i)$ and $\delta(p_i, y_i) \cap F \ne \emptyset$. Assume that a fixed choice of p_i has been made for any i in $\{1, 2, \ldots, n\}$. We prove that $p_i \ne p_j$ for $i \ne j$. Suppose by contradiction that $p_i = p_j$ for some $i \ne j$. Then the NFA M accepts both strings $x_i y_j$ and $x_j y_i$ which contradicts the assumption that the set $\{(x_i, y_i) \mid 1 \le i \le n\}$ is a fooling set for the language L. Hence the NFA M has at least n states. □

Example 1. Let $n \ge 1$, let $L_n = \{w \in \{a, b\}^* \mid \#_a(w) \equiv 0 \bmod n\}$, and let $\mathcal{A}_n = \{(a^i, a^{n-i}) \mid i = 1, 2, \ldots, n\}$. Note that for any i and j in $\{1, 2, \ldots, n\}$, (1) $a^i a^{n-i} \in L_n$, and (2) if $i \ne j$ then, w.l.o.g., $i < j$, so $0^i 0^{n-j} \notin L_n$. Hence the set $\mathcal{A}_n$ is a fooling set for the language L_n, and so any NFA for the language L_n needs at least n states. □

We start our investigation with two propositions.

Proposition 1. *For any m in $\{1,2\}$, there is a 1-state NFA D_m such that minimal NFAs for the complement of the language $L(D_m)$ have m states.*

Proof. Let $\Sigma = \{a,b\}$. Consider the following 1-state NFAs:
  $D_1 = (\{s\}, \Sigma, \delta_1, s, \{s\})$ with $\delta_1(s, X) = \{s\}$ for any $X \in \Sigma$,
  $D_2 = (\{s\}, \Sigma, \delta_2, s, \{s\})$ with $\delta_2(s, a) = \{s\}$ and $\delta_2(s, b) = \emptyset$.
The NFAs D_1 and D_2 do satisfy the proposition since the complement of the language $L(D_1)$ is the empty language, and the set of pairs of strings $\{(\varepsilon, b), (b, \varepsilon)\}$ is a fooling set for the complement of the language $L(D_2)$. □

Proposition 2. *For any integer $n \geq 2$, there is a minimal NFA N of n states such that minimal NFAs for the complement of the language $L(N)$ have n states.*

Proof. Let n be arbitrary but fixed integer with $n \geq 2$. Let $\Sigma = \{a, b\}$.
Define an n-state NFA $N = (Q, \Sigma, \delta, n, F)$, see Fig. 4, where $Q = \{1, 2, \ldots, n\}$, $F = \{2, 3, \ldots, n\}$, and for any $i \in Q$,
  $\delta(1, a) = \delta(1, b) = \{2\}$,
  $\delta(i, a) = \{i - 1\}$ and $\delta(i, b) = \{1\}$ if $i > 1$.

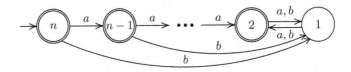

Fig. 4. The nondeterministic finite automaton N

We are going to show that (a) the NFA N is a minimal NFA for the language $L(N)$; (b) the language $L^c(N)$ is accepted by an n-state DFA; (c) any NFA for the language $L^c(N)$ needs at least n states. Then, the proposition follows.
  Consider the set of pairs $\mathcal{A} = \{(a^{i-1}, a^{n-i}b) \mid i = 1, 2, \ldots, n\}$. The set $\mathcal{A}$ is a fooling set for the language $L(N)$ because for any i and j in $\{1, 2, \ldots, n\}$,
(1) $a^{i-1}a^{n-i}b \in L(N)$ since the string $a^{n-1}b$ is accepted by the NFA N, and
(2) if $i < j$, then $a^{i-1}a^{n-j}b \notin L(N)$ since any string $a^l b$ with $0 \leq l < n-1$ is not accepted by the NFA N. By Lemma 1, any NFA for the language $L(N)$ needs at least n states which proves (a).
  To prove (b) note that the NFA N is, in fact, deterministic, and so after exchanging the accepting and the rejecting states we obtain an n-state DFA for the language $L^c(N)$.
  Finally, consider the set of pairs $\mathcal{B} = \{(a^{i-1}, a^{n-i}) \mid i = 1, 2, \ldots, n\}$. The set $\mathcal{B}$ is a fooling set for the language $L^c(N)$ because for any i and j in $\{1, 2, \ldots, n\}$,
(1) $a^{i-1}a^{n-i} \in L^c(N)$ since the string a^{n-1} is not accepted by the NFA N, and
(2) if $i < j$, then $a^{i-1}a^{n-j} \notin L^c(N)$ since any string a^l with $0 \leq l < n-1$ is accepted by the NFA N. By Lemma 1, any NFA for the language $L^c(N)$ needs at least n states and our proof is complete. □

The following theorem is proved in [16].

Theorem 2 ([16]). *For any positive integer n, there exists a binary NFA M of n states such that any NFA for the complement of the language $L(M)$ needs at least 2^n states.*   □

In the next theorem, we show that the nondeterministic state complexity of complements of n-state NFA languages may be arbitrary between $n + 1$ and $2^n - 1$.

Theorem 3. *For any integers n and m with $3 \le n+1 \le m \le 2^n - 1$, there exists a minimal NFA M of n states such that minimal NFAs for the complement of the language $L(M)$ have m states.*

Proof. Let n and m be arbitrary but fixed integers such that $3 \le n + 1 \le m \le 2^n - 1$. Then m can be expressed as $m = n + k$ for an integer k with $1 \le k \le 2^n - 1 - n$. Let $\Sigma = \{a, b\} \cup \{c_1, c_2, \ldots, c_k\} \cup \{d_1, d_2, \ldots, d_k\}$ be a $(2k + 2)$-letter alphabet. We are going to define a minimal n-state NFA M over the alphabet Σ such that minimal NFAs for the language $L^c(M)$ have $n+k$ states. To this aim let $S_1, S_2, \ldots, S_{2^n-1-n}$ be a sequence of subsets of the set $\{1, 2, \ldots, n\}$ that contain at least two elements and are ordered in such a way that for any i and j in $\{1, 2, \ldots, 2^n - 1 - n\}$, the following two conditions hold:

(1) if $\max S_i < \max S_j$, then $i < j$;
(2) if $\max S_i = \max S_j$ and $1 \in S_i \setminus S_j$, then $i < j$,

i.e., the subsets are ordered according to their maxima, and if two sets have the same maximum, then all sets that contain the state 1 precede the sets that do not contain the state 1. Clearly, there are several such orderings, we choose one of them. Note that $S_1 = \{1, 2\}$. For example, the subsets of $\{1, 2, 3, 4\}$ that contain at least two elements could be ordered as follows: $S_1 = \{1, 2\}$, $S_2 = \{1, 3\}, S_3 = \{1, 2, 3\}, S_4 = \{2, 3\}, S_5 = \{1, 4\}, S_6 = \{1, 2, 4\}, S_7 = \{1, 3, 4\}, S_8 = \{1, 2, 3, 4\}, S_9 = \{2, 4\}, S_{10} = \{3, 4\}, S_{11} = \{2, 3, 4\}$.

Define an n-state NFA $M = (Q, \Sigma, \delta, n, F)$, where $Q = \{1, 2, \ldots, n\}$, $F = \{2, 3, \ldots, n\}$, and for any $i \in Q$ and any $j \in \{1, 2, \ldots, k\}$,

$$\delta(i, X) = \begin{cases} \{1, 2\}, & \text{if } i = 1 \text{ and } X = a, \\ \{i - 1\}, & \text{if } i > 1 \text{ and } X = a, \\ \{2\}, & \text{if } i = 1 \text{ and } X = b, \\ \{1\}, & \text{if } i > 1 \text{ and } X = b, \\ S_j, & \text{if } i = 1 \text{ and } X = c_j, \\ \{1\}, & \text{if } i > 1 \text{ and } X = c_j, \\ \{1\}, & \text{if } i \in S_j \text{ and } X = d_j, \\ \{2\}, & \text{if } i \notin S_j \text{ and } X = d_j. \end{cases}$$

We will show that:

(a) the NFA M is a minimal NFA for the language $L(M)$;
(b) the language $L^c(M)$ can be accepted by an $(n + k)$-state DFA;
(c) any NFA for the language $L^c(M)$ needs at least $n + k$ states.

Then, the theorem follows immediately.

To prove (a) consider the following set of pairs of strings

$$\mathcal{A} = \{(a^{i-1}, a^{n-i}b) \mid i = 1, 2, \ldots, n\}.$$

The set $\mathcal{A}$ is a fooling set for $L(M)$ because for any i and j in $\{1, 2, \ldots, n\}$,

(1) $a^{i-1}a^{n-i}b \in L(M)$ since the string $a^{n-1}b$ is accepted by the NFA M, and

(2) if $i < j$, then $a^{i-1}a^{n-j}b \notin L(M)$ since for any l with $0 \leq l < n-1$, the string $a^l b$ is not accepted by the NFA M.

By Lemma 1, any NFA for $L(M)$ needs at least n states which proves (a).

To prove (b) let $M' = (2^Q, \Sigma, \delta', \{n\}, F')$ be the DFA obtained from the NFA M by the subset construction. Let $\mathcal{R}$ be the following system of sets

$$\mathcal{R} = \{\{1\}, \{2\}, \ldots, \{n\}, S_1, S_2, \ldots, S_k\}.$$

Note that the initial state $\{n\}$ of the DFA M' and the state $S_1 = \{1, 2\}$ belong to the system $\mathcal{R}$. We are going to prove that any set in $\mathcal{R}$ is a reachable state of the DFA M' and no other states are reachable in the DFA M'. Clearly, any set of the system $\mathcal{R}$ is reachable since we have $\{i\} = \delta'(\{n\}, a^{n-i})$ for $i = 1, 2, \ldots, n$, and $S_j = \delta'(\{1\}, c_j)$ for $j = 1, 2, \ldots, k$. To prove that no other subset of the set Q is a reachable state of the DFA M' it is sufficient to show that for any state R in $\mathcal{R}$ and any symbol X in Σ, the state $\delta'(R, X)$ is a member of the system $\mathcal{R}$. There are three cases:

(i) $R = \{1\}$. Then we have $(j = 1, 2, \ldots, k)$:

$$\delta'(\{1\}, X) = \begin{cases} \{1, 2\}, & \text{if } X = a, \\ \{2\}, & \text{if } X = b, \\ S_j, & \text{if } X = c_j, \\ \{1\}, & \text{if } 1 \in S_j \text{ and } X = d_j, \\ \{2\}, & \text{if } 1 \notin S_j \text{ and } X = d_j. \end{cases}$$

Since all sets on the right are in the system $\mathcal{R}$, we are ready in this case.

(ii) $R = \{i\}$ for an $i \neq 1$. Then for any X in Σ, the set $\delta'(\{i\}, X)$ is a singleton set and so is in $\mathcal{R}$.

(iii) $R = S_j$ for a j in $\{1, 2, \ldots, k\}$. Then the set $\delta'(S_j, a)$ is a subset of the set $\{1, 2, \ldots, \max S_k - 1\}$ or equals $\{1, 2\}$. Since the sets $S_1, S_2, \ldots, S_k$ are ordered according to their maxima, any subset of $\{1, 2, \ldots, \max S_k - 1\}$ is in the system $\mathcal{R}$. Next, the set $\delta'(S_j, b)$ is equal either to $\{1\}$ or to $\{1, 2\}$, and the set $\delta'(S_j, d_l)$, $l = 1, 2, \ldots, k$, is equal either to $\{1\}$, or to $\{2\}$, or to $\{1, 2\}$. Finally, the set $\delta'(S_j, c_l)$, $l = 1, 2, \ldots, k$, is equal either to $\{1\}$ or to $S_l \cup \{1\}$. Since the set $S_l \cup \{1\}$ precedes the set S_l or equals S_l, we are ready in this case.

Thus we have shown that the DFA M' obtained from the NFA M by the subset construction has exactly $n + k$ reachable states. After exchanging the accepting and the rejecting states of the DFA M' we obtain an $(n + k)$−state DFA for the language $L^c(M)$ which proves (b).

To prove (c) consider the following sets of pairs of strings

$$\mathcal{B} = \{(a^{i-1}, a^{n-i}) \mid i = 1, 2, \ldots, n\},$$

$$\mathcal{C} = \{(a^{n-1}c_j, d_j) \mid j = 1, 2, \ldots, k\}.$$

We will show that the set $\mathcal{B} \cup \mathcal{C}$ is a fooling set for the language $L^c(M)$.

(1) For any $i \in \{1, 2, \ldots, n\}$, the string $a^{i-1}a^{n-i}$ is in the language $L^c(M)$ since the string a^{n-1} is not accepted by the NFA M.

For any $j \in \{1, 2, \ldots, k\}$, the string $a^{n-1}c_j d_j$ is in the language $L^c(M)$ since

$$\delta(n, a^{n-1}) = \{1\}, \quad \delta(\{1\}, c_j) = S_j, \quad \delta(S_j, d_j) = \{1\}, \text{ and } 1 \notin F,$$

and so the string $a^{n-1}c_j d_j$ is not accepted by the NFA M.

(2) If $1 \leq i < s \leq n$, then the string $a^{i-1}a^{n-s}$ is not in the language $L^c(M)$ since the NFA M accepts any string a^l with $0 \leq l < n - 1$.

Next, if $1 \leq j, t \leq k$ and $j \neq t$, then, w.l.o.g., there is a state p in Q such that $p \in S_j$ and $p \notin S_t$. Thus,

$$p \in \delta(n, a^{n-1}c_j) \text{ and } 2 \in \delta(p, d_t),$$

and so the string $a^{n-1}c_j d_t$ is accepted by the NFA M, i.e., is not in the language $L^c(M)$.

Finally, if $i \in \{1, 2, \ldots, n\}$ and $j \in \{1, 2, \ldots, k\}$, then the string $a^{n-1}c_j a^{n-i}$ is not in the language $L^c(M)$ since $\delta(n, a^{n-1}c_j) = S_j$, the size of the set S_j is at least two, and the string a^{n-i} is not accepted by the NFA M starting in state $n - i + 1$ but it is accepted by M starting in any other state.

Thus the set $\mathcal{B} \cup \mathcal{C}$ is a fooling set for the language $L^c(M)$. By Lemma 1, any NFA for the language $L^c(M)$ needs at least $n + k$ states which completes our proof. $\square$

Corollary 1. *For any positive integers r and s with $\log r \leq s \leq r$, there exists a minimal NFA E of r states such that minimal NFAs for the complement of the language $L(E)$ have s states.*

Proof. Let r and s be arbitrary but fixed positive integers with $\log r \leq s \leq r$. Then we have

$$s \leq r \leq 2^s,$$

and by the above results, there is a minimal s-state NFA S such that a minimal NFA, say R, for the language $L^c(S)$ has r states. Set $E = R$. Then the NFA E is a minimal r-state NFA for the language $L^c(S)$, and minimal NFAs for the complement of the language $L^c(S)$, i.e., for $L^c(E)$, have s states. $\square$

Hence, we have shown the following result.

Theorem 4. *For any positive integers n and m with $\log n \leq m \leq 2^n$, there exists a minimal NFA M of n states such that minimal NFAs for the complement of the language $L(M)$ have m states.* $\square$

5   Conclusions

In this paper, we obtained several results concerning the state complexity of concatenation and the nondeterministic state complexity of complementation of regular languages.

In the case of concatenation, we showed that the upper bounds $m2^n - k2^{n-1}$ on the concatenation of an m-state DFA language and an n-state DFA language, where k is the number of the accepting states in the m-state automaton, are tight for any integer k with $0 < k < m$. To prove the result, we used a three-letter alphabet. In the case of $m = 3$, $k = 2$, and $n = 2$, the upper bound can be reached by the concatenation of two binary languages. The problem remains open for a binary alphabet and larger values of m, k, n.

In the case of complementation, we showed that for any positive integers n and m with $\log n \leq m \leq 2^n$, there exists a minimal NFA M of n states such that minimal NFAs for the complement of the language $L(M)$ have m states. However, the input alphabet size grows exponentially with n. We conjecture that the input alphabet could be decreased at least to linear size.

Further investigations may concern the deterministic concatenation and the nondeterministic complementation of finite languages.

Acknowledgements

We would like to thank Professor Geffert for proposing the problem on the nondeterministic complementation and for our helpful discussions on the topic. We are also very grateful to the referees for their corrections and suggestions.

References

1. J.C. Birget, Intersection and union of regular languages and state complexity, *Inform. Process. Lett.* **43** (1992) 185–190.

2. J.C. Birget, Partial orders on words, minimal elements of regular languages, and state complexity, *Theoret. Comput. Sci.* **119** (1993) 267–291.

3. C. Câmpeanu, K. Culik II, K. Salomaa, and S. Yu, State complexity of basic operations on finite languages, in: O. Boldt, H. Jürgensen (Eds.), *Proc. 4th International Workshop on Implementing Automata (WIA'99)*, LNCS 2214, Springer-Verlag, Heidelberg, 2001, pp. 60–70.

4. C. Câmpeanu, K. Salomaa, and S. Yu, Tight lower bound for the state complexity of shuffle of regular languages, *J. Autom. Lang. Comb.* **7** (2002) 303–310.

5. M. Chrobak, Finite automata and unary languages, *Theoret. Comput. Sci.* **47** (1986) 149–158.

6. M. Domaratzki, State complexity and proportional removals, *J. Autom. Lang. Comb.* **7** (2002) 455–468.

7. I. Glaister, J. Shallit, A lower bound technique for the size of nondeterministic finite automata, *Inform. Process. Lett.* **59** (1996) 75–77.

8. M. Holzer, K. Salomaa, and S. Yu, On the state complexity of k-entry deterministic finite automata, *J. Autom. Lang. Comb.* **6** (2001) 453–466.

9. M. Holzer, M. Kutrib, State complexity of basic operations on nondeterministic finite automata, in: J.M. Champarnaud, D. Maurel (Eds.), *Implementation and Application of Automata (CIAA 2002)*, LNCS 2608, Springer-Verlag, Heidelberg, 2003, pp. 148–157.

10. M. Holzer, M. Kutrib, Unary language operations and their nondeterministic state complexity, in: M. Ito, M. Toyama (Eds.), *Developments in Language Theory (DLT 2002)*, LNCS 2450, Springer-Verlag, Heidelberg, 2003, pp. 162–172.

11. M. Holzer, M. Kutrib, Nondeterministic descriptional complexity of regular languages, *Internat. J. Found. Comput. Sci.* **14** (2003) 1087-1102.

12. J. Hromkovič, *Communication Complexity and Parallel Computing*, Springer-Verlag, Berlin, Heidelberg, 1997.

13. J. Hromkovič, Descriptional complexity of finite automata: concepts and open problems, *J. Autom. Lang. Comb.* **7** (2002) 519–531.

14. J. Hromkovič, S. Seibert, J. Karhumäki, H. Klauck, and G. Schnitger, Communication complexity method for measuring nondeterminism in finite automata, *Inform. and Comput.* **172** (2002) 202–217.

15. G. Jirásková, Note on minimal automata and uniform communication protocols, in: C. Martin-Vide, V. Mitrana (Eds.), *Grammars and Automata for String Processing: From Mathematics and Computer Science to Biology, and Back,* Taylor and Francis, London, 2003, pp. 163–170.

16. G. Jirásková, State complexity of some operations on regular languages, in: E. Csuhaj-Varjú, C. Kintala, D. Wotschke, Gy. Vaszil (Eds.), *Proc. 5th Workshop Descriptional Complexity of Formal Systems,* MTA SZTAKI, Budapest, 2003, pp. 114–125.

17. E. Leiss, Succinct representation of regular languages by boolean automata, *Theoret. Comput. Sci.* **13** (1981) 323–330.

18. O.B. Lupanov, A comparison of two types of finite automata, *Problemy Kibernetiki,* **9** (1963) 321-326 (in Russian).

19. F.R. Moore, On the bounds for state-set size in the proofs of equivalence between deterministic, nondeterministic, and two-way finite automata, *IEEE Trans. Comput.* **20** (1971) 1211–1214.

20. G. Pighizzini, Unary language concatenation and its state complexity, in: S. Yu, A. Pun (Eds.), *Implementation and Application of Automata: 5th International Conference, CIAA 2000,* LNCS 2088, Springer-Verlag, 2001, pp. 252–262.

21. G. Pighizzini, J. Shallit, Unary language operations, state complexity and Jacobsthal's function, *Internat. J. Found. Comput. Sci.* **13** (2002) 145–159.

22. M. Rabin, D. Scott, Finite automata and their decision problems, *IBM Res. Develop.* **3** (1959) 114–129.

23. W.J. Sakoda, M. Sipser, Nondeterminism and the size of two-way finite automata, in: *Proc. 10th Annual ACM Symp. on Theory of Computing,* 1978, pp. 275–286.

24. M. Sipser, *Introduction to the theory of computation,* PWS, Boston, 1997.

25. S. Yu, Q. Zhuang, and K. Salomaa, The state complexity of some basic operations on regular languages, *Theoret. Comput. Sci.* **125** (1994) 315–328.

26. S. Yu, Chapter 2: Regular languages, in: G. Rozenberg, A. Salomaa, (Eds.), *Handbook of Formal Languages - Vol. I,* Springer-Verlag, Berlin, New York, pp. 41–110.

27. S. Yu, A renaissance of automata theory? *Bull. Eur. Assoc. Theor. Comput. Sci. EATCS* **72** (2000) 270–272.

28. S. Yu, State complexity of finite and infinite regular languages, *Bull. Eur. Assoc. Theor. Comput. Sci. EATCS* **76** (2000) 270–272.

29. S. Yu, State complexity of regular languages, *J. Autom. Lang. Comb.* **6** (2001) 221–234.

Minimal Unambiguous εNFA

Sebastian John

Technical University Berlin, IV, Computer Science
sebc@cs.tu-berlin.de

Abstract. A nondeterministic finite automaton with ε-transitions (εNFA) accepts a regular language. Among the εNFA accepting a certain language some are more compact than others. This essay treats the problem of how to compactify a given εNFA by reducing the number of transitions. Compared to the standard techniques to minimize deterministic complete finite automata (complete DFA) two novel features matter in compactifying εNFA: the principle of transition partition and the principle of transition union. An algorithm for compactifying εNFA is presented that exploits the union principle. This algorithm has the following property: if the algorithm returns an unambiguous automaton, then this automaton is the transition minimal εNFA.

1 Introduction

Minimization of finite automata is important for theoretical and practical reasons. In several application domains only small automata and their representations yield feasible solutions for practical problems. Basic algorithms for the problem of minimizing deterministic finite automata (DFA) have been published 50 years ago [10, 15, 17]. About succinctness, the feature of nondeterminism introduced in [21] allows to give much more compact automata. A nondeterministic finite automaton (NFA) may be smaller than a DFA by an exponential factor [16]. This even holds for unambiguous NFA [23, 26, 22]; ie NFA, which have at most one accepting computation for every word.

This essay treats the problem of how to compactify a given nondeterministic finite automaton with ε-transitions (εNFA). In general, the problem to compute a state minimal εNFA from a given εNFA is PSPACE-complete, by reduction to a problem given in [1, 6, p. 174], whereas in the deterministic case the problem to compute minimal complete DFA can be solved in time $\mathcal{O}(n \log n)$ [8] — a DFA is complete if each state has a transition for all inputs. Hereby, the minimal complete DFA is unique up to isomorphism [10, 17] and the number of states and the number of transitions are simultaneously minimized. A state minimal complete DFA is a transition minimal complete DFA, and vice versa. This does not hold for NFA and εNFA.

Essentially, there are three ways to define a minimization problem for NFA resp. εNFA: to minimize the number of states or the number of transitions or a sophisticated weighted sum of both. All of them can be solved by an exhaustive search algorithm in time $2^{\mathcal{O}(n^2)}$. In the formal language community, it is traditional to minimize the number of states. The approaches to this problem, that

M. Domaratzki et al. (Eds.): CIAA 2004, LNCS 3317, pp. 190–201, 2005.

work by searching a minimal subautomaton, started with [5]. Many algorithms and heuristics have been proposed by [12, 13, 3, 4, 2, 14].

Another approach to reduce the number of states is due to [25, 20], where the minimization techniques for complete DFA are applied [9, 18, 19]. According to their reduction criteria, a NFA is most compact if there are no equivalent states. But in general, this does not mean state minimization, because there may be NFA accepting the same language using a smaller number of states.

Contrary, this essay investigates transition minimization. We do so mainly for three reasons: the size of an automaton is primarily influenced by the number of transitions, eg regarding an adjacency list, which is an efficient linear representation of an automaton. Secondly, the minimal unambiguous ε-complete εNFA is unique up to isomorphism. And finally, our algorithm to reduce εNFA with respect to the number of transitions performs better than the best known algorithms to compute state minimal NFA. The problem to compute a transition minimal εNFA from a given εNFA is PSPACE-complete by reduction to a problem described in [1, 6, p. 174]. The time complexity for our algorithm depends on the time needed to compute NFA equivalences or NFA complements. At the time, we therefore obtain a bound of $\mathcal{O}(2^n)$ for the running time of the algorithm.

The essay proceeds as follows. Section 2 introduces the formalism of εNFA, explains how the compactness of an εNFA is measured and defines the problem, to be solved. Section 3 elaborates the theory necessary to reduce the number of transitions. This theory and the proofs of the theorems are presented in more detail and with examples in [11]. Section 4 presents the algorithm, proves its correctness and determines its complexity. In Section 5 we conclude with final remarks.

In the sequel, $\mathbb{N}$ denotes the set of natural numbers including 0, Σ is the set of input symbols, Σ^* the set of finite words over Σ including the empty word λ. Variables $u, v, w \in \Sigma^*$ stand for words, $P, F \subseteq \Sigma^*$ for sets of words, A, B for automata, $s, t \in T$ for transitions, and $p \in T^*$ for finite paths with $p = p_1...p_n$ and $n \in \mathbb{N}$. By default, indices are omitted if it is clear from the context, what is meant.

2   Problem

Definition 1. *An εNFA $A = (Q, \Sigma, I, F, E, T)$ is given by*

- *a finite set of states Q*
- *a finite set of input symbols Σ*
- *a set of initial states $I \subseteq Q$*
- *a set of final states $F \subseteq Q$*
- *a set of ε-transitions $E \subseteq Q \times Q$*
- *a set of transitions $T \subseteq Q \times \Sigma \times Q$*

A word $w \in \Sigma^*$, including the empty word $\lambda \in \Sigma^*$, is accepted by the automaton, $w \in L(A)$, if there is a path from an initial state via the automaton's transitions to a final state yielding w. We come back to that point later. Two εNFA A and B are *equivalent* if and only if $L(A) = L(B)$. Among the εNFA accepting the same language there are some that are more compact than others. In our case, the measurement of compactness is based on the number of transitions. More precisely, on the number of transitions not counting ε-transitions. For εNFA A and B, the term "A is more compact than B", for short $A < B$, is defined by:

Definition 2 (Compactness). $A < B :\Longleftrightarrow L(A) = L(B)$ and $|T_A| < |T_B|$

Problem : The problem is to find an algorithm, that computes a most compact automaton, ie: to compute from any given εNFA A an εNFA B with $L(A) = L(B)$ such that $C \not< B$ for all εNFA C.

Theorem 1 (Main Theorem). *There is an algorithm with running time $\mathcal{O}(2^n)$ that does always find an εNFA at least as compact as the input εNFA. The algorithm returns an εNFA, which is transition minimal if unambiguous.*

3   Theory

3.1   Acceptance Criterium

Words are accepted by an automaton along transition paths from initial to final states. We make this more precise by introducing a follow–relation and a label–path homomorphism in contrast to a direct definition as it is commonly used (eg [24, 9]).

The follow–relation $\longrightarrow$ expresses the connectivity of transitions within an εNFA A. For $s, t \in T$, the statement $s \longrightarrow t$ displays that s is connected via states and ε-transitions to t. For convenience, we add a new transition $t_0 \notin T$, set $T_0 := T \cup \{t_0\}$ and define the follow–relation $\longrightarrow$ on $T_0 \times T_0$. We denote the source state and the target state of a transition t as $source(t)$ and $target(t)$:

Definition 3 (follow–relation). *For $s, t \in T$:*

- $s \longrightarrow t :\Leftrightarrow target(s) \; E^* \; source(t)$
- $t_0 \longrightarrow t :\Leftrightarrow$ *There is an initial state $q \in I$ with $q \; E^* \; source(t)$*
- $s \longrightarrow t_0 :\Leftrightarrow$ *There is a final state $q \in F$ with $target(s) \; E^* \; q$*

Transitions t with $t_0 \longrightarrow t$ are called initial transitions, transitions s with $s \longrightarrow t_0$ are called final transitions.

A path $p \in T^*$ is a sequence $p = t_1...t_n$ with $n \in \mathbb{N}$ of transitions $t_i \in T$ connected by the follow–relation each labeled $l(t_i) \in \Sigma$. The word yielding from the path is given by the label–path homomorphism $l : T_0^* \to \Sigma^*$ with $l(p) = l(t_1)...l(t_n)$. More precisely, t_0 transitions are allowed to be at the beginning or at the end or both for the purpose of accepting paths:

Definition 4 (label–path homomorphism). $l(stp) := l(s)l(tp) \; \Leftrightarrow \; s \longrightarrow t$ *with $l(\lambda) := \lambda$ and $l(t_0) := \lambda$.*

Note, that the definition incorporates the connectivity via the follow–relation, elsewhere l is partially undefined.

Proposition 1. $\forall p \in T^* : |l(p)| = |p|$

The accepted language $L(A)$ of an εNFA A, given in the notion of the follow–relation and the label–path homomorphism l, is defined on paths p of connected transitions from an initial to a final transition yielding words w according to l:

Definition 5. $L(A) = \{w \in \Sigma^* \mid$ *there is a path* $p \in T^*$ *with* $l(t_0 p t_0) = w\}$

An εNFA A is unambiguous if and only if for each $w \in L(A)$ there is exactly one path p with $l(t_0 p t_0) = w$.

Regarding the definition of the unambiguousness of an εNFA, arbitrary many ε-transitions are not relevant with respect to this essay. That point would otherwise provoke to distinct strong and weak unambiguousness by the means of ε-transitions.

The information given by the follow–relation of an automaton A is sufficient to reconstruct an automaton that accepts the language $L(A)$. This reconstruction is not unique, but can be done canonically or small regarding the number of states and ε-transitions.

Fact : From any follow–relation an εNFA can be reconstructed.

For convenience, we assume in the following, without the loss of generality, that every εNFA considered has only productive transitions $t \in T$ — there is a linear time algorithm to eliminate every non-productive transition. A transition is productive if and only if it is connected to an initial and a final state over a path of other transitions possibly including ε-transitions, ie: it might be responsible for the acceptance of at least one word of the language. Thus, in the following, for all εNFA considered, and transitions $t \in T$ it holds: $t_0 \longrightarrow^+ t \longrightarrow^+ t_0$.

3.2   Future and Past

In this section, we will determine the semantics of the transitions by exploring what a transition $t \in T$ is responsible for — the future $\varphi(t)$ and the past $\pi(t)$. Similar ideas for states already appeared in [12, 6, 2].

Along a path to accept a word w, there is a transition t processing one of the letters of w. The letters before are part of the past $\pi(t)$. The letters, which are to be processed, belong to future $\varphi(t)$, whereby the present $l(t)$ is part of both $\pi(t)$ and $\varphi(t)$. This reflects the setting of the transition t among the others:

Definition 6 (future and past). $\varphi, \pi : T \to \Sigma^*$

- $\varphi(t) = \{w \in \Sigma^* \mid$ *there is a path p with $l(p t_0) = w$ and $p_1 = t\}$*
- $\pi(t) = \{w \in \Sigma^* \mid$ *there is a path p with $l(t_0 p) = w$ and $p_{|w|} = t\}$*

We define the language $M{:}1$ of words of $M \subseteq \Sigma^*$ without the last letter and $1{:}M$ without the first letter:

Definition 7. $M{:}1 := \{w \in \Sigma^* \mid wa \in M\}$ *and* $1{:}M := \{w \in \Sigma^* \mid aw \in M\}$

According to *future* $\varphi(t)$ and *past* $\pi(t)$ there are the *strict future* $1{:}\varphi(t)$ and the *strict past* $\pi(t){:}1$ each without the *present* $l(t)$. Because the present $l(t)$ of a transition t is unique, we observe obviously, that past is strict past combined with the present and analogously future is present combined with strict future:

Proposition 2. $\pi(t) = \pi(t){:}1\,l(t)$ and $\varphi(t) = l(t)\,1{:}\varphi(t)$

By a little more algebraic investigation of the label–path homomorphism l, we get for all transitions t, all words $w, v \in \Sigma^*$ and all $a \in \Sigma$ that:

Lemma 1. $vaw \in L(A)$ $\Leftrightarrow$ $\exists\, t \in T : va \in \pi(t)$ and $aw \in \varphi(t)$

In case that the εNFA is unambiguous, the property holds for exactly one $t \in T$.

The accepted language of an εNFA A is completely determined by its future and past and from its strict future and strict past:

Proposition 3. $L(A) = \displaystyle\bigcup_{s \to_A t} \pi(s)\varphi(t) = \bigcup_{t \in T} \pi(t){:}1\,l(t)\,1{:}\varphi(t)$

More central is the point that future φ and past π of an εNFA may be obtained by a *fixpoint* construction as they fulfill the equation system if we set $\varphi(t_0) := \{\lambda\} =: \pi(t_0)$:

Lemma 2 (fixpoint). $\varphi(s) = \displaystyle\bigcup_{s \to_A t} l(s)\varphi(t)$ and $\pi(t) = \bigcup_{s \to_A t} \pi(s)l(t)$

The Fixpoint Lemma implies directly a correspondence between the follow–relation and the future and past:

Corollary 1. For transitions s and t with same label $l(s) = l(t)$ it holds:

$s \longrightarrow = t \longrightarrow$ implies $\varphi(s) = \varphi(t)$ and $\longrightarrow s = \longrightarrow t$ implies $\pi(s) = \pi(t)$

3.3   Slicing

Central to the Minimizing Theorem 2 is the notion of slicing a regular language. Slices are unified to most compact slices, $S^{\mathcal{T}}$, which forms a compact εNFA.

Definition 8 (slice). Given a regular language $L \subseteq \Sigma^*$. For all $P, F \subseteq \Sigma^*$, $a \in \Sigma$:

(P, a, F) is a slice of L $:\Leftrightarrow$ $P \neq \emptyset$ and $F \neq \emptyset$ and $PaF \subseteq L$

A slicing of L is a set of slices of L. In particular, let S be the set of all slices of L. We define a partial order on S:

$(P_1, a, F_1) \leq (P_2, a, F_2)$ $:\Leftrightarrow$ $P_1 \subseteq P_2$ and $F_1 \subseteq F_2$

We define $S^{\mathcal{T}} \subseteq S$, the set of maximal slices of L, by

$S^{\mathcal{T}} := \{(P, a, F) \in S \mid$ there is no $(P', a, F') \in S$ with $(P, a, F) < (P', a, F')\}$

Lemma 3. Given the set of all slices S of a regular language L, every linearly ordered set $X \subseteq S$ has a maximum in S, which is:

$$\left(\bigcup_{(P,a,F) \in X} P, \; a, \; \bigcup_{(P,a,F) \in X} F \right)$$

Proof: Let us assume the settings $\cup P := \bigcup_{(P,a,F) \in X} P$ and $\cup F = \bigcup_{(P,a,F) \in X} F$. First, we show that we have defined a slice of L. Because future F and past P of a slice $(P, a, F) \in X$ are not empty, the unions $\cup P$ and $\cup F$ are not empty, either.

It remains to show $\cup Pa\cup F \subseteq L$. Every $w \in \cup Pa\cup F$ is split into subwords $w_1 \in \cup P$ and $w_2 \in \cup F$ with $w = w_1 a w_2$, those come out of slices $x, y \in X$ with $w_1 \in P_x$ and $w_2 \in F_y$. These slices are ordered. We assume without the loss of generality that $x \leq y$, which implies $w_1 \in P_x \subseteq P_y$ and $w_1 a w_2 \in P_y a F_y \subseteq L$. So, $w = w_1 a w_2 \in L$ and consequently $\cup Pa\cup F \subseteq L$.   □

Due to the fact that every slice is part of a maximal linearly ordered set, we have:

Corollary 2. $\forall x \in S, \exists y \in S^T : x \leq y$

In the following, we want to read an automaton out of a slicing of L. In order to do so, we transform every slice into a transition. Usually, there are more than a finite number of slices. So, let us relax the finiteness of εNFA for the moment. We define the automaton A_S from the slicing S of L via the follow–relation. The other automata are subautomata of A_S, especially the ones corresponding to the finite slicings, which are subsets of S; eg S^T is a finite slicing of a regular language L. We come back to this point within the Minimizing Theorem 2.

Definition 9 $(A_S, A_{S^T}, A_{\bar{F}})$. *Assume $t_0 \notin S$ and $S_0 := S \cup \{t_0\}$. The follow– relation $\longrightarrow \subseteq S_0 \times S_0$ is defined for all slices (P_1, a, F_1) and $(P_2, b, F_2) \in S$:*

$$
\begin{aligned}
(P_1, a, F_1) &\longrightarrow (P_2, b, F_2) &:\Leftrightarrow& \; P_1 a \subseteq P_2 \text{ and } bF_2 \subseteq F_1 \\
t_0 &\longrightarrow (P_2, b, F_2) &:\Leftrightarrow& \; \lambda \in P_2 \\
(P_1, a, F_1) &\longrightarrow t_0 &:\Leftrightarrow& \; \lambda \in F_1 \\
[\quad t_0 &\longrightarrow t_0 &:\Leftrightarrow& \; \lambda \in L \quad]
\end{aligned}
$$

The last case fits if λ is not excluded from L from the beginning.

Lemma 4. $L(A_{S'}) \subseteq L$ for each slicing $S' \subseteq S$.

Sketch of proof: Let $w = a_1 \dots a_n \in L(A_{S'})$. There is a path $p \in T^*$ with $l(t_0 p t_0) = w$. Examining the path $p = p_1 \dots p_n$, it sequences slices of the form $p_i = (P_i, a_i, F_i) \in S$ with the initial slice p_1 and final slice p_n due to $\lambda \in P_1$ and $\lambda \in F_n$. The follow–relation implies $a_1 \in P_1 a_1 \subseteq P_2$ and by the induction principle $a_1 \dots a_n \in P_n a_n$. Together with $\lambda \in F_n$, we get $w = a_1 \dots a_n \in P_n a_n F_n \subseteq L$.   □

Lemma 5. *The regular language L is accepted by A_S and A_{S^T}:*

$$L(A_S) = L \text{ and } L(A_{S^T}) = L$$

Sketch of proof: Let $w = a_1 \dots a_n \in L$ we prove by induction:
$L \subseteq L(A_S)$:   Let $p_k = (\{a_1 \dots a_{k-1}\}, a_k, \{a_{k+1} \dots a_n\}) = (P_k, a_k, F_k) \in S$. The sequence $p = p_1 \dots p_n$ is an accepting path in A_S.
$L \subseteq L(A_{S^T})$:   By Corollary 2 there is, for each slice p_k, a slice $p_k^* = (P_k^*, a_k, F_k^*) \in S^T$ with $p_k \leq p_k^*$. That forms an accepting path $p^* = p_1^* \dots p_n^*$. To prove that, we use intermediate slices $(\tilde{P}_{k+1}, a_{k+1}, \tilde{F}_{k+1}) = (P_k^* a_k, a_{k+1}, \{w \mid a_{k+1} w \in F_k^*\})$ to analyze $a_{k+1} F_{k+1}^* - F_k^*$ in order to prove $p_k^* \longrightarrow p_{k+1}^*$.   □

Lemma 6. *Given a regular language L and a slicing $S' \subseteq S$ of L. Within the εNFA $A_{S'}$ we observe that for all slices $(P, a, F) \in S'$, which are transitions in $A_{S'}$, it holds:*

$- \; \pi(P,a,F) \subseteq Pa$ and $\varphi(P,a,F) \subseteq aF$

Moreover, if $S' = S$ or $S' = S^T$:

$- \; \pi(P,a,F) = Pa$ and $\varphi(P,a,F) = aF$

Sketch of proof: By induction on the word length, we reason about the follow–relation. In case of π, consider the predecessors introduced by the fix point lemma, 2, and show that $\pi(P,a,F) = \bigcup_{(\tilde{P},b,\tilde{F}) \to (P,a,F)} \pi(\tilde{P},b,\tilde{F})a$, and finally $\tilde{P}b \subseteq P$ if $(\tilde{P},b,\tilde{F}) \to (P,a,F)$. A proof works analogously for φ.

The second part uses, in addition to the idea in the part above, an idea similar to the one of the proof of Lemma 5: For each slice $(P,a,F) \in S$ analyse $(\{w|wb \in P\},b,aF)$—which has also a maximum in S^T in case $S' = S^T$—being connected to (P,a,F) by the follow–relation. $\qquad \square$

3.4   Minimal Unambiguous εNFA

The following theorem is presented in the style of [9, 18, 19].

Theorem 2. *The three following statements are equivalent for languages $L \subseteq \Sigma^*$ if the slicing S^T of L induces an unambiguous εNFA A_{S^T}:*

- *L is accepted by an εNFA*
- *$L = L(A_{\bar{F}})$ for some finite slicing $\bar{F} \subseteq S$*
- *S^T is finite*

Furthermore it holds:

- $|S^T| \leq |\bar{F}| \leq |T_A|$

Corollary 3. *An unambiguous εNFA A_{S^T} is transition minimal.*

Proof: (1) $\to$ (2) : Let A be an εNFA with $L = L(A)$. For transitions $t \in T$ we define $\bar{t} := (\pi(t){:}1, l(t), 1{:}\varphi(t))$ to construct a finite slicing $\bar{F} = \{\bar{t}|t \in T\}$ — Proposition 3 includes $\pi(t){:}1\, l(t)1{:}\varphi(t) \subseteq L$. And $\bar{F}$ is finite: $|\bar{F}| \leq |T|$.

It remains to show, that $L = L(A_{\bar{F}})$: We show for transitions s and $t \in T_{0A}$ that $s \longrightarrow_A t$ implies $\bar{s} \longrightarrow \bar{t}$ provided that $\bar{t}_0 := t_0$. Hence, every accepting path of A is an accepting path of $A_{\bar{F}}$, ie: $L = L(A) \subseteq L(A_{\bar{F}}) \subseteq L$, and by Corollary 4 then $L(A_{\bar{F}}) = L$.

Assume $s \longrightarrow_A t$. By the Fix Point Lemma 2, we get $\pi(s)l(t) \subseteq \pi(t)$. Therefore $\pi(s){:}1l(s) \overset{P.2}{=} \pi(s) = \pi(s)l(t){:}1 \subseteq \pi(t){:}1$. That means $\pi(s){:}1l(s) \subseteq \pi(t){:}1$ and similarly $l(t)1{:}\varphi(t) \subseteq 1{:}\varphi(s)$, which implies $\bar{s} \longrightarrow \bar{t}$ by the definition of the follow relation, 9. The cases of t_0 are easy to show.

(2) $\to$ (3) : Assume a finite slicing $\bar{F} \subseteq S$ with $L(A_{\bar{F}}) = L$. By the Lemma 2 we know $\forall x \in \bar{F} \subseteq S, \exists\, y \in S^T : x \leq y$. Hence, we are allowed to assume a function $f : \bar{F} \to S^T$ with $x \leq f(x) \in S^T$. We show that f is surjective.

For all slices $(P,a,F) \in S^T$ there are $w_1 \in P$ and $w_2 \in F$ with $w_1 a w_2 \in PaF \subseteq L = L(A_{\bar{F}})$. This implies by Lemma 1 and 6 that there is a slice $(\tilde{P},a,\tilde{F})$ in the finite slicing $\bar{F}$ with $w_1 a \in \pi_{\bar{F}}(\tilde{P},a,\tilde{F}) \subseteq \tilde{P}a \subseteq Pa = \pi_{S^T}(P,a,F)$ and $aw_2 \in \varphi_{\bar{F}}(\tilde{P},a,\tilde{F}) \subseteq a\tilde{F} \subseteq aF = \varphi_{S^T}(P,a,F)$.

Applying the function f to the slice $(\tilde{P}, a, \tilde{F})$ we will prove that we get the same slice, which we have started with. For that purpose, we assume a slice (P', a, F') with $f(\tilde{P}, a, \tilde{F}) = (P', a, F')$ and we are going to show that $(P, a, F) = (P', a, F')$. For that slice holds $(\tilde{P}, a, \tilde{F}) \leq (P', a, F')$ and therefore $w_1 a \in \tilde{P} a \subseteq P' a = \pi_{S\mathcal{T}}(P', a, F')$ and $a w_2 \in a \tilde{F} \subseteq a F' = \varphi_{S\mathcal{T}}(P', a, F')$. That means we have found to (P, a, F) another slice (P', a, F') responsible to accept the word wav. But for unambiguous $A_{S\mathcal{T}}$ there can be only one slice, by Lemma 1. Thus it must be that $(P, a, F) = (P', a, F') = f(\tilde{P}, a, \tilde{F})$. We conclude that f is surjective, ie: $f(\bar{F}) = S^{\mathcal{T}}$, from which it follows that $|S^{\mathcal{T}}| \leq |\bar{F}|$ and therefore $S^{\mathcal{T}}$ is finite.

(3) $\to$ (1) : We take $A_{S\mathcal{T}}$ for that automaton into account. Because of Lemma 5 it is $L(A_{S\mathcal{T}}) = L$.

4   The Algorithm

In this section, an algorithm is outlined to minimize an εNFA A. It reduces the set of transitions $T_0 = \{t_0, t_1, \ldots, t_n\}$. The algorithm is given in pseudo code. Takes as input a boolean adjacency matrix $A : T_0 \times T_0 \to \{0, 1\}$ representing the follow–relation of the input automaton, ie: $A(s, t) = 1 \Leftrightarrow s \longrightarrow_A t$. Those prerequisites are fixed in the declaration (line 0-1).

The algorithm proceeds in two phases. The first pass (line 2-8), which we might name ε-completion, introduces ε-transitions without changing the original regular language. That the language doesn't change is assured by the test $L(A) = L(A_0)$ in line 6. The second pass (line 9-13) eliminates superfluous transitions in order to reduce the εNFA A. Afterwards, the algorithm returns a result in A, which is the automaton with the remaining transitions.

Algorithm

```
(0)   T₀ = [0, 1, ..., n] ;        ≙ {t₀, t₁, ..., tₙ}
(1)   A : T₀ × T₀ → {0, 1} ;       ≙ A(s, t) = 1 ⇔ s ⟶_A t
(2)   A₀ = A ;
(3)   for s = 0 to n do
(4)       for t = 0 to n do
(5)           A(s, t) = 1 ;
(6)           if L(A₀) ≠ L(A) then A(s, t) = 0
(7)       end
(8)   end ;
(9)   for s = 1 to n do
(10)      for t = s + 1 to n do
(11)          if l(s) = l(t) and A(s, _) = A(t, _) then delete(s)
(12)      end
(13)  end
```

Theorem 3. *The algorithm on input of an εNFA A outputs an εNFA B, so that $L(A) = L(B)$ and $B \leq A$. Moreover, if B is unambiguous then B is transition minimal.*

We prove this theorem in the following subsection.

4.1   Correctness

We shall now be concerned with the correctness of the algorithm. Within the first pass we are adding ε-transition to the automaton. As a result there are more paths possible to accept the words of L. The sole chance to change the language is to accept more words, which is exactly ruled out by the test in line (6) of the algorithm. Moreover, we have

Proposition 4. *It is sufficient to check $L(A) \not\subseteq L(A_0)$ with regard to line (6).*

The second pass eliminates superfluous transitions if there is still an equivalent transition within the automaton covering all accepting paths of the transition. Hence, it still holds $L(A_0) = L(A)$ after the second pass. In fact, the only chance to fail the invariant $L(A_0) = L(A)$ is in line (5), that is instantly corrected in line (6) thereafter.

We are deleting transitions; none are added, ie: $A \leq A_0$. We have sketched that the algorithm is correct in the sense that it still returns an automaton, which accepts the same language compared to the input automaton, having a smaller or equal number of transitions.

Let us now investigate the algorithm's minimization property, ie the fact, that the returned automaton is transition minimal if it is unambiguous. For that purpose, we use the notations of the Theorem 2. Then each transition $t \in T_A$ has got assigned the strict future F_t and the strict past P_t, yielding slice $\bar{t} = (P_t, a, F_t)$ according to the automaton A's finite slicing $\bar{F}$, which is mapped via function f to $S^{\mathcal{T}}$ — recall the construction of the function f of the Theorem 2:

$$\bar{t} = (P_t, a, F_t) \in \bar{F} \quad \text{and} \quad f(\bar{t}) \in S^{\mathcal{T}}$$

Consider the first pass, the ε-completion, in which ε-transitions are placed if and only if the language is not changed. At least this is the case if and only if their correspondent transitions $f(\bar{s})$ and $f(\bar{t})$, with respect to the automaton according to $S^{\mathcal{T}}$, are connected $f(\bar{s}) \longrightarrow_{S^{\mathcal{T}}} f(\bar{t})$. We observe:

Lemma 7. $f(\bar{s}) \longrightarrow_{S^{\mathcal{T}}} f(\bar{t})$ *implies* $s \longrightarrow_A t$

Proof: By the setting of f in Theorem 2 it is $\bar{s} \leq f(\bar{s}) = (P_s, a, F_s)$ and $\bar{t} \leq f(\bar{t}) = (P_t, b, F_t)$, which implies $\pi(s) = (\pi(s){:}1)a \subseteq P_s a$ and $\varphi(t) = b(1{:}\varphi(t)) \subseteq bF_t \subseteq F_s$. We conclude $\pi(s)\varphi(t) \subseteq P_s a F_s \subseteq L$. In that case, the algorithm connects s and t by an ε-transition, which does not change the original language $L(A) = L$ we have started with.

Via the proof of Lemma 5 it also holds: $s \longrightarrow_A t \implies f(\bar{s}) \longrightarrow_{S^{\mathcal{T}}} f(\bar{t})$ in every stage of the algorithm. That is why we obtain after the first pass:

Corollary 4. $s \longrightarrow_A t$ *if and only if* $f(\bar{s}) \longrightarrow_{S^{\mathcal{T}}} f(\bar{t})$

The second pass of the algorithm deletes all except one of equivalent transitions. Two transitions s and t are equivalent if and only if there is a semantically more compact transition $x \in S^{\mathcal{T}}$ with $\bar{s} \leq x \geq \bar{t}$. Actually, this transition is $f(\bar{s}) = x = f(\bar{t})$ — see Lemma 8. We define:

Definition 10. $s \equiv t \ :\Longleftrightarrow\ f(\bar{s}) = f(\bar{t})$

Within the proof it turns out that after the first pass of the algorithm the semantics of the transitions in automaton A in terms of future and past are the same as in the automaton according to S^T. The deletion of transitions cleans up by dropping the superfluous material. It results in an automaton with equal many transitions having equal semantics, compared to the one of $f(\bar{F}) = S^T$, if S^T is unambiguous.

Lemma 8. $f(\bar{s}) = f(\bar{t})$ *if and only if* $l(s) = l(t)$ *and* $s \longrightarrow_A = t \longrightarrow_A$

Sketch of proof: Slices are equal iff future and past are equal—show $\pi(\bar{s}) = \pi(f(\bar{s}))$ and $\varphi(\bar{s}) = \varphi(f(\bar{s}))$ by maintaining Corollary 4. It is sufficient to check $s \longrightarrow_A = t \longrightarrow_A$ because of ϵ-completeness. □

This completes the correctness proof as the algorithm computes $f(\bar{F})$ from the input automaton. If S^T is unambiguous, it holds that $f(\bar{F}) = S^T$. Thus the result is transition minimal. If S^T is not unambiguous, the algorithm returns a subautomaton $f(\bar{F}) \subseteq S^T$. Considering all this, and Lemma 8, we conclude:

Corollary 5. S^T *forms a unambiguous εNFA:*

- If there is a minimal unambiguous εNFA, then the algorithm returns it.
- The minimal unambiguous ϵ-complete εNFA is unique upto isomorphism.

Corollary 6.

- If the algorithm returns an ambiguous εNFA then a minimal εNFA is a subautomaton thereof.

4.2   Complexity

We consider the deterministic worst case time complexity of the algorithm. Let $t(n)$ be the deterministic time complexity for the test whether $L(A) = L(B)$ or not for two εNFA A and B. Then the algorithm runs in deterministic time $\mathcal{O}(n^2 t(n) + n^3)$. At the time one only knows $t(n) \in \mathcal{O}(2^n)$. Therefore the running time of the algorithm is in

$$\mathcal{O}(n^2 2^n + n^3) \subseteq 2^{\mathcal{O}(n)}$$

The observation in Proposition 4 is interesting because it allows us to speed up the first pass. Instead of the equivalence test, we should better run an implication test:

$$L(A) \subseteq L(A_0) \Leftrightarrow L(A) \cap \neg L(A_0) = \emptyset$$

Here the most time consuming operation is the complement $\neg L(A_0) = L(\neg A_0)$ —the automaton has to be made complete and deterministic via the power set construction [21] in order to complement it—but this expression only depends on A_0 and can be precomputed. Hence, the implication test has to do the complement operation just once. In every test, to compute the intersection takes $\mathcal{O}(n^2)$ steps, combined with the test of emptiness, $\mathcal{O}(n)$. Let $t(n)$ the deterministic time complexity to compute the complement. It is $t(n) \in \mathcal{O}(2^n)$ [7]. Hence, the worst case time complexity with this optimization is

$$\mathcal{O}(t(n) + n^2(n^2 + n) + n^3) \subseteq \mathcal{O}(2^n + n^4 + 2n^3) = \mathcal{O}(2^n)$$

Moreover, there is a rich variety of possibilities to further optimize the running time of the algorithm. But this is out of the scope for this paper. Finally, it is worth to mention. that the test whether the returned automaton is unambiguous and therefore transition minimal is easy to check in deterministic time $\mathcal{O}(n^2)$, eg [24, p. 97].

5   Conclusion

Minimization of εNFA was investigated, in particular the theory and an algorithm was developed to reduce the number of transitions of a given εNFA. In general, this problem is PSPACE-complete. The algorithm presented reduces the problem of transition minimization polynomially to NFA equivalences, or alternatively to NFA complements; and runs in deterministic time $\mathcal{O}(2^n)$.

Generally observed, the union principle was exploited. By this means, two transitions t_1 and t_2 are equivalent if there is a semantically more compact transition t with $t_1 \leq t \geq t_2$. The algorithm unions the transitions such that $t_1 \cup t_2 \leq t$. Essentially, the reduction is based on partial orders; as opposed to state equivalences in the deterministic case of DFA. The fact that states resp. transitions in NFA are no objects of equivalence classes, is the main difference to other work.

The union principle is sufficient to reduce εNFA to minimal unambiguous εNFA. In other cases, the minimal εNFA it not unambiguous, a partition principle may be applicable, eg a transition t is superfluous if it can be partitioned into t_1 and t_2 with $t = t_1 \cup t_2$ such that there are more compact transitions t_1^c and t_2^c with $t_1 \leq t_1^c$ and $t_2 \leq t_2^c$.

It remains the main open question for further work whether the union and the partition principle together are sufficient to minimize the number of transitions of an εNFA, in general.

Acknowledgements. Stephan Weber and Arfst Nickelsen are gratefully thanked for their fruitful discussions on the subject. And the referees for their interesting remarks.

References

1. Alfred V. Aho, John E. Hopcroft, and Jeffrey D. Ullman. *The Design and Anlalysis of Computer Algorithms.* Addison-Wesley, Reading, Massachusetts, 1974.
2. A. Arnold, A. Dicky, and M. Nivat. A note about minimal non-deterministic automata. *Bulletin of the European Association for Theoretical Computer Science,* 47:166–169, 1992.
3. Wilfried Brauer. *Automatentheorie.* Teuber, Stuttgart, 1984.
4. Wilfried Brauer. On minimizing finite automata. *Bulletin of the European Association for Teoretical Computer Science (EATCS),* 35:113–116, 1988.
5. Janusz A. Brzozowski. Canonical regular expressions and minimal state graphs for definite events. In *Mathematical Theory of Automata,* pages 529–561. Polytechnic Press, Polytechnic Institute of Brooklyn, New York, 1962.

6. Michael R. Garey and David S. Johnson. *Computers and Intractability: A Guide to the Theory of NP-completeness*. W.H. Freeman and Co, 1979.
7. Markus Holzer and Martin Kutrib. State complexity of basic operations on nondeterministic finite automata. In *Implementation and Application of Automata (CIAA '02), LNCS 2608*, pages 151–160, 2002.
8. John E. Hopcroft. An n log n algorithm for minimizing states in a finite automaton. In *Proc. International Symposium on Theory of Machines and Computations, Technion, Haifa (IL)*, pages 189–196, 1971.
9. John E. Hopcroft and Jeffrey D. Ullman. *Introduction to Automata Theory, Languages, and Computation*. Addison-Wesley, 1979.
10. David A. Huffman. The synthesis of sequential switching circuits. *Journal of the Franklin Institute*, 257(3-4):161–190, 275–303, 1954.
11. Sebastian John. Minimal unambiguous eNFA. Technical report, TR-2003-22, Technical University Berlin.
12. Tsunehiko Kameda and Peter Weiner. On the state minimization of nondeterministic finite automata. In *IEEE Transactions on Computers*, volume C-19, pages 617–627, 1970.
13. J. Kim. State minimization of nondeterministic machines. Technical report, RC 4896, IBM Thomas J. Watson Research Center, 1974.
14. Oliver Matz and Andreas Potthoff. Computing small nondeterministic finite automata. In *Proc. Workshop on Tools and Algorithms for the Construction and Analysis of Systems*, pages 74–88, 1995.
15. Georg H. Mealy. Method for synthesizing sequential circuits. *Bell System Technical Journal*, 34:1045–1079, 1955.
16. A.R. Meyer and M.J. Fischer. Economy of description by automata, grammars, and formal systems. In *Proc. 12th Annual Symposium on Switching and Automata Theory*, pages 188–191, 1971.
17. Edward F. Moore. Gedanken-experiments on sequential machines. *Automata Studies, Annals of Mathematics Series*, 34:129–153, 1956.
18. J. Myhill. Finite automata and the representation of events. Technical report, WADC TR-57-624, Wright Patterson Air Force Base, Ohio, USA, 1957.
19. Anil Nerode. Linear automaton transformations. In *Proc. American Mathematical Society, 9*, pages 514–544, 1958.
20. Siegfried Neuber and Peter H. Starke. Über Homomorphie und Reduktion bei nicht-deterministischen Automaten. *EIK: Elektronische Informationsverarbeitung und Kybernetik*, 3:351–362, 1967.
21. Michael O. Rabin and Dana S. Scott. Finite automata and their decision problems. *IBM Journal of Research and Development*, 3:114–125, 1959.
22. Bala Ravikumar and Oscar H. Ibarra. Relating the type of ambiguity of finite automata to the succinctness of their representation. *SIAM Journal on Computing*, 18(6):1263–1282, 1989.
23. Erik M. Schmidt. Succinctness of descriptions of context-free, regular, and finite languages. Technical Report DAIMI PB-84, Department of Computer Science, University of Aarhus, Denmark, 1978.
24. Seppo Sippu and Eljas Soisalon-Soininen. *Parsing Theory, Vol. I: Languages and Parsing*. EATCS Monographs on Theoretical Computer Science. Springer, 1988.
25. Peter H. Starke. Einige Bemerkungen über nicht-deterministische Automaten. *EIK: Elektronische Informationsverarbeitung und Kybernetik*, 2:61–82, 1966.
26. Richard E. Stearns and Harry B. Hunt, III. On the equivalence and containment problems for unambiguous regular expressions, grammars, and automata. In *IEEE: 22nd Annual Symposium on Foundations of Computer Science*, pages 74–81, 1981.

Substitutions, Trajectories and Noisy Channels

Lila Kari[1], Stavros Konstantinidis[2], and Petr Sosík[1,3,⋆]

[1] Department of Computer Science, The University of Western Ontario, London,
ON, Canada, N6A 5B7
{lila, sosik}@csd.uwo.ca
[2] Dept. of Mathematics and Computing Science, Saint Mary's University, Halifax,
Nova Scotia, B3H 3C3 Canada
s.konstantinidis@stmarys.ca
[3] Institute of Computer Science, Silesian University, Opava, Czech Republic

Abstract. The word substitutions are binary word operations which
can be basically interpreted as a deletion followed by insertion, with some
restrictions applied. Besides being itself an interesting topic in formal
language theory, they have been naturally applied to modelling noisy
channels. We introduce the concept of *substitution on trajectories* which
generalizes a class of substitution operations. Within this framework, we
study their closure properties and decision questions related to language
equations. We also discuss applications of substitution on trajectories in
modelling complex channels and a cryptanalysis problem.

1 Introduction

There are two basic forms of the word substitution operation. The *substitution in
α by β* means to substitute certain letters of the word α by the letters of β. The
substitution in α of β means to substitute the letters of β within α by other letters,
provided that β is scattered within α. In both cases the overall length of α is not
changed. Also, we assume that a letter must not be substituted by the same letter.

These two operations are closely related and, indeed, we prove in Section 3
that they are mutual left inverses. Their motivation comes from coding theory
where they have been used to model certain noisy channels [7]. The natural idea
is to assume that during a transfer through a noisy channel, some letters of the
transferred word can de distorted — replaced by different letters. This can be
modelled by a substitution operation extended to sets of words. This approach
also allows one to take into the account that certain substitutions are more likely
than others. Hence the algebraic, closure and other properties of the substitution
operation are of interest, to study how a set of messages (=language) can change
when transferred through a noisy channel.

In this paper we generalize the idea of substitution using the syntactical
constraints — *trajectories*. The *shuffle on trajectories* as a generalization of sequential insertion has been studied since 1996 [15]. Recently also its inverse —

⋆ Corresponding author.

the *deletion on trajectories* has been introduced [1, 9]. A *trajectory* acts as a syntactical condition restricting the positions of letters within the word where an operation places its effect. Hence the shuffle and deletion on trajectories can be understood as meta-operations, defining a whole class of insertion/deletion operations due to the set of trajectories at hand. This idea turned out to be fruitful, with several interesting consequences and applications [1, 2, 3, 4, 10, 14].

In Section 3 we introduce on a similar basis the *substitution and difference on trajectories*. From the point of view of noisy channels, the application of trajectories allows one to restrict positions of errors within words, their frequency etc. We then study the closure properties of substitution on trajectories in Section 4 and basic decision questions connected with them in Section 5. In Section 6 we discuss a few applications of the substitution on trajectories in modelling complex noisy channels and a cryptanalysis problem. In the former case, the channels involved permit only substitution errors. This restriction allows us to improve the time complexity of the problem of whether a given regular language is error-detecting with respect to a given channel [13]. Due to the page limitations, some proofs are omitted and can be found in [11].

2   Definitions

An *alphabet* is a finite and nonempty set of symbols. In the sequel we shall use a fixed alphabet Σ. Σ is assumed to be non-singleton, if not stated otherwise. The set of all words (over Σ) is denoted by Σ^*. This set includes the *empty word* λ. The length of a word w is denoted by $|w|$. $|w|_x$ denotes the number of occurrences of x within w, for $w, x \in \Sigma^*$.

For a nonnegative integer n and a word w, we use w^n to denote the word that consists of n concatenated copies of w. The *Hamming distance* $H(u, v)$ between two words u and v of the same length is the number of corresponding positions in which u and v differ. For example, $H(abba, aaaa) = 2$.

A language L is a set of words, or equivalently a subset of Σ^*. If n is a nonnegative integer, we write L^n for the language consisting of all words of the form $w_1 \cdots w_n$ such that each w_i is in L. We also write L^* for the language $L^0 \cup L^1 \cup L^2 \cup \cdots$ and L^+ for the language $L^* - \{\lambda\}$. The notation L^c represents the complement of the language L, that is, $L^c = \Sigma^* - L$.

A nondeterministic finite automaton, a *NFA* for short, is a quintuple $A = (S, \Sigma, s_0, F, P)$ such that S is the finite and nonempty set of states, s_0 is the start state, F is the set of final states, and P is the set of productions of the form $sx \to t$, where s and t are states in S, and x is a symbol in Σ. The language accepted by the automaton A is denoted by $L(A)$. The *size* $|A|$ of the automaton A is the number $|S| + |P|$.

A *binary word operation* is a mapping $\diamondsuit : \Sigma^* \times \Sigma^* \to 2^{\Sigma^*}$, where 2^{Σ^*} is the set of all subsets of Σ^*. For any languages X and Y, we define

$$X \diamondsuit Y = \bigcup_{u \in X, v \in Y} u \diamondsuit v. \tag{1}$$

The left and the right inverse $\Diamond^l$ and $\Diamond^r$ of $\Diamond$, respectively, are defined as

$$w \in (x \Diamond v) \text{ iff } x \in (w \Diamond^l v) \text{ iff } v \in (x \Diamond^r w), \text{ for all } v, x, w \in \Sigma^*.$$

Moreover, the word operation $\Diamond'$ defined by $u \Diamond' v = v \Diamond u$ is called reversed $\Diamond$. If x and y are symbols in $\{l, r, '\}$, the notation $\Diamond^{xy}$ represents the operation $(\Diamond^x)^y$. Using the above definitions, one can establish identities between operations of the form $\Diamond^{xy}$.

Lemma 1. *(i)* $\Diamond^{ll} = \Diamond^{rr} = \Diamond'' = \Diamond$,
(ii) $\Diamond^{rl} = \Diamond^{r'} = \Diamond^{lr}$,
(iii) $\Diamond^{lr} = \Diamond^{l'} = \Diamond^{rl}$.

Bellow we list several binary word operations together with their left and right inverses.

Catenation: [1] $u \cdot v = \{uv\}$, with $\cdot^l = \longrightarrow_{rq}$ and $\cdot^r = \longrightarrow_{lq}$.
Left quotient: $u \longrightarrow_{lq} v = \{w\}$ if $u = vw$, with $\longrightarrow_{lq}^l = \cdot'$ and $\longrightarrow_{lq}^r = \cdot$.
Right quotient: $u \longrightarrow_{rq} v = \{w\}$ if $u = wv$, with $\longrightarrow_{rq}^l = \cdot$ and $\longrightarrow_{rq}^r = \longrightarrow_{lq}'$.
Shuffle (or scattered insertion): $u \sqcup\!\sqcup v = \{u_1 v_1 \cdots u_k v_k u_{k+1} \mid k \geq 1,$
    $u = u_1 \cdots u_k u_{k+1}, v = v_1 \cdots v_k\}$, with $\sqcup\!\sqcup^l = \leadsto$ and $\sqcup\!\sqcup^r = \leadsto'$.
Scattered deletion: $u \leadsto v = \{u_1 \cdots u_k u_{k+1} \mid k \geq 1, u = u_1 v_1 \cdots u_k v_k u_{k+1}, v =$
    $v_1 \cdots v_k\}$, with $\leadsto^l = \sqcup\!\sqcup$ and $\leadsto^r = \leadsto$.

3   Substitution on Trajectories

Based on the previously studied concept of the insertion and deletion on trajectories, we consider a generalization of three natural binary word operations which are used to model certain noisy channels [7]. Generally, *channel* [13] is a binary relation $\gamma \subseteq \Sigma^* \times \Sigma^*$ such that (u, u) is in γ for every word u in the input domain of γ – this domain is the set $\{u \mid (u, v) \in \gamma \text{ for some word } v\}$. The fact that (u, v) is in γ means that the word v can be received from u via the channel γ. In [7], certain channels with insertion, deletion and substitution errors are characterized via word operations. For instance, the channel with at most m insertion errors is the set of pairs $\{(u, v) \mid v \in u \sqcup\!\sqcup (\Sigma^0 \cup \ldots \cup \Sigma^m)\}$. The following definitions allow one to characterize channels with substitution errors.

Definition 1. *If $u, v \in \Sigma^*$ then we define the substitution in u by v as*

$$u \bowtie v = \{u_1 v_1 u_2 v_2 \ldots u_k v_k u_{k+1} \mid k \geq 0, u = u_1 a_1 u_2 a_2 \ldots u_k a_k u_{k+1},$$
$$v = v_1 \ldots v_k, a_i, v_i \in \Sigma, 1 \leq i \leq k, a_i \neq v_i, \forall i, 1 \leq i \leq k\}.$$

The case $k = 0$ corresponds to $v = \lambda$ when no substitution is performed.

---
[1] We shall also write uv for $u \cdot v$.

Definition 2. *If $u, v \in \Sigma^*$ then we define the* substitution in u of v *as*

$$u \triangle v = \{u_1 a_1 u_2 a_2 \ldots u_k a_k u_{k+1} \mid k \geq 0, \ u = u_1 v_1 u_2 v_2 \ldots u_k v_k u_{k+1},$$
$$v = v_1 \ldots v_k, a_i, v_i \in \Sigma, 1 \leq i \leq k, \ a_i \neq v_i, \forall i, 1 \leq i \leq k\}.$$

Definition 3. *Let $u, v \in \Sigma^*$, $|u| = |v|$, let $H(u,v)$ be the Hamming distance of u and v. We define*

$$u \triangleright v = \{v_1 v_2 \ldots v_k \mid k = H(u,v), \ u = u_1 a_1 \ldots u_k a_k u_{k+1},$$
$$v = u_1 v_1 \ldots u_k v_k u_{k+1}, a_i, v_i \in \Sigma, 1 \leq i \leq k, \ a_i \neq v_i, \forall i, 1 \leq i \leq k\}.$$

The above definitions are due to [7], where it is also shown that the left-and the right-inverse of $\bowtie$ are $\triangle$ and $\triangleright$, respectively. Given two binary word operations $\Diamond_1, \Diamond_2$, their composition $(\Diamond_1 \Diamond_2)$ is defined as

$$w \in u(\Diamond_1 \Diamond_2)v \iff w \in (u \Diamond_1 v_1) \Diamond_2 v_2, \quad v = v_1 v_2,$$

for all $u, v, w \in \Sigma^*$. Then it is among others shown that:

(i) The channel with at most m substitution and insertion errors is equal to
$\{(u,v) \mid v \in u(\triangle \sqcup\!\sqcup)(\Sigma^0 \cup \ldots \cup \Sigma^m)\}$.
(ii) The channel with at most m substitution and deletion errors is equal to
$\{(u,v) \mid v \in u(\leadsto\!\bowtie)(\Sigma^0 \cup \ldots \cup \Sigma^m)\}$.

Moreover, further consequences including composition of channels, inversion of channels etc. are derived. The above substitution operations can be generalized using trajectories as follows.

Definition 4. *For a trajectory $t \in V^*$ and $u, v \in \Sigma^*$ we define the* substitution in u by v on trajectory t *as*

$$u \bowtie_t v = \{u_1 v_1 u_2 v_2 \ldots u_k v_k u_{k+1} \mid k \geq 0, \ u = u_1 a_1 \ldots u_k a_k u_{k+1}, \ v = v_1 \ldots v_k,$$
$$t = 0^{j_1} 1 0^{j_2} 1 \ldots 0^{j_k} 1 0^{j_{k+1}}, \ a_i, v_i \in \Sigma, 1 \leq i \leq k, \ a_i \neq v_i, \forall i, 1 \leq i \leq k,$$
$$j_i = |u_i|, 1 \leq i \leq k+1\}.$$

Definition 5. *For a trajectory $t \in V^*$ and $u, v \in \Sigma^*$ we define the* substitution in u of v on trajectory t *as*

$$u \triangle_t v = \{u_1 a_1 u_2 a_2 \ldots u_k a_k u_{k+1} \mid k \geq 0, \ u = u_1 v_1 \ldots u_k v_k u_{k+1}, \ v = v_1 \ldots v_k,$$
$$t = 0^{j_1} 1 0^{j_2} 1 \ldots 0^{j_k} 1 0^{j_{k+1}}, \ a_i, v_i \in \Sigma, 1 \leq i \leq k, \ a_i \neq v_i, \forall i, 1 \leq i \leq k,$$
$$j_i = |u_i|, 1 \leq i \leq k+1\}.$$

Definition 6. *For a trajectory $t \in V^*$ and $u, v \in \Sigma^*$ we define the* right difference of u and v on trajectory t *as*

$$u \triangleright_t v = \{v_1 v_2 \ldots v_k \mid k \geq 0, \ u = u_1 a_1 \ldots u_k a_k u_{k+1}, \ v = u_1 v_1 \ldots u_k v_k u_{k+1},$$
$$t = 0^{j_1} 1 0^{j_2} 1 \ldots 0^{j_k} 1 0^{j_{k+1}}, \ a_i, v_i \in \Sigma, 1 \leq i \leq k, \ a_i \neq v_i, \forall i, 1 \leq i \leq k,$$
$$j_i = |u_i|, 1 \leq i \leq k+1\}.$$

These operations can be generalized to sets of trajectories in the natural way:

$$u \bowtie_T v = \bigcup_{t \in T} u \bowtie_t v, \quad u \triangle_T v = \bigcup_{t \in T} u \triangle_t v \text{ and } u \triangleright_T v = \bigcup_{t \in T} u \triangleright_t v.$$

Example 1. Let $T = V^*$, i.e. the set T contains all the possible trajectories. Then $\bowtie_T = \bowtie$, $\triangle_T = \triangle$ and $\triangleright_T = \triangleright$.

One can observe that similarly as in [7], the above defined substitution on trajectories could be used to characterize channels where errors occur in certain parts of words only, or with a certain frequency and so on. If we replace the language $\Sigma^0 \cup \ldots \cup \Sigma^m$ in the above examples by a more specific one, we can also model channels where errors may depend on the content of the message. In the sequel we study various properties of the above defined substitution operations.

Lemma 2. *For a set of trajectories T and words $u, v \in \Sigma^*$, the following holds:*

(i) $\bowtie_T^l = \triangle_T$ *and* $\bowtie_T^r = \triangleright_T$,
(ii) $\triangle_T^l = \bowtie_T$ *and* $\triangle_T^r = \triangleright_T'$,
(iii) $\triangleright_T^l = \triangle_T'$ *and* $\triangleright_T^r = \bowtie_T$.

4   Closure Properties

Before addressing the closure properties of substitution, we show first that any (not necessarily recursively enumerable) language over a two letter alphabet can be obtained as a result of substitution.

Lemma 3. *For an arbitrary language $L \subseteq \{a, b\}^*$ there exists a set of trajectories T such that*

(i) $L = a^* \bowtie_T b^*$,
(ii) $L = a^* \triangle_T a^*$.

Proof. Let $T = \phi(L)$, $\phi : \{a, b\}^* \longrightarrow V^*$ being a coding morphism such that $\phi(a) = 0$, $\phi(b) = 1$. The statements follow easily by definition. □

Similarly as in the case of shuffle and deletion on trajectories [1, 15, 9], the substitution on trajectories can be characterized by simpler language operations.

Lemma 4. *Let $\Diamond_T$ be any of the operations $\bowtie_T$, $\triangle_T$, $\triangleright_T$. Then there exists a finite substitution h_1, morphisms h_2, g and a regular language R such that for all languages $L_1, L_2 \subseteq \Sigma^*$, and for all sets of trajectories $T \subseteq V^*$,*

$$L_1 \Diamond_T L_2 = g((h_1(L_1) \sqcup \sqcup h_2(L_2) \sqcup \sqcup T) \cap R). \tag{2}$$

The previous lemmata allow us to make statements about closure properties of the substitution operations now.

Theorem 1. *For a set of trajectories $T \subseteq V^*$, the following three statements are equivalent.*

(i) T is a regular language.
(ii) $L_1 \bowtie_T L_2$ is a regular language for all $L_1, L_2 \subseteq \Sigma^*$.
(iii) $L_1 \triangle_T L_2$ is a regular language for all $L_1, L_2 \subseteq \Sigma^*$.

Proof. The implications (i) $\Rightarrow$ (ii) and (i) $\Rightarrow$ (iii) follow by Lemma 4 due to the closure of the class of regular languages with respect to shuffle, finite substitution, morphisms and intersection. Alternatively, one can give a polynomial-time construction of an NFA which accepts the language $L_1 \bowtie_T L_2$ or $L_1 \triangle_T L_2$, respectively.

To show the implication (ii) $\Rightarrow$ (i), assume that $L_1 \bowtie_T L_2$ is a regular language for all $L_1, L_2 \subseteq \Sigma^*$. Let $a, b \in \Sigma$ without loss of generality, then also $L = a^* \bowtie_T b^*$ is a regular language, and $T = \phi^{-1}(L)$, ϕ being the coding defined in the proof of Lemma 3. Consequently, T is regular. The implication (iii) $\Rightarrow$ (i) can be shown analogously. □

Theorem 2. *For all regular set of trajectories $T \subseteq V^*$ and regular languages $L_1, L_2 \subseteq \Sigma^*$, $L_1 \triangleright_T L_2$ is a regular language.*

Proof. The same as the proof of Theorem 1, (i) $\Rightarrow$ (ii). □

Theorem 3. *Let $\Diamond_T$ be any of the operations $\bowtie_T$, $\triangle_T$, $\triangleright_T$.*

(i) Let any two of the languages L_1, L_2, T be regular and the third one be context-free. Then $L_1 \Diamond_T L_2$ is a context-free language.
(ii) Let any two of the languages L_1, L_2, T be context-free and the third one be regular. Then $L_1 \Diamond_T L_2$ is a non-context-free language for some triples (L_1, L_2, T).

We note that in the case of Theorem 3 (ii), one can obtain e.g. languages of the form $a^n b^n c^n$.

5   Decision Problems

In this section we study three elementary types of decision problems for language equations of the form $L_1 \Diamond_T L_2 = R$, where $\Diamond_T$ is one of the operations $\bowtie_T$, $\triangle_T$, $\triangleright_T$. These problems, studied already for various binary word operations in [6, 1, 9, 5] and others, are stated as follows. First, given L_1, L_2 and R, one asks whether the above equation holds true. Second, the existence of a solution L_1 to the equation is questioned, when L_1 is unknown (the left operand problem). Third, the same problem is stated for the right operand L_2. All these problems have their variants when one of L_1, L_2 (the unknown language in the case of the operand problems) consists of a single word.

We focus now on the case when L_1, L_2 and T are all regular languages, hence they are defined by means of NFA's accepting them. Then $L_1 \Diamond_T L_2$ is also a regular language by Theorems 1, 2, $\Diamond_T$ being any of the operations $\bowtie_T$, $\triangle_T$, $\triangleright_T$. Immediately we obtain the following result.

Theorem 4. *The following problems are both decidable if the operation $\Diamond_T$ is one of $\bowtie_T$, $\triangle_T$, $\triangleright_T$, T being a regular set of trajectories:*

(i) *For given regular languages L_1, L_2, R, is $L_1 \Diamond_T L_2 = R$?*

(ii) *For given regular languages L_1, R and a word $w \in \Sigma^*$, is $L_1 \Diamond_T w = R$?*

Also the decidability of the left and the right operand problems for languages are straightforward consequences of the results in Section 4 and some previously known facts about language equations [6].

Theorem 5. *Let $\Diamond_T$ be one of the operations $\bowtie_T$, $\triangle_T$, $\triangleright_T$. The problem "Does there exist a solution X to the equation $X \Diamond_T L = R$?" (left-operand problem) is decidable for regular languages L, R and a regular set of trajectories T.*

Proof. Due to [6], if a solution to the equation $X \Diamond_T L = R$ exists, then also $X_{\max} = (R^c \Diamond_T^l L)^c$ is also a solution, $\Diamond_T$ being an invertible binary word operation. In fact, $X_{\max}$ is the maximum (with respect to the subset relation) of all the sets X such that $X \Diamond_T L \subseteq R$. We can conclude that a solution X exists iff

$$(R^c \Diamond_T^l L)^c \Diamond_T L = R. \tag{3}$$

holds. Observe that if $\Diamond_T$ is one of $\bowtie_T$, $\triangle_T$, $\triangleright_T$, then $\Diamond_T^l$ is $\triangle_T$, $\bowtie_T$ or $\triangle_T'$, respectively, by Lemma 2. Hence the left side of the equation (3) represents an effectively constructible regular language by Theorems 1, 2. Consequently, the validity of (3) is decidable and moreover the maximal solution $X_{\max} = (R^c \Diamond_T^l L)^c$ can be effectively found if one exists. $\square$

Theorem 6. *Let $\Diamond_T$ be one of the operations $\bowtie_T$, $\triangle_T$, $\triangleright_T$. The problem "Does there exist a solution X to the equation $L \Diamond_T X = R$?" (right-operand problem) is decidable for regular languages L, R and a regular set of trajectories T.*

Proof. Analogous as in the previous case. $\square$

Theorem 7. *Let $\Diamond_T$ be one of the operations $\bowtie_T$, $\triangle_T$, $\triangleright_T$. The problem "Does there exist a word w such that $w \Diamond_T L = R$?" is decidable for regular languages L, R and a regular set of trajectories T.*

Proof. Assume that $\Diamond_T$ is one of $\bowtie_T$, $\triangle_T$, $\triangleright_T$. Observe first that if $y \in w \Diamond_T x$ for some $w, x, y \in \Sigma^*$, then $|y| \leq |w|$. Therefore, if R is infinite, then there cannot exist a solution w of a finite length satisfying $w \Diamond_T L = R$. Hence for an infinite R the problem is trivial.

Assume now that R is finite. As shown in [6], the regular set $X_{\max} = (R^c \Diamond_T^l L)^c$ is the maximal set with the property $X \Diamond_T L \subseteq R$. Hence w is a solution of $w \Diamond_T L = R$ iff

(i) $w \Diamond_T L \subseteq R$, i.e. $w \in X_{\max}$, and
(ii) $w \Diamond_T L \not\subseteq R$.

Moreover, (ii) is satisfied iff $w \Diamond_T L \not\subseteq R_1$ for all $R_1 \subset R$, and hence $w \notin (R_1^c \Diamond_T^l L)^c$. Hence we can conclude that the set S of all singleton solutions to the equation $w \Diamond_T L = R$ can be expressed as

$$S = (R^c \Diamond_T^l L)^c - \bigcup_{R_1 \subset R} (R_1^c \Diamond_T^l L)^c.$$

Since we assume that R is finite, the set S is regular and effectively constructible by Lemma 2, Theorems 1, 2 and closure of the class of regular languages under finite union and complement. Hence it is also decidable whether S is empty or not, and eventually all its elements can be effectively listed. $\qquad\square$

Theorem 8. *Let $\Diamond_T$ be one of the operations $\bowtie_T, \triangle_T, \triangleright_T$. The problem "Does there exist a word w such that $L \Diamond_T w = R$?" is decidable for regular languages L, R and a regular set of trajectories T.*

Proof. Assume first that $\Diamond_T$ is one of $\bowtie_T, \triangle_T$. Observe that if $y \in x \Diamond_T w$ for some $w, x, y \in \Sigma^*$, then $|y| \geq |w|$. Therefore, if a solution w to the equation $L \Diamond_T w = R$ exists, then $|w| \leq k$, where $k = \min\{|y| \mid y \in R\}$. Hence, to verify whether a solution exists or not, it suffices to test all the words from $\Sigma^0 \cup \Sigma^1 \cup \ldots \cup \Sigma^k$.

Focus now on the operation $\triangleright_T$. Analogously to the case of Theorem 7, we can deduce that there is no word w satisfying $L \triangleright_T w = R$, if R is infinite. Furthermore, the set $X_{\max} = (L \triangleright_T^r R^c)^c = (L \bowtie_T R^c)^c$ is the maximal set with the property $L \triangleright_T X \subseteq R$. The same arguments as in the proof of Theorem 7 allow one to express the set of all singleton solutions as

$$S = (L \bowtie_T R^c)^c - \bigcup_{R_1 \subset R} (L \bowtie_T R_1^c)^c.$$

For a finite R, the set S is regular and effectively constructible, hence we can decide whether it contains at least one solution. $\qquad\square$

We add that in the above cases of the left and the right operand problems, if there exists a solution, then at least one can be effectively found. Moreover, in the case of their singleton variants, all the singleton solutions can be effectively enumerated.

6   Applications

In this section we discuss a few applications of the substitution-on-trajectories operation in modelling certain noisy channels and a cryptanalysis problem. In the former case, we revisit a decidability question involving the property of error-detection.

For positive integers m and l, with $m < l$, consider the SID channel [12] that permits at most m substitution errors in any l (or less) consecutive symbols of any input message. Using the operation $\bowtie_T$, this channel is defined as the set of pairs of words (u, v) such that u is in $v \bowtie_T \Sigma^*$, where T is the set of all trajectories t such that, for any subword s of t, if $|s| \leq l$ then $|s|_1 \leq m$. In general, following the notation of [7], for any trajectory set T we shall denote by $[\bowtie_T \Sigma^*]$ the channel $\{(u, v) \mid v \in u \bowtie_T \Sigma^*\}$. In the context of noisy channels, the concept of error-detection is fundamental [13]. A language L is called *error-detecting for* a channel γ, if γ cannot transform a word in L_λ to another word in L_λ; that is, if $u, v \in L_\lambda$ and $(u, v) \in \gamma$ then $u = v$. Here L_λ is the language $L \cup \{\lambda\}$. The empty word in this definition is needed in case the channel permits symbols to be inserted into, or deleted from, messages – see [13] for details. In our case, where only substitution errors are permitted, the above definition remains valid if we replace L_λ with L.

In [13] it is shown that, given a rational relation γ and a regular language L, we can decide in polynomial time whether L is error-detecting for γ. Here we take advantage of the fact that the channels $[\bowtie_T \Sigma^*]$ permit only substitution errors and improve the time complexity of the above result.

Theorem 9. *The following problem is decidable in time $O(|A|^2|T|)$.*
  Input: NFA A over Σ and NFA T over $\{0, 1\}$.
  Output: Y/N, depending on whether $L(A)$ is error-detecting for $[\bowtie_T \Sigma^*]$.

Proof. In [8] it is shown that given an NFA A, one can construct the NFA A^σ, in time $O(|A|^2)$, such that the alphabet of A^σ is $E = \Sigma \times \Sigma$ and the language accepted by A^σ consists of all the words of the form $(x_1, y_1) \cdots (x_n, y_n)$, with each $(x_i, y_i) \in E$, such that $x_1 \cdots x_n \neq y_1 \cdots y_n$ and the words $x_1 \cdots x_n$ and $y_1 \cdots y_n$ are in $L(A)$. Let ϕ be the morphism of E into $\{0, 1\}$ such that $\phi(x, y) = 0$ iff $x = y$. One can verify that $L(A)$ is error-detecting for $[\bowtie_T \Sigma^*]$ iff the language $\phi(L(A^\sigma)) \cap L(T)$ is empty. Using this observation, the required algorithm consists of the following steps: (i) Construct the NFA A^σ from A. (ii) Construct the NFA $\phi(A^\sigma)$ by simply replacing each transition $s(x, y) \to t$ of A^c with $s\phi(x, y) \to t$. (iii) Use a product construction on $\phi(A^\sigma)$ and T to obtain an NFA B accepting $\phi(L(A^\sigma)) \cap L(T)$. (iv) Perform a depth first search algorithm on the graph of B to test whether there is a path from the start state to a final state.   □

We close this section with a cryptanalysis application of the operation $\bowtie_T$. Let V be a set of candidate binary messages (words over $\{0, 1\}$) and let K be a set of possible binary keys. An unknown message v in V is encrypted as $v \oplus t$, where t is an unknown key in K, and $\oplus$ is the exclusive-OR logic operation. Let e be an observed encrypted message and let T be a set of possible guesses for t, with $T \subseteq K$. We want to find the subset X of V for which $X \oplus T = e$, that is, the possible original messages that can be encrypted as e using the keys we have guessed in T. In general T can be infinite and given, for instance, by a regular expression describing the possible pattern of the key. We can model this problem using the following observation whose proof is based on the definitions of the operations $\bowtie_T$ and $\oplus$, and is left to the reader.

Lemma 5. *For every word v and trajectory t, $v \bowtie_t \Sigma^* = \{v \oplus t\}$.*

By the above lemma, we have that the equation $X \oplus T = e$ is equivalent to $X \bowtie_T \Sigma^* = e$. By Theorem 5, we can decide whether there is a solution for this equation and, in this case, find the maximal solution $X_{\max}$. In particular, $X_{\max} = (e^c \triangle_T \Sigma^*)^c$. Hence, one needs to compute the set $M \cap X_{\max}$. Most likely, for a general T, this problem is intractable. On the other hand, this method provides an alternate way to approach the problem.

Acknowledgements

Research was partially supported by the Canada Research Chair Grant to L.K., NSERC Discovery Grants R2824A01 to L.K. and R220259 to S.K., and by the Grant Agency of Czech Republic Grant 201/02/P079 to P.S.

References

1. M. Domaratzki, Deletion along trajectories. *Theoretical Computer Science* **320** (2004), 293–313.
2. M. Domaratzki, *Splicing on Routes versus Shuffle and Deletion Along Trajectories.* Tech. report 2003-471, School of Computing, Queen's University, 2003.
3. M. Domaratzki, *Decidability of Trajectory-Based Equations.* Tech. report 2003-472, School of Computing, Queen's University, 2003, and to appear in the proceedings of MFCS 2004.
4. M. Domaratzki, A. Mateescu, K. Salomaa, S. Yu, Deletion on Trajectories and Commutative Closure. In T. Harju and J. Karhumaki, eds., *WORDS'03: 4th International Conference on Combinatorics on Words.* TUCS General Publication No. 27, Aug. 2003, 309–319.
5. M. Ito, L. Kari, G. Thierrin, Shuffle and scattered deletion closure of languages. *Theoretical Computer Science* **245** (2000), 115–133.
6. L. Kari, On language equations with invertible operations, *Theoretical Computer Science* **132** (1994), 129–150.
7. L. Kari, S. Konstantinidis, Language equations, maximality and error detection. Submitted.
8. L. Kari, S. Konstantinidis, S. Perron, G. Wozniak, J. Xu, *Finite-state error/edit-systems and difference measures for languages and words.* Dept. of Math. and Computing Sci. Tech. Report No. 2003-01, Saint Mary's University, Canada, 2003.
9. L. Kari, P. Sosík, *Language deletion on trajectories.* Dept. of Computer Science technical report No. 606, University of Western Ontario, London, 2003, and submitted for publication.
10. L. Kari, S. Konstantinidis, P. Sosík, Preventing undesirable bonds between DNA codewords. In C. Feretti, G. Mauri, C. Zandron (Eds.), *DNA 10, Tenth International Meeting on DNA Computing.* University of Milano–Bicocca, 2004, 375–384.
11. L. Kari, S. Konstantinidis, P. Sosík, *Substitution on Trajectories.* In J. Karhumäki, H. Maurer, G. Paun, G. Rozenberg (Eds.), *Theory Is Forever – Essays Dedicated to Arto Salomaa on the Occasion of His 70th Birthday. LNCS* **3113**, 2004, 145–158.

12. S. Konstantinidis, An algebra of discrete channels that involve combinations of three basic error types. *Information and Computation* **167** (2001), 120–131.

13. S. Konstantinidis, Transducers and the properties of error detection, error correction and finite-delay decodability. *J. Universal Comp. Science* **8** (2002), 278–291.

14. A. Mateescu, A. Salomaa, Nondeterministic trajectories. *Formal and Natural Computing: Essays Dedicated to Grzegorz Rozenberg, LNCS* **2300** (2002), 96-106.

15. A. Mateescu, G. Rozenberg, A. Salomaa, Shuffle on trajectories: syntactic constraints, TUCS Technical Report No. 41, Turku Centre for Computer Science, 1996, and *Theoretical Computer Science* **197** (1998), 1–56.

16. G. Rozenberg, A. Salomaa (eds.), *Handbook of Formal Languages,* Springer-Verlag, Berlin, 1997.

State Complexity and the Monoid of Transformations of a Finite Set

Bryan Krawetz[1], John Lawrence[2], and Jeffrey Shallit[3]

[1] School of Computer Science, University of Waterloo
bakrawet@alumni.uwaterloo.ca
[2] School of Computer Science, University of Waterloo
shallit@graceland.uwaterloo.ca
[3] Department of Pure Mathematics, University of Waterloo
jwlaren@math.uwaterloo.ca

Abstract. In this paper we consider the state complexity of an operation on formal languages, $\text{root}(L)$. This naturally entails the discussion of the monoid of transformations of a finite set. We obtain good upper and lower bounds on the state complexity of $\text{root}(L)$ over alphabets of all sizes. As well, we present an application of these results to the problem of 2DFA-DFA conversion.

1 Introduction

A *deterministic finite automaton*, or *DFA*, is a 5-tuple $\mathcal{A} = (Q, \Sigma, \delta, q_0, F)$, where Q is a finite non-empty set of states, Σ is the finite input alphabet, $\delta : Q \times \Sigma \to Q$ is the transition function, $q_0 \in Q$ is the initial state, and $F \subseteq Q$ is the set of final states. We assume that δ is defined on all elements of its domain. The domain of δ can be extended in the obvious way to $Q \times \Sigma^*$, where Σ^* is the free monoid over the alphabet Σ. For a DFA $\mathcal{A}$, the set $L(\mathcal{A}) = \{w \in \Sigma^* \ : \ \delta(q_0, w) \in F\}$ is said to be the language *recognized* by $\mathcal{A}$.

The *state complexity* of a regular language $L \subseteq \Sigma^*$, denoted $\text{sc}(L)$, is defined as the number of states in the smallest DFA recognizing L. We may extend this concept to consider the state complexity of an operation on regular languages, that is, the complexity of the resulting language relative to the complexity of the operand languages. The state complexity of basic operations, such as union, intersection, and concatenation, have been studied extensively by Yu et al. [16, 17].

In this paper we examine the less familiar operation, $\text{root}(L)$, given by

$$\text{root}(L) = \{w \in \Sigma^* : \exists n \geq 1 \text{ such that } w^n \in L\} \ .$$

In pursuit of good bounds on the state complexity of $\text{root}(L)$, we study its realtionship to the connections between algebra and finite automata.

For a finite set Q, a function $f : Q \to Q$ is called a *transformation*. We denote the set of all transformations of Q by Q^Q. For $f, g \in Q^Q$, their composition is written fg, and is given by $(fg)(q) = g(f(q))$, for all $q \in Q$. Together, Q^Q and the composition operator form a monoid.

M. Domaratzki et al. (Eds.): CIAA 2004, LNCS 3317, pp. 213–224, 2005.

Transformations and their monoids have been studied in some detail by Dénes (whose work is summarized in [4]), and Salomaa [13, 14]. Dénes investigates several algebraic and combinatorial properties of transformations, while much of Salomaa's work is concerned with subsets that generate the full monoid of transformations.

In Theorem 1, we will show that transformations of the states in a DFA recognizing a language L can be used to construct a DFA to recognize root(L). This establishes the connection between transformations and root(L), which we will explore. As well, it shows that root(L) is a regularity-preserving operation, that is, if L is regular, then root(L) is regular.

Let L be a language and let $\mathcal{A} = (Q, \Sigma, \delta, q_0, F)$ be a DFA such that $L = L(\mathcal{A})$. For $w \in \Sigma^*$, define $\delta_w(q) = \delta(q, w)$, for all $q \in Q$. Then δ_w is a transformation of Q. If we denote the empty word by ϵ, then δ_ϵ is the identity transformation.

Theorem 1. *For a language L and a DFA $\mathcal{A} = (Q, \Sigma, \delta, q_0, F)$ with $L = L(\mathcal{A})$, define the DFA $\mathcal{A}' = (Q^Q, \Sigma, \delta', q_0', F')$ where $q_0' = \delta_\epsilon$, $F' = \{f : \exists n \geq 1 \text{ such that } f^n(q_0) \in F\}$, and δ' is given by*

$$\delta'(f, a) = f\delta_a, \text{ for all } f \in Q^Q \text{ and } a \in \Sigma .$$

Then root(L) $= L(\mathcal{A}')$.

Proof. An easy induction on the length of $w \in \Sigma^*$ shows that $\delta'(q_0', w) = \delta_w$. Then $x \in$ root(L) $\Leftrightarrow \exists n \geq 1 : x^n \in L \Leftrightarrow \delta_x \in F' \Leftrightarrow \delta'(q_0', x) \in F'$.

Zhang [18] used a similar technique to characterize regularity-preserving operations. To recognize the image of a language under an operation, Zhang constructs a new DFA with states based on Boolean matrices. These matrices represent the transformations of states in the original DFA.

Corollary 1. *For a regular language L, if sc(L) $= n$ then sc(root(L)) $\leq n^n$.*

Proof. This is immediate from the construction given in Theorem 1.

Corollary 1 gives us our first bound on the state complexity of root(L). In the remainder of this paper we improve this upper bound, and give a non-trivial lower bound for the worst-case blow-up of the state complexity of root(L), for alphabets of all sizes. These upper and lower bounds demonstrate that a simple, intuitive operation can increase the state complexity of a language from n to nearly n^n, even over binary alphabets. Our most important results are given in Corollary 3, Corollary 4, and Theorem 6.

2   Unary Languages

For the sake of completeness, we examine the state complexity of root(L) in the unary case. Due to the simpler structure of unary languages, sc(root(L)) can be determined without investigating the transformations of states. It turns out that sc(root(L)) is bounded by the complexity of the original language.

Proposition 1. *If L is a unary regular language, then $\mathrm{sc}(\mathrm{root}(L)) \leq \mathrm{sc}(L)$. This bound is tight.*

The idea of the following proof is that given a particular DFA recognizing L, we can modify it by adding states to the set of final states. The resulting DFA will recognize the language $\mathrm{root}(L)$.

Proof. Let $\Sigma = \{a\}$ be the alphabet of L. Since L is regular and unary, there exists a DFA $\mathcal{A}$ recognizing L, such that $\mathcal{A} = (\{q_0, \ldots, q_{n-1}\}, \{a\}, \delta, q_0, F)$, where $\delta(q_i, a) = q_{i+1}$, for all $0 \leq i < n-1$, and $\delta(q_{n-1}, a) = q_j$, for some $0 \leq j \leq n-1$. We call the states $q_0, \ldots, q_{j-1}$ the *tail*, and the states $q_j, \ldots, q_{n-1}$ the *loop*.

Notice that $\mathrm{root}(L) = \{a^s \in \Sigma^* : s \mid t, a^t \in L\}$. For all strings $a^t \in L$, we have some $k \geq 0$ and some $b \leq n-1$ such that $t = kl + b$, where $l = n - j$ is the number of states in the loop. Let $s = lm + c$ for some $m \geq 0$ and some $0 \leq c < l$. Then

$$
\begin{aligned}
s \mid t &\Leftrightarrow \exists r \;:\; lk + b = r(lm + c) \\
&\Leftrightarrow \exists r \;:\; lk - rlm = rc - b \\
&\Leftrightarrow \exists r \;:\; \gcd(l, -lm) \mid rc - b \qquad \text{(by Theorem 4.3.1 of [1])} \\
&\Leftrightarrow \exists r \;:\; l \mid rc - b \\
&\Leftrightarrow \exists r, v \;:\; rc - b = lv \\
&\Leftrightarrow \exists r, v \;:\; rc - lv = b \\
&\Leftrightarrow \gcd(l, c) \mid b \;. \qquad \text{(by Theorem 4.3.1 of [1])}
\end{aligned}
$$

Thus, a number of the form $kl + b$, where $k \geq 0$ and $b \leq n-1$, has the divisors

$$\{lm + c \in \mathbb{Z} : m \geq 0, \gcd(l, c) \mid b\} \;.$$

So for each $a^t \in L$, the divisors of $t = kl + b$ can be recognized by changing the corresponding states into final states. Therefore, $\mathrm{sc}(\mathrm{root}(L)) \leq \mathrm{sc}(L)$.

To show this bound is tight, for $n \geq 2$ consider the language $L_n = \{a^{n-2}\}$. Under the Myhill-Nerode equivalence relation [7], no two strings in the set $\{\epsilon, a, a^2, \ldots, a^{n-1}\}$ are equivalent. All other strings in Σ^* are equivalent to a^{n-1}. Hence $\mathrm{sc}(L_n) = n$. Furthermore, since a^{n-2} is the longest word in $\mathrm{root}(L_n)$, $\delta(q_0, a^{n-2})$ cannot be a state in the loop. It follows that we require exactly $n-1$ states in the tail plus a single, non-final state in the loop. Hence $\mathrm{sc}(\mathrm{root}(L_n)) = n$. Therefore the bound is tight.

3   Languages on Larger Alphabets

For a regular language L and its minimal DFA $\mathcal{A} = (Q, \Sigma, \delta, q_0, F)$, Theorem 1 describes how to construct an automaton $\mathcal{A}'$ to recognize $\mathrm{root}(L)$. The automaton $\mathcal{A}'$ has all transformations of Q as its states. However, it is easy to see that the only reachable states are compositions of the transformations $\delta_\epsilon, \delta_{a_1}, \ldots, \delta_{a_m}$, where each $a_i \in \Sigma$. The elements $\delta_\epsilon, \delta_{a_1}, \ldots, \delta_{a_m}$, and all of their compositions form the *transition monoid* of $\mathcal{A}$. We can now state the following improvement of the upper bound on the state complexity of $\mathrm{root}(L)$.

Corollary 2. *For a regular language L, let $\mathcal{A}$ be the smallest DFA recognizing L. Then if M is the transition monoid of $\mathcal{A}$, we have that $\mathrm{sc}(\mathrm{root}(L)) \leq |M|$.*

Proof. In Theorem 1, the only reachable states in the construction of $\mathcal{A}'$ are those that belong to the transition monoid of $\mathcal{A}$.

Define $Z_n = \{1, 2, \ldots, n\}$. Now define $T_n = Z_n^{Z_n}$, the set of transformations of Z_n, and $S_n \subseteq T_n$ as the set of permutations of Z_n. For $\gamma \in T_n$ we write

$$\gamma = \begin{pmatrix} 1 & 2 & \cdots & n \\ \gamma(1) & \gamma(2) & \cdots & \gamma(n) \end{pmatrix} .$$

Definition 1. *If $M \subseteq T_n$ is the set of all compositions of the transformations $f_1, \ldots, f_m \in T_n$, then we say that $\{f_1, \ldots, f_m\}$ generates M.*

The relationship between the state complexity of a language and the transition monoid of its minimal DFA naturally leads to the question: for a positive integer m, how large a submonoid of T_n can be generated by m elements? In connection with the study of Landau's function (for a survey see [12]), Szalay [15] showed that, for $m = 1$, the largest submonoid of T_n has size

$$\exp\left\{ \sqrt{n\left(\log n + \log\log n - 1 + \frac{\log\log n - 2 + o(1)}{\log n}\right)} \right\} .$$

When $m \geq 3$, the result, as follows, is well known.

Definition 2. *For $\gamma \in T_n$, define the* image *of γ by $\mathrm{img}(\gamma) = \{y \in Z_n : y = \gamma(z),\ z \in Z_n\}$.*

Definition 3. *For $\gamma \in T_n$, define the* rank *of γ as the number of distinct elements in the image of γ, and denote it by $\mathrm{rank}(\gamma)$.*

Lemma 1. *Let $n \geq 3$. Suppose $H \subseteq T_n$ such that H generates T_n. Then $|H| \geq 3$. Furthermore, $|H| = 3$ if and only if H can be written in the form $H = \{\alpha, \beta, \gamma\}$, where $\{\alpha, \beta\}$ generates S_n and $\mathrm{rank}(\gamma) = n - 1$.*

For a proof of this lemma, see Dénes [3]. This shows that the largest submonoid generated by three elements has the full size n^n.

Only recently has there been any study of the largest submonoid on two generators. Significant progress has been made in this area by Holzer and König [5, 6], and, independently, by Krawetz, Lawrence, and Shallit [9]. The results of Holzer and König are summarized here.

Let k, l be coprime integers with $k, l \geq 2$, and $k + l = n$. Furthermore, let $\alpha = (1\ 2\ \cdots\ k)(k+1\ k+2\ \cdots\ n)$ be a permutation of Z_n composed of two cycles, one of length k, the other of length l. Define $U_{k,l}$ to be the set of all transformations $\gamma \in T_n$ where exactly one of the following is true:

1. $\gamma = \alpha^m$ for some positive integer m;
2. For some $i \in \{1, \ldots, k\}$ and some $j \in \{k+1, \ldots, n\}$ we have that $\gamma(i) = \gamma(j)$ and for some $m \in \{k+1, \ldots, n\}$ we have that $m \notin \text{img}(\gamma)$.

Let $\pi_1 = (1\ 2\ \cdots\ k)$ be an element of S_{n-1}, and let $\pi_2 \in S_{n-1}$ be a permutation such that π_1 and π_2 generate S_{n-1}. Now define $\beta \in T_n$ by

$$\beta = \begin{pmatrix} 1 & 2 & \cdots & n-1 & n \\ \pi_2(1) & \pi_2(2) & \cdots & \pi_2(n-1) & \pi_2(1) \end{pmatrix} .$$

Lemma 2 (Holzer and König). *The set $U_{k,l}$ is a submonoid of T_n and is generated by $\{\alpha, \beta\}$.*

It is worth noting that in their definition of $U_{k,l}$, Holzer and König allow $k = 1$ and $l = 1$. They show implicitly, however, that the size of the monoid in these degenerate cases is too small to be of any consequence here.

Theorem 2 (Holzer and König). *For $n \geq 7$, there exist coprime integers k,l such that $n = k + l$ and $|U_{k,l}| \geq S(n)$, where*

$$S(n) = n^n \left(1 - \sqrt{2} \left(\frac{2}{e} \right)^{\frac{n}{2}} e^{\frac{1}{12}} - \sqrt{8} \frac{1}{\sqrt{n}} e^{\frac{1}{12}} \right) .$$

In addition to a lower bound on the size of the largest two-generated monoid, Theorem 2 proves the existence of a sequence of two-generated monoids whose size approaches n^n as n tends toward infinity. Similar results were obtained independently by Krawetz, Lawrence, and Shallit [9]. More recently, Holzer and König [6] proved the following result regarding the maximality of monoids of the form $U_{k,l}$.

Theorem 3 (Holzer and König). *For all prime numbers $n \geq 7$, there exist coprime integers $k,l \geq 2$ such that $k + l = n$ and $U_{k,l}$ is the largest two-generated submonoid of T_n.*

They also stated the following conjecture.

Conjecture 1 (Holzer and König). For any $n \geq 7$, there exist coprime integers $k,l \geq 2$ such that $k + l = n$ and $U_{k,l}$ is the largest two-generated submonoid of T_n.

In Corollary 2, we established the relationship between the state complexity of $\text{root}(L)$ and the size of the transition monoid of the minimal DFA recognizing L. We now show that we can construct a language based on a particular monoid, so that we may take advantage of Theorems 2 and 3. By associating an alphabet with the generators of a monoid, we can define a transition function for a DFA. We can then complete the definition of the DFA by choosing a start state and a set of final states. We give the DFA construction more formally below.

Let n, m be integers with $n, m \geq 1$. Let $X = \{\alpha_1, \ldots, \alpha_m\}$ be a set of transformations in T_n. Finally, let $M \subseteq T_n$ denote the monoid generated by X. Then a *DFA based on X* is a DFA $\mathcal{M} = (Z_n, \Sigma, \delta, z_0, F)$ where: $|\Sigma| \geq m$; $z_0 \in Z_n$; $F \subseteq Z_n$; and for some map $\Psi : \Sigma \to X \cup \{\delta_\epsilon\}$ that is surjective on X, δ is given by $\delta_a = \Psi(a)$, for all $a \in \Sigma$.

Proposition 2. *Let $M = (Z_n, \Sigma, \delta, z_0, F)$ be a DFA. Then M is the transition monoid of $\mathcal{M}$ if and only if $\mathcal{M}$ is based on X, for some $X \subseteq T_n$ that generates M.*

Proof. For a DFA $\mathcal{M}$ based on X, it is immediate from the construction that M is the transition monoid of $\mathcal{M}$. For any DFA $\mathcal{M}$ that has M as its transition monoid, the set $\{\delta_a \in T_n : a \in \Sigma\}$ will generate M. We can then take Ψ given by $\Psi(a) = \delta_a$, for all $a \in \Sigma$.

Let $\mathcal{A}_{\Psi,X} = (Z_n, \Sigma, \delta, z_0, F)$ denote the DFA based on X when $z_0 = 1$, $F = \{1\}$, and Ψ is bijective on an m-element subset of Σ, with all other elements of Σ mapped to δ_ϵ. It is easily seen that if Ψ_1 and Ψ_2 are maps over the same domain, then $\mathcal{A}_{\Psi_1,X}$ is isomorphic to $\mathcal{A}_{\Psi_2,X}$, up to a renaming of the states and alphabet symbols. For this reason, we denote this DFA simply by $\mathcal{A}_{\Sigma,X}$.

Example 1. Let $Y = \{\alpha, \beta\}$, where

$$\alpha = \begin{pmatrix} 1\ 2\ 3\ 4\ 5 \\ 2\ 1\ 4\ 5\ 3 \end{pmatrix}, \text{ and } \beta = \begin{pmatrix} 1\ 2\ 3\ 4\ 5 \\ 2\ 3\ 4\ 1\ 2 \end{pmatrix} .$$

Define Φ by $\Phi(a) = \alpha$ and $\Phi(b) = \beta$. Then Fig. 1 depicts the DFA $\mathcal{A}_{\Phi,Y}$.

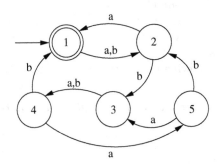

Fig. 1. The automaton $\mathcal{A}_{\Phi,Y}$

For a set X of transformations in T_n, let $M(X)$ denote the monoid generated by X. We now state the following important result concerning the state complexity of root(L).

Theorem 4. *Let X be a set of transformations in T_n. If $U_{k,l} \subseteq M(X)$ for some coprime integers $k \geq 2$ and $l \geq 3$, with $k + l = n$, then the minimal DFA recognizing* root$(L(\mathcal{A}_{\Sigma,X}))$ *has* $|M(X)| - \binom{n}{2}$ *states.*

Before we can prove this theorem, we must provide a few more definitions and lemmas.

Definition 4. *Let $\rho \in T_n$. For any i, j, k, if $\rho(i) = k = \rho(j)$ implies that $i = j$, then we say that k is unique.*

Definition 5. *Let $\rho \in T_n$ have rank 2, with $\text{img}(\rho) = \{i, j\}$. Then by the complement of ρ, we mean the transformation $\overline{\rho} \in T_n$, where*

$$\overline{\rho}(k) = \begin{cases} i, & \text{if } \rho(k) = j; \\ j, & \text{if } \rho(k) = i \ . \end{cases}$$

For example, if $\rho = \begin{pmatrix} 1\,2\,3 \ \cdots \ n-1\,n \\ 3\,3\,2 \ \cdots \quad\ 2 \quad 2 \end{pmatrix}$, then $\overline{\rho} = \begin{pmatrix} 1\,2\,3 \ \cdots \ n-1\,n \\ 2\,2\,3 \ \cdots \quad\ 3 \quad 3 \end{pmatrix}$. In general, it is easy to see that ρ and $\overline{\rho}$ have the same rank, and that $\overline{\overline{\rho}} = \rho$.

For a set of transformations $X \subseteq T_n$, let $\mathcal{M} = (Z_n, \Sigma, \delta, z_0, F)$ be an automaton based on X. We define the DFA $\mathcal{M}^*$ as follows. Let $\delta'(\eta, a) = \eta \delta_a$ for all $\eta \in M(X)$ and $a \in \Sigma$. Also, let $F' = \{\eta \in M(X) : \eta^n(z_0) = F \text{ for some } n \geq 1\}$. Then define $\mathcal{M}^* = (M(X), \Sigma, \delta', \delta_\epsilon, F')$. It follows that $L(\mathcal{M}^*) = \text{root}(L(\mathcal{M}))$.

In order to analyze the state complexity of the language $L(\mathcal{M}^*)$, we must identify the equivalent states of $\mathcal{M}^*$. For $\eta, \theta \in M(X)$, note that η and θ are equivalent states if and only if for all $w \in \Sigma^*$ we have $\delta'(\eta, w) \in F' \Leftrightarrow \delta'(\theta, w) \in F'$. However, since $\delta'(\eta, w) = \eta \delta_w$, this is equivalent to saying that η and θ are equivalent states if and only if for all $\rho \in M(X)$ we have $\eta \rho \in F' \Leftrightarrow \theta \rho \in F'$.

Lemma 3. *Let $X \subseteq T_n$, and let $\mathcal{M} = (Z_n, \Sigma, \delta, z_0, F)$ be an automaton based on X such that $z_0 \in F$. Let $\eta, \theta \in M(X)$, with $\text{rank}(\eta) = 2$. If $\eta(z_0)$ is unique for η, and $\overline{\eta} = \theta$, then η and θ are equivalent states in $\mathcal{M}^*$.*

Lemma 4. *Let $X \subseteq T_n$, and let $\mathcal{M} = (Z_n, \Sigma, \delta, z_0, F)$ be an automaton based on X, such that $z_0 \notin F$. Let $\eta, \theta \in M(X)$, with $\eta(z_0)$ unique for η, $\text{rank}(\eta) = 2$, and $\text{img}(\eta) = \text{img}(\theta)$. If $\theta(z_0) = \eta(z_0)$, and if $\theta(z) = \eta(z_0)$ implies that $z \in F$, then η and θ are equivalent states in $\mathcal{M}^*$.*

The proofs of Lemmas 3 and 4 have been omitted due to space constraints.

Now that we have seen some examples of equivalent states in $\mathcal{M}^*$ in the general case, we restrict our focus. For the remainder of this section, let Y be a set of transformations in T_n such that $U_{k,l} \subseteq M(Y)$, for some coprime integers $k \geq 2$ and $l \geq 3$, with $k + l = n$.

Lemma 5. *Let $\eta, \theta \in M(Y)$, with $\eta \neq \theta$. If $\text{rank}(\eta) = 1$, then η and θ are not equivalent states in $\mathcal{A}^*_{\Sigma,Y}$.*

Proof. Since η has rank 1, we have that $\text{img}(\eta) = \{z_1\}$ for some z_1. If $\eta(1) \neq \theta(1)$, then take $\rho \in U_{k,l}$ such that $\rho(z_1) = 2$, and $\rho(z) = 1$, for all $z \neq z_1$. Then $\text{img}(\eta\rho) = \{2\}$, so that $\eta\rho \notin F'$. But $\theta\rho(1) = 1$, so that $\theta\rho \in F'$. Hence η and θ are not equivalent. If $\eta(1) = \theta(1)$, then $\text{rank}(\theta) \neq 1$ so that for some $z_2 \neq 1$ we have $\theta(z_2) \neq z_1$. Take $\rho \in U_{k,l}$ such that $\rho(\theta(z_2)) = 1$, and $\rho(z) = z_2$, for all $z \neq \theta(z_2)$. Then $\text{img}(\eta\rho) = \{z_2\}$, so that $\eta\rho \notin F'$. But $(\theta\rho)^2(1) = 1$, so that $\theta\rho \in F'$. Hence η and θ are not equivalent.

Lemma 6. *For $\eta, \theta \in M(Y)$ with $\eta \neq \theta$, let η have rank 2. Then η and θ are equivalent states in $\mathcal{A}^*_{\Sigma,Y}$ if and only if $\eta(1)$ is unique for η, and $\overline{\eta} = \theta$.*

The proof of Lemma 6 has been omitted due to space constraints.

Lemma 7. *Let η, $\theta \in M(Y)$, with $\eta \neq \theta$. If η, θ have rank ≥ 3, then η and θ are not equivalent states in $\mathcal{A}^*_{\Sigma,Y}$.*

Proof. Since $\eta \neq \theta$, there exists some $z_1 \in Z_n$ such that $\eta(z_1) \neq \theta(z_1)$. Let $z_2 = \eta(z_1)$. Take $\rho \in U_{k,l}$ such that $\rho(z_2) = 1$, and $\rho(z) = 2$, for all $z \neq z_2$. Now, since rank$(\eta) \geq 3$, we have rank$(\eta\rho) = 2$. If $\eta\rho(1)$ is not unique, then by Lemma 6, $\eta\rho$ and $\theta\rho$ are not equivalent. Hence η and θ are not equivalent. If $\eta\rho(1)$ is unique, it must be that $z_1 = 1$. Furthermore, since rank$(\theta) \geq 3$, we cannot have $\theta(z) = z_2$ for all $z \neq 1$, so we cannot have $\theta\rho(z) = 1$ for all $z \neq 1$. Therefore $\theta\rho \neq \overline{\eta\rho}$. Then by Lemma 6, $\eta\rho$ and $\theta\rho$ are not equivalent. Hence η and θ are not equivalent. $\blacksquare$

We are now ready to prove Theorem 4.

Proof (Theorem 4). Lemmas 5 – 7 cover all possible cases for $\eta, \theta \in M(X)$, $\eta \neq \theta$. Therefore, two states are equivalent if and only if they satisfy the hypothesis of Lemma 6. There are $\binom{n}{2}$ such equivalence classes in $M(X)$, each containing exactly 2 elements. All other elements of $M(X)$ are in equivalence classes by themselves. It follows that the minimal DFA recognizing root$(L(\mathcal{A}_{\Sigma,X}))$ has $|M(X)| - \binom{n}{2}$ states. $\blacksquare$

Now that we have established a close relationship between sc(root(L)) and the transition monoid of the minimal automaton recognizing L, we can take advantage of results concerning the size of the largest monoids. The following corollary gives a lower bound on sc(root(L)) for alphabets of size two. It also proves the existence of a sequence of regular binary languages with state complexity n whose roots have state complexity approaching n^n as n increases without bound.

We now state our first main result.

Corollary 3. *For $n \geq 7$, there exists a regular language L over an alphabet of size 2, with sc(L) $\leq n$, such that*

$$\text{sc}(\text{root}(L)) \geq n^n \left(1 - \sqrt{2}\left(\frac{2}{e}\right)^{\frac{n}{2}} e^{\frac{1}{12}} - \sqrt{8}\frac{1}{\sqrt{n}}e^{\frac{1}{12}}\right) - \binom{n}{2}.$$

Proof. The result follows from a combination of Theorem 2 and Theorem 4. $\blacksquare$

Our results from Theorem 4 do not apply when $l = 2$. Unfortunately, Theorem 3 does not exclude this possibility. To guarantee that this fact is of no consequence, we must show that not only is the monoid $U_{n-2,2}$ never the largest, but that it is also at least $\binom{n}{2}$ smaller than the largest monoid. The following lemma deals with this.

Lemma 8. *For $n \geq 7$, we have that*

$$|U_{2,n-2}| - |U_{n-2,2}| \geq \binom{n}{2}.$$

The proof of Lemma 8 has been omitted due to space constraints.

In the construction of the DFA $\mathcal{A}_{\Sigma,Y}$, the choice of start and final states is optimal. The following theorem shows that for any other DFA with the same transition function, another assignment of start and final states will not increase the state complexity of the language it recognizes.

Theorem 5. *Let* $\mathcal{M} = (Z_n, \Sigma, \delta, z_0, G)$ *be an automaton based on* Y. *Then* $sc(\mathrm{root}(L(\mathcal{M}))) \leq sc(\mathrm{root}(L(\mathcal{A}_{\Sigma,Y})))$.

Proof. If $z_0 \in G$, then Lemma 3 applies. It follows that there are at least $\binom{n}{2}$ pairs of equivalent states in M^*. If $z_0 \notin G$, then Lemma 4 applies, and again we have at least $\binom{n}{2}$ pairs of equivalent states in M^*. In either case, this gives

$$sc(\mathrm{root}(L(\mathcal{M}))) \leq |M(Y)| - \binom{n}{2} = sc(\mathrm{root}(L(\mathcal{A}_{\Sigma,Y}))) .$$

We now state our second main result.

Corollary 4. *For prime numbers* $n \geq 7$, *there exist positive, coprime integers* $k \geq 2$, $l \geq 3$, *with* $k + l = n$, *such that if* L *is a language over an alphabet of size 2 and* $sc(L) \leq n$, *then* $sc(\mathrm{root}(L)) \leq |U_{k,l}| - \binom{n}{2}$. *Furthermore, this bound is tight.*

Proof. Let U' denote the largest two-generated submonoid of T_n. Then by Theorem 3 and Lemma 8, we have that $U' = U_{k',l'}$ for some coprime integers $k' \geq 2$, $l' \geq 3$ with $k' + l' = n$.

Let $\mathcal{M}$ be the smallest DFA recognizing L, and let M be the transition monoid of $\mathcal{M}$. If M is of the form $U_{k,l}$, with $k \geq 2$, $l \geq 3$, then it follows from Theorem 5 that $sc(\mathrm{root}(L)) \leq |U_{k,l}| - \binom{n}{2}$. Hence $sc(\mathrm{root}(L)) \leq |U'| - \binom{n}{2}$. If M is of the form $U_{k,l}$, with $k = n - 2$, $l = 2$, then by Corollary 2 and Lemma 8 we have $sc(\mathrm{root}(L)) \leq |U_{n-2,2}| \leq |U_{2,n-2}| - \binom{n}{2} \leq |U'| - \binom{n}{2}$.

To deal with the case where M is not isomorphic to a $U_{k,l}$ monoid, the result of Theorem 3 is not quite strong enough. However, by re-visiting the proof given by Holzer and König, we can obtain the following improvement [8]:

For all prime numbers $n \geq 7$, there exist coprime integers $k, l \geq 2$ such that $k + l = n$ and $U_{k,l}$ is the largest two-generated submonoid of T_n. Furthermore, if V is the largest two-generated submonoid of T_n such that V is not isomorphic to $U_{k'',l''}$ for some appropriate k'' and l'', then $|U_{k,l}| - |V| \geq \binom{n}{2}$. Then it follows that

$$sc(\mathrm{root}(L)) \leq |M| \leq |U_{k,l}| - \binom{n}{2} .$$

The fact that the bound is tight is an immediate consequence of Theorem 4.

If Conjecture 1 is true, then for all $n \geq 7$ (prime or composite), the construction $\mathcal{A}_{\Sigma,X}$ will yield a language that is within $\binom{n}{2}$ of the upper bound on the state complexity of $\mathrm{root}(L)$. We conjecture that this construction will actually reach the upper bound.

Conjecture 2. For any integer $n \geq 7$, there exist positive, coprime integers $k \geq 2$, $l \geq 3$, with $k + l = n$, such that if L is a language over an alphabet of size 2, with $\mathrm{sc}(L) \leq n$, then $\mathrm{sc}(\mathrm{root}(L)) \leq |U_{k,l}| - \binom{n}{2}$. This bound is tight.

Since the results concerning the largest monoid on 3 or more generators are specific, we can obtain much better bounds on the state complexity of $\mathrm{root}(L)$ for alphabets of size at least 3.

Lemma 9. *For $n \geq 1$, if $M \subseteq T_n$ is a monoid such that $|M| > n^n - \binom{n}{2}$, then $M = T_n$.*

Proof. For $1 \leq n \leq 3$, the result can easily be verified computationally, so assume that $n \geq 4$.

Since $|M| > |T_n| - \binom{n}{2}$, there are at most $\binom{n}{2} - 1$ elements of T_n missing from M. There are $\binom{n}{2}$ transpositions in T_n. Then it follows that M must contain at least one transposition. Also, there are $(n-1)!$ permutations of Z_n whose cycle structure consists of a single cycle with length n. Since $n \geq 4$, we have that $(n-1)! \geq \binom{n}{2}$. Again, considering the size of M, it follows that M must contain at least one n-cycle. Hence $S_n \subseteq M$.

Now consider the transformations in T_n with rank $n-1$. For a transformation to have rank $n - 1$, two elements of Z_n must have the same image; this can be done in $\binom{n}{2}$ ways. Furthermore, we must have that one element of Z_n is missing from the image; this can be done in n ways. Finally, the $n - 1$ elements of the image can be arranged in $(n - 1)!$ ways. This gives a total of $\binom{n}{2} \cdot n!$. It follows that M must contain at least one transformation of rank $n-1$. Then by Lemma 1, we have that $M = T_n$.

We now state our third main result.

Theorem 6. *Let Σ be an alphabet of size $m \geq 3$. For $n \geq 1$, if L is a language over Σ with $\mathrm{sc}(L) \leq n$, then $\mathrm{sc}(\mathrm{root}(L)) \leq n^n - \binom{n}{2}$. Furthermore, this bound is tight.*

Proof. Define M to be the transition monoid of the smallest DFA recognizing L. If $|M| \leq n^n - \binom{n}{2}$, then certainly $\mathrm{sc}(\mathrm{root}(L)) \leq n^n - \binom{n}{2}$. So suppose that $|M| > n^n - \binom{n}{2}$. Then it follows from Lemma 9 that $M = T_n$.

For $1 \leq n \leq 6$, it has been verified computationally that if the transition monoid of the minimal DFA recognizing L is T_n, then $\mathrm{sc}(\mathrm{root}(L)) = n^n - \binom{n}{2}$. For $n \geq 7$, if the transition monoid is T_n, then clearly $U_{k,l} \subseteq T_n$ for some suitable k, l so that Theorem 4 applies, and hence $\mathrm{sc}(\mathrm{root}(L)) = n^n - \binom{n}{2}$.

To show that the bound is tight, it suffices to show that for any n there exists a language L over Σ such that the transition monoid of the minimal DFA recognizing L is T_n. Let X be a set of transformations such that $|X| = m$ and X generates T_n. For $n \in \{1, 2\}$, the fact that such an X exists is obvious. For $n \geq 3$, the existence of X follows from Lemma 1. Then the language $L(\mathcal{A}_{\Sigma,X})$ gives the desired result.

4   An Application to 2DFA-DFA Conversion

Conversion between different types of automata is a well-studied topic in computer science. In this section, we discuss how the bounds on the state complexity of root(L) can be used to improve results concerning the conversion from a two-way deterministic automaton (2DFA) to a DFA. Specifically, we concern ourselves with 2DFA with end-markers. For a complete definition of a 2DFA with end-markers and its accepted language see [2].

Previous results concerning 2DFA-DFA conversion have been obtained by Meyer and Fischer [10] who constructed a sequence of languages recognizable by an n-state 2DFA and with state complexity of $n^{\Theta(n)}$. Moore [11] also demonstrated a sequence with a similar bound. Our construction is as follows.

For a language L with state complexity n, it is possible to recognize root(L) using a 2DFA with $2n$ states. The idea is to construct a 2DFA to simulate the behaviour of the minimal DFA for L, but with that added ability to suspend computation when the end of input reaches a non-final state q of the DFA. At this point, the 2DFA rewinds to the beginning of input, then resumes computation from state q. After t passes, a word w reaches a final state in the DFA if and only if $w^t \in L$.

Let $\Sigma = \{0, 1\}$. For sufficiently large n, choose the integers k and l as per Theorem 2, and let $X_n \subset T_n$ be a two-element set generating $U_{k,l}$. Since $L(\mathcal{A}_{\Sigma,X_n})$ has state complexity n, it follows from the previous paragraph that the language $L_n = \text{root}(L(\mathcal{A}_{\Sigma,X_n}))$ can be recognized by an n-state 2DFA. Then, by applying Theorems 2 and 4, we get

$$\text{sc}(L_n) \geq S\left(\frac{n}{2}\right) - \frac{1}{8}n^2 \ ,$$

where $S(n)$ is defined as in Theorem 2.

This gives us another example of a language with an $n^{\Theta(n)}$ blow-up in the number of states. Furthermore, it can be shown that this example provides an improvement of

$$\Theta\left(n^{\frac{5}{2}}\right) \quad \text{and} \quad \Theta\left(\left(\frac{25}{32}\right)^{\frac{1}{10}n} n^{\frac{3}{10}n}\right) \ ,$$

over the Moore and Meyer-Fischer examples, respectively. A more detailed treatment of this discussion is given in [8].

References

1. E. Bach, and J. Shallit. *Algorithmic Number Theory, Volume 1: Efficient Algorithms.* The MIT Press, 1996.
2. J.-C. Birget. State-complexity of finite-state devices, state compressibility and incompressibility. *Math. Systems Theory* **26** (1993), 237–269.
3. J. Dénes. On transformations, transformation-semigroups and graphs. In *Theory of Graphs: Proc. Colloq. Graph Theory (1966).* pp 65–75. Academic Press, 1968.

4. J. Dénes. On a generalization of permutations: some properties of transformations. In *Permutations: Actes du Colloque sur Les Permutations, (1972)*, pp. 117–120. Gauthier-Villars, 1972.

5. M. Holzer, and B. König. On deterministic finite automata and syntactic monoid size. In *Proc. DLT 2002*, Vol. 2450 of *LNCS*, pp. 258–269. Springer-Verlag, 2003.

6. M. Holzer, and B. König. On deterministic finite automata and syntactic monoid size, continued. In *Proc. DLT 2003*, Vol. 2710 of *LNCS*, pp. 349–360. Springer-Verlag, 2003.

7. J. E. Hopcroft, and J. D. Ullman. *Introduction to Automata Theory, Languages, and Computation*. Addison-Wesley, 1979.

8. B. Krawetz. Monoids and the state complexity of the operation root(L). Master's thesis, University of Waterloo, 2003. Available at http://www.math.uwaterloo.ca/~shallit/krawetz.ps.

9. B. Krawetz, J. Lawrence, and J. Shallit. State complexity and the monoid of transformations of a finite set. Preprint. Available at http://arxiv.org/math/0306416v1.

10. A. R. Meyer, and M. J. Fischer. Economy of description by automata, grammars, and formal systems. In *Proc. 12th IEEE Symp. Switching and Automata Theory*, pp. 188–190, 1971.

11. F. R. Moore. On the bounds for state-set size in the proofs of equivalence between deterministic, nondeterministic and two-way finite automata. *IEEE Trans. Comput.* **20** (1971), 1211–1214.

12. J.-L. Nicolas. On Landau's function $g(n)$. In R. L. Graham, and J. Nesetril (eds.), *The Mathematics of Paul Erdös*, pp. 228–240. Springer-Verlag, 1997.

13. A. Salomaa. On basic groups for the set of functions over a finite domain. *Ann. Acad. Scient. Fenn.*, Ser A. I. 338 (1963).

14. A. Salomaa. Composition sequences for functions over a finite domain. *Theoret. Comp. Sci.* **292** (2003), 263–281.

15. M. Szalay. On the maximal order in S_n and S_n^*. *Acta Arith.* **37** (1980), 321–331.

16. S. Yu. State complexity of regular languages. *J. Aut. Lang. and Comb.* **6** (2001), 221–234.

17. S. Yu, Q. Zhuang, and K. Salomaa. The state complexities of some basic operations on regular languages. *Theoret. Comp. Sci.* **125** (1994), 315–328.

18. G.-Q. Zhang. Automata, boolean matrices, and ultimate periodicity. *Inform. Comput.* **152** (1999), 138–154.

An Application of Quantum Finite Automata to Interactive Proof Systems*
(Extended Abstract)

Harumichi Nishimura and Tomoyuki Yamakami

Department of Computer Science, Trent University,
Peterborough, Ontario, Canada K9J 7B8

Abstract. Quantum finite automata have been studied intensively since their introduction in late 1990s. This paper seeks their direct application to interactive proof systems in which a mighty quantum prover communicates with a quantum-automaton verifier through a common communication cell.

Keywords: quantum finite automaton, quantum interactive proof system, quantum measurement, quantum circuit.

1 Development of Quantum Finite Automata

A quantum-mechanical computing device has drawn wide attention since the pioneering work of Feynman, Benioff, and Deutsch in the 1980s. Moore and Crutchfield [14] as well as Kondacs and Watrous [13] introduced the notion of a *quantum finite automaton* (*qfa*, in short) as a simple but natural model of a quantum computer equipped with finite-dimensional quantum memory space. A qfa performs a series of unitary operations as its head scans input symbols and the qfa eventually enters accepting or rejecting states when it halts. Any entry of such a unitary operator is a complex number, called a *(transition) amplitude*. A quantum computation is seen as an evolution of a quantum superposition of the machine's configurations, where a configuration is a pair of an inner state and a head position of the machine. A quantum evolution is reversible in nature. A special operation called a *measurement* is performed to "observe" whether the qfa enters an accepting state, a rejecting state, or a non-halting state. Of all the variations of qfa's discussed in the past literature, we shall focus our study only on the original models of Moore and Crutchfield and of Kondacs and Watrous for our application to interactive proof systems.

Kondacs and Watrous [13] defined a *1-way quantum finite automaton* (*1qfa*, in short) as well as a *2-way quantum finite automaton* (*2qfa*, in short) that performs a projection measurement at every step. In the model of Moore and Crutchfield, however, a 1-way qfa is measured only once when the head scans the right-end marker. Their model is often referred to as a *measure-once 1-way*

---

* This work was supported in part by the Natural Sciences and Engineering Research Council of Canada.

M. Domaratzki et al. (Eds.): CIAA 2004, LNCS 3317, pp. 225–236, 2005.

quantum finite automaton (mo-1qfa, in short) and the qfa model of Kondacs and Watrous is by contrast called a *measure-many 1-way quantum finite automaton*. As Brodsky and Pippenger [4] showed, mo-1qfa's are so restrictive that they are fundamentally equivalent in power to "permutation" automata, which recognize exactly group languages. On the contrary, Kondacs and Watrous [13] proved that a 2qfa can recognize a certain non-regular language in worst-case linear time by exploiting its quantum superposition. The power of a qfa may vary in general depending on restrictions of its behaviors: for instance, head move, measurement, mixed quantum state, etc.

We are particularly interested in a qfa whose error probability is bounded above by a certain constant $\epsilon \in [0, 1/2)$ independent of input lengths. Such a qfa is conventionally called *bounded error*. We use the notation 1QFA (2QFA, resp.) to denote the class of all languages recognized by bounded-error 1qfa's (2qfa's, resp.) with arbitrary complex amplitudes. Similarly, let MO-1QFA be the class of all languages recognized by bounded-error mo-1qfa's. Moreover, 2QFA(*poly-time*) denotes the collection of all languages recognized by expected polynomial-time 2qfa's with bounded error, where an *expected polynomial-time 2qfa* is a 2qfa whose average running time on each input of length n is bounded above by a fixed polynomial in n. When all amplitudes are drawn from a designated amplitude set K, we emphatically write 2QFA_K and $2\text{QFA}_K(\textit{poly-time})$. For comparison, we write REG for the class of all regular languages. How powerful is a 2qfa? It directly follows from [18] that any bounded-error 2qfa with $\mathbb{A}$-amplitudes[1] can be simulated on a certain probabilistic Turing machine (PTM, in short) using $O(\log n)$-space with unbounded error. Since any unbounded-error $s(n)$-space PTM can be simulated deterministically in time $2^{O(s(n))}$ [3], we conclude that $2\text{QFA}_\mathbb{A} \subseteq \text{P}$. For an overview of qfa's, see the textbook, e.g., [10].

In this paper, we seek an application of qfa's to an interactive proof system, which can be viewed as a two-player game between the players called a prover and a verifier. Throughout the paper, we study the computational power of several variations of such systems. In the following section, we take a quick tour of the notion of interactive proof systems.

2   Basics of Interactive Proof Systems

In mid 1980s, Goldwasser, Micali, and Rackoff [8] and independently Babai [2] introduced the notion of a so-called (single-prover) *interactive proof system (IP system*, in short), which can be viewed as a two-player game in which a player P, called a *prover*, who has unlimited computational power, tries to convince or fool the other player V, called a *verifier*, who runs a randomized algorithm. These two players can access a given input and share a common communication bulletin board on which they can communicate with each other by posting their messages in turn. The goal of the verifier is to decide whether the input is in a given language L with designated accuracy. We say that *L has an IP system* (P, V)

---

[1] The set $\mathbb{A}$ consists of all algebraic complex numbers.

(or an IP system (P, V) *recognizes* L) if there exists an error bound $\epsilon \in [0, 1/2)$ such that the following two conditions hold: (1) if the input x belongs to L, then the "honest" prover P convinces the verifier V to accept x with probability $\geq 1 - \epsilon$ and (2) if the input x is not in L, then the verifier V rejects x with probability $\geq 1 - \epsilon$ even though it plays against any "dishonest" prover. Because of their close connection to cryptography, program checking, and list decoding, the IP systems have become one of the major research topics in computational complexity theory.

When a verifier is a polynomial-time PTM, Shamir [17] proved that the corresponding IP systems exactly characterize the complexity class PSPACE. This demonstrates the power of interactions made between mighty provers and polynomial-time PTM verifiers.

The major difference between the models of Goldwasser et al. [8] and of Babai [2] is the amount of the verifier's private information that is revealed to the prover. Goldwasser et al. considered the IP systems whose verifiers can hide his probabilistic moves from provers to prevent any malicious attack of the provers. Babai, by contrast, considered the IP systems in which verifiers' moves are completely known to provers. Although he named his IP system an *Arthur-Merlin game*, it is also known as an IP system with "public coins." Despite the difference of the models, Goldwasser and Sipser [9] proved that the classes of all languages recognized by both IP systems with polynomial-time PTM verifiers coincide.

In early 1990s, Dwork and Stockmeyer [7] focused their research on IP systems with weak verifiers, particularly, bounded-error *2-way probabilistic finite automaton* (*2pfa*, in short) verifiers that "privately" flip fair coins. For later use, let IP($2pfa$) be the class consisting of all languages recognized by IP systems with 2pfa verifiers and let IP($2pfa, poly\text{-}time$) be the subclass of IP($2pfa$) where the verifiers run in expected polynomial time. When the verifiers flip only "public coins," we write AM($2pfa$) and AM($2pfa, poly\text{-}time$) instead. Dwork and Stockmeyer showed without any unproven assumption that the IP systems with 2pfa verifiers are more powerful than 2pfa's alone (which are viewed as IP systems without any prover). Moreover, they showed the existence of an IP system with a private-coin 2pfa verifier that is more powerful than any IP system with a 2pfa verifier who flips coins only publicly. The IP systems of Dwork and Stockmeyer are seen as a special case of a much broader concept of space-bounded IP systems. See [5] for their overview.

Recently, a quantum analogue of an IP system was introduced by Watrous [19] under the term (single-prover) *quantum interactive proof system* (*QIP system*, in short). The QIP systems with uniform polynomial-size quantum-circuit verifiers exhibit significant computational power of recognizing every language in PSPACE by exchanging only three messages between a prover and a verifier [11, 19]. The study of QIP systems, including their variants (such as multi-prover model and zero-knowledge model), has become a major topic in quantum complexity theory. In particular, quantum analogues of Babai's Merlin-Arthur games, called *quantum Merlin-Arthur games* have drawn significant attention.

3   An Application of QFAs to QIP Systems

Following the success of IP systems with 2pfa verifiers, we wish to apply qfa's to QIP systems. A purpose of our study is to examine the power of interaction when a weak verifier, represented by a qfa, meets with a mighty prover. The main goal of our study is (i) to investigate the roles of the interactions between a prover and a weak verifier, (ii) to understand the influence of various restrictions and extensions of QIP systems, and (iii) to study the QIP systems in a broader but general framework. When the power of verifiers are limited, we can prove without any unproven assumption the separations and collapses of certain complexity classes defined by QIP systems with such weak verifiers.

We first give a "basic" definition of a QIP system whose verifier is a qfa. Our basic definition is a natural concoction of the IP model of Dwork and Stockmeyer [7] and the qfa model of Kondacs and Watrous [13]. In the subsequent section, we discuss a major difference between our QIP systems and the circuit-based QIP systems of Watrous [19]. We shall later restrict the behaviors of a prover and a verifier to obtain several variants of our basic QIP systems since these restricted models have never been addressed in the literature.

Let $\mathbb{Q}$ and $\mathbb{C}$ be respectively the sets of all rational numbers and of all complex numbers. Let $\mathbb{N}$ be the set of all natural numbers (i.e., nonnegative integers) and set $\mathbb{N}^+ = \mathbb{N} \setminus \{0\}$. For any $n \in \mathbb{N}$, $\mathbb{Z}_n$ denotes the set $\{0, 1, 2, \ldots, n-1\}$. By $\tilde{\mathbb{C}}$, we denote the set of all *polynomial-time approximable*[2] complex numbers. Our alphabet Σ is an arbitrary finite set throughout this paper. Opposed to the notation Σ^*, Σ^∞ stands for the collection of all infinite sequences, each of which consists of symbols from Σ.

We assume the reader's familiarity with basic concepts of quantum computation. Conventionally, the notation (P, V) is used to denote the QIP system with the prover P and the verifier V. In such a QIP system (P, V), the 2qfa verifier V is specified by a finite set Q of verifier's inner states, a finite input alphabet Σ, a finite communication alphabet Γ, and a verifier's transition function δ. The set Q is the union of three mutually disjoint subsets Q_{non}, Q_{acc}, and Q_{rej}, where any state in Q_{non}, Q_{acc}, and Q_{rej} are respectively called a *non-halting state*, an *accepting state*, and a *rejecting state*. Accepting states and rejecting states are simply called *halting states*. In particular, Q_{non} has the so-called *initial inner state* q_0. The input tape is indexed by natural numbers (the first cell is indexed 0). The two designated symbols ¢ and \$ not in Σ, called respectively the *left-end marker*[3] and the *right-end marker*, mark the left end and the right end of the input. For convenience, set $\check{\Sigma} = \Sigma \cup \{¢, \$\}$ and assume that Γ contains a special symbol #. At the beginning of the computation, an input string x over Σ of length n is written orderly from the first cell to the nth cell of the input tape. The tape head initially scans the left-end marker. The communication cell holds

---

[2] A complex number is called *polynomial-time approximable* if its real parts and imaginary parts are deterministically approximated to within 2^{-n} in polynomial time.

[3] For certain variants of qfa's, the left-end marker is redundant. See, e.g., [1].

only a symbol in Γ and initially the symbol $\#$ is written in the cell. Similar to the original definition of [13], our input tape is *circular*; that is, whenever the verifier's head scanning $\mathcal{C}$ ($\$$, resp.) on the input tape moves to the left (right, resp.), the head reaches to the right end (resp. left end) of the input tape.

A *configuration* of the verifier V on an input of length n is represented by a triplet $(q, \gamma, k) \in Q \times \Gamma \times \mathbb{Z}_{n+2}$, which indicates that the verifier is in state q, the content of the communication cell is γ, and the verifier's head position is k on the input tape. A *superposition* of the verifier's configurations is a vector in the *verifier's configuration space*, that is, the finite dimensional Hilbert space $\mathcal{H}_n$ spanned by the computational basis $\{|q, \gamma, k\rangle \mid (q, \gamma, k) \in Q \times \Gamma \times \mathbb{Z}_{n+2}\}$. The *verifier's transition function* δ is a map from $Q \times \check{\Sigma} \times \Gamma \times Q \times \Gamma \times \{0, \pm 1\}$ to $\mathbb{C}$ and is interpreted as follows. For any $q, q' \in Q$, $\sigma \in \check{\Sigma}$, $\gamma, \gamma' \in \Gamma$, and $d \in \{0, \pm 1\}$, the complex number $\delta(q, \sigma, \gamma, q', \gamma', d)$ specifies the transition amplitude with which the verifier V scanning symbol σ on the input tape and symbol γ on the communication cell in state q changes q to q', replaces γ with γ', and moves the machine's head on the input tape in direction d.

For any input x of length n, δ induces the unitary operator U_δ^x on $\mathcal{H}_n$ defined by $U_\delta^x |q, \gamma, k\rangle = \sum_{q', \gamma', d} \delta(q, x_k, \gamma, q', \gamma', d) |q', \gamma', k + d \pmod{n + 2}\rangle$, where x_k denotes the kth symbol in x. The verifier is called *well-formed* if U_δ^x is unitary on $\mathcal{H}_n$. Since we are interested only in well-formed verifiers, we henceforth assume that all verifiers are well-formed.

For every input x of length n, the 2qfa verifier V starts with the superposition $|q_0, \#, 0\rangle$. A single step of the verifier on input x consists of the following process. First, V applies his operation U_δ^x to an existing superposition $|\phi\rangle$ and then $U_\delta^x |\phi\rangle$ becomes the new superposition $|\phi'\rangle$. Let $W_{acc} = \text{span}\{|q, \gamma, \xi\rangle \mid (q, \gamma, \xi) \in Q_{acc} \times \Gamma \times \mathbb{Z}_{n+2}\}$, $W_{rej} = \text{span}\{|q, \gamma, \xi\rangle \mid (q, \gamma, \xi) \in Q_{rej} \times \Gamma \times \mathbb{Z}_{n+2}\}$, and $W_{non} = \text{span}\{|q, \gamma, \xi\rangle \mid (q, \gamma, \xi) \in Q_{non} \times \Gamma \times \mathbb{Z}_{n+2}\}$. Moreover, let $k_{acc}, k_{rej},$ and k_{non} be respectively the positive numbers representing "accept," "reject," and "non halt." The new superposition $|\phi'\rangle$ is then measured by the observable $k_{acc} E_{acc} + k_{rej} E_{rej} + k_{non} E_{non}$, where $E_{acc}, E_{rej},$ and E_{non} are respectively the projection operators on $W_{acc}, W_{rej},$ and W_{non}. Assuming that $|\phi'\rangle$ is expressed as $|\psi_1\rangle + |\psi_2\rangle + |\psi_3\rangle$ for certain vectors $|\psi_1\rangle \in W_{acc}, |\psi_2\rangle \in W_{rej},$ and $|\psi_3\rangle \in W_{non}$, we say that, at this step, V *accepts* x with probability $\||\psi_1\rangle\|^2$ and *rejects* x with probability $\||\psi_2\rangle\|^2$. Only the non-halting superposition $|\psi_3\rangle$ continues to the next step and V is said to *continue (to the next step) with probability $\||\psi_3\rangle\|^2$*. In particular, if the verifier is a 1qfa, then the verifier's transition function δ must satisfy the following two additional conditions: (i) for every $q, q' \in Q$, $\sigma \in \check{\Sigma}$, and $\gamma, \gamma' \in \Gamma$, $\delta(q, \sigma, \gamma, q', \gamma', d) = 0$ if $d \neq 1$ (i.e., the head always moves to the right) and (ii) the verifier must enter halting states exactly when or before the verifier scans the left end-marker $\$$.

In contrast to the verifier, the prover P has an infinite private tape and accesses an input x and a communication cell. Let Δ be a finite set of the prover's tape alphabet, which includes the blank symbol $\#$. The *prover's configuration space* is the Hilbert space spanned by the computational basis $\{|\gamma\rangle |y\rangle \mid (\gamma, y) \in \Gamma \times \Delta_{fin}^\infty\}$, where $\Delta_{fin}^\infty = \Delta^* \times \{\#\}^\infty$. We require the prover to alter only a finite segment of his private tape at each step. Formally, the prover P on input x is specified by a series of unitary operators $\{U_{P,i}^x\}_{i\in\mathbb{N}^+}$, each of which acts on the prover's configuration space, such that $U_{P,i}^x$ is of the form $V_{P,i}^x \otimes I$, where $\dim(V_{P,i}^x)$ is finite and I is the identity operator. Such a series of operators is sometimes called the *prover's strategy*. For any function k from $\mathbb{N}^2$ to $\mathbb{N}$, we call the prover $k(n,i)$-*space bounded* if the prover uses at most the first $k(n,i)$ cells of his private tape; that is, at the ith step, $V_{P,i}^x$ is applied only to the first $k(n,i)$ cells in addition to the communication cell. If the prover has a string y in his private tape and scans symbol γ in the communication cell, then he applies $U_{P,i}^x$ to the quantum state $|\gamma\rangle|y\rangle$ at the ith step. If $U_{P,i}^x|\gamma\rangle|y\rangle = \sum_{\gamma',y'} \alpha_{\gamma',y'}^i |\gamma'\rangle|y'\rangle$, then the prover changes y into y' and replaces γ by γ' with amplitude $\alpha_{y',\gamma'}^i$.

The *computation* of the QIP system (P,V) on input x starts with the initial configuration of V with the prover's private tape consisting of all blank symbols. The two players apply their unitary operators U_δ^x and $\{U_{P,i}^x\}_{i\in\mathbb{N}^+}$ in turn starting with the verifier's move. A measurement is made after every move of the verifier to determine whether V is in a halting state. Each computation path therefore ends exactly when V enters a certain halting state along this path. As the running time of the QIP system, we count the number of steps taken by the verifier and the prover. We define the probability that (P,V) *accepts* (*rejects*, resp.) the input x as the limit, as $t \to \infty$, of the probability that V accepts (rejects, resp.) x in at most t steps. We say that V *always halts with probability* 1 if, for every input x and every prover P^*, (P^*,V) reaches halting states with probability 1. In general, V may not always halt with probability 1.

Let L be any language and a, b be any two real numbers in the unit interval $[0,1]$. Let (P,V) be any QIP system. We say that L has an (a,b)-*QIP system* (P,V) (or (P,V) *recognizes* L) if the following two conditions hold:

1. (completeness) for every $x \in L$, (P,V) accepts x with probability at least a, and
2. (soundness) for any $x \notin L$ and any prover P^*, (P^*,V) rejects[4] x with probability at least b.

For convenience, we use the same notation (P,V) to mean a QIP system and also a protocol taken by the prover P and the verifier V.

Adapting Condon's [5] notational convention, we write $\text{QIP}_{a,b}(\langle\mathcal{R}\rangle)$, where $\langle\mathcal{R}\rangle$ is a set of restrictions, to denote the collection of all languages recognized by certain (a,b)-QIP systems with the restrictions specified by $\langle\mathcal{R}\rangle$. Let $\text{QIP}(\langle\mathcal{R}\rangle)$ be $\bigcup_{\epsilon>0} \text{QIP}_{1/2+\epsilon,1/2+\epsilon}(\langle\mathcal{R}\rangle)$. If in addition the verifier's amplitudes are restricted to an amplitude set K (but there is no restriction for the prover), then we rather write $\text{QIP}_K(\langle\mathcal{R}\rangle)$. Although it is possible to consider a wide variety of QIP systems by choosing different $\langle\mathcal{R}\rangle$, we focus mostly on the following four basic restrictions: $\langle mo\text{-}1qfa\rangle$ ("measure-once" 1qfa verifiers), $\langle 1qfa\rangle$ ("measure-many" 1qfa verifiers), $\langle 2qfa\rangle$ ("measure-many" 2qfa verifiers), and $\langle poly\text{-}time\rangle$

---

[4] The QIP system may increase its power if we instead require (P^*,V) to *accept* x with probability $\leq 1 - b$ for any prover P^*. See, e.g., [7] for the classical case.

(expected polynomial running time). For instance, QIP($2qfa$, *poly-time*) denotes the language class defined by QIP systems with expected polynomial-time 2qfa verifiers.

4   A Comparison with Circuit Based QIP Systems

We briefly discuss the major difference between our automaton-based QIP systems and circuit-based QIP systems in which a prover and a verifier are viewed as series of quantum circuits intertwined each other in turn, sharing only message qubits. We assume the reader's familiarity with Watrous's circuit-based QIP model [19].

In the circuit-based model of Watrous, the measurement of the output qubit is performed only once at the end of the verifier's computation since any measurement during the computation can be postponed (see, e.g., [15]). This is possible because the verifier has private qubits and his running time is bounded. However, since our qfa verifier has no private tape and may not halt within a finite number of steps, if we want to simulate the qfa verifier on a quantum circuit, then we need to measure a certain number of qubits (as a halting flag) after each move of the verifier.

A verifier in the circuit-based model is allowed to carry out a large number of basic unitary operations in a single interaction round while a qfa verifier in our model is constantly attacked by a malicious prover after every step of the verifier. Therefore, such a malicious prover may exercise more influence on the verifier in our QIP model than in the circuit-based model. Later in Section 9, we shall introduce a variant of our basic QIP systems that allow a verifier to make a series of transitions without communicating with a prover.

5   A QFA Verifier Against a Mighty Prover

Following the definition of a QIP system with a qfa verifier, we demonstrate how well a qfa verifier plays against a powerful prover. We begin with the case of 1qfa verifiers. It is well-known in [13] that 1QFA $\subsetneq$ REG. In the following theorem, we show that the interaction between a prover and a 1qfa verifier truly enhances the power of recognizing languages.

Theorem 1. 1QFA $\subsetneq$ QIP($1qfa$) = REG.

Note that the first inequality of Theorem 1 follows from the last equality since 1QFA $\neq$ REG. In particular, to show the inclusion QIP($1qfa$) $\subseteq$ REG, we need Lemmas 1 and 2. For convenience, we first introduce a restricted QIP system. Let s and t be any functions from $\mathbb{N}$ to $\mathbb{N}$. A $(t(n), s(n))$-*bounded QIP system* is obtained from a QIP system by forcing the QIP protocol to "terminate" after $t(|x|)$ steps by collapsing any non-halting state to the special output symbol "*I don't know*" and by using only $s(|x|)$-space bounded provers. A language has a $(t(n), s(n))$-bounded QIP system if the system satisfies the completeness and soundness conditions of Section 3 with error probability at most $\epsilon \in [0, 1/2)$.

Lemma 1. *Let L be any language in* QIP(1qfa)*. There exists a constant $c \in \mathbb{N}^+$ such that L has a $(n + 2, c)$-bounded QIP system with a 1qfa verifier.*

Lemma 1 can be seen as a special case of Lemma 3. Lemma 2 relates to the notion of *1-tiling complexity* [6]. For any language L over alphabet Σ and any number $n \in \mathbb{N}$, we define the finite binary matrix $M_L(n)$ whose rows and columns are indexed by the strings in $\Sigma^{\leq n}$ in the following fashion: any (x, y)-entry of $M_L(n)$ is 1 if $xy \in L$ and 0 otherwise. A *1-tiling* of $M_L(n)$ is a set S of M_L's submatrices M such that (i) all the entries of $M_L(n)$ are specified by a certain index set $R \times C$, where $R, C \subseteq \Sigma^{\leq n}$, (ii) all the entries of M have the same value 1, and (iii) every 1-valued entry of $M_L(n)$ is covered by at least one element of S. The *1-tiling complexity* of L is the function $T_L^1(n)$ whose value is the minimal size of a 1-tiling of $M_L(n)$.

Lemma 2. *Let L be any language and let $\epsilon \in [0, 1/2)$. If a $(n + 2, c)$-bounded QIP system (P, V) with a 1qfa verifier recognizes L with error probability at most ϵ, then the 1-tiling complexity of L is at most $[2(1 + 2d^2)/(1 - 2\epsilon)]^{2d+1}$, where $d = |Q||\Gamma||\Delta|^c$ for the set Q of the verifier's inner states, the prover's tape alphabet Δ, and the communication alphabet Γ.*

We return to the proof of Theorem 1. Recall that a language is regular if and only if its 1-tiling complexity is bounded above by a certain constant [6]. Since Lemma 2 implies that every language in QIP(1qfa) has $O(1)$ 1-tiling complexity, we conclude that QIP(1qfa) $\subseteq$ REG. This completes the proof.

Next, we turn our interest to 2qfa verifiers. Consider the complexity classes QIP(2qfa) and QIP(2qfa, *poly-time*). We begin with our main result: QIP(2qfa, *poly-time*) is located between 2QFA(*poly-time*) and NP with an appropriate choice of amplitudes. This can be compared with the result of Dwork and Stockmeyer [7] that REG $\subsetneq$ IP(2pfa, *poly-time*) $\subseteq$ PSPACE. Note that REG $\subsetneq$ 2QFA(*poly-time*) [13] and 2QFA(*poly-time*) $\subseteq$ QIP(2qfa, *poly-time*).

Theorem 2. QIP$_{\tilde{\mathbb{C}}}$(2qfa, *poly-time*) $\subseteq$ NP.

A key idea for the proof of Theorem 2 is to bound the prover's configuration space. Similar to Lemma 1, we can prove the following.

Lemma 3. *Every language in* QIP(2qfa, poly-time) *has a $(t(n), c \log n + c)$-bounded QIP system for a certain polynomial t and a certain constant $c > 0$.*

Lemma 3 directly comes from the following claim, which is proven in a fashion similar to [12–Lemma 9].

Lemma 4. *Let (P, V) be any QIP system with a 2qfa (1qfa, resp.) verifier and let Q, Γ be respectively the sets of all inner states and of all communication symbols. There is a prover P' that satisfies the following conditions: for every input x, (i) the prover's ith operation $U_{P', i}^x$ is $|Q||\Gamma|(|x|+2)$-dimensional ($|Q||\Gamma|$-dimensional, resp.) unitary operator, where $i \in \mathbb{N}^+$, and (ii) the probability of accepting x by (P', V) is exactly equal to the one by (P, V).*

We therefore pay our attention only to $(n^{O(1)}, O(\log(n)))$-bounded QIP systems. To simulate such a system, we need to approximate the prover's unitary operations using a fixed universal set of quantum gates. Lemma 5 relates to an upper bound of the number of quantum gates necessary to approximate a given unitary operator. The lemma is explicitly stated in [16]. We fix an appropriate universal set consisting of the Controlled-NOT gate and a finite number of single-qubit gates, with $\tilde{\mathbb{C}}$-amplitudes, that generate a dense subset of SU(2) with their inverse.

Lemma 5. *For every sufficiently large $k \in \mathbb{N}^+$, every k-qubit unitary operator U_k, and every $\epsilon > 0$, there exists a quantum circuit C acting on k qubits such that C has size at most $2^{3k} \log^3 (1/\epsilon)$ and $\|U(C) - U_k\| < \epsilon$, where $U(C)$ is the unitary operator associated with C, where $\|A\| = \sup_{|\phi\rangle \neq 0} \|A|\phi\rangle\|/\||\phi\rangle\|$.*

A quantum circuit can be further encoded into a binary string, provided that the encoding length is at least the size of the quantum circuit. Such an encoding proves the following proposition for any polynomial-time computable increasing functions $t(n)$ and $s(n)$.

Proposition 1. *Any language that has a $(t(n), s(n))$-bounded QIP system with $\tilde{\mathbb{C}}$-amplitudes belongs to* NTIME$(n^{O(1)}t(n)2^{O(s(n))} \log^{O(1)} t(n))$.

Theorem 2 follows immediately from Proposition 1 together with Lemma 3.

Proposition 2. QIP($2qfa$) *and* QIP($2qfa, poly\text{-}time$) *are closed under union.*

6   How Often Is Measurement Performed?

A measurement is one of the most fundamental operations in quantum computation. Although a measurement is necessary to "know" the content of a quantum state, the measurement collapses the quantum state and thus causes a quantum computation irreversible. We make a brief comparison between mo-1qfa verifiers and 1qfa verifiers. As mentioned in Section 1, mo-1qfa's and 1qfa's are quite different in power because the numbers of measurement operations are different.

Theorem 3. MO-1QFA $\subsetneqq$ QIP($mo\text{-}1qfa$) $\subsetneqq$ QIP($1qfa$).

Theorem 3 is a direct consequence of Proposition 3 because MO-1QFA and REG are known to be closed under complementation[5] [4].

Proposition 3. QIP($mo\text{-}1qfa$) *is not closed under complementation.*

To prove Proposition 3, it suffices to show an counter example that $\{a\}^* \setminus \{\lambda\} \in$ QIP($mo\text{-}1qfa$) and $\{\lambda\} \notin$ QIP($mo\text{-}1qfa$). More generally, we can claim that no finite language belongs to QIP($mo\text{-}1qfa$). This claim is a consequence of the following lemma, which shows a more general limit of QIP systems with mo-1qfa verifiers.

---

[5] A complexity class $\mathcal{C}$ is *closed under complementation* if, for any language A over alphabet Σ in $\mathcal{C}$, its complement $\Sigma^* \setminus A$ also is in $\mathcal{C}$.

Lemma 6. *Let L be a language and M be its minimal automaton. Assume that there exist an input symbol a, an accepting state q_1, and a rejecting state q_2 satisfying: (1) if M reads a in the state q_1, then M enters the state q_2 and (2) if M reads a in the state q_2, then M stays in the state q_2. The language L is then outside of $\mathrm{QIP}(mo\text{-}1qfa)$.*

7   Is a Quantum Prover Stronger Than a Classical One?

Our prover can perform any operation that quantum physics allows. If the prover is limited to wield only "classical" power, we call such a prover "classical." More precisely, a prover is *classical* if the prover's move is dictated by a unitary operator whose entries are either 0s or 1s. By contrast, we sometimes refer to any standard prover as a *quantum prover*. Intuitively, more powerful the prover becomes, more easily may the weak verifier be convinced as well as fooled. Hereafter, the restriction $\langle c\text{-}prover \rangle$ means that a prover is forced to be classical.

Proposition 4. $\mathrm{QIP}(1qfa) \subseteq \mathrm{QIP}(1qfa, c\text{-}prover)$.

Next, we consider the complexity class $\mathrm{QIP}(2qfa, poly\text{-}time, c\text{-}prover)$. Since $\mathrm{QIP}(2qfa, poly\text{-}time, c\text{-}prover)$ contains $\mathrm{2QFA}(poly\text{-}time)$, we immediately obtain $\mathrm{REG} \subsetneq \mathrm{QIP}(2qfa, poly\text{-}time, c\text{-}prover)$. Moreover, using classical provers, we can show that $\mathrm{QIP}(2qfa, poly\text{-}time, c\text{-}prover)$ contains the non-regular language $Center = \{x \mid \exists y, z[|y| = |z| \wedge x = y1z]\}$. More strongly, $Center$ can be recognized by a certain QIP system with a 2qfa verifier that runs in *worst-case* polynomial time. Since no IP system with an expected polynomial-time 2pfa verifier recognizes $Center$ with public coins [7], we therefore attain the following separation.

Theorem 4. $\mathrm{QIP}(2qfa, poly\text{-}time, c\text{-}prover) \not\subseteq \mathrm{AM}(2pfa, poly\text{-}time)$.

8   What if a Verifier Reveals His Private Information?

The strength of a prover's strategy hinges on the amount of the information that a verifier knowingly reveals. The classical notion of "public coins" means that the complete information of the verifier's configurations is given to a prover. When the verifier reveals his choice of next moves, the prover can calculate the verifier's current configuration and even predict the verifier's next move. This paper considers only its straightforward analogy in the quantum setting. We call such a system *public*. Formally, we introduce a *public QIP system* as follows.

Definition 1. *A QIP system (P, V) with the qfa verifier V is called public if the verifier V writes his choice of inner state and head direction in the communication cell at every step; that is, the verifier's transition function δ satisfies that, for any x, q, γ, and k, $U_\delta^x |q, \gamma, k\rangle = \sum_{q', \xi, d} \delta(q, x_k, \gamma, q', \xi, d)|q', \xi, k+d \,(\mathrm{mod}\; n+2)\rangle$, where $\xi = (q', d)$ whenever q' is a non-halting state.*

To emphasize the public QIP system, we use the restriction $\langle public \rangle$. We obtain the following separation results. Let 1RFA denote the class of all languages recognized by *1-way reversible finite automata* (i.e., 1qfa's whose transition amplitudes are drawn from $\{0, 1\}$).

Proposition 5. $1RFA \subsetneq QIP_{1,1}(1qfa, public) \nsubseteq 1QFA$.

9   How Many Interactions Are Necessary?

In the previous sections, we have shown that quantum interaction between a prover and a verifier clearly enhances the qfa's ability to recognize languages. Since our original definition allows a verifier to communicate with a prover at every step, it is natural to ask whether such interactions are necessary. In this section, we carefully examine the number of interactions performed in a QIP system. To study the number of interactions, we need to modify our original definition of QIP systems with qfa verifiers. Ideally, the prover changes the symbol in the communication cell only when the verifier asks the prover to do so. For such a modification, we first look into the IP systems of Dwork and Stockmeyer [7]. In their system, a verifier is allowed to do computation silently with no communication with a prover at any chosen step. The verifier communicates with the prover only when the help of the prover is needed. We can view the verifier's silent mode as follows: if the verifier V does not want to communicate with the prover, he writes a special communication symbol in the communication cell to signal the prover that he does not need any help from the prover. We use the communication symbol $\#$ to condition that the prover is not allowed to alter the content of the communication cell.

We introduce a new QIP system. To avoid any messy technicality, we rather take a simple approach: we prohibit any malicious prover to cheat a verifier by altering the symbol $\#$ willfully. Formally, we require the prover's operation $\{U_{P,i}^x\}_{i \in \mathbb{N}^+}$ to satisfy that, for every $i \in \mathbb{N}^+$ and every $y \in \Delta_{fin}^\infty$ that appears on the prover's tape with a non-zero amplitude after the previous operation $U_{P,i-1}^x$ (if $i \geq 2$), there is a certain pure quantum state $|\psi_{y,i}\rangle$ in the Hilbert space $span\{\Delta_{fin}^\infty\}$ for which $U_{P,i}^x|\#\rangle|y\rangle = |\#\rangle|\psi_{y,i}\rangle$. Since the verifier can make several moves without any direct interaction with the prover, this new model is in essence close to the circuit-based QIP model discussed in Section 4. We call our new model an *interaction-bounded QIP system*. For comparison, we use the notation $QIP^\#(1qfa)$ to denote the class of all languages recognized by certain interaction-bounded QIP systems. Since $QIP^\#(1qfa)$ includes $QIP(1qfa)$, our interaction-bounded QIP systems can also recognize the regular languages.

Lemma 7. $REG \subseteq QIP^\#(1qfa)$.

We need to clarify the meaning of the number of interactions. Here, the *number of interactions* means the maximum number of steps at which the verifier writes any symbol except for $\#$ in the communication cell along any computation path. Let $QIP_k^\#(1qfa)$ be the class of all languages recognized by interaction-bounded QIP systems which conduct interactions at most k times.

Theorem 5. $1\mathrm{QFA} \subsetneq \mathrm{QIP}_1^{\#}(1qfa) \subsetneq \mathrm{QIP}^{\#}(1qfa)$.

Final Note. All the proofs omitted from this extended abstract will appear in its forthcoming complete version.

References

1. A. Ambainis, M. Beaudry, M. Golovkins, A. Ķikusts, M. Mercer, and D. Thérien. Algebraic results on quantum automata. In *Proc. 21st STACS*, Lecture Notes in Comput. Sci., Vol.2996, pp.93–104, 2004.
2. L. Babai. Trading group theory for randomness. In *Proc. 17th STOC*, pp.421–429, 1985.
3. A. Borodin, S. Cook, and N. Pippenger. Parallel computation for well-endowed rings and space-bounded probabilistic machines. *Inform. Control* **58** (1983) 113–136.
4. A. Brodsky and N. Pippenger. Characterizations of 1-way quantum finite automata. *SIAM J. Comput.* **31** (2002) 1456–1478.
5. A. Condon. The complexity of space bounded interactive proof systems. In *Complexity Theory: Current Research* (eds. Ambos-Spies, et al.), Cambridge University Press, pp.147–189, 1993.
6. A. Condon, L. Hellerstein, S. Pottle, and A. Wigderson. On the power of finite automata with both nondeterministic and probabilistic states. *SIAM J. Comput.* **27** (1998) 739–762.
7. C. Dwork and L. Stockmeyer. Finite state verifiers I: the power of interaction. *J. ACM* **39** (1992) 800–828.
8. S. Goldwasser, S. Micali and C. Rackoff. The knowledge complexity of interactive proof systems. *SIAM J. Comput.* **18** (1989) 186–208.
9. S. Goldwasser and M. Sipser. Private coins versus public coins in interactive proof systems. In *Proc. 18th STOC*, pp.59–68, 1986.
10. J. Gruska. *Quantum Computing*. McGraw Hill. 1999.
11. A. Kitaev and J. Watrous. Parallelization, amplification, and exponential time simulation of quantum interactive proof systems. In *Proc. 32nd STOC*, pp.608–617, 2000.
12. H. Kobayashi and K. Matsumoto. Quantum multi-prover interactive proof systems with limited prior entanglement. *J. Comput. Syst. Sci.* **66** (2003) 429–450.
13. A. Kondacs and J. Watrous. On the power of quantum finite state automata. In *Proc. 38th FOCS*, pp.66–75, 1997.
14. C. Moore and J. Crutchfield. Quantum automata and quantum grammars. *Theor. Comput. Sci.* **237** (2000) 275–306
15. M. A. Nielsen and I. L. Chuang. *Quantum Computation and Quantum Information*. Cambridge University Press, 2000.
16. H. Nishimura and T. Yamakami. Polynomial time quantum computation with advice. *Inform. Process. Lett.* **90** (2004) 195–204.
17. A. Shamir. IP=PSPACE. *J. ACM* **39** (1992) 869–877.
18. J. Watrous. On quantum and classical space-bounded processes with algebraic transition amplitudes. In *Proc. 40th FOCS*, pp.341–351, 1999.
19. J. Watrous. PSPACE has constant-round quantum interactive proof systems. *Theor. Comput. Sci.* **292** (2003) 575–588.

Time and Space Efficient Algorithms for Constrained Sequence Alignment

Z.S. Peng and H.F. Ting

Department of Computer Science,
The University of Hong Kong, Hong Kong
{zspeng, hfting}@cs.hku.hk

Abstract. In this paper, we study the constrained sequence alignment problem, which is a generalization of the classical sequence alignment problem with the additional constraint that some characters in the alignment must be positioned at the same columns. The problem finds important applications in Bioinformatics. Our major result is an $O(\ell n^2)$-time and $O(\ell n)$-space algorithm for constructing an optimal constrained alignment of two sequences where n is the length of the longer sequence and ℓ is the length of the constraint. Our algorithm matches the best known time complexity and reduces the best known space complexity by a factor of n for solving the problem. We also apply our technique to design time and space efficient heuristic and approximation algorithm for aligning multiple sequences.

1 Introduction

In Bioinformatics, sequence alignment is a useful method for measuring the similarity of DNA sequences. By constructing an alignment of the DNA sequences of different species, Biologists may obtain important information on the evolutionary history of these species or discover conserved regions in their genomes. For the Pairwise Sequence Alignment problem (PSA), which asks for aligning only two sequences, there are polynomial-time algorithms for constructing optimal solutions [3, 11]. For the Multiple Sequence Alignment problem (MSA), which aligns more than two sequences, we know that the problem is NP-complete [10, 8], and there are many heuristics [5, 4, 7] and approximation algorithms [12, 2, 9] for constructing good, but not necessary optimal, solutions.

Existing sequence alignment programs do not allow users to use their biological knowledge to improve the quality of the alignment. For example, it is generally agreed that in the alignment of RNase sequences, three active-site residues His12, Lys41 and His119 should be aligned in the same columns. However, most sequence alignment programs mis-align these important residues. To solve this problem, Tang *et al.* [1] formulated the Constrained Sequence Alignment problem, which is a natural generalization of the classical sequence alignment problem. The new problem has an additional input of a constrained sequence, which imposes a structure on the alignment by requiring every character in the constrained sequence to appear in the same column of the alignment. They gave an algorithm for

M. Domaratzki et al. (Eds.): CIAA 2004, LNCS 3317, pp. 237–246, 2005.

the Constrained Pairwise Sequence Alignment problem (CPSA) (i.e., constructing constrained alignment of two sequences) that runs in $O(\ell n^4)$) time and uses $O(\ell n^4)$ space where n is the length of the longer input sequence and ℓ is the length of the constrained sequence. They also proposed the *progressive alignment* heuristic for the Constrained Multiple Sequence Alignment (CMSA) problem, which basically uses an optimal algorithm for CPSA to align pairs of input sequences progressively. Using the $O(\ell n^4)$-time and $O(\ell n^4)$-space algorithm for CPSA to implement the heuristic gives an $O(\ell k n^4)$ time and $O(\ell n^4)$ space complexity, where k is the number of sequences to be aligned.

In [6], Chin *et al.* gave an $O(\ell n^2)$-time and $O(\ell n^2)$-space algorithm for CPSA. When applying this algorithm to the progressive alignment heuristic, they reduced both the time and space complexity of the heuristic by a factor of n^2. They also gave an approximation algorithm, called Center-star, for CMSA which runs in $O(\ell C k^2 n^2)$ time and uses $O(\ell k^2 n^2)$ memory space, and guarantees that the distance score of the alignment returned by the algorithm is always at most $(2 - 2/k)$ times the distance score of the optimal alignment. Here, C is a constant depending on the input sequences. Experiments showed that the quality of the alignment returned by Center-Star is 15%–30% better than that of the progressive alignment heuristic.

Both the progressive alignment heuristic and Center-star are not practical because of their huge $O(\ell k^2 n^2)$ memory space requirement. The DNA sequences that we study in Bioinformatics are usually more than 1M characters long. Thus, to align four such sequences with a constrained sequence of 4 characters, we need at least $2^{16} Gb = 65536Gb$ of memory. Note that a typical workstation is equipped with at most 4Gb memory.

The major result of this paper is an $O(\ell n^2)$-time and $O(\ell n)$-space algorithm for the CPSA problem. Note that we have reduced the space requirement by a factor of n without increasing the time complexity. This algorithm immediately enables us to reduce the space requirement of the progressive alignment heuristic from $O(\ell n^2)$ to $O(\ell n)$. Furthermore, we adapt our space-saving technique so as to reduce the space complexity of Center-star to $O(\ell k^2 n)$ without increasing its time complexity. These improvements are very important practically. Now, to align four DNA sequences of 1M long with a constrained sequence of 4 characters, we need only 64Mb of memory, which is well within the capability of a typical workstation.

The organization of this paper is as follows. In Section 2, we give the definitions and notations that are used in our discussion. In Sections 3 and 4, we describe our algorithm for the CPSA problem and analyze its time and space complexity. We show how to adapt our technique to reduce the space complexity of Center-Star in Section 5.

2   Definitions and Notations

Let Σ be a finite set of characters which does not include '␣', the space character. We are given a distance function $\delta : (\Sigma \cup \{␣\}) \times (\Sigma \cup \{␣\}) \to \Re$ such that any two characters a, b in $\Sigma \cup \{\_\}$ have distance $\delta(a, b)$. We assume that $\delta(\_, \_) = 0$. (Intuitively, the distance $\delta(a, b)$ measures the *mutation* distance between characters a, b.) For any sequence $S = S[1]S[2] \cdots S[n]$ over Σ, let $|S|$ denote its length n, and for any $1 \leq i \leq j \leq n$, let $S[i..j]$ denote the substring $S[i]S[i+1] \cdots S[j]$. To simplify our discussion, we let $S[i..j]$ be the empty sequence if $i > j$.

Let S and S' be any two sequences over Σ. A *sequence alignment* of S and S' is given by an alignment matrix, which has two rows and $w \geq \max\{|S|, |S'|\}$ columns, such that when we remove all the spaces in the first (resp. second) row, we get S (resp. S'). Let P be a common subsequence of S and S' (i.e., P is a subsequence of S and is also a subsequence of S'). A *constrained sequence alignment* (CSA) of S and S' with respect to P is an alignment A of S and S' with the following additional property: there are $|P|$ columns $c_1, c_2, \ldots c_{|P|}$ in A such that for all $1 \leq j \leq |P|$, we have $A[1, c_j] = A[2, c_j] = P[j]$. Figure 1 gives an example.

S1: IN-YRWRCKNQN--LRTTF ANV-N-CGNQS I RCP HNRT--NCHRS R--VPLL HCDL--P

S2: INNYQ-RCKNQNTFLL-TF-NVVNVCGNP N--CP S NKTR KNCH-S GS QVP--HCNLTTP

P: CKCCC

Fig. 1. An example on constrained sequence alignment

Define $\delta(A) = \sum_{1 \leq j \leq w} \delta(A[1, j], A[2, j])$ to be the *score* of the alignment A. We say that A is optimal if it has the smallest score among all CSAs of S and S' with respect to P. We let $\delta_{\text{opt}}(S, S', P)$ denote the score of an optimal CSA. To unify our discussion, we let $\delta_{\text{opt}}(S, S', P) = \infty$ if P is not a common subsequence of S and S'.

We generalize sequence alignment to multiple sequences naturally. Consider $k > 2$ sequences $S_1, S_2, \ldots, S_k$ over Σ. A sequence alignment of $S_1, S_2, \ldots, S_k$ is given by an alignment matrix of k rows and $w \geq \max\{|S_1|, |S_2|, \ldots, |S_k|\}$ columns such that for any $1 \leq i \leq k$, if we remove all the space characters in row i, we get the sequence S_i. Let P be a common subsequence of $S_1, S_2, \ldots, S_k$. A constrained sequence alignment (CSA) of $S_1, S_2, \ldots, S_k$ with respect to P is an alignment A of $S_1, S_2, \ldots, S_k$ with the following property: there are $|P|$ columns $c_1, c_2, \ldots c_{|P|}$ in A such that for all $1 \leq j \leq |P|$, we have $A[1, c_j] = A[2, c_j] = \cdots = A[k, c_j] = P[j]$. Define the *sum-of-pair* score of A, or simply the score of A, to be

$$\delta(A) = \sum_{1 \leq p < q \leq k} \sum_{1 \leq j \leq w} \delta(A[p, j], A[q, j]).$$

We say that A is optimal if $\delta(A)$ has the smallest value. The score of an optimal CSA is denoted as $\delta_{\text{opt}}(S_1, S_2, \ldots, S_k; P)$.

3   Two Useful Formulas

Let $S = S[1..m]$ and $S' = S'[1..n]$ be two sequences of m and n characters over Σ. Let $P = P[1..\ell]$ be a common subsequence of S and S'. In the next two sections, we describe an algorithm for computing an optimal CSA of S and S' with respect to P. Our algorithm is recursive and it needs to compute all optimal CSAs of $S[1..i]$ and $S'[1..j]$ with respect to $P[1..k]$ for some i, j, k. It also needs to compute all optimal CSAs of $S[i..m]$ and $S'[j..n]$ with respect to $P[k..\ell]$. Below, we state two useful formulas that are important for us to find these optimal alignments efficiently.

For any $0 \le i \le m$, $0 \le j \le n$, and $0 \le k \le \ell$, let $D(i, j, k)$ be the score of an optimal alignment of $S[1..i]$ and $S'[1..j]$ with respect to $P[1..k]$. In other words, $D(i, j, k) = \delta_{\mathrm{opt}}(S[1..i], S'[1..j]; P[1..k])$. Recall that $\delta_{\mathrm{opt}}(S[1..i], S'[1..j]; P[1..k]) = \infty$ if $P[1..k]$ is not a common subsequence of $S[1..i]$ and $S'[1..j]$. In [6], Chin *et al.* gave a formula that relates with different $D(i, j, k)$:

Formula I:

$$
D(i, j, k) = \min \begin{cases}
D(i-1, j-1, k-1) + \delta(S[i], S'[j]) & \text{if } S[i] = S'[j] = P[k], \\
D(i-1, j-1, k) + \delta(S[i], S'[j]) & \text{if } i, j \ge 1, \\
D(i-1, j, k) + \delta(S[i], \textvisiblespace) & \text{if } i \ge 1, \\
D(i, j-1, k) + \delta(\textvisiblespace, S'[j]) & \text{if } j \ge 1.
\end{cases}
$$

Furthermore, we have $D(0,0,0) = 0$, and $D(i,0,k) = \infty$ and $D(0,j,k) = \infty$ for all $0 \le k \le \ell$, $0 \le i \le m$, and $0 \le j \le n$. (Recall that $\textvisiblespace$ is the space character.)

The above formula is useful for computing the score of alignment for sequences $S[1..i]$, $S'[1..j]$, $P[1..k]$. To handle alignments for sequences $S[i..m]$, $S'[j..n]$, $P[k..\ell]$, we need the following lemma.

Lemma 1. *For any $1 \le i \le m+1$, $1 \le j \le n+1$, and $1 \le k \le \ell + 1$, let $Q(i, j, k) = \delta_{\mathrm{opt}}(S[i..m], S'[j..n]; P[k..\ell])$. We have*
Formula II:

$$
Q(i, j, k) = \min \begin{cases}
Q(i+1, j+1, k+1) + \delta(S[i], S'[j]) & \text{if } S[i] = S'[j] = P[k], \\
Q(i+1, j+1, k) + \delta(S[i], S'[j]) & \text{if } i \le m \text{ and } j \le n, \\
Q(i+1, j, k) + \delta(S[i], \textvisiblespace) & \text{if } i \le m, \\
Q(i, j+1, k) + \delta(\textvisiblespace, S'[j]) & \text{if } j \le n,
\end{cases}
$$

with the boundary conditions (i) $Q(m+1, n+1, \ell+1) = 0$, and (ii) $Q(i, n+1, k) = \infty$ and $Q(m+1, j, k) = \infty$ for all $1 \le k \le \ell+1$, $1 \le i \le m+1$, and $1 \le j \le n+1$.

Proof. We consider the construction of an optimal constrained sequence alignment A of $S[i..m]$ and $S'[j..n]$ with respect to $P[k..\ell]$. Note that $\delta(A) = Q[i, j, k]$. There are four possibilities:

- If $S[i] = S'[j] = P[k]$, A can align $S[i], S'[j]$ and $P[k]$ at the same column, and the remaining columns of A form an optimal alignment of $S[i+1..m]$ and $S'[j+1..n]$ with respect to $P[k+1..\ell]$. In this case, $\delta(A) = Q[i+1, j+1, k+1] + \delta(S[i], S'[j])$.

- If $i \leq m, j \leq n$, A can align $S[i]$ and $S'[j]$ at the same column, and the remaining columns of A form an optimal alignment of $S[i+1..m]$ and $S'[j+1..n]$ with respect to $P[k..\ell]$; in this case, $\delta(A) = Q[i+1, j+1, k] + \delta(S[i], S'[j])$.
- If $i \leq m$, then A can align $S[i]$ with a space, and the remaining columns of A form an optimal alignment of $S[i+1..m]$ and $S'[j..n]$ with respect to $P[k..\ell]$; in this case, $\delta(A) = Q(i+1, j, k) + \delta(S[i], \_)$.
- If $j \leq n$, then A can align $S'[j]$ with a space, and the remaining columns of A form an optimal alignment of $S[i..m]$ and $S'[j+1..n]$ with respect to $P[k..\ell]$; in this case, $\delta(A) = Q(i, j+1, k) + \delta(\_, S'[j])$.

Obviously, $\delta(A)$ must be equal to the minimum of these four values.   □

4   An Optimal CSA Algorithm for Two Sequences

In this section, we describe an algorithm for constructing an optimal alignment of $S = S[1..m]$ and $S' = S'[1..n]$ with respect to $P = P[1..\ell]$. We need the following lemma, which gives a structural property about the alignment.

Lemma 2. *Let i be any integer in $[1, m]$, the set of integers between 1 and m. Then $\delta_{\text{opt}}(S[1..m], S'[1..n], P[1..\ell])$ is equal to*

$$\min_{\substack{0 \leq j \leq n \\ 0 \leq k \leq \ell}} \{\delta_{\text{opt}}(S[1..i], S'[1..j]; P[1..k]) + \delta_{\text{opt}}(S[i+1..m], S[j+1..n]; P[k+1..\ell])\}$$

Proof. Consider an optimal CSA A of S and S' with respect to P. Recall that A has two rows, and after throwing all the space characters in the first row, we get S. Suppose the ith character of S, i.e., $S[i]$, is at the pth column of the first row. In other words, $S[i] = A[1, p]$. Now, we consider S' and the second row of A. Suppose that $S'[1..j]$ falls into the first p columns of the second row. Furthermore, suppose that $c_1, c_2, \ldots, c_\ell$ are the ℓ columns in the CSA A such that $A[1, c_h] = A[2, c_h] = P[h](1 \leq h \leq \ell)$, and that either $k = 0$ or $1 \leq k \leq p \leq \ell$. Then, the first p columns of A form a CSA A_1 of $S[1..i]$ and $S'[1..j]$ with respect to $P[1..k]$, and the remaining columns form a CSA A_2 of $S[i+1..m]$ and $S'[j+1..n]$ with respect to $P[k+1..\ell]$. Because of the optimality of A, we conclude that A_1 and A_2 must be optimal.   □

We give below our recursive algorithm for finding an optimal CSA of S and S' with respect to P.

Algorithm CSA$(S[1..m], S'[1..n], P[1..\ell])$
begin
S1: Find the pair $(j, k) \in [1, n] \times [1, \ell]$ such that $\delta_{\text{opt}}(S[1..m/2], S'[1..j]; P[1..k])$
    $+\delta_{\text{opt}}(S[m/2+1..m], S'[j+1..n]; P[k+1..\ell])$ is minimum;
S2: Call recursively **CSA**$(S[1..m/2], S'[1..j], P[1..k])$ to find an optimal alignment A_1 of $S[1..m/2]$ and $S'[1..j]$ with respect to $P[1..k]$.
S3: Call recursively **CSA**$(S[m/2+1..m], S'[j+1..n], P[k+1..\ell])$ to find an optimal alignment A_2 of $S[m/2+1..m]$ and $S'[j+1..n]$ with respect to $P[k+1..\ell]$.
S4: Return A_1A_2.
end

Note that Steps S2, S3 and S4 are straightforward. The following lemma gives the details of Step S1.

Lemma 3. *We can finish Step 1 using $O(\ell mn)$ time and $O(\ell n)$ space.*

Proof. Recall that in Section 3, we have $D(i, j, k) = \delta_{\mathrm{opt}}(S[1..i], S'[1..j]; P[1..k])$ and $Q(i, j, k) = \delta_{\mathrm{opt}}(S[i..m], S'[j..n]; P[k..\ell])$. For any $0 \le p \le m$, let

$$D[p, *, *] = \{D[i, j, k] \mid i = p, 0 \le j \le n, 0 \le k \le \ell\}.$$

For any $1 \le p \le m + 1$, let

$$Q[p, *, *] = \{Q[i, j, k] \mid i = p, 1 \le j \le n + 1, 1 \le k \le \ell + 1\}.$$

It is easy to see that if we are given $D[m/2, *, *]$ and $Q[m/2 + 1, *, *]$, we can find the pair (j, k) required in Step 1 using $O(\ell n)$ time.

Note that we know all the values in $D[0, *, *]$, and from Formula I, we know that for any $p > 0$, we can compute $D[p, j, k]$ from $D[p - 1, j - 1, k - 1]$, $D[p-1, j-1, k]$, $D[p, j-1, k]$ and $D[p-1, j, k]$ in constant time. Thus, we can compute $D[1, *, *]$ from $D[0, *, *]$, and in general, $D[p, *, *]$ from $D[p-1, *, *]$ by applying Formula I to find sequentially $D[p, 0, 0]$, $D[p, 2, 0], \ldots, D[p, 1, 1], D[p, 1, 2]$, $\ldots, D[p, n, \ell]$. The total time taken is $O(\ell n)$. It follows that we can compute $D[m/2, *, *]$ iteratively from $D[0, *, *]$, $D[1, *, *], \ldots, D[m/2 - 1, *, *]$ using totally $O(\ell mn)$ time. Since we can reuse the space after each iteration, the total space needed is $O(\ell n)$.

Similarly, we can apply Formula II to find $Q[m/2 + 1, *, *]$ using the same time and space complexity. The lemma follows.   □

Now, we are ready to analyze the time and space complexity of our algorithm.

Theorem 1. *The algorithm* CSA *runs in $O(\ell mn)$ time and uses $O(\ell n)$ space.*

Proof. Let $T(m, n, \ell)$ and $S(m, n, \ell)$ be the worst case time and space complexity of CSA for finding an optimal constrained sequence alignment of two sequences with length m and n with respect to a common subsequence with length ℓ. First, we analyse the space complexity. We will prove by induction that $S(m, n, \ell) = O(\ell n)$. By Lemma 3, Step 1 uses $O(\ell n)$ space. Step 2 and Step 3 use respectively $S(m/2, j, k)$ and $S(m/2, n - j, \ell - k)$ space. Note that we can reuse the space after each step. Hence, we have

$$S(m, n, \ell) \le \max\{O(\ell n), O(kj), O((\ell - j)(n - j))\} = O(\ell n).$$

Now, we consider the time. By Lemma 3, Step 1 takes at most $c\ell mn$ time for some constant c. We prove below by induction that the running time of the whole algorithm is at most double the running time of Step 1. In other words, $T(m, n, \ell) \le 2cmn\ell$.

As mentioned above, Step 1 runs in $c\ell mn$ time. Steps 2 and 3 call CSA recursively, each take $T(m/2, n, \ell)$ time. Hence, we have the following recurrence:

$$\begin{aligned} T(m, n, \ell) &\leq c\ell mn + T(m/2, j, k) + T(m/2, n-j, \ell-k) \\ &\leq c\ell mn + 2c \cdot \frac{m}{2} jk + 2c \cdot \frac{m}{2}(n-j)(\ell-k) \\ &\leq (c + 2 \cdot \frac{c}{2})mn\ell \\ &\leq 2cmn\ell. \end{aligned}$$

The theorem is proved.   □

5   An Approximating CSA Algorithm for Multiple Sequences

In this section, we describe how to adapt our space-saving technique to reduce the space complexity of the Center-star approximation algorithm of Chin $et\,al.$, which constructs a constrained sequence alignment of $S = \{S_1, S_2, \ldots, S_k\}$ with respect to P in $O(\ell Ck^2n^2)$ time and $O(\ell k^2n^2)$ space, where $\ell = |P|$, C is some constant depending on input, and $n = \max\{|S_1|, |S_2|, \ldots, |S_k|\}$. The alignment constructed by the algorithm is guaranteed to have a score no greater than $(2 - 2/k)$ times that of an optimal alignment. We show below how to implement this algorithm such that the space complexity is reduced to $O(\ell k^2n)$ while the time complexity is still $O(\ell Ck^2n^2)$.

5.1   The Center-Star Algorithm

To describe the Center-star algorithm, we need some definitions. Let S be any sequence in $\mathcal{S}$. Let S' be another sequence, and A be a constrained sequence alignment of S and S' with respect to P. We say that in A, the ith character of S is aligned with the jth character of P if at some column p of A, $S[i] = A[1, p] = A[2, p] = P[j]$ and after removing all spaces in the first row of A, $A[1, p]$ becomes the ith character of S. We say that A aligns S to P at positions $1 \leq c_1 < c_2 < \cdots < c_\ell$ if for all $1 \leq j \leq \ell$, the c_jth character of S is aligned with the jth character of P in A. We let $A_{\mathrm{opt}}(S, S', P, (c_1, c_2, \ldots, c_\ell))$ denote the optimal CSA of S and S' with respect to P that aligns S with P at $(c_1, c_2, \ldots, c_\ell)$.

Now, we are ready to describe the Center-star algorithm. To find a CSA of $S_1, S_2, \ldots, S_k$ with respect to P, it executes the following two steps:

1. Find $S^* \in \mathcal{S} = \{S_1, S_2, \ldots, S_k\}$ and list of positions $(c_1, c_2, \ldots, c_\ell)$ such that $\sum_{S' \in \mathcal{S}} \delta(A_{\mathrm{opt}}(S^*, S', P, (c_1, c_2, \ldots, c_\ell)))$ is minimum.
2. Merging the $k - 1$ alignments $A_{\mathrm{opt}}(S^*, S', P, (c_1, c_2, \ldots, c_\ell))$ $(S' \in \mathcal{S} - S^*)$ into an alignment of sequences $S_1, S_2, \ldots, S_k$ with respect to P by adding spaces at the appropriate positions.

It is easy to see that the most time and space consuming computation in the algorithm is to find $A_{\mathrm{opt}}(S, S', P, (c_1, c_2, \ldots, c_\ell))$. Chin $et\,al.$ showed that such optimal alignment can be found in $O(\ell n^2)$ time and $O(\ell n^2)$ space. (Recall that $n = \max\{|S_1|, |S_2|, \ldots, |S_k|\}$.) In the next section, we apply our technique to reduce the space complexity from $O(\ell n^2)$ to $O(\ell n)$, while keeping the time complexity to be $O(\ell n^2)$. It follows that our implementation reduces the overall space complexity of the Center-star algorithm from $O(\ell k^2 n^2)$ to $O(\ell k^2 n)$ without increasing the time complexity. We refer to [6] for more details on the complexity analysis of the Center-star algorithm.

5.2   Reducing the Space Complexity

Let $S = S[1..m]$, $S' = S'[1..n]$ and $P = P[1..\ell]$. Let $\delta_{opt}(S, S', P, (c_1, c_2, \ldots, c_\ell))$ denote the score of the optimal constrained sequence alignment of S and S' with respect to P that aligns S to P at position $(c_1, c_2, \ldots, c_\ell)$. To simplify discussion, we let $\delta_{opt}(S, S', P, (c_1, c_2, \ldots, c_\ell)) = \infty$ if no such alignment is possible. We need the following lemma.

Lemma 4. *Let* $i \in [1, m]$. $\delta_{opt}(S[1..m], S[1..n], P[1..\ell], (c_1, c_2, \ldots, c_\ell))$ *equals*

$$\min_{0 \leq j \leq n, 0 \leq k \leq \ell} \delta_{opt}(S[1..i], S[1..j], P[1..k], (c_1, c_2, \ldots, c_k)) +$$

$$\delta_{opt}(S[i+1..m], S[j+1..n], P[k+1..\ell], (c_{k+1}, c_{k+2}, \ldots, c_\ell))$$

Proof. Similar to the proof of Lemma 2. □

The above lemma suggests immediately the a recursive algorithm for finding $A_{opt}(S, S', P, (c_1, c_2, \ldots, c_\ell))$, which is given in Figure 2. To execute Step S1 effi-

---

Algorithm CSAP($S[1..m], S'[1..n], P[1..\ell], (c_1, c_2, \ldots, c_\ell)$)

begin

S1: Find the j, k such that the sum of $\delta_{opt}(S[1..m/2], S'[1..j], P[1..k], (c_1, \ldots, c_k))$
     and $\delta_{opt}(S[m/2+1..m], S'[j+1..n], P[k+1..\ell], (c_{k+1}, \ldots, c_\ell))$ is minimum;

S2: Call recursively CSAP($S[1..m/2], S'[1..j], P[1..k], (c_1, \ldots, c_k)$) to find the optimal alignment A_1

S3: Call recursively CSAP($S[m/2+1..m], S'[j+1..n], P[k+1..\ell], (c_{k+1}, \ldots, c_\ell)$) to find the optimal alignment A_2

S4: Return $A_1 A_2$.

end

Fig. 2. Algorithm for constructing an optimal CSA with position constraints

ciently, we need two formulas similar to Formulas I and II. The first one is given in [6].

For any $0 \leq i \leq m$, $0 \leq j \leq n$, $0 \leq k \leq \ell$, let

$$D'(i, j, k) = \delta_{opt}(S[1..i], S'[1..j], P[1..k], (c_1, c_2, \ldots, c_k)).$$

For any $1 \le i \le m+1$, $1 \le j \le n+1$, $1 \le k \le \ell+1$, let

$$Q'(i,j,k) = \delta_{\text{opt}}(S[i..m], S'[j..n], P[k..\ell], (c_k, c_{k+1}, \ldots, c_\ell)).$$

We have

$$D'(i,j,k) = \min \begin{cases} D'(i-1,j-1,k-1) + \delta(S[i], S'[j]) & \text{if } c_k = i \text{ and} \\ & S[i] = S'[j] = P[k], \\ D'(i-1,j-1,k) + \delta(S[i], S'[j]) & \text{if } i,j \ge 1, \\ D'(i-1,j,k) + \delta(S[i], \text{\textvisiblespace}) & \text{if } i \ge 1, \\ D'(i,j-1,k) + \delta(\text{\textvisiblespace}, S'[j]) & \text{if } j \ge 1. \end{cases}$$

and

$$Q'(i,j,k) = \min \begin{cases} Q'(i+1,j+1,k+1) + \delta(S[i], S'[j]) & \text{if } c_k = i \text{ and} \\ & S[i] = S'[j] = P[k], \\ Q'(i+1,j+1,k) + \delta(S[i], S'[j]) & \text{if } i \le m \text{ and } j \le n, \\ Q'(i+1,j,k) + \delta(S[i], \text{\textvisiblespace}) & \text{if } i \le m, \\ Q'(i,j+1,k) + \delta(\text{\textvisiblespace}, S'[j]) & \text{if } j \le n, \end{cases}$$

with the boundary conditions

- $D'(0,0,0) = 0$, $D'(i,0,k) = \infty$ and $D'(0,j,k) = \infty$ for all $0 \le k \le \ell$, $0 \le i \le m$, $0 \le j \le n$, and
- $Q'(m+1,n+1,\ell+1) = 0$, and $Q'(i,n+1,k) = \infty$ and $Q'(m+1,j,k) = \infty$ for all $1 \le k \le \ell+1$, $1 \le i \le m+1$, $1 \le j \le n+1$.

Given these formulas, we can apply the technique used in Section 4 to implement Step 1 of CSAP efficiently.

Theorem 2. *We can finish Step 1 of* CSAP *in* $O(\ell n^2)$ *time and* $O(\ell n)$ *space. Furthermore,* CSAP *runs in* $O(\ell n^2)$ *time and used* $O(\ell n)$ *space.*

Proof. Similar to the proofs of Lemma 3 and Theorem 1.   □

References

1. C.Y. Tang, C.L. Lu, M.D.T. Chang, Y.T. Tsai, Y.J. Sun, K.M. Chao, J.M. Chang, Y.H. Chiou, C.M. Wu, H.T. Chang, and W.I. Chou. Constrained multiple sequence alignment tool development and its application to RNase family alignment. In *Proceedings of the First IEEE Computer Society Bioinformatics Conference*, pages 127–137, 2002.
2. D. Gusfield. Efficient methods for multiple sequence alignment with guaranteed error bounds. *Bulletin of Mathematical Biology*, 30:141–154, 1993.
3. D. Gusfield. *Algorithms on strings, trees, and sequence.* Cambridge University Press, British, 1999.
4. D. Higgins and P. Sharpe. CLUSTAL: a package for performing multiple sequence alignment on a microcomputer. *Gene*, 73:237–244, 1988.

5. F. Corpet. Multiple sequence alignment with hierarchical clustering. *Nucleic Acids Research*, 16:10881–10890, 1988.

6. F.Y.L. Chin, N.L. Ho, T.W. Lam, W.H. Wong, and M.Y. Chan. Efficient constrained multiple sequence alignment with performance guarantee. In *Proceedings of the IEEE Computational Systems Bioinformatics Conference*, pages 337–346, 2003.

7. J.D. Thompson, D.G. Higgins, and T.J. Gibson. CLUSTAL W: Improving the sensitivity of progressive multiple sequence alignment through sequence weighting, position-specific gap penalties and weight matrix choice. *Nucleic Acids Research*, 22(22):4673–4680, 1994.

8. L. Wang and T. Jiang. On the complexity of multiple sequence alignment. *Journal of Computational Biology*, 1:337–348, 1994.

9. P.A. Pevzner. Multiple alignment, communication cost, and graph matching. *SIAM Journal on Applied Mathematics*, 52:1763–1779, 1992.

10. P. Bonizzoni and G.D. Vedova. The complexity of multiple sequence alignment with *SP*-score that is a metric. *Theoretical Computer Science*, 259:63–79, 2001.

11. S. Needleman and C. Wunsch. A general method applicable to the search for similarities in the amino acid sequence of two proteins. *Journal of Molecular Evolution*, 48:443–453, 1970.

12. V. Bafna, E.L. Lawler, and P.A. Pevzner. Approximation algorithms for multiple sequence alignment. *Theoretical Computer Science*, 182:233–244, 1997.

Stochastic Context-Free Graph Grammars for Glycoprotein Modelling

Baozhen Shan

Dept. Computer Science, Univ. of Western Ontario,
London, ON, Canada N6A 5B7
bxshan@csd.uwo.ca

Abstract. The rapid progress in proteomics has generated an increased interest in the full characterization of glycoproteins. Tandem mass spectrometry is a useful technique. One common problem of current bioinformatics tools for automated interpretation of tandem mass spectra of glycoproteins is that they often give many candidates of oligosaccharide structures with very close scores. We propose an alternative approach in which stochastic context-free graph grammars are used to model oligosaccharide structures. Our stochastic model receives as input structures of known glycans in the library to train the probability parameters of the grammar. After training, the method uses the learned rules to predict the structure of glycan given a composition of unknown glycoprotein. Preliminary results show that integrating such modelling with the automated interpretation software program, GlycoMaster, can very accurately elucidate oligosaccharide structures with tandem mass spectra. This paper describes the stochastic graph grammars modelling glycoproteins.

1 Introduction

The rapid progress in proteomics has generated an increased interest in the full characterization of glycoproteins. The elucidation of glycoprotein structures and functions remains one of the most challenging tasks in proteomics [11]. Tandem mass spectrometry has been recognized as a useful technique for the determination of the oligosaccharide structures [2]. In the current practice of glycoprotein structural determination by MS/MS, purified glycoproteins are digested into glycopeptides, short peptides linked to oligosaccharides, with enzymes like trypsin. Then tandem mass spectra are measured for glycopeptides with a tandem mass spectrometer. Finally, the spectra are interpreted by computer software to determine the structures of oligosaccharides [29].

Current bioinformatics tools for automated interpretation of tandem mass spectra of glycoproteins [9, 13, 14, 24] apply the approaches similar to *de novo* sequencing for protein identification [3, 6, 22], which compute directly from the MS/MS spectra. However, unlike DNA and proteins where sequence is linear and provides nearly all the primary structure, oligosaccharides of glycoproteins are characterized by their two dimentional sequence, linkage and stereochemistry. One common problem of current computer softwares is that they often

M. Domaratzki et al. (Eds.): CIAA 2004, LNCS 3317, pp. 247–258, 2005.
© Springer-Verlag Berlin Heidelberg 2005

give many candidates with close scores for a MS/MS spectrum. Typically, those candidates have same composition (numbers of each monosaccharide contained in a glycan) with different sequence structures. Therefore, current bioinformatics tools can accurately compute compositions of oligosaccharides from tandem mass spectra. However, it seems not feasible to directly interpret branched oligosaccharide tandem mass spectra, because different branched structures with same composition often give very similar spectra experimentally.

Definition 1. *Given a composition of a glycoprotein, modelling problem is to determine the most possible structure of the glycan.*

There are two kinds of approaches reported to tackle such problem. One is instrumental approach in which the ring-cleavage fragmentation provide linkage information [16]. However, very few such experiments have successfully been reported due to the limitation of fragmentation in MS/MS spectrometer [22]. The other is catalog-library approach [19, 28]. Often, oligosaccharides released from a family of glycoproteins are composed of a small finite set of monosaccharides. In this regard, the numerous oligosaccharide species are analogous to the products found in syntheses involving combinnatorial libraries. Structure similarities exist between different oligosaccharides, because specific substructural motifs are preserved among different compounds. Such motif information is very useful to determine branched structures. However, this requires directly compare spectra. To the best of our knowledge, no such bioinformatics tool has been reported.

We proposed an alternative approach to this problem in which stochastic context-free graph grammars are used to model oligosaccharide structures, and developed a software tool which uses information from more than one spectrum by referencing databases of glycoproteins [27]. Applying stochastic grammars is based on the observation that the family of structures of glycoproteins are derived from a common precursor oligosaccharide by a network of competing biosynthetic pathways. Intuitively, we could use a prior probability distribution of structures. Production rules of the grammars model glycosylation reactions at each step in biosynthesis pathways.

Our software first compute structural candidates from the tandem mass spectrum. Then, stochastic graph grammars are used to refine candidates. The stochastic model is trained by structures of known glycans in the library. Then, for each composition computed from tandem mass spectrum of unknown glycoprotein, it gives the most possible structures of the oligosaccharide. In this paper, we describe the stochastic graph grammars used in our approach.

2   Related Works

A grammar consists of a set of variables, some terminal and some non-terminal. Specifically, a starting nonterminal S is contained in a grammar. The nonterminals are rewritten according to a set of production rules. A stochastic grammar is a variant of a grammar in which each production is associated with a probability, a real number between 0 and 1. The probability of the derivation will be the product of the probabilities of all productions used in the derivation.

Stochastic grammars are getting more interest in bioinformatics. Hidden Markov Model (HMM) approaches were introduced to the analysis of molecular sequences by Churchill [7], who analyzed regions of varying G+C content in single DNA sequences. They were extensively used for gene finding [4, 20, 21]. Hidden Markov model and evolutionary trees were used in protein secondary structure prediction and other comparative sequence analyses [15, 23].

Stochastic context-free grammars (SCFGs) are succefully used to model a family of homologous RNA sequence and secondary structure prediction [25, 25]. Context-free grammars are ideal to model interactions of nucleotides in RNA molecules. The rewriting rules (with probabilities) can be used to specify nested correlations of residues in an RNA sequence and therefore how the sequence is structurally formed. For RNA stem-loops these SCFGs have provided a general modelling approach that permits effective construction of algorithmic solutions to the RNA structure determination problems.

However, above sequence grammars are hard to describe full relationship among objects in biology. Formally, a context-sensitive grammar is required to model RNA pseudoknotted structures [5]. Stochastic Ranked Node Rewriting Tree Grammars are needed to predict protein beta-parallel structure [1], which can handle a complicated combination of anti-parallel and parallel dependencies.

Stochastic graph grammars active area of research [26]. They were successfully used to represent chemical compounds and to model the evolution of developmental pathways [10, 12]. Stochastic graph grammars defined a probability distribution over graphs and were used to generate graphs according to that distribution and to determine the probability of a given graph which may be new or unseen. As compact grammatical representations of sets of graphs or probability distributions over graphs, the application of stochastic graphs grammars to situation where the relationships between biological objects can be described using graphs.

3   Graph Grammars

Let Σ be an alphabet of node labels and Γ an alphabet of edge labels. A graph over Σ and Γ is a tuple $G = (V, E, \lambda)$, where V is a finite nonempty set of nodes, E is a finite set of edges $E \subseteq \{(v, \gamma, w) | v, w \in V, v \neq w, \gamma \in \Gamma\}$, and λ: $V \to \Sigma, E \to \Gamma$ is a labelling function for each node and each edge.

The set of all graphs over Σ and Γ is denoted $GR_{\Sigma,\Gamma}$. A subset of $GR_{\Sigma,\Gamma}$ is called a *graph language*.

A production of a node replacement grammar will be of the form $X \to (D, C)$ where X is a nonterminal node label, D is a graph, and C is a set of connection instructions. In a node-replacement graph grammar, anode of a given graph is replaced by a new subgraph, which is connected to the remainder of the graph by new edges, depending on how the node was connected to it. These node replacements are controlled by the productions (or replacement rules) of the grammars. In this paper, the context-free node-replacement graph grammars are used, in which the result of the replacements does not depend on the order in which they are applied [26]. The replacement of nodes is specified by a finite number of productions and the embedding mechanism is specified by a finite number of connections.

4   Our Contributions

4.1   Biosynthetic Pathways and Graph Grammar

Oligosaccharides are composed of monosaccharides by glycosylation. In mammalian glycoproteins, common monosaccharide are Xylose (Xyl), Fucose (Fuc), Galactose (Gal), Mannose (Man), Glucose (Glu), N-acetyl-glucosamine (Glc-NAc), N-acetyl-galactosamine (GalNAc) and N-acetylneuraminic acid (NueAc). In mass spectrometry, galactose, mannose and glucose are undistinguishable, and so are N-acetyl-glucosamine and N-acetyl-galactosamine. In this paper, the structures are simplified with square corresponding to N-acetyl-glucosamine and N-acetyl-galactosamine, and cycle corresponding to galactose, mannose and glucose. A structural representation for a glycan ($GlcNAc_4Gal_3FucXyl$) of a peanut peroxidase is shown in Fig. 1.

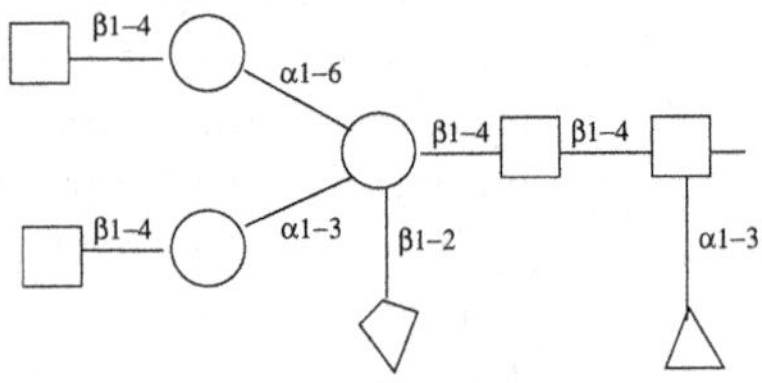

Fig. 1. A structural representation of a glycan

We focus on the most abundant, N-linked "complex-type" glycoproteins, oligosaccharides of which are characterized [11] by sharing a common trimannosyl-chitobiose core (Fig. 2a) and the presence of variable numbers of antennae (Fig. 2b, c). The dotted line in Fig. 2b stands for optional attachment of monosaccharides to the core structure. That is, GlcNAc and Xyl may also be attached to the core. The core is often modified by the addition of Fuc to GlcNAc. Further biosynthetic processing converts the small pool of "core plus stubs" into an extensive array of mature oligosaccharides.

Although the biosynthesis of "complex-type" oligosaccharides follows a complex multistep pathway, the family of structures are derived from a common precursor oligosaccharide by a network of competing biosynthetic pathways. So, there is a distribution among the glycan structures in a glycoprotein family, which can be described by graph grammars. Specifically, stochastic context-free node-replacement graph grammars are used to model glycoproteins. An oligosaccharide of N-linked glycoprotein is abstracted as an connected graph with vertex

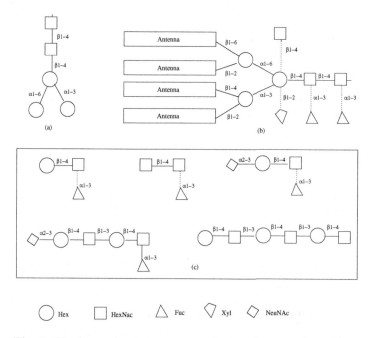

Fig. 2. The frequent substructures and core of mammalian glycans

labels and edges representing sugar types (e.g., Man, GlcNAc) and glycosidic linkages (e.g., α 2-3, β 1-4). The graph representation is typically a rooted tree with labelled nodes and labelled edges. Each node has only one parent and at most four children. The edge is labelled from the numbering position of child to that of parent. α and β stand for structurally in-planar and out-planar respectively. The glycosylation reactions that make up the biosynthetic pathways are abstracted as production rules of the graph grammars (Fig. 3) with the form (M, D, E) where M (capital letter) is "mother" graph which consists of one node only, D is "daughter" graphs and E is connecting embedding. Glycosylation is modelled as graph rewriting. Rewriting rules from the graph grammar are used to transform the graph.

As a test case, tandem mass spectra of cationic isozyme peanut peroxidases were used in this paper. Only four symbols, Hex (h), HexNAc (n), Xyl (x), and Fuc (f) are needed to represent their glycan structures. Based on above observation, we have

Lemma 1. *Let* $\Sigma = \{Hex, Xyl, Fuc, HexNAc, NeuNac\}$ *be an alphabet of node labels and* $\Gamma = \{\alpha i - j, \beta i - j\}$, $i, j \in \{1, 2, 3, 4, 6\}$ *an alphabet of edge labels. A glycan structure is represented as a graph* S *over* Σ *and* Γ *s.t.* $S = (V, E, \lambda)$, *where* V *is a finite nonempty set of nodes,* E *is a finite set of edges* $E \subseteq \{(v, \gamma, w) | v, w \in V, v \neq w, \gamma \in \Gamma\}$, *and* $\lambda \colon V \to \Sigma, E \to \Gamma$ *is a labelling function for each node and each edge.*

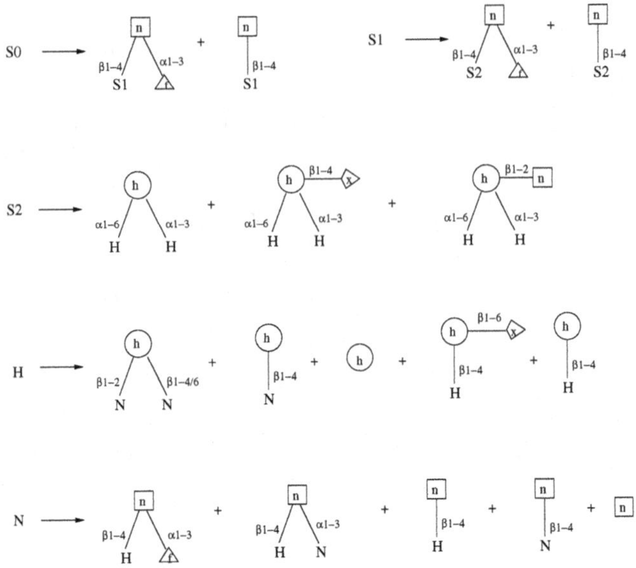

Fig. 3. The productions of the graph grammar

Lemma 2. *Let G be a graph grammar $G = (\Sigma, \Delta, \Gamma, P, S_0)$ where Σ is the alphabet of node labels, $\Delta \subseteq \Sigma$ is the alphabet of terminal node labels, Γ is alphabet of edge labels, P is the finite set of productions listed in Fig. 3, and S_0 is the initial nonterminal, and S be a family of glycan structures. $S = L(G)$, where $L(G) = \{H \mid S_0 \Rightarrow *H\}$.*

Parsing of the structure in Fig. 1 is shown in Fig. 4. The structure corresponds to two derivations, $S_0 S_1 S_2 H H N N$ and $S_0 S_1 S_2 H N H N$.

4.2   Expression Probability of Glycoprotein

In theory, the entire human genome sequence, coupled with methods to measure the expression level of each gene, provides tools for thorough study of glycan biosynthesis. The development of sophisticated computational algorithms should allow glycosylation-specific effects on gene expression to be deconvoluted from irrelevant secondary effects. So, there is a distribution among the glycan structures in a glycoprotein family, which can be described by graph grammars.

Definition 2. *Let P be a set of production rules. Probability of a graph s is defined as*

$$pr(s) = \sum_{d \in D} \prod_{p_i \in d} pr_i \,, \tag{1}$$

where pr_i be the probability of a production rule $p_i \in P$, D be a set of derivation paths to a graph s.

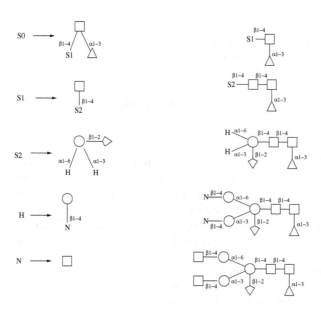

Fig. 4. An example of structure parsing

Lemma 3. *Given a composition of glycan, expression levels of structures can be described by stochastic graph grammars*

4.3 Training

Training approach is based on parsing the input graph that minimizes the derivation length of the graph and then estimating probabilities on productions [8]. For a known glycoprotein, the structure of its glycan is represented as a graph s. The algorithm *Parsing* takes as an input a graph s and the grammars G defined in Fig. 3. Specifically, starting from S_0 the algorithm searches compatible production to the substructure in the graph starting from root, and replaces it; Then, find productions for new nonterminal nodes. The parsing order for nonterminal nodes is not considered, because given a structure, different derivations have same numbers of productions just with different orders. For simplicity, depth first approach is used. Finally, the algorithm gives as output a set of derivations D with minimal length. Each $d \in D$ has same the number for each production.

Algorithm Parsing(G, s)
    Input: G (Graph grammar), s(structure graph)
    Output: D (a set of derivations)

1. *Enqueue*$(N, root_s)$
2. **while not** *Empty*(N)
3. $v \leftarrow Dequeue(N)$
4.   **for** each child c of v

5. $Enqueue(T)$
6.   **while not** $Empty(T)$
7. $t \leftarrow Dequeue(T)$
8.   **if** t is not a leaf node
9. $Enqueue(N, t)$
10.   Find q of (v, q) //based on children
11. $Enqueue(D, (v, q))$
12. **return** D

The algorithm *Learning* takes as input a set of structures S and a set of production rules G. It first parses each graph $s \in S$ to find one of the derivations with the minimum number of productions, then updates the count of each production used in that derivation. Finally, it computes the probability for each production, which is the ratio of $count_{(n,q)}$, the number of production (n, q) used in all graph parsing, to $count_n$, total number for that nonterminal node n.

Algorithm Learning(G, S)
    Input: G (production rules), S (set of structure)
    Output: Pr (set of probabilities of productions)

1. **for** each $(p, q) \in G$
2. $count_{(p,q)} \leftarrow 0$
3. **for** each structure $s \in S$
4. $D \leftarrow \text{Parsing}(G, s)$
5.   **for** each $(p, q) \in D$
6. $count_{(p,q)} \leftarrow count_{(p,q)} + 1$
7. **for** each nonterminal node $n \in G$
8. $count_n \leftarrow 0$
9.   **for** each q s.t. $(n, q) \in G$
10. $count_n \leftarrow count_n + count_{(n,q)}$
11.   **for** each q s.t. $(n, q) \in G$
12. $pr_{(n,q)} \leftarrow count_{(n,q)}/count_n$
13. $Pr \leftarrow Pr \cup \{pr_{(n,q)}\}$
14. **return** Pr

4.4   Predicting

After training, given a composition the algorithm starts from starting symbol S_0 to generate derivations by applying production rules continuously. Because graph grammars may be ambiguous, a structure may have multiple derivations and thus the probability is the sum of all distinct derivations. Finally, structures with desired probabilities are the output.

The computation of such probability is very expensive (exponential time complexity). Heuristic dynamic programming technique was used in this paper. We assume the structures are derived with most probably glycosylation in a network of competing biosynthetic pathways. So, derivations with i productions is computed by the most probably derivation with $i - 1$ productions and *ith* productions.

Theorem 1. *Let $P(i)$ be optimal probability of derivation with first i productions applied, and $p(i, k)$ be a probability of ith production which applies to kth nonterminal node contained in the derivation with first $i - 1$ productions.*

$$P(i) = maxP(i - 1) \times p(i, k) \tag{2}$$

In order to improve the accuracy of prediction, J derivations are considered for each length of derivation.

Theorem 2. *Let $P(i, j)$ be optimal probability of jth derivation ($j = 1$ to J) with first i productions applied, and $p(i, m, k)$ be a probability of ith production which applies to kth nonterminal node contained in mth optimal derivation with first $i - 1$ productions.*

$$P(i, j) = max_{m=1toJ}P(i - 1, m) \times p(i, m, k). \tag{3}$$

Algorithm: Predicting(G, c)
    Input: G (production rules), c (composition)
    Output: $S(c)$ (a set of candidates of structure)

1. $N_{1,1}, N_{1,2} \leftarrow \{S_0\}$
2. $i \leftarrow 1$, $count_1 \leftarrow 2$
3. **do** $i \leftarrow i + 1$, $j \leftarrow 0$
4.   **for** $k = 1$ to J
5.   **for** each $n \in N_{i-1,k}$
6.   **for** each $(n, q) \in G$ s.t. (n, q) is valid for c
7. $j \leftarrow j + 1$
8. $parent_{i,j} \leftarrow p_{i-1,k}$ // for backtracking
9. $d_{i,j} \leftarrow (n, q)$
10. $N_{i,j} \leftarrow N_{(i-1,k)} \cup \{n1\}$ s.t. $(n1 \in q)$
11. $pr_{i,j} \leftarrow pr_{(n,q)} \times pr_{i-1,k}$
12.   **if** hit composition **then** $D \leftarrow D \cup \{d_{i,j}\}$
13. $count_i \leftarrow j$
14. **while** $count_i \geq 1$
15. **for** each $d \in D$
16. $s \leftarrow backtracking(d)$
17.   **if** $s \notin S(c)$ **then** $S(c) \leftarrow S(c) \cup \{s\}$
18.   **else** sum the probability
19. **return** $S(c)$

Predicting, starts from starting symbol, S_0, to generate derivations by applying production rules (line 1-2). $N_{i,j}$ is a set of nonterminal nodes contained in jth derivation with i productions. Derivation paths are getting longer and longer, which correspond to larger and larger substructures, by continuing applying production rules (line 3-14). $d_{i,j}$ is ith production of jth derivation with i length. Whenever the derivation reach the desired composition (line 12), it is added to the set of valid derivations, D. When generating graphs, production rule is applied non-terminal nodes from leftmost to rightmost with shortest distance from the root node, and independently of all other productions in the derivation. Thus the probability, $pr_{i,j}$, of the derivation is obtained by multiplying the probabilities of all productions used. Because graph grammars may be ambiguous, a structure may have multiple derivations and thus the probability is the sum of all distinct derivations (line 15-19). Finally, structures with desired probabilities are the output. The time complexity becomes $O(n^2)$.

4.5   Application

Such grammars modelling glycoproteins were integrated with GlycoMaster, a software automated interpreting tandem mass spectra of glycoprotein [27]. In an tandem mass spectrum, each connected subcomponent of the glycan may yield a specific m/z. A matching score can be attributed to a subcomponent according to the peak that matches the subcomponent mass. If no peak matches, a negative score is given. GlycoMaster outputs a structure that has the optimal total subcomponent matching scores with the input mass spectrum. For branched oligosaccharides, GlycoMaster gives multiple candidates of structure with similar score. The stochastic graph grammars were used to refine outputs of GlycoMaster. Practically, refining process is simplified. For each composition, the software parses the candidates and computes the most possible structures.

5   Preliminary Results

The tandem mass spectra in our experiment were obtained by using Q-TOF2 in the positive ion nano ESI tandem mass mode with borosilicate nano tips.

Our modelling was experimented with the cationic peanut peroxidase. The known glycopeptides in the database [17] were used for training. Our software was tested using ten samples. The ten glycopeptide samples are cationic isozyme peanut peroxidase with tryptic digestion. Spectra of the samples were obtained by Q-TOF2 as described above. Correctness of automated interpretation is evaluated by comparing with manual analysis [34]. The structures computed by GlycoMaster without referring the stochastic graph grammars for eight out of ten samples are the same as deduced form of manual interpretation. The software integrating with the grammars gave nine same structures as manual interpretation. In this initial set of experiments, all the structures are N-linked structures and the number of monomers ranged from 6 to 15.

The preliminary experiments show conclusions following.

– Stochastic context-free graph grammars can be used to model glycoproteins. They capture major characteristics of biosynthetic pathways. Such stochastic grammars are very useful in predicting the structures given the compositions of unknown oligosaccharides.

- Integrating the grammar modelling with GlycoMaster can very accurately determine the most probable structures of N-linked glycans from the MS/MS spectrum of the glycopeptide.
- Because we use a sophisticated heuristic algorithm instead of enumerating all possible structures, the software works well even for large size polysaccharides.

6 Future Works

Stochastic context-free graph grammars provide useful information for elucidation of oligosaccharide tandem mass spectra. More libraries of tandem mass spectra of glycoproteins and quick library-searching techniques are needed. Specifically, bioinformatics tools must be developed to allow the facile comparison of tandem mass spectrometeric data from unknown and known structures.

References

1. Abe, N. and Mamitsuka, H.: Predicting protein secondary structure using stochastic tree grammars. Machine Learning **29** (1997) 275-301
2. Aebersold, K. and Mann, M.: Mass spectrometry-based protemics. Nature **422** (2003) 198-207
3. Bartels, C.: Fast algorithm for peptide sequencing by mass spectroscopy. Biomed. Environ. Mass Spectrom. **19** (1990) 363-368
4. Burge, C. and Karlin, S.: Prediction of complete gene structures in human genomic DNA. J. Mol. Biol. **268** (1997) 78-94
5. Cai L., Malmberg, R.L., and Wu Y.: Stochastic modeling of RNA pseudoknotted structures: a grammatical approach. Bioinformatics **19** (2003):i66-i73
6. Chen T. *et al.*: A dynamic programming approach to *de novo* peptide sequencing via tandem mass spectrometry. J. Comp. Biology **8** (2001) 325-337
7. Churchill, G. A.: Stochastic models for heterogeneous DNA sequences. Bull. Math. Biol. **51** (1989) 79-94
8. Cook, D.J. and Holder, L.B.: Graph-Based Data Mining. IEEE Intelligent Systems **15** (2000) 32-41
9. Cooper, C.A., Gasteiger, E. and Packer, N.H.: GlycoMod - A software tool for determining glycosylation compositions from mass spectrometric data. Proteomics **1** (2000) 340-349
10. Dehaspe, L., Toivonen, H. and King, R.D.: Finding Frequent Substructures in Chemical Compounds. In *Proceeding of the Fourth International Conference of Knowledge Discovery and Data Mining* (1998) 30-36
11. Dell, Anne and Morris, Howard R.: Glycoprotein Structure Determination by Mass Spectrometry. Science **291** (2001) 2351-2356
12. Dupplaw, D. and Lewis, P.H.: Content-Based Image Retrievel with Scale-spaced Object Trees. In *Proceedings of Storage and Retrieval for Media Databases* **3972** (2000)253-261
13. Ethier, M., Saba, J.A., Ens, W., Standing, K.G. and Perreault, H.: Automated structural assignment of derived complex N-linked oligosaccharides from tandem mass spectra. Rapid Commun. Mass Spectrom. **16** (2002) 1743-1754

14. Gaucher, S.P., Morrow, J. and Leary, J.A.: A saccharide topology analysis tool used in combination with tandem mass spectrometry *Anal. Chem.* **72** (2000) 2231-2236

15. Goldman, N., Thorne, J.L. and Jones, D.T.: Using Evolutionary Trees in Protein Secondary Structure Prediction and Other Comparative Sequence Analyses. J. Mol. Biol. **263** (1996) 196-208

16. Harvey, D. H.: Collision-induced fragmentation of underivatized N-linked carbohydrates ionized by electrospray. J. Mass Spectrom. **35** (2000) 1178-1190

17. KEGG LIGAND Database (Japan) http://www.genome.ad.jp/ligand/

18. Knudsen, B. and Hein, J.: RNA Secondary structure prediction using stochastic context-free grammars and evolutionary history. Bioinformatics **15** (1999) 446-454

19. Konig, S. and Leary J.A.: Evidence for linkage position determination in cobalt coordinated pentasaccharides using ion trap mass spectrometry. J. Am. Soc. Mass Spectrom. **9** (1999) 1125-1134

20. Krogh, A., I. Saira Mian and David Haussler: A hidden Markov model that finds genes in E.coli DNA. Nuc. Ac. Res. **22** (1994) 4768-4778

21. Lukashin, A. V. and Bodovsky, M.: GenMark.hmm: new solutions for gene finding. Nuc. Ac. Res. **26** (1998) 1107-1115

22. Ma, B. *et al.*: PEAKS: Powerful Software for Peptide *De Novo* Sequencing by MS/MS. Commun. Mass Spectrom **268** (1997) 78-94

23. Mamitsuka, H. and Abe, N.: Predicting Location and Structure of Beta-Sheet Regions Using Stochastic Tree Grammars. ISMB-94 **17** (2003) 2337-2342

24. Mizuno, Y. and Sasagawa, T.: An automated interpretation of MALDI/TOF post-source decay spectra of oligosaccharides. 1. Automated Peak Assignment. Anal. Chem. **71** (1999) 4764-4771

25. Rivas, Elena and Eddy, Sean R.: The language of RNA: a formal grammar that includes pseudoknots. Bioinformatics **16** (2000) 334-340

26. Rozenberg, G. editor.: Handbook of Graph Grammars and Computing by Graph Transformation. World Scientific (1997)

27. Shan, B., Zhang, K., Ma, B., Zhang, C. and Lajorie, G.: Automated structural elucidation of glycopeptides from MS/MS spectra. In 52nd ASMS Conference. (2004)(to be appeared)

28. Tseng, K. *et al.*: Catalog-Library Approach for the Rapid and Sensitive Structural Elucidation of Oligosaccharides. Anal. Chem. **71** (1999)3747-3754

29. Zala, Joseph: Mass Spectrometry of Oligosaccharides. Mass Spectrometry Reviews (2004) 23161-227

30. Clarke, F., Ekeland, I.: Nonlinear oscillations and boundary-value problems for Hamiltonian systems. Arch. Rat. Mech. Anal. **78** (1982) 315–333

31. Clarke, F., Ekeland, I.: Solutions périodiques, du période donnée, des équations hamiltoniennes. Note CRAS Paris **287** (1978) 1013–1015

32. Michalek, R., Tarantello, G.: Subharmonic solutions with prescribed minimal period for nonautonomous Hamiltonian systems. J. Diff. Eq. **72** (1988) 28–55

33. Tarantello, G.: Subharmonic solutions for Hamiltonian systems via a $\mathbb{Z}_p$ pseudoindex theory. Annali di Matematica Pura (to appear)

34. Zhang, C., Doherty-Kirby, A., Huystee, R. B., and Lajoie, G.:Investigation of Cationic Peanut Peroxidase Glycans by Electrospray Ionization Mass Spectrometry. Phytochemistry (2004) (accepted).

Parametric Weighted Finite Automata for Figure Drawing

German Tischler

Universität Würzburg, Lehrstuhl für Informatik II, Am Hubland,
97074 Würzburg, Germany
tischler@informatik.uni-wuerzburg.de
http://www2.informatik.uni-wuerzburg.de/staff/tischler

Abstract. Weighted finite automata (WFA) are nondeterministic finite automata labeled with real weights on their edges and states. They compute real functions on the unit interval. Parametric weighted finite automata (PWFA) are weighted finite automata with a multi-dimensional codomain. The only completely smooth functions computable by WFA are polynomials, while PWFA are also able to compute the sine, cosine, exponential and logarithmic function. We will present methods for constructing PWFA computing basic shapes, Catmull-Rom splines, Bezier polynomials and B-splines. We show how these possibilities can be combined to obtain a figure drawing framework that is based on a very simple automaton model that has only the operations of sum, multiplication by a constant and iteration.

1 Introduction

A definition of weighted finite automata (WFA), as it is used in this paper, can be found in [5]. WFA compute real functions, their domain is the set of words of infinite length over $\Sigma = \{0, 1, \ldots, k\}$, where $k \in \mathbb{N}$ is usually at least 1. Every domain word $w = w_0 w_1 \ldots$ is interpreted as the number $0.w_0 w_1 \ldots$, so for $k \geq 1$ WFA compute real functions on the unit interval $[0; 1]$. It was shown in [5] that WFA can compute every real polynomial on $[0; 1]$ and that the set of WFA-computable functions is closed under sum, difference and product. On the other hand it was proven in [6] that polynomials are the only completely smooth functions (having all derivatives in some open interval containing properly the closed unit interval) computable by WFA. It is simple to show though that it is possible to define non-polynomial functions with WFA that are differentiable infinitely often almost everywhere in $[0; 1]$. The most popular application of WFA so far was image compression, see for example [4].

Parametric weighted finite automata (PWFA) were defined in [1]. They are generalized WFA that are parameterized with a natural number d called their dimension. They can be seen as d simultaneously running versions of the same WFA that are only differing in their initial distribution. Therefore a PWFA of dimension d computes a d-dimensional real function on Σ^*. The set of functions

M. Domaratzki et al. (Eds.): CIAA 2004, LNCS 3317, pp. 259–268, 2005.

in $\mathbb{R}^2$ interpreted as (x, y) that are computable by PWFA contains the sine, cosine and exponential function as well as all corresponding inverse functions obtainable by swapping x and y in the result vectors. All this was shown in [1].

Here we show that the set of sets definable by PWFA is closed under set union, affine transformation and restriction of the domain language to any regular language. These results will be, as far as they are relevant for figure drawing, described shortly in this paper; the proof details can be found in [9]. We will show that certain kinds of spline functions are computable by PWFA. This includes Bezier polynomials[8], Catmull-Rom splines[3] and B-splines[2].

2   Properties of PWFA

A PWFA P is a quintuple (Q, Σ, W, I, F) where

1. Q is a finite set of states
2. $\Sigma = \{0, 1, \ldots, l-1\}$ is a finite alphabet
3. $W = \{A_0, A_1, \ldots, A_{l-1}\}, A_i \in \mathbb{R}^{|Q| \times |Q|}$ is the set of transition matrices
4. $I = (I_0 I_1 \ldots I_{d-1}), I_i \in \mathbb{R}^{|Q|}$ are the d initial distributions; the I_i are the rows of the matrix I
5. $F \in \mathbb{R}^{|Q|}$ is the final distribution

For every word $w = w_0 w_1 \ldots w_{n-1} \in \Sigma^*$ of finite length, P computes a result vector defined as

$$f_P(w) = I \prod_{i=0}^{n-1} A_{w_i} F . \tag{1}$$

The set $S(P)$ the automaton computes is

$$S(P) = \bigcap_{n=0}^{\infty} \overline{S_{\geq n}(P)} \tag{2}$$

with

$$S_{\geq n}(P) = \bigcup_{i=n}^{\infty} S_i(P) \tag{3}$$

and

$$S_i(P) = \{f_P(w) | w \in \Sigma^i\} \tag{4}$$

where the overline notation in equation 2 denotes the topological closure of the set under the line. Input words of WFA are interpreted as real numbers. For a PWFA the input word has no such interpretation; we solely consider the computed set $S(P)$. Figure 1 provides a small example.

The following properties are provided here, because most of them are used later on in the paper.

Theorem 1. *Let X and Y be PWFA with $d_X = d_Y$. Then $S(X) \cup S(Y)$ is computable by a PWFA.*   □

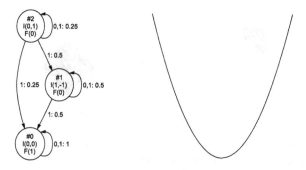

Fig. 1. An automaton computing the set $\{(x, x^2-x)|x \in [0;1]\}$ is shown on the left. The set it computes is visualized on the right. The states are labeled with their number, the initial distribution for each dimension and the final distribution. The edges are labeled with the corresponding weights. Edges that carry weight 0 are not shown

Fig. 2. Closure under set union: if there are automata for painting figure a (e.g. a set $[v, w] \times [x, y]$ for real intervals $[v, w]$ and $[x, y]$ interpreted as a filled rectangle) and figure b (set that denotes a filled circle), then there is an automaton that produces the merged figure

This property is visualized in figure 2. The proof is constructive and can be found in [9]. In the worst case the union automaton has a state set that has cardinality $|Q_X| + |Q_Y| + d$.

A PWFA can be seen as a structure that contains a certain set of functions. In particular every state represents a function that the automaton computes in a dimension that has it's initial distribution set to 1 for this state and zero for all other states. We call this function f_{P_i}. Thus choosing initial distribution I_k for dimension k means that the automaton computes the function

$$\tilde{f}_{P_k} = \sum_{i=0}^{|Q_P|-1} I_k(i) f_{P_i} \tag{5}$$

in dimension k. The set of WFA-computable functions is closed under addition, subtraction and multiplication, so it forms a commutative, associative ring with identity element. This ring contains polynomials and characteristic functions of closed intervals $J = [a; b] \subseteq [0; 1]$ if a and b have finite representations in any g-

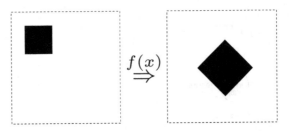

Fig. 3. Closure under affine transformation: the square on the left side is moved, rotated and scaled to obtain the square on the right side

adic system for $g \geq 2$. This implies that PWFA can represent Bezier polynomials, Catmull-Rom splines and certain B-splines.

We say a vector produced by a PWFA is useless, if it does not contribute to the computed set. All PWFA known to be relevant for figure drawing do not produce useless vectors. Another useful property for figure drawing is the following:

Theorem 2. *Let A be PWFA of dimension d that does not compute an infinite number of useless vectors and $f(x) = Bx + c$ any affine transformation on $\mathbb{R}^d$. Then the set $f(S(A))$ is computable by a PWFA.*   □

As above the proof is constructive and can be found in [9]. The multiplicative part can be implemented by substituting the matrix I_P by BI_P and the additive part by the introduction of one additional state, so any affine transformation can be applied to a PWFA by adding no more than one state.

Another interesting property of PWFA is that the restriction of their input language to any regular set instead of Σ^* is still PWFA-computable.

Theorem 3. *Let P be a PWFA and $R \subseteq \Sigma_P^*$ regular. There is a PWFA P' that computes the set $S(P')$ with $S_i(P')$ as defined in equation 4 replaced by $S_i(P') = \{f_P(w)|w \in R \cap \Sigma^i\}$*   □

The construction used in the proof[9] generates an automaton P' that has $O(|Q_P| \cdot |Q_{D_R}|)$ states, where D_R is the deterministic minimal automaton of the language R. This enables us to remove certain parts of the output set, figure 4 shows an example. The set $R_{\frac{-7}{64}}$ is the set of words that represent numbers in $\left[\frac{1}{8}, \frac{7}{8}\right]$. It is regular and can be written as

$$R_{\frac{-7}{64}} = ((((001 + 01) + 10) + 110)((0 + 1)*)) \tag{6}$$

in the notation used in [7]. This set describes values z with $z^2 - z \leq \frac{-7}{64}$. Although the construction of an automaton for a given set R is simple, the inference of such a set to restrict a PWFA produced set to a specific subset is usually not. In the simple example above it requires the solution of the quadratic polynomial $z^2 - z - \frac{7}{64}$ and even here the value $-\frac{7}{64}$ was chosen so that it produces roots with a short finite binary representation ($\frac{1}{8} = 0.001$ and $\frac{7}{8} = 0.111$). In other cases

Fig. 4. Regular restriction of the input language: figure $(x(z), y(z)) = (z^3 - z^2, z^2 - z)$, $z \in [0; 1]$ for Σ^* (left) and for $R_{\frac{-7}{64}}$ (right)

we can show that some desirable restrictions of the output of a PWFA cannot be achieved by a regular restriction of the input set. The exponential function in [1] e.g. cannot be restricted to the domain of non-negative real numbers using a regular restriction, because the required language is not regular. As this property is apparently hard to control, it appears less helpful for figure drawing than the closure under set union and affine transformation.

3   Figure Drawing with PWFA

We will show that a simple figure drawing framework that uses only a single PWFA for rendering can be constructed. It includes the drawing of rectangles, filled rectangles, circles, filled circles and some splines and thus also applications for these splines like the construction of font shapes.

The computation of circles with PWFA was introduced in [1]. It is done by constructing an automaton along the formula

$$\text{unitcircle} = \bigcup_{k=0}^{\infty} \begin{pmatrix} 1 & 0 \\ 0 & 1 \end{pmatrix} \begin{pmatrix} 0.8 & 0.6 \\ -0.6 & 0.8 \end{pmatrix}^k \begin{pmatrix} 1 \\ 0 \end{pmatrix}. \tag{7}$$

This can be extended to the production of circular discs with an arbitrary inner and outer radius. The automaton in figure 5 shows this. An automaton that implements equation 7 is contained with the states 0 and 1. It is also simple to form unfilled and filled rectangles, figure 6 shows an automaton that draws an unfilled square. Color images can be implemented by adding more dimensions, for example one more for gray-level images or three more for color images in RGB or YCbCr mode. In addition to such simple geometric forms PWFA can also display some splines.

This includes the Catmull-Rom splines introduced in [3]. These splines are interpolating control points with piecewise cubic polynomials. The control points are equally spaced; we assume that we have values of a curve at the points $\{0, 1, \ldots, k-1\}$. The resulting curve is built from k pieces. It is C^∞ (differentiable infinitely often) between the control points and C^1 (is differentiable) at the control points, the second derivative is linear interpolated. The Catmull-Rom spline is a special case of the Hermite cubic curve

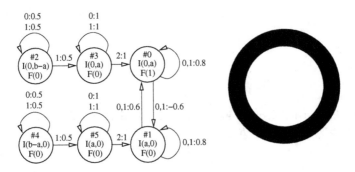

Fig. 5. PWFA computing circular disc with inner radius a and outer radius b (left) and the image it produces for $a = 0.55$ and $b = 0.75$ (right)

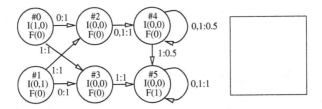

Fig. 6. PWFA computing unit square (left) and the image it produces (right)

$$h(t) = (2t^3 - 3t^2 + 1)p_0 + (t^3 - 2t^2 + t)m_0 + \\ (-2t^3 + 3t^2)p_1 + (t^3 - t^2)m_1 \tag{8}$$

that is a curve with two control points p_0 and p_1 and the tangents m_0 and m_1 at these control points. For the Catmull-Rom spline the tangents are computed using the control points p_{-1} and p_2, so the tangents do not have to be provided explicitly. Every Catmull-Rom spline with $k = 2^n, n \in \mathbb{N}$ control points can be implemented by a PWFA with

$$|Q| = 2\left(\frac{k}{2} + \frac{k}{4} + \ldots + 1\right) + 4 = 2k + 2 \tag{9}$$

states. This is clear from figure 7. There are 4 states that represent the cubic polynomial (states 0 to 3) and two decision trees for the x (states 4 to 6) and y (states 7 to 9) components. If k is not a power of 2, the number of states necessary is at most $2\left(2^{\lfloor \log_2 k \rfloor} + \lfloor \log_2 k \rfloor\right) + 4$. The cubic polynomial sub-automaton is shared between all segments of the spline.

Bezier polynomials can also be computed by PWFA. The point-set B defined by a Bezier polynomial b of degree k and dimension d is given in virtue of it's control-point vector

$$((b_{0,0}, b_{0,1}, \ldots, b_{0,d-1}), \ldots, (b_{k,0}, b_{k,1}, \ldots, b_{k,d-1}))$$

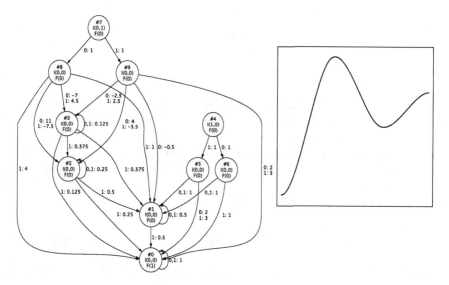

Fig. 7. PWFA computing a Catmull-Rom spline for the control-vector (0 4 2 3) (left) and the image it produces (right)

as

$$B = \bigcup_{z \in [0;1]} b(z) \tag{10}$$

with

$$b(z)(j) = \sum_{i=0}^{k} \binom{k}{i} z^i (1-z)^{k-i} b_{i,j} \text{ for } j = 0, 1, \ldots, d-1 . \tag{11}$$

All dimensions are computed by evaluating a polynomial and all these polynomials have at most degree k, so every Bezier polynomial of degree k can be represented as a PWFA with $k+1$ states. The curve in figure 4 is an example of a Bezier polynomial for the control-point vector

$$((0,0), (-1/3, 0), (-1/3, -1/3), (0,0)) .$$

Similar to the construction of PWFA for the Catmull-Rom spline it is possible to construct automata that produce several Bezier polynomials of the same degree while reusing the states that build the polynomial. The number of states necessary to draw a set of l Bezier polynomials of degree k with dimension d is thus at most $k + 1 + d(2^{\log_2 \lfloor l \rfloor} + \log_2 \lfloor l \rfloor)$.

Both Bezier polynomials and Catmull-Rom splines are by construction C^1 everywhere and C^∞ almost everywhere. This leaves no other possibility as to break up a spline into several pieces, if it is desired that the curve is not smooth at some point, for example the shape of the letter T. It is also hard to control the behavior of the curve between it's control points. B-splines overcome some of these problems. They can be defined inductively as

$$B_{i,1}(x) = \begin{cases} 1 & \text{for } t_i \leq x \leq t_{i+1} \\ 0 & \text{otherwise} \end{cases} \tag{12}$$

$$B_{i,k}(x) = \frac{x - t_i}{t_{i+k-1} - t_i} B_{i,k-1}(x) + \frac{t_{i+k} - x}{t_{i+k} - t_{i+1}} B_{i+1,k-1}(x) \tag{13}$$

where $t = (t_i), i \in \mathbb{Z}$ is called the knot vector. We first observe that B-splines are computable by PWFA, if the characteristic functions of the knot intervals $[t_i; t_{i+1}]$ are PWFA-computable. The equations 12 and 13 are apparently functionally invariant against translation and dilation of the knot vector, so we have some limited influence on the PWFA computability of a given B-spline. This implies that B-splines with $t_{i+1} - t_i = \frac{p_i}{q_i} c$ for $p_i \in \mathbb{Z}, q_i \in \mathbb{N}^+$ and $c \in \mathbb{R}$ for all $i \in \mathbb{Z}$ are PWFA-computable. We can write

$$\begin{aligned} B_{i,k} &= \{ (x, B_{i,k}(x)) | \, x \in \mathbb{R} \} \\ &= \{ (\text{LCM}(q_j)(x - t_0)/c, B_{i,k} \, (\text{LCM}(q_j)(x - t_0)/c)) \, | x \in \mathbb{R} \} \end{aligned} \tag{14}$$

where $\text{LCM}(q_j)$ denotes the least common multiple of all relevant $q_j \in \mathbb{N}^+$ and substitute the knot vector $t_i, i \in \mathbb{Z}$ by $t'_i = \frac{\text{LCM}(q_j)(t_i - t_0)}{c}, i \in \mathbb{Z}$. The number of relevant q_j is finite for every finite set of B-splines of a certain degree k, because they are all only depending on a finite set a knots in the knot vector. After this transformation, the relevant knots are all integers. We can divide the knot vector by $2^{\lceil \log_2 t'_{\max} \rceil}$, where $t'_{\max}$ is the maximum relevant knot value, to get a WFA friendly input. The B-spline will then be evaluated on the interval $[0; 2^{-\lceil \log_2 t'_{\max} \rceil}]$.

The construction of PWFA that compute uniform (that means $t_{i+1} - t_i = t_{i+2} - t_{i+1}$ for all $i \in \mathbb{Z}$) B-splines is simple. As in [8], we substitute $u = \frac{x - t_i}{L} = \frac{x}{L} - i$ under the assumption of $t_i = iL$. We then derive an algebraic form of the B-spline as a function of $(i + u)L$. In case of the uniform linear B-spline we get

$$U_{i,2}((i + u)L) = \begin{cases} u & 0 \leq u \leq 1 \\ 2 - u & 1 \leq u \leq 2 \end{cases}. \tag{15}$$

There are as many cases as the degree of the B-spline. These cases correspond to the leafs of a complete binary tree with depth $\lceil \log_2(k) \rceil - 1$. One level can be saved, because there are two outgoing edges from each tree leaf. Figure 8 shows an example for the uniform linear B-spline. The tree consists only of state 2. If z is the input word, the automaton computes the function $f(z) := 2z$ for $0 \leq z \leq 0.5$ and $f(z) := 2(1 - z)$ for $0.5 \leq z \leq 1$ in the y component. This differs from equation 15, because the reading of the first symbol that is used to decide which case the automaton is to compute equals a variable substitution. In the first case the substitution is $u \mapsto x$, in the second it is $u \mapsto x+1$ etc. The scaling with 2 is due to the fact that the automaton has already made one transition through the binary tree, when it enters the spline computation. If k is a power of 2, there is a PWFA with $2k - 1$ states that computes the uniform B-spline $U_{0,k}$, otherwise a few additional states are needed to control the behavior of the automaton for leafs of the complete binary tree that do not carry any case of the algebraic formulation

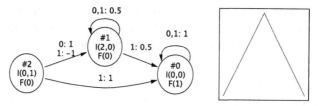

Fig. 8. PWFA computing a uniform linear B-spline $B_{0,2}$ ($t_0 = 0, t_1 = 1, t_2 = 2$) (left) and the image it produces in $[0; 2] \times [0; 1]$ (right)

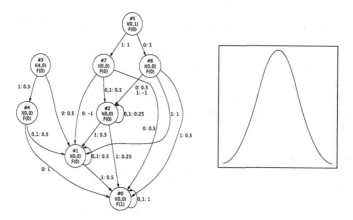

Fig. 9. PWFA computing a uniform quadratic B-spline $B_{0,3}$ ($t_0 = 0, t_1 = 1, t_2 = 2, t_3 = 3$) (left) and the image it produces in $[0; 3] \times [0; 0.75]$ (right)

of the B-spline. For the uniform quadratic B-spline we could for example let the automaton produce the first case again for the non-existent fourth case that exists in the complete binary tree with 2 leafs. Figure 9 shows this. States 0, 1 and 2 build a quadratic polynomial. States 5, 6 and 7 build the complete binary tree for the three cases of the quadratic B-spline, the fourth, non-existent state is mapped to the first case. States 3 and 4 control the x-component of the result vectors. It produces the same values for $00w$ as for $11w$ for all $w \in \Sigma^*$. Usually B-splines are used in linear combinations to build splines. An extension of a PWFA that computes a uniform B-spline $B_{i,k}$ to one that computes a finite linear combination of uniform B-splines $B_{j,k}, j \in \mathbb{Z}$ with the same knot vector, can be done by assigning all appropriate B-spline cases to the corresponding binary tree leafs. In case of the linear uniform B-spline leaf i would carry two algebraic expressions $U_{i,2}$ and $U_{i+1,2}$ multiplied by the coefficient from the linear combination.

4 Conclusion

We showed that basic figures can be drawn with PWFA. This includes simple shapes as rectangles and circles but also more complex shapes such as Catmull-

Rom splines, Bezier polynomials and some B-splines. All these objects can be combined in one automaton. During the decoding of the automaton the only arithmetic operations needed are addition, multiplication by a constant and iteration.

References

1. J. Albert, J. Kari, *Parametric Weighted Finite Automata and Iterated Function Systems* Proceedings L'Ingenieur et les Fractales - Fractals in Engineering, Delft, 248-255, 1999.
2. C. de Boor, *A practical guide to splines* Springer-Verlag New York Heidelberg Berlin, 1978.
3. E. Catmull, R. Rom, *A class of Local Interpolating Splines* in Barnill R.E. and R.F. Riesenfeld (eds.), Computer Aided Geometric Design, Academic Press, New York, 1974.
4. K. Culik II, J. Kari, *Inference Algorithms for WFA and Image Compression* in Y. Fisher (ed.), Fractal Image Compression. Springer Verlag Berlin, Heidelberg, New York, 1995.
5. K. Culik II, J. Karhumäki, *Finite automata computing real functions* SIAM Journal on Computing 23/4, 789-814, 1994.
6. D. Derencourt, J. Karhumäki, M. Latteux, A. Terlutte, *On Computational Power of Weighted Finite Automata* Lecture Notes in Computer Science 629, 236-245, 1992
7. J.H. Hopcroft, J.D. Ullman, *Introduction to automata theory, languages and computation* Addison Wesley, 1979.
8. T. Pavlidis, *Algorithms for graphics and image processing* Computer science press, 1982.
9. G. Tischler, *Properties and applications of parametric weighted finite automata* submitted.

Regional Finite-State Error Repair*

Manuel Vilares[1], Juan Otero[1], and Jorge Graña[2]

[1] Department of Computer Science, University of Vigo,
Campus As Lagoas s/n, 32004 Orense, Spain
{vilares, jop}@uvigo.es
[2] Department of Computer Science, University of A Coruña,
Campus de Elviña s/n, 15071 A Coruña, Spain
grana@udc.es

Abstract. We describe an algorithm to deal with error repair over finite-state architectures. Such a technique is of interest in spelling correction as well as approximate string matching in a variety of applications related to natural language processing, such as information extraction/recovery or answer searching, where error-tolerant recognition allows misspelled input words to be integrated in the computational process. Our proposal relies on a regional least-cost repair strategy, dynamically gathering all relevant information in the context of the error location. The system guarantees asymptotic equivalence with global repair strategies.

1   Introduction

An ongoing question in natural language processing (NLP) is how to recover ungrammatical structures for processing text. Focusing on spelling correction tasks, there are few things more frustrating than spending a great deal of time debugging typing or other errors in order to ensure the accuracy of NLP tools over large amount of data. As a consequence, although it is one of the oldest applications to be considered in the field of NLP [4], there is an increased interest in devising new techniques in this area.

In this regard, previous proposals extend the repair region to the entire string, complemented with the consideration of thresholds on an editing distance [7, 8]. This global approach, which seems to be universally accepted, has probably been favored by the consideration of English, a non-concatenative language with a reduced variety of morphological associated processes [11], as running language. However, the application of this kind of techniques to highly inflectional languages such as Latin ones [1], or agglutinative languages such as Turkish [10], could fail to take advantage of the underlying grammatical structure, leading to a significant loss of efficiency.

* Research partially supported by the Spanish Government under projects TIC2000-0370-C02-01 and HP2002-0081, and the Autonomous Government of Galicia under projects PGIDIT03SIN30501PR and PGIDIT02SIN01E.

M. Domaratzki et al. (Eds.): CIAA 2004, LNCS 3317, pp. 269–280, 2005.

In this context, we are interested in exploring regional repair techniques, introducing proper tasks for error location and repair region estimation. Our aim is to avoid examining the entire word, in contrast to global algorithms that expend equal effort on all parts of the word, including those containing no errors.

2   The Operational Model

Our aim is to parse a word $w_{1..n} = w_1 \ldots w_n$ according to a regular grammar $\mathcal{G} = (N, \Sigma, P, S)$, where N is the set of non-terminals, Σ the set of terminal symbols, P the rules and S the start symbol. We denote by w_0 (resp. w_{n+1}) the position in the string, $w_{1..n}$, previous to w_1 (resp. following w_n). We generate from $\mathcal{G}$ a *numbered minimal acyclic finite state automaton* for the language $\mathcal{L}(\mathcal{G})$. In practice, we choose a device [6] generated using GALENA [3]. A *finite automaton* (FA) is a 5-tuple $\mathcal{A} = (\mathcal{Q}, \Sigma, \delta, q_0, \mathcal{Q}_f)$ where: $\mathcal{Q}$ is the set of states, Σ the set of input symbols, δ is a function of $\mathcal{Q} \times \Sigma$ into $2^{\mathcal{Q}}$ defining the transitions of the automaton, q_0 the initial state and $\mathcal{Q}_f$ the set of final states. We denote $\delta(q, a)$ by $q.a$, and we say that the FA is *deterministic* when, in any case, $\mid q.a \mid \leq 1$. The notation is transitive, so $q.w$ denotes the state reached by using the transitions labelled by each letter w_i, $i \in \{1, \ldots, n\}$ of w. Therefore, w is *accepted* iff $q_0.w \in \mathcal{Q}_f$, that is, the *language accepted by* $\mathcal{A}$ is defined as $\mathcal{L}(\mathcal{A}) = \{w, \text{ such that } q_0.w \in \mathcal{Q}_f\}$. An FA is *acyclic* when the underlying graph is. We talk about a *path in the* FA to refer to a sequence of states $\{q_1, \ldots, q_n\}$, such that $\forall i \in \{1, \ldots, n-1\}$, $\exists a_i \in \Sigma$, $q_i.a_i = q_{i+1}$.

In order to reduce the memory requirements, we minimize the FA [2]. So, we say that two FAs are *equivalent* iff they recognize the same language. Two states, p and q, are *equivalent* iff the FA with p as initial state and the one that starts in q recognize the same language. An FA is *minimal* iff no pair in $\mathcal{Q}$ is equivalent.

It is important to note that although the standard recognition process is deterministic, the repair process could introduce non-determinism by exploring alternatives associated to possibly more than one recovery strategy. So, in order to get polynomial complexity, we avoid duplicating intermediate computations in the repair of $w_{1..n} \in \Sigma^+$, storing them in a table $\mathcal{I}$ of *items*, $\mathcal{I} = \{[q, i], q \in \mathcal{Q}, i \in [1, n+1]\}$, where $[q, i]$ looks for the suffix $w_{i..n}$ to be analyzed from $q \in \mathcal{Q}$.

We describe our proposal using *parsing schemata* [9], a triple $\langle \mathcal{I}, \mathcal{H}, \mathcal{D} \rangle$, with $\mathcal{H} = \{[a, i], a = w_i\}$ an initial set of items called *hypothesis* that encodes the word to be recognized[1], and $\mathcal{D}$ a set of *deduction steps* that allow new items to be derived from already known items. Deduction steps are of the form $\{\eta_1, \ldots, \eta_k \vdash \xi \,/\, conds\}$, meaning that if all antecedents η_i are present and the conditions $conds$ are satisfied, then the consequent ξ is generated. In our case, $\mathcal{D} = \mathcal{D}^{\text{Init}} \cup \mathcal{D}^{\text{Shift}}$, where:

$$\mathcal{D}^{\text{Init}} = \{\vdash [q_0, 1]\} \qquad \mathcal{D}^{\text{Shift}} = \{[p, i] \vdash [q, i+1] \,/\, \exists [a, i] \in \mathcal{H}, \ q = p.a\}$$

---

[1] A word $w_{1...n} \in \Sigma^+$, $n \geq 1$ is represented by $\{[w_1, 1], [w_2, 2], \ldots, [w_n, n]\}$.

The recognition associates a set of items S_p^w, called *itemset*, to each $p \in \mathcal{Q}$; and applies these deduction steps until no new application is possible. The word is recognized iff a *final item* $[q_f, n+1]$, $q_f \in \mathcal{Q}_f$ has been generated. We can assume, without lost of generality, that $\mathcal{Q}_f = \{q_f\}$, and that exists an only transition from (resp. to) q_0 (resp. q_f). To get it, we augment the original FA with two states becoming the new initial and final states, and relied to the original ones through empty transitions, a concession to the minimality.

3   The Edit Distance

The *edit distance* [5] between two strings measures the minimum number of editing operations of insertion, deletion, replacement of a symbol, and transposition of adjacent symbols that are needed to convert one string into another. Let $x_{1..m}$ (resp. $y_{1..n}$) be the misspelled string (resp. a possible partial candidate string), the edit distance, $ed(x, y)$ is computed as follows:

$$
ed(x_{i+1}, y_{j+1}) =
\begin{cases}
ed(x_i, y_j) & \text{iff } x_{i+1} = y_{j+1} \\
& \text{(last characters are the same)} \\
1 + \min\{\ ed(x_{i-1}, y_{j-1}), \\
\qquad\quad ed(x_{i+1}, y_j), \\
\qquad\quad ed(x_i, y_{j+1})\} & \text{iff } x_i = y_{j+1}, x_{i+1} = y_j \\
& \text{(last two characters transposed)} \\
1 + \min\{\ ed(x_i, y_j), \\
\qquad\quad ed(x_{i+1}, y_j), \\
\qquad\quad ed(x_i, y_{j+1})\} & \text{otherwise}
\end{cases}
$$

$$ed(x_0, y_j) = j \qquad\qquad 1 \le j \le n$$
$$ed(x_i, y_0) = i \qquad\qquad 1 \le i \le m$$

where x_0 (resp. y_0) is ε. We can now extend the concept of language accepted by an FA $\mathcal{A}$, $\mathcal{L}(\mathcal{A})$, to define the *language accepted by an FA $\mathcal{A}$ with an error threshold* $\tau > 0$ as $\mathcal{L}_\tau(\mathcal{A}) = \{x, \text{ such that } ed(x, y) \le \tau, y \in \mathcal{L}(\mathcal{A})\}$. We shall consider the edit distance as a common metrical basis in order to allow an objective comparison to be made between our proposal and previous ones.

4   Regional Least-Cost Error Repair

We talk about the *error* in a portion of the word to mean the difference between what was intended and what actually appears in the word. So, we can talk about the *point of error* as the point at which the difference occurs.

Definition 1. *Let $\mathcal{A} = (\mathcal{Q}, \Sigma, \delta, q_0, \mathcal{Q}_f)$ be an FA, and let $w_{1..n}$ be a word. We say that w_i is a point of error iff it verifies the following conditions:*

$$(1) \quad q_0.w_{1..i-1} = q \qquad (2) \quad q.w_i \notin \mathcal{Q}$$

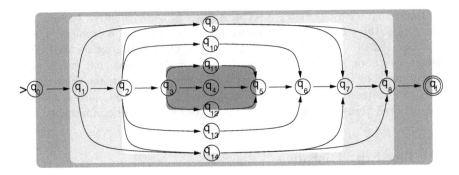

Fig. 1. The concept of region applied to error repair

The point of error is fixed by the recognizer and it provides the starting point for the repair, in which the following step consists in locating the origin of that error. We aim to limit the impact on the prefix already analyzed, focusing on the context close to the point of error and saving on computational effort. To do so, we first introduce a collection of topological properties that we illustrate in Fig. 1.

Definition 2. *Let* $\mathcal{A} = (\mathcal{Q}, \Sigma, \delta, q_0, \mathcal{Q}_f)$ *be an* FA, *and let* $p, q \in \mathcal{Q}$. *We say that* p *is lesser than* q *iff there exists a path* $\{p, \ldots, q\}$. *We denote that by* $p < q$.

We have, in Fig. 1, that $q_i < q_{i+1}$, $\forall i \in \{1, \ldots, 7\}$. Our order is induced by the transitional formalism, which results in a well defined relation since our FA is acyclic. In this sense, we can also give a direction to the paths.

Definition 3. *Let* $\mathcal{A} = (\mathcal{Q}, \Sigma, \delta, q_0, \mathcal{Q}_f)$ *be an* FA, *we say that* $q_s \in \mathcal{Q}$ *(resp.* q_d*) is a* source *(resp.* drain*) state for any path in* $\mathcal{A}$, $\{q_1, \ldots, q_m\}$, *iff* $\exists a \in \Sigma$, *such that* $q_1 = q_s.a$ *(resp.* $q_m.a = q_d$*).*

Intuitively, we talk about source (resp. drain) states on out-coming (resp. incoming) transitions, which orientates the paths from sources to drains. So, in Fig. 1, q_1 (resp. q_8) is a source (resp. drain) for paths $\{q_9\}$, $\{q_2, q_{10}, q_6, q_7\}$, $\{q_2, q_3, q_{11}, q_5, q_6, q_7\}$ or $\{q_2, q_3, q_4, q_5, q_6, q_7\}$. We can now consider a coverage for FAs by introducing the concept of *region*.

Definition 4. *Let* $\mathcal{A} = (\mathcal{Q}, \Sigma, \delta, q_0, \mathcal{Q}_f)$ *be an* FA, *a pair* (q_s, q_d), $q_s, q_d \in \mathcal{Q}$ *is a region in* $\mathcal{A}$, *denoted by* $\mathcal{R}_{q_s}^{q_d}(\mathcal{A})$, *iff it verifies that*

(1) $q_s = q_0$ **and** $q_d = q_f$ *(the global* FA*)*
   or
(2) $\{\forall \rho, \ source(\rho) = q_s\} \Rightarrow drain(\rho) = q_d$ **and** $| \{\forall \rho, \ source(\rho) = q_s\} | > 1$

which we write as $\mathcal{R}_{q_s}^{q_d}$ *when the context is clear. We also denote* paths$(\mathcal{R}_{q_s}^{q_d}) = \{\rho / source(\rho) = q_s, \ drain(\rho) = q_d\}$ *and, given* $q \in \mathcal{Q}$, *we say that* $q \in \mathcal{R}_{q_s}^{q_d}$ *iff* $\exists \rho \in paths(\mathcal{R}_{q_s}^{q_d})$, $q \in \rho$.

This allows us to ensure that any state, with the exception of q_0 and q_f, is included in a region. Applied to Fig. 1, the regions are $\mathcal{A} = \mathcal{R}_{q_0}^{q_f}$, $\mathcal{R}_{q_1}^{q_8}$, $\mathcal{R}_{q_2}^{q_7}$ and $\mathcal{R}_{q_3}^{q_5}$, with $\{q_4, q_{11}, q_{12}\} \subset \mathcal{R}_{q_3}^{q_5} \not\ni q_3$ and $\mathcal{R}_{q_2}^{q_7} \ni q_9 \notin \mathcal{R}_{q_3}^{q_5}$. In a region, all prefixes computed before the source can be combined with any suffix from the drain through the paths between both. This provides a criterion to place around a state a zone for which any change in it has no effect on its context.

Definition 5. *Let $\mathcal{A} = (\mathcal{Q}, \Sigma, \delta, q_0, \mathcal{Q}_f)$ be an* FA, *we say that a region $\mathcal{R}_{q_s}^{q_d}$ is the minimal region in $\mathcal{A}$ containing $p \in \mathcal{Q}$ iff it verifies that $q_s \geq p_s$ (resp. $q_d \leq p_d$), $\forall \mathcal{R}_{p_s}^{p_d} \ni p$. We denote it as $\mathcal{M}(\mathcal{A}, p)$, or simply $\mathcal{M}(p)$ when the context is clear.*

In Fig. 1, $\mathcal{M}(q_4) = \mathcal{M}(q_{11}) = \mathcal{R}_{q_3}^{q_5}$ and $\mathcal{M}(q_3) = \mathcal{M}(q_9) = \mathcal{R}_{q_2}^{q_7}$. At this point, it is trivial to prove the following lemma, which guarantees the consistency of the previous concept based on the uniqueness of a minimal region.

Lemma 1. *Let $\mathcal{A} = (\mathcal{Q}, \Sigma, \delta, q_0, \mathcal{Q}_f)$ be an* FA, *then $p \in \mathcal{Q} \setminus \{q_0, q_f\} \Rightarrow \exists \mathcal{M}(p)$.*

Proof. Trivial from definition 5.

We can now formally introduce the concept of *point of detection*, the point at which the recognizer detects that there is an error and calls the repair algorithm.

Definition 6. *Let $\mathcal{A} = (\mathcal{Q}, \Sigma, \delta, q_0, \mathcal{Q}_f)$ be an* FA, *and let w_j be a point of error in $w_{1..n} \in \Sigma^+$. We say that w_i is a point of detection associated to w_j iff:*

$$\exists q_d > q_0.w_{1..j}, \; \mathcal{M}(q_0.w_{1..j}) = \mathcal{R}_{q_0.w_{1..i}}^{q_d}$$

We denote this by detection$(w_j) = w_i$, *and we say that $\mathcal{M}(q_0.w_{1..j})$ is the region defining the point of detection w_i.*

In our example in Fig. 1, if we assume w_j to be a point of error such that $q_{10} = q_0.w_{1..j}$, we conclude that $w_i = $ detection(w_j) if $q_2 = q_0.w_{1..i}$ since $\mathcal{M}(q_{10}) = \mathcal{R}_{q_2}^{q_7}$. So, the error is located in the immediate left recognition context, given by the closest source. However, we also need to locate it from an operational viewpoint, as an item in the computational process.

Definition 7. *Let $\mathcal{A} = (\mathcal{Q}, \Sigma, \delta, q_0, \mathcal{Q}_f)$ be an* FA, *let w_j be a point of error in $w_{1..n} \in \Sigma^+$, and let w_i be a point of detection associated to w_j. We say that $[q, j] \in S_q^w$ is an error item iff $q_0.w_{j-1} = q$; and we say that $[p, i] \in S_p^w$ is a detection item associated to w_j iff $q_0.w_{i-1} = p$.*

Following our running example in Fig. 1, $[q_2, i]$ is a detection item for the error item $[q_{10}, j]$. Intuitively, we talk about error and detection items when they represent states in the FA concerned with the recognition of points of error and detection, respectively. Once we have identified the beginning of the repair region from both the topological and the operational viewpoint, we can now apply the *modifications* intended to recover the recognition process from an error.

Definition 8. *Let* $\mathcal{A} = (\mathcal{Q}, \Sigma, \delta, q_0, \mathcal{Q}_f)$ *be an* FA, *a modification to* $w_{1..n} \in \Sigma^+$ *is a series of edit operations,* $\{E_i\}_{i=1}^n$, *in which each* E_i *is applied to* w_i *and possibly consists of a sequence of insertions before* w_i, *replacement or deletion of* w_i, *or transposition with* w_{i+1}. *We denote it by* $M(w)$.

We now use the topological structure to restrict the notion of modification, introducing the concept of *error repair*. Intuitively, we look for conditions that guarantee the ability to recover the standard recognition, at the same time as they allow us to isolate repair branches by using the concept of path in a region.

Definition 9. *Let* $\mathcal{A} = (\mathcal{Q}, \Sigma, \delta, q_0, \mathcal{Q}_f)$ *be an* FA, $x_{1..m}$ *a prefix in* $\mathcal{L}(\mathcal{A})$, *and* $w \in \Sigma^+$, *such that* xw *is not a prefix in* $\mathcal{L}(\mathcal{A})$. *We define a repair of* w *following* x *as* $M(w)$, *so that:*

(1) $\mathcal{M}(q_0.x_{1..m}) = \mathcal{R}_{q_s}^{q_d}$ *(minimal region including the point of error,* $x_{1..m}$ *)*
(2) $\exists\{q_0.x_{1..i} = q_s.x_i, \ldots, q_s.x_{i..m}.M(w)\} \in paths(\mathcal{R}_{q_s}^{q_d})$

We denote it by repair(x, w), *and* $\mathcal{R}_{q_s}^{q_d}$ *by* scope(M).

However, the notion of *repair*(x, w) is not sufficient for our purposes, since our aim is to extend the recovery process to consider all possible repairs associated to a given point of error, which implies simultaneously considering different prefixes.

Definition 10. *Let* $\mathcal{A} = (\mathcal{Q}, \Sigma, \delta, q_0, \mathcal{Q}_f)$ *be an* FA *and let* $y_i \in y_{1..n}$ *be a point of error, we define the* set of repairs *for* y_i, *as*

$$\text{repair}(y_i) = \{xM(w) \in repair(x, w)/w_1 = detection(y_i)\}$$

We now need a mechanism to filter out undesirable repair processes, in order to reduce the computational charges. To do so, we should introduce comparison criteria to select only those repairs with minimal cost.

Definition 11. *For each* $a, b \in \Sigma$ *we assume insert,* $I(a)$; *delete,* $D(a)$, *replace,* $R(a, b)$, *and transpose,* $T(a, b)$, *costs. The cost of a modification* $M(w_{1..n})$ *is given by* $\text{cost}(M(w_{1..n})) = \Sigma_{j \in J_{-\!|}} I(a_j) + \Sigma_{i=1}^n (\Sigma_{j \in J_i} I(a_j) + D(w_i) + R(w_i, b) + T(w_i, w_{i+1}))$, *where* $\{a_j, \ j \in J_i\}$ *is the set of insertions applied before* w_i; $w_{n+1} =\dashv$ *the end of the input and* $T_{w_n, \dashv} = 0$.

In order to take edit distance as the error metric for measuring the quality of a repair, it is sufficient to consider discrete costs $I(a) = D(a) = 1$, $\forall a \in \Sigma$ and $R(a, b) = T(a, b) = 1$, $\forall a, b \in \Sigma$, $a \neq b$. On the other hand, when several repairs are available on different points of detection, we need a condition to ensure that only those with the same minimal cost are taken into account, looking for the best repair quality. However, this is not in contradiction with the consideration of error thresholds or alternative error metrics.

Definition 12. *Let* $\mathcal{A} = (\mathcal{Q}, \Sigma, \delta, q_0, \mathcal{Q}_f)$ *be an* FA *and let* $y_i \in y_{1..n}$ *be a point of error, we define the* set of regional repairs *for* y_i, *as follows:*

$$regional(y_i) = \left\{ xM(w) \in repair(y_i) \; \middle/ \; \begin{array}{l} cost(M) \leq cost(M'), \ \forall M' \in repair(x, w) \\ cost(M) = \min_{L \in repair(y_i)} \{cost(L)\} \end{array} \right\}$$

It is also necessary to take into account the possibility of cascaded errors, that is, errors precipitated by a previous erroneous repair diagnosis. Prior to dealing with the problem, we need to establish the existing relationship between the regional repairs for a given point of error and future points of error.

Definition 13. *Let* $\mathcal{A} = (\mathcal{Q}, \Sigma, \delta, q_0, \mathcal{Q}_f)$ *be an* FA *and let* w_i, w_j *be points of error in* $w_{1..n} \in \Sigma^+$, $j > i$. *We define the set of viable repairs for* w_i *in* w_j, *as*

$$viable(w_i, w_j) = \{xM(y) \in regional(w_i)/xM(y) \ldots w_j \ prefix \ for \ \mathcal{L}(\mathcal{A})\}$$

Intuitively, the repairs in $viable(w_i, w_j)$ are the only ones capable of ensuring the continuity of the recognition in $w_{i..j}$ and, therefore, the only possible repairs at the origin of the phenomenon of cascaded errors.

Definition 14. *Let* w_i *be a point of error for* $w_{1..n} \in \Sigma^+$, *we say that a point of error* w_k, $k > j$ *is a point of error precipitated by* w_j *iff*

$$\forall xM(y) \in viable(w_j, w_k), \ \exists \mathcal{R}^{q_d}_{q_0.w_{1..i}} \ defining \ w_i = detection(w_j)$$

such that $scope(M) \subset \mathcal{R}^{q_d}_{q_0.w_{1..i}}$.

In practice, a point of error w_k is precipitated by the result of previous repairs on a point of error w_j, when the region defining the point of detection for w_k summarizes all viable repairs for w_j in w_k. This implies that the information compiled from those repair regions has not been sufficient to give continuity to a recognition process locating the new error in a region containing the preceding ones and, therefore, depending on them. That is, the underlying grammatical structure suggests that the origin of the current error could be a mistaken treatment of past errors. Otherwise, the location would be fixed in a zone not depending on these previous repairs.

5   The Algorithm

We propose that the repair be obtained by searching the FA itself to find a suitable configuration to allow the recognition to continue, a classic approach in error repair. However, in the state of the art there is no theoretical size limit for the repair region, but only for the edit distance on corrections in it. So, in order to avoid distortions due to unsafe error location, the authors make use of global algorithms limiting the computations by a threshold on the edit distance. This allows them to restrict the section of the FA to be explored by pruning either all repair paths which are more distant from the input than the threshold [7], or those not maintaining a minimal distance no bigger than the threshold [8].

However, the fact that we are not profiting from the linguistic knowledge present in the FA to locate the error and to delimit its impact may lead to suboptimal computational costs or to precipitating new errors. We eliminate this problem by a construction where all repair phases are dynamically guided by the FA itself and, therefore, inspired by the underlying grammatical structure.

5.1   A Simple Case

We assume that we are dealing with the first error detected in a word $w_{1..n} \in \Sigma^+$. The major features of the algorithm involve beginning with the error item, whose error counter is zero. So, we extend the item structure, $[p, i, e]$, where e is now the error counter accumulated in the recognition of w at position w_i in state p.

We refer again to Fig. 1. So, given an error item, $[q_{10} = q_0.w_{1..j}, j, e_j]$, the system locates the corresponding detection item, $[q_2 = q_0.w_{1..i}, i, e_i]$, by using a pointer on $\mathcal{M}(q_{10}) = \mathcal{R}_{q_2}^{q_7}$. We then apply all possible transitions in this region beginning at both, the point of error and the its associated point of detection, which corresponds to the following deduction steps in error mode, $\mathcal{D}_{error} = \mathcal{D}_{error}^{Shift} \cup \mathcal{D}_{error}^{Insert} \cup \mathcal{D}_{error}^{Delete} \cup \mathcal{D}_{error}^{Replace} \cup \mathcal{D}_{error}^{Transpose}$:

$$\mathcal{D}_{error}^{Shift} = \{[p, i, e] \vdash [q, i+1, e], \; \exists [a, i] \in \mathcal{H}, \; q = p.a\}$$

$$\mathcal{D}_{error}^{Insert} = \{[p, i, e] \vdash [p, i+1, e+I(a)], \; \not\exists p.a\}$$

$$\mathcal{D}_{error}^{Delete} = \{[p, i, e] \vdash [q, i-1, e+D(w_i)] \; \Big/ \; \begin{array}{l} \mathcal{M}(q_0.w_{1..j}) = \mathcal{R}_{q_s}^{q_d} \\ p.w_i = q_d \in \mathcal{R}_{q_s}^{q_d} \text{ or } q = q_d \end{array} \}$$

$$\mathcal{D}_{error}^{Replace} = \{[p, i, e] \vdash [q, i+1, e+R(w_i, a)], \; \Big/ \; \begin{array}{l} \mathcal{M}(q_0.w_{1..j}) = \mathcal{R}_{q_s}^{q_d} \\ p.a = q \in \mathcal{R}_{q_s}^{q_d} \text{ or } q = q_d \end{array} \}$$

$$\mathcal{D}_{error}^{Transpose} = \{[p, i, e] \vdash [q, i+2, e+T(w_i, w_{i+1})] \; \Big/ \; \begin{array}{l} \mathcal{M}(q_0.w_{1..j}) = \mathcal{R}_{q_s}^{q_d} \\ p.w_i.w_{i+1} = q \in \mathcal{R}_{q_s}^{q_d} \text{ or } q = q_d \end{array} \}$$

where $w_{1..j}$ looks for the current point of error. Note that, in any case, the error hypotheses apply on transitions behind the repair region. The process continues until a repair covers the repair region, accepting a character in the remaining string. Returning to Fig. 1, the scope of repair for the error detected at $w_i \in detection(w_j)$ is $\mathcal{M}(q_{10}) = \mathcal{R}_{q_2}^{q_7}$, the region defining the detection item $[q_2 = q_0.w_{1..i}, i, e_i]$. Once this has been performed on each recognition branch, we select the regional repairs and the process goes back to standard mode.

5.2   The General Case

We now assume that the repair process is not the first one in the word and, therefore, can modify a previous one. This arises when we realize that we come back to a detection item for which some recognition branch includes a previous repair process. To illustrate such a case, we return to Fig. 1 assuming $[q_{10} = q_0.w_{1..k}, k, e_k]$ and $[q_8 = q_0.w_{1..l}, l, e_l]$ to be points of error. As a consequence, $[q_8 = q_0.w_{1..l}, l, e_l]$ would be precipitated by $[q_{10} = q_0.w_{1..k}, k, e_k]$ since $\mathcal{A} = \mathcal{R}_{q_0}^{q_f}$ defining $w_0 = detection(w_l)$ includes $\mathcal{R}_{q_2=q_0.w_{1..j}}^{q_7}$, the scope of a previous repair.

To deal with precipitated errors, the algorithm re-takes the previous error counters, adding the cost of the new repair hypotheses to profit from the experience gained from previous recovery phases. At this point, regional repairs have two important properties. First, they are independent of the FA construction and secondly, there is no loss of efficiency in relation to global repair approaches.

Lemma 2. *(The Expansion Lemma) Let $\mathcal{A} = (\mathcal{Q}, \Sigma, \delta, q_0, \mathcal{Q}_f)$ be an FA and let w_k, w_l be points of error in $w_{1..n} \in \Sigma^+$, such that w_l is precipitated by w_k, then:*

$$q_0.w_{1..i} < q_0.w_{1..j}, \; \mathcal{M}(q_0.w_l) = \mathcal{R}_{q_0.w_{1..i}}^{q_d}, \; w_j = y_1, \; xM(y) \in viable(w_k, w_l)$$

Proof. Let $w_j \in \Sigma$, such that $w_j = y_1$, $xM(y) \in viable(w_k, w_l)$ be a point of detection for w_k, for which some recognition branch derived from a repair in $regional(w_k)$ has successfully arrived at w_l. Let also w_l be a point of error precipitated by $xM(y) \in viable(w_k, w_l)$. By definition 14, we can affirm that

$$scope(M) \subset \mathcal{M}(q_0.w_l) = \mathcal{R}^{q_d}_{q_0.w_{1..i}}$$

Given that $scope(M)$ is the lowest region summarizing $q_0.w_{1..j}$, it follows that $q_0.w_{1..i} < q_0.w_{1..j}$. We conclude the proof by extending it to all repairs in $viable(w_k, w_l)$. □

Intuitively, we prove that the state associated to the point of detection in a cascaded error is lesser than the one associated to the source of the scope in the repairs precipitating it. As a consequence, the minimal possible scope of a repair for the cascaded error includes any scope of those previous repairs.

Corollary 1. *Let $\mathcal{A} = (\mathcal{Q}, \Sigma, \delta, q_0, \mathcal{Q}_f)$ be an FA and let w_k, w_l be points of error in $w_{1..n} \in \Sigma^+$, such that w_l is precipitated by w_k, then*

$$max\{scope(M), \ M \in viable(w_k, w_l)\} \subset max\{scope(\tilde{M}), \ \tilde{M} \in regional(w_l)\}$$

Proof. It immediately follows from lemma 2. □

This allows us to get an asymptotic behavior close to global repair methods. That is, the algorithm ensures a quality comparable to global strategies, but at the cost of a local one. This has profound implications for the efficiency, measured by time, the simplicity and the power of computing regional repairs.

Lemma 3. *Let $\mathcal{A} = (\mathcal{Q}, \Sigma, \delta, q_0, \mathcal{Q}_f)$ be an FA and let w_i be a point of error in $w_{1..n} \in \Sigma^+$, the time bound for the regional repair is, in the worst case,*

$$\mathcal{O}(\frac{n!}{\tau! * (n - \tau)!} * (n + \tau) * 2^\tau * fan\text{-}out_\mu^\tau)$$

where τ and fan-out$_\mu$ are, respectively, the maximal error counter computed and the maximal fan-out of the automaton in the scope of the repairs considered.

Proof. Here, the proof is a simple extrapolation of the estimation proposed for the Savary's algorithm [8]. In the worst case, there are at most $n!/(\tau! * (n - \tau)!)$ possible distributions of τ modifications over n word positions. For each distribution $(1 + 2 * fan\text{-}out_\mu)^\tau$ paths at most are followed, each path being of length $n + \tau$ at most. So, the worst case complexity is the one proposed. □

However, this lemma does not yet determine the relation with classic global approaches [7, 8], as is our aim, but only an average case estimation of our own time complexity. To reach this, we extend the repair region to the total FA.

Corollary 2. *Let $\mathcal{A} = (\mathcal{Q}, \Sigma, \delta, q_0, \mathcal{Q}_f)$ be an FA and let w_i be a point of error in $w_{1..n} \in \Sigma^+$, the time bound for the regional repair is, in the worst case, the same reached for a global approach.*

Proof. It immediately follows from the previous lemma 3 and corollary 1, as well as [8]. In effect, in the worst case, the scope of the repair is the global FA.   □

Taking into account the kind of proof applied on lemma 3, this implies that our technique has the same time complexity claimed for Savary's global one [8], in the best of our knowledge the most efficient proposal on spelling correction.

6   Practical Aspects

Our aim here is to validate the practical interest of our proposal in relation to classic global ones, trying to corroborate the theoretical results previously advanced. We think that it is an objective criterion for measuring the quality of a repair algorithm, since the point of reference is a technique that guarantees the best quality for a given error metric when all contextual information is available. So, we have compared our algorithm with the Savary's global approach [8]. The restrictions imposed on the length of this paper limit our present discussion to some relevant practical details.

6.1   The Running Languages

We choose to work with languages with a great variety of morphological processes, which make them adequate for our description. In particular, the first preliminary practical tests have been performed on Spanish. The most outstanding features are to be found in verbs, with their highly complex conjugation paradigm, as well as in complex gender and number inflection.

We have taken for Spanish a lexicon with 514,781 different words, to illustrate our work. This lexicon is recognized by an FA containing 58,170 states connected by 153,599 transitions, of sufficient size to allow us to consider this automaton as a representative starting point for our purposes. From this lexicon, we have selected a representative sample of morphological errors for practical evaluation of the algorithm. This sample has the same distribution observed in the original lexicon in terms of lengths of the words dealt with. This is of some importance since, as the authors claim, the efficiency of previous proposals depends on these factors [7, 8], which makes no practical sense. No other dependencies have been detected at morphological level and, therefore, they have not been considered. In each length-category, errors have been randomly generated in a number and position in the input string.

6.2   Preliminary Experimental Results

We are interested in both computational and quality aspects. In this sense, we consider the concept of item previously defined in order to measure the computational effort. To take into account data related to the performance from both the user's and the system's viewpoint, we have introduced the following two measures, for a given word, w, containing an error:

$$performance(w) = \frac{useful\ items}{total\ items} \qquad recall(w) = \frac{proposed\ corrections}{total\ corrections}$$

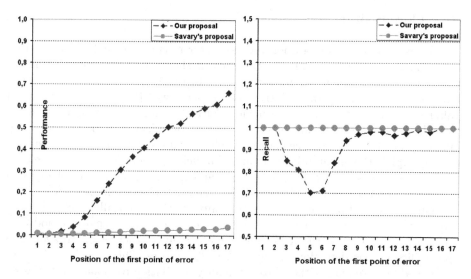

Fig. 2. Performance and recall results

that we complement with a global measure on the *precision* of the error repair approach in each case, that is, the rate reflecting when the algorithm provides the correction attended by the user. We use the term *useful items* to refer to the number of generated items that finally contribute to the obtaining of a repair, and *total items* to refer to the number of these structures generated during the process. We denote by *proposed corrections* the number of corrections provided by the algorithm, and by *total corrections* the number of possible ones, in absolute terms.

The practical results shown in Fig. 2 appear to corroborate that not only the performance in our case is better than Savary's, but also that the difference existing between them increases with the location of the first point of error. With respect to the recall relation, Savary's algorithm shows a constant graph since the approach applied is global and, consequently, the set of corrections provided is always the entire one for a fixed error counter. In our proposal, the results prove that the recall is smaller than that for Savary's, which illustrates the gain in computational efficiency in comparison with the global method. Finally, the precision of the regional (resp. the global) method is of 77% (resp. 81%). We must remember that here we are only taking into account morphological information, which has an impact on precision for a regional approach, but not for a global one, which always provides all possible repair alternatives. So, a precision measure represents a disadvantage for our proposal since we base efficiency on limitation of the search space. The future integration of linguistic information from both syntactic and semantic viewpoints should significantly reduce this gap in precision, which is less than 4%, or may even eliminate it.

7   Conclusion

As an extension of a recognition process, error repair is strongly influenced by the underlying grammatical structure, which should be taken into account in order to design efficient handling strategies. In this sense, spelling correction in NLP on FAs applies on states distributed in such a way that the number of path alternatives usually becomes exponential with the length of the input string.

These considerations are of importance in practical systems because they impact both the performance and the implementation techniques. So, most proposals exploit the apparently structural simplicity at word level to apply global techniques that examine the entire word and make a minimum of changes to repair all possible errors, which can be extremely time-consuming on a FA.

Our proposal drastically reduces this impact by dynamically graduating the size of the error repair zone. We describe a least-cost error repair method able to recover and resume the recognition at the point of each error, to avoid the possibility of non-detection of any subsequent errors. This translates into an improved performance without loss of quality in relation to global strategies.

References

1. J.P. Chanod and P. Tapanainen. Creating a tagset, lexicon and guesser for a French tagger. In *ACL SIGDAT Workshop on From Texts to Tags: Issues in Multilingual Language Analysis*, pages 58–64, University College, Dublin, Ireland, 1995.
2. J. Daciuk, S. Mihov, B.W. Watson, and R.E. Watson. Incremental construction of minimal acyclic finite-state automata. *Computational Linguistics*, 26(1):3–16, 2000.
3. J. Graña, F.M. Barcala, and M.A. Alonso. Compilation methods of minimal acyclic automata for large dictionaries. *Lecture Notes in Computer Science*, 2494:135–148, 2002.
4. K. Kukich. Techniques for automatically correcting words in text. *ACM Computing Surveys*, 24(4):377–439, 1988.
5. V.I. Levenshtein. Binary codes capable of correcting deletions, insertions and reversals. *Doklady Akademii Nauk SSSR*, 163(4):845–848, 1965.
6. C.L. Lucchesi and T. Kowaltowski. Applications of finite automata representing large vocabularies. *Software-Practice and Experience*, 23(1):15–30, January 1993.
7. K. Oflazer. Error-tolerant finite-state recognition with applications to morphological analysis and spelling correction. *Computational Linguistics*, 22(1):73–89, 1996.
8. A. Savary. Typographical nearest-neighbor search in a finite-state lexicon and its application to spelling correction. *Lecture Notes in Computer Science*, 2494:251–260, 2001.
9. K. Sikkel. *Parsing Schemata*. PhD thesis, Univ. of Twente, The Netherlands, 1993.
10. A. Solak and K. Oflazer. Design and implementation of a spelling checker for Turkish. *Literary and Linguistic Computing*, 8(3), 1993.
11. Richard Sproat. *Morphology and Computation*. The MIT Press, Cambridge, Massachusetts, 1992.

Approximating Dependency Grammars Through Intersection of Regular Languages

Anssi Yli-Jyrä

Department of General Linguistics, University of Helsinki,
P.O. Box 9, FIN-00014 University of Helsinki, Finland
anssi.yli-jyra@helsinki.fi

Abstract. The paper formulates projective dependency grammars in terms of constraints on a string based encoding of dependency trees and develops an approach to obtain a *regular approximation* for these grammars. In the approach, dependency analyses are encoded with balanced bracketing that encodes dependency relations among the words of the analyzed sentence. The brackets, thus, indicate dependencies rather than delimit phrases. The encoding allows expressing dependency rules (in the sense of Hays and Gaifman) using a semi-Dyck language and a so-called *context restriction operation*. When the semi-Dyck language in the representation is replaced with a regular restriction of it, we obtain an approximation for the original dependency grammar.

1   Introduction

Simple and efficient approaches to the task of dependency parsing, where dependency analyses are assigned to sentences, has recently attracted considerable attention ([1,2] *etc.*). In this paper, we will show that parsing with ambiguous projective dependency grammars is an intersection problem. With a certain restriction, this leads to a linear-time parser, implementable with finite automata.

A dependency analysis consists of a dependency tree (D-tree) whose nodes are, as assumed in this paper, words in a sentence. A D-tree shows which words are related to which other words and in what way. It shows the structure of the sentence in terms of hierarchical links between its actual elements. D-trees can be visualized using tree diagrams such as the one in Fig. 1.

det   subj   pred   det   obj
that   man   ate   an   apple

Fig. 1. A D-tree consists of dependency links drawn above a sentence. (This example is borrowed from (Oflazer 2003), but the arrows are drawn here in the opposite direction.)

The links denote syntactic dependencies and are represented by arcs with arrows and category labels. If $X \rightarrowtail Y$ is an arc between two words X and Y,

M. Domaratzki et al. (Eds.): CIAA 2004, LNCS 3317, pp. 281–292, 2005.

we will say that Y depends immediately on X (or, conversely, X governs Y immediately), and that Y is an immediate syntactic dependent of X (or, X is the immediate syntactic governor of Y). In the D-tree, there is a unique non-governed word called the *root*. The category label of each link indicates *how* Y is dependent on X. Word Y can be *e.g.* a subject (subj), a object (obj) or a determiner (det) of X. (*Cf.* [3], p.14,23)

A D-tree is said to be *planar* (more precisely, *semi-planar*) if the links do not cross each other when drawn above the sentence [4]. Thus, the example in Fig. 1 is planar. A planar D-tree D is *projective* [5,6] if it remains planar (Fig. 2) even if we add the so-called *left wall* node (//////) that governs the root of D (*cf.* [7], pages 99–100).

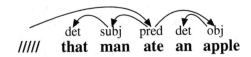

det   subj   pred det obj

//////   **that man ate an apple**

Fig. 2. The D-tree of Fig. 1 maintains planarity when the wall node is added

In this paper, we will present a regular approximation of grammars that generate only projective dependency trees. The approximation is based on a new formulation of the Hays [8] and Gaifman [9] dependency grammars. The formulation represents dependency trees as bracketed strings. The correspondence between tree diagrams and their bracket-encoding is best understood through an example, such as the one shown in Fig. 3.

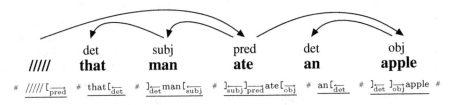

Fig. 3. The correspondence between a tree diagram and its encoding as a string. In order to facilitate reading, brackets belonging to the same tree node have been grouped with an underline that is not part of the encoding

The string encoding of a D-tree involves the words of a sentence, labeled square brackets, a symbol (#) for word boundaries, and the wall node //////. Each bracket belongs to the word (or to the wall) within the closest surrounding word boundaries. The wall node ////// is not needed to enforce projectivity, but it will make all the word nodes have a governor link, which slightly simplifies the representation.

In the encoding, each arc of the D-tree is split into two parts. An opening bracket [(with an additional label as a subscript) indicates the left end of the arc, and a closing bracket] (with an additional label as a subscript) indicates the right end of the arc. The substring between these brackets must contain a balanced bracketing. A pair of matching brackets always indicate a link between two words in the sentence.

Let Λ be the set of category labels in D-trees. For each category label $a \in \Lambda$, the string encoding has two different labels for brackets. If *e.g.* 'subject' is a label in the D-tree, '$\overrightarrow{\text{subject}}$' and '$\overleftarrow{\text{subject}}$' are possible labels of brackets in the string encoding. Using the bracket label '$\overrightarrow{\text{subject}}$' indicates that the subject is at the closing bracket and using the bracket label '$\overleftarrow{\text{subject}}$' indicates that the subject is at the opening bracket.

The first important contribution of this paper is to point out certain less obvious properties of Robinson's [10] set of axioms for projective D-trees:

- The usual projectivity condition [6] is stronger than her fourth axiom.
- Her axioms do not themselves imply treeness (*cf. vs.* [11], p.4).
- Robinson premised the acyclicity property, but this nuance of the axiom set is often disregarded (*cf. e.g.* [12, 11, 2]).
- Antisymmetricity is a necessary consequence of non-crossing brackets that represent dependencies and a simple local condition.
- Projectivity follows from the placement and the uniqueness of the root node, irreflexivity, and non-crossing brackets.

The second important contribution of this paper is a reformulation of the generative dependency rules of the Hays and Gaifman dependency grammars (HGDG) as properties of bracketed string languages. The grammar representation makes use of a semi-Dyck language (*cf.* [13]) in order to capture non-local properties of bracketed strings. Because HGDGs generate context-free languages [9], we get from the intersection of these constraints a homomorphic representation for context-free languages. This new characterization resembles the famous Chomsky-Schützenberger theorem [14] that says that every context-free language is a homomorphic image of an intersection of a semi-Dyck language and a regular language.

Finally, the third important contribution of this paper is to present a linear-time parseable non-deterministic dependency grammar with restriction to limited projective dependency trees. This is obtained by replacing the semi-Dyck language with a regular language. A regular approximation for the semi-Dyck language can handle only limited balanced bracketing. Consequently, the intersection of constraints becomes a regular subset approximation for the grammar that does not limit the depth of balanced bracketing. The regular approximation grammar obtained can obviously be applied to sentences in linear time. In contrast to typical linear-time deterministic dependency parsers, our approach leaves the ambiguity unsolved. Moreover, our approach can be used for enumeration of valid D-trees and sentences.

2   Some Related Work

The applicability of finite-state methods to automatic syntactic analysis of natural language has been investigated in different approaches [15]. In pure *finite-state approaches*, finite-state devices are combined so that the whole system could be represented by a single finite-state machine, although it may be of an impractical size. In *extended finite-state approaches*, finite-state devices are used as basic components, but they are combined in such a way that the finite-state nature of the whole system is not necessarily retained.

Oflazer [2] has presented an interesting extended finite-state approach for dependency parsing of natural language. In particular, the string encoding used in our approach can be seen as a notational variant of Oflazer's representation. The representation used by Oflazer encodes the example in Fig. 1 as the string

<00(that)0d> <D0(man)0s> <S0(ate)00> <01(an)1d> <Do(apple)00>

where the stacked "brackets" d,D, O,o and s,S (corresponding to our $[\overleftarrow{\text{det}},]\overleftarrow{\text{det}}$, $[\overrightarrow{\text{obj}},]\overrightarrow{\text{obj}}, [\overleftarrow{\text{subj}},]\overleftarrow{\text{subj}})$ are stored into so-called *channels*.

There exist cubic-time dependency parsers for HGDGs [16]. Most phrase types can be produced with a parser with quadratic time complexity [17]. Deterministic linear time dependency parsers have been studied *e.g.* in [1]. Constraint-based approaches to dependency parsing include Constraint Dependency Grammar [18] and Topological Dependency Grammar [19], which can actually generate non-context-free languages. Other approaches to assigning dependency structures to sentences include many lexicalized grammar formalisms that will not be listed here.

3   Hays and Gaifman Dependency Grammars

Tesnière's work [20] pioneered dependency-syntax grammars (DG). A formulation of more restricted dependency grammars given by Hays [8] and Gaifman [9] is only loosely related to Tesnière's theory, but it is still very influential in practical DG implementations. Their dependency grammar, HGDG, contains three kinds of rules by which the dependency analysis for a particular language is done:

1. Rules of the form $X(\star)$ that state that elements of the *word category* X may govern the sentence. (We adopt a short-hand notation $\star(\{X_1, X_2, \ldots, X_n\})$ for the set of these rules.)
2. Rules giving for every word category X the list of words belonging to it. These are of the form $X : \{w_1, w_2, \ldots, w_n\}$.
3. Rules which give for each word category X those categories which may derive directly from it with their relative positions. For each X there is a finite number of rules of the type $X(V_1 V_2 \ldots V_n \star Y_1 Y_2 \ldots Y_m)$. An application of this rule means that in the D-tree a word of the category X immediately governs words of categories $V_1, V_2, \ldots, V_n$ on the left of X and words of the categories $Y_1, Y_2, \ldots, Y_m$ on the right. The governed words occur in the order in which their categories are specified in the rule. These rules are called *dependency rules*.

For details of the semantics of HGDGs, the reader is referred to Gaifman [9].

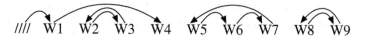

Fig. 4. A D-graph that conforms to Robinson's four axioms but violates acyclicity. The Harper, Hays, Lecerf and Ihm projectivity accepts the cycles at W5-W9, but not at W2-W3

3.1 Axiomatization of Projective Dependency Trees

A famous mathematical axiomatization of the D-graphs generated by HGDGs is given by Robinson [10]. This axiomatization is usually regarded as a set consisting of the following axioms:

1. There is one and only one word that is independent.
2. All other words are immediately governed by some word.
3. No word depends immediately (i.e. directly) on more than one other word.
4. If word A depends immediately on word B and some word C intervenes between them (in the linear order of the words in the sentence), then C depends immediately on A or B <u>or some other intervening element.</u>

It should be noted that Robinson's fourth axiom is not equivalent to the usual condition of *projectivity* in the sense of Harper, Hays, Lecerf and Ihm (*cf.* [6]). The projectivity condition drops the underlined part in the fourth axiom and says instead that C depends transitively on A or B. In contrast to what is claimed in [1], neither of these conditions imply non-existence of cycles longer than one or two edges (Fig. 4). The reader can now easily proof that acyclicity and connectedness of the dependency trees are not consequences of Robinson's set of axioms, contrary to what is often suggested [12, 11, 2]. It is often forgotten that Robinson included a crucial premise according to which the transitive closure of the immediate dependency relation will be (i) *irreflexive i.e.* without trivial cycles and (ii) *antisymmetric i.e.* without other cycles. When these extra requirements are taken as additional axioms, we are restricted to acyclic structures and the extended axiom set describes exactly the set of projective dependency trees.

4 The Essentials of the New Representation

4.1 The Alphabet

Assume that Λ is the set of category labels. We define four disjoint bracket sets as follows:

$$B_L = \{\,[_{\overrightarrow{a}} \mid a \in \Lambda\}; \qquad\qquad B_r = \{\,]_{\overrightarrow{a}} \mid a \in \Lambda\};$$
$$B_l = \{\,[_{\overleftarrow{a}} \mid a \in \Lambda\}; \qquad\qquad B_R = \{\,]_{\overleftarrow{a}} \mid a \in \Lambda\}.$$

The brackets with capital L and R subscripts attach to the governor and the brackets with small l and r subscripts to the dependent member of the pair.

We will assume that Σ is the alphabet for building strings. It is the union of a number of disjoint subsets, namely the set of *word tokens* W, the *labeled left square brackets* $B_L \cup B_l$, the *labeled right square brackets* $B_R \cup B_r$, and the set of other special symbols $\{\#, ///// \}$.

The first string homomorphism $g : \Sigma^* \rightarrow \Sigma'^*$, where $[,] \notin \Sigma$ and $\Sigma' = \Sigma - (B_L \cup B_l \cup B_R \cup B_r) \cup \{[,]\}$, is defined in such a way that it essentially replaces labeled brackets with the corresponding unlabeled ones. The second string homomorphism $h : \Sigma'^* \rightarrow W^*$ is defined in such a way that it deletes from the strings all other symbols except the words W.

Obviously, the inverse homomorphism h^{-1} can be used to freely inject symbols $\{\#, /////, [,] \}$ into strings of W^*, and g^{-1} to replace $[$ and $]$ with various left and right square brackets. To parse a string $w \in W^+$, we will intersect the inverse homomorphic image $g^{-1}(h^{-1}(w))$ with the grammar G that is an intersection $C_1 \cap C_2 \cap \cdots C_n$ of constraint languages.

4.2   The Context Restriction Operation

A *context restriction of a center* $\mathcal{X}$ *in contexts* $\mathfrak{C}_1, \mathfrak{C}_2, \cdots, \mathfrak{C}_n$ is an operation whose first argument $\mathcal{X}$ is a subset of Σ^* and each context $\mathfrak{C}_i$, $1 \leq i \leq n$, is of the form $\mathcal{V}_i \underline{\quad} \mathcal{Y}_i$, where $\mathcal{V}_i, \mathcal{Y}_i \subseteq \Sigma^*$. The operation is expressed using a notation

$$\mathcal{X} \Rightarrow \mathcal{V}_1 \underline{\quad} \mathcal{Y}_1, \mathcal{V}_2 \underline{\quad} \mathcal{Y}_2, \ldots, \mathcal{V}_n \underline{\quad} \mathcal{Y}_n.$$

and it defines the set of all strings $w \in \Sigma^*$ such that, for every possible $v, y \in \Sigma^*$ and $x \in \mathcal{X}$, for which $w = vxy$, there exists some context $\mathcal{V}_i \underline{\quad} \mathcal{Y}_i$, $1 \leq i \leq n$, where both $v \in \Sigma^* \mathcal{V}_i$ and $y \in \mathcal{Y}_i \Sigma^*$.

If all the languages involved in a context restriction are regular, the operation defines a regular language. In case $n = 1$, the language expressed by the operation is $\Sigma^* - ((\Sigma^* - \Sigma^* \mathcal{V}_1) \mathcal{X} \Sigma^* \cup \Sigma^* \mathcal{X} (\Sigma^* - \mathcal{Y}_1 \Sigma^*))$. Context restrictions with multiple contexts can also be routinely compiled into finite automata [21].

4.3   The Semi-Dyck Derivative and Its Regular Approximations

The *semi-Dyck language* (*cf.* [13]) over the alphabet $\{ [,] \}$ is the language D_1 generated by the context-free grammar with single nonterminal S, two terminals $[,]$ and the productions $S \rightarrow \epsilon \mid S [S] S$. The regular language $D_{1,d}$ is an approximation of D_1, where the *depth d of bracketing* is bounded:

$$D_{1,d} = \begin{cases} \epsilon & \text{if } d = 0 \\ (D_{1,d-1} \cup ([D_{1,d-1}]))^* & \text{if } d > 0 \end{cases}$$

Let $f : \Sigma^* \rightarrow (B_L \cup B_r \cup B_l \cup B_R)^*$ be a string homomorphism that deletes all the other symbols except the square brackets. Obviously, the inverse homomorphism f^{-1} can be used to insert other symbols into the strings of square brackets.

The variable Δ can be given different kinds of values in the following ways:

$$\Delta \;\leftarrow\; f^{-1}(g^{-1}(D_1)) \tag{1}$$

$$\Delta \;\leftarrow\; f^{-1}(g^{-1}(D_{1,d})) \tag{2}$$

Assignment (1) makes Δ a context-free language and (2) makes it regular. The choice between (1) and (2) will determine whether the grammar in this paper gives exactly the power of HGDGs or whether it admits only a regular approximation for them. Our motivation to use variable Δ is that, in the second case, we actually get a neat finite-state equivalent formalism for a *regular subset* of context-free sets whose dependency structures are naturally described by non-finite-state formalisms.

In both cases, the language Δ is more liberal with respect to bracket labels compared to a semi-Dyck language based on an equivalent number of terminal symbols. Later on in this paper we will, however, employ a technique presented by Wrathall [22] in order to enforce matching bracket labels in aid of variable Δ and the context restriction operation (Wrathall used more elementary operations instead of context restriction).

Note that when Δ is defined to be a context-free derivative of the semi-Dyck language D, the obtained grammar representation will not be regular. Although context-free languages in general are not closed under relative complement that is used in context restrictions, all the constraints and their intersection will be context-free languages because of the "backbone" of balanced bracketing.

5   The Axiomatization of Bracketed Dependency Trees

5.1   The Basic Set of Strings with Balanced Brackets

In our encoding of D-trees, the sentence begins and ends with a word boundary # (3a), and the bracketing must be balanced (3b). These axioms are expressed as constraints:

$$\#\Sigma^*\#; \qquad\qquad\qquad \Delta. \tag{3}$$

Moreover, between each two word boundaries there exists at least one word, and two words are always separated by a word boundary. These axioms are expressed by the following regular constraint languages:

$$\Sigma^* - \Sigma^*\# \left(\Sigma - (W \cup \{/\!/\!/\!/\!/\})\right)^* \# \Sigma^*; \tag{4}$$

$$\Sigma^* - \Sigma^* \left(W \cup \{/\!/\!/\!/\!/\}\right) \left(\Sigma - \{\#\}\right)^* \left(W \cup \{/\!/\!/\!/\!/\}\right) \Sigma^* .$$

In addition, the matching brackets must have equivalent labels. This is done through the following constraints that are inserted for each bracket label (*i.e.* word category) $a \in \Lambda$ (*cf.* [22]):

$$[_{\overrightarrow{a}} \;\Rightarrow\; \underline{\quad} \;\Delta\;]_{\overrightarrow{a}}; \qquad\qquad [_{\overleftarrow{a}} \;\Rightarrow\; \underline{\quad} \;\Delta\;]_{\overleftarrow{a}}. \tag{5}$$

5.2   The Properties of Projective Dependency Trees

We will now implement each of the requirements stated by Robinson by means of language properties. Our convention to use the wall node causes some unimportant modifications.

1. There is one and only one node that is independent, *i.e.*

$$\Sigma^* \# (\Sigma - \{\#\} \cup B_l \cup B_r)^* \# \Sigma^*; \quad (6)$$

$$\Sigma^* - \Sigma^* \# (\Sigma - \{\#\} \cup B_l \cup B_r)^* \# (\Sigma^* \#)^* (\Sigma - \{\#\} \cup B_l \cup B_r)^* \# \Sigma^*. \quad (7)$$

2. All word nodes except the wall node (//////) are immediately governed by some node:

$$W \Rightarrow (B_r \cup B_l)(\Sigma - \{\#\})^* \underline{\quad} , \underline{\quad} (\Sigma - \{\#\})^* (B_r \cup B_l). \quad (8)$$

3. No word depends immediately on more than one other word, *i.e.*

$$\Sigma^* - \Sigma^* (B_r \cup B_l)(\Sigma - \{\#\})^* (B_r \cup B_l) \Sigma^*. \quad (9)$$

4. There are no trivial cycles (irreflexivity), *i.e.*

$$\Sigma^* - \Sigma^* (B_l \cup B_L)(\Sigma - \{\#\})^* (B_r \cup B_R) \Sigma^*. \quad (10)$$

5. If Robinson's fourth axiom is violated between two words A and B, where A is immediately dependent on B, then at least one of the following cases must hold:

   (a) An intervening word C is the root of the sentence. This case can be excluded with the following constraint that requires that the root (in practice, the wall) is not an intervening word:

$$\# \; ///// \; \Sigma^*. \quad (11)$$

   (b) An intervening word C is one of the independent words of the sentence ($\longrightarrow$ multiple roots). This case is excluded by Constraint (7).
   (c) An intervening word C is dependent on itself ($\longrightarrow$ violates irreflexivity). This case is excluded by Constraint (10).
   (d) An intervening word C is governed by a word that is not A, B, C nor any other intervening word ($\longrightarrow$ a crossing edge). This case is excluded by Constraint (3b).

6. The simplest kind of nontrivial cycle contains two adjacent words. Such a case occurs if the bracketing has either of the following two patterns:

$$\cdots \# \; E \; [_{\overleftarrow{X}} \; [_{\overrightarrow{Y}} \; \# \;]_{\overrightarrow{Y}}]_{\overleftarrow{X}} \; F \; \# \cdots \quad \text{or}$$
$$\cdots \# \; F \; [_{\overrightarrow{Y}} \; [_{\overleftarrow{X}} \; \# \;]_{\overleftarrow{X}}]_{\overrightarrow{Y}} \; E \; \# \cdots$$

Observe that at the word F, the bracket indicating the category of the word itself is not adjacent to it. This means that the link from F to its governor is shorter than a link to one of its dependents that is in the same direction as the governor. In fact, every cycle containing at least two words must have such a word F. There are also other situations where the bracket indicating the category of a word is not adjacent to the word itself. These are exactly those cases in which an intervening element C governs two linked words A or B.

$$\Sigma^* - \Sigma^*(B_L B_l \cup B_r B_R)\Sigma^*. \tag{12}$$

Due to Constraint (10) we can adopt a convention that places closing brackets on the left side of each word and opening brackets on the right side by saying that

$$(W \cup \{/////\}) \Rightarrow \# (B_R \cup B_r)^* \underline{\quad} (B_L \cup B_l)^* \#. \tag{13}$$

Because the bracketing used in the encoding is balanced, the bracket corresponding to the longest link will be placed closest to the word, and the bracket corresponding to the shortest link will be placed closest to the word boundary $\#$. This conforms the same order that is used by Oflazer [2–page 524] when he allocates so called *channel symbol slots* in his representation.

6   The New Representation for the Grammars

We will now re-express all the rules of HGDGs using context restrictions. The rule listing the categories that can be independent is of the form $\star(\{X_1, X_2, \ldots, X_n\})$. This is expressed through the following regular constraint

$$///// \Rightarrow \underline{\quad} \# \; \{[_{\overrightarrow{X_1}}, [_{\overrightarrow{X_2}}, \cdots, [_{\overrightarrow{X_n}}\} \; \#. \tag{14}$$

The rules listing words $\{w_1, w_2, \ldots, w_n\}$ in each category X are of the form $X : \{w_1, w_2, \ldots, w_n\}$. In the presence of (13), these rules can be expressed by the following constraints:

$$[_{\overleftarrow{X}} \Rightarrow \{w_1, w_2, \ldots, w_n\} \underline{\quad}; \qquad]_{\overrightarrow{X}} \Rightarrow \underline{\quad} \{w_1, w_2, \ldots, w_n\}. \tag{15}$$

Each dependency rule $X(V_1 V_2 \ldots V_n \star Y_1 Y_2 \ldots Y_m)$ specifying a set of dependents for category X corresponds to the context $\mathfrak{C}_{(V_1 V_2 \ldots V_n \star Y_1 Y_2 \ldots Y_m)}$:

$$\# \;]_{\overleftarrow{V_n}}]_{\overleftarrow{V_{n-1}}} \cdots]_{\overleftarrow{V_1}} \; W^* \underline{\quad} W^* \; [_{\overrightarrow{Y_m}} [_{\overrightarrow{Y_{m-1}}} \cdots]_{\overrightarrow{Y_1}} \; \#.$$

When a word category X has n such contexts $\mathfrak{C}_1, \mathfrak{C}_2, \ldots, \mathfrak{C}_n$, their union corresponds to the following regular context restriction:

$$\{ \;]_{\overrightarrow{X}}, [_{\overleftarrow{X}} \; \} \Rightarrow \mathfrak{C}_1, \mathfrak{C}_2, \ldots, \mathfrak{C}_n. \tag{16}$$

For example, the dependency rule

bitransitive(subject $\star$ object indirect-object)

will be represented using the following context restriction[1]:

$$\{ \;]_{\overrightarrow{\text{bitransitive}}}, [_{\overleftarrow{\text{bitransitive}}} \; \} \Rightarrow \# \;]_{\overleftarrow{\text{subject}}} \; W^* \underline{\quad} W^* \; [_{\overrightarrow{\text{indirect-object}}} [_{\overrightarrow{\text{object}}} \#.$$

---

[1] In the expression, the opening bracket for the indirect-object precedes the bracket of the object, because matching brackets obey the LIFO discipline.

7 Discussion on Practical Applicability

As to the regular approximation that is obtained when an approximation $D_{1,d}$ of D_1 is assigned to the variable Δ, the most important practical question is: Can we actually use the obtained finite-state grammar to parse natural language sentences efficiently and accurately?

Parsing of the obtained approximation grammars means computing the intersection of the language $g^{-1}(h^{-1}(w))$ and the grammar constraints. Such a system can be seen as a special variant of Finite-State Intersection Grammar (FSIG) (cf. [15]), where the most striking problem has been to prevent intermediate results from blowing up in size when the intersection is computed. However, we have some reasons to be more optimistic with the current grammars than with FSIGs in general:

1. There are examples of so-far more successful extended finite-state approaches [2] (cf. also [15]), where bracketing at different depths is elaborated incrementally, according to a Bottom-Up or Top-Down parsing strategy. It seems that such strategies could be implemented also in the framework of FSIG by splitting each context restriction into sub-constraints [21].
2. The bracketing employed here represents local context-free trees, which gives rise to new ambiguity packing methods [23] based on parallel decompositions of automata. This may lead to improvements that narrow the distance between techniques for parsing through finite-state intersection and parsing with Chart-like data structures.
3. Most of the constraint languages presented here are locally testable, which entails that their intersection can be done without considerable difficulties. In our initial experiments, we applied them first and enforced the non-local constraints (3b) and (5) in a later stage.

At this stage our experiments are still very limited and they merely highlight that the proposed representation is implementable and can be used both in parsing and enumeration of valid sentences. We extracted two kinds of grammars from a portion of the Danish Dependency Treebank [24] (the second, smaller grammar was mainly hand-crafted). As word categories, we used syntactic functions in the first grammar and words themselves in the second one. These grammars represented two (almost) extreme ways to make generalizations from the available data. In both cases, the grammar constraints were given in a script to the XFST program [25]. Compiling a grammar with a few hundred rules into a set of separate automata took only one second. Intersection during parsing of both grammars was also quite fast because the constraint automata were small and only a few of them contributed to parsing of the actual input sentence.

In the bracketing scheme presented of the current paper, the number of dependents per node contributes directly to the depth of nested brackets. It is, however, possible to optimize bracketing depth in such cases by using so-called reduced bracketing. Accordingly, the bracketing of Fig. 3 can be replaced with the following bracketing:

/////[→pred # that[→det # →det] man ⟨→subj # →subj→pred] ate[→obj # an ⟨→det # →det→obj] apple

Due to space limitations the intricate details of reduced dependency bracketing cannot be handled here. A scheme for reduced bracketing of dependencies and its extension to non-projective dependency trees appear in [26]. The problems related to grammar induction or extraction and accuracy cannot be discussed here in depth due to space limitations.

Acknowledgments

I would like to thank Kimmo Koskenniemi, Lauri Carlson and the three anonymous referees for valuable comments on earlier versions of this article. The work was funded by NorFA under the author's personal Ph.D. scholarship (ref.nr. 010529).

References

1. Nivre, J.: An efficient algorithm for projective dependency parsing. In: 8th Int'l Workshop on Parsing Technologies (IWPT 03), Nancy, France (2003)
2. Oflazer, K.: Dependency parsing with an extended finite-state approach. Computational Linguistics **29** (2003)
3. Mel'čuk, I.A.: Dependency Syntax: Theory and Practice. State University of New York Press, Albany (1988)
4. Sleator, D., Temperley, D.: Parsing English with a link grammar. In: 3rd International Workshop on Parsing Technologies. (1993) 277–291
5. Ihm, P., Lecerf, Y.: Éléments pour une grammaire générale'des langues projectives. Technical Report EUR 210.f, Centre de Traitement de l'Information Scientifique – CETIS (1963)
6. Marcus, S.: Algebraic Linguistics; Analytical Models. Academic Press, New York and London (1967)
7. Höfler, S.: Link2tree: A dependency-constituency converter. Lizentiatsarbeit, Institute of Computational Linguistics, University of Zürich (2002)
8. Hays, D.G.: Dependency theory: A formalism and some observations. Language **40** (1964) 511–525
9. Gaifman, H.: Dependency systems and phrase-structure systems. Information and Control **8** (1965) 304–37
10. Robinson, J.J.: Dependency structures and transformational rules. Language **46** (1970) 259–285
11. Debusmann, R.: An introduction to dependency grammar. Hausarbeit für das Hauptseminar *Dependenzgrammatik* SoSe 99. Univeristät des Saarlandes (2000)
12. Lai, T.B.Y., Huang, C.: Functional constraints in dependency grammar. In: GLDV'99. Multilinguale Corpora: Codierung, Structurierung, Analyse. 11. Jahrestagung der Gesellschaft für Linguistische Daten Verarbeitung, 8.-10.7.1999, Frankfurt a/M (1999) 235–244
13. Harrison, M.A.: Introduction to Formal Language Theory. Reading, MA, Addison-Wesley (1978)
14. Chomsky, N., Schützenberger, M.P.: The algebraic theory of context-free languages. In Brafford, P., Hirschberg, D., eds.: Computer Programming and Formal Systems. North-Holland, Amsterdam (1963) 118–161

15. Roche, E., Schabes, Y., eds.: Finite-state language processing. A Bradford Book, MIT Press, Cambridge, MA (1997)

16. Lombardo, V., Lesmo, L.: An Earley-type recognizer for dependency grammar. In: 16th COLING. Volume 2., Copenhagen (1996) 723–728

17. Elworthy, D.: A finite state parser with dependency structure output. In: Proceedings of International Workshop on Parsing Technologies. (2000)

18. Maruyama, H.: Structural disambiguation with constraint propagation. In: Proceedings of the 28th ACL (ACL-90), Pittsburgh, PA (1990) 31–38

19. Duchier, D.: Lexicalized syntax and topology for non-projective dependency grammar. In: Joint Conference on Formal Grammars and Mathematics of Language FGMOL'01, Helsinki (2001)

20. Tesnière, L.: Éléments de Syntaxe Structurale. Editions Klincksieck, Paris (1959)

21. Yli-Jyrä, A., Koskenniemi, K.: Compiling contextual restrictions on strings into finite-state automata. In: The Eindhoven FASTAR Days, Technische Universiteit Eindhoven, Eindhoven, The Netherlands (2004)

22. Wrathall, C.: Characterizations of the Dyck sets. R.A.I.R.O. Informatique théorique/Theoretical Computer Science **11** (1977) 53–62

23. Yli-Jyrä, A.: Simplification of intermediate results during intersection of multiple weighted automata. In Droste, M., Vogler, H., eds.: "Weighted Automata — Theory and Applications", Dresden, Germany (2004) 46–48

24. Kromann, M.T., Mikkelsen, L., Lynge, S.K.: The Danish Dependency Treebank Website. Dept. of Computational Linguistics, Copenhagen Business School. http://www.id.cbs.dk/~mtk/treebank (2003)

25. Beesley, K.R., Karttunen, L.: Finite State Morphology. CSLI Studies in Computational Linguistics. CSLI Publications (2003)

26. Yli-Jyrä, A.: Axiomatization of restricted non-projective dependency trees through finite-state constraints that analyse crossing bracketings. In Kruijff, G.J.M., Duchier, D., eds.: Proceedings of the Workshop of Recent Advances in Dependency Grammar, COLING'04 Workshop. (2004) 33–40

On the Equivalence-Checking Problem for a Model of Programs Related With Multi-tape Automata*

Vladimir Zakharov and Ivan Zakharyaschev

Moscow State University, Moscow, Russia
zakh@cs.msu.su

Abstract. We study the equivalence-checking problem for a formal model of computer programs which is used for the purpose of verification. In this model programs are viewed as deterministic finite automata operating on Kripke structures defined in the framework of dynamic logics. When a transition relation in such structures is functional and weakly directed, the result of a program execution does not depend on the order in which basic statements are applied to data states. The models of programs with commuting statements have a close relationship to multi-tape finite automata. We consider the case when evaluation functions which specify truth-values of basic predicates in programs are monotonic. This corresponds to multi-tape automata operating on binary words of the type 0^*1^*. The main theorem states that the equivalence-checking problem in the model of programs with commuting and monotonic statements is decidable in polynomial time.

In this paper we study the equivalence-checking problem for a formal model of computer programs which may be of practical use for the purpose of verification. In the framework of this model programs are viewed as deterministic finite automata operating on Kripke structures. One of the point in favor of this formalism is that the semantics of programs can be conveniently specified by means of dynamic logic formulae. Depending on these specifications (axioms) one faces models of programs with decidable as well as undecidable equivalence-checking problem (see [7, 13] for a survey). In [12] it was developed some uniform approach to the designing of efficient (polynomial time) decision procedures for the equivalence-checking problem for such programs. The main limitation of this approach is that it is insensitive to specific features of evaluation functions in Kripke structures; these functions specify truth values of basic predicates occurring in programs. Meanwhile, in some models the characteristic properties of evaluation functions are of primary importance for decidability and complexity of the equivalence-checking problem.

We demonstrate this effect by considering the equivalence-checking problem for a model $\mathcal{M}_{cm}$ of deterministic imperative programs with commuting and

---

* Research supported by the RFBR grant 03-01-00132.

M. Domaratzki et al. (Eds.): CIAA 2004, LNCS 3317, pp. 293–305, 2005.

monotonic statements. Commutativity of statements means that the result of a computation does not depend on a relative order in which these statements are applied to data. In [12] it was demonstrated that the equivalence-checking problem for a model $\mathcal{M}_c$ of deterministic programs with commuting statements is decidable in time $O(n^2)$. Monotonicity refers to the property of predicates to preserve *true* value in any computation since they are evaluated to *true* — this indicates some kind of progress in program runs. The equivalence-checking problem for the model of programs with commuting and monotonic statements was studied in [10, 11]. In [11] the problem is shown to be decidable, although no complexity results are obtained. The decision procedure developed in [11] involves an exhaustive search in the set of all paths of some bounded length in programs under consideration. When developing our decision technique we introduce some new data structure for succinct representation of compatible paths in programs and this yields a polynomial time decision procedure for the equivalence-checking problem.

Commutativity and monotonicity can be expressed in terms of dynamic logic axioms. By making small changes in the monotonicity axioms, one falls into the model $\mathcal{M}_{\mathrm{dmta}}$ of programs whose expressive power is exactly the same as that of deterministic multi-tape automata (DMTAs). The equivalence-checking problem for DMTAs is one of the famous problems in automata theory. After numerous attempts [1, 9, 6] it was finally solved in [4], though the complexity of this problem is still unclear. We may assume that the equivalence-checking problem for programs with commuting and monotonic statements is intermediate in its complexity between the same problems for two known models of programs $\mathcal{M}_c$ and $\mathcal{M}_{\mathrm{dmta}}$. And it is reasonable to suggest that studying this problem for $\mathcal{M}_{\mathrm{cm}}$ furnishes some new information on decision problems for DMTAs.

The paper is organized as follows. In Sect. 1, we define formally the syntax and semantics of propositional sequential programs (PSPs) and set an equivalence-checking problem. In Sect. 2, the model $\mathcal{M}_{\mathrm{cm}}$ which captures the semantics of programs with commuting and monotonic statements is introduced. We also discuss in some details the relationships between programs with commuting and monotonic statements and DMTAs. In Sect. 3, we introduce the concept of a cut of compatible paths in programs. Paths α_1 and α_2 in programs π_1 and π_2 are called compatible if there exists a Kripke structure M such that both paths are traversed when π_1 and π_2 are executed on M. If π_1 and π_2 have different behaviors, then this difference manifests itself in at least one pair of compatible paths. A cut $G(\alpha_1, \alpha_2)$ is an encoding of α_1 and α_2 into a small data structure which carries enough information for constructing compatible extensions of α_1 and α_2. We develop a technique for deducing one cut from another and show that equivalence of programs with commuting and monotonic statements can be checked by manipulating cuts. Section 4 presents a decision procedure for the equivalence-checking problem, which is the main result of this paper. The complexity of this procedure is polynomial of the size of programs to be analyzed, but the degree of the polynomial is a function of the cardinality of the alphabets of basic statements and predicates used in programs. Finally, we discuss to what extent the technique developed in this paper could be generalized. As an example, we show that it can be adapted for the equivalence-checking of DMTAs operating on "monotonic" binary words of the type 0*1*.

1   Preliminaries

In this section we define the syntax and the semantics of propositional sequential programs (PSPs).

Fix two finite alphabets $\mathcal{A} = \{a_1, \ldots, a_r\}$, $\mathcal{P} = \{p_1, \ldots, p_k\}$. In what follows r and k denote the cardinality of alphabets $\mathcal{A}$ and $\mathcal{P}$ respectively. The elements of $\mathcal{A}$ are called *basic statements*. Intuitively, each basic statement stands for some assignment statement in imperative program. The elements of $\mathcal{P}$ are called *basic predicates*. They stand for elementary built-in relations on program data. Each basic predicate may be evaluated by 0 (false) or 1 (true). A tuple $\langle \delta_1, \ldots, \delta_k \rangle$ of truth-values of basic predicates is called a *condition*. The set of all conditions is denoted by $\mathcal{C}$. It is clear that $|\mathcal{C}| = 2^k$. We write $\Delta_1, \Delta_2, \ldots$ for generic elements from $\mathcal{C}$. Given a condition $\Delta = \langle \delta_1, \ldots, \delta_k \rangle$ and an integer i, $1 \leq i \leq k$, we denote by $\Delta[i]$ a truth-value δ_i of the predicate p_i. We also define a partial order relation $\preceq$ on the set of conditions: $\Delta' \preceq \Delta'' \iff \forall i : 1 \leq i \leq k : \Delta'[i] \leq \Delta''[i]$.

Definition 1. *A* propositional sequential program *(PSP, for short) is a finite transition system $\pi = \langle V, \mathbf{entry}, \mathbf{exit}, T, B \rangle$, where*

- *V is a non-empty set of* program points;
- *$\mathbf{entry}$ is the* initial point *of the program;*
- *$\mathbf{exit}$ is the* terminal point *of the program;*
- *$T: (V - \{\mathbf{exit}\}) \times \mathcal{C} \to V$ is a (total) transition function;*
- *$B: (V - \{\mathbf{exit}\}) \to \mathcal{A}$ is a (total) binding function.*

A transition function represents the control flow of a program, whereas a binding function associates with each point some basic statement. A PSP may also be thought of as a deterministic finite state automaton operating over the input alphabet $\mathcal{C}$ and the output alphabet $\mathcal{A}$. By the *size* $|\pi|$ of a program π we mean the cardinality of the set V.

Let $\pi = \langle V, \mathbf{entry}, \mathbf{exit}, T, B \rangle$ be a PSP. A finite or infinite sequence of pairs

$$\alpha = (v_1, \Delta_1), (v_2, \Delta_2), \ldots, (v_i, \Delta_i), (v_{i+1}, \Delta_{i+1}), \ldots, \qquad (1)$$

such that $v_i \in V$, $\Delta_i \in \mathcal{C}$, and $v_{i+1} = T(v_i, \Delta_i)$ hold for every i, $i \geq 1$, is called a *path* from a point v_1 in π. If α ends with a pair (v_n, Δ_n) then we say that α *reaches* a point $v_{n+1} = T(v_n, \Delta_n)$. If $v_1 = \mathbf{entry}$ then α is called an *initial path*. A path is called *acyclic* if no points occur in this path more than once. If α is finite then we write $|\alpha|$ for its *length*. We use a notation $\alpha|^n$, $n > 0$, for the prefix of α of the length n.

The semantics of PSPs is defined with the help of Kripke structures in the framework of dynamic logics.

Definition 2. *A* Kripke structure *is a quadruple* $M = \langle S, s_0, R, \xi \rangle$, *where*

- *S is a non-empty set of* data states;
- *$s_0 \in S$ is a distinguished* initial state;
- *R: $\mathcal{A} \times S \to S$ is a (total)* updating function;
- *$\xi: S \to \mathcal{C}$ is a (total)* evaluation function.

An updating function R is used for the interpretation of basic statements: a data state $R(a, s)$ is the result of application of a statement a to a data state s. An evaluation function ξ is used for the interpretation of basic predicates: given a data state s, an evaluation $\xi(s)$ returns a tuple of truth-values for all basic predicates on s. In fact, a Kripke structure M can also be viewed as a deterministic (possibly infinite state) automaton operating over the input alphabet $\mathcal{A}$ and the output alphabet $\mathcal{C}$. It is in this way semantics of PSPs was defined in [2].

Let π be a PSP, and M be a Kripke structure. The *run* of π on M is a sequence (finite or infinite) of triples

$$r(\pi, M) = (v_1, s_1, \Delta_1), (v_2, s_2, \Delta_2), \ldots, (v_i, s_i, \Delta_i), (v_{i+1}, s_{i+1}, \Delta_{i+1}), \cdots , \quad (2)$$

such that

1. $v_1 = \mathbf{entry}$, s_1 is the initial state of M;
2. $\Delta_i = \xi(s_i)$, $v_{i+1} = T(v_i, \Delta_i)$, $s_{i+1} = R(B(v_i), s_i)$ hold for every i, $i \geq 1$;
3. the sequence $r(\pi, M)$ either is infinite (in this case we say that the run *loops* and yields no results), or ends with a triple (v_n, s_n, Δ_n) such that $T(v_n, \Delta_n) = \mathbf{exit}$ (in this case we say that the run *terminates* with a result $s_{n+1} = R(B(v_n), s_n)$).

We denote by $[r(\pi, M)]$ the result of a run $r(\pi, M)$ assuming that the result is undefined when $r(\pi, M)$ loops.

Given a run of the form (2), it is clear that the sequence

$$\alpha = (v_1, \Delta_1), (v_2, \Delta_2), \ldots, (v_i, \Delta_i), (v_{i+1}, \Delta_{i+1}), \cdots$$

is an initial path in π; we say that α *is associated* with the run (2).

In what follows when referring to a *model of programs* $\mathcal{M}$ we mean the set of all PSPs over fixed alphabets $\mathcal{A}, \mathcal{P}$ whose semantics is specified by the set $\mathcal{M}$ of Kripke structures.

Definition 3. *Given a model of programs* $\mathcal{M}$, *PSPs π_1 and π_2 are said to be equivalent ($\pi_1 \sim_{\mathcal{M}} \pi_2$ in symbols) if $[r(\pi_1, M)] = [r(\pi_2, M)]$ holds for every structure M from $\mathcal{M}$.*

The equivalence-checking problem for a model of programs $\mathcal{M}$ is specified as follows: given a pair of PSPs π_1 and π_2, check whether $\pi_1 \sim_{\mathcal{M}} \pi_2$ holds.

2   Programs with Commuting and Monotonic Statements

In this paper we focus on the equivalence-checking problem for the model of programs which captures at the propositional level the semantics of programs with commuting and monotonic statements. Given a structure $M = \langle S, s_0, R, \xi \rangle$, we say that

- updating function R is *commutative* if $R(a, R(b, s)) = R(b, R(a, s))$ holds for every pair of basic statements a and b and any data state s;
- evaluation function ξ is *monotonic* if $\xi(s) \preceq \xi(R(a, s))$ holds for every basic statement a and data state s.

The set $\mathcal{M}_c$ of Kripke structures with commutative updating functions is completely characterized by dynamic logic axioms: $\langle a_i \rangle Q \leftrightarrow [a_i] Q$ and $\langle a_i; a_j \rangle Q \leftrightarrow \langle a_j; a_i \rangle Q$, $1 \leq i, j \leq r$. When assuming $|\mathcal{A}| = |\mathcal{P}| = k$ and restricting our consideration only to such evaluation functions ξ that for every basic statement a_i and data state s, conditions $\xi(s)$ and $\xi(R(a_i, s))$ may differ only in the i-th position (in truth values for the basic predicate p_i corresponding to a_i), we obtain a model $\mathcal{M}_{\mathrm{dmta}}$ which is a submodel of $\mathcal{M}_c$. This model is distinguished with help of axioms $p_j \leftrightarrow \langle a_i \rangle p_j$, $1 \leq i, j \leq k$, $i \neq j$. In [10] it was shown that $\mathcal{M}_{\mathrm{dmta}}$ has the same expressive power as deterministic k-tape automata.

Denote by $\mathcal{M}_{\mathrm{cm}}$ the submodel $\mathcal{M}_c$ which consists of all structures with commutative updating functions and monotonic evaluations. The model $\mathcal{M}_{\mathrm{cm}}$ is separated from $\mathcal{M}_c$ with help of axioms $p_j \rightarrow \langle a_i \rangle p_j$, $1 \leq i, j \leq k$. Since these axioms are closely related with those used for specification of $\mathcal{M}_{dmta}$, there is a hope that results obtained for $\mathcal{M}_{\mathrm{cm}}$ furnish some information on the complexity of decision problems for DMTAs. The aim of this paper is to study the equivalence-checking problem for $\mathcal{M}_{\mathrm{cm}}$. We begin with reducing this problem to the equivalence-checking problem for the subclass $\mathcal{M}_{\mathbb{N}}$ whose structures have a data space and an updating function in common.

Let $\mathbb{N} = \{0, 1, 2, \dots\}$ be the set of all non-negative integers. We use two operations on $\mathbb{N}$: addition $+$, and truncated subtraction $\dot{-}$, where

$$n \dot{-} m = \begin{cases} n - m, & \text{if } n \geq m, \\ 0 & \text{otherwise.} \end{cases}$$

We consider r-dimensional integer vector space $\mathbb{N}^r$ as a common data space for structures from $\mathcal{M}_{\mathbb{N}}$. Generic elements of $\mathbb{N}^r$ are denoted by $\mathbf{d}$ (possibly with indices). We write $\mathbf{0}$ for the vector $\langle 0, 0, \dots 0 \rangle$ and use $+$ and $\dot{-}$ for the componentwise summation and truncated subtraction on vectors from $\mathbb{N}^r$. A partial order relation $\leq$ on $\mathbb{N}^r$ is defined as usual: $\mathbf{d}_1 \leq \mathbf{d}_2 \iff \exists \mathbf{d}_0 \in \mathbb{N}^r : \mathbf{d}_2 = \mathbf{d}_1 + \mathbf{d}_0$. By the *norm* $\|\mathbf{d}\|$ of a vector $\mathbf{d}$ we mean the sum of all its components.

To introduce a common updating function R we relate each basic statement a_i, $1 \leq i \leq r$, with a unit vector $[a_i] = \langle 0, 0, \dots, 1, \dots 0 \rangle$ which has a single non-zero component 1 at the position i. Then R is specified as follows: $R(a_i, \mathbf{d}) = \mathbf{d} + [a_i]$ for every basic statement a_i and data state $\mathbf{d}$.

The model $\mathcal{M}_{\mathbb{N}}$ consists of all structures $M_\xi = \langle \mathbb{N}^r, \mathbf{0}, R, \xi \rangle$, where ξ is a monotonic evaluation function on $\mathbb{N}^r$. It is easy to see that any M_ξ is a commutative and monotonic structure. Let π', π'' be any pair of PSPs. Since any structure M from $\mathcal{M}_{\mathrm{cm}}$ is a homomorphic image of some structure M_ξ from $\mathcal{M}_{\mathbb{N}}$, we have

Proposition 1. $\pi' \sim_{\mathcal{M}_{\mathrm{cm}}} \pi'' \iff \pi' \sim_{\mathcal{M}_{\mathbb{N}}} \pi''$.

Our next step is to reduce the class of programs under consideration to those whose syntactic structure is most suitable for efficient equivalence-checking. We say that an initial path α in PSP π is *executable* if it is a prefix of some path associated with the run of π on some structure $M_\xi \in \mathcal{M}_{\mathbb{N}}$. It is easy to see that a path (1) is executable iff $\Delta_i \preceq \Delta_{i+1}$ holds for every $i \geq 0$. It should be noted also that due to monotonicity of evaluation functions each predicate p_j, $1 \leq j \leq k$, changes its value at most once along every executable path. Therefore every executable path (1) contains at most k pairwise different conditions. A PSP π is called *free* if every path in π from **entry** to **exit** is executable.

Proposition 2. *For every PSP π there exists a PSP π_0 that is free and such that $\pi \sim_{\mathcal{M}_{\mathbb{N}}} \pi_0$ and $|\pi_0| \leq 2^k |\pi|$.*

Proof. Given a PSP $\pi = \langle V, \mathbf{entry}, \mathbf{exit}, T, B \rangle$, we introduce a new distinguished point **loop** and consider a PSP $\pi' = \langle V', \mathbf{entry'}, \mathbf{exit}, T', B' \rangle$ such that $V' = \{(v, \Delta) : v \in V - \{\mathbf{exit}\}, \Delta \in \mathcal{C}\} \cup \{\mathbf{exit}, \mathbf{loop}\}$, $\mathbf{entry'} = (\mathbf{entry}, \langle 0, 0, \ldots, 0 \rangle)$, $B'((v, \Delta)) = B(v)$ (here $B'(\mathbf{loop})$ is irrelevant), and T' is defined as follows

$$
T'((v, \Delta), \Delta') = \begin{cases} (T(v, \Delta'), \Delta'), & \text{if } \Delta \preceq \Delta' \text{ and } T(v, \Delta') \neq \mathbf{exit}, \\ \mathbf{exit}, & \text{if } \Delta \preceq \Delta' \text{ and } T(v, \Delta') = \mathbf{exit}, \\ \mathbf{loop} & \text{otherwise.} \end{cases}
$$

$$T'(\mathbf{loop}, \Delta) = \mathbf{loop} \text{ for all } \Delta \in \mathcal{C}.$$

It should be noticed that π' has exactly the same set of executable paths as π, and therefore $\pi' \sim_{\mathcal{M}_{\mathbb{N}}} \pi$. A PSP π_0 is obtained from π' by directing to **loop** all transitions that do not belong to any path from **entry** to **exit**. Also, this doesn't affect the set of terminating runs of π'. Hence, $\pi_0 \sim_{\mathcal{M}_{\mathbb{N}}} \pi$. $\square$

Proposition 3. *Let π_0 be a free PSP, and u', u'' be two points that belong to some path from **entry** to **exit**. Then there are at most $|\pi_0|^k$ acyclic paths in π_0 from u' to u''.*

Proof. The length of any acyclic path in π_0 doesn't exceed $|\pi_0|$. Since π_0 is a deterministic PSP, any acyclic path (1) that begins from u' and reaches u'' is completely characterized by the sequence of conditions $\Delta_0, \Delta_1, \ldots, \Delta_i$. Since π_0 is a free PSP, such path is a suffix of some executable path. Therefore, as it was noted above, each predicate p_j, $1 \leq j \leq k$, changes its value at most once along every such path. This implies that the cardinality of the set of all acyclic paths from u' to u'' does not exceed $|\pi_0|^k$. $\square$

3   Compatible Paths and Cuts

Now we restrict our consideration only to free PSPs. Free PSPs enable us to check the equivalence by examining paths in programs instead of runs on structures. Our next step is to reduce the equivalence-checking of free PSPs π_1 and π_2 to the analysis of compatible paths in π_1 and π_2. Initial paths α_1 and α_2 in π_1 and π_2 are called *compatible* if both paths are executable on the same structure $M_\xi \in \mathcal{M}_{\mathbb{IN}}$. It is worth noting that if π_1 and π_2 have different behaviors then this difference manifests itself in at least one pair of compatible paths. This is a reason for developing an effective means for the analysis of compatible paths.

We begin with bringing into use some suitable notation for operating with paths in free PSPs. When considering a finite path α, $|\alpha| = n$, of the form (1) in a PSP π, we write $u(\alpha)$ for the point reached by this path (i.e., $u(\alpha) = T(v_n, \Delta_n)$). Furthermore, for every $i, 1 \leq i \leq n$, we denote by $\Delta(\alpha, i)$ the condition Δ_i which fires the i-th transition along this path, and write $\mathbf{d}(\alpha, i)$ for the vector $[B(v_1)] + [B(v_2)] + \cdots + [B(v_i)]$ which is the data state "computed" at the i-th transition. A vector $\mathbf{d}(\alpha, i)$ may be viewed as the intermediate result of the run of π along α. To complete the picture we will assume that $\mathbf{d}(\alpha, 0) = \mathbf{0}$.

The following proposition delivers a straightforward criterion for checking compatibility of finite initial paths in free PSPs.

Proposition 4. *Initial paths α_1 and α_2 in free PSPs π_1 and π_2 are compatible iff the following implications*

$$\mathbf{d}(\alpha_1, i-1) \leq \mathbf{d}(\alpha_2, j-1) \implies \Delta(\alpha_1, i) \preceq \Delta(\alpha_2, j),$$
$$\mathbf{d}(\alpha_2, j-1) \leq \mathbf{d}(\alpha_1, i-1) \implies \Delta(\alpha_2, j) \preceq \Delta(\alpha_1, i)$$

hold for every pair i, j such that $1 \leq i \leq |\alpha_1|$, $1 \leq j \leq |\alpha_2|$.

Proof. If α_1 and α_2 are compatible then, by definition, there exists some $M_\xi \in \mathcal{M}_{\mathbb{IN}}$ such, that $\Delta(\alpha_1, i) = \xi(\mathbf{d}(\alpha_1, i-1))$ and $\Delta(\alpha_2, j) = \xi(\mathbf{d}(\alpha_1, j-1))$ hold for all i, j, $1 \leq i \leq |\alpha_1|$, $1 \leq j \leq |\alpha_2|$. The implications above just reflect the fact that the evaluation function ξ is monotonic.

On the other hand, as it can be seen from the definition of a run of a PSP, a path α_q, $q = 1, 2$, is executable on M_ξ iff $\xi(\mathbf{d}(\alpha_q, i-1)) = \Delta_i$ holds for every $1 \leq i \leq |\alpha_q|$. The implications above guarantee that the set of equations

$$\xi(\mathbf{d}(\alpha_1, i-1)) = \Delta(\alpha_1, i), \qquad 1 \leq i \leq |\alpha_1|,$$
$$\xi(\mathbf{d}(\alpha_2, j-1)) = \Delta(\alpha_2, j), \qquad 1 \leq j \leq |\alpha_2|,$$

specifies consistently a monotonic evaluation ξ, such that both paths α_1 and α_2 are executable on the structure M_ξ. □

Proposition 4 is not quite efficient for generating compatible paths since keeping track of all transitions along paths is both time- and space-consuming. This can be alleviated significantly if we take into account that, due to monotonicity of evaluation functions, conditions change at most k times along every executable path.

Assume that paths α_1 and α_2 in free PSPs π_1 and π_2 have the same length (i.e. $|\alpha_1| = |\alpha_2| = n$). Then for every such pair of paths we define the *cut* of α_1, α_2 as a sextuple

$$G(\alpha_1, \alpha_2) = (u(\alpha_1), u(\alpha_2), \mathbf{d}_1, \mathbf{d}_2, c_1, c_2) ,$$

where $\mathbf{d}_1 = \mathbf{d}(\alpha_1, n) \overset{\text{·}}{-} \mathbf{d}(\alpha_2, n)$, $\mathbf{d}_2 = \mathbf{d}(\alpha_2, n) \overset{\text{·}}{-} \mathbf{d}(\alpha_1, n)$, and c_1 and c_2 are *constraints* induced by α_1 and α_2 as follows:

$$c_1 = \{\langle \hat{\mathbf{d}}_i, \Delta(\alpha_1, i)\rangle \; : i = 1, \text{ or } i > 1 \text{ and } \Delta(\alpha_1, i) \neq \Delta(\alpha_1, i-1),$$
$$\hat{\mathbf{d}}_i = \mathbf{d}(\alpha_1, i-1) \overset{\text{·}}{-} \mathbf{d}(\alpha_2, n), 1 \leq i \leq n\}$$
$$c_2 = \{\langle \hat{\mathbf{d}}_j, \Delta(\alpha_2, j)\rangle \; : j = 1, \text{ or } j > 1 \text{ and } \Delta(\alpha_2, j) \neq \Delta(\alpha_2, j-1),$$
$$\hat{\mathbf{d}}_j = \mathbf{d}(\alpha_2, j-1) \overset{\text{·}}{-} \mathbf{d}(\alpha_1, n), 1 \leq j \leq n\}$$

Intuitively, a cut $G(\alpha_1, \alpha_2)$ is a specific data structure which carries all necessary information for constructing compatible extensions of paths α_1 and α_2. Vectors $\mathbf{d}_1$ and $\mathbf{d}_2$ indicate the discrepancy of the paths, i.e. how much differ the intermediate results of the runs along α_1 and α_2. These results coincide iff $\mathbf{d}_1 = \mathbf{d}_2 = \mathbf{0}$. It follows immediately from the definition of $G(\alpha_1, \alpha_2)$ that vectors $\mathbf{d}_1$ and $\mathbf{d}_2$ are always orthogonal and $\|\mathbf{d}_1\| = \|\mathbf{d}_2\|$. The latter is due to the fact that $\|\mathbf{d}(\alpha_1, n)\| = \|\mathbf{d}(\alpha_2, n)\| = n$. Constraints c_1, c_2 provide the requirements to be satisfied by every pair of compatible extensions of the paths α_1, α_2. Since every path in a free PSP contains at most k pairwise different conditions, each constraint c_q, $q = 1, 2$, contains at most k pairs of the form $\langle \hat{\mathbf{d}}, \Delta \rangle$ and every such vector $\hat{\mathbf{d}}$ obeys the relation $\hat{\mathbf{d}} \leq \mathbf{d}_q$. Hence, if four components $u_1, u_2, \mathbf{d}_1, \mathbf{d}_2$ of a cut are fixed then no more than $\|\mathbf{d}_1\|^{2kr}$ different cuts of the form $(u_1, u_2, \mathbf{d}_1, \mathbf{d}_2, c_1, c_2)$ are possible for pairs of paths in PSPs π_2, π_2.

Propositions 5 and 6 below elucidate the intended meaning of cuts. Denote by $\mathcal{C}(c)$ the set of all conditions occurred in a constraint c.

Proposition 5. *Let α_1 and α_2 be a pair of compatible paths of the same length in free PSPs π_1 and π_2, and $G(\alpha_1, \alpha_2) = (u_1, u_2, \mathbf{d}_1, \mathbf{d}_2, c_1, c_2)$ be the cut of α_1, α_2. Then paths $\alpha'_1 = \alpha_1, (u_1, \Delta_1)$ and $\alpha'_2 = \alpha_2, (u_2, \Delta_2)$ are compatible iff conditions Δ_1 and Δ_2 meet the following requirements ($q = 1, 2$):*

Req 1: $\mathbf{d}_1 = \mathbf{d}_2 \implies \Delta_1 = \Delta_2$;
Req 2: *the relationship $\Delta \preceq \Delta_q$ holds for every pair $\langle \mathbf{0}, \Delta \rangle$ in c_{3-q}.*

Furthermore, the cut $G(\alpha'_1, \alpha'_2) = (u'_1, u'_2, \mathbf{d}'_1, \mathbf{d}'_2, c'_1, c'_2)$ of the paths α'_1 and α'_2 can be obtained as follows ($q = 1, 2$):

$$u'_q = T_{\pi_q}(u_q, \Delta_q), \tag{3}$$

$$\mathbf{d}'_q = (\mathbf{d}_q + [B_{\pi_q}(u_q)]) \overset{\text{·}}{-} [B_{\pi_{3-q}}(u_{3-q})], \tag{4}$$

$$c'_q = \{\langle \mathbf{d}', \Delta\rangle : \langle \hat{\mathbf{d}}, \Delta \rangle \in c_q, \mathbf{d}' = \hat{\mathbf{d}} \overset{\text{·}}{-} [B_{\pi_{3-q}}(u_{3-q})]\} \cup c_q^{new}, \tag{5}$$

where

$$c_q^{new} = \begin{cases} (\mathbf{d}_q \overset{\text{·}}{-} [B_{\pi_{3-q}}(u_{3-q})], \Delta_q), & \text{if } \Delta_q \notin \mathcal{C}(c_q), \\ \emptyset & \text{otherwise.} \end{cases}$$

Proof. ($\Rightarrow$) Suppose α_1' and α_2' are executable on some $M_\xi \in \mathcal{M}_{\mathbb{N}}$. Then $\mathbf{d}_1 = \mathbf{d}_2$ implies $\mathbf{d}(\alpha_1, n) = \mathbf{d}(\alpha_2, n)$, where $n = |\alpha_1| = |\alpha_2|$, which, in turn, implies $\Delta_1 = \xi(\mathbf{d}(\alpha_1, n)) = \xi(\mathbf{d}(\alpha_2, n)) = \Delta_2$. (**Req 1** proved.) Also, if $\langle \mathbf{0}, \Delta \rangle \in c_{3-q}$ then, by definition of constraints, there exists $i, 1 \le i \le n$, such that $\Delta = \Delta(\alpha_{3-q}, i)$ and $\mathbf{d}(\alpha_{3-q}, i - 1) \le \mathbf{d}(\alpha_q, n)$. Then **Req 2** follows from Proposition 4.

($\Leftarrow$) Since vectors $\mathbf{d}_1$ and $\mathbf{d}_2$ are always orthogonal, **Req 1** gives the same effect as the pair of implications from Proposition 4 for the case $i = j = m$, where $m = |\alpha_1'| = |\alpha_2'|$. If $i < m$ and $\mathbf{d}(\alpha_1, i - 1) \le \mathbf{d}(\alpha_2, m - 1)$ then, by definition of c_1, the pair $\langle \mathbf{0}, \Delta \rangle$ belongs to c_1. Therefore, **Req 2** gives the same effect as all those implications from Proposition 4 that correspond to the cases when $i < |\alpha_1'|$ and $j = |\alpha_2'|$. The same arguments are applicable to the case when $i = |\alpha_1'|$ and $j < |\alpha_2'|$. The implications from Proposition 4 corresponding to the cases when $i < |\alpha_1'|$ and $j < |\alpha_2'|$ also hold due to the compatibility of α_1 and α_2. Thus, by Proposition 4, the paths α_1' and α_2' are compatible as well.

Equalities (3)–(5) follow immediately from the definition of a cut. $\square$

Proposition 6. *Let α_1 and α_2 be a pair of compatible paths of the same length n in free PSPs π_1 and π_2. Let $G(\alpha_1, \alpha_2) = (v_n^1, v_n^2, \mathbf{d}_1, \mathbf{d}_2, c_1, c_2)$ be the cut of α_1 and α_2. Suppose that $\alpha_1' = (v_n^1, \Delta_0), (v_{n+1}^1, \Delta_1), \ldots, (u_{n+m}^1, \Delta_m)$ is a path in π_1 from the point v_n^1. Then the paths $\alpha^1 \alpha_1'$ and α_2 are compatible iff α_1' satisfies the requirement below:*

Req 3:   *the implication $(\hat{\mathbf{d}} \le \mathbf{d}_1 + [B(v_n^1)] + \cdots + [B(v_{n+i-1}^1)]) \Rightarrow (\Delta \preceq \Delta_i)$*
holds for every pair $(\hat{\mathbf{d}}, \Delta)$ from c_2 and for every i, $0 \le i \le m$.

Proof. The arguments are similar to those used in the proof of Proposition 5. $\square$

Thus, Propositions 5 and 6 testify that a cut $G(\alpha_1, \alpha_2)$ is all we need to know about paths α_1 and α_2 to yield all their compatible extensions. Given a cut $G = (u_1, u_2, \mathbf{d}_1, \mathbf{d}_2, c_1, c_2)$, we say, with Propositions 5 and 6 in mind, that

1. a pair of conditions (Δ_1, Δ_2) is *G-admissible* if both conditions Δ_1 and Δ_2 satisfy **Req 1** and **Req 2**;
2. a point w in PSP π_1 is *G-accessible* from u_1 if there exists a path α_1' in π_1 which reaches w and satisfies **Req 3**.

It should be readily apparent that the *G*-admissability of a pair (Δ_1, Δ_2) can be checked in time $O(rk^2)$. And when checking the *G*-accessibility of a point w from u_1, one should take into account the following simple consideration.

Remark 1. If w is *G*-accessible from u_1 then w can be reached as well by some acyclic path which satisfies **Req 3**.

The reason for this is the fact that in free PSPs the sequence of conditions in every path is non-decreasing. Hence, all cycles can be eliminated from a path without violating **Req 3**. Because of this, for checking the *G*-accessibility of w it is sufficient to inspect all acyclic paths from u_1 to w. By Proposition 3, the amount of such paths is bounded by $|\pi_1|^k$ and for each of them **Req 3** can be verified in time $O(rk|\pi_1| \log \|\mathbf{d}_2\|)$. Thus, we arrive at the following proposition.

Proposition 7. *Let $G = (u_1, u_2, \mathbf{d}_1, \mathbf{d}_2, c_1, c_2)$ be the cut of a pair of compatible paths in free PSPs π_1 and π_2. Let w be a point in π_1. Then the G-accessibility of w from u_1 can be checked within a time $O(rk|\pi_1|^{k+1} \log \|\mathbf{d}_2\|)$.*

By introducing the concepts of compatible paths and cuts we get a possibility to offer a criterion for the equivalence of free PSPs on $\mathcal{M}_{\mathbb{N}}$.

Theorem 1. *Let π_1 and π_2 be free PSPs. Then π_1 and π_2 are <u>not</u> equivalent on $\mathcal{M}_{\mathbb{N}}$ iff there exists a pair of compatible paths α_1 and α_2 whose cut $G(\alpha_1, \alpha_2) = (u_1, u_2, \mathbf{d}_1, \mathbf{d}_2, c_1, c_2)$ complies with at least one of the following four demands:*
  Dem 1. $u_1 = u_2 = \mathbf{exit}$ and $\mathbf{d}_1 \neq \mathbf{d}_2$;
  Dem 2. one of the points (say, u_1) is $\mathbf{exit}$, whereas the other (u_2) is not;
  Dem 3. one of the points (say, u_2) is $\mathbf{loop}$, whereas $\mathbf{exit}$ is $G(\alpha_1, \alpha_2)$-accessible from the other (u_1);
  Dem 4. the relationship $\|\mathbf{d}_1\| > \max(|\pi_1|, |\pi_2|)$ holds and at least in one of PSPs π_q, $q = 1, 2$, the point $\mathbf{exit}$ is $G(\alpha_1, \alpha_2)$-accessible from u_q.

Proof. ($\Rightarrow$) Suppose that $[r(\pi_1, M_\xi)] \neq [r(\pi_2, M_\xi)]$ holds for some evaluation ξ. We may assume w.l.o.g. that $r(\pi_1, M_\xi)$ terminates and it is no longer than $r(\pi_2, M_\xi)$. Denote its length by n. Let α_1 and α_2 be paths in π_1 and π_2 associated, respectively, with the runs $r(\pi_1, M_\xi)$ and $r(\pi_2, M_\xi)$. Then behaviors of π_1 and π_2 on M_ξ fall into one of the two following cases.

1. Both runs $r(\pi_1, M_\xi)$ and $r(\pi_2, M_\xi)$ terminate and have the same length n. Since $\mathbf{d}(\alpha_1, n) = [r(\pi_1, M_\xi)]$ and $\mathbf{d}(\alpha_2, n) = [r(\pi_2, M_\xi)]$, the cut $G(\alpha_1, \alpha_2) = (\mathbf{exit}, \mathbf{exit}, \mathbf{d}_1, \mathbf{d}_2, c_1, c_2)$ is such that $\mathbf{d}_1 \neq \mathbf{d}_2$.
2. The run $r(\pi_2, M_\xi)$ is infinite, or has a length exceeding that of $r(\pi_1, M_\xi)$. Then $G(\alpha_1, \alpha_2|^n) = (\mathbf{exit}, u_2, \mathbf{d}_1, \mathbf{d}_2, c_1, c_2)$ and $u_2 \neq \mathbf{exit}$.

($\Leftarrow$) Let $G(\alpha_1, \alpha_2) = (u_1, u_2, \mathbf{d}_1, \mathbf{d}_2, c_1, c_2)$ be a cut of some compatible paths α_1 and α_2 in PSPs π_1 and π_2 respectively, and let $|\alpha_1| = |\alpha_2| = n$. Suppose

1. $u_1 = u_2 = \mathbf{exit}$ and $\mathbf{d}_1 \neq \mathbf{d}_2$. Let M_ξ be some common structure the paths α_1 and α_2 are executable on. Then $\mathbf{d}(\alpha_1, n) = [r(\pi_1, M_\xi)]$ and $\mathbf{d}(\alpha_2, n) = [r(\pi_2, M_\xi)]$. Since $\mathbf{d}_1 = \mathbf{d}(\alpha_1, n) \doteq \mathbf{d}(\alpha_2, n)$ and $\mathbf{d}_2 = \mathbf{d}(\alpha_2, n) \doteq \mathbf{d}(\alpha_1, n)$, it follows herefrom that $[r(\pi_1, M_\xi)] \neq [r(\pi_2, M_\xi)]$.
2. $u_1 = \mathbf{exit}$ and $u_2 \neq \mathbf{exit}$. Let M_ξ be a structure the paths α_1 and α_2 are executable on. Then either the run $r(\pi_2, M_\xi)$ is infinite, or it terminates after m steps, $m > n$. The latter means that $\|[r(\pi_2, M_\xi)]\| > \|[r(\pi_2, M_\xi)]\|$. Thus, in both cases $[r(\pi_1, M_\xi)] \neq [r(\pi_2, M_\xi)]$.
3. $u_2 = \mathbf{loop}$ and $u_1 \neq \mathbf{loop}$. If $\mathbf{exit}$ is $G(\alpha_1, \alpha_2)$-accessible from u_1 then, by Proposition 6, there exist compatible paths $\alpha_1\alpha_1'$ and α_2 such that $\alpha_1\alpha_1'$ reaches $\mathbf{exit}$ and α_2 reaches $\mathbf{loop}$. They are associated with runs $r(\pi_1, M_\xi)$ and $r(\pi_2, M_\xi)$ on some common structure M_ξ yielding different results.
4. $\|\mathbf{d}_1\| > \max(|\pi_1|, |\pi_2|)$ and $\mathbf{exit}$ is $G(\alpha_1, \alpha_2)$-accessible from u_1. By Remark 1, $\mathbf{exit}$ can be reached from u_1 by some path α_1' such that α_1' satisfies **Req 3** and $|\alpha_1'| = m < |\pi_1|$. By Proposition 6, paths $\alpha_1\alpha_1'$ and α_2 are compatible and, hence, they are executable on the same structure M_ξ. Clearly,

$\alpha_1\alpha_1'$ is associated with a terminated run $r(\pi_1, M_\xi)$. Consider the case when $r(\pi_2, M_\xi)$ is a terminated run of the same length as $r(\pi_1, M_\xi)$ (in other cases it immediately follows that $[r(\pi_1, M_\xi)] \neq [r(\pi_2, M_\xi)])$ and let $\alpha_2\alpha_2'$ be the path associated with $r(\pi_2, M_\xi)$. Then the relationships

$$[r(\pi_1, M_\xi)] = \mathbf{d}(\alpha_1, n) + \mathbf{d}(\alpha_1', m), \quad [r(\pi_2, M_\xi)] = \mathbf{d}(\alpha_2, n) + \mathbf{d}(\alpha_2', m),$$
$$\|\mathbf{d}(\alpha_1, n) \doteq \mathbf{d}(\alpha_2, n)\| = \|\mathbf{d}_1\| > |\pi_1|, \|\mathbf{d}(\alpha_2', m)\| = \|\mathbf{d}(\alpha_1', m)\| < |\pi_1|$$

imply $\|[r(\pi_1, M_\xi)] \doteq [r(\pi_2, M_\xi)]\| > 0$. The latter means that $[r(\pi_1, M_\xi)] \neq [r(\pi_2, M_\xi)]$. $\qquad\square$

4   Decision Procedure and Complexity

As it follows from Theorem 1, to detect non-equivalence of free PSPs π_1 and π_2 it will suffice to check those cuts $G = (u_1, u_2, \mathbf{d}_1, \mathbf{d}_2, c_1, c_2)$ of compatible paths in these programs, whose discrepancy indicated by $\mathbf{d}_1$ and $\mathbf{d}_2$ is small enough, or to be more precise, $\|\mathbf{d}_1\| = \|\mathbf{d}_2\| \leq \max(|\pi_1|, |\pi_2|)$. In the data space $\mathbb{N}^r$ the number of vectors whose norm does not exceed some fixed value n is bounded by n^r. As noted above, the number of cuts having the same pair of points u_1, u_2 and the same pair of vectors $\mathbf{d}_1, \mathbf{d}_2$, $\|\mathbf{d}_1\| = \|\mathbf{d}_2\| \leq n$, does not exceed n^{2kr}. Proposition 5 provides us with a simple technique for generating the cuts of all pairs of compatible paths, and Propositions 6, 7 give us an effective means for checking G-accessibility of **exit**.

Equivalence-checking procedure. Let π_1 and π_2 be free PSPs whose size does not exceed N. Starting with the initial cut $G_0 = (\mathbf{entry}, \mathbf{entry}, \mathbf{0}, \mathbf{0}, \emptyset, \emptyset)$ generate a set of cuts in accordance with the instructions:

1. given a cut G, build, using the requirements **Req 1** and **Req 2**, the set of G-admissible pairs of conditions (Δ_1, Δ_2);
2. for every G-admissible pair of conditions (Δ_1, Δ_2) construct, using relationships (3)–(5), a cut G'.

For every new cut $G' = (u_1', u_2', \mathbf{d}_1', \mathbf{d}_2', c_1', c_2')$ check whether any of the demands **Dem 1–4** is met (when checking **Dem 3** and **Dem 4** use the requirement **Req 3** and Propositions 6, 7 for examining G-accessibility of **exit** from u_1 or u_2). If one of the demands is satisfied then stop and reject programs π_1, π_2 as non-equivalent. As soon as all constructed cuts are checked and no new cuts emerge, stop and accept programs π_1, π_2 as equivalent.

Note, that, by Propositions 7, the number of cuts that do not comply with **Dem 4** is less than $n^{2+2r+2kr}$. This guarantees termination of the procedure. Theorem 1, coupled with Propositions 3–7, guarantees correctness, completeness and effectiveness of the procedure above. By combining these considerations with Propositions 1 and 2, we arrive at the main result of this paper.

Theorem 2. *The equivalence-checking problem for PSPs operating on Kripke structures with commutative updating functions and monotonic evaluation functions is decidable in time $n^{O(kr)}$, where n is the size of programs to be analyzed,* *r and k are the cardinalities of the sets of basic statements and basic predicates used in the programs.*

5 Discussion

Our approach to the designing of polynomial time equivalence-checking algorithms can be adapted to other models of programs with commuting or partially commuting statements. The key to the decision procedures lies within the concept of cut which makes it possible to reduce the analysis of program runs to the manipulations with a limited number of cuts. This can be achieved when the set of evaluation functions ξ used in Kripke structures M_ξ have a finite or regular behavior along all paths in a program.

We think that our approach can not be applied directly to the equivalence-checking problem for M_{dmta}. Although it is possible to extend easily the concept of compatible runs and cuts to this model, we do not see any way to estimate the number of cuts to be checked in order to detect non-equivalence of PSPs. Nevertheless, if we consider the equivalence-checking problem for DMTAs operating on some specific tuples of words then our approach can be applicable sometimes. For example, it can be used in efficient equivalence-checking of DMTAs operating on the words 0*1*. With only slight modifications of Propositions 2 and **Req 1** the algorithm presented above can be transformed into a new decision procedure for the model $M_{dmta} \cap M_{cm}$; the complexity of this procedure will be polynomial of the DMTAs size and exponential of the number of tapes.

Acknowledgement. We thank anonymous referees for their stimulating criticism on the submitted version of this paper.

References

1. Bird M., The equivalence problem for deterministic two-tape automata, *J. Comput. Syst. Sci.*, 1973, **7**, p.218-236.
2. Glushkov V.M., Letichevskii A.A., Theory of algorithms and discrete processors, *Advances in Information System Science*, 1969, **1**, N 1.
3. Harel D., Dynamic logics. In *Handbook of Philosophical Logics*, D.Gabbay and F.Guenthner (eds.), 1984, p.497-604.
4. Harju T., Karhumaki J., The equivalence of multi-tape finite automata. *Theoret. Comput. Sci.*, 1991, **78**, p.347-355.
5. Ianov Iu I., On the equivalence and transformation of program schemes *Communications of the ACM*, 1:10 (1958), 8–12.
6. Kinber E., The inclusion problem for some classes of deterministic multitape automata. *Theoret. Comput. Sci.*, 1983, **26**, p.1-24.
7. Kotov V.E., Sabelfeld V.K., Theory of program schemata, Nauka, 1991, 246p. (in Russian)
8. Letichevsky A.A., On the equivalence of automata over semigroup, *Theoretic Cybernetics*, 1970, **6**, p.3-71 (in Russian).

9. Lewis H.R., A new decidable problem with applications. In *Proceedings of 18th FOCS Conference*, 1979, p.62-73.
10. Podlovchenko R.I., On the decidability of the equivalence problem on a class of program schemata having monotonic and partially commuting statements. *Programming and Software Engineering*, 1990, N 5, p.3-12 (in Russian).
11. Podlovchenko R.I., On Program Schemes with Commuting and Monotone Operators *Programming and Computer Software*, 2003, **29**, N 5, p. 270–276
12. Zakharov V.A., An efficient and unified approach to the decidability of equivalence of propositional program schemes. *Automata, Languages and Programming* (Proceedings of ICALP'98, Aalborg, Denmark, July 13-17, 1998), LNCS 1443, 247–258.
13. Zakharov V.A., The equivalence problem for computational models: decidable and undecidable cases. *Machines, Computations, and Undecidability* (Proceedings of MCU 2001), Chisinau, Moldavia, May 23-27, 2001), LNCS 2055, 133–153.

Tight Bounds for NFA to DFCA Transformations for Binary Alphabets

Cezar Câmpeanu[1],* and Andrei Păun[2]

[1] Department of Computer Science and Information Technology,
University of Prince Edward Island, Charlottetown, P.E.I., Canada C1A 4P3
cezar@sun11.math.upei.ca
[2] Department of Computer Science, College of Engineering and Science,
Louisiana Tech University, Ruston, P.O. Box 10348, Louisiana, LA-71272 USA
apaun@latech.edu

Abstract. In this paper we prove a lower bound for the maximum state complexity of Deterministic Finite Cover Automata (DFCAs) obtained from Non-deterministic Finite Automata (NFAs) of a given state complexity n, in case of a binary alphabet. We show, for binary alphabets, that the difference between maximum blow-up state complexity of DFA and DFCA can be as small as $2^{\lceil \frac{n}{2} \rceil - 2}$ compared to the number of states of the minimal DFA. We conjecture that the lower bound given in the paper is also the upper bound.

1 Introduction

State complexity of deterministic automata is important because it gives an accurate estimate of the memory space needed to store the automaton. In case of finite languages, DFCA reduces this space by taking into account the length of the longest word in the language, so that in practice the amount of memory necessary to store such a structure is significantly reduced. In [1] and [2] it is proved that for a given finite language the state complexity of a minimal DFCA is always less than or equal to the state complexity of a DFA recognizing the same language. Using this idea, it is interesting to know whether this improvement can always be significant or not in the number of states of the automaton, since transforming a DFA to a DFCA is also time consuming.

The main purpose of this paper is to study the state complexity of the transformation from NFA to DFCA.

In [3] it is given an upper bound for converting NFA to minimal DFA for finite languages and non-unary alphabets, and it is proved that the upper bound is reached in case of a binary alphabet. However, in the general case there is no result about the structure of states/transitions of these automata.

* The first author is supported by Natural Sciences and Engineering Research Council of Canada (NSERC) grant UPEI-600089 and the second author is supported by a LATECH-CenIT grant.

M. Domaratzki et al. (Eds.): CIAA 2004, LNCS 3317, pp. 306–307, 2005.

We focus mainly on the binary case proving that in the worst case the minimal number of states of a minimal DFCA for a finite language L generated by an n-state NFA can be at least as high as $2^{n-t} - 2^{t-2} + 2^t - 1$, where $t = \lceil \frac{n}{2} \rceil$. Notice that this bound is just with 2^{t-2} lower than the bound obtained in [3] for the worst case transformation from NFA to DFA.

2   The Lower Bound for the Worst Case DFCA Complexity

Let $LB(n) = \begin{cases} 2^{t-1} + 2^{t-2} + 2^t - 1, & \text{if } n \text{ is even,} \\ 2^{t-2} + 2^t - 1, & \text{if } n \text{ is odd.} \end{cases}$

Theorem 1. *For each integer $n > 1$, there exists a finite language $L \subseteq \{a,b\}$ such that L is accepted by a minimal acyclic n-state NFA, and any complete DFCA for L has at least $LB(n)$ states.*

Proof. Let $\Sigma = \{a,b\}$. We consider the language $L_n = L'_n \cup L''_n$, $L'_n = \{w \mid w = w_1 b, |w| = t\}$, $L''_n = \{w \mid w = uava$, such that $|w| < n$, and $|v| = \lfloor \frac{n}{2} \rfloor - 2\}$.

The language L_n is accepted by the nondeterministic automaton with n states $0, 1, ..., n-1$ presented in Figure 1 ($f = n-1$).

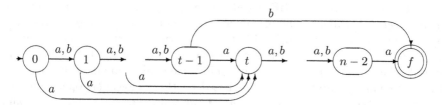

Fig. 1. An example of NFA for which the DFCA reaches $LB(n)$ states

We have proved that for an NFA with n states accepting a finite language over a binary alphabet the equivalent minimal DFCA has at least $2^{\lceil \frac{n}{2} \rceil - 2}$ less states than the number of states of the minimal DFA.

References

1. Cezar Câmpeanu and Andrei Păun, Counting The Number of Minimal DFCA Obtained by Merging States, *International Journal of Foundations of Computer Science*, Vol. 14, No 6, December (2003) 995 – 1006.
2. Cezar Câmpeanu, Nicolae Sântean, and Sheng Yu, Finite Languages and Cover Automata, *Theoretical Computer Science*, 267, 1-2 (2001), 3 – 16.
3. Kai Salomaa, Sheng Yu, NFA to DFA transformations for finite languages over arbitrary alphabets, *Journal of Automata, Languages and Combinatorics*, Vol **2**, 1997, 177 – 186.
4. Sheng Yu, Regular Languages, In: A. SALOMAA AND G. ROZENBERG (eds.), *Handbook of Formal Languages*. Springer Verlag, Berlin, 1997, 41 – 110.

Simulating the Process of Gene Assembly in Ciliates

Liliana Cojocaru

Rovira i Virgili University of Tarragona,
Pl. Imperial Tarraco 1, 43005, Spain
liliana.cojocaru@estudiants.urv.es

Abstract. *Ciliates* are protozoic organisms having two types of nuclei: micronuclei (that store the DNA) and macronuclei (that provide the RNA). Another feature that makes them distinct is the phenomenon of transformation of micronuclear genes into macronuclear genes during their sexual reproduction, called the *Gene Assembly Process in Ciliates* (GAPC). *Parallel Communicating Finite Transducer Systems* (PCFTS) are translating devices composed of several finite transducers that work in parallel in a synchronized manner. They communicate with each other by states and by the output tapes. In this paper we present a simulation of the molecular operations performed during GAPC with PCFTS.

Micronuclear genes are composed of combinations of residual segments, i.e. *Internal Eliminated Segments* (IES) and active segments, i.e. *Macronuclear Destinated Segments* (MDS). The prominent feature of GAPC consists in the very spectacular manner in which, during the transformation of micronuclear genes into macronuclear genes, the MDS regions are spliced and the IES portions are excised. The splicing process is carried on in some weaker points of the micronuclear gene, named *pointers*, and it is based on three molecular operations: *ld*, *hi*, and *dlad*. Let Π be the (finite) *pointers alphabet*. For $p, r \in \Pi$, $p \neq r$, and $\pi \in \Pi^*$, these operations have been mathematically formalized in [3] as follows:

1. the $\mathbf{ld}_p$ operation on $\pi = \pi_1 pp\pi_2$ is defined as $\mathbf{ld}_p(\pi) = \pi_1\pi_2$,
2. the $\mathbf{hi}_p$ operation on $\pi = \pi_1 p\pi_2\bar{p}\pi_3$ is defined as $\mathbf{hi}_p(\pi) = \pi_1\mathbf{rs}(\pi_2)\pi_3$, where $\mathbf{rs}(\pi_2)$ is the *reversed switch* of π_2, i.e. $\mathbf{rs}(qr...t) = \bar{t}...\bar{r}\bar{q}$, for $q, r, ..., t \in \Pi$,
3. the $\mathbf{dlad}_{p,r}$ operation on $\pi = \pi_1 p\pi_2 r\pi_3 p\pi_4 r\pi_5$ is $\mathbf{dlad}_{p,r}(\pi) = \pi_1\pi_4\pi_3\pi_2\pi_5$.

A generalization of these operations for the case when $p, r \in \Pi^+$ can be found in [1], i.e. the extended version of this paper. PCFTS have been introduced in [2], with linguistic proposes. Next, we present a PCFTS with two components, that works on *legal* strings ([3]) and simulates the $\mathbf{hi}_p$ operation. Let $T = (\Pi, \Pi, T_1, T_2, K)$ be a $rpcft(2)$ ([2]), and q_0/s_0 be the initial state of T_1/T_2. The δ mappings[1], for a given $p \in \Pi$ and any $y \in \Pi$, are defined below:

$1.\delta_1(q_0, y) = \{(q_0, \lambda), (K_2, \bar{y})^\flat\}$ $2.\delta_1(q_0, p) = \{(q_p, \lambda)\}$ $3.\delta_1(q_0, \lambda) = \{(q_0, \lambda)\}$
$4.\delta_1(s_{[0]}, \lambda) = \{(s_{[\bar{0}]}, \lambda), (s_f, \lambda)\}$ $5.\delta_1(q_p, y) = \{(q_{[p]}, \bar{y})\}$ $6.\delta_1(s_{[0]}, \bar{p}) = \{(q_{\bar{p}}, \lambda)\}$
$7.\delta_1(q_{\bar{p}}, \lambda) = \{(q_{\bar{p}}, \lambda), (q_f, \lambda)\}$ $8.\delta_1(q_{pp}, \lambda) = \{(q_f, \lambda)\}$ $9.\delta_1(s_f, \lambda) = \{(s_f, \lambda)\}$
$10.\delta_1(q_{\bar{p}}, y) = \{(q_{pp}, y)\}^\diamond$ $11.\delta_1(q_{pp}, y) = \{(q_{pp}, y)\}^\diamond$

---

[1] Here each $\flat$ marks the condition $y \neq p$, and each $\diamond$ marks the condition $y \notin \{p, \bar{p}\}$.

M. Domaratzki et al. (Eds.): CIAA 2004, LNCS 3317, pp. 308–309, 2005.
© Springer-Verlag Berlin Heidelberg 2005

1. $\delta_2(s_0, \lambda) = \{(s_0, \lambda), (K_1, \lambda)\}$ 2. $\delta_2(s_0, y) = \{(s_1, y)\}^\flat$ 3. $\delta_2(s_1, y) = \{(s_1, y)\}^\flat$,
4. $\delta_2(q_{[p]}, \lambda) = \{(s_{[0]}, \lambda)\}$ 5. $\delta_2(s_2, y) = \{(s_2, y)\}$ 6. $\delta_2(s_{[\bar{0}]}, \lambda) = \{(s_{[0]}, \lambda)\}$,
7. $\delta_2(s_1, p) = \{(s_2, p), (K_1, \lambda)\}$ 8. $\delta_2(q_f, y) = \{(q_f, \lambda)\}^\flat$.

Briefly, the system works as follows: in the beginning, only the first transducer T_1 reads pointers without any output. When p is found, the state q_0 is changed into the state q_p and, in the next step, the second transducer T_2 is obliged to query T_1, otherwise T_1 will not be able to continue the computation in the state $q_{[p]}$. In this moment the system begins to compute $\mathbf{rs}(\pi_2)$. The result is always yielded on the output tape of T_1, and ends when $\bar{p}$ is found. From now on both transducers synchronously yield on the first tape the string π_3 and on the second tape the string π_1. When this procedure ends too, T_2 asks for the content of the first tape in order to have on the second tape the result of the $\mathbf{hi}_p$ operation, i.e. $\pi_1\mathbf{rs}(\pi_2)\pi_3$. The final system state is (q_0, q_f), when the long distance pair $(p, \bar{p})$ is found. For the case when only the pointer p is found the system ends in (s_f, s_2), while in the case when p is not found the system ends in (q_0, s_1). In both last cases the input string is entirely outputted on the tape of T_2.

A $rpcft(2)$ that simulates the $\mathbf{dlad}_{p,r}$ operation, presented also in [1], works as follows: firstly only T_1 reads pointers without any output. When the first occurrence of p is found, the current state of T_1 is changed into s_p. From now on T_1 outputs the string π_2. When the first occurrence of r is found, the state s_p is changed into s_r. In this moment, T_2 has to query T_1, otherwise T_1 will be blocked in the state s_r. The content of the first output tape is discharged into the output tape of T_2 in order to give freedom to T_1 to yield on its tape the string π_3. When the second occurrence of p is found, T_1 asks for the content of the second output tape in order to compute the sequence $\pi_3\pi_2$, and to give freedom to T_2 to output the sequence $\pi_1\pi_4$. This is the moment when T_2 starts to read symbols. Simultaneously, T_1 yields the sequence $\pi_3\pi_2\pi_5$. At the end of the computation the content of the first output tape is discharged into the second one in order to obtain the result of the $\mathbf{dlad}_{p,r}$ operation, i.e. $\pi_1\pi_4\pi_3\pi_2\pi_5$.

The above examples show that PCFTS with two components are description-ally very efficient to simulate complex molecular operations. They also can be used to check whether a strategy for a realistic MDS descriptor ([3]) is successful, i.e., at the end of all possible applications of $\mathbf{ld}$, $\mathbf{hi}$ and $\mathbf{dlad}$ operations, the input is reduced into the empty string, according to the chosen strategy.

References

1. Cojocaru, L.: On the Molecular Operations Performed During the Gene Assembly Process in Ciliates. In: Proceedings of ECAI 2004 - Workshop on Symbolic Networks, Valencia, Spain, 22-27 August (2004) 27-39
2. Csuhaj-Varjú, E., Martín-Vide, C., Mitrana, V.: Parallel Communicating Finite Transducer Systems. In: Language and Computers: Studies in Practical Linguistics, No. 47 (2002) 9-23
3. Ehrenfeucht, A., Harju, T., Petre, I., Prescott, D.M., Rozenberg, G.: Computation in Living Cells, Gene Assembly in Ciliates. Springer-Verlag, Berlin Heidelberg New York (2004)

A BDD-Like Implementation of an Automata Package

Jean-Michel Couvreur

LSV, ENS Cachan, Cachan, France
couvreur@lsv.ens-cachan.fr

Finite Automata are basic structures that appear in many areas of Computer Science and other disciplines. The emergence of new tools based on automata for the manipulation of infinite structures [4, 5, 1] makes a crucial challenge of improving the efficiency of automata packages. The present work is motivated by model-checking problems. where most of the algorithms are based on fixed point computations that share many identical subcomputations. A promising track is the realization of a BDD-like package because BDDs have proved these capability to take advantage of this aspect when using cache technique. Since Bryant's original publication of BDD algorithms [2], there has been a great deal of research in the area. One of the most powerful applications of BDDs has been symbolic model checking, used to formally verify digital circuits and other finite state systems [3]. A BDD package is based on an efficient implementation of the if-then-else (ITE) operator. It uses essentially two principles:

- (1) a hash table, called unique table, maintains a strong canonical form in BDDs and stores a forest of BDDs sharing common substructures,
- (2) a hash table, called computed cache, keeps subresults when evaluating a recursive ITE operation.

Applying the BDD principle to automata is not that easy. Thus a solution to our problem has to design new principles to overcome the following difficulties: define a strong canonical form for automata, handle a forest of automata sharing common substructures, design a constant time procedure to check automata equality and an efficient hash function. Notice that classic notion of minimal automata are far from solving these problems. One needs to design a new structure, well-adapted to substructures sharing and a new algorithm transforming an automaton into this new structure, guaranteeing a strong canonical form.

In this paper we propose a data structure, called shared automata, for representing deterministic finite automata. Informally, a shared automaton codes a strongly connected component of an automaton and its exit states. Thus, an automaton may be considered as an acyclic graph of shared automata. This representation is well-adapted to substructure sharing between automata. We have designed an incremental algorithm based on this decomposition producing shared automata where states respect some canonical order. During the canonisation of an automaton, produced shared automata are stored in a unique table, guaranteeing a strong canonical form like for BDDs. In our system, automata operations, as set operations, are obtained when computing on-the-fly a non canonical representation of the result while applying the canonical algorithm.

M. Domaratzki et al. (Eds.): CIAA 2004, LNCS 3317, pp. 310–311, 2005.

Table 1. Experimentation results for some Petri nets

Model	| {Place} |	| {Transition} |	LASH	PresTaf
LEA	30	35	6min 36s	1min 13s
Manufacturing System	14	13	9min 37s	1min 4s
CSM	13	8	14min 38s	1min 2s
PNCSA	31	36	66min	3min22
ConsProd	18	14	1316min	3min55

During this evaluation, subresults are stored in a computer cache, avoiding unnecessary re-evaluation of subexpressions. We experimentally compare PresTaf, a direct implementation of the Presburger arithmetic built on the shared automata package, and the Presburger package LASH [5] based on standard automata algorithms. The goal of this experimentation is to evaluate the benefits that shared automata techniques can bring to systems using standard automata algorithms. Comparison with other kind of Presburger package is out of the scope of our experimentation. We chose a classic problem verification: the backward symbolic state space exploration for Petri nets. Experimental results (see Table 1) show the great benefit of the new canonical structure applied to this kind of problems. As BDD [6], the main factor of this benefit is the computed cache. Indeed, the iterations of a state space exploration share many subproblems.

References

1. S. Bardin, A. Finkel, J. Leroux, and L. Petrucci. FAST: Fast Acceleration of Symbolic Transition systems. In *CAV '03*, volume 2725 of *LNCS*, pages 118–121, 2003.
2. R. Bryant. Graph based algorithms for boolean function manipulation. *IEEE Transactions on Computers*, 35(8):677–691, 1986.
3. J. R. Burch, E. M. Clarke, K. L. McMillan, D. L. Dill, and L. J. Hwang. Symbolic Model Checking: 10e20 states and beyond. *Information and Computation*, 98(2):97–109, 1998.
4. J. Elgaard, N. Klarlund, and A. Moller. Mona 1.x: new techniques for WS1S and WS2S. In *CAV '98*, volume 1427 of *LNCS*, 1998.
5. P. Wolper and B. Boigelot. On the construction of automata from linear arithmetic constraints. In *TACAS'00*, volume 1785 of *LNCS*, pages 1–19, 2000.
6. B. Yang, R. E. Bryant, D. R. O'Hallaron, A. Biere, O. Coudert, G. Janssen, R. K. Ranjan, and F. Somenzi. A performance study of BDD-based model checking. In *FMCAD'98*, pages 255–289, 1998.

Approximation to the Smallest Regular Expression for a Given Regular Language

Manuel Delgado and José Morais*

Departamento de Matemática e CMUP, Universidade do Porto,
Rua do Campo Alegre, 687, 4169-007 Porto, Portugal
mdelgado@fc.up.pt
jjoao@netcabo.pt

Abstract. A regular expression that represents the language accepted by a given finite automaton can be obtained using the the state elimination algorithm. The order of vertex removal affects the size of the resulting expression. We use here an heuristic to compute an approximation to the order of vertex removal that leads to the smallest regular expression obtainable this way.

1   Introduction and Motivation

The *size* of a regular expression is the number of occurrences of alphabetical symbols in it. A representation of a regular language through a small sized expression is in general preferable to a representation of the same language through an expression of bigger size. This is clearly the case when one wants to perform computations with the expression. The interest of the first author in this problem arose when, to solve a problem in finite semigroup theory, he needed to compute the commutative image of a regular language. He kept the interest in this problem even after developing an algorithm to perform the needed computations without passing through a regular expression [1]. In that paper the reader may find a brief description of the state elimination algorithm as well as more formal definition of *generalized transition graph* (GTG), which is similar to that of a finite automaton, but the edges are labeled with regular expressions instead of just letters. To learn more on the mentioned problem in finite semigroup theory we suggest the paper [2], where computations with the transformation monoids $\mathcal{POI}_n$ and $\mathcal{POPI}_n$ have been performed. These monoids, for $n = 4$ and $n = 5$, will be used in the table below.

We remark that to compute a regular expression for the language of a deterministic automaton it is in general a good idea to start minimizing the automaton given, since the minimal automaton obtained is quite often much smaller than

---

* Both authors gratefully acknowledge support of FCT and the POCTI program through CMUP.

M. Domaratzki et al. (Eds.): CIAA 2004, LNCS 3317, pp. 312–314, 2005.

the original one. In a recent GAP [4] package by S. Linton and the authors [3] an efficient algorithm to minimize a deterministic automaton is implemented.

Next we present an heuristic that attempts to remove the vertices in an order leading to the smallest result.

2   Heuristic

We define the *weight of a* GTG as the sum of the sizes of all regular expressions labeling the edges of the GTG. The *weight of a vertex* is defined as the weight that will be added to the weight of the GTG by the removal of that vertex. Using the convention $\sum_{k=1}^{0} a_k = 0$, one may easily check that the weight of a vertex x can be computed by the formula

$$\sum_{k=1}^{In}(W_{in}(k) \times (Out - 1)) \;+\; \sum_{k=1}^{Out}(W_{out}(k) \times (In - 1)) \;+\; W_{loop} \times (In \times Out - 1)$$

where In is the number of edges (not loops) that go into x, Out is the number of edges (not loops) that go out from x, $W_{in}(k)$ is the size of the label of the kth edge that goes into x, $W_{out}(k)$ is the size of the label of the kth edge that goes out from x and W_{loop} is the size of the label of the loop around x.

Our approach to the problem of computing small expressions is to remove, at each step, one of the least weighted vertices. Notice that using the above formula, the time consumed to compute the weight of a vertex is not relevant.

The following table, produced using automata obtained from Cayley graphs of certain transformation monoids already referred, shows that the usage of this heuristic gives quite satisfactory results. The computations have been achieved using GAP [4] (to deal with monoids) and the GAP package [3]. (The time is measured in GAP units, in a Pentium IV 2.6 GHz.)

Automaton	States	Alph.	Exp. without heuristic		Exp. with heuristic	
			size	time	size	time
$Min(\mathcal{POI}_4[1,20])$	16	4	1807	40	491	30
$Min(\mathcal{POI}_5[1,125])$	32	5	107438	270	8602	130
$Min(\mathcal{POPI}_4[1,60])$	33	2	8381	40	704	30
$Min(\mathcal{POPI}_5[1,70])$	81	2	398620	340	11528	260

Unfortunately, "less weight" does not necessarily mean "better choice". To deal with this problem we have also implemented a function that uses a lookahead approach. It takes two additional arguments: lk and nv and it "looks ahead" lk steps, by at each step computing the nv least weighted vertices and repeating the process for the GTG obtained by removing each of these nv. This approach leads in general to considerably better results, but the time consumed is higher.

References

1. Delgado, M.: Computing commutative images of rational languages and applications. Theor. Inform. Appl. **35** (2001) 419–435
2. Delgado, M. and Fernandes,V. H.: Abelian kernels of some monoids of injective partial transformations and an application. Semigroup Forum **61** (2000) 435–452
3. Delgado, M., Linton, S. and Morais, J.: Automata: A GAP [4] package. Accepted. http://www.fc.up.pt/cmup/mdelgado/automata.
4. The GAP Group: GAP – Groups, Algorithms, and Programming. Version 4.4, 2004, http://www.gap-system.org.

Algebraic Hierarchical Decomposition of Finite State Automata: Comparison of Implementations for Krohn-Rhodes Theory

Attila Egri-Nagy and Chrystopher L. Nehaniv

University of Hertfordshire, School of Computer Science,
College Lane, Hatfield, Herts AL10 9AB, United Kingdom
{A.Nagy, C.L.Nehaniv}@herts.ac.uk

The hierarchical algebraic decomposition of finite state automata (Krohn-Rhodes Theory) has been a mathematical theory without any computational implementations until the present paper, although several possible and promising practical applications, such as automated object-oriented programming in software development [5], formal methods for understanding in artificial intelligence [6], and a widely applicable integer-valued complexity measure [8, 7], have been described. As a remedy for the situation, our new implementation, described here, is freely available [2] as open-source software. We also present two different computer algebraic implementations of the Krohn-Rhodes decomposition, the $V \cup T$ and holonomy decompositions [4, 3], and compare their efficiency in terms of the number of hierarchical levels in the resulting cascade decompositions.

The difficulties of computational implementations of the Krohn-Rhodes decomposition come from the fact that mathematical proofs do not consider computational feasibility, i.e. the space and time complexity of the required calculations. This problem is especially acute in semigroup theory, where semigroups have so many elements. We represent a semigroup by a set of generators (the transformations induced by the input symbols of the automaton) instead of by a Cayley-table, finite presentation, or explicit enumeration of all elements; transformations are represented as mappings on the set $\mathbf{n} = \{1, \ldots, n\}$. This internal representation is still human-readable as well since it coincides with the mathematical notation. Transformations are stored as 1-dimensional arrays. The content of the cell with index i is the image of i. This way the multiplication of transformations can be done in time linear in n, the number of states. As usual, for getting fast set operations, subsets are represented as bitvectors encoding characteristic functions. For deciding whether element is contained in a set or not, hashtables are used.

Two different decompositions have been implemented in this work. The $V \cup T$ technique and the holonomy decomposition were chosen since they are inherently different, representing distinct classes of algorithms, and their proofs are close to an algorithmic description. The $V \cup T$ method is one of the earliest proof techniques [4]. It works with semigroups and uses the right regular representation for the resulting cascaded components. The main idea of the algorithm is that we iteratively decompose the semigroup into two possibly overlapping subsemigroups (a left-ideal and a proper subsemigroup). The iteration ends when the

M. Domaratzki et al. (Eds.): CIAA 2004, LNCS 3317, pp. 315–316, 2005.

components are left-simple or cyclic semigroups. The list of the components in order form the cascaded product. The inefficiency of the $V \cup T$ algorithm originates from the iterative step: V and T may overlap and thus subcomponents may appear again and again. Therefore the standard $V \cup T$ technique cannot be used for practical purposes: due to its redundancy it may produce even more components than the order of the characteristic semigroup (e.g. the full transformation on 4 points has $4^4 = 256$ elements and its decomposition has 401 components). Getting more elements than n^n for an automaton with n states is far from being efficient. We implemented the $V \cup T$ method as a package [2] for GAP [1].

The holonomy method works by the detailed study of how the characteristic monoid of an automaton acts on the automaton's state set. It looks for and cascades holonomy groups, i.e. subgroups of the characteristic monoid permuting certain sets of subsets of the state set. Isomorphic holonomy groups under a certain equivalance relation may be represented together thus avoiding repetitions in the wreath product. Therefore the holonomy algorithm was chosen and further optimized by using a more direct constructive method for holonomy groups instead of brute force breadth-first search based implementation. Due to the experimental nature of the method, it was implemented as standalone software [2].

References

1. GAP – Groups, Algorithms, and Programming, a system for computational discrete algebra Version 4.3. (http://www.gap-system.org)., 2002.
2. Attila Egri-Nagy and Chrystopher L. Nehaniv. GrasperMachine, Computational Semigroup Theory for Formal Models of Understanding, experimental software packages. (http://graspermachine.sf.net)., 2003.
3. Samuel Eilenberg. *Automata, Languages and Machines*, volume B. Academic Press, 1976.
4. Kenneth Krohn, John L. Rhodes, and Bret R. Tilson. *Algebraic Theory of Machines, Languages, and Semigroups* (M. A. Arbib, ed.), chapter 5, The Prime Decomposition Theorem of the Algebraic Theory of Machines, pages 81–125. Academic Press, 1968.
5. Chrystopher L. Nehaniv. Algebraic engineering of understanding: Global hierarchical coordinates on computation for the manipulation of data, knowledge, and process. In *Proc. 18th Annual International Computer Software and Applications Conference (COMPSAC 94)*, pages 418–425. IEEE Computer Society Press, 1994.
6. Chrystopher L. Nehaniv. Algebra and formal models of understanding. In Masami Ito, editor, *Semigroups, Formal Languages and Computer Systems*, volume 960, pages 145–154. Kyoto Research Institute for Mathematics Sciences, RIMS Kokyuroku, August 1996.
7. Chrystopher L. Nehaniv and John L. Rhodes. The evolution and understanding of hierarchical complexity in biology from an algebraic perspective. *Artificial Life*, 6:45–67, 2000.
8. John L. Rhodes. *Applications of Automata Theory and Algebra via the Mathematical Theory of Complexity to Finite-State Physics, Biology, Philosophy, Games, and Codes.* (Univ. California Berkeley Math Library 1971), unpublished book.

Does Hausdorff Dimension Measure Texture Complexity?*

Mark G. Eramian and Matthew Drotar

Department of Computer Science, The University of Saskatchewan,
57 Campus Drive, Saskatoon, Saskatchewan S7N 5A9
eramian@cs.usask.ca

It has been suggested by Jürgensen and Staiger [1] that local Hausdorff dimension is representative of local image texture complexity, or "messiness". If true, this could be a useful local texture feature in computer vision applications such as image segmentation and object classification. In this study we investigate whether the interpretation of Hausdorff dimension as a measure of texture complexity corresponds to reality, that is, human perception of texture complexity. Jürgensen and Staiger consider black and white images described by finite-state and closed ω-languages [1]. The (local) Hausdorff dimension of an ω-language can be computed from its corresponding automaton. Thus, we are interested in the relationship between the Hausdorff dimension of ω-languages which describe black and white texture images and the perceived texture complexity of the image described.

Culik II and Kari were the first to investigate binary and greyscale image compression using automata [2, 3]. Staiger showed that the entropy of regular ω-languages is computable from the transition matrix of the automaton of such a language [4] and that entropy coincides with the Hausdorff dimension for finite-state and closed ω-languages [5]. Jürgensen and Staiger postulated that the Hausdorff dimension of a language would be a good measure of the complexity of a texture generated by a corresponding automaton [6]. Subsequently they defined the local Hausdorff dimension and postulated that a map of local Hausdorff dimension for an image would be a good method of illustrating how relative image texture complexity varied over the image [1].

We conducted an experiment to test the supposed correlation between Hausdorff dimension and perceived texture complexity. Surveys were distributed in which participants were asked to rank two sets of texture images according to their "complexity". Some images were common to both sets. Participants were also asked to directly compare five pairs of images and indicate which they believed to be more complex, or whether they believed them to be of the same complexity. The texture images were obtained by randomly generating automaton transition matrices and selecting automata that generated suitable images. All images used were generated by automata having only a single strongly con-

---

* This research was funded in part by NSERC grant RGPIN262027-03 (M. G. Eramian), in part by an NSERC Undergraduate Research Award (M. Drotar) and in part by institutional grants from the University of Saskatchewan.

M. Domaratzki et al. (Eds.): CIAA 2004, LNCS 3317, pp. 317–318, 2005.

nected component, thus ensuring that local entropy over each image was constant [1]. We received about 100 responses to the survey.

Analysis of the data indicates that there appears to be no significant correlation between Hausdorff dimension and perceived texture complexity. There was little agreement among participants over how the images should be ranked; moreover about 73% of respondents gave different relative rankings to the same two images in different sets suggesting that context may influence perceived texture complexity. There was also little agreement over the relative complexity of the directly compared pairs of images. In three of the five cases, the majority of respondents perceived that image A was more complex than image B when in fact, in all five pairs, image A had the lower Hausdorff dimension. Finally, for no pair did a majority of the participants believe that the images were of the same complexity, despite the fact that each pair of images had nearly equal Hausdorff dimension.

Our conclusion from this study must be that Hausdorff dimension appears to be unsuitable for characterizing image texture complexity.

References

1. Jürgensen, H., Staiger, L.: Local Hausdorff dimension. Acta Informatica **32** (1995) 491–507
2. Culik II, K., Kari, J.: Inference algorithms for WFA and image compression. In Fisher, Y., ed.: Fractal Image Encoding and Analysis, Springer-Verlag (1998)
3. Culik II, K., Valenta, V.: Finite automata based compression of bi-level and simple color images. Comput. and Graphics **21** (1997) 61–68
4. Staiger, L.: The Hausdorff dimension of ω-languages is computable. EATCS Bulletin **66** (1998) 178–182
5. Staiger, L.: Combinatorial properties of the Hausdorff dimension. J. Statistical Planning Inference **23** (1989) 95–100
6. Jürgensen, H., Staiger, L.: Local Hausdorff dimension and quadtrees. Technical Report 259, University of Western Ontario, Department of Computer Science (1991)

Combining Regular Expressions with (Near-)Optimal Brzozowski Automata

Michiel Frishert and Bruce W. Watson

Technische Universiteit Eindhoven,
Department of Mathematics and Computer Science,
P.O.Box 513, NL-5600 MB Eindhoven, The Netherlands
michiel@michielfrishert.com, bruce@bruce-watson.com

Derivatives of regular expressions were first introduced by Brzozowski in [1]. By recursively computing all derivatives of a regular expression, and associating a state with each unique derivative, a deterministic finite automaton can be constructed. Convergence of this process is guaranteed if uniqueness of regular expressions is recognized modulo associativity, commutativity, and idempotence of the union operator. Additionaly, through simplification based on the identities for regular expressions, the number of derivatives can be further reduced.

Alternative approaches to computing the derivatives automaton that we have found either store duplicate copies of the parse trees, or compute and then determinize the (non-deterministic) partial derivatives automaton. An implementation using an approach similar to ours was published by Mark Hopkins in a 1993 note on the comp.compilers newsgroup, see [2].

Regular expressions are commonly represented as parse trees, and computation of derivatives can easily be implemented using such trees. The regular expression represented by a subtree of a parse tree is called a *subexpression*. Due to the nature of the Brzozowski derivatives, the same subexpression is often contained in more than one derivative. Such common subexpressions can be removed through the process of *global common subexpression elimination* (GCSE).

Our implementation uses n-ary parse trees rather than binary parse trees. This avoids the need of binary trees to keep the tree left (or right) heavy and sorted for fast equivalence detection. When creating a new node in the parse tree, with a given set (or list) of child nodes, we test for equivalent nodes by checking the parents of one of the child nodes. By storing the set of parents for each node in the parse tree, and through hash tables this can be done in near-constant time.

The n-ary parse tree along with GCSE ensure that equivalence is detected modulo associativity, idempotence and commutativity, which guarantees termination of the algorithm. Rewrite rules are used to implement simplification through the identities. The generic rewrite system allows us to add additional rewrite rules if desired. The rewrite rules are applied before GCSE.

Derivatives can be computed in two fashions: lazily (top-down), or eagerly (bottom-up). The first approach derivatives are computed as they are needed to find the derivatives of the parse tree root. The second approach computes derivatives for all subexpressions as they become available from parsing. In many cases, the exact same set of derivatives are computed in both methods, because

M. Domaratzki et al. (Eds.): CIAA 2004, LNCS 3317, pp. 319–320, 2005.

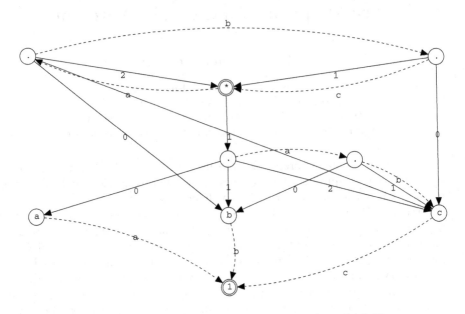

Fig. 1. Combined Parse Trees for the Derivatives of $(abc)^*$

the derivatives of a regular expression are defined in terms of the derivatives of its subexpressions. For the top-down approach there are cases where we can avoid computing the derivatives of subexpressions as follows: for each node in the parse tree we maintain a first-symbol set, which is the set of symbols for which that node will have a non-empty derivative. This can be computed directly from the parse tree. We only compute derivatives for those symbols in the first-symbol set. The improvement becomes obvious for example for the intersection of regular expressions ab and cd. Because the intersection of their first-symbol sets is empty, we do not compute derivatives of ab or cd, or for their subexpressions in turn. This benefits only the top-down approach, as the bottom-up approach already computes the derivatives of both subexpressions before ever encountering the node intersecting the two.

Figure 1 shows the combined parse graph for the derivatives of $(abc)^*$. Solid, straight lines form the parse graph, while dashed, curved lines represent the derivatives relations. The numbered edges indicate the order of concatenation in the parse graph.

References

1. Brzozowski, J.A.: Derivatives of Regular Expressions. Communications of the ACM **11** (1964) 481–494
2. Hopkins, M.: Regular expression software. Posted to the comp.compilers newsgroup (1994) ftp://iecc.com/pub/file/regex.tar.gz.

From Automata to Semilinear Sets: A Logical Solution for Sets $\mathcal{L}(\mathcal{C}, \mathcal{P})$

Denis Lugiez

Laboratoire d'Informatique Fondamentale (LIF) de Marseille,
Université de Provence – CMI, 39, rue Joliot-Curie F-13453 Marseille Cedex 13
lugiez@cmi.univ-mrs.fr[**]

Abstract. We give a logical characterization of semilinear sets L of the form $\mathcal{L}(\mathcal{C}, \mathcal{P})$ that can be checked in double exponential time from an automaton $\mathcal{A}$ accepting L. Sets $\mathcal{C}$ and $\mathcal{P}$ such $L = \mathcal{L}(\mathcal{C}, \mathcal{P})$ are computed during the verification process.

Presburger Arithmetic, Semilinear Sets and Automata. Presburger arithmetic is the first-order theory of addition of natural numbers $\mathcal{N}$. A set $L = \{\vec{x} \mid \vec{x} = \vec{b} + \Sigma_{i=1}^{i=k} \lambda_i \, \vec{p}_i, \lambda_i \in \mathcal{N}\} \subseteq \mathcal{N}^p$ is a linear set denoted by $L(\vec{b}, \mathcal{P})$ ($\mathcal{P}$ is the set of periods) and a semilinear set is a finite union of linear sets. $L(\mathcal{C}, \mathcal{P})$ denotes the semilinear set $\bigcup_{\vec{c} \in \mathcal{C}} \mathcal{L}(\vec{c}, \mathcal{P})$ i.e. a finite union of linear sets with the same periods. If Σ is the alphabet of p-tuples on the alphabet $0, 1$, finite state automata on Σ accepts sets of representation of p-tuples of natural numbers. Semilinear sets are the models of Presburger arithmetic formulas and the representation of semilinear sets are regular languages of Σ^*, but a regular language may not represent a semilinear set. Muchnik characterizes the automata that represents the model of a Presburger formula [Muc03]. Unfortunately, there is no simple way to extract the semilinear set from this characterization whereas the ability of computing the semilinear set from the automaton is an interesting feature for the verification of infinite state systems [RV02, BW02]. Moreover, to decide if an automaton represents a semilinear set may require a tower of 4 exponentials. We prove that a semilinear representation can be extracted from another characteristic formula in double exponential time for semilinear sets of the form $L(\mathcal{C}, \mathcal{P}) = \bigcup_{\vec{c} \in \mathcal{C}} \mathcal{L}(\vec{c}, \mathcal{P})$. Recently, Leroux [Ler03] has given an algorithm to reconstruct an unquantified formula from the automaton that accepts its solutions, which covers different sets and Latour [Lat04] has done the same for integer convex polyhedra which is a special case of our result.

Semilinear Sets $L(\mathcal{C}, \mathcal{P})$. Let $L \subseteq \mathcal{N}^p$, an element $\vec{x} \in L$ is *reducible* in L iff either $\vec{x} = 0$ or there exist $\vec{x}_1 \in L, \vec{x}_2 \in L$ such that $\vec{x} = \vec{x}_1 + \vec{x}_2$ and $\vec{x}_1, \vec{x}_2 \neq 0$.

[**] The complete version of this paper is available as [Lug04]. This work was done while on sabbatical leave at LSV, UMR 8643, ENS de Cachan, 61 avenue du Président Wilson, 94235 CACHAN Cedex, FRANCE.

A element $\vec{x} \neq 0$ is *irreducible* iff it is not reducible. Let $\mathcal{I}r(L)$ be the set of irreducible elements of L. Let $Add(L)$ be the set $\{\vec{z} \mid \forall \vec{x} \in L, \vec{x} + \vec{z} \in L\}$.

Proposition 1. *A set L is a semilinear set of the form $L(\mathcal{C}, \mathcal{P})$ iff (i) $\mathcal{I}r(Add(L))$ is finite, (ii) $\exists C \in \mathcal{N}$ such that $\forall \vec{x} \; [\vec{x} > C \implies \exists \vec{z}, \vec{x}' \; (\vec{z} \in Add(L) \wedge \vec{x}' \in L \wedge \vec{x} = \vec{x}' + \vec{z})]$. If (i) and (ii) holds then $L = L(\mathcal{C}, \mathcal{I}r(Add(L)))$ for $\mathcal{C} = \{\vec{x} \mid |\vec{x}| \leq C\}$.*

Given an automaton $\mathcal{A}$ such that $L = L(\mathcal{A})$ the conditions (i),(ii) can be checked in double exponential time.

Expressivity of semilinear sets $L(\mathcal{C}, \mathcal{P})$. For each integer convex polyhedron P there is a set $\mathcal{L}(\mathcal{C}, \mathcal{P})$ that is equal to P [SCH86] (the set of periods $\mathcal{P}$ is the Hilbert basis of the polyhedron). More general sets can be represented: Let (C) be a conjunction (C) of inequalities $\Sigma_{i=1}^{i=p} a_{i,j} x_i \geq d_j$ $j \in J$ and moduli equations $\Sigma_{i=1}^{i=p} b_{i,k} x_i \equiv c_k \mod m_k$ $k \in K$ where $a_{i,j}, b_{i,k}, d_j$ are integers (possibly negative ones), c_k, m_k are positive integers.

Proposition 2. *The set of solutions of (C) is a semilinear set $\mathcal{L}(\mathcal{C}, \mathcal{P})$.*

This holds also for a disjunction of conjunctions that differ in the terms d_j's and c_k's only, like in $(C) \vee (C')$ where C is defined by $x + y \geq 1 \wedge 3x \equiv 1 \mod 4$ and (C') is defined by $x + y \geq 2 \wedge 3x \equiv 2 \mod 4$.

Therefore, given an automaton accepting sets of (binary representations) of natural numbers, it is decidable if this set is the set of solutions of a conjunction of inequalities and moduli equations (and we can compute a equivalent semilinear set representing the set of solutions).

References

[BW02]   B. Boigelot and P. Wolper. Representing arithmetic constraints with finite automata: An overview. In P.J. Stuckey, editor, *Proc. ICLP*, number 2401 in LNCS, pages 1–19. Springer-Verlag, 2002.

[Lat04]   L. Latour. From automata to formulas: Convex integer polyhedra.In *Proc. 19th LICS*. IEEE, 2004. to appear.

[Ler03]   Jerome Leroux. *Algorithmique de la verification des systèmes à compteurs. Approximation et accélération. Implémentation de l'outil FAST*. PhD thesis, ENS-Cachan, December 2003. http://www.lsv.ens-cachan.fr/Publis/PAPERS/Leroux-these.ps.

[Lug04]   D. Lugiez. From automata to semilinear sets: a solution for polyhedra and even more general sets. Technical report, LIF, 2004. available from http://www.lif.univ-mrs.fr/

[Muc03]   A. Muchnik. The definable criterion for definability in Presburger arithmetic and its applications. *Th. Comp. Science*, 290:1433–1444, 2003.

[RV02]   T. Rybina and A. Voronkov. Using canonical representation of solutions to speed-up infinite-state model-checking. In *14th Int. Conf., CAV*, volume 2404 of *LNCS*, pages 386–400. Springer-Verlag, 2002.

[SCH86]   A. Schrijver. *Theory of Linear and Integer Programming*. John Wiley and sons, New-York, 1986.

Myhill-Nerode Theorem for Sequential Transducers over Unique GCD-Monoids

Andreas Maletti[*]

Faculty of Computer Science, Dresden University of Technology,
D–01062 Dresden, Germany
maletti@tcs.inf.tu-dresden.de

Abstract. We generalize the classical MYHILL-NERODE theorem for finite automata to the setting of sequential transducers over unique GCD-
monoids, which are cancellative monoids in which every two non-zero
elements admit a unique greatest common (left) divisor. We prove that
a given formal power series is sequential, if and only if it is directed
and our MYHILL-NERODE equivalence relation has finite index. As in
the classical case, our MYHILL-NERODE equivalence relation also admits
the construction of a minimal (with respect to the number of states)
sequential transducer recognizing the given formal power series.

Deterministic finite automata and sequential transducers are applied, for example, in lexical analysis, digital image manipulation, and speech processing [2]. In
the latter application area also very large sequential transducers, *i.e.*, transducers having several million states, over various monoids are encountered [2], so
without minimization algorithms [4] the applicability of sequential transducers
would be severely hampered.

In [2,3] efficient algorithms for the minimization of sequential transducers
are presented in case the weight is taken out of the monoid $(\Delta^*, \cdot, \varepsilon)$ or out of
the monoid $(\mathbb{R}_+, +, 0)$. A MYHILL-NERODE theorem also allowing minimization
is well-known for sequential transducers over groups [1].

We use $(A, \odot, \mathbf{1}, \mathbf{0})$ to denote a monoid with the absorbing element $\mathbf{0}$. A
unique GCD-monoid is a cancellation monoid $(A, \odot, \mathbf{1}, \mathbf{0})$ in which (i) $a|\mathbf{1}$ im-
plies $a = \mathbf{1}$, (ii) a greatest common divisor (gcd) exists for every two non-zero
elements, and (iii) a least common multiple (lcm) exists for every two non-zero
elements having a common multiple. Unique GCD-monoids exist in abundance
(e.g., $(\mathbb{N} \cup \{\infty\}, +, 0, \infty)$ and $(\mathbb{N}, \cdot, 1, 0)$ as well as the monoids mentioned in the
previous paragraph).

A *sequential transducer* (ST) is a tuple $M = (Q, q_0, F, \Sigma, \delta, \mathcal{A}, a_0, \mu)$ where
(i) Q is a finite set, (ii) $q_0 \in Q$, (iii) $F \subseteq Q$, (iv) Σ is an alphabet,
(v) $\delta \colon Q \times \Sigma \longrightarrow Q$, (vi) $\mathcal{A} = (A, \odot, \mathbf{1}, \mathbf{0})$ is a monoid, (vii) $a_0 \in A \setminus \{\mathbf{0}\}$,
and (viii) $\mu \colon Q \times \Sigma \longrightarrow A$. For every $q \in Q$ the mappings $\widehat{\delta}_q \colon \Sigma^* \longrightarrow Q$ and
$\widehat{\mu}_q \colon \Sigma^* \longrightarrow A$ are recursively defined by (i) $\widehat{\delta}_q(\varepsilon) = q$ and $\widehat{\mu}_q(\varepsilon) = \mathbf{1}$, and

[*] Financially supported by the German Research Foundation (DFG, GK 334/3).

M. Domaratzki et al. (Eds.): CIAA 2004, LNCS 3317, pp. 323–324, 2005.
© Springer-Verlag Berlin Heidelberg 2005

for every $w \in \Sigma^*$ and $\sigma \in \Sigma$ by (ii) $\widehat{\delta}_q(w \cdot \sigma) = \delta(\widehat{\delta}_q(w), \sigma)$ and $\widehat{\mu}_q(w \cdot \sigma) = \widehat{\mu}_q(w) \odot \mu(\widehat{\delta}_q(w), \sigma)$. Finally, the power series $S_M \in A\langle\!\langle \Sigma^* \rangle\!\rangle$ recognized by M is then defined to be $(S_M, w) = a_0 \odot \widehat{\mu}_{q_0}(w)$, if $\widehat{\delta}_{q_0}(w) \in F$, otherwise $\mathbf{0}$. We call a power series $S \in A\langle\!\langle \Sigma^* \rangle\!\rangle$ *sequential* (with respect to $\mathcal{A}$), if there exists a sequential transducer M such that $S = S_M$.

In the following, let $\mathcal{A} = (A, \odot, \mathbf{1}, \mathbf{0})$ be a unique GCD-monoid, $M = (Q, q_0, F, \Sigma, \delta, \mathcal{A}, a_0, \mu)$ be a ST, and $S \in A\langle\!\langle \Sigma^* \rangle\!\rangle$. Moreover, we use $g(w) = \gcd_{u \in \Sigma^*, w \cdot u \in \mathrm{supp}(S)}(S, w \cdot u)$ for every $w \in \Sigma^*$. If $(S, w) = g(w)$ for all $w \in \mathrm{supp}(S)$, then S is called *directed*.

Definition 1. *The ST M is normalized, if there exists $\perp \in Q \setminus (F \cup \{q_0\})$ such that $\delta(\perp, \sigma) = \perp$ for every $\sigma \in \Sigma$ and $\mu(q, \sigma) = \mathbf{0} \iff \delta(q, \sigma) = \perp$ for every $q \in Q$.*

Definition 2. *We define the* MYHILL-NERODE *relation $\equiv_S \subseteq \Sigma^* \times \Sigma^*$ by $w_1 \equiv_S w_2$, iff there exist $a_1, a_2 \in A \setminus \{\mathbf{0}\}$ such that for every $w \in \Sigma^*$*

$$w_1 \cdot w \in \mathrm{supp}(S) \iff w_2 \cdot w \in \mathrm{supp}(S) \text{ and } a_1^{-1} g(w_1 \cdot w) = a_2^{-1} g(w_2 \cdot w).$$

Proposition 1. *If S is directed and $\equiv_S$ has finite index, then there exists a sequential transducer M with $\mathrm{index}(\equiv_S)$ states such that $S_M = S$.*

Proof. In the proof we write $[w]$ and $[\Sigma^*]$ instead of $[w]_{\equiv_S}$ and $[\Sigma^*]_{\equiv_S}$. Let $M = (Q, q_0, F, \Sigma, \delta, \mathcal{A}, a_0, \mu)$ where for every $w \in \Sigma^*$ and $\sigma \in \Sigma$

(i) $Q = [\Sigma^*]$, $q_0 = [\varepsilon]$, $F = \{ [w] \mid w \in \mathrm{supp}(S) \}$,
(ii) $\delta([w], \sigma) = [w \cdot \sigma]$, $a_0 = g(\varepsilon)$, and $\mu([w], \sigma) = g(w)^{-1} \odot g(w \cdot \sigma)$.

Moreover, the constructed ST is minimal with respect to the number of states amongst all normalized deterministic ST computing S.

Theorem 1. *The following are equivalent.*

(i) *S is directed and $\equiv_S$ has finite index.*
(ii) *S is sequential.*

References

1. Jack W. Carlyle and Azaria Paz. Realizations by stochastic finite automaton. *Journal of Computer and System Sciences*, 5(1):26–40, 1971.
2. Mehryar Mohri. Finite-state transducers in language and speech processing. *Computational Linguistics*, 23(2):269–311, 1997.
3. Mehryar Mohri. Minimization algorithms for sequential transducers. *Theoretical Computer Science*, 234(1–2):177–201, 2000.
4. Marcel P. Schützenberger and Christophe Reutenauer. Minimization of rational word functions. *SIAM Journal of Computing*, 20(4):669–685, 1991.

Minimalizations of NFA Using the Universal Automaton

Libor Polák*

Department of Mathematics, Masaryk University,
Janáčkovo nám 2a, 662 95 Brno, Czech Republic
polak@math.muni.cz

In this contribution we shall see how our (algebraic) approach to the so-called universal automaton of a given regular language helps to understand the process of the minimalization of a NFA. The minimality is meant with respect to the number of states. Although it is known that the problem is PSPACE-complete (see [5]) one can propose algorithms of not too high complexities to compute relatively good approximations.

The universal automaton was considered implicitly already by Conway in [3]. Its significance for the problem of the minimalization of a NFA was stated by Arnold, Dicky and Nivat in [1] where the authors proved that an arbitrary minimal NFA for a given regular language L is isomorphic to a subautomaton of the universal automaton $\mathcal{U}$ for L. They credit that result to Carrez [2]. In fact, also the calculations of Kameda and Weiner in [6] were done implicitly in $\mathcal{U}$.

Our view on the universal automaton is based on author's paper [8]. The methods of several previous works on minimalizations of NFA can be modified so that they fit in our approach. We formulate various conditions on sets of states of the universal automaton $\mathcal{U}$ and we investigate the relationships between them. Any such set of states P determines an automaton $\mathcal{U}_P$. The conditions (L) and (B) determine those sets in a unique way, so they form bases for concrete implementations. A checking of the conditions with the exception of "$\mathcal{U}_P$ accepts L" leads to polynomial time algorithms with respect to the dimension of the so-called universal matrix for L.

Let $\mathsf{D} = \{u^{-1}L \mid u \in A^*\} = \{u_1^{-1}L, \ldots, u_n^{-1}L\}$, $\widehat{\mathsf{D}} = \{Lv^{-1} \mid v \in A^*\} = \{Lv_1^{-1}, \ldots, Lv_m^{-1}\}$, $\mathsf{U} = \{ w_1^{-1}L \cap \cdots \cap w_k^{-1}L \mid k \geq 0, \ w_1, \ldots, w_k \in A^* \}$. Let $B = (\beta_{ij})$ be a matrix of type m/n with entries from $\{0,1\}$ where $\beta_{ij} = 1$ if and only if $u_j v_i \in L$. This matrix is called the *basic matrix* of the language L. Adding to the columns of B new ones which are componentwise meets of sets of columns of B ($0 \wedge 0 = 0 \wedge 1 = 1 \wedge 0 = 0$, $1 \wedge 1 = 1$) we get the matrix U which is called the *universal matrix* of L. Note that the states of the minimal complete deterministic automaton of L correspond to the columns of B and the states of the universal automaton of L correspond to the columns of U. Moreover, we can easily compute unions and intersections of states of $\mathcal{U}$ using the matrix U.

Let $\mathcal{U} = (\mathsf{U}, A, E, I, T)$ be the universal automaton of a regular language $L \subseteq A^*$. Each $P \subseteq \mathsf{U}$ induces a subautomaton $\mathcal{U}_P = (P, A, E_P, I \cap P, T \cap P)$ of

---

* Supported by the Ministry of Education of the Czech Republic under the project MSM 143100009.

M. Domaratzki et al. (Eds.): CIAA 2004, LNCS 3317, pp. 325–326, 2005.

$\mathcal{U}$ where $E_P = \{(p, a, q) \in E \mid p, q \in P\}$. Clearly, the language accepted by $\mathcal{U}_P$ is a subset of L. We can formulate several conditions on a subset P of U:

(A) the automaton $\mathcal{U}_P$ accepts the language L,
(C) the automaton $\mathcal{U}_P$ is complete, i.e. $(\forall p \in P)(\forall a \in A)(\exists q \in P)\, q \subseteq a^{-1}p$,
(I) the initial state is covered, i.e. $L = \bigcup \{p \in P \mid p \subseteq L\}$,
(D) closeness with respect to derivatives, i.e. $(\forall p \in P)(\forall a \in A)\, a^{-1}p \in P$,
(K) (Kiel) $(\forall p \in P)(\forall a \in A)\, a^{-1}p = \bigcup \{q \in P \mid q \subseteq a^{-1}p\}$,
(W) (Waterloo) $(\forall q \in \mathsf{D})\, q = \bigcup \{p \in P \mid p \subseteq q\}$,
(LM) the local minimality, i.e. $P \models (A)$ but for each $p \in P$ we have $P\backslash\{p\} \models \neg(A)$,
(L) (Lille) $P_l = \{\, p \in \mathsf{D} \mid p \text{ is union-irreducible in } (\mathsf{D}, \subseteq),\ p \neq \emptyset \,\}$,
(B) (Brno) $P_b = \{\, \bigcap \{u_j^{-1}L \mid \beta_{ij} = 1\} \mid Lv_i^{-1} \text{ union-irreducible in } (\widehat{\mathsf{D}}, \subseteq) \,\}$.

We also put $P_0 = \{\, q \in \mathsf{D} \mid q \neq \bigcup \{r \in \mathsf{U} \mid r \subseteq q,\ r \neq q\} \,\}$.
The following results relate the above conditions.

Theorem 1. *The following implications between our conditions hold.*
  (i) (D) $\Longrightarrow$ (K) & (C).
  (ii) (L) $\Longrightarrow$ (I) & (K) $\Longrightarrow$ (A) $\Longrightarrow$ (W).
Moreover, (iii) P_b satisfies (A).
  (iv) Both P_l and P_b satisfy the condition (LM).
  (v) For each $P \subseteq \mathsf{U}$ satisfying (A) we have $P_0 \subseteq P$.
  (vi) None of the implications in (i) and (ii) can be reversed.

Compact proofs, algorithms for constructing the matrices B and U, several examples and exact lines to the related works [4, 6, 7, 10] can be find in [9].

References

1. Arnold, A., Dicky, A. and Nivat, M.; A note about minimal non-deterministic automata, Bull. EATCS 47, pp. 166-169 (1992)
2. Carrez, C.; On the minimalization of non-deterministic automaton, Laboratoire de Calcul de la Faculté des Sciences de l'Université de Lille, 1970
3. Conway, J.H.; *Regular Algebra and Finite Machines*, Chapman and Hall, Ltd., 1971
4. Denis, F., Lemay, A. and Terlutte, A.; Residual finite state automata, Fundam. Inform. 51, No.4, pp. 339–368 (2002)
5. Jiang, Tao and Ravikumar, B.; A note on the space complexity of some decision problems for finite automata. Inf. Process. Lett. 40, No.1, pp. 25–31 (1991)
6. Kameda, T. and Weiner, P.; On the state minimization of nondeterministic finite automata, IEEE Transactions on Computers, Vol. C-19, No. 7, pp. 617–627 (1970)
7. Matz, O. and Potthoff, A.; Computing small nondeterministic finite automata, *Proc. Workshop on Tools and Algorithms for the Construction and Analysis of Systems 1995*, BRICS Lecture Notes, pp. 74–88
8. Polák, L.; Syntactic semiring and universal automaton, *Proc. Developments in Language Theory, Szeged 2003*, Springer LNCS, Vol. 2710, pp. 411–422 (2003)
9. Polák, L.; Minimalization of NFA using the universal automaton, *Preproc. Descriptional Complexity of Formal Systems, London (Canada) 2004*, pp. 238–249 (2004)
10. Tamm, H. and Ukkonen, E.; Bideterministic automata and minimal representations of regular languages, *Proc. CIAA, Santa Barbara (USA) 2003*, Springer LNCS, Vol. 2759, pp. 61–71 (2003)

Two-Dimensional Pattern Matching by Two-Dimensional Online Tessellation Automata*

Tomáš Polcar and Bořivoj Melichar

Department of Computer Science and Engineering,
Faculty of Electrical Engineering, Czech Technical University,
Karlovo nám. 13, 121 35 Prague 2, Czech Republic
{polcart, melichar}@fel.cvut.cz

Abstract. A new method that transforms a special type of non-deterministic two-dimensional online tesselation automata into deterministic ones is presented. This transformation is then used in a new general approach to exact and approximate two-dimensional pattern matching based on two-dimensional online tessellation automata that generalizes pattern matching approach based on finite automata well known from one-dimensional case.

Two-dimensional pattern matching is a natural extension of a well known pattern matching problem into two dimensions. The fundamental version is a seeking of rectangular patterns in rectangular text.

Let us suppose squared pattern P of size (m, m), squared text T of size (n, n), and $\sigma = \min(|A|, m^2)$, where $|A|$ is the size of the alphabet A. The first linear time two-dimensional exact pattern matching algorithm, which takes $\mathcal{O}\left((m^2 + n^2)\log\sigma\right)$ time, was introduced by Bird [1]. Using two-dimensional periodicity, Galil and Park [2] proposed the truly alphabet independent algorithm, which requires $\mathcal{O}\left(m^2 + n^2\right)$ time. Two-dimensional online tessellation automata were introduced by Inoue and Nakamura [3]. An algorithm for two-dimensional pattern matching using these automata, which simulates the algorithm of Bird [1], was given by Toda, Inoue, and Takanami [4]. The best result in the pattern matching with at most k substitutions gave Amir and Landau [5] achieving $\mathcal{O}\left((k + \log\sigma)n^2\right)$ using $\mathcal{O}\left(n^2\right)$ space.

A nondeterministic (deterministic) two-dimensional online tessellation automaton, referred as 2OTA (2DOTA), is a 5-tuple $\mathcal{A} = (A, Q, \delta, q_0, F)$ where A is the input alphabet, Q is the finite set of states, $\delta : Q \times Q \times A \to \mathcal{P}(Q)$ ($\delta : Q \times Q \times A \to Q$) is the transition function, $q_0 \in Q$ is the initial state, $F \subseteq Q$ is the set of final states.

Inoue and Nakamura [3] showed that 2OTA are more powerful than 2DOTA, because there is at least one 2OTA accepting language that is not recognizable

---

* This research has been partially supported by by FRVŠ grant No. 2060/04, by CTU grant No. CTU0409213, and by Ministry of Education, Youth, and Sports of the Czech Republic under research program No. J04/98:212300014.

M. Domaratzki et al. (Eds.): CIAA 2004, LNCS 3317, pp. 327–328, 2005.

by any 2DOTA. It means that it is not possible to create a universal algorithm for 2OTA to 2DOTA transformation.

Fortunately, this algorithm can be constructed for a special type of 2OTA by generalization of the subset construction, which is well know from one-dimensional case. It means that states of the created 2DOTA will be formed by sets of states of original 2OTA. Since this construction is based on the simulation of nondeterministic automata in a deterministic way, these automata will be called *simulatable* 2OTA. A simulatable 2OTA $\mathcal{A} = (A, Q, \delta, q_0, F)$ can be transformed into equivalent 2DOTA $\mathcal{A}' = (A, Q', \delta', q_0', F')$ as follows: $Q' = \mathcal{P}(Q)$, $\delta'(p, q, a) = \bigcup_{o \in p} \bigcup_{r \in q} \delta(o, r, a)\ \forall p, q \in Q',\ \forall a \in A,\ q_0' = \{q_0\}$, $F' = \{q \mid q \in Q', q \cap F \neq \emptyset\}$.

The pattern matching than works in three independent phases. At first, a 2OTA for given pattern and pattern matching problem is constructed. This is the only step that differs for different pattern matching problems because each problem requires special automaton. After that, this automaton is transformed into equivalent 2DOTA. At last, deterministic automaton reads the input text and whenever it reaches a final state it reports an occurrence of the pattern.

The biggest advantage of this approach is the fact that the matching phase is really fast. It requires $\mathcal{O}(n^2)$ time for the text of size (n, n) with very small hidden constant. Moreover, the time complexity of the preprocessing phase depends only on the size of the pattern, size of the alphabet, the number of allowed errors, and the type of used error distance. Disadvantage is that the preprocessing phase is exponential with the size of the pattern. For pattern of size (m, m) it is $\mathcal{O}(|A|2^{m^2})$ in case of exact pattern matching and $\mathcal{O}(|A|2^{k^2m^2})$ in case of pattern matching with at most k substitutions. Thus this pattern matching algorithm is very useful in case that the text is much greater than the size of the pattern $(m \ll n)$, or when the pattern is searched in many input texts. The extra space required by presented algorithm is $\mathcal{O}(|A|2^{m^2} + n)$ in case of exact pattern matching, and $\mathcal{O}(|A|2^{k^2m^2} + n)$ in case of pattern matching with at most k substitutions.

References

1. Bird, R.S.: Two dimensional pattern matching. Information Processing Letters **6** (1977) 168–170
2. Galil, Z., Park, K.: Truly alphabet-independent two-dimensional pattern matching. In: Proceedings of the 33rd IEEE Annual Symposium on Foundations of Computer Science. (1992) 247–256
3. Inoue, K., Nakamura, A.: Some properties of two-dimensional on-line tessellation acceptors. Information Sciences **13** (1977) 95–121
4. Toda, M., Inoue, K., Takanami, I.: Two-dimensional pattern matching by two-dimensional on-line tesselation acceptors. Theoretical Computer Science **24** (1983) 179–194
5. Amir, A., Landau, G.: Fast parallel and serial multidimensional approximate array matching. Theor. Comput. Sci. **81** (1991) 97–115

Size Reduction of Multitape Automata

Hellis Tamm*, Matti Nykänen, and Esko Ukkonen

Department of Computer Science,
P.O. Box 68, 00014 University of Helsinki, Finland
{hellis.tamm, matti.nykanen, esko.ukkonen}@cs.helsinki.fi

Several models of multitape automata have been introduced over the years. Here we consider a modified version of the Rabin-Scott model [2] motivated by the needs of developing a string manipulating database system of [1]. We present an algorithm to reduce the size of a multitape automaton in this model. The algorithm uses certain local transformations that change the order in which transitions concerning different tapes occur in the automaton graph, and merge suitable states together into a single state. Although the resulting automaton is not necessarily minimal, the size of the automaton may be reduced considerably as the example below indicates.

An n-tape automaton A is given by a quintuple $(Q, \Sigma, \delta, I, F)$ where Q is a finite set of *states*, Σ is the *input alphabet*, $\delta : Q \times \Sigma_{\{1,...,n\}} \to 2^Q$ is the *transition function* where $\Sigma_{\{1,...,n\}} = \{a_i \mid a \in \Sigma, i \in \{1, ..., n\}\}$, $I \subseteq Q$ is the set of *initial states* and $F \subseteq Q$ is the set of *final states*.

Our reduction algorithm is based on the following four language preserving automaton transformations.

Swap Upwards. Let $q' \in Q$ be a non-initial and non-final state with $k \geq 1$ incoming and one outgoing transition. Let the transitions associated with q' be $q_1 \overset{(a_1)_{i_1}}{\longrightarrow} q', ..., q_k \overset{(a_k)_{i_k}}{\longrightarrow} q'$ and $q' \overset{b_j}{\longrightarrow} q$, such that j refers to a tape that is different from all tapes $i_l, l \in \{1, ..., k\}$. Then q' and its incoming and outgoing transitions can be removed and replaced with new non-initial and non-final states $q'_1, ..., q'_k$ and transitions $q_1 \overset{b_j}{\longrightarrow} q'_1, ..., q_k \overset{b_j}{\longrightarrow} q'_k$, and $q'_1 \overset{(a_1)_{i_1}}{\longrightarrow} q, ..., q'_k \overset{(a_k)_{i_k}}{\longrightarrow} q$.

Sink Combine. Let $q_1, ..., q_k$ be some non-initial states of A, all having exactly one incoming transition labelled a_i from a state q of A where q is different from all $q_i, i \in \{1, ..., k\}$. Then $q_1, ..., q_k$ can be combined into one state q', meaning that $q_1, ..., q_k$ and their incoming and outgoing transitions are removed and replaced by a new non-initial state q' which is final if and only if any of $q_1, ..., q_k$ is final, with all outgoing transitions of $q_1, ..., q_k$ now leaving q', and a transition $q \overset{a_i}{\longrightarrow} q'$.

Symmetric operations *Swap Downwards* and *Source Combine* are defined similarly.

Based on these transformations we have designed an algorithm to reduce the size of an n-tape automaton A. For a given automaton tape, Swap Upwards and Sink Combine transformations are performed on one copy of A, and Swap Downwards and Source Combine transformations are performed on another copy of A. Transformations are carried out locally only in places where certain con-

---

* Supported by the Academy of Finland grant 201560.

M. Domaratzki et al. (Eds.): CIAA 2004, LNCS 3317, pp. 329–330, 2005.
© Springer-Verlag Berlin Heidelberg 2005

330   H. Tamm, M. Nykänen, and E. Ukkonen

ditions hold implying that the size of the automaton will be reduced by them. The smaller of the aforementioned two automata is retained, and the process is repeated using the next tape, until no more reduction can be achieved for any tape. The algorithm runs in $O(N^4)$ time where N is the number of states of the automaton.

An example. Let $L_k = \{ww^R \mid w \in \{0,1\}^k\}$ where $k \geq 1$. Let A_k be a 2-tape automaton accepting all tuples (w_1, w_2) such that $w_1 \in L_k^*$ and w_2 is a string of the same length as w_1, consisting of 0's; A_k is created in a certain way, exemplified for $k = 2$ by the leftmost automaton shown below.

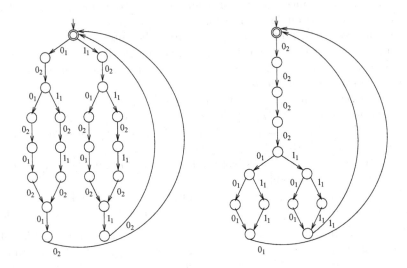

The result of applying the reduction algorithm on A_k with $7 \times 2^k - 7$ states is the automaton A_{kred} with $3 \times 2^k + 2k - 3$ states. The automaton A_{2red} is shown above at right. For example, for $k = 5$, from the 217 states of A_5, 114 states are eliminated.

Detailed description and an application of the reduction algorithm can be found in [3] where this algorithm combined with the classical DFA minimization procedure is used to reduce the size of multitape automata generated from alignment declarations of [1].

References

1. Grahne, G., Hakli, R., Nykänen, M., Tamm, H., and Ukkonen, E. Design and implementation of a string database query language. *Inform. Syst.* **28**, (2003), 311-337.
2. Rabin, M.O., and Scott, D. Finite automata and their decision problems. *IBM J. Res. Develop.* **3**, (1959), 114-125.
3. Tamm, H. On minimality and size reduction of one-tape and multitape finite automata. PhD thesis (in preparation), Department of Computer Science, University of Helsinki, Finland.

Testability of Oracle Automata*

Gaoyan Xie, Cheng Li, and Zhe Dang**

School of Electrical Engineering and Computer Science,
Washington State University,
Pullman, WA 99164, USA

An *oracle finite automaton* (OFA) is a finite/Buchi automaton augmented with a finite number of unbounded, one-way, and writable query tapes. By each transition, an OFA can read an input symbol, append a symbol to the end of a query tape, erase the content of a query tape, or query an *oracle* with the content of a query tape (called a *query string*). Here, an *oracle O* is a language in some language class $\mathcal{O}$ (all oracles in the OFA must be in the same language class $\mathcal{O}$, and we denote such OFAs with $\text{OFA}^{\mathcal{O}}$). The name of "oracle" comes from the fact that, except for its language class, the definition of O is not given. However, the oracle O can always be queried with the answer whether a query string w is in O.

Obviously, for the OFA defined above, its emptiness problem (whether an OFA accepts an empty language) can not be solved by simply analyzing the OFA's transition graph, since whether a transition can be chosen during its execution may depend on the results of queries to its oracles. We solve the problem by first computing a number, called a *query bound*, from the specification of the OFA and the language class $\mathcal{O}$ of its oracles such that querying the oracles with query strings not longer than the query bound is sufficient to answer its emptiness problem. Once the query bound is computable, we say that the emptiness problem is solvable or, more accurately, testable.

Our results focus on establishing conditions on the language class $\mathcal{O}$ and on the OFA such that the emptiness problem is testable. Specifically, we consider cases when $\mathcal{O}$ is the class of languages accepted by nondeterministic finite automata with n states ($\text{FA}(n)$), accepted by nondeterministic pushdown automata with n states ($\text{PDA}(n)$), or is the class of commutative semilinear languages with characteristic n ($\text{LIN}(n)$, defined in the full paper). We also consider cases when the OFA is in some restricted forms: *positive* (a "no" answer from a query always makes the OFA crash), *memoryless* (a query tape is always erased immediately after being used to query an oracle), or *prefix-closed* (if a query string is a word of an oracle then all prefixes of the query string are also words of the oracle). We say that an OFA is *k-query* if it never queries its oracles more than k times during its executions, and an OFA is *single* if it has only one oracle. Most of our testability results also demonstrate respective query bounds explicitly. For instance, consider an OFA M with an oracle O drawn from $\text{PDA}(n)$ whose stack alphabet is Σ. Then, in general, the emptiness problem for M is not testable.

---

* The research was supported in part by NSF Grant CCF-0430531.
** Corresponding author (zdang@eecs.wsu.edu).

M. Domaratzki et al. (Eds.): CIAA 2004, LNCS 3317, pp. 331–332, 2005.

However, the problem becomes testable with a query bound $2^{O(|M|^2 \cdot n^2 \cdot |\Sigma|)}$ when M is restricted to each of the following cases: (1) $M^{\mathrm{PDA}(n)}$ is positive, single, and prefix-closed; (2) $M^{\mathrm{PDA}(n)}$ is positive, single, and 1-query; (3) $M^{\mathrm{PDA}(n)}$ is positive, single, and memoryless; (4) $M^{\mathrm{PDA}(n)}$ is $M^{\mathrm{DPDA}(n)}$ and single.

We also generalize our testability results on OFA to oracle Buchi automata (ω-OFA). For instance, consider an ω-OFA M with oracles drawn from $\mathrm{LIN}(n)$. In general, the emptiness problem for M is not testable. However, the problem becomes testable with a query bound $O(n^{k \cdot |M|^k})$ when M is k-query. The query bound becomes $O(n^{|M|})$ when M is memoryless and single.

Using standard automata-theoretic approaches [7], we can show that various verification problems (such as *reachability, safety, LTL model-checking*, etc.) for an (ω-) oracle automaton can be reduced to its emptiness problem. And this result can immediately find applications in the automatic verification of systems containing some unspecified/partially specified components, which can not be solved either by algorithmic analysis techniques (like model-checking [1, 7, 2]) or traditional software testing techniques (like black-box testing [4]). With the oracle finite automata introduced in this paper, the expected behaviors of an unspecified/partially specified component can be modeled as an oracle; the communications between the system and the component can be modeled as queries to the oracle and the query results are obtained by testing the component. With the testability results of oracle automata obtained in this paper, the various verification problems (as mentioned earlier) concerning systems with unspecified/partially specified component can be solved through both algorithmic analysis and black-box testing. And this approach fits nicely within the current trend [5, 3, 6] of seeking innovative ways to combine model-checking with software testing techniques.

References

1. E. M. Clarke, E. A. Emerson, and A. P. Sistla. Automatic verification of finite-state concurrent systems using temporal logic specifications. *TOPLAS* 8(2):244–263, 1986.
2. E. M. Clarke, O. Grumberg, and D. A. Peled. *Model Checking*. The MIT Press, 1999.
3. Alex Groce, Doron Peled, and Mihalis Yannakakis. Amc: An adaptive model checker. *CAV'02*, LNCS 2404, pp. 521–525, Springer, 2002.
4. D. Lee and M. Yannakakis. Principles and methods of testing finite state machines - A survey. *Proceedings of the IEEE* 84: 1090–1126, 1996.
5. Doron Peled. Model checking and testing combined. *ICALP'03*, LNCS 2719, pp. 47–63, Springer, 2003.
6. Doron Peled, Moshe Y. Vardi, and Mihalis Yannakakis. Black box checking. *FORTE/PSTV'99*, pp. 225–240, 1999.
7. M. Y. Vardi and P. Wolper. An automata-theoretic approach to automatic program verification. *LICS'86*, pp. 332–344, 1986.

Magic Numbers for Symmetric Difference NFAs

Lynette van Zijl*

Department of Computer Science, Stellenbosch University, South Africa
lynette@cs.sun.ac.za

Iwama et al [1] showed that there exists an n-state binary nondeterministic finite automaton such that its equivalent minimal deterministic finite automaton has exactly $2^n - \alpha$ states, for all $n \geq 7$ and $5 \leq \alpha \leq 2n - 2$, subject to certain coprimality conditions. We investigate the same question for both unary and binary symmetric difference nondeterministic finite automata [2]. In the binary case, we show that for any $n \geq 4$, there is an n-state $\oplus$-NFA which needs $2^{n-1} + 2^{k-1} - 1$ states, for $2 < k \leq n-1$. In the unary case, we prove the following result for a large practical subclass of unary symmetric difference nondeterministic finite automata: For all $n \geq 2$, we show that there are many values of α such that there is no n-state unary symmetric difference nondeterministic finite automaton with an equivalent deterministic finite automaton with $2^n - \alpha$ states, where $0 < \alpha < 2^{n-1}$. For each $n \geq 2$, we quantify such values of α precisely.

$\oplus$-NFAs were defined in [2]; suffice it to say that $\oplus$-NFAs are NFAs with the union operation in the subset construction replaced with the symmetric difference operation.

In the unary case, we prove the following theorem:

Theorem 1. *(a) For any $n \geq 2$, there is an n-state unary $\oplus$-NFA with nonsingular characteristic matrix which needs $2^n - 1$ deterministic states.*
(b) For any $n \geq 2$, let $n = n_1 + n_2 + \ldots + n_j$, and let

$$B = \{lcm(2^{n_1} - 1, 2^{n_2} - 1, \ldots, 2^{n_j} - 1)\}.$$

If M is an n-state unary $\oplus$-NFA with nonsingular characteristic matrix whose minimal $\oplus$-DFA has b states with $2^{n-1} \leq b \leq 2^n - 1$, then $b \in B$.

□

Experimentation on smaller values of n indicated that there are always n-state unary $\oplus$-NFAs such that their $\oplus$-DFAs with $lcm(2^{n_1}-1, 2^{n_2}-1, \ldots, 2^{n_j}-1)$ states are minimal, and we give the following conjecture:

Conjecture 1. For any $n \geq 2$, there is an n-state unary $\oplus$-NFA which needs $lcm(2^{n_1} - 1, 2^{n_2} - 1, \ldots, 2^{n_j} - 1) > 2^{n-1}$ deterministic states, where $n = n_1 + n_2 + \ldots + n_j$.

□

We now consider binary $\oplus$-NFAs:

Theorem 2. *For any $n \geq 4$, there is a binary n-state $\oplus$-NFA M which needs $2^{n-1} + 2^{k-1} - 1$ states, for $2 < k \leq n - 1$.*

---

* This research was supported by NRF grant #2053436.

M. Domaratzki et al. (Eds.): CIAA 2004, LNCS 3317, pp. 333–334, 2005.
© Springer-Verlag Berlin Heidelberg 2005

Proof. By construction. Construct $M = (Q, \{a, b\}, \delta, \{q_0\}, F, \oplus)$ such that $Q = \{q_0, q_1, \ldots, q_{n-1}\}$. Let $\delta(q_{n-1}, a) = \emptyset$, and set up δ over a for states q_0 to q_{n-2} so that the characteristic polynomial $c_a(X)$ is primitive and irreducible seen over the states q_0 to q_{n-2}. Then M'_a has exactly $2^{n-1} - 1$ reachable states, in a single cycle. Also, state q_{n-1} does not occur as a constituent part of any of the states in M'_a.

Now construct the transition table for the alphabet symbol b in such a manner that b will generate a cycle of length $2^k - 1$, starting at state q_0, so that this cycle shares exactly $2^{k-1} - 1$ states with M'_a, and exactly 2^{k-1} of the states in M'_b contains q_{n-1}: Let $\delta(q_{n-1}, b) = \emptyset$. For any k, choose $c_b(X)$ over state q_0 to q_{k-1} to be a primitive irreducible polynomial, and construct the transition function accordingly. For states q_k to q_{n-1}, let the transition function go to the empty set. Now add state q_{n-1} to every set which is not the empty set.

From the construction of M, we know that none of the states in the a-cycle of M' contains q_{n-1}, while 2^{k-1} of the states in the b-cycle contain q_{n-1}. The other $2^{k-1} - 1$ states in the b-cycle are those that intersect with the a-cycle. We now choose our final state as q_{n-1}.

To show minimality, we show that for any two states $Y \neq Z$ in M', there is a word $w \in \mathcal{L}$ such that $\delta'(Y, w)$ leads to a final state, but $\delta'(Z, w)$ does not. If Y is from the a-cycle and Z from the b-cycle (excluding intersection points), then Y is nonfinal and Z final and they cannot be equivalent. If both Y and Z are from the b-cycle, then there is some p such that such that $\delta'(Y, b^p)$ leads to a final state, while $\delta'(Z, b^p)$ does not and hence Y and Z cannot be equivalent. If both Y and Z are from the a-cycle, there must be at least one value p such that $\delta'(Y, b^p)$ leads to a final state, but $\delta'(Z, b^p)$ does not. Again Y and Z cannot be equivalent, and the proof holds. $\qquad\square$

Future work on this topic includes an analysis of the behaviour of traditional unary NFAs. Another area for future work is an investigation of magic numbers for unary $\oplus$-NFAs with singular characteristic matrices. Empirical results in [3] seem to indicate that there will be few if any values of α such that this class of unary NFAs needs $2^n - \alpha$ deterministic states, where $2^{n-1} < \alpha \leq 2^n - 1$.

References

1. Iwama, K., Matsuura, A., Paterson, M.: A Family of NFAs which need $2^n - \alpha$ Deterministic States. Theoretical Computer Science **301** (2003), 451–462.
2. Van Zijl, L., Random Number Generation with Symmetric Difference NFAs. *Proceedings of CIAA2001*, Pretoria, South Africa, July 2001. Lecture Notes in Computer Science **2494** (2002) 263–273.
3. Van Zijl, L., Nondeterminism and Succinctly Representable Regular Languages. *Proceedings of SAICSIT'2002*, ACM International Conference Proceedings Series (2002), 212–223.

Author Index

Lecture Notes in Computer Science

For information about Vols. 1–3261

please contact your bookseller or Springer